Politics and Policy in American States and Communities

EIGHTH EDITION

Dennis L. Dresang
University of Wisconsin—Madison

James J. Gosling
University of Utah

Boston   Columbus   Indianapolis   New York   San Francisco   Upper Saddle River
Amsterdam   Cape Town   Dubai   London   Madrid   Milan   Munich   Paris   Montreal   Toronto
Delhi   Mexico City   São Paulo   Sydney   Hong Kong   Seoul   Singapore   Taipei   Tokyo

For Maxine

Dennis L. Dresang

For Amy, David and Michael

James J. Gosling

Executive Editor: Reid Hester
Executive Marketing Manager: Wendy Gordon
Supplements Editor: Corey Kahn
Production Manager: Denise Phillip
Project Coordination, Text Design, and Electronic Page Makeup: PreMediaGlobal
Cover Design Manager: John Callahan

Cover Designer: Kay Petronio
Cover Image: Getty Images, Inc.
Photo Researcher: Connie Gardner
Senior Manufacturing Buyer: Dennis J. Para
Printer/Binder: Quebecor World/Taunton
Cover Printer: Lehigh-Phoenix Color/Hagerstown

Credits and acknowledgments borrowed from other sources and reproduced, with permission, in this textbook appear on the appropriate pages within the text.

Library of Congress Cataloging-in-Publication Data
Dresang, Dennis L.
  Politics and policy in American states and communities/Dennis L. Dresang, James J. Gosling.—8th ed.
    p. cm.
  Includes bibliographical references and index.
  ISBN-13: 978-0-205-25159-9
  ISBN-10: 0-205-25159-5
  1. State governments—United States. 2. Local government—United States. I. Gosling, James J. II. Title.
  JK2408.D68 2013
  320.80973—dc23

                                                                              2011050880

10 9 8 7 6 5 4 3 2 1—RNT—15 14 13 12

Photo Credits: Page 4: Louisiana Department of Wildlife and Fisheries; 6: © moodboard/Corbis RF; 8: © Chris Faytok/Star Ledger/Corbis; 33: © Alan Schein Photography/Corbis; 94: © Mario Anzuoni/Reuters/Corbis; 97: © Kevin Fleming/Corbis; 108: © Ed Quinn/Corbis; 127: © Gail Oskin/WireImage/Getty Images; 160: © Jim West/Corbis; 163: © John Hart/AP Photo; 170: © Philip James Corwin/Corbis; 195: © Linda Stelter/Newhouse News Service/Birmingham News/Landov; 203: © Frances M. Roberts/Newscom; 205: © Elaine Thompson/AP Images; 226: © Jose Sanchez/AP Photo; 235: © David Allio/Corbis; 251: © Philip Gould/Corbis; 275: © Steven Georges/Press-Telegram/Corbis; 288: © Topeka Capital- Journal, Anthony S. Bush/AP Images; 307: © Getty Images News; 324: © Reuters/Corbis; 364: © Steve Starr/Corbis; 369: © Peter Turnley/Corbis; 395: © Jeff Miller/University of Wisconsin, Madison; 412: © JP Laffont/Sygma/Corbis; 447: © Nik Wheeler/Corbis.

ISBN-10: 0-205-25159-5
ISBN-13: 978-0-205-25159-9

Contents

Preface

S tates and communities provide essential public services that have been threatened because of the financial crises that began in 2008. Mortgage foreclosures and lower incomes obviously hurt families. In addition, there are losses from the taxes on income, sales, and property that pay for government operations. When police officers, firefighters, sanitation workers, public school teachers, and other employees have to be laid off, basic functions are threatened and the country's unemployment woes increase. Local officials are critical players in projects to employ people and to address the needs for repairing roads and bridges, moving to renewable energy sources, and improving health care.

Governments of states, communities, and tribes are fundamental to governance in the United States and directly affect our daily lives. The ways in which states and local governments respond to the challenges of the early twenty-first century are critical not only for current concerns but also for the future. We have been pleased to see the increased interest in and appreciation of politics and policy making in states and communities over the past two decades. Those who understand governance at the grassroots have a more accurate picture of the United States than if they only focus on what happens in Washington, D.C.

BASIC PERSPECTIVE AND FEATURES

Our own experiences, both as professors and as officials in state and local government, prompted us to write this book. We were concerned that students—and citizens—typically have a low level of knowledge about the governments that affect them so directly. It was out of this concern that we developed our face-to-face approach in which we relate politics, institutions, and policies to the interactions that each of us has with state and local government officials and employees. We found that our students better understood concepts, theories, and institutions if they were able to draw on connections to their own lives and experiences such as being pulled over for speeding; getting a fishing license; having trash collected, streets cleaned, and snow plowed; or going to a public school. Face-to-face interactions raise questions about the authority, discretion, and resources of public employees and about an individual's attitude toward government and politics. These interactions provide the foundation and the inspiration for this text.

The uniqueness of this book is not only its perspective, but also its coverage. We discuss intergovernmental relations extensively. We also include tribal governments in our discussions of institutions and policies. This text provides analyses of the historic bases of federalism and of contemporary changes in state, local, and tribal relationships.

In addition to making information and scholarship current, this edition includes the following important features:

- Discussion of the critical issues of today: economic, health, and education
- Analysis of the debate over federal and state health care reforms, with special attention given to the enactment of the federal 2010 Patient Protection and Affordable Care Act
- Discussion of the use of recall elections and referenda by public employee unions threatened with revocation of collective bargaining rights
- Exploration of the increased use of social media in campaigning
- Consideration of the recent controversies regarding the death penalty and methods of execution
- Analysis of the emergence of the federal government as a major player in education policy
- Review of educational policy alternatives initiated by states, including those in reaction to their experiences in implementing the federal government's No Child Left Behind Act

Those who have used previous editions have praised the attention to policy making and to major policy issues. They also cite the pedagogical tools in each chapter, such as the learning objectives at the beginning and the opening vignettes, case studies, tables, glossary, summary, and references. Particularly popular are the debate forums and the Internet suggestions that are included in each of the substantive chapters.

Professor Gosling wishes to thank Charlene Orchard, a doctoral student at the University of Utah, for updating tables and figures from the Seventh Edition, as well as contributing suggested revisions to the text.

An Instructor's Manual/Test Bank is available for qualified adopters of *Politics and Policy in American States and Communities*. The test bank is designed to reinforce and test students' knowledge of the themes and concepts of the text. The test bank contains multiple-choice, short answer, true/false, and essay questions. Integrated into the text itself are a number of instructional aids, including learning objectives, suggestions for discussion, and glossaries, as well as Internet and dialogue boxes described above. Also available are PowerPoint presentations that instructors may want to consider using.

Students who want to reinforce their learning may take advantage of MySearchLab with Pearson eText. This book-specific website features a full, interactive eText; complete overviews of the entire writing and research process; and chapter-specific content, such as learning objectives, quizzes, media, and flashcards to enrich learning and help students succeed. To order this book with MySearchLab access at no extra charge, use ISBN 0-205-89549-2.

DENNIS L. DRESANG
JAMES J. GOSLING

1

Face-to-Face Governance

LEARNING OBJECTIVES

- Appreciate the relevance of state and local governments to everyday life.
- Understand the nature and patterns of face-to-face interactions between individuals and public officials.
- Know how the capacities of governments affect face-to-face interactions.
- Know how public participation and attitudes affect face-to-face interactions.

You just passed a car and are driving 75 mph in a 65-mph zone. You spot a patrol car parked behind some bushes on the side of the road. Although you brake and slow down, you are sure the officer saw you speeding. The patrol car pulls onto the road with its lights flashing. You have butterflies in your stomach, and it seems like your heart is stuck in your throat. You pull over and stop. The officer says that she clocked you going 10 mph over the speed limit and asks for your driver's license. She goes back to her car and, after what seems like an eternity, hands you a warning ticket. You get a stern lecture about the importance of obeying traffic laws and are sent on your way.

The officer clearly could have given you a ticket but decided instead to give you only a warning. Perhaps she was satisfied when you slowed down, or maybe she was lenient because you were passing another car. It could be that you weren't going so far over the speed limit that you were creating a hazard. You were respectful and didn't get angry. She might have let you off because you seemed penitent and didn't come across as arrogant and irresponsible. Whatever the reason, you are relieved the officer chose to excuse you.

State, local, and tribal governments are about face-to-face interactions. Governments are not impersonal, abstract institutions that hover over society. Instead, they consist of people who are in positions of authority, who solve problems and provide services that involve and affect other people. Sometimes the interaction allows someone to do something (e.g., drive a vehicle), sometimes it regulates (e.g., stopping individuals from disturbing the peace), and sometimes it provides services (e.g., disposing of trash and maintaining safe, pleasant neighborhoods).

The face-to-face interactions between citizens and the governments in states and communities are the central focus of this book. We will examine what government officials do and how we experience government in our lives. For example, if police officers respond to a complaint about a noisy party, we need to understand what authorizes these government officials to enter private property and curtail the activities of citizens. We need to understand the discretion and the limits that guide these officers in law enforcement. Citizens can seek the services of the police to maintain order and to help with emergencies, but citizens can also be constrained or restrained by police or even subjected to their brutality. This book explains the forces that determine the nature of the interactions among police, courts, legislative bodies, governors, mayors, political parties, interest groups, and individual citizens.

Understanding face-to-face interactions with government also requires a discussion of how the more than 87,000 different jurisdictions in the United States relate to one another. Take, for example, the law that limits drinking to people age 21 or older. State governments adopted this law because the federal government threatened to withhold millions of dollars in transportation funds to any state that did not have such a law. States rely on police departments, which are part of local governments, to enforce the law. Some local governments require their officers to check the age of all young adults they see drinking or are suspected of drinking. Other police departments are given discretion to enforce this law within the context of other goals they are pursuing, such as combating crimes of violence and fostering cooperation and peace within the community.

The focus on interaction includes attention to the processes through which individuals become government officials. As citizens, we determine who gets elected and, indirectly, appointed to public offices. How people get their jobs affects how they behave. Supporters influence elected officials. Appointed officials are concerned about the criteria on which the appointment is based and the judgments of whoever has authority to fire them.

The bottom-up or face-to-face perspective of this text is an examination of what various governments do; how and why they do it; how individuals and groups can influence the goals and behaviors of governments; and, perhaps most important, how they affect us. Throughout this book we will be ever mindful of the purpose and relevance of government and politics.

The call for reinventing government, popular in the 1990s, came in reaction to cases where governments passed regulations and engaged in activities that did not address the real needs and concerns of people.[1] The reinventing government movement argued that citizens should be viewed as customers of government. Governments should be serving their citizens the way one might expect a private business to meet customer demands and wishes.

We do not assume that all state and local (including tribal) governments are currently customer-oriented. We certainly do not assume that all citizens are active in efforts to shape and influence their governments. We are quite aware of government agencies that seem to be enforcing rules and following procedures in an apparently mindless, purposeless manner. We realize that some public officials engage in corruption and make decisions that favor those who are willing and able to pay, rather than those who elected them to office. We know full well that less than one-fourth of those eligible to vote typically cast ballots in local elections. A good turnout in highly visible gubernatorial and presidential contests is only 50 to 60 percent of the electorate. Although meetings of school boards, city councils, and legislatures are open to the public, few people—even when they are affected by the decisions that will be made—make the effort to attend. The major purpose of our focus on face-to-face interaction is not to romanticize or to idealize it, but rather to recognize its importance in understanding the role of state and local governments in our lives, and in knowing how our actions and inaction can affect them.

SCOPE

State and local governments touch almost every aspect of our lives. Those who want to become teachers, lawyers, doctors, architects, barbers, undertakers, and members of many other professions and crafts must secure licenses from the states in which they intend to work. If you wish to operate a restaurant or a bar or if you want to build or remodel a home or a shop, you must get appropriate licenses and permits from local governments. If you have complaints as a client, a patient, or a customer, you can seek redress before boards, agencies, and—if necessary—the courts of state and local governments.

Local governments determine how land may be used. For urban areas, land-use regulation is critical to traffic flow, business location, the existence of parks and green spaces, and the character of neighborhoods. For rural areas, the concerns are access to roads and to water. There are restrictions on whether an area may be used for agriculture, industrial development, or waste disposal. Everyone meets face to face with local government officials regarding issues of housing, employment, education, and recreation.

State governments and school districts have primary responsibility for education. States have established colleges and universities. Local school districts provide education from kindergarten through high school and sometimes through technical and vocational schools and two-year community colleges. Teachers must seek certification from officials in a state agency. Parents and students deal with school administrators, school board members, and sometimes state officials over issues of cost, curriculum, graduation requirements, and the like. Federal efforts to shape education are often regarded as intrusions, whereas local efforts are natural.

The federal government can pass laws and establish programs that supersede state and local laws. The U.S. Supreme Court voids some of these mandates on the grounds that the Constitution limits the extent to which federal actions trump those at the state and local levels. Even when federal laws do prevail, the federal government—as a practical matter—lets state and local governments be the primary actors in many areas of domestic policy. When the federal government gets involved, such as in health and welfare policies and in transportation programs, it works jointly with states and localities to fund and set policy guidelines. Washington relies almost entirely on state and local officials to do the actual work and administration. In an area such as drug enforcement, where both the federal and state governments pass laws, the general pattern is that much of the actual work (other than interdicting drugs entering the United States) is done by local officials. Likewise, except for military and diplomatic action abroad, domestic security in the aftermath of the terrorist attack on September 11, 2001, relies heavily on local police officers, firefighters, and public health personnel. When hurricanes strike, rivers flood, or an epidemic occurs, local workers are on the frontline, hopefully with adequate support from the federal or state governments.

Governments are problem solvers. The scope of governments, especially state and local governments, varies with the problems of society. We are far from the mythical period in

Rescue workers in the aftermath of Hurricane Ike, which hit U.S. communities on the coast of the Gulf of Mexico in September 2008. State and local governments are the first responders to natural disasters and terrorist attacks.

which individuals and families were largely self-sufficient and governments were tiny in staff, budget, and scope of responsibilities. Individuals and groups have become interdependent, calling on government to enforce contracts and to resolve conflicts. They also petition government for financial assistance and tax breaks.

Technological advances have profound effects on the relationships between governments and the governed. At the turn of the twentieth century, state governments had to respond to potentials for abuse that accompanied the development of the railroad and the availability of electricity, gas, and telephones. States established regulatory commissions to make sure transportation, energy, and communications companies made these important resources available to everyone. Companies were forced to provide at least a minimum quality of safety and service without charging unreasonable prices. In the early twenty-first century, governments are wrestling with the implications of other technologies. Policymakers are concerned about protecting rights of privacy threatened by computer technology; coping with the social costs of workers laid off because a plant replaces them with robots or tasks are outsourced abroad; adjusting to the high costs of energy; and protecting the copyrighted work of musicians, artists, and authors. Medical personnel can use the Internet to receive data from a remote area in a neighboring state and send a diagnosis and prescription, but sometimes they are prevented from doing so because of state licensing requirements. Different suppliers of electricity can use the same wires, thus allowing for competition where before only monopolies were possible. The scandals involving major corporations, which came to light in 2002, included charges that some companies manipulated sources of power available to certain states as a way of artificially raising prices and profits.

Governments face a challenging and changing scope of issues. Unfortunately, capacity does not always match responsibility.

CAPACITY

One cannot precisely measure the capacities of state and local governments. Nonetheless, it is safe to say that governments, especially since the 1960s, have greatly increased their ability to deal with problems and challenges. The fundamental components of capacity for governments are as follows.

1. Legal Authority. A major difference between public and private organizations is that the public organizations make and enforce laws. Parking longer than you should on a city street or at a city meter can earn you a ticket. Parking on private property when you should not requires the landowner to inform city authorities that you are trespassing before any legal action can be taken. Laws empower government officials. At the same time, laws limit government officials. A police officer may not arrest you for drinking at age 20 unless a law prohibits drinking at that age.

2. Human Resources. Governments are labor intensive. State and local government bodies consist primarily of professionals and paraprofessionals. Some government jobs are low skilled, such as garbage collecting and park maintenance, but most government employees are teachers, social workers, police officers, analysts, attorneys, accountants, and the like. Able, competent personnel are essential to effective government.

3. Financial Resources. Like any organization, governments need money. State and local governments must pay salaries, maintain buildings, construct and repair roads, and make welfare payments. Fiscal capacity includes the stability of revenue sources. States that rely heavily on income or sales taxes, for example, are somewhat at the mercy of the health of the economy. As the economy slows down, and thus tax revenue based on income and sales decreases, expenses—especially those that are welfare- and crime-related—usually go up. State and local governments depend on federal money. Local governments also depend on money from the state. The generosity of governments toward one another has varied considerably over time.

Several events in the 1960s converged to prompt state and local governments to become more relevant to the concerns of the people and to enhance their capacity to provide services and solve problems. For the first half of the twentieth century, many state governments were dominated by rural interests and thus had a rural agenda, despite the rapid emergence of urban areas after World War II. Governments that did not respond to emerging concerns did not attract the talent and attention of serious politicians and professionals. To put it in stark terms, irrelevance led to incompetence. In 1962, the U.S. Supreme Court ruled that state legislatures had to be based on the principle of one-person, one-vote.[2] This effectively ended the pattern in which state legislative districts were based on geography, not population. States had been inattentive to urban issues until their legislatures became more fairly representative. In part, this neglect of an increasingly important and complicated part of our society became dramatically evident in the urban riots that occurred throughout the country in the 1960s. Similarly, national commissions and task forces created in response to the Russian launching of *Sputnik* and the initial failures of the U.S. space efforts dramatized the failure of states and local school districts to provide quality education, especially in math and science.

In the 1970s and 1980s, every major institution of state government underwent change and development.[3] A flurry of state constitutional conventions and commissions emerged. Task forces drew legislative districts to conform to the Supreme Court mandate to have each district in a state consist of the same number of eligible voters. Legislatures acquired staff members to help with policy analysis and oversight. Governors and state agencies were empowered to exercise more policy discretion and to manage government more

A police officer in Mounds View, Minnesota, giving a teenager a ticket. What prompts public officials to exercise their authority? Police officers do not ticket every motorist who exceeds the speed limit or violates some other regulation.

efficiently. Likewise, states gave local governments more authority to address the specific issues of their respective communities.

The agendas of state and local governments became relevant for the first time in decades. State legislatures, with increased representation and power for urban areas, passed legislation and appropriated funds to respond to critical needs. School districts consolidated to serve both rural and urban communities more effectively. Likewise, other local government units formally and informally agreed on ways to work together to solve common problems. The federal government emphasized the issues of poverty and urban communities, and provided funds to encourage and facilitate state and local action.

Not surprisingly, talented, committed people found that these developments made state and local governments attractive arenas for making their own contributions. Reforms of institutions enhanced opportunities for serious and capable people to have meaningful and rewarding careers. The commitment of public funds made change and innovation possible.

This is not to say that the increase in the capacities of state and local governments was ubiquitous or that these governments are now fully able to solve all the issues before them. Although new funds were available in the 1960s and 1970s, a major problem since then has been a cut in federal monies and voter reaction against local property tax increases. Revenue problems have been made worse by increases in cost, especially for health care, energy, and fuel.

An increase in financial resources does not always provide an increased capacity to solve problems, but it usually helps. When the federal government made major new financial commitments to domestic problems in the early 1960s, it severely limited the discretion and authority of state and local governments to use the funds. Officials in Washington, D.C., did not trust the ability, and sometimes the intentions, of state and local governments. Thus, federal funds came with strict and detailed instructions about how the money could be spent. With money came mandates.

In the 1970s, President Richard M. Nixon successfully urged Congress to continue sending more money to state and local governments but with fewer strings. In another pattern, President Ronald Reagan decreased the flow of federal money but at the same time gave state and local officials more discretion and more responsibility for domestic programs. Obviously, state and local officials preferred the Nixon approach. An issue of growing concern has been the increase in unfunded federal mandates—laws and regulations that state and local government must obey, although they receive no money to help with the costs incurred. The twenty-first century began with state and local governments pinched between these conflicting demands, which were exacerbated by security needs after the September 11, 2001, terrorist attack and the sharp rise in energy costs, on the one hand, and an economic recession and drastic increase in federal debt, on the other. The home mortgage crisis in 2008 added to the woes of local governments because the crisis decreased property tax revenues but not the need for government services.

The limits on government capacity to solve problems can lead to face-to-face interactions that are frustrating and even hostile. Failures in public school classrooms have prompted some parents to seek private alternatives, some to demand reforms in public schools, and some to give up hope for a promising future for their children. Contamination from hazardous waste, acts of violent crime, and streets that always seem to need repair can lead to frustration and even cynicism. A fundamental principle of democracy is that the governed be given an opportunity to influence their government. How citizens react to their governments, both generally and in specific cases, is important to the dynamics of the face-to-face interaction.

PARTICIPATION

There are many more opportunities for us to participate directly in community governance than in the operation of the federal government. Each of us has the opportunity to vote at the federal level for a president and vice president, two senators, and one representative. In contrast, we elect not only legislators, governors, and lieutenant governors to state government, but also a number of constitutional officers such as attorneys general; treasurers; secretaries of state; and, depending on the state, up to 11 other officers. In addition, there are elections for city offices, county offices, courts, school boards, and a variety of other local governments. Throughout the United States, there are over 7,000 state legislators and hundreds of thousands of local officials. It is almost inevitable that everyone will meet face to face with someone elected to a state or local office, and it is quite probable that a friend, neighbor, or relative will hold an elective office. And electing people to office is not the only form of democracy in states and communities.

California, Oregon, and 19 other states allow their citizens the opportunity to enact laws directly by voting on ballot proposals without going through the legislature or the governor. Every state government provides for advisory referenda, which aim at influencing elected officials. Voters in almost every community must directly authorize their governments to borrow money and sometimes to exceed established limits in taxing or spending.

In many New England and Midwestern communities, town meetings are held at least once a year. Anyone who attends and is eligible to vote can take part in the discussions and vote on the motions that are offered. State and local government agencies hold hearings for public comment before making policy decisions or rulings. Federal and local laws that require environmental impact statements—studies that describe the effects of proposed projects—allow groups to get the courts to halt a project if all the procedures for public disclosure and public participation have not been followed. As the scope of government has extended to include complex issues requiring professional and technical expertise, the concern about citizen access and citizen participation has increased rather than decreased. (See the Debating the Issues box.) Especially with issues such as hazardous waste disposal, the insistence on the opportunity for citizen involvement can block decisions and resolutions. Nonetheless, the commitment to a participatory process continues.

Participation in elections, hearings, and court actions includes both individuals and groups. The power of collective action lies in the sincerity and intensity of what is shared. Groups can impress politicians with their numbers, and they can pool resources needed for taking effective action. This can include hiring a professional lobbyist to track the progress of a proposal and to intervene with arguments and information at critical points. State and local governments also encounter ad hoc, grass-roots groups and neighborhood organizations that form to express concern about a specific issue or incident. These groups may not become a permanent part of the political landscape, but they can have a major impact on setting the agenda and shaping a particular policy.[4]

Whether people participate in political action depends on how intensely they feel about an issue and whether they believe they can have an impact. The latter factor is referred to as efficacy. Members of minority groups that have been excluded from economic, educational, and political opportunities typically have a low sense of efficacy. They can feel apathetic and cynical toward government.[5] They tend to feel more like the subjects of government than like citizens or participants.

Voter from the floor at a New Hampshire town meeting addressing a question to the moderator. When do individuals participate in government? Only a minority take advantage of the many opportunities to elect officials or to influence policies.

DEBATING THE ISSUES

Should citizens or experts make policy?

Expert: Citizens do not have the background to make informed decisions about complicated issues such as where to build a road, how to dispose of hazardous waste, or what to include in school programs. Citizen involvement makes policy making a popularity contest rather than a selection of a sound choice.

Citizen: Government in a democracy is supposed to respond to the needs and concerns of citizens. Experts, who know how to build a safe road, what to do with hazardous waste, and how to teach students, should be implementing what citizens want—not telling us what we want!

Expert: And just who is a "citizen"? You are all approaching this from your own individual, selfish interests. No one speaks for the general good. At least we can be objective!

Citizen: The answer is simple: majority opinion rules.

Expert: But what about those who do not get involved? Only a minority of citizens vote, attend hearings, or make their views known.

How would you respond? Are there ways of reconciling these positions?

Another situation in which those legally eligible to participate in government do not bother to try occurs when a community has been ruled, formally or informally, by a particular family or group of families.[6] A community power elite may be wealthy and have high social status. The power may be personal or come from historic links with a political machine in the state or county. In some towns or villages, a single company or factory so dominates the economy of the area that it greatly influences what happens politically. Usually it takes an external economic or political force or an internal fragmentation within the power elite to provide meaningful opportunities for the general population to participate in community governance.

The way people feel about specific issues and about government affects their face-to-face interaction with public officials. If the attitude toward government is hostility, apathy, or cynicism, messages to and from government are going to be far different than if the orientation is one of cooperation, concern, and efficacy. Most people have distinct views of the different levels of government. Confidence in the federal government varies widely over the years. On the other hand, support for state and local governments is relatively stable, suggesting the importance of face-to-face relationships.[7]

Tables 1.1 and 1.2 are summary presentations of the central focus of this book, the face-to-face interactions between the public and state and local governments. Table 1.1 juxtaposes the major functions of government with the major needs and concerns of the governed. This table views state and local government as a dialogue between citizen needs and government functions. Government affects us and we affect it. The emergency services provided by government are available to each of us. We use city streets and sidewalks, county roads, and state highways. If you cannot get to campus or to work because your street does not get plowed

Table 1.1   Bases for Face-to-Face Interactions

Government Function	Citizen Needs
Service	Emergencies, education, transportation, recreation
Regulation	Safety, law and order, environmental protection
Adjudication	Conflict resolution
Legislation	New policy development, information, and clarification of existing policies
Revenue	Income, fairness, understandability

Table 1.2   Types of Face-to-Face Interactions

		Citizen Cooperation	
		Low	High
Government Discretion	**Low**	Confrontational	Rule compliance
	High	Arbitrary	Responsive

after a snowstorm, you need to be able to bring this to the attention of city officials and to get results. That will probably happen via a personal contact either over the phone, electronically by e-mail or twitter, or face to face.

Government officials usually initiate the face-to-face contact if the matter is one of regulation rather than of service. This may occur when a building inspector arrives to be sure safety codes are being followed as you are putting an addition on your house. Police officers engage in many face-to-face interactions as they do their work.

Courtrooms are arenas of numerous face-to-face interactions as judges and juries settle disputes over family matters and contracts and as they determine guilt or innocence in criminal trials. Individuals and their attorneys confront one another in a courtroom. They face the jury and the judge and plead their case. The presentation is important. Rarely do the facts speak for themselves. Jurors must determine who seems credible as well as which arguments are most persuasive.

The legislative function of government is also about meeting the personal needs of citizens. Candidates for legislative office make this point when they meet voters in a neighbor's home, in a shopping center, or at the local school. While legislation must be written in general terms to address new issues or to change existing policies, the genesis of legislation is often a particular problem or opportunity. Legislators, in addition to deliberating on proposed laws, spend much of their time doing casework and serving the needs of individual constituents who have a question, need clarification, or want prompt action from a government agency.

Finally, state and local governments have face-to-face interactions with citizens as taxpayers. When our income is effectively lowered because of the various taxes we have to pay, we are likely to be attentive and concerned. Tax collectors spend considerable time answering questions from individuals who want to be sure they understand the tax bill and who insist that they pay no more than their fair share. If there is a big increase in your property tax bill, you will undoubtedly want to know why. You will want to know if others in your neighborhood—especially the ones right across the street who just finished an expensive remodeling project—had similar increases in their tax bills. You can get the information you want and, if you are so inclined, lodge a protest by paying a visit to the city or county tax office.

In some sense Table 1.1 presents an ideal, conceptual portrait. Not reflected, for example, is a government agency so intent on serving its own needs that it protects or expands its jurisdiction and its rules without regard for its contribution to society. Agencies charged with ensuring that buildings are safe sometimes promulgate standards that may relate only remotely to a highly improbable hazard, but that nonetheless force builders to incur extra expenses to comply with rules. Sometimes a township or village fights annexation into a city, thereby thwarting efforts that might provide more efficient and effective services in a metropolitan area.

Table 1.1 does not reflect the debate about whether citizen needs are appropriately met by government services or regulation. A central issue in the abortion controversy, for example, is whether government should require what women do with their health and their bodies. Since the establishment of the United States, the electorate has wrestled with questions about when it is appropriate to rely on government subsidies and regulations to influence the behavior and development of the economy.

The major types of face-to-face interactions are presented in Table 1.2. Again, the intent is to provide a conceptual framework, not to describe every possible situation. Table 1.2 is based on what citizens and governments bring to their interactions. It is critical that citizens approach government with an attitude that is highly cooperative. Government officials, on the other hand, may have no leeway or discretion as they provide services, collect taxes, and enforce regulations. At the opposite end of the continuum, government officials may be able to empathize with individuals and to solve problems with specific or unique circumstances in mind.

As conveyed in the *responsive* cell in Table 1.2, the face-to-face interaction may be one in which government and citizens are responsive to the needs and resources of one another. A school district, for example, may be faced with an alarming increase in student violence. To ensure safety for individual students and still provide a quality education, school officials, parents, students, and the community generally have to identify what can and should be done. The school cannot act in isolation.

The *rule compliance* cell describes circumstances in which government strictly enforces rules, and citizens cooperate. For example, it is important for tax administration to be consistent and rule-oriented, and for citizens to be compliant. The alternatives are corruption. Tax collectors would act differently toward friends, relatives, business partners, and those willing to make side payments. Or there might be tax evasion, in which citizens cheat by concealing information about their income, sales, or property. Likewise, compliance with clear, firm rules and directions is essential in many traffic situations if drivers are to move through an area in a safe and relatively smooth manner.

The *arbitrary* cell includes deplorable situations in which a government official may be unpredictable or whimsical, or may disadvantage some people because of race, religion, gender, or other characteristics. This kind of behavior does not generate much respect, even among those who are favored. Neither government nor citizens can expect support from one another in this situation.

The *confrontational* cell describes a setting in which government officials are limited by rules or resources and cannot respond to the needs and wishes of the governed. Citizens do not identify positively with the government and what it is or is not doing. The result is hostility and confrontation between citizens and government. The situation may be issue-specific and result in protests like those in the 1960s over racial discrimination and environmental pollution. Confrontation between government and citizens may also focus on certain segments of a community such as poor people, racial minorities, or college students.

The grass-roots interactions between governments and the governed are diverse. They depend on the responsibilities of government, the concerns and attitudes of citizens, and the authority and resources that state and local officials have available to them. Succeeding chapters discuss the key influences that determine the various patterns of face-to-face interactions.

Your Face-to-Face Interactions with State and Local Government. Use the following questions to place yourself in one or more of the quadrants of Table 1.2. You may have had experiences with state and local government officials that fit more than one type of interaction. In answering the questions, think of specific examples as well as your general feelings.

1. Do you think of government as a problem solver or as a rule enforcer? Can you provide any personal examples?
2. Do government officials treat you and others as part of stereotypes—for example, students, women, racial groups?
3. Do you think your vote really matters?
4. Can you influence elected officials by sending them an e-mail or talking with them?
5. Have you ever been treated unfairly by a government official? Do you think, generally, that unfair treatment is likely?

PLAN OF THIS BOOK

The chapters of this book are organized in sections that describe the institutions, processes, and policy concerns of state and local governments, and that discuss in more detail the face-to-face interactions that comprise governance at the grass-roots level. Chapter 2 begins a section that lays the foundation for a close examination of the operations of state and local governments. This chapter discusses the resources and traditions of state and local governments and the current challenges they face. The other chapters in this section provide a legal and institutional framework. Chapter 3 discusses the role of the federal government and the relationships among federal, state, tribal, and local governmental units in the United States. Chapter 4 deals with constitutions, charters, treaties, and other sources of governmental authority. Chapter 5 presents an overview of policy making, with an emphasis on legislation in state governments.

The next section looks at the major ways in which citizens become actors in the policy process. Chapter 6 discusses the ad hoc, neighborhood, and informal forms of participation; Chapter 7, the role and nature of formal interest groups; and Chapter 8, the electoral process, including political parties and campaigns.

The next section focuses on the other set of actors in the face-to-face interactions, that is, the institutions of state and local governments. Chapters 9 through 13 describe chief executives, legislative bodies, bureaucracies, and courts. As Chapter 11 points out, some local governments, like most school boards and county boards, combine executive and legislative responsibilities in the same body. The chapters on institutions discuss the sources of authority for each institution, how they exercise that authority, how they relate to one another, and how they interact with the governed. Figure 1.1 shows the general structure of state government institutions. The chart applies to most state governments. There are exceptions, of course, to this general structure. Nebraska, for example, has only one legislative house, whereas the other 49 states have two. Likewise, as will be explained in Chapter 13, most judges in state courts are elected, although some governors appoint some or all of their respective state's judges.

Chapter 14 begins a section that discusses how governments address major problems and opportunities. In Chapters 14–18, we examine crime, education, welfare, health, the environment, economic development, and fiscal policies. Each chapter describes major

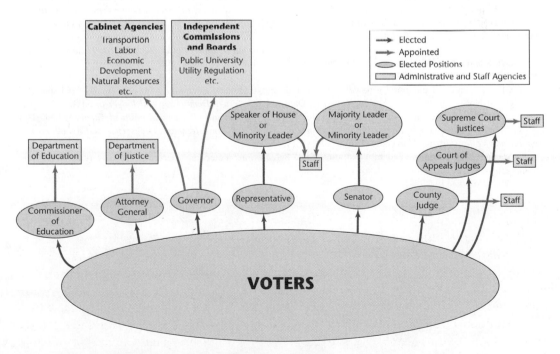

Figure 1.1 General Organization of State Governments

issues of concern and how citizens and their governments struggle to resolve these issues. We invite readers to apply the general lessons of the first four sections of this text to understand how their respective states and communities are responding to the challenges of specific policy issues.

Discussion Questions

1. Identify instances of interaction between yourself and officials of state and local governments. Describe the purposes of these interactions. Were these experiences friendly and did they result in problem resolution, or were they hostile and did they result in frustration?

2. Define government capacity, and explain how it affects face-to-face interactions.

3. How and why do people get involved in politics?

4. How are people's attitudes toward government or their expectations of government likely to affect their interactions with public officials?

Endnotes

1. David Osborne and Ted Gaebler, *Reinventing Government: How the Entrepreneurial Spirit Is Transforming the Public Sector* (Reading, Mass.: Addison-Wesley, 1992).

2. *Baker v. Carr,* 369 U.S. 186 (1962).

3. Alan Rosenthal, *Legislative Life: People, Process and Performance in the States* (New York: Harper & Row, 1981); James L. Garnett, *Reorganizing State Government: The Executive Branch* (Boulder, Colo.: Westview, 1981); Larry Sabato, *Goodbye to Good-Time Charlie: The American Governor Transformed,* 2d ed. (Washington, D.C.: Congressional Quarterly, 1983); Robert A. Kagan et al., "The Evolution of State Supreme Courts," *Michigan Law Review* 76 (1978), 961–1005.

4. Sidney Verba, Kay Lehman Scholzman, and Henry E. Brady, *Voice and Equality: Civic Voluntarism in American Politics* (Cambridge, Mass.: Harvard University Press, 1995); Laura R. Woliver, *From Outrage to Action: The Politics of Grass-Roots Dissent* (Urbana: University of Illinois Press, 1993); Matthew A. Crenson, *Neighborhood Politics* (Cambridge, Mass.: Harvard University Press, 1983).

5. Thomas Cavanagh, "Black Political Participation," in *A Common Destiny: Blacks and American Society,* ed. Gerald David Jaynes and Robin Williams Jr. (Washington, D.C.: National Academy Press, 1989); Hanes Walton, *Black Politics* (Philadelphia, Pa.: Lippincott, 1972).

6. Classic studies of community power elites include Floyd Hunter, *Community Power Structure* (Chapel Hill: University of North Carolina Press, 1953); Robert A. Dahl, *Who Governs? Democracy and Power in an American City* (New Haven, Conn.: Yale University Press, 1961); Nelson Polsby, *Community Power and Political Theory,* 2d ed. (New Haven, Conn.: Yale University Press, 1961); John Gaventa, *Power and Powerlessness: Quiescence and Rebellion in an Appalachian Valley* (Urbana: University of Illinois Press, 1980).

7. Stephen J. Farnsworth, "Federal Frustration, State Satisfaction? Voters and Decentralized Governmental Power," *Publius* 29, no. 3 (1999), 75–88.

2

State Diversity, Growth and Decline, and the Contemporary Urban Dilemma

LEARNING OBJECTIVES

- Understand the distinctive patterns of political culture and economics at work in each region of the United States that influence the political debate over public policy.
- Know how political cultures affect the face-to-face interaction of residents and government representatives.
- Identify patterns of interregional growth and interregional decline, and understand the implications of both.
- Understand the relationship of growing interstate competition over economic development and the increased activism of states in domestic policy making.

Andrea was born and raised in Salem, Oregon, and attended the University of Oregon in nearby Eugene. She enjoyed the walkable neighborhoods with their adjoining blocks of specialty shops, cafés, and parks. She loved the clean air and the environmental consciousness of western Oregonians, sharing their interest in conserving natural resources and managing growth in the public interest. After graduation, she was offered an electrical engineering job in a growing high-tech company in Las Vegas. Finding the position too attractive to turn down, she moved to Las Vegas and began work, joining the nearly 60,000 newcomers who pour into the greater Las Vegas area each year and making it the fastest growing metropolitan area in the United States. Andrea quickly came to appreciate how different Las Vegas is from Salem and Eugene. She realized immediately that she needed her car to get to the galleria and strip malls, which had replaced the neighborhood shops just a few blocks away. As land developers and home builders extended living opportunities well into the desert and the foothills of Las Vegas, people became even more dependent on their automobiles, increasing traffic congestion and air pollution. But, beyond that, she sensed a different public attitude about community interests and the role of government. People seemed to prefer a minimal role for government, fitting nicely with Nevada's low tax effort. Las Vegas seemed to retain much of the individualism of the Wild West. Andrea felt strangely out of place.

Face-to-face interactions between individuals and their governments take place in a variety of settings. Issues differ from one community to another. So do the traditions and resources that affect the discretion available to government officials and the attitudes that citizens have about their governments. An important and fascinating dimension of the study of state and local governments is to appreciate the different cultural, economic, and sociological contexts in which politics and governance occur.

The states are indeed diverse. California, Utah, West Virginia, Wisconsin—each state's name evokes a panoply of images. California conjures up visions of packed six-lane freeways, San Francisco and the Golden Gate Bridge, the Los Angeles riots, the high-tech Silicon Valley, Napa Valley vineyards, the deterioration of once-proud public schools, the property tax rollback of Proposition 13, and the glamour of Hollywood. Utah prompts images of the Mormon Church, large families, the Great Salt Lake, conservative Republican government, world-class skiing, national parks, and wide-open spaces. Thoughts of West Virginia turn to coal mining, scenic rolling hills and mountainous areas, industrial smokestacks, and unemployed workers. Wisconsin is associated with dairy products, German heritage, beer, tourism, and heavy manufacturing.

Significant diversity exists not only *among* the states, but *within* many states as well. Rural northern Wisconsin, with its lakes and tourist resorts, is vastly different from highly urbanized and blue-collar southeastern Wisconsin, which has Milwaukee at its functional, if not geographic, center. Both differ from the agriculturally rich southwestern and south central parts of the state, with their hundreds of miles of dairy farms and cornfields. Similarly, Kentucky's northern industrial belt can be contrasted with the rural bluegrass countryside of its southern part. Chicago, with its ethnic neighborhoods and large predominantly black sections, can be contrasted with the conservative, rural communities of central and southern Illinois, which are typified by national Republican leaders' concern about whether a political initiative "will play in Peoria." Northern Virginia, which seems an extended suburb of the District of Columbia, has little in common with the rest of the state. Its ways are northern, and its transitory population comes from throughout the United States. Its focus is on national affairs and politics, far removed from the concerns of its capital, Richmond.

Florida provides another significant illustration of intrastate diversity. Although Tallahassee leans toward the Deep South both socially and culturally, the coastal areas of central Florida have lost much of their Southern flavor because relocated senior citizens from the North and hordes of tourists add other mores and accents. Southernmost Florida, particularly the greater Miami area, has a decidedly Hispanic cast, dominated by its Cuban influence. Miami supports over 10,000 Cuban-owned businesses. More Cubans now reside in the Miami metropolitan area than in any city other than Havana. In central Florida, the increasing numbers of Puerto Ricans reflect the diversity within the Hispanic community.

Out West, arid eastern Oregon and Washington look and feel different from the much more heavily populated coastal areas, and their politics reflect their physical, social, and cultural differences. The frontier mentality of resource use, characteristic of the eastern slope, contrasts with the conservationist ethos of the Pacific Coast's metropolitan centers. Northern Idaho is influenced more by Spokane, Washington, than by Boise. A bit farther south, the influence of Salt Lake City's Mormon Church extends to the Mormon-dominant areas of southern Idaho and northern Arizona.

Several factors contribute to this interstate and intrastate diversity. Most significant among them are patterns of settlement, patterns of immigration and migration, topography and natural resources, economics, demography, religion, political movements, and political culture. Although these factors have promoted diversity, several have contributed to a nationalization of the states, rendering them more similar.

Economic development has extended its reach to all sections of the nation. No longer are the nation's economic fortunes disproportionately tied to the industrial sections of the Northeast, the Midwestern Great Lakes states, and California. The South and the West have come alive economically, providing the greatest post–World War II employment growth this country has known.

People followed job opportunities, setting off episodic migrations from the Northeast and Midwest to the South and the West. They were joined by people who worked and raised their families in the Northeast or the Midwest but for retirement sought out warmer weather and lower taxes. Northeasterners and Midwesterners became Southerners and Westerners, bringing with them their accumulated experiences and perspectives, and their distinctive regional accents. This influx of people, together with the Sunbelt's comparatively higher birthrate, produced population growth that outstripped that of the rest of the nation.

Television has weakened cultural differences among regions, but it has not eliminated them, and the increasing use of the Internet is extending this trend. For the most part, all Americans, wherever they may reside, receive the same national network programming. They view the same primetime entertainment, the same daytime soaps, and the same national news. Their own local news frequently is read by television newscasters whose speech betrays no regional identity.

In addition, the very business of state and local government is becoming more alike. State and local policymakers increasingly face common problems, and in their attempts to address them, differences in per capita state and local spending have flattened somewhat over the past few decades. Significant disparities still exist, but the gaps among regions are narrowing. Since the mid-1960s, per capita state and local spending has declined as a percentage of the U.S. average in the Far West, Southwest, Intermountain, Plains, and Great Lakes regions, and it has increased in the New England, Mid-Atlantic, and Southeast regions.[1]

Population growth can account for some of this change. Unless government spending rises fast enough to keep pace with rapidly growing populations, per capita spending declines. Although the South, like the West, has experienced marked population growth, many Southern states have made a concerted effort to increase spending in excess of what would be needed merely to provide existing services to their new residents. State initiatives to improve the quality of primary and secondary education have typified those efforts. Despite notable progress, however, most Southern states still spend less per capita than does California.[2]

State and local governments also increasingly find themselves in competition with each other for economic development. States compete with other states, and local governments compete with each other, both inside and outside their own state's borders. They want to retain the industry and jobs they have while attracting more. To be attractive in this competitive arena, they strive to play on their strengths and remedy their shortcomings, which bring about a certain amount of national leveling.

VALUES

Regardless of the section of the country, state, or community in which a person lives, Americans share values coming out of the collective national experience. These values, many articulated during the colonial era and having their roots in Western liberal political thought, continue to affect the way we look at government and the way we think about our relationship to it, and to define public problems.

These values provide an important common foundation for how individuals approach and interact with state and local governments. Because the U.S. Constitution and state constitutions were created or have been interpreted in accordance with these values, they strengthen public policy making at all levels in this country. At the same time, citizens apply them in making judgments about what government legitimately should do.

These deeply rooted, most basic American values include:

1. Popular Sovereignty. Popular sovereignty holds that political power resides in the people, not in the government itself. Government exists at the people's behest, and they can replace their elected representatives.

2. Limited Government. The traditional conception of **limited government** held that government should be limited in what it can do and in how it can affect the lives of its citizenry. Limited government aims to prevent government authority and discretion from being exercised arbitrarily or tyrannically. With the passage of time, especially following the Great Depression, public sentiment shifted toward giving government more range to design and fund programs that meet heightened public needs, as long as those programs and the government officials responsible for them are ultimately controlled by the people. The Reagan administration (1981–1988) championed a growing public sentiment at the time that government had to make a strong case for intervention, and that when it chose to act, its programs operated efficiently and effectively. The Clinton administration (1993–2000) gave government more latitude in making the case for action in the public interest. Although the Bush administration (2001–2008) echoed the ideological themes championed by President Reagan, America's war against terrorism has prompted both expanded government intervention in society and markedly increased spending on homeland security. Governors, mayors, and other state and local political leaders may lean toward one or another of these orientations, but they also share an adherence to the doctrine of limited government.

3. The Rule of Law. The concept of the **rule of law** is that the law applies to all equally. Regardless of personal circumstances, everyone, including government officials, is under the law, and all acts of government must be justified as consistent with the law.

---

popular sovereignty A value underlying the idea that political power resides in the people, not in government itself.

limited government A value underlying the idea that government should be limited in what it can do—in how it can affect the lives of its citizenry.

rule of law The concept that law applies to all equally, and that all acts of government must be justified under the law.

4. Individual Liberty. The principle of **individual liberty** holds that each individual is in the best position to decide what is in his or her own best interest. Government has the rightful obligation to protect the rights of people to pursue those interests, as long as that pursuit does not infringe on the liberty of another. Government action must be consistent with ensuring life, liberty, and the pursuit of happiness.

5. Equality. The principle of **equality** stipulates that all people have the right to equal protection under the law and that one person's vote counts the same as another's, regardless of personal circumstances.

6. Equality of Opportunity. Equality of opportunity is a principle that evolved well after ratification of the U.S. Constitution. It had its roots in the aftermath of the Civil War and has been interpreted and strengthened by U.S. Supreme Court decisions. This key American value holds that all individuals should possess an equal opportunity to get ahead in life, and that artificial barriers (for example, race or gender) should not disadvantage them in their quest. At the same time, Americans agree less about whether certain citizens, because of past discrimination, should be given preference over others in hiring or government contracts. Nonetheless, few would demur from the principle of providing equal opportunity and rewarding performance.

Americans also have a can-do attitude. We believe that problems are there for the solving. American know-how, characterized by inventiveness and tenacity, stands ready to confront any challenge. To foreign observers, this national confidence may seem brash or even foolish, but to us it represents possibility—the possibility of betterment and advancement.

POLITICAL CULTURES

Along with these basic values, Americans are influenced by the **political cultures** in which they were raised and live. These political cultures are products of accumulated historical experiences, tradition, patterns of immigration and migration, and religious identities. They shape political attitudes, views of the appropriate role of government in society, the relative priorities placed on public programs, and avenues for political participation. Political culture differs regionally and even within states of the same region, and it affects the attitudes and behaviors of both citizens and government officials.

---

individual liberty The principle underlying the idea that individuals are free to decide what is in their best interest, and that government has the obligation to protect the rights of people to pursue those interests, as long as that pursuit does not infringe on the liberty of another.

equality The principle that all people have the right to equal protection under the law.

equality of opportunity A value underlying the idea that all persons should possess an equal opportunity to get ahead in life, and that artificial barriers (for example, race or gender) should not disadvantage them in their quest.

political culture The combined effects of historical experiences, tradition, patterns of immigration and migration, and religious identities that shape political attitudes, views of the appropriate role of government in society, the relative priorities placed on public programs, and avenues for political participation.

Political scientist Daniel Elazar has conceptualized and identified three political cultures that can be found throughout the United States: individualistic, moralistic, and traditionalistic.[3]

• An *individualistic* political culture values politics as a means to improve a person's economic and social position. Individuals attempt to use government for their own ends, and those purposes at times may best be served through government restraint, by keeping government out of the way and letting the private marketplace allocate value. At other times, the politically influential have no reservation about championing government policies, such as a tax break, that benefit them and those like them. In a similar vein, they think it is totally appropriate to award government jobs, where permitted, to loyal political supporters. Both examples point to tangible individualized benefits resulting from successful political competition.

• A *moralistic* political culture accords government a positive role in society. Government intervention is seen as good precisely because it can advance the collective public welfare. Government can act to put the public interest over narrow personal interest. It can come to the assistance of those who are disadvantaged in the economic and social marketplace. A moralistic political culture encourages broad participation, including the voice of common folks, in determining what is in the public interest. Accordingly, the political debate focuses around issues rather than interests or personalities.

• A *traditionalistic* political culture is oriented toward protecting the interests of traditional elites, and that often entails preserving the status quo. Hierarchies are maintained, and the general public defers to traditional elites. As a result, mass participation tends to be low in comparison to the other two cultures.

These political cultures in the United States have their roots in colonial America. The commercial centers of the Atlantic Coast, notably New York, Philadelphia, and Baltimore, fostered a climate of individualism, favoring individual advancement over the public good. Traders actively competed for entrepreneurial opportunities. In that competition, individuals looked to government to either stay out of the way or selectively protect their commercial interests. A moralistic political culture emerged from Puritanism and New England's strong tradition of local government acting on behalf of the common interest, as articulated in town meetings. Finally, the privilege and segregation of the Southern plantation gave rise to a traditionalistic political culture built on deference and preservation of the status quo.

With westward migration, these cultures spread well beyond the original 13 colonies, to be mixed with the values and traditions of newly arrived immigrants. Migrating colonists often brought their distinctive political cultures to different parts of the same state. The proclivities of immigrants variously reinforced or competed with those of the early settlers. Regions experiencing little migration maintained their original political cultures.

The South, with its long tradition of isolation, had preserved a deeply imbued traditionalism, which has only been broken down over the past 40 years. Scandinavian immigration to Minnesota and North Dakota, along with German immigration to Wisconsin, reinforced the moralist leanings of those states' original migrant settlers. Both the Scandinavian and German social and political inheritance valued a positive role for government in society, a collective sense that government can improve the overall quality of life. The moralist traditions of the German Social Democratic Party readily took root in Milwaukee, and the citizenry elected a long string of Socialist mayors up to 1958. Migration from the Middle Atlantic states spread the ethos of individualism westward along the southern-tier Great Lakes states, and a heavy southern European immigration reinforced it.

As noted earlier, different parts of the same state have evolved different political cultures. Traditionalism still holds sway in northwestern Florida, including the capital city of Tallahassee, but the political culture of southern Florida, dominated by Miami, reflects the individualism of its Cuban immigrants. Similarly, the moralism of the San Francisco Bay Area can be contrasted with the individualism of southern California. Figure 2.1 shows Elazar's identification of political cultures across the United States.

Elazar's typology of political cultures provides a general expectation of the types of face-to-face interactions we can find in different states and their localities. Figure 2.2 illustrates how the different types of political culture relate to face-to-face interactions.

Those areas that have moralistic cultures prescribe a role for government in which public resources are actively used to address a fairly wide range of public problems. Citizens see government as a positive force and generally support enabling public officials. This type of political culture converges with the *responsive* category of face-to-face interactions, with high citizen cooperation and high government discretion.

The *compliant* pattern of citizen–government interaction fits the description of traditionalist political culture. Here citizens support the existing ways in which governments have operated. Governments do not seek or use much discretion.

A political culture that prizes individuals and a limited role for government can foster both confrontational and arbitrary face-to-face interactions. They can turn confrontational when public officials and their employees possess little discretion to interpret or bend the rules to fit individual circumstances. In these cases, people who look to government to advance their interests or to get out of the way altogether, depending on the circumstances, can be quick to take umbrage at what they see as unresponsiveness to their situations. Alternatively, when greater government discretion is present, individualism can lead to an arbitrariness of decision making. Rather than finding government broadly responsive to the public, a narrower particularistic responsiveness can be found in individualistic political cultures, one that often takes the appearance of *arbitrary* choice.

Culture describes general patterns and tendencies rather than the full universe of discrete acts. Elazar did not intend to account for the behavior of every community or every political actor in a geographic region. Likewise, we certainly do not consider the political culture of an area to exclude the possibility of face-to-face interactions that don't "fit." This caveat aside, political cultures do differ between regions and do affect the behaviors of both citizens and officials.

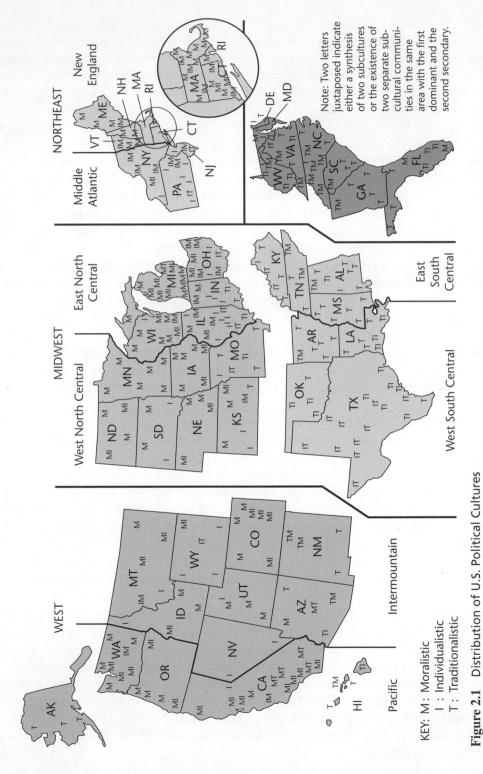

Figure 2.1 Distribution of U.S. Political Cultures

Source: Daniel J. Elazar, *American Federalism: A View from the States,* 2d ed. (New York: Harper & Row, 1972), p. 107. Reprinted with permission of Pearson Education, Inc.

KEY: M : Moralistic
I : Individualistic
T : Traditionalistic

Note: Two letters juxtaposed indicate either a synthesis of two subcultures or the existence of two separate subcultural communities in the same area with the first dominant and the second secondary.

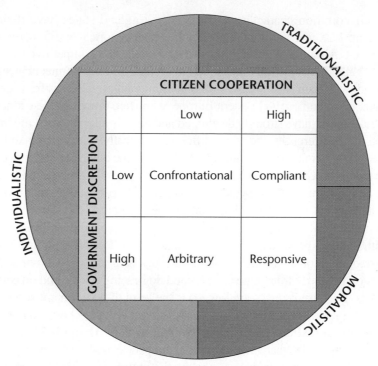

Figure 2.2 Political Culture and Face-to-Face Interactions

AN INTRODUCTORY TOUR OF THE STATES

The U.S. Census Bureau identifies four regions nationally: the Northeast, the South, the Midwest, and the West. Each has its own identifiable regional subdivisions. The following provides a social, economic, and political overview of the states.

The Northeast

The Northeast comprises New England and the Middle Atlantic states. The New England states share many common characteristics that give the area a regional distinctiveness, including early colonial settlement, strong local governments, ethnic-based politics, and strong regional identity. The concept of "I'm a New Englander" is embedded in all the region's residents, perhaps with the exception of those living in the southwestern third of Connecticut, who identify more with New York City. In comparison, not many Californians would take pride in identifying themselves as Westerners. They consider themselves Californians, or perhaps even northern or southern Californians, symbolizing the split identity of that state.

Politics in New England is serious business. It is a preoccupation not characteristic of any other region, and it has deep historical roots dating back to the local town meeting in colonial times. New Englanders expect to participate in political decision making, and they do so both locally and at the state level. New England has regional voter turnout second only to that of the Plains states.[4]

Despite their common characteristics, the New England states have their differences. Maine, New Hampshire, and Vermont retain much of their historical tradition, remaining largely rural and Protestant. Although New Hampshire has developed a competitive two-party system, Democrats have gained a decided advantage in Maine and Vermont. Connecticut, Massachusetts, and Rhode Island, with their much larger Catholic immigrant populations from Ireland, French-speaking Canada, and southern and eastern Europe, who were drawn by the economic promises of early industrialization, have strongly developed and heavily supported Democratic parties.[5]

Beyond political differences, the states differ economically. Maine is ranked in the bottom half of the states on per capita personal income. In contrast, the other five states in the region rank high in the top half, with Connecticut, Massachusetts, and New Hampshire all in the top 10.[6]

Residents of New England are taxed fairly heavily. Property taxes are among the highest in the nation, and all but New Hampshire rank in the top half of the states in per capita state and local revenue.[7] New Hampshire is the maverick when it comes to state taxation—ranking forty-eighth among the states in per capita state tax collections and last in state taxation per $100 of personal income.[8] It has neither a state personal income tax nor a state sales tax. Instead, it relies on revenues from state lotteries and dog-racing tracks, and on earnings from its state liquor stores. Because its taxes are low, so is the level of government services it provides. Among the New England states, New Hampshire is lowest in state school aid per pupil.[9] Former Massachusetts Governor Michael Dukakis, reflecting on New Hampshire's economic growth spurt in the mid-1980s, stated that, although New Hampshire might be "a nice place for talented young workers to live, its services were so shabby that it wasn't a nice place in which to be old or sick or handicapped or uneducated or down and out."[10] Vermont, although sharing many of the same topographical and social features as New Hampshire, provides a marked contrast. Vermont taxes and spends at much higher levels than does its eastern neighbor, consistently ranking among the top five states nationally in per capita spending and tax collection.[11]

The Middle Atlantic states—New York, New Jersey, and Pennsylvania—are part of the nation's "Foundry," as author Joel Garreau describes them in *The Nine Nations of North America*.[12] They are heavily populated and urban, heavily industrial, and energy dependent. In their large, older metropolitan areas, they share many of the problems of congestion, pollution, and infrastructure decay. They are also wealthier than most other parts of the United States, especially New Jersey and New York, which rank second and fifth, respectively, on per capita personal income. Pennsylvania ranks eighteenth. New York and New Jersey take advantage of that higher ability to pay: both states rank in the top ten nationally on per capita state and local revenues. New York tops the nation in its use of the personal income tax.

Politically, Democrats hold sway in New Jersey and New York, clearly benefiting from the strength and influence of organized labor. Although unions exercise considerable influence in Pennsylvania as well, the parties are more competitive there, even though Democrats have the edge.[13] Interest groups play a major part in Middle Atlantic politics, but voter turnout falls below the national median.

The South

There are different ways of identifying which states the South comprises. The South can be limited to the 11 states that formed the Confederacy: Alabama, Arkansas, Florida, Georgia, Louisiana, Mississippi, North Carolina, South Carolina, Tennessee, Texas, and Virginia. The

U.S. Bureau of the Census adds Delaware, Kentucky, Maryland, Oklahoma, and West Virginia to the list. Others might include the border state of Missouri. In fact, even though Kentucky and Missouri never seceded from the Union, their stars are included in the Confederacy's flag, representing their attempt at secession.

Despite the homogenizing influences of slavery and the Civil War, significant differences exist between Southern states such as Alabama, Arkansas, Georgia, Mississippi, North Carolina, South Carolina, and Tennessee, on the one hand, and Delaware, Florida, Maryland, and Virginia, on the other. The former epitomize the Deep South. They consistently rank toward the bottom on per capita income, state and local revenues, and state and local spending, as well as on levels of education[14] and unionization, with Alabama breaking ranks on unionization and tending toward the middle. They rank near the top on the percentage of the population living in poverty[15] and on infant mortality.[16] Politically, the Deep South states tend to have low voter turnout. The Democratic Party continues its dominance in state legislative races in Alabama, Arkansas, Mississippi, North Carolina, and West Virginia. The Republicans have maintained a slight edge in Tennessee and continue to have a solid advantage in Georgia and South Carolina. Regardless of the party in power, government functions are more centralized at the state level in the Deep South than in any other region nationally. Consequently, local governments tend to be weak.

In contrast, the states of Delaware, Florida, Maryland, and Virginia are more closely akin to their northern neighbors economically and socially. Politically, they have somewhat more competitive parties—except for Maryland, which is firmly in Democratic hands—but they do not differ that much on voter participation. Republicans have gained a decided advantage in Florida and Virginia.

Of the four West South Central states (Arkansas, Louisiana, Oklahoma, and Texas), Arkansas and Louisiana are the most similar socially and economically to the states of the Deep South. Arkansas ranks forty-fifth among the states in per capita personal income, and Louisiana is thirty-second. Like the other Southern states, both have a low percentage of unionized workers. Both states have increasingly developed competitive political parties, though Democrats maintain the advantage in Arkansas, and Republicans have gained the edge in Louisiana, led by their young rising star, Governor Bobby Jindal. In Louisiana, personalities have been as important as, and some say more important than, the issues.

Oklahoma and Texas, despite their significant economic and population growth over the past two decades, politically and socially fit in with the other Southern states. Although the Republican Party has realized gains in Oklahoma, producing a highly competitive party system, the biggest change has taken place in Texas, where the party system has evolved from Republican dominance to a competitive party system. Of the two, Texas taxes and spends at levels more in line with the rest of the South than with states farther north. Like the Southern states, both rank low on unionization.

Arkansas and Texas offer interesting contrasts. Although Arkansas's per capita personal income is 12 percent lower than that of Texas, Arkansas makes a much greater effort to generate taxes in support of public services. While Texas ranks 44th in state tax collections per $100 of personal income, Arkansas ranks 22nd.[17]

Several states classified as Southern have split personalities and allegiances. Virginia, West Virginia, Kentucky, and Florida are good examples. Northern Virginia has very little in common with most of the rest of the state. It is really an extended suburb of the District of Columbia, with per capita income well in excess of the state median. In contrast, southern Virginia, with its higher concentration of African Americans, rural areas, and lower per capita income, retains its Southern ways. Northern West Virginia is also a much different place from the rest of the state. With its industrial smokestacks and predominantly blue-collar work force, it resembles Pittsburgh or Youngstown, both economically and socially, more than it does Dixie. Given northern West Virginia's heavy industrial base, together with the coal mines of its southeast, it is not surprising that West Virginia, as a state, ranks far above its southern neighbors in unionization. Kentucky likewise has its northern industrial belt, which resembles that of Cincinnati or Dayton more than the blue-grass horse country of its central and southern part. Finally, south Florida, with its transplanted population and its heavy Cuban influence, is hardly reminiscent of the Old South. Party competition is stronger in south Florida than in the rest of the state, and its ethnic-based politics more resembles Chicago's than Tallahassee's.

The Midwest

The Midwest is the least homogeneous of the four regions. The Census Bureau divides the Midwest into two parts: the East North Central states (Ohio, Indiana, Illinois, Michigan, and Wisconsin) and the West North Central states (Minnesota, Iowa, Missouri, North Dakota, South Dakota, Nebraska, and Kansas). Another way of looking at the Midwest is to divide the states into the Midwestern Great Lakes states and the Plains states, which entails adding Minnesota to the East North Central division. This latter categorization makes sense given Minnesota's shared political culture with Wisconsin, deeply embedded in the farmer and labor Progressive tradition. Minnesota's politics today, with its pronounced Democratic leanings, more closely resembles Wisconsin's than that of its western or southern neighbors. Politics in Wisconsin and Minnesota are highly issue-oriented, reflecting the political heritage of their German and Scandinavian settlers. Voter turnout has been high in both states historically. Both states also have highly professional, well-paid bureaucracies. Wisconsin's political parties are more competitive than those of Minnesota.

Of the other Great Lakes states, Michigan is closer to Wisconsin and Minnesota in its politics. Michigan's politics also tend to be largely issue-oriented, reflecting similar patterns of ethnic in-migration, but its politics reflect a stronger management–labor cleavage than is found in the other two states. Its powerful labor unions, dominated by the United Auto Workers (UAW), significantly influence the policy positions taken by Michigan Democrats. After all, Michigan has the nation's sixth largest percentage of workers belonging to labor unions. Yet its rural and suburban areas have traditionally been the strongholds of the Republican Party, giving it a competitive party system statewide. It also enjoys high voter turnout.

Minnesota, Wisconsin, and Michigan tax and spend more heavily than their Great Lakes neighbors, again a likely product of a political culture that views government as playing a positive role in society by promoting the common good. When per capita state tax collections are used as a measure, Minnesota, Wisconsin, and Michigan rank in the top 20 nationally. In contrast, Illinois, Indiana, and Ohio rank in the bottom half of the states.

Illinois, Indiana, and Ohio share a different political culture from that of Minnesota, Wisconsin, and Michigan, one that is less concerned about how government can be used to improve the general welfare and that views politics as just another means by which individuals can improve their economic and social position. Such an environment fosters greater political patronage and corruption than is found in the more public-regarding cultures of Minnesota, Wisconsin, and Michigan. Although Republicans made advances in Ohio, the rise of Democrats in this swing state has produced a competitive party system. Both parties tend to be more interested in winning control of government to dispense its favors to the faithful than to enact a substantive policy agenda. Voter turnout is highest in the western Great Lakes states.

The Plains states comprise America's breadbasket. Its flat and fertile terrain yields a bounty of wheat to the north, and corn and soybeans to the south, and although only a small percentage of its residents are engaged in farming, the region is highly dependent economically on agriculture. Many of its major industries are involved in the production of agricultural supplies and machinery and in food processing. Commercial enterprises, such as banking and insurance, also have a significant agricultural and agribusiness base. Businesses in small-town, rural areas rise and fall with the economic welfare of agriculture. Per capita income for the region, as an average, falls toward the middle nationally.

The Plains states lack the major population centers of the Midwestern Great Lakes states. Kansas City and Des Moines dominate the region as centers of commerce and culture. Socially, the Plains states tend to be conservative and pragmatic. Missouri's state motto, "The Show Me State," could be applied to the region as a whole. Residents of the homogeneous Plains states prize the traditional values of hard work, family, and religion. The crime rate is lower than the national average, the divorce rate is well below the national average, and the abortion rate is less than the national average.[18]

Politically, the Plains states were significantly affected by the Populist movement of the late-nineteenth century. The Populist creed was built on active political participation by the populace as a whole, not just by the influential elites in society or those who happen to be organized into interest groups. That heritage is evident today because the Plains states continue to have the highest voter turnout of any region in the country. Another legacy of the Populist era is institutionalized direct democracy, in the form of the direct initiative and popular referendum, in which residents can petition to get propositions on the statewide ballot and enact them into law directly, without approval of the governor or legislature. Among the Plains states, Missouri, Nebraska, North Dakota, and South Dakota possess both the direct initiative and popular referendum.[19] In terms of party politics, the Plains are among the most Republican in the nation, with their state legislatures under strong control of the Republican Party.

The West

Western states make up two geographical divisions: the Intermountain states (Montana, Idaho, Wyoming, Colorado, New Mexico, Arizona, Utah, and Nevada) and the Pacific states (Washington, Oregon, and California). For convenience, the U.S. Bureau of the Census adds Alaska and Hawaii, but they probably should be treated as distinct and unique cases.

The Intermountain states are part of what Garreau refers to as the Empty Quarter of North America. This region can be differentiated from others on the basis of its sparse and diffused population, huge empty spaces, mineral resources, and uneven distribution of water. In addition, much of its land is owned and managed by the federal government. The federal government owns 86 percent of the land in Nevada and *at least* 43 percent in every other Intermountain state.[20] Federally held lands include national parks, national forests, national wildlife refuges, public lands (some of which are leased for grazing rights), and Indian reservations. This sizable federal presence has generated controversy in several of the states because a growing number of residents view this land as a potentially valuable tax resource and strive to obtain more local control over the region's future. Even beyond issues of land ownership and management, Intermountain residents do not like outsiders telling them what they can and cannot do. The successful movement to reinstate a national 65-mph speed limit on interstate highways had its impetus in the Intermountain states.

Environmental issues also divide residents of this region. The lines have been drawn between developers and preservationists on issues involving mining, environmental damage, and water diversion, but a clear majority sympathizes with development and the economic benefits that accompany it. However, national conservation groups and a majority in Congress see themselves as protectors of a national treasury belonging to all the people, not just those in the Intermountain states.

Given the controversy surrounding issues related to rapid development, politics in the region tend to be issue-oriented, but with a thick symbolic wrapping. Strong feelings on the public debate in the northern tier states bring voters to the polls in high percentages, contributing to a regional average that is in third place nationally, behind the Plains states and New England.

Although political scientists have traditionally classified the Intermountain states as two-party competitive—except for New Mexico and Colorado, which is given a sizable Democratic advantage—the Republicans have been able to hold onto the gains they made in the 1980s and 1990s in several Intermountain states, capitalizing on the region's aversion to government intervention in society and the economy. Idaho, Utah, and Wyoming have become Republican strongholds, but Democrats have improved their position in Arizona, even though Republicans hold a moderate advantage.

Except for New Mexico, all the Intermountain states possess the direct initiative and popular referendum. However, as in the Plains states, the mechanisms of direct democracy are not used as much as they are in the Pacific states.

Major political battles take place in the Pacific states over direct initiative propositions, which had their birth in the West Coast's Progressive Era early in the twentieth century. The political contests begin with petition drives aimed at getting the requisite number of signatures to qualify propositions on the statewide ballot and continue up to the general election, as supporters and opponents of initiatives work to see their positions prevail. Voters in the Pacific states make extensive use of the initiative. Between 1981 and 1999, for example, California alone voted on more initiatives than the voters of all the Intermountain and Plains states combined. Oregon was a close second nationally.[21] And the issues dealt with were far from insignificant, involving questions of tax limitation, abortion, legalization of marijuana, and the quarantine of AIDS patients.

Due significantly to the popular use of the direct initiative, political party organizations are weak in the Pacific states, especially in California and Oregon, but the parties themselves are competitive. Democrats in California have a decided advantage in legislative elections, but Republicans have managed to win the governorship for most of the 1980s and 1990s. The exception is Democrat Gray Davis, who won convincingly in 1998, putting both the legislature and the governorship in Democratic hands. Davis's victory in 2002 was a much narrower win over a weak Republican candidate. Davis's growing unpopularity led to his recall one year later, and voters later selected moderate Republican Arnold Schwarzenegger to replace him. Schwarzenegger won reelection easily in 2006. In 2010, however, Democrat Edmund G. "Jerry" Brown soundly defeated Republican Meg Whitman for the governorship.

California stands out as the behemoth of West Coast politics. But California's politics are far from homogeneous. If an imaginary line were drawn south of Santa Barbara, California could be divided into two discrete states politically: the one south of the line being politically conservative, Republican, and growth-oriented (despite an already considerable concentration), and the one north being much more liberal, Democratic, and preservation-oriented. Among the several factors dividing northern and southern California, a significant one is water. Northern California is water rich, and southern California is water poor. Obviously the south would like to divert more of the north's water, but the political intransigence of the north has forced southern California to look east for its water—water that is diverted from Utah and Arizona.

Washington and Oregon clearly resemble northern California in their politics. Garreau places Washington, Oregon, and northern California together socially and politically into what he calls Ecotopia, with San Francisco as its capital. Southern California is included within Mexamerica, with Los Angeles as its capital, dramatizing the social and political chasm between the two California state regions.

California traditionally has been the strongest of the three states economically, benefiting from a well-developed, highly diversified economy. That diversity—spanning high-technology industry, agriculture and agribusiness, service industries, and government employment—cushioned California against national economic shocks, including the Great Recession. Washington and Oregon are less diversified. Washington has been highly dependent on the fortunes of the aerospace industry, but has also been attracting a broad array of high-technology companies which are capitalizing on the increasing use of digital technologies by all sectors of the economy. The resulting increase in diversity has helped to make the state's economy more resilient. Oregon continues to be dependent on the wood products industry and has been negatively impacted by the slowdown in the housing market that began in 2006 and that has been exacerbated by the Great Recession. Of the three, Oregon is the poorest, ranking twenty-eighth in per capita personal income. California ranks eleventh and Washington ranks fourteenth nationally. All three states rank in the top half nationally on per capita state and local general expenditures, consistent with their longstanding commitment in support of public services.

Alaska and Hawaii

As mentioned earlier, Alaska and Hawaii each represent unique cases among the states. Alaska, with its sparse population, has by far the greatest per capita costs of state and local government of any state in the union, at over twice the national average. Alaska's ability to finance government spending is mostly tied to the price of oil and natural gas because half of Alaska's state tax revenues come from the severance tax (a tax applied when these resources are extracted, or severed, from the land). To compensate for the higher costs of government, Alaska's median household income is consistently among the highest in the country. Faced with major economic problems tied to the depressed price of oil in the mid- to late 1990s, Alaska's government was forced to engage in cutback management. Yet with the price of oil and natural gas increasing sharply in the mid- to late 2000s, state government in Alaska was awash in revenues. The Alaska state legislature began its 2006 session with a projected revenue surplus nearing $1 billion, which grew in subsequent years.[22] But toward the end of the decade, the sharply falling price of oil significantly reduced the revenue flow for oil-producing states such as Alaska. In the fall of 2010, Alaska's Department of Revenue projected that increasing demand for oil would drive prices up in fiscal year (FY) 2012 and beyond.

Largely a land of first-generation immigrants, Alaska has a competitive two-party system, which has also experienced a growth of alternative parties during the 1990s, most notably the Greens and Libertarians. Republicans, however, maintain an advantage. Voter turnout is surprisingly high in Alaska, given its diffuse population. Alaskans also possess the initiative and the popular referendum but have not used them to a significant extent.

Hawaii's economy is more diversified than Alaska's, although it relies primarily on agriculture and tourism. Tourism is its biggest business, and Hawaii has the second highest percentage of unionized workers in the nation. Its per capita income is higher than the national average, with an overall ranking of 11 in 2009. It spends slightly above the national average on a per capita basis. Hawaii provides the lowest property tax support for education in the nation but is above the national average in per pupil state school aid, consistent with Hawaii's tradition of highly centralized government services.

Hawaii's politics have a decided racial element[23]: Asian Americans hold most of the major political offices in Hawaii, and Asian Americans, 37 percent of the state's population, make up 42 percent of its registered voters.[24] After having a long-term lock on both the legislature and the governor's office, Democrats lost the governorship in 2002, raising Republican hopes for a more competitive party system. Although the Republican governor won reelection in 2006, Democrats expanded their legislative majority in the 2006 and 2008 elections, leading to the election of Democrat Neil Abercrombie as governor in 2010. Voter turnout in Hawaii is below the national average.

METROPOLITAN DEVELOPMENT

The United States has become an urbanized nation. Almost 80 percent of people in the United States live in metropolitan areas—areas that differ in their political culture, racial and ethnic composition, and economic base. Despite these differences, the metropolitan areas of America are in some ways becoming more alike. The major metropolitan areas of New York, Los Angeles, Chicago, San Francisco, Philadelphia, Detroit, and Boston—which together make up one-quarter of America's population—are experiencing increasingly similar social problems. But so are other metropolitan population centers such as Nashville, Salt Lake City, San Antonio, and Phoenix.

The geographic, residential, social, and economic faces of metropolitan America have changed and continue to change. Up to the Civil War, only eight cities had populations over 100,000. The major population centers along the Atlantic Coast seaboard prospered as leading mercantile centers engaged in shipping brokering, wholesaling, and banking.

The Emergence of the City

The decades after the Civil War were marked by rapid urban expansion that accompanied industrialization.[25] The modern American city emerged between 1860 and 1910; 50 cities had populations over 100,000 by 1910. Foreign immigrants swelled the ranks of city dwellers. Nearly 12 million immigrants came to the United States between 1870 and the beginning of the twentieth century. The foreign-born poured in from Germany, Poland, Italy, and Ireland. Ethnic-based neighborhoods sprang up as the new arrivals sought housing and support from family members who preceded them. By 1910, large ethnic enclaves had developed in most Northern industrial cities. Significant among them were the German community in Milwaukee, the Polish in Chicago, and the Irish in Boston. New York became the home of immigrants from many European nations, containing more foreign-born residents than any other city in the world. Large Italian neighborhoods could readily be distinguished from German and Irish ones.

The period from 1910 to 1950 saw dramatic growth in the population of the major industrial cities of the North, including New York, Boston, Chicago, Detroit, Philadelphia, Pittsburgh, St. Louis, Cleveland, and Milwaukee. That growth was aided by a large-scale migration of Southern blacks to the major industrial cities of the Northeast and Midwest. The growing mechanization of agriculture displaced many rural poor, who headed north, looking for industrial jobs and a better life. African Americans living along the southern Atlantic Coast settled in cities such as Philadelphia, Newark, Jersey City, New York, and Boston. Residents of the South Central states of Alabama, Mississippi, Tennessee, Arkansas, and Louisiana commonly followed the Mississippi River north to the Midwestern population centers of St. Louis, Cincinnati, Kansas City, Chicago, and Detroit. African Americans from Oklahoma and Texas headed west, primarily attracted to the growing cities of California like Oakland and the other affordable East Bay cities in the northern part of the state, and to Los Angeles and several surrounding communities in the south.

As had the European immigrants before them, the newly arrived African Americans tended to cluster together in definable neighborhoods mostly because of their desire for connection, their limited financial resources, restrictive zoning ordinances, and racial discrimination in housing. These factors, particularly the last named, also limited their mobility. Fledgling African American neighborhoods extended their reach into previously all-white areas, prompting many white residents to move to other parts of the city or to the suburbs. Yet flight to the suburbs was nothing new; it had its origins in the nineteenth century when rail transportation made it possible for the upper class to build new housing outside a growing inner urban core that became home to working-class European immigrants, who were viewed by the social elite as little more than riffraff. The prosperity of the 1920s provided the economic means for another exodus from the city. This time, however, out-migration was not limited to the upper class; the better off among the middle class joined in increasing numbers to escape the growing congestion, noise, dirt, and ethnic conflict of the industrial cities. The automobile made it possible for more people to live in new-found suburban serenity and commute to their city jobs. Already by 1930 the suburbs were growing faster than the cities.

The Rise of the Suburbs

Migration to the suburbs jumped dramatically again after World War II. Federal insurance programs carrying subsidized mortgage rates made home ownership available to more and more young families, who often chose to start their new lives in the suburbs. The National Defense Highway Act, enacted in the aftermath of the Soviet Union's successful launch of the *Sputnik* satellite in 1957, provided a major transfusion of federal funds to expand the nation's primary routes and the Interstate Highway System, greatly facilitating suburban commuting. For the first time, in 1963, more metropolitan-area residents lived in the suburbs than in the cities.

Suburban growth has continued unabated, right up to the present. In all parts of the nation, the suburbs of metropolitan areas have grown faster than their major cities. In fact while suburban areas grew, many central cities declined. Population and jobs were lost from many of the older, industrial cities of the Northeast and Midwest. Their greater metropolitan areas, however, typically continued to show modest growth because central-city decline was offset by the growth of surrounding communities and unincorporated areas. Although people moved their residences to the suburbs in the early stages of post–World War II suburbanization, their jobs remained in the city. They could live with others who looked like them and who shared their values, returning to the city for work, shopping, and cultural and athletic events. Nearby suburban malls, with their compactness and variety, proved to be attractive alternatives to shopping downtown. The trade-off for suburbanites was the daily commute to work, but improved highways, with free-flowing traffic in the early years, rendered it tolerable.

Racism also fostered suburbanization. For many whites, the suburbs provided refuge from the growing presence of minorities, whose numbers increased in inner-city areas, and whose widening residential spread was viewed by whites with alarm. Suburban communities also meant suburban schools—schools that were less crowded, contained fewer minority children, and were often newer than urban schools.

The 1960s brought with them another significant development: job opportunities followed people to the suburbs. Industries, looking for cheap land and hospitable surroundings, commonly chose to expand their operations outside central cities. They also increasingly relocated existing plants and businesses to the suburbs. Instead of attempting to modernize outmoded central-city plants, industrial developers often opted to build new state-of-the-art facilities on readily available and inexpensive suburban lands. These new locations commonly increased operating efficiencies, whether because of the move from multistory buildings to single-story, or the decreased transportation costs arising from closer proximity to major state and interstate highways.

As a result of these forces, suburban blue-collar jobs rose by almost 30 percent during the 1960s, while similar jobs declined by 13 percent in major cities. White-collar employment in the suburbs grew at an even faster rate, increasing by almost 70 percent, compared to a modest increase of 7 percent in the cities.[26]

This **migration of jobs** to the suburbs attracted even more suburban residential growth in the decades ahead. New housing developments sprang up almost overnight. They were quickly joined by new shopping complexes, medical buildings, parks, golf courses, and health and racket clubs. Suburban life became even more self-contained. Except for professional sporting events and cultural activities, the cities provided little allure to many new suburbanites. In fact, cities posed increasing threats. Rising crime and deteriorating city centers kept people away.

The Third Wave: Contemporary Edge Cities

It was not unusual for suburban communities, particularly those in the West and the South, to double or triple their population between 1970 and 1990. But such suburban growth was not limited to existing suburban cities and villages. Unincorporated areas blossomed, to be annexed by existing communities or to become cities and villages in their own right. Undeveloped land shrank dramatically or ceased to exist altogether. In many areas, development stretched almost uninterrupted across previously existing farmlands, orchards, and even desert terrain. These populous and commercially busy extensions into the frontier suggest something new, something different from the traditional suburban bedroom community. They do *not* resemble the old downtowns. They have developed an identity all their own—one characterized by planned residential developments, campus-like corporate offices and high-tech centers, and grand shopping plazas or tree-filled galleries. Joel Garreau refers to them as edge cities, the third wave of reaching for new frontiers, following the push to the cities and then to the suburbs.[27]

These new edge cities are at the forefront of contemporary metropolitan growth. They have become the new metropolitan cores, tied together by freeways, jetways, and communications

A suburban development. While planned developments can facilitate the provision of efficient government services, the emergence of numerous suburbs presents major challenges to officials in metropolitan areas.

job migration The movement of jobs from one location to another, usually applied to the movement of groups cross-regionally.

links. According to Garreau, two-thirds of U.S. office facilities are in edge cities, and four-fifths have been created since 1970.[28] New upscale residential developments, or planned communities, as they are called, put commuters in close proximity to their employment and recreation. Others commute from outside edge cities, replacing the old commute downtown. In edge cities, traffic bustles in all directions during extended rush-hour periods, unlike the unidirectional commute downtown or back to the suburbs.

To qualify as an edge city, an area must:

1. Have 5 million or more square feet of leasable office space (more, for example, than downtown Memphis has).
2. Have 600,000 or more square feet of leasable retail space.
3. Have more jobs than bedrooms.
4. Be perceived by the population as an identifiable place.
5. Look nothing like it did 30 years ago.[29]

Prominent examples of edge cities include the far East Bay area of San Francisco, stretching from the Concord/Walnut Creek area to the Pleasanton/Livermore area; Orange County, with Irvine at its center in southern California; the Tyson's Corner/Merrifield area of Fairfax County near Washington, D.C.; the Schaumberg/O'Hare Airport area north of Chicago; the Perimeter Center area, at the northern tip of Atlanta's beltway; and Boston's high-tech corridor in the area around Route 128 and the Massachusetts Turnpike.

Although these newer metropolitan centers retain their glitter, a number of the aging, traditional suburbs have begun to take on the characteristics of older cities. The once-new residential and commercial areas have deteriorated with age. Their more affluent residents have moved out, in search of environments more in tune with their social status. In their place have come the less advantaged, looking to improve their own living conditions. The conventional portrait of the white, middle-class suburb is no longer contemporary. Older, working-class suburbs, whether they be integrated or the providence of a dominant racial or ethnic group, can be found in diverse metropolitan areas throughout the United States.

City Gentrification

Countering this broad push outward is a smaller yet vibrant return to the central city in many metropolitan areas across the United States. And the characteristics of those moving downtown are changing. Although the poorer areas of central cities still attract newcomers looking for cheap housing and a job, or for the social connections and support that ethnic neighborhoods provide, others look to downtown as an escape from the life of a commuter. Increasingly, young professionals are trading their congested commute for a place closer to work and to the social and cultural amenities that cities offer. In so doing, they are moving into neighborhoods on the fringe of business centers—raising housing and rental prices, and displacing poorer residents from those areas.

City policymakers are doing what they can to make central cities more attractive to professionals with economic means. Mayors and city councils have increasingly come to support a wide array of urban rejuvenation projects, prominently including sports stadiums, convention and performing arts centers, and pedestrian malls. Policymakers in a number of cities have combined these efforts with an emphasis on historic preservation.

Denver offers a prime example. The Rockies' new baseball stadium, Coors Field, serves as an anchor for downtown redevelopment. Located in a once-dilapidated fringe area that many referred to as Skid Row, the new ballpark in LoDo (lower downtown), as it is now called, is in the middle of a bustling mixed-use neighborhood of shops, restaurants, and loft conversions. It is a neighborhood that has retained the historic flavor of its original architecture.

The economic effects of this transition have been remarkable. In the late 1980s, property went for about $10 a foot. A decade later it cost more than $80 a foot, with vacancies few and far between.[30] Businesses and residents who can afford to pay higher prices have benefited from this urban gentrification. Those who cannot pay find themselves displaced and searching for affordable housing—some joining the ranks of the homeless. The city's treasury benefited from a greatly expanded property tax base.

Similar developments have taken place in other urban centers, including those of Baltimore, Cleveland, Detroit, Salt Lake City, Phoenix, and Seattle, to name a few prominent examples. In each case, it has been the goal of policymakers to attract people downtown for recreation and business, and to provide the infrastructure that lures them to live there. Urban policymakers realize that trade-offs exist in city life. Convenience and proximity to attractions compete with the higher crime and noise found in central cities. Mayors and councils are hoping that pedestrian-friendly development and more aggressive neighborhood policing efforts shift that balance in favor of downtown reinvigoration.

Exploring the Web

Positioning on Growth

Should local governments plan and regulate growth in their communities, or should that be left to individual choices and market forces?

■ Check out the American Planning Association's website, www.planning.org, to learn how professional planners approach this issue. You may even want to see about educational opportunities and the careers for planners.

■ Contrast the views of the Sierra Club (www.sierraclub.org), which opposes unplanned growth that results in urban sprawl, and two groups promoting economic development: the Council for Urban Economic Development (www.cued.org) and the National Association of Development Organizations (www.nado.org). These last two groups bring together the interests of cities and counties, chambers of commerce, real estate developers, utilities, banks, and other prodevelopment groups.

■ Look at the websites of two organizations, the International Downtown Association (www.ida-downtown.org) and the Congress for the New Urbanism (www.cnu.org), both of which support development but want it to occur in ways that promote compact, walkable, mixed-use neighborhoods (with shops, offices, and homes interspersed) and offer access to mass transit.

PATTERNS OF INTERREGIONAL GROWTH AND DECLINE

Over 50 percent of the people in the United States today live in the suburbs, another 30 percent live in the central cities of metropolitan areas, and the remainder live outside metropolitan areas altogether. Many of these major cities continue to lose population to the suburbs and edge cities, and to other sections of the nation. Major cities affected include those in the industrial Northeast and Midwest. Table 2.1 shows the extent of that loss. Buffalo, Cleveland, Detroit, Pittsburgh, and St. Louis lost about 40 percent of their populations between 1970 and 2010. Whether efforts to rejuvenate downtown areas and attract an inward flow of young professionals will be successful in reversing this trend remains to be seen.

Racial and ethnic minorities were the ones most likely to stay in the declining cities, as Table 2.2 suggests. They often lacked the resources and opportunities that could allow them

Table 2.1 Population Decline in Major Cities

City	1970	2010	Percentage Change
Baltimore, Md.	905,000	637,418	−30
Buffalo, N.Y.	463,000	270,240	−42
Chicago, Ill.	3,369,000	2,851,268	−15
Cleveland, Ohio	751,000	431,369	−43
Detroit, Mich.	1,514,000	911,921	−40
Milwaukee, Wis.	717,000	605,013	−16
Newark, N.J.	382,000	278,154	−27
Philadelphia, Pa.	1,949,000	1,547,297	−21
Pittsburgh, Pa.	520,000	311,647	−40
St. Louis, Mo.	622,000	356,587	−43

Source: Bureau of the Census, U.S. Department of Commerce.

Table 2.2 African Americans as Percentage of a City Population

City	1970	2010	Percentage Change
Baltimore, Md.	46	64	39
Buffalo, N.Y.	20	39	95
Chicago, Ill.	33	33	0
Cleveland, Ohio	38	53	40
Detroit, Mich.	44	83	89
Milwaukee, Wis.	15	40	167
Newark, N.J.	54	52	−4
Philadelphia, Pa.	34	43	26
Pittsburgh, Pa.	20	26	30
St. Louis, Mo.	41	44	7

Source: Bureau of the Census, U.S. Department of Commerce.

to join the exodus. Although consistent statistical breakdowns on race and ethnicity are not available dating back to 1970, longitudinal data do exist for African Americans and are made available after each decennial census. The percentage of African Americans increased in nearly all of the listed cities experiencing population decline. They increased their percentage of Milwaukee's population by 167 percent between 1970 and 2010, the greatest relative increase of any city listed. Detroit's African American residents increased their relative population share by 89 percent over those years, comprising over four-fifths of Detroit's population by 2010.

As jobs dried up at home, many Americans pulled up stakes and sought employment opportunities in those sections of the country experiencing the greatest economic growth. For Northerners, that meant heading to the West and the South (Figure 2.3). Three states—California, Florida, and Texas—accounted for about half the population growth in the United States between 1970 and 2010.

The deep national recession of 1981–1982 took its toll on industrial jobs in the upper Midwest as demands for pig iron, steel, rubber, glass, industrial machinery, and automobiles and other vehicles fell off precipitously. The Midwest lost almost 1.2 million jobs between 1980 and 1983 alone, with five East North Central states accounting for 986,000 lost jobs: Illinois (319,000), Ohio (274,000), Michigan (220,000), Indiana (100,000), and

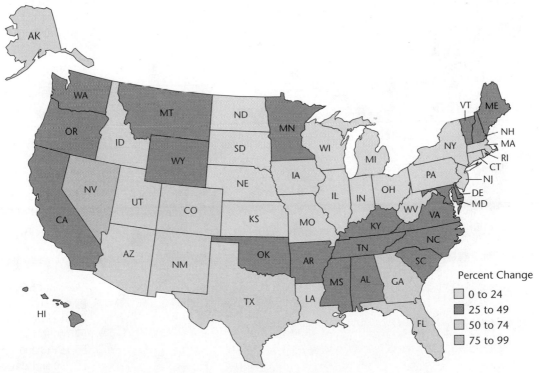

Figure 2.3 Change in Total Population, 1970–2010
Source: Bureau of the Census, U.S. Department of Commerce.

Wisconsin (73,000). Outside the Midwest, other states suffering sizable employment reductions included Pennsylvania (229,000), West Virginia (64,000), and Kentucky (62,000)[31] (see Figure 2.4).

At the same time that unemployment reached new highs since that of the Great Depression in the industrial states of the Snowbelt, business was booming in the energy-producing states that did not rely on coal. Laid-off steel and auto workers from Pennsylvania and Michigan flocked to oilfield jobs, where many employers paid $3,000 a month. Opportunities in the oil and natural gas industries appeared almost unlimited in the early 1980s as rapidly rising prices encouraged exploration and production. The energy boom meant prosperity for states such as Alaska, Texas, Louisiana, Oklahoma, and Wyoming. The highest riders were clearly Alaska, Texas, and Louisiana. Rapidly expanding severance tax revenues swelled their state treasuries. For them, it was a period of boom compared to the bust conditions in the North's heavy industrial belt.

An upturn in the nation's economy reawakened demand for industrial products. Many of the states hardest hit by the 1981–1982 recession had turned things around by the mid-1980s. For example, Pennsylvania's unemployment rate dropped from a high of 11.8 percent in 1983 to 6.8 percent in 1986. Michigan's rate fell from its 1982 high of 15.5 percent

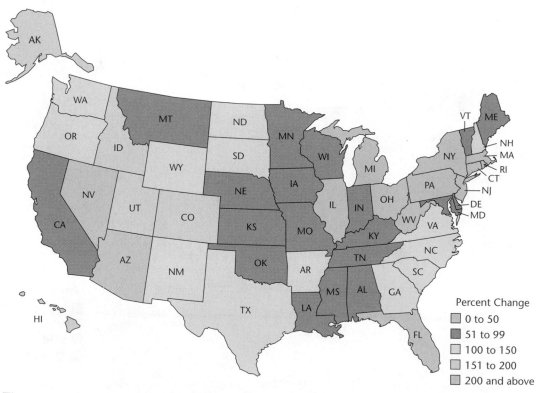

Figure 2.4 Change in Non-Farm Employment, 1970–2010
Source: Bureau of the Census, U.S. Department of Commerce.

to 8.8 percent in 1986. Ohio's fell from 12.5 to 8.1 percent, and Wisconsin's dropped from 10.7 to 7.0 percent. West Virginia's employment picture also brightened somewhat from its 1983 unemployment high of 18 percent, but the continued depressed price of coal kept it from dropping any lower than 11.8 percent in 1986.[32]

Just as fortunes improved for the industrial states, they worsened for both the energy-producing and agricultural states. The downturn in agriculture—associated with reduced international demand, depressed commodity prices, and high levels of farm debt—proved to be shorter than that facing the energy-related industries. Yet the mid-decade agricultural recession hit farmers hard, depressing the fortunes of both farmers and those in agribusiness. The U.S. dollar's weakness toward the end of the decade and into the 1990s, however, made American agricultural commodities and farm implements more financially attractive in international markets, and thus improved agriculture's economic condition. For the energy-producing states, the breakdown of cartelized price controls on oil resulted in a sinking price of oil, which dropped from a January 1985 high of $27 per barrel to a 1987 low of $15 per barrel.

Despite the effects of fluctuating energy prices, the West and the South enjoyed an underlying stability of economic and population growth during the 1970s and 1980s. And as shown in Figure 2.5, the West continued to lead the nation in growth during the 2000s.

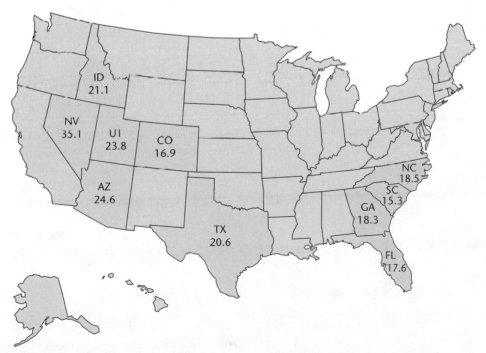

Figure 2.5 The 10 Fastest Growing States in the 2000s, Percentage Population Change: 2000–2010
Source: Bureau of the Census, U.S. Department of Commerce.

The West especially had its share of economic success stories. Several of the nation's fastest growing metropolitan areas during the past three decades have built their expansion on the fortunes of high technology. Austin, Texas, is no longer considered just a university town; it has become a major technology center of the Southwest, having attracted Texas Instruments, Motorola, Data General, Tracor, and IBM. Its metropolitan population grew from 360,000 in 1970 to over 1.7 million by 2009, a striking increase of 374 percent. Metropolitan San Jose, in the heart of California's Silicon Valley, has accumulated the highest concentration of high-technology industries in the world, including Apple, Cisco Systems, Intel, National Semiconductor, IBM, Hewlett-Packard, Lockheed, Oracle, and Yahoo. Between 1970 and 2009, the San Jose metropolitan area added almost 750,000 residents. These examples could readily be expanded to include other Western high-technology growth centers such as Albuquerque, Colorado Springs, and Tucson.

In addition to these prominent economic success stories, most major Western cities and their metropolitan areas have continued to grow (see Table 2.3). Those cities remaining relatively flat in population, such as San Francisco and Seattle, have done so essentially because they ran out of land available for expansion. Their greater metropolitan areas, however, which have the physical potential to accommodate development, have experienced tremendous growth.

Table 2.3   Centers of Population Growth

	City			Metropolitan Area		
	1970	**2009**	**Percentage Change**	**1970**	**2009**	**Percentage Change**
Albuquerque, N.Mex.	245,000	529,219	116	316,000	857,903	171
Austin, Tex.	254,000	786,386	210	360,000	1,705,075	374
Bakersfield, Calif.	70,000	324,463	364	330,000	807,407	145
Colorado Springs, Colo.	136,000	399,827	194	236,000	626,227	165
Dallas, Tex.	844,000	1,299,542	54	2,352,000	6,447,615	174
El Paso, Tex.	322,000	620,456	93	359,000	751,296	109
Fresno, Calif.	166,000	479,918	189	413,000	915,267	122
Houston, Tex.	1,234,000	2,257,926	83	1,891,000	5,867,489	210
Las Vegas, Nev.	126,000	567,641	351	273,000	1,902,834	597
Modesto, Calif.	62,000	202,743	227	195,000	510,385	162
Phoenix, Ariz.	584,000	1,593,659	173	971,000	4,364,094	349
Sacramento, Calif.	257,000	466,676	82	848,000	2,127,355	151
San Antonio, Tex.	654,000	1,373,668	110	888,000	2,072,128	133
San Diego, Calif.	697,000	1,306,300	87	1,358,000	3,053,793	125
Stockton, Calif.	110,000	287,578	161	291,000	674,860	132
Tucson, Ariz.	263,000	543,910	107	352,000	1,020,200	190

Source: Bureau of the Census, U.S. Department of Commerce.

The greatest growth in the West has taken place in its small and midsize communities. For evidence one need simply look at the California cities and metropolitan areas of Bakersfield, Fresno, Modesto, Sacramento, and Stockton. Arizona, Nevada, and Texas offer other illustrations of marked population growth in the West.

Suburban Phoenix provides a dramatic example of metropolitan growth. Whereas the population of Phoenix more than doubled, adding over a million residents between 1970 and 2009, its greater metropolitan area grew by 349 percent, adding 3.4 million residents, led by the suburban communities of Mesa, Tempe, and Scottsdale. The Las Vegas metropolitan area, Nevada's largest, also experienced remarkable population growth during the same period—expanding by a staggering 597 percent and adding over 1.6 million residents. Like California, Texas offers several areas of notable growth, with the greatest occurring in the Dallas–Fort Worth and Houston areas. The Dallas–Fort Worth area added almost 4.1 million residents between 1970 and 2009. The fastest growth took place in its suburban communities of Plano, Arlington, and Garland. In comparison, Houston's metropolitan area increased by 210 percent, adding almost 4 million residents; however, most of that increase occurred before declining oil prices in the mid-1980s dulled the economic attractiveness of the Houston area.

Outside the West, Florida has seen the greatest population growth, and it has been widespread and predominantly suburban. The largest population increases have occurred in the Miami–Fort Lauderdale–Hollywood area, the Tampa–Clearwater–St. Petersburg area, the Orlando area, and the West Palm Beach–Boca Raton–Del Ray area. Yet the fastest growth could be found in the Fort Myers–Cape Coral and the Fort Pierce areas.

Just as the 1981–1982 recession contributed to America's economic and demographic reshaping, the 1990–1991 recession showed signs of playing a similar role. Although less severe than that of the early 1980s, it was broader in its impact. Whereas the 1981–1982 recession hit production workers the hardest, that of the early 1990s cut across a much wider range of industries and occupations. It also affected more states. Only a few states, most prominently those of the Intermountain region, were immune from its effects. Of all regions of the country, the New England and Middle Atlantic states suffered the most. With the exception of Maine, they all can be found in the bottom 10 states on nonfarm employment growth and real gross state product. Other states hurt by the 1990–1991 recession include Delaware, Maryland, Missouri, Oklahoma, South Carolina, and Virginia. Unlike the 1981–1982 recession, the industrial Great Lakes states, with the exception of Ohio, fared much better than their Northeastern counterparts. In fact, Wisconsin and Indiana were among the better economic performers nationally.

The surprise of the 1990–1991 recession was the performance of California, whose economic diversity has traditionally insulated its residents from national economic downturns. California joined the Northeastern states toward the bottom on all indicators of economic well-being, including growth of employment, gross state product, and personal income. Despite signs of limited recovery by mid-decade, some of California's recession refugees headed east to take advantage of the economic prosperity of the Intermountain states.[33] Moderately strong recovery in the second half of the 1990s once again attracted a net influx of residents into California.

Faced with a recession-induced imbalance between revenues and budgeted expenditures, 29 states were forced to reduce their enacted budgets during FY 1990–1991. That number rose to 35 during the following year, evidence of the widespread recessionary impact.[34] States also had to increase taxes to keep budgets in balance. California led the nation, increasing taxes and fees by $7.3 billion in FY 1991 and by $9.1 billion in FY 1992.

By 1998, states were accumulating large end-of-year surpluses and were cutting taxes instead of raising them. Surpluses as a percentage of expenditures ranged from nearly 6 percent to 9 percent between FY 1998 and FY 2000, despite widespread state actions to cut taxes in a period of strong economic growth. Between 1998 and 2000 alone, tax cuts amounted to over $17 billion, though state budgets increased by about 6 percent during that same time.[35]

The national recession of 2001 changed things. Since state legislatures enacted budgets for FY 2002, 40 states had to address budget shortfalls totaling nearly $40 billion. State legislatures were forced to cut spending and raise taxes. Slow economic growth continued to put pressure on state budgets in 2003.[36] State legislatures made $12 billion in additional cuts during the course of FY 2003, after they had adopted what they thought were balanced budgets.[37]

A strong national economic recovery provided a much brighter revenue picture. By 2006, state budgets were healthier than they had been in five years. No state ended FY 2005 with a deficit, and year-end aggregate balances totaled $37 billion.[38]

By the time legislatures convened in early 2007 to consider gubernatorial budget recommendations for FY 2008, economic storm clouds began to gather on the horizon. Leading economic indicators declined and the housing industry weakened. New home construction and sales of existing homes both fell in 2006, leading to an even sharper drop in 2007, when they fell an average of 17 percent from their peak in 2006. Homeowners, many with subprime and adjustable-rate loans, increasingly found themselves with homes worth less than what they owed on their mortgages. They were increasingly delinquent, or in default, in their mortgage payments, and facing foreclosure. In fact, foreclosures totaled 2.2 million nationwide in 2007, up by 70 percent from 2006. Foreclosures rose to 3 million in 2008, up by 81 percent from 2007 and by a dramatic 225 percent from 2006.[39] And rising foreclosures in neighborhoods, with the commonly associated neglect of the foreclosed properties, contributed to further price declines. Areas especially hard hit included Las Vegas; California's desert valleys east of Los Angeles and its midstate central valley communities such as Fresno and Stockton; southern Florida; and metropolitan Phoenix and Denver.

In this precarious economic setting, state legislatures were forced to use a combination of spending cuts and revenue increases to close a nearly $75 billion budget gap for FY 2009 and a $89.3 billion gap for FY 2010.[40] Projections by legislative fiscal officers pointed to the need to reduce revenue shortfalls for FY 2011 by another $89.9 billion across the states, with the biggest percentage shortfalls relative to budget expected in Illinois (12.2 percent) and Alabama (8 percent).[41]

DEBATING THE ISSUES

Is immigration a good or bad thing?

Some Americans view immigration as posing a threat to America's traditional way of life. They see immigrants either as becoming dependent on public welfare or taking jobs from native-born citizens. Others look at immigration much more positively. For them, it embodies the pursuit of the American dream. Immigrants do take jobs, but some bring highly technical skills with them to help meet the expanding needs of the U.S. information industries, while other, less-skilled newcomers willingly take jobs toward the bottom of the employment chain—jobs often disdained by the native born.

Studies show that both perspectives have some validity. Immigrants initially are more dependent on public assistance than are Americans born in this country. Yet as they establish themselves in the United States, that dependence declines. And after 20 years, the earning power of immigrants parallels that of the natives.

With the immigrant population swelling in states such as California, New York, Florida, Texas, and Illinois, how do you view immigrants?

Is continued immigration at the current pace in the nation's best interest? What about your state's interest?

Explore these questions on the Internet:
Center for Immigration Studies, *www.cis.org*
National Immigration Forum, *www.immigrationforum.org*
Center for Migration Studies, *http://cmsny.org*

THE NEW IMMIGRATION AND METROPOLITAN GROWTH

Along with interregional migration, immigration again must be examined as a significant force promoting metropolitan-area population growth. Approximately 1 million people gain permanent residency in the United States every year; add to that another half million illegal immigrants. Thus, the U.S. economy has to absorb 1.5 million new residents a year.[42] Illegal aliens alone comprise about 5 percent of America's work force, largely filling low-wage jobs. Illegal immigrants hold half of the jobs in agriculture, one-quarter of the jobs in construction and groundskeeping, and one-fifth of those in food service.[43] Three-fourths of the U.S. immigrant population resides in just six states: California, New York, Texas, Florida, New Jersey, and Illinois.

Although the federal government has the authority to set immigration policy nationally, immigrant flows into the United States burden state and local governments. Immigrants place additional demands on public treasuries, putting pressure on welfare, social services, medical assistance, and schools. With them comes increased demand for bilingual education, and, given the range of languages spoken, the attendant costs are significant. Rising social problems can also accompany increased immigration. Existing residents may look at immigrants as new competitors in an already tight job market. In addition, the strains of enculturation can prompt newly arrived youth to coalesce into gangs in order to survive in a multiracial and multi-ethnic urban environment. Nevertheless, numerous success stories abound of immigrants who work hard and educate their children.

Concerns about the social and fiscal costs of illegal immigration prompted California voters in 1994 to pass a ballot initiative, Proposition 187, denying public services to nearly 1.5 million illegal aliens. A federal court, however, ruled California's new law unconstitutional. A stream of recent legislation will likely test constitutional standards once again. In 2006, Arizona and Illinois passed laws requiring U.S. citizenship or legal immigrant status to receive state-financed health benefits. Kansas passed legislation limiting public services and benefits to legal residents of the state. Wisconsin did the same, but Governor Jim Doyle, a Democrat, vetoed the Republican-controlled legislature's action. In 2010, Arizona broke new ground on the immigration issue when it passed a law making failure to carry immigration-status documentation a crime and giving police broad powers to detain any person suspected of being in the country illegally. Even though the Arizona law is being challenged in court at the time of this writing, other states are grappling with similar legislation. In 2011, Georgia, South Carolina, and Utah passed laws giving more power to police to check whether individuals are illegal immigrants. Indiana's legislation penalizes employers who knowingly hire illegals and denies unemployment benefits to illegal immigrants. An Alabama measure was also signed into law in 2011 requiring public schools to determine the immigration status of students.

THE CONSEQUENCES OF GROWTH AND DECLINE

Economic growth means a bigger tax base for state and local governments. New and expanded industries and businesses not only mean new jobs for an area, they also mean an enlarged property base to be taxed by local jurisdictions. The new jobs generate increased personal income that can be subject to state and local income taxes. A significant influx of new workers often requires new housing developments to accommodate them. Local governments, in turn, are able to tax these new properties and structures. As residential areas grow, retail establishments crop up to serve the expanded community, further broadening the property tax base. That commercial activity enriches state and local sales tax coffers. Thus, economic growth means not only public revenue enhancement but also rising demands for expanded government services. Residential and commercial growth requires major investment in the infrastructure, including streets, sewers, sidewalks, traffic signals, and parks. Growth also brings demands for expanded public services, such as police and fire protection, street cleaning and maintenance, and garbage collection. Residential growth puts pressure on the schools, frequently requiring the construction of new schools or the expansion of existing ones.

These associated costs of growth can be met as long as sufficient revenue expansion accompanies that growth. Rising employment provides the financial means. But what happens when population increases without adequate jobs to employ prospective workers?

Dependence on public services rises, but personal income does not. Without good jobs, new residents are unable to buy new homes or make other major purchases. Thus, population growth, by itself, is not a panacea. Government officials seek employment-led population growth.

In comparison, **declining jurisdictions** see their tax bases shrink. Individuals displaced from their jobs often go elsewhere to seek employment. Those who have not been attached to the labor force tend to stay behind, continuing their dependence on government programs and increasing the relative percentage of those who are receiving but not contributing commensurately. At the same time, declining jurisdictions usually are unable to reduce the costs of government in proportion to employment and population loss. They are left with fixed overhead costs—most of them in personnel—that support declining levels of services. Ironically, cities losing population usually have ample low-cost housing available, reflecting dampened demand. Low-cost housing proves attractive to the disadvantaged, who are frequently minorities and immigrants seeking new opportunity. This offsetting population growth, however, places added demands on an already overextended public treasury. Facing declining revenues and stable or rising public expenditures, local governments are confronted with a dilemma. They need to increase taxes to balance their budgets, but tax increases make them even less attractive for economic development and the jobs that come with it.

The suburbs and edge cities of the United States appear to have a considerable advantage in this competition for economic development. In a real sense, the rich get richer, and the problems mount for those jurisdictions with low budgets. Yet recent history suggests that there may be limits to growth. Growth at the extreme means congestion, increased pollution, crowded classrooms, and heightened stress of daily living. These unwanted conditions of the sought-after good life may prompt a search for a better alternative. It is unlikely the escape will be back to the city, with its own congestion and crime. The more likely scenario is that people will look for a new frontier, pushing edge cities even farther out, or they will turn to presently underpopulated, pristine areas that hold the promise of an improved quality of life. Continued technological advances in communications and transportation may make that a reality for those who can make the transition. Some will remain where they are out of choice; others will stay put because they lack the resources or opportunities that make mobility possible. Unfortunately, there are few signs that life will get better for those remaining behind.

SUMMARY AND CONCLUSIONS

The states are diverse, having been shaped by their historical patterns of settlement, patterns of immigration and migration, topography and natural resources, economics, demography, religious leanings, political movements, and political culture. Despite that diversity, Americans subscribe to a set of deep-rooted values, including popular sovereignty, limited government, the rule of law, individual liberty, equality, and equality of opportunity.

---

declining jurisdictions Governmental jurisdictions facing the loss of population and employment, usually accompanied by a declining tax base.

These values provide a normative foundation that underlies public policy making at all levels of American government.

Americans are influenced by the political cultures in which they were raised and live. Political culture shapes how residents view the appropriate role of government, how they prioritize government programs, and the extent to which they participate in politics. Although political cultures can be found to vary regionally, they can also differ among states within the same region and even within the same state, reflecting distinctive experiences and traditions.

Regardless of these regional and interstate differences, the United States has become an urbanized nation. Three out of four people in the United States live in metropolitan areas—areas that differ in their political cultures, economies, and racial and ethnic composition. The path to metropolitan development has followed four phases: our nation's early rural roots, the building of great cities, the rise of the suburbs, and the recent emergence of edge cities.

Suburban and edge-city growth has come at the expense of many cities. People and jobs have migrated from center cities to outlying areas, leaving cities with reduced levels of personal income, higher concentrations of minority populations, reduced resources to support government programs, and increased crime. The large cities of the Northeast and the industrial Midwest have lost population and jobs to the growing areas of the Sunbelt—the West and the South. Three states alone—California, Florida, and Texas—accounted for about half the population growth in the United States between 1970 and 2010.

The 1990–1991 recession and its slow-growth recovery weakened California's magnetic attractiveness. The New England and Mid-Atlantic states also were hard hit. In contrast, the Intermountain states were relatively insulated from the national recession, leading the nation in economic growth. Strong post recessionary growth turned the fiscal situation around in most states by the mid-1990s, and continued prosperity allowed many states to accumulate reserves and cut taxes throughout the remainder of the decade. The recession of 2001 changed things, plunging many states into budget shortfalls—a phenomenon that continued into 2003. As the economy recovered, so did state revenues. By mid-decade, states had turned budget shortfalls into budget surpluses. However, fortunes reversed in many states toward the decade's end, when a sagging national economy, falling home prices, and rising mortgage defaults sent state budgets in a good part of the nation back into revenue shortfalls. The Great Recession of 2007–2009 impacted the states in both the short term, from the downturn in the housing market, and the long term, from high and sustained unemployment.

Along with interregional migration, immigration is another contemporary force promoting metropolitan-area growth. That immigration has been concentrated in six states: California, New York, Texas, Florida, New Jersey, and Illinois, in descending order. For California, an influx of immigrants has added to the state's current economic and social problems because these new arrivals have added pressures on welfare, social services, medical assistance programs, and schools.

State and local governments want population growth led by economic development. Expanded employment provides the revenues necessary for governments to meet the increased service needs of a growing populace. Population growth without economic development places additional unfunded burdens on government. Employment and population loss results in reduced tax revenues. Declining jurisdictions, facing fixed overhead costs, are unable to reduce the costs of government in proportion to their loss in revenue.

The suburbs and edge cities of the United States have enjoyed an advantage in the competition for economic development—an advantage that is likely to continue. Advances in communications and transportation will probably continue to push development outward, toward a new frontier, for those who have the resources or opportunities to make the transition. Some will remain where they are out of choice; others will stay put because they lack a viable option.

Discussion Questions

1. Discuss the concept of political culture and describe prominent regional differences. Discuss the roots of these observed differences.

2. In what ways are the states becoming more alike? What elements of distinctiveness remain?

3. What factors have prompted dramatic population and employment growth in the South and West since 1970? Has that growth come at the expense of the North and East?

4. What trade-offs do local governments face when their local economies and populations grow? What significant changes have occurred within metropolitan areas since World War II? With what effects and implications?

Glossary

declining jurisdictions 45
equality 19
equality of opportunity 19

individual liberty 19
job migration 33
limited government 18

political culture 19
popular sovereignty 18
rule of law 18

Endnotes

1. *Statistical Abstract of the United States*, 2011 and previous editions (Washington, D.C.: Bureau of the Census, U.S. Department of Commerce).

2. United States Census Bureau, The 2011 Statistical Abstract, 258, http://www.census.gov/compendia/statab/2011/tables/11s0258.pdf.

3. Daniel J. Elazar, *American Federalism: A View from the States*, 2d ed. (New York: Harper & Row, 1972), 84–85.

4. *Statistical Abstract of the United States*, 2008, 257. This source also is used for subsequent references to voter turnout by state.

5. John F. Bibby, *Politics, Parties, and Elections in America*, 5th ed. (New York: Wadsworth Publishing Company, 2002). This source also is used for subsequent references to the relative competitiveness of political parties among the states, updated by an analysis of the 2008 general election.

6. *Statistical Abstract of the United States*, 2011, 445. This source also is used for subsequent references to state rankings on per capita personal income.

7. *Abstract of the United States*, 2008, 273–274. This source also is used for subsequent references to state rankings on per capita state and local revenue.

8. See Table 18.2 of this text. This source also is used for subsequent references to rankings on per capita state tax collections and per $100 of personal income.

9. *Digest of Education Statistics*, 2001 (Washington, D.C.: National Center for Education Statistics, U.S. Department of Education, 2001), Table 159. This source also is used for subsequent references to state ranking on per pupil state school aid.

10. Quoted in Joel Garreau, *The Nine Nations of North America* (Boston, Mass.: Houghton Mifflin, 1981), 28.

11. See Tables 18.1 and 18.2 of this text. Table 18.2 also is used for subsequent references to rankings of state tax effort.

12. Garreau, *The Nine Nations of North America*, 49–97.

13. *Statistical Abstract of the United States*, 2008, 424. This source also is used for subsequent references to the percentage of workers who are unionized, by state.

14. *Statistical Abstract of the United States*, 2008, 147.

15. Ibid., 457. This source is also used for subsequent references to the percentage of the population living in poverty.

16. *Statistical Abstract of the United States*, 2008, 82. This source also is used for subsequent references to state rankings on infant mortality rate.

17. National Conference of State Legislatures, "Ranking of State-Local Revenue and Expenditure Data," http://www.ncsl.org/default.aspx?tabid=12627.

18. U.S. Federal Bureau of Investigation, *Crime in the United States*, 2006, www.fbi.gov/ucr/ucr.htm.

19. Initiative and Referendum Institute, http://www.iandrinstitute.org.

20. Garreau, *The Nine Nations of North America*, 120.

21. *Initiative & Referendum Analysis*, 2 (June 1992) (Princeton, N.J.: Public Affairs Research Institute of New Jersey, Inc.), 1; *State Legislatures* 18, no. 12 (December 1992), 12–15; *State Legislatures* 22, no. 10 (December 1996), 17; National Conference of State Legislatures, www.ncsl.org.

22. Alaska Department of Revenue, *Fall 2010 Revenue Sources Book*, http://www.tax.alaska.gov/programs/document-viewer/viewer.aspx?2136f.

23. Garreau, *The Nine Nations of North America*, 120.

24. Bureau of the Census, U.S. Department of Commerce, "Voting and Registration in the Election of November 2008," http://www.census.gov/hhes/www/socdemo/voting/publications/p20/2008/tables.html.

25. This discussion of the growth of citizens and their metropolitan areas is derived from the following sources: Howard Chudacoff, *The Evolution of American Urban Society* (Englewood Cliffs, N.J.: Prentice-Hall, 1975); Constance M. Green, *American Cities in the Growth of the Nation* (London: Athlene Publishing, 1957); Lawrence J. R. Herson and John M. Bolland, *The Urban Web: Politics, Policy, and Theory* (Chicago, Ill.: Nelson-Hall Publishers, 1990), 43–65; and Sam Bass Warner Jr., *The Urban Wilderness: A History of the American City* (New York: Harper & Row, 1972).

26. Richard D. Bingham, *State and Local Government in an Urban Society* (New York: Random House, 1986), 30.

27. Joel Garreau, *Edge City: Life on the New Frontier* (New York: Doubleday, 1991).

28. Ibid., 5.

29. Ibid. 6–7.

30. Laura Loyacono, "Look What's Happening to Downtown," *State Legislatures*, 25, no. 6 (June 1999), 27.

31. *Statistical Abstract of the United States*, 1987, 395.

32. Ibid., 393; Bureau of Labor Statistics, U.S. Department of Labor, telephone inquiry for 1986 data.

33. Brian Cromwell, "California's Neighbors," *Federal Reserve Bank of San Francisco Weekly Letter*, no. 93–94 (October 8, 1993).

34. *Fiscal Survey of the States*, 1992 (Washington, D.C.: National Association of State Budget Officers, April 1992), 4.

35. *Fiscal Survey of the States*, 1999 (Washington, D.C.: National Association of State Budget Officers, December 1999), vii–viii.

36. *Fiscal Survey of the States*, 2002 (Washington, D.C.: National Association of State Budget Directors, May 2002).

37. *Budgeting Amidst Fiscal Uncertainty* (Washington, D.C.: National Association of State Budget Officers, 2004), 5.

38. National Conference of State Legislatures, *State Budget Actions: FY 2005 and FY 2006*, www.ncsl.org/ programs/ fiscal/sba05sum.htm.

39. RealtyTrac, www.realtytrac.com.

40. National Conference of State Legislatures, "State Budget Update: November 2010," http://www.ncsl.org/default.aspx?tabid=21829.

41. National Conference of State Legislatures, "State Budget Update: March 2011," http://www.ncsl.org/default.aspx?tabid=22549.

42. Center for Immigration Studies, Current Numbers, June 2006, www.cis.org/CurrentNumbers.

43. Michael Sandler, "Committing a Hiring Offense," *CQ Weekly* 64, no. 21 (May 22, 2006): 1391–1397.

3

Federalism and Intergovernmental Relations

In 2008 Massachusetts Governor Deval Patrick signed legislation into law that allowed same-sex residents of other states to be legally married in Massachusetts. Bill and John made the trip from Nebraska to be married by a municipal judge in Boston. Their marriage remained legally recognized in Massachusetts, but once they returned home to Lincoln, their union had no legal standing in their home state, in spite of the U.S. Constitution's guarantee that states will give "full faith and credit" to legal public acts taken in other states. Complicating matters here is the federal Defense of Marriage Act, passed by Congress and signed into law by President Bill Clinton in September 1996, which stipulates that "No state shall be required to give effect to a law of any other state with respect to same-sex marriage." New York, by virtue of an executive order issued by its governor, does recognize same-sex marriages performed in other states. Bill and John, however, are from a state that has chosen not to recognize such marriages. Bill and John plan to test the constitutionality of the federal law allowing states to choose by filing suit in federal district court.

Amerian federalism deals narrowly with the relationship between the national government and the states. Intergovernmental relations broaden the scope to include the relationships of local governments with the federal government and the states. As we shall see, the U.S. Constitution speaks only to federal–state relationships. Both the federal government and the states derive their respective authority from the Constitution. Although national law is supreme under federalism, power is divided under the Constitution between the national government and the states. The U.S. Supreme Court serves as the ultimate arbiter, ensuring that the national government acts within its constitutional grant of authority and does not infringe on the states' prerogatives. Local governments are legal possessions of the states and thus derive their powers from the states. The Constitution makes no reference to local governments at all. In a sense, they are like political subdivisions within a unitary system of government, in which those subdivisions can exercise only those powers expressly granted them by the central government. Most countries, including major powers such as Japan, Great Britain, France, and China, have a unitary system of government. Joining the Unites States as federal systems are Canada, Mexico, Germany, Australia, India, and Switzerland, but the states and the provinces are most independent and strongest in their relationship with the national government in the United States and Canada, respectively.

A certain irony pervades federalism in the United States. Public opinion polls consistently indicate that citizens feel closest to their local governments and believe they get the greatest value for their tax dollar from them. State governments come in second, and the federal government is viewed least favorably. The public also trusts states more than the federal government to administer joint federal–state programs. In a national survey, only 12 percent of those responding agreed with the proposition that the "federal government should not shift responsibilities for programs back to the states, but should continue to manage such programs at the federal level." Most respondents concluded that the "states know what they need better than the federal government does."[1] At the same time, it is clear to observers that from the days of Franklin Roosevelt's New Deal in the 1930s to today, there has been a steady shift of power and responsibility from the states to the federal government. The federal government, largely through presidential initiatives, has been the nation's agenda setter, and Congress has used its power of the purse to create financial incentives for state policymakers to follow the federal government's lead. With ever-expanding congressional grants of authority, federal agencies have enacted administrative regulations detailing the conditions for state participation.

An old adage suggests that where you stand depends on where you sit. Individuals tend to view issues from the vantage point of where they live and how they are situated in life. A certain tension can exist between how individuals view public policies in the abstract and how they look at them when those policies impinge on them directly. For example, public opinion surveys show that most Americans support environmental protection[2]—a fact that did not escape President Bill Clinton in his support of tougher air quality standards and that constrained President George W. Bush in his efforts to open protected federal lands for energy exploration. Yet many individuals are quick to complain if increased environmental standards affect them or their livelihood, whether those effects take the form of increased costs to their small business in meeting tightened emission controls, or the higher costs and increased inconvenience of taking their automobiles to the few shops equipped to perform the new and more costly enhanced emission-control tests.

Issues such as stricter federal controls on landfills, federal rangeland reforms in the West, and perceived inadequacies in the federal government's enforcement of laws against illegal immigration and their consequences for border states capture the increased attention of the popular press as well as publications aimed at state government officials. These contemporary issues follow past federal actions that still evoke the ire of state and local policymakers. Issues that remain particularly sensitive are the National Voter Registration Act, the so-called motor-voter legislation, which required states to register voters at driver's licensing, welfare, and unemployment offices; congressional elimination of the deductibility of state and local taxes; and the Asbestos Hazard Emergency Act, which required school districts to inspect for asbestos in schools and remove it when necessary. In the last instance, school districts objected less to the health-motivated effort and cost involved than they did to the imposition of what they perceived as an unfunded federal mandate.

Those concerned about the federal government continuing to shift the balance of power in its favor cannot help but notice that the 1996 national welfare reform fails to square with that scenario. Instead of accruing greater power and authority over welfare, Congress, with the president's ultimate support, elected to devolve much of the responsibility for designing and administering welfare to the states.

Does federal welfare reform represent a turning point in American federalism? Does it signal the president's and Congress's inclination to limit the growth of federal power, or even to reverse it? Can we expect to see further devolution, along with greater limitations on federal mandates and regulations affecting state and local governments? Or is welfare reform a limited diversion from the steady path of federal preeminence? Although the jury is still out, Congress's passage of the Elementary and Secondary Education Act of 2001, at the strong urging of President George W. Bush, raised the issue about welfare devolution being an anomaly in the path of growing federal power. The act requires all states to employ statewide tests of student proficiency and make the results public. It also mandates that states allow parents of students attending failing schools to transfer their children to better-performing schools.

History suggests that authoritative answers can come only from the president and Congress because they are the prime movers in setting the relative balance of federalism. It is true that the federal courts, and ultimately the U.S. Supreme Court, have influenced the balance in some significant ways, but the most pervasive and enduring force has come from the policy choices of Congress, typically following the president's lead.

Whether individuals and organized interests like the present balance of power between the federal government and the states or prefer to see it adjusted in a certain way depends on both their values and their circumstances. A belief that a strong federal government is necessary to properly assist the less fortunate in society might well outweigh a high-bracket taxpayer's concern over the associated greater costs and possible tax implications. A preference for state over federal legislation and regulation in theory might be tested in application, for example, when industry upstream in a neighboring state continues, with seeming impunity, to contaminate a waterway flowing into one's own state. Generally, however, if individuals or organizations believe that their interests can be advanced more efficiently at the national government level than at the state level, they are more likely to support federal action over state action. Conversely, those who see their interests best protected by the states are likely to champion devolution or decentralization. The power struggle over federalism is an extension of the politics of political power in general because politics is the process by which divergent interests compete over public resources, prescriptions, and proscriptions.

This chapter explores a number of significant influences on American federalism: its constitutional foundations and the Supreme Court's sometimes shifting interpretations thereof, the willingness of presidents and Congress to push the envelope of federal authority, and the reactions of state policymakers to federal initiatives. The chapter also looks at how local governments have been affected not only by the changing relationship between the federal government and the states but also by direct federal and state actions.

CONSTITUTIONAL DEVELOPMENTS

The framers of the U.S. Constitution struggled with the issue of power balance between the federal government and the states. The Federalists, led by James Madison, Alexander Hamilton, and John Jay, pressed the case for a strong national government. They saw the earlier approved Articles of Confederation as inadequate to preserve the survival of their newly independent nation. In the short-lived confederation, the national government possessed only those powers that the states were willing to give it. The confederation could not levy taxes and had to depend on voluntary financial support from its member states. However, it was difficult to get the states to act at all because any legislative measure needed the approval of 9 of the 13 states, and amendments to the Articles required unanimous consent. Filling the void, individual states sought independent trade agreements with foreign nations. They also competed with each other over claims to lands to the west.

The need for a stronger national government became apparent by the mid-1770s, and the states of Massachusetts, Virginia, and Maryland began discussions about how the existing arrangement could be strengthened. That effort led all states, except Rhode Island, to gather together in Philadelphia in 1787 for a Constitutional Convention. Out of that convention emerged the Constitution of the United States, minus the Bill of Rights, which was added in 1791.

The Constitution did not place the federal government over the states; it allocated power between the two, enumerating the respective authority of each and providing a framework under which the national government and the states could exercise implicit prerogatives. The Constitution makes no reference to local governments; Supreme Court decisions have adjudged them to be creatures of the states, possessing only those powers given to them by state law.

Article VI established the U.S. Constitution as the "supreme law of the land," having legal ascendancy over state constitutions and state law. Whenever they conflict, the U.S. Constitution prevails. Article I, Section 8, lists 17 powers expressly given to Congress, including levying taxes, regulating interstate commerce, printing and coining money, and maintaining a national military force. Article I also gives Congress the authority to "make all laws which shall be necessary and proper for carrying into execution the foregoing powers." This **implied powers clause** has served as the basis for Congress's expansion of its enumerated powers.

---

implied powers clause Language in Article I of the U.S. Constitution that gives Congress the authority to "make all laws which shall be necessary and proper for carrying into execution the foregoing powers" (the powers expressly given the federal government by the Constitution).

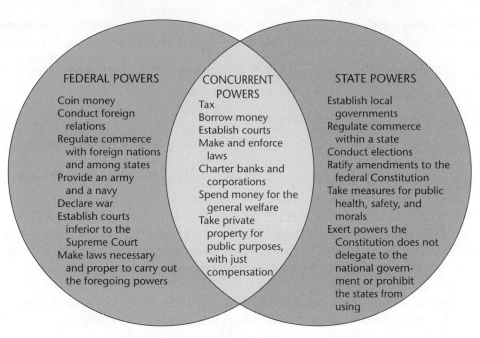

FEDERAL POWERS

Coin money
Conduct foreign
  relations
Regulate commerce
  with foreign nations
  and among states
Provide an army
  and a navy
Declare war
Establish courts
  inferior to the
  Supreme Court
Make laws necessary
  and proper to carry out
  the foregoing powers

**CONCURRENT
POWERS**

Tax
Borrow money
Establish courts
Make and enforce
  laws
Charter banks and
  corporations
Spend money for the
  general welfare
Take private
  property for
  public purposes,
  with just
  compensation

STATE POWERS

Establish local
  governments
Regulate commerce
  within a state
Conduct elections
Ratify amendments to the
  federal Constitution
Take measures for public
  health, safety, and
  morals
Exert powers the
  Constitution does not
  delegate to the
  national govern-
  ment or prohibit
  the states from
  using

Figure 3.1   Distribution of Power under Federalism

The Constitution gives the national government and the states several powers that they both can exercise—the so-called **concurrent powers**. Both are authorized to tax, borrow money, establish courts, make and enforce laws, charter banks and corporations, spend money for the general welfare, and take private property for public purposes after providing just compensation for it (see Figure 3.1).

The Tenth Amendment to the Constitution appears to limit the powers of the federal government in deference to the states, providing that any powers not explicitly given to the national government are "reserved" to the states. A strict interpretation of the reserved powers clause would suggest that the states can constitutionally exercise great discretion in their governance. However, this inherent contradiction between the rightful powers of the federal government and the states has been the subject of several, occasionally divergent, landmark Supreme Court decisions.

The role for the Supreme Court as arbiter was firmly established in *Marbury v. Madison* (1803), in which the Supreme Court invalidated a law of Congress for the first time. Under Chief Justice John Marshall, the Court asserted its authority as the final judicial authority over disputes between the national government and the states. In doing so, the Court relied heavily on Article III, which declares that the "judicial power of the United States shall be vested in one Supreme Court." The chief justice argued that **judicial power** entails the authority to interpret

---

concurrent powers Authority given by the U.S. Constitution to both the federal government and the states to
    exercise governmental power.
judicial power The authority of the U.S. Supreme Court to interpret the constitutionality of laws enacted within the
    United States. This authority was firmly established in the Supreme Court case, *Marbury v. Madison* (1805).

the law, including the highest law of the land, the U.S. Constitution. On balance, the Supreme Court's decisions over the past two centuries have expanded the powers of the federal government in relation to the states. Such major decisions have come in the areas of interstate commerce[3] and civil rights,[4] although not until the mid-twentieth century in the latter case.

Recent Supreme Court Decisions

Recent Supreme Court decisions, on balance, have continued to strengthen the federal government in relation to the states. In fact, two landmark decisions in the 1980s solidified the federal government's preeminent position, that is, at least until the Court appeared to hedge a bit in the mid- to late 1990s. In the first decision, *Garcia v. San Antonio Metropolitan Transit Authority* (1985), the Court ruled in a 5–4 decision that state and local governments must be treated as employers under the National Fair Labor Standards Act because Congress did not explicitly provide an exemption for them. This decision reversed the operating principle that states have sovereignty that automatically protects them from congressional acts that might affect their internal operations.

The *Garcia* ruling sent the message that if the states, "as states," want protection from the national government within the constitutional system, they must look to Congress, not to the courts. As Justice Harry Blackmun, author of the majority opinion, wrote, "State sovereign interests . . . are more properly protected by procedural safeguards inherent in the structure of the federal system than by judicially created limitations on federal power." In effect, the Court suggested that state and local elected officials contact their congressional representatives and work out their differences through the federal legislative process. In response, critics argued that the *Garcia* decision essentially made Congress the arbiter of its own actions.

A subsequent Supreme Court decision, *South Carolina v. Baker* (1988), reinforced the federal government's hegemony over the states and their local jurisdictions. The Court ruled that Congress has the right to tax individuals' earnings derived from interest payments on state and local bonds, overturning the Court's 1895 decision in *Pollock v. Farmers' Loan and Trust Company* and eliminating the longstanding rule that had prohibited federal taxation of interest paid on state and local bonds. Not surprisingly, state and local leaders saw the Court's action as potentially costing their governments billions of dollars in increased interest because they would have to raise the rate of return to keep their debt instruments competitive if the exemption from federal taxation were lost. In addition, they saw this ruling as a power move by the federal government.

In the 1990s, the Supreme Court tempered somewhat the legislative license it gave the federal government. It is not at all clear whether its moderation represents a fundamental rethinking of Tenth Amendment boundaries or merely a cautionary note along the road to continuing federal penetration. In an important 1995 decision, *United States v. Lopez,* the Court appeared to put some new limits on Congress's authority to use the commerce clause in Article I of the Constitution as justification for federal legislation in areas deemed to be reserved to the states. In that decision, the Court struck down a federal law banning gun possession within 1,000 feet of schools. The majority in the 5–4 decision reasoned that the overturned law is a criminal statute that has nothing to do with interstate commerce, broadly conceived. The majority further reasoned that the states had their own legislative means to address the problem, if they so desired. The ruling marked the first time in over 60 years that the Court struck down an act of Congress on the grounds that it exceeded its power under the commerce clause.[5]

Two years later, in the 1997 *Plintz v. United States* case, again by a 5–4 vote, the Supreme Court struck down provisions of the federal Brady Handgun Violence Prevention Act, which required local law enforcement officers to conduct background checks on gun purchasers. Justice Antonin Scalia, writing for the majority, declared that the "federal government may neither issue directives requiring the states to address particular problems, nor command the states' officers, or those of their political subdivisions, to administer or enforce a federal regulatory program."[6] He went on to acknowledge that the federal government can establish federal programs and use federal funds to entice state or local participation, as it does in a wide variety of existing federal programs. The significance of the case lies in the willingness of the Court to limit the federal government's ability to unilaterally transfer federal regulatory activities to the states.

Then, after three straight major decisions that sided with the states, the Court, in 2004, tipped the balance back in the federal government's favor. The case *Alaska Department of Environmental Conservation v. EPA* upheld the federal Environmental Protection Agency's (EPA's) ruling that a zinc mine operator in Alaska must use the best available pollution-reducing technology to power a major expansion of its mining operations. Alaska's environmental protection department had permitted the Red Dog Mine to install a diesel-fired generator that would reduce emissions by 30 percent, compared to a 90 percent reduction that the best available, but more costly, technology could yield. The state agency argued that its approval optimally balanced Alaska's environmental and economic interests. The EPA contended that the department had exceeded its authority under the Clean Air Act of 1990 and that it must require the mining operation to install the more effective technology.

Alaska challenged the ruling but lost in the Ninth Circuit Court in San Francisco. The state appealed to the U.S. Supreme Court, which upheld the lower court's ruling by a 5–4 vote. Justice Ruth Ginsberg delivered the opinion for the majority.

The following year, the Supreme Court acted again in favor of the federal government over a state. The case *Raich v. Gonzales* dealt with the question of whether federal law prevails over state law. In 1996, California voters approved a direct initiative ballot proposition legalizing marijuana for medical use. That law, the Compassionate Use Act, conflicted with the federal Controlled Substances Act, which banned possession of marijuana. The controversy came to a head when agents of the federal Drug Enforcement Administration (DEA) seized physician-prescribed marijuana from a patient's home. An association of medical marijuana users sued the DEA and U.S. Attorney General John Ashcroft in federal district court. The plaintiffs argued that the federal government's actions exceed its powers under the interstate commerce clause of the U.S. Constitution. The district court ruled against the plaintiffs. They appealed the ruling to the Ninth Circuit Court of Appeals, which reversed the district court's ruling. The federal government, in turn, appealed the appeals court's reversal to the U.S. Supreme Court.

The Supreme Court sided with the federal government. In a 6–3 decision, the majority held that Congress did have the authority under the commerce clause to regulate the use of marijuana because local use affected supply and demand in a national marijuana market. The balance point once again appeared to be tipping toward the national government.[7]

Only four months after deciding the *Raich* case, the justices were hearing another case dealing with the federal government's regulatory reach under the Controlled Substances Act. This time the case pitted the federal government against the state of Oregon. In 1994, Oregon voters, also using the direct initiative, authorized physicians to prescribe lethal doses of controlled substances to terminally ill patients. Attorney General Ashcroft took the position that the Oregon statute violated the federal Controlled Substances Act and that assisting with a suicide is not a "legitimate medical purpose." He threatened to revoke the medical licenses of physicians who did so. Oregon sued Ashcroft in federal district court. Both the district court and the Ninth Circuit Court of Appeals found Ashcroft's directive unconstitutional, taking the position that the attorney general exceeded his authority and that it is the states that constitutionally have the legal right to define general standards of medical practice. On appeal, the Supreme Court, in *Gonzales v. Oregon*, sustained the lower courts' rulings—this time deferring to states' rights under the Tenth Amendment of the U.S. Constitution.[8]

It is clear that the U.S. Constitution, and its subsequent interpretation by the federal courts, establishes the legal framework for the relationship between the national government and the states. It does not, however, tell us how far federal and state policymakers are willing to stretch the boundaries of that framework. Nor is it clear that the federal government will actually use the legal authority available to it to enact mandates and limits on state governments. For that dimension, we have to move beyond a discussion of formal and legal federalism and examine the patterns of intergovernmental relations that have evolved.

THE PHASES OF FEDERALISM

Federal–state relations have taken a number of different turns since the Constitution's ratification in 1788, but until recently the overall direction of congressional action has been toward broader intervention by the federal government in affairs traditionally the domain of the states. Five discernible phases (summarized in Table 3.1) merit attention.[9]

Dual Federalism (1787–1932)

During this period in U.S. political history, a clearer separation divided the functional responsibilities of the national government than in later years. The national government largely pursued its enumerated powers, including matters of national defense, foreign affairs, tariffs, interstate commerce, and mail delivery. The states, on the other hand, assumed responsibility for education, social welfare, health, and criminal justice, among other functions. Despite a common understanding of respective service responsibilities, this period was not without contention between the national government and the states.

Slavery and segregation provided the grounds for conflict. In the 1840s and 1850s, the Supreme Court found itself being confronted with questions of slave ownership, the status of fugitive slaves, and whether slaves could be held in the emerging western territories. Most decisions supported the position of the Southern states on the institution of slavery. In one such notable case, *Dred Scott v. Sanford* (1857), the Supreme Court held that slaves were the rightful property of their owners.

Table 3.1 The Phases of Federalism

Phase	Timeline	Significant Characteristics
Dual Federalism	(1787–1932)	• Separation of functional responsibilities between the national government and the states • The national government pursuing its enumerated powers • The states exercising responsibility for their reserved powers • Low levels of federal aid
Cooperative Federalism	(1933–1963)	• Increased federal aid to help the states meet *their own priorities* • Increased programs of direct aid to local governments • Increased federal assistance to deal with record levels of unemployment from the Great Depression • State and local spending from their own revenue sources growing faster than federal grants-in-aid following World War II and a return to normalcy
Centralized Federalism	(1964–1980)	• Articulation of *national* domestic policy goals • Federal funds used as "carrots" to entice state administrative and financial participation in programs aiming to achieve a Great Society • Major expansion of *categorical* grants and associated funding across presidential administrations of different partisan stripes • Significant increase in state aid to local governments
The New Federalism	(1981–1992)	• Dramatic reversal of prior period; reduction of federal grants-in-aid, in constant dollars, during the Reagan administration • Consolidation of categorical grants into block grants, along with elimination of certain existing categorical grants • Executive attempts to sort out the appropriate responsibilities of the national government and the states • Executive attempts to turn back federal program responsibilities to the states
Empathic Federalism	(1993–2000)	• Renewed executive interest in pursuing national domestic policy goals, but with greater flexibility accorded to the states on how to achieve desired outcomes • Increased administrative flexibility accorded to the states • New aid targeted to troubled urban areas • Selective congressional-led devolution of program responsibility to the states
Recentralizing Federalism	(2001–2008)	• Expanded role for federal government in education • Thwarting state initiative in environmental protection • Constraining states in expanding eligibility for the State Children's Health Insurance Program (SCHIP)
Fiscal Stimulus-Centered Federalism Turns to Self-Help Federalism	(2009+)	• Increased federal funding for Medicaid • Expanded aid for local school districts and institutions of higher education • Increased spending on highway and bridge reconstruction and maintenance • Increased capital spending for mass transit and commuter rail • Creation of a state fiscal stabilization fund to reduce the need for state spending cuts and associated employee layoffs, followed by a marked federal pullback

The Civil War tested the concept of national sovereignty. The struggle over secession, precipitated by deep divisions based on the question of slavery, was resolved in favor of the national government. In an 1869 ruling on the issue of secession, Chief Justice Salmon Chase reaffirmed what the Supreme Court viewed as the immutable character of the national union of states:

> The preservation of the states and the maintenance of their governments are as much within the design and care of the constitution as the preservation of the union and the maintenance of the national government. The constitution, in all of its provisions, looks to an indestructible union, composed of indestructible states.[10]

For Justice Chase and the Court, both the national government and the states needed to be strong, each deriving its strength from the Constitution, which is protected by the federal courts. However, the operational balance of power, in the aftermath of the Civil War, would continue to be tested.

In the four years following the Civil War, Congress passed—and the states ratified—three monumental amendments to the U.S. Constitution. The Thirteenth Amendment, ratified in 1865, prohibited slavery within the United States. The Fourteenth Amendment, ratified three years later, guaranteed citizenship to freed slaves and prohibited states from denying any citizen his or her rights of life, liberty, or property without due process of law. In 1869, Congress passed the Fifteenth Amendment barring the states from denying the vote to anyone "on account of race, color, or previous condition of servitude." The states ratified it one year later. (Ironically, however, women were not given the vote until 1920, with the ratification of the Nineteenth Amendment.)

These three amendments suggested that the federal government, through congressional action, would assert itself to protect individual rights, including the rights of African Americans, even if that meant restricting the prerogatives of the states. At the same time, most Southern states quickly enacted legislation, commonly referred to as the Black Codes, which restricted the opportunities of their African American residents. These laws were used to keep African American children out of white-only schools; prevent African Americans from serving on juries; and maintain segregated accommodations such as restaurants, transportation, theaters, and restrooms. Local jurisdictions in the South functionally prevented African Americans from voting by employing poll taxes and difficult literacy tests. Congress struck back, passing the Civil Rights Act of 1875, which specifically granted African Americans equal access to public accommodations. In practice, little changed, and despite appeals for redress, the Supreme Court showed scant interest in getting involved. When it did, it tended to support the position of states' rights, drawing a distinction between the rights of national citizenship and those of state citizenship. In 1883, in the so-called Civil Rights Cases, the Court ruled that Congress's jurisdiction extended only to state and other governmental acts of discrimination against African Americans, not to actions of private entities.[11] Under this interpretation, a restaurant proprietor, for example, could legally refuse to serve African Americans, as could any other retail establishment. Faced with continuing legal challenges, the Supreme Court, in *Plessy v. Ferguson* (1896), with only a single dissenting vote, ruled that "separate but equal" facilities or services met the tests for equal protection called for under the Fourteenth Amendment. Yet as history has demonstrated many times over, segregated facilities and services were separate but rarely equal. Practice fell far short of the promise offered by the three Civil War amendments. The civil rights of African Americans would have to wait until the Civil Rights movement of the 1950s and 1960s secured them.

In contrast, the Supreme Court generally did not restrain the federal government from extending its reach in interstate commerce, monetary and banking policy, and the regulation of industries and the railroads. The federal government was also active in supporting extension of the nation's infrastructure, including rail, port, and canal construction.

Cooperative Federalism (1933–1963)

The Great Depression of the 1930s dealt an unprecedented blow to the economy of the United States. With unemployment topping 20 percent in the depths of the depression, popular demands for government assistance put tremendous pressure on the states' ability to go it alone. The severity of the economic travail forced the states to seek federal assistance in confronting its effects. The activist administration of Franklin Delano Roosevelt proved to be a willing leader in the fight to regain economic prosperity—a goal endorsed by both the national government and the states.

The obstacles to recovery appeared almost overwhelming in 1933. The stock market crash of 1929 sent shockwaves throughout the economy, affirming growing fears that America's economy, which had ridden a crest of speculation, bank failure, and overproduction, was in trouble. No state was immune from the economic fallout.

The Roosevelt administration and the Democrat-controlled Congress responded with a panoply of national initiatives to turn the economy around and *help the states* assist those most hurt by the economic and social disaster. Congress followed the president's urgings and approved emergency grants to assist the states in meeting the escalating costs of unemployment compensation. Despite the Supreme Court's initial resistance, Congress also created over 25 separate programs as part of New Deal legislation, most prominently including job-creating public works programs for adults and youth; matching federal funds in support of state emergency relief efforts; government loans to financial institutions and railroads; and federal aid in support of state-administered social welfare programs assisting dependent children, the elderly, the blind, and farmers. During the last year (1932) of the Hoover administration, the federal government spent $193 million on 12 grant-in-aid programs to state and local governments. In comparison, after the first five years of the New Deal, federal grant-in-aid spending had risen to $2.66 billion and supported 26 programs.[12] Much of that assistance went directly to local governments.

World War II completed the effort to put Americans back to work—in military uniforms or in industries supporting the war effort. Federal spending ballooned during the war years; between 1940 and 1945 alone, federal spending climbed from $9.5 billion to $92.7 billion—a staggering increase of 875 percent.[13] In contrast, the Allied victory allowed federal spending to drop nearly in half by 1950, although U.S. participation in the Korean War notched federal spending up again in the early 1950s. With the end of the Korean War, the U.S. treasury had amassed a level of tax revenues that became available to support domestic programs aimed at assisting the state and local governments to educate and retrain returning veterans, renew downtown areas, provide housing assistance, and expand the nation's interstate highway network. But during the 10 years between 1954 and 1964, the growth in state and local spending actually exceeded the growth in federal spending. In fact, federal spending decreased as a percentage of the gross national product (GNP) because defense spending won a shrinking share of the federal budget.[14]

Local governments faced the greatest challenge in building the infrastructure necessary to support a fast-growing population, expand basic services for growing municipalities and counties, and educate the postwar baby boomers. Population growth created the need for increased state spending in support of state government–administered programs and for increased financial aid to local school districts.

Centralized Federalism (1964–1980)

This period marked a departure from the national government's supportive role in domestic policy making. Instead of assisting the states to develop programs to meet emerging domestic needs, the federal government articulated national policy goals and held out a greatly increased fiscal carrot to entice state participation, which often involved state administration. Domestic policy in the early years of this period can best be characterized by President Lyndon Johnson's call for a **Great Society**, in which government, through the federal partner's lead, established public programs aimed at improving the lot of the underprivileged. President Johnson defined a truly Great Society as one that ensured an adequate quality of life for the less fortunate. Congress responded by creating many new social programs to provide financial aid and medical assistance to the needy, construct low-cost housing, provide compensatory education for the underprivileged, support mass transit, and finance legal counsel for the poor. During the Johnson administration, Congress created over 209 new grant-in-aid programs, each with its own programmatic, administrative, and reporting requirements.[15]

In part, the aggressive and directive approach of the federal government under President Johnson's leadership was a reaction to state and local governments at that time. States were dominated by rural interests and not attentive to the issues of growing urbanization. Governors like George Wallace of Alabama, Lester Maddox of Georgia, and Orval Faubus of Arkansas personified and led state resistance to granting rights and recognizing the needs of African Americans. The institutions of states and cities were generally incapable of addressing the challenges of the mid-twentieth century, as will be explained in Chapters 9 to 13. With good reason, policymakers in Washington, D.C., did not trust state and local officials. National programs were designed to provide very little discretion to subnational governments.

The vast majority of Great Society programs greatly expanded the use of **categorical grants** to distribute federal funds to states or local governments. Categorical grants can be used only for the narrow purposes established by Congress or prescribed in the federal administrative code. Grants are made for specific purposes, such as building bridges, providing medical care for the needy, and subsidizing mass transit. They cannot be diverted

---

Great Society The label given to President Lyndon Johnson's social policy initiatives aimed at improving the lot of the underprivileged.

categorical grants Federal financial aid that can be used only for the specific purposes identified in congressional legislation or prescribed in the federal administrative code.

to any other use. In accepting the grant, state and local governments become obligated to comply with the grant's various requirements, which dictate the purposes to which the funds may be put as well as any conditions attached to their provision.

Categorical grants come in one of two forms: formula grants or project grants. **Formula grants** distribute funds to states and local governments according to a formula approved by Congress. **Project grants** are provided to cover the costs of a specific project and usually are awarded following a review of competing proposals.

Several of the largest categorical grants-in-aid can be classified as entitlement programs: people who qualify for them have an entitlement, or legal right, to receive benefits. For entitlements, the federal treasury must pay the bill regardless of congressional expenditure estimates for the program. In a real sense, then, entitlement spending is uncontrollable unless Congress changes the entitlement by deleting or modifying the statutory authorization; without that congressional action, the resulting costs of entitlements must be covered.

Most grants-in-aid require matching funds from state or local governments as a demonstration of their interest in, and commitment to, the aided program. State and local matching shares typically run from 10 to 50 percent, depending on the program, with the federal government providing the remainder. For some joint state–local programs, the state picks up the full nonfederal share, but for others, the state passes a percentage of the matching costs on to the participating local governments.

Presidential administrations and Congresses following the Johnson years not only continued support for the vast majority of these programs, but significantly increased funding for them as well (Table 3.2). They also added 134 new categorical grant-in-aid programs between 1969 and 1980, perpetuating centralized federalism.[16]

Despite the persistency of this direction, President Richard Nixon, Johnson's successor, added a new twist to federal aid by introducing the block grant. **Block grants** can be used for a number of related purposes consistent with their authorization, and they carry fewer restrictions and administrative regulations. Congress approved three new block grants during the Nixon administration: the now-defunct Comprehensive Employment and Training Act (CETA), which provided job training and public service employment; the Community Development Block Grant, tying together a number of preexisting urban development and renewal programs; and Title XX of the Social Security Act, which consolidated several categorical social service programs into the same grant. With any of the three, the grant recipients could decide how to allocate grant funds among the many possible purposes authorized in the enabling legislation. They could set the relative priorities within the general purposes of the act and thus be responsive to local needs and preferences. Under the Title XX block grant program, for example, one state might decide to place the highest priority on foster care and mental health services, while another might choose to emphasize supportive social services for the aged.

---

formula grants Federal financial aid distributed to states and local governments according to a formula approved by Congress.

project grants Federal financial aid provided to cover the costs of a specific project and usually awarded following a review of competing proposals.

block grants Federal financial aid that can be used for a number of related purposes consistent with congressional authorization.

Table 3.2 Federal Grants-in-Aid to State and Local Governments (in Current Dollars), Selected Years, 1949–2012

Fiscal Year	Amount ($ Billions)	Fiscal Year	Amount ($ Billions)
1949	1.9	1988	115.3
1954	3.1	1990	135.3
1959	6.5	1992	178.1
1964	10.1	1994	210.6
1969	20.2	1996	227.8
1972	34.4	1998	246.1
1974	43.4	2000	285.9
1976	59.1	2002	352.9
1978	77.9	2004	407.5
1980	91.4	2006	434.1
1982	88.1	2008	461.3
1984	97.6	2010	608.4
1986	112.3	2012[e]	584.3

[e] = estimate

Source: Office of Management and Budget, *Historical Tables, Budget of the U.S. Government,* FY 2012, 250–251.

President Nixon also introduced general revenue sharing. In doing so he recognized the dramatic increases in the capacities of state and local governments that had occurred by the 1970s. He was politically and philosophically opposed to heavy involvement by the federal government in economic and social programs, and he was inclined to provide more responsibility and discretion to state and local officials. With revenue sharing, the federal government provided funds, without strings, to state and local governments based on an allocation formula that took into account population, relative income, urbanization, and tax effort. States and local governments that did best under the formula included those with the largest populations, particularly those with higher percentages of poor residents, and those that made the greatest effort to raise their own revenues through taxation.

Revenue sharing no longer exists today. At President Jimmy Carter's recommendation, Congress dropped states from the program in 1980—a time when swelling state surpluses and cuts in state taxes prompted national leaders to question the appropriateness of the federal government sending even more federal resources the states' way. They also increasingly questioned the uses to which the federal funds were put. Revenue sharing for local governments met the fiscal ax in 1986 as part of a deficit reduction measure of the Reagan administration and Congress. During its existence, roughly one-third of revenue sharing went to the states, two-fifths to municipalities, and about one-fourth to counties.[17]

Combining all forms of assistance, federal aid to state and local governments increased by 324 percent from the beginning of the Great Society in 1964 through Nixon's truncated second term in 1974.[18] Even at that pace, state spending actually grew faster during that period. Although matching requirements for the receipt of federal funds pushed up state spending, the states' own financial assistance to local governments proved to be the major force behind rising state spending. Legislatures, often following gubernatorial initiatives, not only expanded state aid in the aggregate, but also used growing revenues to equalize the distribution of major state aid programs such as general school aid, state-shared revenues, and mass transit assistance. As a result, state aid to local governments increased almost 3.5 times in the 10 years between 1964 and 1974.[19] It slowed a bit during the remainder of the decade because both state and local governments increasingly felt the backlash of a growing taxpayer revolt and its demands for tax cuts.

The institution of block grants and revenue sharing has prompted some academic observers to question whether we should speak of a New Federalism associated with the Nixon administration, restricting centralized federalism to the Great Society years. The conventional interpretation, however, argues that although greater flexibility and reduced regulation selectively accompanied block grants and revenue sharing, federal policy leadership pursued through narrow categorical grants and federal regulatory requirements continued as the predominant mode throughout the 1970s. By 1980, categorical grants still comprised nearly four-fifths of all federal grants-in-aid.

The New Federalism (1981–1992)

This period of decentralization and withdrawal represents a reexamination of the federal government's relationship with state and local governments. Some federal programs were eliminated and others were consolidated. In several areas, the federal partner appeared to be drawing back, as part of a conscious policy shift, on its earlier commitments.

The Reagan Years.   President Ronald Reagan was elected in 1980 with what he viewed as a popular mandate to reverse the federal government's course. For Reagan, the reach of the federal government had become too extensive: taxes had to be cut, and the growth in domestic spending, including federal aid to state and local governments, had to be markedly reduced. As he saw it, the Great Society and its aftermath had launched an explosion of a wide range of federal categorical aid programs purportedly in the national interest. Not only had the total number of federal grant-in-aid programs mushroomed to 534 by 1980, at a cost exceeding $90 billion, but the proportion of direct federal to local aid increased from 14 percent of all federal aid in 1968 to 30 percent in 1980.[20] For President Reagan, these trends had to be reversed. The cost of federal aid had to be brought under control, and the states had to be given greater discretion about how the money should be spent. In President Reagan's words:

> Our citizens feel they have lost control of even the most basic decisions made about the essential services of government, such as schools, welfare, roads, and even garbage collection. They are right. A maze of interlocking jurisdictions and levels of government confronts the average citizen in trying to solve even the simplest of problems. They do not know where to turn for answers, who to hold accountable, who to praise, who to blame, who to vote for or against. The main reason for this is the overpowering growth of federal grants-in-aid programs during the past few decades.[21]

Reagan questioned whether the federal government should be involved at all in a number of policy areas. Using the federal budget as a policy tool, he set out to eliminate federal funding for several federal agencies, including the Department of Education, the

Department of Energy, the Economic Development Administration, the Community Services Administration, and the Legal Services Corporation. Programs recommended for elimination prominently included federal operation subsidies for mass transit and Conrail (government-financed commercial rail service), as well as funding for public housing construction and alternative energy technology development. Reagan also sought to reduce the rate of growth for other programs and to consolidate still others into block grants to the states, letting governors and legislatures decide how to allocate funds among the block's many purposes.

Reagan had limited success in getting Congress to go along with his call for outright elimination of federal agencies and programs. Congress agreed to terminate only the Community Services Administration and the Legal Services Corporation. At the programmatic level, Congress ended federal subsidies for Conrail and funding for public housing construction, preferring in the latter case to continue subsidizing low-cost housing in the private marketplace. Reagan did enjoy success, however, in consolidating categorical grants into block grants and in significantly reducing the growth in federal aid to state and local governments, as will be illustrated later in this chapter.

As part of the fiscal year (FY) 1982 block grant reforms, President Reagan proposed the consolidation of 85 existing categorical grants into seven new block grants. Congress changed the package a bit, consolidating 77 categorical grants into nine block grants, including two existing block programs that underwent some modification. In addition, Congress eliminated 43 other categorical grants at the administration's recommendation, including seven programs in energy conservation and regulation, eight in pollution control and abatement, five in migrant and refugee care, six in area and regional development, three in health maintenance, and fourteen in the category of state and local government "capacity building."[22]

The increased discretion available to state and local governments through these block grant programs did not come without a price. Although the 77 categorical grant programs totaled $8.2 billion for FY 1981, the new block grants were funded at $6.1 billion in the next year—a 25 percent reduction.[23] After its initial success, the Reagan administration made 23 additional proposals to expand existing block grants or to consolidate other categorical grants into new block grants. Congress approved only one: it replaced the CETA block grant program with the private business-endorsed Job Training Partnership Act program. State and local officials, though supporting the flexibility that comes with block grants, increasingly saw them as a subterfuge for the Reagan administration's attacks on domestic spending.

President Reagan wanted to go beyond his own efforts to create new block grant programs. In his January 1982 State of the Union address, he proposed a substantive sorting of state and federal responsibilities. Having quickly acquired the name "the big swap," Reagan's proposal called for the federal government to turn over to the states sole responsibility for the nation's basic income maintenance programs, Aid for Families with Dependent Children (AFDC) and food stamps. In exchange, the "feds" would assume full responsibility for Medicaid. In addition, the president's package included fully turning back to the states 61 other grant-in-aid programs, including those in the areas of transportation, education, community development, social services, and general government assistance. Reagan expected that, in some cases, state officials might even decide that, without federal support, the programs were not of sufficient priority to be continued. The states would then assume total responsibility for administering and financing the programs that they elected to continue. To assist them, Reagan called for a comparable amount of federal tax revenue to be returned to the states. Toward that end, a New Federalism Trust Fund would be created, providing a vehicle, during a transitional 10-year period, to help the states pay the costs of their new-found program responsibilities. After the transition, the states would assume full financial responsibility. They would use the transitional period as a time to enact the necessary state revenue increases, filling the gap left by the federal partner. To give them tax room, Reagan proposed a phased reduction of federal excise taxes, which the states were invited to reenact if they so chose.

However, the president's proposal contained little concrete elaboration—a fact that greatly bothered state policymakers. Precise amounts were not mentioned, nor was any sliding schedule provided for federal support over the 10-year period. The concept of program turnbacks met with general sympathy among state governors and legislators, but they shared great concern over how the transitional funding arrangement would work and how the states would ultimately pay the full bill. Top state administrators and affected interest groups promptly turned from a discussion of the relative conceptual and theoretical merits of the proposals to narrow assessments of how their programs would fare under the change. In the public welfare area, for example, interest groups (as well as program-supportive administrators) expressed their concerns that devolution would result in lower benefit rates and stricter eligibility standards.[24]

Another significant issue in the debate over program and revenue devolution dealt with whether the federal government should play the role of fiscal equalizer within the federal system. In other words, is it appropriate for the federal government to step in and ease the disparities in fiscal capacity among the states? The issue of relative fiscal capacity was important because, with program turnbacks, the states would have been in quite different positions in their ability to assume the added fiscal responsibility. Because many of the federal grants-in-aid programs were designed with some measure of fiscal capacity affecting allocations among the states, state officials (particularly through the National Governors' Association [NGA]) demanded that any transitional revenue transfer be allocated, in part, on an equalized basis. But the dilemma still remained about how the less well-off states would be able to pick up the full program costs after the transitional period ended. These nagging, practical concerns took some of the luster off the theoretical attractiveness of devolution.

The big swap and its associated package of program turnbacks never got much beyond the preliminary discussion stage. Although in general agreement over the desirability of realignment, both the states and the Reagan administration got scared off by its fiscal implications. State policymakers were worried about the added fiscal burden that might be imposed, particularly in an environment in which the strength of well-entrenched interest groups would make it very difficult for the states to shed any of the inherited responsibilities. The Reagan administration, in light of the growing national deficit associated with the 1981–1982 recession, appeared to develop serious second thoughts, not only about the fiscal viability of transitional revenue assistance, but also about the extent to which the administration would make major budget cuts in the affected programs as another means of restraining domestic spending and balancing the federal budget. On the administration's side, faced with a worsening budget picture, Reagan became unwilling to make the fiscal concessions that appeared necessary to win gubernatorial backing for his initiative. Improving our military strength and maintaining the integrity of the president's fiscal policy proved to be higher priorities than his New Federalism initiative. Put differently, when the competing priorities of effecting structural reform of federalism and cutting domestic spending came into prospective conflict, reform of federalism was quickly set aside in favor of spending cuts.

Figure 3.2 shows the Reagan administration's success in drastically turning around the pattern of federal assistance inherited from previous administrations. In contrast to annual real-dollar increases, which averaged over 8 percent between 1960 and 1980, federal aid dropped by an annual real-dollar average of 1.7 percent between FY 1980 and FY 1988.[25]

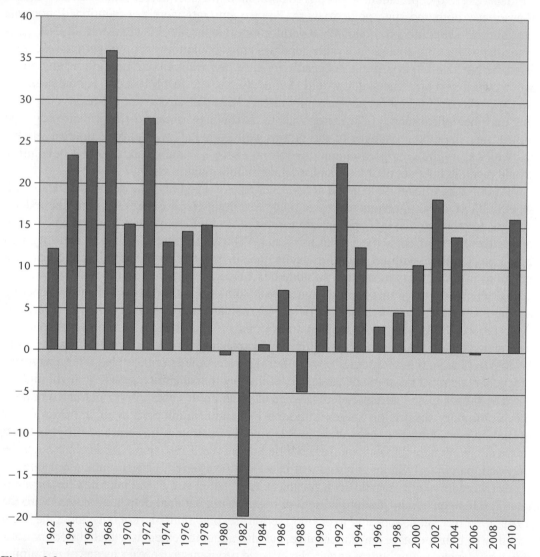

Figure 3.2 Biennial Percentage Change in Federal Aid to State and Local Governments, Selected Years, 1962–2010 (Constant 2000 Dollars)

Source: Office of Management and Budget, *Historical Tables, Budget of the U.S. Government*, Fiscal Year 2011, 249–250.

Direct grants to the states and local units of government, compared to programs directly aiding individuals such as income support and Medicaid, accounted for all of the decline, offset by an increase in constant-dollar spending for aid to individuals.

The George H. W. Bush Years.   In some ways, President George Bush followed the lead of his predecessor. Like Reagan, he continued to seek consolidation of categorical grants into broader block grant programs. In his budget proposals for FY 1992, President Bush offered Congress and the states a $20 billion list of categorical grants from which Congress, after counsel from the states, could choose $15 billion worth for consolidation into a single new block grant. Under his proposal, the states would lose an estimated $27.3 billion in federal funds over five years. The biggest prospective losers through consolidation would have included New York ($3 billion) and Texas and California ($1 billion each). The Bush administration suggested the categorical grants it preferred to see consolidated at reduced funding levels, but invited state policymakers to offer substitutions.

In response to that invitation, the NGA proposed that seven block grants be created from 42 categorical grant programs, totaling $14.1 billion. The National Conference of State Legislatures (NCSL) upped the ante, calling for 12 block grants forged from 85 categorical grants, to the tune of $21.3 billion. Unlike the Bush initiative, both proposals included provisions mandating stable funding for the new block grants, including a prospective adjustment for inflation, an element missing from the administration's initiative.[26]

Local governments failed to share the NGA's or the NCSL's enthusiasm for more block grants. They viewed it as further eroding their influence with the federal government and their already weakened discretion over the allocation of grant funds. They saw block grants as strengthening the hands of governors and state legislatures. Urban cities and counties questioned whether rural-dominated legislatures in many states would respond sympathetically to their needs.

The opposition of local governments, along with the budgetary implications of inflation-proof funding in an environment of growing national deficit, sealed the doom of further block grants. The prospects of increased federal administrative efficiencies and added state decision-making flexibility proved to be insufficiently attractive to mold executive–congressional agreement in the face of strong local opposition. In addition, the states would not lend their endorsement without a guarantee of stable and inflation-proof funding. At the same time, the demand for a guarantee precluded the administration's support, reinforcing the commonly held perception that the prospects for future shrinkage best explained the Bush administration's support of block grants.

Although President Bush, like President Reagan before him, continued to champion the elimination of ideologically objectionable programs, overall federal aid to state and local governments fared far better under Bush than under Reagan. Caught up in the politics of a growing budget deficit with no end in sight, President Bush's sights became fixed on finding a macro-level solution to the pervasive budgetary gridlock.

Toward that end, the president and congressional leadership fashioned the comprehensive deficit reduction package of October 1990, which established separate caps on defense, foreign aid, and discretionary domestic spending through FY 1994. Yet it also added more than $45 billion in budget authority for domestic discretionary spending from FY 1991 to FY 1993 and provided that the cap for domestic discretionary spending be adjusted annually for inflation.[27]

These concessions gave President Bush and Congress additional fiscal room to do more for state and local governments. The tight constraints in place during the Reagan era had been loosened. State and local governments, accordingly, turned to the Bush administration and the Democrat-controlled Congress to make up for lost ground. Despite Bush's conservative rhetoric, federal grants-in-aid, instead of declining in constant dollars as they had done during the Reagan years, rose by nearly a fifth from FY 1991 to FY 1993 (see Figure 3.2). Increases in both discretionary and entitlement-driven aid, particularly Medicaid in the latter category, contributed to the remarkable turnaround in federal assistance. No longer did significant cuts in discretionary aid result in aggregate reduction in federal aid to state and local governments, despite automatic increases in entitlement spending. The spending spigot had once again been turned on.

Empathic Federalism (1993–2000)

From the beginning of his campaign through the early years of his presidency, Bill Clinton expressed empathy toward the state and local governments. As governor of Arkansas, he was on the receiving end of federal retrenchment during the Reagan administration and the first half of the Bush administration. Unlike his recent predecessors, President Clinton called for greater federal leadership to address many of the problems facing the urban areas of America. He also understood that states and local governments were not likely to launch costly new programs without the availability of federal funding.

President Clinton's empathy was constrained by the federal budget deficit he inherited from Republican President Bush and the Democrat-controlled Congress. Having campaigned on a pledge to reduce the deficit and put the breaks on future growth, Clinton found himself in his first term with little fiscal room to undertake new spending initiatives. Yet the Clinton administration needed no reminder that deficit reduction was its top priority because it was President Clinton himself who took the lead in fashioning deficit-reduction legislation. It was also the president who cajoled recalcitrant Democrats into lending their support.

Not all Democrats eagerly jumped on the bandwagon. Some found the $241 billion tax increase, to be paid over four years, just too much to swallow, even though the legislation also would slow down spending by $255 billion over the same period. Others swallowed a little more easily, realizing that most of the income tax increase would come from upper-income taxpayers. But even with active presidential lobbying, the deficit-reduction package passed the House by a mere two votes. Vice President Gore had to break a deadlock in the Senate, giving the president a razor-thin one-vote margin in that chamber. Republicans called for fewer taxes and more spending cuts. They also voiced their belief that the tax increase would dampen economic recovery, costing jobs rather than creating them.

Clinton also won enough support from the Democratic majority in Congress to gain passage of legislation aimed at helping local communities address the problems of their most depressed neighborhoods. Following the president's lead, Congress provided modest funding to support nine so-called **empowerment zones**, with six of the zones to be designated in urban cities and the other three in rural areas. Under the legislation, each city with designated empowerment zones received $100 million to be used to foster economic development and create jobs. Each rural area received $40 million. As part of the application process for designation, local governments had to show how nonfederal resources would be packaged with federal funds to achieve the zone's objectives. Detroit's successful application included a commitment to create over 3,000 jobs within the zone, and a consortium of Detroit-based universities pledged to focus applied research and educational outreach efforts on the zone.[28]

The Democratic majority in Congress followed their president's call again the next year, passing an omnibus crime bill in the waning hours before the August 1994 recess. With most Democrats championing the bill's passage, Republican minority leaders attempted to brand the measure as laden with pork-barrel spending at the very time that more needed to be done to reduce the national budget deficit—a strategy that won over a number of fiscally conservative Democrats. Yet the defection of moderate Republicans, and those who grew increasingly concerned about appearing obstructionist on legislation that the public favored, added enough votes to a solid Democratic block to secure the bill's passage. President Clinton and the Democratic majority's success launched an unprecedented federal venture into fighting crime back home, a domain that has historically been the province of state and local governments.

State and local governments, on the whole, championed the federal government's initiative. State and local policymakers, along with law enforcement leaders, welcomed the sizable financial support. After all, a large share of the $30.2 billion crime bill went to state and local governments. The biggest slice, $8.8 billion, was intended for the addition of approximately 100,000 state and local police officers across the nation, an estimate considered highly inflated by the Republican leadership. Another $7.9 billion went to states in the form of construction grants for prisons and correctional boot camps. The third largest share, $6.9 billion, was to be distributed by formula to local communities in support of crime prevention programs. Smaller amounts were also distributed, including $1.8 billion to reimburse states for the costs of incarcerating illegal aliens convicted of felony offenses, and $1.6 billion to finance the Local Partnership Act (a provision originally rejected by Congress as part of Clinton's economic stimulus package offered early in his administration) that gives cities and towns greater discretion over how to spend the money.

The federal financial help was not without a catch, however. Congress, in writing the authorization, placed a five-year limit on funding, with a descending percentage of federal funds distributed over the period. That meant local governments had to absorb the difference, and ultimately the total loss of federal funds, to keep the newly initiated programs going.

The 1994 election brought an end to the Democratic majority in Congress and put a damper on Congress's inclination to support presidential initiatives to aid state and local governments. A wave of Republican victories gave the Republican Party control of both congressional chambers and left Congress with a decidedly conservative cast. With such a dramatic changeover, it is not surprising that state and local leaders viewed 1994 as the probable last

---

empowerment zones Areas within depressed neighborhoods that Congress has designated as eligible for earmarked federal financial assistance.

hurrah for new federal programs of targeted federal aid. Congressional Republican leaders, especially those in the House, seemed much more intent on devolving federal programs to the states than on adding new ones. In fact, the House Republican Party's Contract with America called for reforming welfare and ending its longstanding entitlement status (under which any-one meeting the eligibility requirements for welfare received benefits, regardless of the cost).

Welfare reform became a Republican-led congressional initiative that finally prevailed in 1996 following two presidential vetoes. Its third try included changes that made it mini-mally acceptable to President Clinton. The new program, entitled Temporary Assistance to Needy Families, lost the entitlement status accorded the AFDC program it replaced, and took the form of an appropriations-limited block grant to support state efforts aimed at moving participants from welfare dependence to work. Supporters hoped that state experi-mentation within the framework of federally imposed upper limits on the duration that recipients could receive benefits would result in a continuation of declining caseloads.

The ingredients appear right for Congress to continue its search for ways to devolve federal program responsibilities to the states while keeping a cap on new federal initiatives. However, the transition from budget deficit to budget surplus gave Congress tempting fiscal flexibility to reverse its course in search of electoral support. In fact, a key part of the 2000 presidential debate centered on whether the federal government should increase its financial support of edu-cation. It also focused on what should be the appropriate balance between federal directives and state autonomy and even whether federal funds should be used to support nonpublic education.

Recentralizing Federalism (2001–2008)

After only a month in office, President George W. Bush committed his administration to a return to the ideals of Reagan's New Federalism. In late February 2001, Bush created a new Interagency Working Group on Federalism. He charged the group with identifying (1) federal endeavors that would be more appropriately carried out by state and local gov-ernments; (2) measures for improving federal responsiveness to state and local concerns; and (3) opportunities for flexible funding, waivers from regulatory requirements, and ini-tiatives that promote state and local innovation and flexibility.[29] Yet the policies he pur-sued during his presidency suggested not a return to greater state discretion in federal–state relations but instead to a recentralization of federal prerogative. The Bush administration variously acted to preempt state policy making, thwart state initiative, limit state program flexibility, and substitute federal priorities for state priorities.

Within five months of assuming office, President Bush began his push for new federal legislation requiring states to test every child in grades 3 through 8 in reading and mathemat-ics proficiency. Not only did the states have to report the results to parents, but they also had to release results by school and school district. The legislation Bush sought required school officials to make annual progress toward meeting student performance requirements or face a series of gradually more stringent sanctions, up to reconstituting schools or closing them. As an intermediate step, the president wanted the legislation to give financial vouchers to par-ents of children attending failing schools, helping them to pay the costs of transferring their children to nonpublic schools, including parochial schools. Although Congress failed to sup-port the proposed voucher initiative, the resulting legislation, entitled No Child Left Behind, did mandate that states allow students attending schools not making adequate yearly progress toward performance goals to transfer to better-performing public schools, and that the school district cover the costs of transportation. And while the resulting legislation increased federal aid to cover the costs of compliance, it represented clear federal intervention in a traditional realm of state policy making. This Bush initiative is discussed in greater detail in Chapter 15.

Environmental policy, covered in Chapter 17, represents an area in which the Bush administration thwarted state initiative. Although 13 states adopted regulatory standards late in Bush's second term in office requiring automobile manufacturers to markedly reduce carbon dioxide emissions for vehicles sold in their states, the U.S. EPA refused to grant the states the required waivers to allow them to put the regulations into effect. The EPA argued that it lacked the legal authority under the Clean Air Act to regulate carbon dioxide emissions from motor vehicles. Subsequently, the U.S. Supreme Court ruled that the federal agency does indeed have that authority.[30] At the time of this writing, it is unclear whether the EPA will choose to exercise that authority and grant the requested waivers.

Another strain in federal–state relations involves the State Children's Health Insurance Program (SCHIP) and centers on whether states have the discretion to determine eligibility standards for participation in the program. SCHIP provides matching federal funds to help states extend health insurance coverage to children living in families whose incomes make them ineligible for Medicaid. In response to state actions to liberalize income ceilings governing eligibility, the Centers for Medicare and Medicaid Services (CMS), the federal agency within the Department of Health and Human Services responsible for the administration of SCHIP, issued a restrictive directive to state program heads. The directive requires that, before states can cover children in families earning more than 250 percent of the poverty line, they must ensure that the program enrolls at least 95 percent of uninsured children living in families with incomes below 200 percent of the poverty line, under the threat of loss of federal funding. In response, the states of New Jersey, New York, Maryland, Illinois, and Washington sued the CMS, maintaining that the directive exceeded the agency's authority to restrict state discretion to determine recipient eligibility and allocate the program's funding. In a report to Congress, the federal General Accountability Office (GAO) supported this claim. In February of 2009, President Obama issued a memorandum to the secretary of Health and Human Services requesting that the requirements be withdrawn. This action followed passage of the Children's Health Insurance Program Reauthorization Act (CHIPRA), which expanded the program to include about 4 million more children and continued coverage through 2013.

The Bush administration declared war on terrorism, and its Homeland Security initiatives reinforced state and local policymakers' concerns that practice might not square with the rhetoric of decentralization and local flexibility. The practical requirements of enhanced security call for increased federal leadership and coordination, especially in the areas of emergency preparedness and response, and protection of critical infrastructure. Nonetheless, state and local officials worried that increased federal direction would come at the expense of lost state and local control and that federal financial support would fail to compensate state and local governments for their added contribution to beefed-up homeland security.

Congress responded to the latter concern in May 2003 by appropriating $20 billion in one-time funds to the states. About half of these funds were earmarked to assist states and local governments to cover costs associated with homeland defense, and the other half intended to help the

DEBATING THE ISSUES

How much should the federal government get involved in education?

The federal government currently plays a minor role in American education, helping to finance programs that largely benefit minority, low-income, and handicapped students. In fact, education is a prime example of a reserved power exercised by the states. The states set overall policy for education, and local school district officials run the schools in accordance with state policy. The federal government is attempting to increase its role in education policy by attaching far-reaching conditions or strings to the aid that it provides. State and local taxpayers pay approximately 91 percent of the elementary and secondary education bill, with the federal government contributing only about 9 percent. That federal share includes funding in support of the No Child Left Behind program, enacted in 2001. A question for many school districts is whether to reject the conditions set by this act and thereby reject the federal funds.

Education has become a central policy issue nationwide. The public, the media, and politicians at all levels of government are expressing increased concern about how well the public schools are educating America's youth. Yet if schools are to be improved, whose responsibility should it be? Should the federal government become more involved, as it has been historically in areas such as welfare and environmental protection? For instance, should the federal government establish national performance standards that all students must meet in order to be promoted from grade to grade, or to graduate? Should the federal government require all teachers to pass subject-matter examinations to test their knowledge of the subjects they teach? Should the federal government create and pay for new programs to assist states and local school districts to improve educational performance? Should it try to inject greater competition in education by requiring states to provide taxpayer-financed vouchers to parents who opt to send their children to private schools? Or should the federal government stay out of the way, perhaps giving the states even greater flexibility to spend the limited federal aid that goes to education?

It is clearly in the national interest for students to perform well in school. But the burning question is: How can improved student performance best be attained? Does the answer lie in tougher standards imposed by the federal government, pushing the boundaries of federalism, or in increased local discretion, including giving schools greater freedom from federal and state regulations?

How would you set the balance?

Take a look at the following Internet resources as you consider your answer:

Center for Education Reform, *http://www.edreform.com*
The Institute for Education Reform, *http://www.calstate.edu/ier*
National Conference of State Legislatures, *http://www.ncsl.org*
The White House, *http://www.whitehouse.gov/issues/education*

states reduce their large budget deficits, occasioned significantly by rapidly increasing Medicaid costs. Although President Bush originally opposed the additional federal assistance, he ultimately agreed to the increase as part of a compromise to win support for his successful tax-cut legislation.

Both the major national associations of governors and big-city mayors welcomed the federal financial assistance for homeland security; at the same time they noted the increased expense that states and cities have been forced to bear in increasing security. The NGA reports that states spent $6 billion of their own funds on homeland security in the 12 months following the September 11, 2001, terrorist attacks and that they could be expected to bear a similar annual financial burden in the years to come. The U.S. Conference of Mayors put the cities' annual share of spending at $2.6 billion.[31]

The mayors of New York City and Washington, D.C., decried cuts in federal Homeland Security Grants for their cities as part of an overall $119 million cut approved by Congress. New York experienced an $83 million reduction, from $207 million in FY 2005 to $124 million in FY 2006, in federal grant funds that the city can use to cover the costs of planning, operations, equipment, training, and administration. Grant funding for the nation's capital declined from $77 million to $76 million. Some areas of the nation, however, received increases, reflecting a reallocation in response to a new needs assessment. The Los Angeles–Long Beach area, for example, got over $11 million more.[32] In effect, local governments experiencing cuts will have no choice but to fill the gap with locally raised revenues—barring increased state support—if they are to maintain the same level of programming. The alternative is doing less.

More recently, as part of his budget recommendations for FY 2009, President Bush proposed a large, $1.9 billion cut (a 47 percent reduction) in federal first-responder grants to state and local governments for security, law enforcement, firefighters, and medical teams responding to emergencies. Bush proposed that the savings be shifted to help fund expanded border security—a pressing national priority.[33]

For overall funding of federal aid during the Bush presidency, see Figure 3.2, which illustrates that constant-dollar federal spending on grants-in-aid to state and local governments essentially flattened out during Bush's second term as president, after having risen substantially during his first term. In fact, you would have to go back to the Reagan years to find more restrictive federal aid.

Fiscal Stimulus-Centered Federalism Turns to Self-Help Federalism (2009+)

Facing the worst recession since the Great Depression, Congress, at the behest of the newly elected President Obama, passed the American Recovery and Reinvestment Act in February 2009. Of the $787 billion stimulus package of tax benefits and spending increases between FY 2009 and FY 2011, $87 billion was earmarked for state Medicaid programs, $40 billion for local school districts and institutions of higher education, $27.5 billion for highways, $17.7 billion for mass transit and commuter rail, and $54 billion in a State Fiscal Stabilization Fund aimed at reducing the need for state spending cuts and associated employee layoffs.[34] Congress enacted the fiscal policy legislation to boost demand in an environment of falling national economic output and resulting state revenue shortfalls that could exceed an accumulated $350 billion by the end of FY 2011 and $103 billion for FY 2012.[35]

Although state and local policy makers have voiced their gratitude for the federal fiscal transfusion, they also realize that the increased federal funding is only a stopgap measure, since it is temporary and does not become part of state and local governments' ongoing budget base. After FY 2011, state and local government officials will be confronted with prospective tax increases or spending cuts to fill budget gaps, unless the hoped-for economic recovery is strong enough to replenish lost revenues or at least significantly reduce the need for politically painful budget actions. Yet for many, the solace of getting needed fiscal help in the short run crowded out anxiety about what the future may hold. And as policy makers in our nation's capital turned their attention to reducing the federal budget deficit and lowering debt, that anxiety deepened.

THE PLIGHT OF LOCAL GOVERNMENTS IN THE FEDERAL SYSTEM

Local governments have found themselves squeezed by fiscal federalism. Because they are legally creatures of the states, they possess only those powers given to them in state constitutions or by acts of state legislatures, which makes them vulnerable. They do not always possess the authority to respond to exigencies not of their own making. For instance, the federal government may reduce financial assistance to cities and counties at the same time that states place limitations on their ability to raise local revenues. Those restrictions commonly limit property tax increases, prompting local governments to look elsewhere for needed revenues. However, local governments can turn only to other revenue mechanisms that states have given them the authority to employ. Local income taxes and sales taxes remain the province of the state, unless the state constitution or statutory law has conferred that authority on municipalities or counties. Both the federal government and the states can mandate that local governments comply with certain policies or administrative requirements, even though that compliance requires additional unplanned local spending.

Since the Reagan administration, local governments have also had to cope with a declining share of federal grants-in-aid as a percentage of locally raised revenue, as Table 3.3 illustrates. However, relative declines in federal aid to local governments can be offset by increases in state aid. But as this table also shows, that did not happen to a significant extent. State aid's share of local general revenue has remained essentially consistent since the beginning of the Reagan years.

It is apparent that local governments have been forced to become more self-reliant. They have increased existing user fees and added new ones. In addition, where they have the option, cities and counties have increasingly turned to the local sales tax and income tax for additional revenue.[36] Despite its relative decline, the property tax still remains the biggest source of local revenues. Confronting citizen opposition to property tax increases, cities and counties are focusing their energies on expanding their local property tax bases, using incentives to attract business and industry to locate and expand within their civic boundaries. Economic development has become the watchword of the day in many communities—development that provides jobs along with an increased tax base.

Table 3.3 Distribution of Local General Revenue, Selected Years, 1902–2006

Year	Amount ($ Millions)	Percentage of Total		
		From Local Source	From Federal Government	From State
1902	854	93.4	0.5	6.1
1922	6,866	91.7	0.2	8.1
1932	5,690	85.7	0.2	14.1
1940	6,939	72.2	4.0	23.8
1950	14,014	68.4	1.5	30.1
1960	33,027	69.4	1.8	28.8
1970	90,916	63.5	3.2	33.3
1980	231,453	55.9	9.1	35.0
1990	512,322	62.8	3.6	33.6
2000	888,865	60.6	3.7	35.7
2002	995,779	60.0	4.3	35.7
2004	1,094,729	60.6	3.7	35.7
2006	1,243,748	61.7	4.4	33.9

Note: Because of rounding, percentages may not add up to 100 percent.
Source: Bureau of the Census, U.S. Department of Commerce.

Local governments have been forced to fend more for themselves over the past two decades. The tight economic times of the early 1990s forced state governments to reexamine their fiscal conditions and more guardedly prioritize their spending. The ensuing economic recovery and strong growth that followed, along with the unexpected windfall of tobacco settlement monies (discussed at length in Chapter 18), gave state policymakers the fiscal flexibility to follow their inherent political inclination to do more for the folks back home. The National Association of State Budget Officers reported that about half the state budget changes for FY 2000 affected local governments. Most of those changes increased aid to education or reduced local property taxes.[37]

The almost magical fiscal conditions in the late 1990s and early 2000 were not sustainable; the 2001 recession and the slow economic growth that followed it forced state legislatures to cut spending and raise taxes in order to comply with their states' balanced budget requirements. As discussed more fully in Chapter 18, strong economic growth toward mid-decade turned revenue shortfalls into budget surpluses in most states. However, the still fresh experience of cutback management prompted governors and state legislatures to exercise greater restraint in increasing state aid to local governments.

With the economy's sharp downward plunge toward the end of the decade, governors and legislatures faced daunting revenue shortfalls even larger than they confronted earlier in the decade. Although federal fiscal stimulus spending temporarily reduced the magnitude of necessary budget cuts, state aid to local governments was forced to share in the budget reductions, at the very time when falling home prices cut into local property tax revenues.[38]

REGULATORY FEDERALISM

Federal aid to state and local governments often comes with strings attached. The federal government may impose conditions on state and local governments that accept its financial assistance. This **regulatory federalism** has become a prominent part of the landscape of fiscal federalism and is most commonly directed at the state partner. It includes a variety of mechanisms aimed at eliciting compliance with federal policy or administrative requirements. The first type of regulatory federalism involves mandates, which require that state or local governments follow the dictates of federal statutes or administrative rules or face sanctions for noncompliance. The second type uses federal funding to bias state or local options in ways that are consistent with federal policy preferences. Noncompliance brings with it the threat of lost federal funds. As a third option, the federal government can partially preempt the states by establishing minimum national standards while continuing to authorize the states to exercise primary regulatory responsibility in the program area, as long as state standards meet or exceed the national minimum. For the states to exercise regulatory authority within these parameters, federal law usually requires the states to submit a plan to the responsible federal agency showing that the states' regulatory requirements conform to federal law. Then, if these mechanisms are ineffective in eliciting uniform compliance or prove to be unduly cumbersome, the federal government can impose financial penalties or turn to outright preemption, enacting laws or regulations that take precedence over state laws or regulations. Penalties can be assessed directly against the regulated program or against a different program when Congress believes that action provides a more effective penalty. This latter instance involves the use of so-called crossover sanctions. Let's look at each in turn.

Mandates

Congress can impose mandates on states and local governments without giving them the funds required to pay for the added costs these direct orders impose. In one of its most highly publicized mandates, Congress amended the Fair Labor Standards Act to extend federal minimum wage and hour requirements to state and local public employees. Upon legal challenge by the League of Cities, the U.S. Supreme Court initially ruled that Congress could not order the states to do something that fell within the states' constitutionally protected reserved powers. The Court subsequently reversed that decision[39] in its 1985 ruling in *Garcia v. San Antonio Transit Authority.*

More recent mandates have provoked the ire of policymakers in many states. The National Voter Registration Act of 1993, for example, requires that states allow residents to register to vote when they apply for a driver's license. It also mandates that voter registration be made available at public assistance offices, including those serving people on welfare, the unemployed, and the disabled. Another significant mandate, included in the Americans with Disabilities Act of 1990, requires that state and local governments modify their government facilities to make them accessible to individuals with disabilities.

State and local policymakers have become increasingly vocal in their opposition to unfunded mandates. The Republican NGA, under the leadership of its chairperson, Utah

---

regulatory federalism A variety of mechanisms employed by the federal government to enlist state compliance with federal policy or administrative requirements, including mandates, financial sanctions, and preemption.

governor Mike Leavitt, championed relief from unfunded mandates. Responding to intense feelings back home, the Republican leadership in the U.S. House of Representatives incorporated mandate reform in their 1994 Contract with America, requiring the Congressional Budget Office to disclose the costs of legislative mandates on state and local governments. The proposal also called for tougher procedural obstacles for mandates to overcome in the legislative process. President Clinton, in his 1995 State of the Union address, chimed in his support for mandate reform. Congress, in this environment of bipartisan support, approved the proposal, which Clinton signed into law in March 1995.

Although legislation has been proposed to require federal funding for any mandate that Congress imposes on state or local governments, no bill has passed either chamber. The costs of such a provision and its likely negative effect on the federal budget deficit greatly mitigate its prospects of passage. Yet mounting opposition to mandates in state capitols and city halls will keep the issue of federal funding of its mandates in the policy limelight. As governors and state legislative leaders press their case for federal mandate reform, it is likely that local executive and legislative leaders will become more vocal about relief from mounting state-imposed mandates in their petitions.

Penalties to Bias Options

President Reagan's Presidential Commission on Drunk Driving, in its 1983 Final Report, called for the states to adopt 21 as the minimum age for purchasing and possessing alcoholic beverages. Rather than require states to adopt such laws, and thus raising the issue of its authority to mandate state legislation in a traditional area of reserved power, Congress employed a cross-over sanction, making full receipt of federal highway funding contingent on state enactment of such legislation. States that failed to enact the 21-year-old minimum drinking age within two years of passage of the federal legislation faced having their federal highway funds reduced by 5 percent for the first year of noncompliance and 10 percent for the second year and each year beyond. Future compliance, after the deadlines, would not result in a retroactive restoration of withheld funds. After some initial recalcitrance, all states have complied.

In a similar vein, Congress passed legislation in 1974, during a national energy crisis, which gave the federal Department of Transportation authority to disapprove a state's federally aided highway projects if its legislature did not adopt a maximum 55 mph speed limit. All states complied within a mere two months, but their enforcement of the law, despite required speed monitoring, has been spotty at best. In 1987, with the Reagan administration's endorsement, Congress increased the national speed limit to 65 mph on rural portions of the interstate and on other designated four-lane highways outside metropolitan areas. Congress later allowed states to set even higher limits.

Partial Preemption

The area of environmental regulation provides many examples of the federal government's increasingly strengthened use of partial preemption. In fact, the Water Quality Act of 1965 was the first federal statutory act to employ partial preemption as a federal regulatory tool. That legislation made it clear that the federal government was ultimately responsible for ensuring water quality across the nation, but the states were allowed to exercise responsibility for administration and enforcement over water quality as long as they complied with the requirements of the federal act, which merely mandated that states adopt their own standards "applicable to interstate waters or portions thereof within each state," accompanied by implementation and enforcement plans.[40] If states dragged their feet in setting standards, the legislation authorized the federal government to promulgate standards in place of state discretion. Nevertheless, fewer than 30 states had enacted acceptable plans within five years of the act's passage.[41] In response, rather than preempting the states altogether, Congress passed the Water Control Act of 1972, signed into law by President Nixon. It set minimum national standards for discharge of effluent into a waterway. States, however, could enact more restrictive standards. In either case, the states were delegated authority to administer and enforce the requirements. If they demurred, the federal EPA could step in and assume direct regulatory control. In 1974, Congress went even further, requiring the EPA to set maximum allowable levels for several chemical and bacteriological pollutants in the nation's waterways, which the states then were expected to enforce. As with the earlier legislation, if the states chose not to play that role, the EPA could assume direct control.

Outright Preemption

Outright federal preemption has been the exception rather than the rule within regulatory federalism, but Congress has resorted to it when other mechanisms have not worked effectively. The regulation of motor carriers provides a salient example.

Prior to enactment of the Surface Transportation Assistance Act of 1982, states could set limits on trucks' fully loaded weight, length, and width. As a variant of partial preemption, a state's maximum limits had to fall within the allowed federal maximum limits. Yet each state was free, within those outer limits, to enact lower maximum limits consistent with its policy preferences. This system produced nonuniform requirements among the states, which prompted the trucking industry to push for uniformity. Their argument was simple: nonuniformity impeded the efficient movement of interstate transport. Instead of using the threat of sanctions to induce the states to adopt higher uniform maximum limits, Congress chose to preempt the states' rights to set limits on motor carriers traveling the interstate highways or designated primary routes. Preemption held the promise of a swift and sure removal of a perceived impediment to economically rational truck transport.[42] Subsequent amendments to the law have continued the federal preemption in this area.

In another example, Congress enacted legislation in August 1994 that prohibited the states from regulating routes and rates in intrastate trucking. That legislation, which took effect January 1, 1995, followed more than a decade after the federal deregulation of interstate trucking. Although the state governments can no longer regulate the routes over which commercial motor carriers can carry goods, or the prices they charge for that service, the states can continue to regulate motor carriers to ensure compliance with safety and insurance requirements.

The No Child Left Behind legislation provides a recent example of outright federal preemption. In this law, Congress gave parents of children attending public schools that fail to make adequate yearly progress toward meeting performance standards the right to transfer their children to another public school in the district. The federal mandate requires the school district to provide transportation.

RELATIONS AMONG THE STATES

In addition to the hierarchical relationships inherent in fiscal federalism and regulatory federalism, the states also cooperate with each other on the horizontal plane of interstate relations. The framers of the Constitution, realizing that citizens of the United States would move and transact business across state lines, recognized the need for reciprocal treatment among the states. They set out to establish a constitutional balance between the rights of individuals to exercise their personal liberty and their ability to escape responsibility for their actions in one state by simply moving to another. As a result, they created Article IV, which addresses the following provisions governing interstate relations: full faith and credit, privileges and immunities, extradition, and interstate compacts.

Full Faith and Credit

The Constitution stipulates that "full faith and credit shall be given in each state to the public acts, records, and judicial proceedings of every other state." Thus, official records registered in one state, such as birth certificates, must be accepted as valid records of birth in other states. Similarly, courts in one state must accept the court records of other states, in effect also accepting the associated judicial decisions. If this were not the case, a person would need only to cross state lines to escape the consequences of a court judgment ordered in his or her former state.

The dominant current controversy over Article IV's full faith and credit provision surrounds the issue of same-sex marriage. In December 2003, the Massachusetts State Supreme Court ruled that same-sex couples residing in Massachusetts cannot be denied the right to marry under that state's constitution. Massachusetts appealed the decision to the U.S. Supreme Court, which refused in November 2004 to overturn the state court's ruling. The Massachusetts legislature in September 2005 defeated a proposed amendment to the state constitution that would have banned same-sex marriages and instead create civil unions. Governor Deval Patrick in August 2008 signed into law legislation that allowed same-sex residents of other states to be legally married in Massachusetts. Beyond Massachusetts, same-sex marriage is legal in Connecticut, Iowa, Vermont, Rhode Island, and New York. State supreme court orders authorized same-sex marriages in Connecticut (in 2008) and in Iowa (in 2009). Vermont in 2009 became the first state to legalize same-sex marriage by legislation, but it took an override of the governor's veto to accomplish the feat. After failing to pass a marriage bill early in 2011, Rhode Island's legislature passed, and the governor signed, a civil unions bill in June, which gave same-sex couples many of the rights and benefits that the state provides married couples. On June 24, 2011, New York Governor Andrew M. Cuomo's signature approved legislation legalizing same-sex marriage, making New York the largest state where gay and lesbian couples are able to wed. The legality of same-sex marriage in these states raises the issue of whether other states must legally recognize them when the married partners move and become residents elsewhere. In response to this conundrum but not resolving it, a number of states have enacted statues defining marriage as being between one man and one woman.

Complicating matters is the fact that Congress passed the federal Defense of Marriage Act (DOMA) in 1996, which President Bill Clinton signed into law. The act stipulates that "No state shall be required to give effect to a law of any other state with respect to

Exploring the Web

Organizing for Competition

Federal legislation and regulation can affect both state and local governments. Thus, it should not be surprising that state and local governments form associations to promote their interests when dealing with the federal government.

■ At the state level, the NGA (www.nga.org) represents the interests of our nation's governors, while the NCSL (www.ncsl.org) pursues the interests of state legislators. Check out their websites and become familiar with the major issues of concern to the states. Take a look at current issues of the NGA's publications, *Legislative Updates* and *Legislative Priorities,* and the NCSL's *State-Federal News.*

■ Local governments are not to be outdone by their state counterparts. Cities, towns, and counties have their own associations. The following shows the major organizations and the interests they represent:

Organization	Interest
U.S. Conference of Mayors (www.usmayors.org)	Big Cities
National League of Cities (www.nlc.org)	Medium/Small Cities
National Association of Towns (www.natat.org)	Towns and Townships
National Association of Counties (www.naco.org)	Counties

Each site alerts members and the public to its association's legislative priorities. Check out, for example, the Mayors' *Washington Update,* the Counties' *Legislative Alert,* or the Towns' *Washington Report.*

same-sex marriage." It also defines marriage as between a man and a woman. By the end of 2008, a total of 40 states had passed legislation modeled after DOMA. Absent amending the U.S. Constitution to define marriage in a way that would render same-sex marriage illegal in all states, the U.S. Supreme Court may ultimately decide the constitutionality of DOMA as it relates to full faith and credit.

Privileges and Immunities

Article IV also states that "the citizens of each state shall be entitled to all privileges and immunities of citizens in the several states." People can move freely among the states, changing their residence from one state to another, owning property in one state while maintaining a primary domicile in another, and conducting business across state lines. In doing so, the Constitution provides that a state should not discriminate against legal residents of other states living or owning property or businesses in that state. For example, a state could not legally establish two rates for its income tax—one for new residents and another for existing residents who had lived in the state for a minimum period of time.

In practice, however, the courts have allowed limitations. States do treat newcomers differently in certain cases. Persons holding professional or occupational licenses in their old state must meet the requirements for licensure in their new state if they want to practice or work in that state. They can also face a requirement that they reside in their new state for a specified time before they can become licensed. Such residency requirements also commonly apply to college and university students who are attending public higher education in one state but hold legal residence in another. Before they can qualify for the lower resident tuition amounts, they have to meet several requirements intended to demonstrate that they are in that state to establish permanent residence, not merely to get an education before returning to their home state. The courts have also allowed states to charge out-of-state residents higher fees to use public property or facilities. Nonresidents are commonly charged higher fees for the privilege of hunting or fishing within a state's borders or for camping or hiking in a state park, based on the rationale that residents have already at least partially supported these public resources through state taxes.

Extradition

The Constitution also reads that "a person in any state with treason, felony, or other crime who shall flee from justice and be found in another state, shall on the demand of the executive authority from the state from which he fled, be delivered up, to be removed to the state having jurisdiction of the crime." Thus, if someone commits a murder in Wisconsin, flees to North Dakota, and is arrested there, the governor of Wisconsin can request that the accused murderer be returned to Wisconsin for trial. Requests for extradition are generally honored; a clear norm of reciprocity exists among the nation's governors.

Interstate Compacts

The Constitution provides that states can enter into compacts with other states, but that these agreements must be approved by Congress. Although Congress has readily approved them, it has the authority to withhold its approval if it believes that a proposed compact infringes on the inherent powers of the national government. Existing compacts prominently apply to areas such as the use of water flowing across state borders, the conservation of natural resources crossing state lines, the supervision of prison inmates on parole, the exchange of information about motor vehicle operator moving violations, and the handling of interstate tax matters, to name a few.

RELATIONS WITH INDIAN NATIONS

Treaties between the federal government and American Indian nations directly affect 34 states. Most of these states are west of the Mississippi River, but New York, Michigan, Florida, Connecticut, and Wisconsin are also included. Although the treaties were between

Table 3.4 Federal Policies toward Indian Nations

Timeline	Policies
Up to 1830	Mix conquest and coexistence. Make treaties.
1830–1871	Force all tribes to move west of the Mississippi River. Make treaties.
1871–1934	Assimilate American Indians into white culture.
1934–1953	Respect tribal customs and government. Encourage economic self-determination.
1953–1973	Terminate legal status of tribes. Ignore treaty provisions.
1973–present	Recognize tribes and treaty rights. Encourage constitutions and self-determination.

two nations, the United States and an American Indian tribal nation, invariably the tribal leaders signed because of actual or threatened military defeat. The legal status of the various tribes in the United States is that of a **domestic dependent nation**, where they retain their individual identity and sovereignty, but must rely on the federal government for the interpretation and application of treaty provisions. State and local governments are clearly affected by the federal–tribal relations but have little influence and almost no legal authority over these relations.

The policy approach of the federal government toward American Indians has varied widely (Table 3.4). From 1830 to 1871, a major goal was to move all American Indians to land west of the Mississippi. The policy between 1871 and 1934 was to assimilate American Indians into the white culture of the United States. From 1934 until 1953 and then again from 1973 to today, the formal policy was to respect tribal customs, strengthen tribal governments, and promote economic self-determination. Between 1953 and 1973, the federal government terminated the legal status of some of the tribes, ended services to them, and refused to recognize their treaty rights. This generated protests and led to a resumption of the general policy begun in 1934.[43] While some would argue that the federal government has not been serious or effective enough in supporting treaty rights and self-determination, the current policy received new emphasis with the inclusion of tribes in steps to devolve responsibilities from Washington to states and local communities.

States are not parties to the treaties between the Unites States and American Indian nations and have no direct legal authority over tribes. The federal government has granted some powers, in several specific areas, to states. The Indian Gaming Regulatory Act of 1988, for example, gives state governments limited authority to negotiate agreements, called **compacts**, with tribes who wish to operate casino gambling. Also, in 1953, Congress passed Public Law 280, which allows some states to pursue Indians suspected of criminal behavior even if they are on reservation land.

For the most part, however, federal–tribal relations provide given constraints and opportunities as states and communities engage in planning and problem solving. The two most important features of federal–tribal relations for state and local governments are land rights

---

domestic dependent nation A type of sovereignty that makes a Native American tribe in the United States outside the authority of state governments but reliant on the federal government for the definition of tribal authority.

compact A formal legal agreement between a state and a tribe.

and treaty provisions for hunting, fishing, and gathering. Tribes have **reservation land** and **trust land**, neither of which is subject to taxation or regulation by state or local governments. Reservation land is designated in a treaty. Tribes can acquire trust land by purchasing or otherwise securing ownership of a parcel and then seeking to have it placed in trust status by the secretary of the Department of the Interior. The general policy of the department is to grant the request if a tribe had once lived on the land and currently has a legal deed to it. Trust land has the potential for disrupting a community's development plans or taking part of its tax base. For example, a tribe can purchase land in a metropolitan area, get it placed in trust, and then build a casino on it, despite objections by city authorities that a casino does not fit with development plans and that the casino cannot be taxed or regulated. Indian nations typically build and maintain cooperative relations with local governments, but there are some unresolved disputes when tribal rights and local development plans clash.

Hunting, fishing, and gathering activities have important cultural and religious significance for many American Indian nations. Treaty provisions giving rights to tribes to hunt, fish, and gather wild rice or berries on their own land and on public lands and waterways in land they once owned are crucial for tribal identity and dignity. These treaty rights supersede regulations enacted for environmental and recreational purposes. Non-American Indian anglers and hunters sometimes protest that American Indians have special privileges. Environmental planners worry about the potential implications of unregulated American Indian activity. In 1999, for example, the Makah tribe in the Northwest celebrated the successful capture and killing of a whale. While the tribe applauded the preservation of an important cultural tradition, some wildlife advocates bemoaned the treaty rights that allowed the destruction of a valued animal. Treaty rights are fundamentally between tribes and the federal government because they are the parties that signed the treaties. Nonetheless, these issues invariably affect states and local communities.

SUMMARY AND CONCLUSIONS

The U.S. Supreme Court's rulings over the past two centuries have greatly expanded the powers of the national government in relation to the states, particularly in the areas of interstate commerce and civil rights. However, the national government's penetration into areas of traditional state prerogative has largely been the product of federal legislation, characteristically in response to presidential initiatives. Federal grants-in-aid became the fiscal carrot to win state cooperation toward realizing national domestic policy goals. The states accepted the trade-off of federal policy leadership in exchange for financial support in addressing public problems facing the states. The federal government increasingly utilized the categorical grant as the primary instrument to meet states' needs.

---

reservation land Land designated in a treaty that is under the authority of a Native American nation and is exempt from most state laws and taxes.

trust land Land owned by a Native American nation and designated by the federal Bureau of Indian Affairs as exempt from most state laws and taxes.

Following nearly two decades of federal program initiatives and rising federal spending, Ronald Reagan's election to the presidency marked the beginning of a period of reexamination of the federal government's relationship with state and local governments. For Reagan, the reach of the federal government had become too extensive. He successfully sought to cut taxes and reduce the growth in domestic spending, including real-dollar decreases in federal aid to state and local governments. Along with these reductions, the Reagan administration proposed returning the responsibility for several federal programs to the states, as well as giving them greater discretion in setting spending priorities for others. He achieved only modest success in both respects. President Bill Clinton promised a return to greater federal leadership in domestic policy making. He also called for greater state and local discretion in determining how to reach national goals. Welfare reform, which eliminated AFDC's entitlement status and substituted an appropriations-capped program of block grants to the states, gave state officials considerable flexibility in administering their new welfare programs and experimenting with ways to move recipients from welfare to work. Congress, however, had more to do with shaping the new legislation than did the president. With Republican majorities in control of both chambers of Congress, Washington looked more to decentralization and devolution than to augmenting federal assistance to state and local governments.

The George W. Bush administration sent mixed signals on federalism, promising a return to Reaganite ideals while expanding federal involvement in educational policy and homeland security. Bush's successor, Barack Obama, inherited a deteriorating economy that quickly fell into the deepest recession since the Great Depression. The Obama administration's attention turned to providing financial assistance to state and local governments as a means of boosting economic demand and offsetting a portion of the budgetary cuts that state and local government officials would have been forced to make.

Since the late 1970s, local governments have found themselves squeezed by fiscal federalism. With their reliance on property taxes, local governments have been caught between taxpayer revolts and cutbacks in federal financial assistance, prompting them to seek other forms of revenue expansion, including increased reliance on user fees and local income and sales taxes, where permitted by state law. They have turned to the states for increased financial aid, and the states have responded when their own fiscal condition has allowed. Nevertheless, it is clear that local governments have been forced to become more self-reliant.

Federal aid to state and local governments frequently comes with strings attached, as regulatory requirements often accompany financial assistance. Regulatory federalism can include mandates that give direct orders from the federal government, penalties imposed by the federal government to bias state and local options, partial federal preemption, or outright federal preemption.

In addition to the hierarchical relationships inherent in fiscal and regulatory federalism, the U.S. Constitution requires that the states themselves cooperate with each other on the horizontal plane of intergovernmental relations to ensure that citizens are not inappropriately discriminated against as they move or establish business enterprises across state lines. Conversely, interstate cooperation addresses limiting the extent to which residents of one state can escape responsibility for their illegal actions by simply moving or fleeing to another state.

Discussion Questions

1. How has the inherent tension between the implied powers of the national government and the inherent powers of the states been interpreted over time by the courts? What significance do these interpretations since 1980 hold for the states?

2. Compare and contrast the five phases of federalism. What factors have influenced the national government's changing involvement in the affairs of the states, and how have the states responded?

3. Discuss the various ways in which the federal government has shared its financial resources with state and local government over time. Include in your discussion any relationship between the form of assistance and differing views about the appropriate role of government in society in general, and about the appropriate role of the federal government in particular.

4. Discuss the options that the federal government has to elicit state compliance with national policy objectives, and provide examples of how each one has been used.

5. To what extent is it accurate to portray local units of government as particularly squeezed by the fiscal policies of the federal government and the states?

Glossary

block grants 61
categorical grants 60
compact 82
concurrent powers 53
domestic dependent nation 82

empowerment zones 69
formula grants 61
Great Society 60
implied powers clause 52
judicial power 53

project grants 61
regulatory federalism 76
reservation land 83
trust land 83

Endnotes

1. "The Dimming American Dream," *State Legislatures* 21, no. 7 (July/August 1995), 7.

2. "Public Views of the Environment," *Congressional Quarterly Weekly* Report 53, no. 24 (July 17, 1995), 1697.

3. *McCulloch v. Maryland*, 17 U.S. 316 (1819); *National Relations Board v. Jones and Laughlin Steel Corporation*, 301 U.S. 1 (1937); *E.E.O.C. v. Wyoming*, 460 U.S. 226 (1983).

4. *Brown v. Board of Education of Topeka, Kansas*, 347 U.S. 483 (1954); *Harper v. Virginia State Board of Elections*, 383 U.S. 663 (1966); *South Carolina v. Katzerback*, 383 U.S. 301 (1966).

5. David G. Savage, "High Court Bolsters States' Rights," *State Legislatures* 23, no. 8 (September 1997), 11–13.

6. Council of State Governments, "Supreme Court Confirms the Role of States in U.S. Federalism System," *Issue Alerts* (July 25, 1997).

7. OYEZ, *Raich v. Gonzales*, 545 U.S. 03-1454 (2005).

8. OYEZ, *Gonzales v. Oregon,* 546 U.S. 04-623 (2006).

9. This categorization in part uses a modified framework developed by Thomas R. Dye in *Politics in States and Communities,* 6th ed. (Englewood Cliffs, N.J.: Prentice Hall, 1988), 70–72.

10. *Texas v. White,* 7 Wallace 700 (1869).

11. 109 U.S. 3 (1883).

12. Ann O'M. Bowman and Richard C. Kearney *State and Local Government* (Boston, Mass.: Houghton Mifflin, 1990), 38.

13. James J. Gosling, *Budgetary Politics in American Governments,* 4th ed. (New York: Routledge, 2006), 81.

14. Ibid., 85.

15. Jeffrey R. Henig, *Public Policy and Federalism* (New York: St. Martin's Press, 1985), 16.

16. Charles A. Bowsher, "Federal Cutbacks Strengthen State Role," *State Government News* (February 1986), 18.

17. *The National Journal* 19, no. 5 (11 April 1987), 862–863.

18. *Significant Features of Fiscal Federalism*, 1988 ed., 2 (Washington, D.C.: Advisory Commission on Intergovernmental Relations, 1988), 32–33.

19. *Significant Features of Fiscal Federalism,* 1989 ed., vol. 2 (Washington, D.C.: Advisory Commission on Intergovernmental Relations), 20.

20. Bowsher, "Federal Cutbacks Strengthen State Role," 18.

21. Ronald Reagan, State of the Union Address, January 26, 1982.

22. Susan Golonka, "Whatever Happened to Federalism?" *Intergovernmental Perspective* 8, no. 1 (Winter 1982), 5.

23. David B. Walker, Albert J. Richter, and Cynthia Cates Colella, "The First Ten Months: Grant-in-Aid, Regulatory, and Other Changes," *Intergovernmental Perspective* 8, no. 1 (Winter 1982), 5.

24. George E. Peterson, "Federalism and the States: An Experiment in Decentralization," in *Reagan Record,* ed. John L. Palmer and Isabel V. Sawhill (Cambridge, Mass.: Ballinger, 1984), 224–226.

25. *Historical Tables, Budget of the U.S. Government, Fiscal Year* 2003 (Washington, D.C.: Office of Management and Budget, 2002) 217–218.

26. Bruce D. McDowell, "Grant Reform Reconsidered," *Intergovernmental Perspective* 17, no. 3 (Summer 1991), 8–11.

27. Gosling, *Budgetary Politics in American Governments*, 147.

28. David C. Saffell and Harry Basehart, *Governing States and Cities* (New York: McGraw-Hill, 1979), 46.

29. Ruben Barrales, "Federalism in the Bush Administration," *Spectrum*, Summer 2001, 5–6.

30. *Massachusetts et al. v. Environmental Protection Agency et al.*, 549 US 05-1120 (2007).

31. *The National Strategy for Homeland Security* (Washington, D.C.: The White House, 2003), 64–65.

32. Dan Eggen and Mary Beth Sheridan, "Anti-Terror Funding Cut in D.C. and New York," *The Washington Post*, June 1, 2006, www.Washingtonpost.com. Accessed April 9, 2009.

33. Spencer S. Hsu, "Local Security Grants Cut by Nearly Half," *Washington Post*, February 5, 2008, A13.

34. Farhana Hossain et al, "The Stimulus Plan: How to Spend $787 Billion, *The New York Times*, April 7, 2009, http://projects.nytimes.com/44th_president/stimulus.

35. Donald J. Boyd, "What Will Happen to State Budgets When the Money Runs Out? (Albany, N.Y.: The Nelson A. Rockefeller Institute of Government, February 19, 2009). Elizabeth McNichol, Phil Oliff, and Nicholas Johnson, "States Continue to Feel Recession's Impact," Center on Budget and Policy Priorities, June 17, 2011, www.cbpp.org.

36. Gosling, *Budgetary Politics in American Governments*, 195–202.

37. *Fiscal Survey of the States*, 1999 (Washington, D.C.: National Association of State Budget Officers, December 1999), 3.

38. *Fiscal Survey of the States*, 2008 (Washington, D.C.: National Association of State Budget Officers, December 2008), 9–13.

39. *National League of Cities v. Usery*, 426 U.S. 833 (1976).

40. *Water Quality Act of 1965,* 79 Stat. 903, 33 U.S.C., 1151 et seq.

41. John J. Harrigan, *Politics and Policy in States and Communities,* 4th ed. (New York: HarperCollins, 1991), 466.

42. James J. Gosling, "Transportation Policy and the Ironies of Intergovernmental Relations," in *The Midwest Response to the New Federalism,* ed. Peter K. Eisinger and William Gormley (Madison: University of Wisconsin Press, 1988), 250–259.

43. Sharon O'Brien, *American Indian Tribal Governments* (Norman: University of Oklahoma Press, 1989), 261–297.

CHAPTER 4

Constitutions and Charters

LEARNING OBJECTIVES

- Understand how state and tribal constitutions and municipal and school charters establish basic individual rights and the fundamental rules of the game for governance.
- Appreciate the effects of regional historical developments on state constitutions.
- Know the common, basic provisions of constitutions.
- Recognize the major types of local governments.

In 2004, a total of 27 states amended their constitutions to ban same-sex marriages and, in most cases, civil unions that provide rights and responsibilities similar to those in a marriage relationship. Supreme courts in Massachusetts, Iowa, and California have interpreted their respective state constitutions to provide same-sex couples with the right to marry. Voters in California amended their constitution in 2008 to overturn their supreme court and deny same-sex couples the right to marry. In August 2010 a federal judge ruled that the California vote violated the equal protection clause of the Fourteenth Amendment to the U.S. Constitution. California halted marrying same-sex couples while the federal ruling was being appealed. High courts in Maryland, New York, and Washington ruled that their constitutions do not provide a constitutional right or prohibition regarding same-sex marriage, leaving it to the legislature and governor to address this issue. In 2011, New York passed a law authorizing same-sex marriage. State constitutions, in other words, are key in defining rights, and in doing so these documents may not conflict with the U.S. Constitution.

Landlords and tenants typically sign contracts that specify what the landlord must do to maintain the property, what the tenant must *not* do to the property, the rate of the rent and when it must be paid, and what limits there are to the tenant's behavior (i.e., having pets, raising children, inviting guests, producing noise).

- Contracts are fundamental to our social and business relationships.
- Contracts are agreements that specify what the respective parties must do, may do, and must not do.

- Contracts can bind heirs and successors.
- In anticipation of potential changes in circumstances, processes exist for amending, replacing, and even voiding contracts.

Similarly, citizens enter into a fundamental agreement with one another about what their government must do, may do, and must not do, and about what obligations individuals have toward government. That agreement is a constitution. A **constitution** differs from a contract in that it is not an agreement establishing a relationship between two different parties; instead, it is a document that stipulates how all citizens will be governed.

Constitutions, like contracts, set forth the basic rules of the game. A constitution describes in some detail the institutions and processes of the government. It also specifies what the government is empowered to do (i.e., seize private property with just compensation when necessary for the common good) and what it may not do (i.e., force individuals to practice a certain religion). Many countries consider marriage a religious act and outside the scope of government authority or concern. This would translate into a constitutional provision that limited government to recognizing agreements between two individuals to share responsibilities and obligations, but would not have governments conferring marital status on the couple.

Every state has a constitution, as does the federal government. Most American Indian tribes, under pressure from the federal government, have adopted constitutions similar to those of state governments but with some adaptations designed to preserve important tribal traditions.

Local governments, however, are creatures of state governments. The institutions, processes, and scope of authority of local governments are set by state statutes and by **charters** issued by state governments. States establish counties, school districts, and water districts. As people settle in an area, they need to have a city, town, or village government. However, a group of people cannot, on their own, agree to be a city and agree on how that city or school district will be run. To have legal authority, individuals who want to have their own city or school district must secure formal recognition from the state. Once they do so, and depending on the type of local government they qualify to be, state laws will provide them with a charter that gives authority to make certain laws, provide specific services, collect taxes or fees, and perhaps even enforce their laws. Since 1992, state governments have allowed for the creation of charter schools—public schools with their own individual "constitutions"—giving them the authority to act differently from other public schools.

State constitutions and the laws establishing local public authorities are critical to the face-to-face interaction between individuals and governments. These laws affect the authority and discretion of public officials. School officials are limited in the problems that they can solve in part because school districts are limited by state government in what they can do. Public school officials may want to provide funds to a farm family that has been

---

constitution Written document establishing the basic authority, rules, and procedures for national, state, and tribal governments.

charters State or local laws that establish the basic authority, rules, and procedures for municipal governments and, in some cases, schools.

devastated by a storm, but they cannot do so unless a law authorizing that expenditure was passed in accordance with the provisions of the charter or law establishing that school. A police officer may be convinced that a sex offender who has just been released from prison is going to repeat the crime, but the state (and federal) constitution requires due process before anyone can be detained or incarcerated. Discretion is a function of what is allowed. Constitutions and charters provide and limit legal capacity or authority.

HISTORY OF STATE CONSTITUTIONS

Constitutions are legal documents of fundamental importance in the United States. It must be acknowledged that constitutions are also political documents. The battles at constitutional conventions and the drives for and against constitutional change reflect not only differences in philosophies but conflicts between major groups in society. Constitutions make relatively dry reading material. The history of constitution writing, on the other hand, is fascinating.

The First State Constitutions: Guarantee Individual Rights, Weaken Executive Powers

The 13 original states had constitutions before the United States did. To define the institutions and processes of government, officials in the new states modified their colonial charters. The charters, which were only about five pages each, formally defined the governing authority granted by the British throne to the governors of each colony. These included provisions for a legislative body to advise the governor and pass laws in certain areas, subject to the governor's veto. The modifications made to create state constitutions obviously removed references to the British monarch. They also weakened the executive branch of government and strengthened the legislature. The founders designed their new state legislatures to be the dominant institution, in large part as a response to what they regarded as tyranny and oppression by British governors.

The state constitutions also included a **bill of rights**, identifying some basic individual liberties—such as freedom of expression and the right to due process when accused of a crime—that government had to recognize.[1] Colonial charters did not include a bill of rights. A major concern of those writing the first state constitutions was to limit the scope and powers of government. All the original state constitutions included sections that protected individual rights from government intrusion.

The authors of state constitutions drew from the political philosophies of John Locke and Jean-Jacques Rousseau, who were prominent at the time.[2] These authors are identified with social contract theory, which views a government as the result of an agreement, implicit or explicit, among individuals about how they are going to work together to serve their common interests without unnecessarily sacrificing certain basic interests and rights they have as individuals. Constitutions come fairly close to being empirical examples of such contracts.

---

bill of rights Provisions in a constitution that prohibit government from restricting certain individual liberties.

Despite the egalitarian, democratic rhetoric that goes with social contract theory and the American Revolution, the initial constitutions were highly elitist. Only white males who owned property could vote or hold office. Government, like other institutions of status and authority, was considered the responsibility and the province of wealthy, well-educated, white men. A more accessible and responsive form of government came later, in response to the demands from those excluded.

The Federal Constitution: Strengthen National Government

As Chapter 3 explained, the U.S. Constitution contains ambiguities and contradictions in provisions that describe the relative powers and roles of the national government and the state governments. That disparity has led to a dynamic relationship between the two levels of government. In general, federal constitutional developments have established a clear legal supremacy of the national government, although the U.S. Supreme Court has placed limits on how extensively Washington, D.C., can control the state.

The dominant legal position of the national government has had important effects on state constitutions written after the ratification of the U.S. Constitution in 1787. When the first state constitutions were written, a major concern was *limiting* the power and discretion of government. When states sent delegates to Philadelphia to repair the flaws in the Articles of Confederation, the major concern was *empowering* the national government. Not part of the original Constitution, the Bill of Rights was drafted to address concerns about the scope of federal power, and some reluctant, skeptical states made the addition of those first 10 amendments their condition for ratifying the Constitution.

The original emphasis on empowerment not only laid the groundwork for the legal supremacy of the national government, but also affected the constitutions of states that joined the United States after the adoption of the U.S. Constitution. No longer were existing states coming together to form a union. Instead, territories were seeking to join an existing union. The body with the authority to accept new states was the national government, rather than the existing state governments. Thus, the national government determined the criteria for joining and judged whether those criteria had been met. One criterion was an acceptable state constitution. Not surprisingly, Congress and the president made sure that new states had constitutions similar to those of existing states.

Northwest Ordinance of 1787: Copy Original Constitutions and Add States

One of the final legislative acts of the national Congress under the Articles of Confederation was to pass the **Northwest Ordinance of 1787**. This law continued to be recognized by the federal government under the U.S. Constitution. The Northwest

---

Northwest Ordinance of 1787 Law passed by Congress under the Articles of Confederation that established the process by which the territories of Ohio, Indiana, Illinois, Michigan, and Wisconsin would be governed and admitted as states.

Ordinance was a response to demands by settlers, in what is now Ohio, that they be under the services and protection of the U.S. government and that they be recognized as a state. The easy part was to establish basic institutions and principles for governing the area as a territory. The demands for statehood, however, raised more troubling issues. The 13 original states feared a loss of relative power, and they were not certain they had the resources to serve the needs of populations on the expanding frontier. Congress, however, felt that the added resources of an expanded United States offset these concerns.[3]

The Northwest Ordinance established a framework for adding what are now the states of Ohio, Illinois, Indiana, Michigan, and Wisconsin to the United States. It also set precedents for the other states that would follow. The ordinance took the fundamental step of recognizing that a territory governed by the United States could be admitted to the federation as a state, equal in status to existing states. A key criterion for admission stated in the ordinance was the presence of at least 60,000 free inhabitants. Slaves and Native Americans did not count. The basic text of the Northwest Ordinance follows:

1. Congress shall appoint a governor, a secretary, and three judges for the Northwest Territory. These officials shall adopt suitable laws from the original states. When the territory has five thousand free male inhabitants of full age, they shall be allowed to elect representatives. These, together with the governor and a legislative council of five, shall form a general assembly to make laws for the territory.
2. The inhabitants shall be entitled to the benefits of trial by jury and other judicial proceedings according to the common law.
3. Religion, morality, and knowledge being necessary to good government and the happiness of mankind, schools and the means of education shall forever be encouraged.
4. There shall be formed in the said territory not less than three nor more than five States. . . . And, whenever any of the said States shall have sixty thousand free inhabitants therein, such State shall be admitted, by its delegates, into the Congress of the United States, on an equal footing with the original States.
5. There shall be neither slavery nor involuntary servitude in the said territory, otherwise than in the punishment of crimes whereof the party shall have been duly convicted.

When Congress considered petitions from these states for admission to the United States, it insisted that the petitioners have a constitution that was consistent with those of the original states and that was compatible with the U.S. Constitution. This requirement was relatively easy to meet. The common pattern of initial migration to the Northwest Territory was from the original states, primarily New York and Massachusetts, as well as individuals coming directly from Europe.[4] Not surprisingly, the new state constitutions read almost exactly the same as those of New York and Massachusetts. The executive, legislative, and judicial institutions of state government had common designs among all the states. Differences were minor.

The original states all limited suffrage to white males who owned at least enough property to be liable to taxation. Ohio began the move to allow all white men to vote, even if they did not own property. Because almost all white male adults at the time owned some property, that change was more revolutionary in concept than in practical terms.

Some of the state constitutional conventions and referenda were accompanied by heated debates over banking regulations, the salaries of judges, and "radical" proposals to allow women the right to own property. The discussions of appropriate constitutions were consistent with the individualistic and moralistic political cultures of the Northeast and Midwest. The role of government and the responsibilities of the governed were central concerns. The final outcome of these debates in the newer states was the adoption of constitutions that mimicked those of the original states.[5]

Civil War: Dispute Slavery and Settle Sovereignty

States that emerged out of the Louisiana Purchase and further expansion westward followed a pattern similar to that set in the Northwest Ordinance. Statehood required white settlement and the adoption of an acceptable constitution. The major issue of contention in the establishment of state constitutions was whether they would allow for an expansion of slavery. Here, too, the dominant political culture was evident. The traditionalist South favored control by existing elites, rather than changes designed to enfranchise and empower everyone. The national movement to curtail and abolish slavery continued to grow, however. Supporters of this movement objected to the admission of states that allowed slavery. Delegates from the South denied that the federal government had the right to dictate whether a state might allow slavery and sought new allies in additional states that permitted individuals to own slaves.

The famous Missouri Compromise of 1820–1821 supposedly settled the issue of slavery in state constitutions. Missouri had a well-established tradition of slavery. Slave owners pointed to the promise in the Louisiana Purchase treaty of 1803 that they would not be deprived of their slave "property." At the same time that Missouri petitioned for admission to the United States, Maine, too, sought statehood.[6] Henry Clay, as speaker of the House of Representatives, ended the bitter debate generated by Missouri's petition for statehood by authoring a compromise that admitted Missouri as a slave state and Maine as a free state. Part of this compromise was an agreement that no more states that might come from the Louisiana Purchase territory be admitted as slave states.

The latter provision was violated in 1854 when Kansas and Nebraska were admitted as states. Senator Stephen A. Douglas from Illinois was eager to get Nebraska and Kansas admitted, in part to foster development of a transcontinental railroad that would lead to the emergence of Chicago as a hub. He convinced President Franklin Pierce and enough members of Congress to set the Missouri Compromise aside so that Kansas could be admitted as a slave state and Nebraska as a free state.[7] This infuriated those opposed to slavery. They organized a new party, the Republican Party, which immediately gained dominance in states throughout the North.

Although the emotional issue of slavery was the specific concern, the Civil War was fought in large part over whether the federal government could force states to include certain provisions in their constitutions. The Civil War also addressed the question of whether states that were part of the Union could unilaterally secede.[8] In the end, the arguments were settled in favor of a preeminent federal government. The disputes were resolved on the basis of military and economic strength, not just logic and persuasion.

When Southern states seceded, they adopted new constitutions that tied them to the Confederacy. The basic governmental institutions of the executive, legislative, and judicial branches provided for the same separation of powers authorized in the national Constitution, but the relationships between state governments and the national one were clearly more voluntary. The secessionist states preferred a **confederation**, similar to the loose union of the original states prior to the 1787 U.S. Constitution.

When the Civil War was over, the federal government forced the states of the Confederacy to rewrite their constitutions. One demand, of course, was that the new constitutions outlaw slavery. The writing of these constitutions was fraught with tensions between the vanquished traditional elites, the newly enfranchised former slaves, and carpetbaggers from the North. The highest level of state constitutional changes in history characterized the decade that followed the Civil War. Twenty-seven constitutions were entirely or substantially rewritten.

Arkansas represents a typical example. In 1864, under military occupation, the state adopted a new constitution to replace the constitution it established in 1861, when Arkansas joined the Confederate States of America. The 1864 constitution was essentially the same as its predecessor, except that it made slavery illegal and pledged allegiance to the United States of America. Four years later, Arkansas adopted what it referred to as the **Carpetbag Constitution**. Carpetbaggers were opportunists who came from one state to get a government position in another state. Nine Arkansans—three of whom had been slaves—gathered as a constitutional convention to write a document that conformed to federal requirements specified in the Reconstruction Act of 1867. Accordingly, the 1868 Arkansas constitution explicitly extended the franchise to African American men and took the vote away from former Confederates. The constitution eliminated all distinctions in the law based on race. In addition, those at the convention drew legislative district boundaries to favor counties with large African American populations.

The Carpetbag Constitution of 1868 did not last long. African Americans simply did not have the socioeconomic and political power to sustain control of state government. The federal government, as is frequently the case, had the legal authority to continue to force states to follow a particular course, but it lacked the will and the administrative capacity to ensure full compliance. Whites in Arkansas took advantage of federal inattention and of African American disorganization. They reasserted control of state government. To consolidate that control, they wrote another constitution.

The Arkansas Constitution of 1874, which has been amended but is still in force, established a weak and limited state government.[9] The office of governor was made weak by limiting it to two-year terms and by having judges and cabinet officers elected rather than appointed by the governor. The legislature was restricted to meeting for one 60-day

---

confederation A league of independent states loosely united in a common government. Examples include the United States after the Revolutionary War and before the adoption of the current U.S. Constitution, and the Southern states that seceded from the Union and then were defeated in the Civil War.

Carpetbag Constitution A state constitution established during the aftermath of the Civil War in the former Confederacy by individuals who came from Northern states and acquired positions of formal authority.

period every other year. The constitution is very detailed in describing what may and may not be authorized, especially in spending and taxing. Like other former Confederate states, Arkansas consciously weakened the voting power of African Americans by requiring literacy tests that were administered in such a way that they kept even highly educated African Americans from registering to vote. The 1874 constitution, in short, made state government weak and thereby enhanced the importance of social status and economic wealth, rather than government authority, to wield power and influence.

Expansion West and Progressive Reforms: Allow Direct Democracy

State governments in the North and Midwest were also in disarray after the Civil War. Corruption and incompetence were rampant. The culprits north of the Mason–Dixon line were political machines, not carpetbaggers. Bosses of machines relied heavily on bloc voting of neighborhoods and small towns of new immigrants from non-English-speaking countries in Europe. In return for supporting the machine, these communities could count on getting basic city services and government jobs.

The reaction to machine politics and patronage was the **Progressive Movement**, which took off at the turn of the century. The main objective of the Progressive Movement was to destroy political machines by opening the political process to individual citizens and to grassroots movements. This enhanced the participatory features of the political culture. Progressives favored the nomination of candidates for elective office through an open primary system rather than negotiations among a handful of bosses behind closed doors. Reformers also sought to curtail the patronage powers of governors and mayors by electing more agency heads, by creating citizen boards and commissions to run some agencies, and by requiring candidates to pass an examination for government jobs. The movement also favored empowering voters through several processes: (1) initiative (citizens can vote for a policy change without involving the governor or legislation), (2) referendum (legislatures submit policy changes to voters for their

Rally on the constitutional ban
of same-sex marriages.

Progressive Movement A popular reaction against machine politics and corruption that was located primarily in Northern and Western states and began in the 1890s. Progressives favored open government, party primaries, and citizen control of agencies.

approval or rejection), and (3) recall (voters can remove an elected official from office in the middle of a term).[10] All of these reforms will be discussed in more detail in other chapters.

The Progressives affected state constitutions in the Northeast and Midwest through amendments. The newer states in the West incorporated Progressive reforms into their constitutions either as they joined the Union or shortly thereafter. Like other states, those in the West borrowed heavily from existing constitutions when they wrote theirs. The noticeable difference is the influence of the Progressive Movement and the provision for direct democracy processes.[11]

When they joined the United States, Western states entered into compacts that provided federal rights to land. In 1993, Alaska's governor Walter Hickel, who had been secretary of the Interior (the department that administers federal lands) under President Nixon, sued the federal government for allegedly not abiding by the compact accompanying Alaska's statehood in 1959. That compact designated over 100 million acres in Alaska for federal parks, refuges, and wilderness areas and then stipulated that state government receive 90 percent of any mineral revenues that came from those lands. Governor Hickel calculated that the federal government owed $29 billion because of the oil extracted from Alaska. Federal courts determine the merits and the enforceability of such compacts. In this case, lower courts ruled against Alaska and the U.S. Supreme Court refused to accept an appeal.

Hawaii: A Special Case

Each state has a unique and rich history. Hawaii was a kingdom ruled by an absolute monarch through the reign of Kamehameha the Great (1782–1819).[12] One of the contemporary effects of this legacy is that Hawaii's constitution provides for more centralized governance than any other state. Public education, police and fire protection, library services, and health and welfare programs that are commonly run by local governments are run directly by state government in Hawaii.

The federal government continued the pattern of central rule when it ruled Hawaii as a territory (1900–1959). Out of deference to the monarchical tradition, the federal government established a governing structure based on an executive that was considerably more powerful than was common in state governments. The plantation economy of Hawaii provided little need for local governments. Each plantation took care of its own need for police and fire protection and other basic services. Plantations and churches provided education and social service for the families of workers. Powerful plantation owners were not eager for government duplication or interference.[13] The constitution adopted in 1956 as Hawaii joined the United States retained the centralization that had already characterized governance of the islands.

Another unique feature of Hawaii's constitution is the special attention to the welfare of native Hawaiians. A "native Hawaiian" is defined as someone who is at least 50 percent descended from the islands' indigenous inhabitants. These individuals have land rights that are specially protected, and they benefit from a fund based on the income from land designated originally by the federal government—and now state government—for this purpose.[14] Native Hawaiians are a minority of the population on the islands that bear their name, and their rights and political power continue to be an issue.

Tribal Constitutions

Treaties between the federal government and the various American Indian nations continue to define the fundamental relationships between these governments and the rights of tribes and of individual American Indians. As pointed out in Chapter 2, federal policy toward American Indians has varied over time.

Since Congress passed the Indian Self-Determination and Education Assistance Act in 1975, the emphasis has been on recognizing and strengthening tribal governments. This policy, which builds on a similar approach that lasted from 1934 to 1953, is consistent with the general devolution approach that the federal government has been taking toward relations with state and local governments. One of the primary ways in which the federal government is trying to strengthen tribal governments is to encourage the adoption of constitutions. The Bureau of Indian Affairs offers assistance in writing the constitutions. Other federal agencies, such as the Environmental Protection Agency (EPA), are willing to devolve some of their authority to tribes that have constitutions.

Tribal constitutions read very much like state constitutions, with preambles that espouse principles of democracy and provisions that call for a separation of powers among executive, legislative, and judicial branches. The typical tribal constitution is very short and basic, and it usually provides for a single-house legislature and for the rights of tribal members to recall their elected leaders and to pass legislation through the direct initiative (a process explained in Chapter 6).[15] An important and unique constitutional issue for tribes is the definition of citizenship or membership in the tribe. The criterion for official or enrolled membership is a minimum percentage of an individual's ancestors that can be traced to the tribe. Some tribes allocate specific seats in their legislatures for members who do not live on their respective reservations. Some nations struggle with the formal provisions of their constitutions and the informal but real power of their elders, clans, and traditions.[16]

National Government Changes: Intervening on Behalf of Individuals

The interest of Washington, D.C., in a state constitution does not end with the admission of a territory to the United States. States historically preceded the national government in making a commitment to protect individual rights, but since the Civil War, the national government has frequently been the primary champion of these rights. The Fourteenth Amendment to the U.S. Constitution, ratified in the aftermath of the Civil War, specifically authorizes the national government to intervene on behalf of individuals who are mistreated by their states. Section I of the Fourteenth Amendment reads:

> No state shall make or enforce any law which shall abridge the privileges or immunities of citizens of the United States; nor shall any State deprive any person of life, liberty, or property, without due process of law; nor deny to any person within its jurisdiction the equal protection of the laws.

Initially, the concern was that former Confederate states would pass laws that disadvantaged former slaves. That concern was fundamental in the famous *Brown v. Board of Education of Topeka* (1954) case, in which the U.S. Supreme Court ruled that states had to integrate their schools racially and rejected the notion that racially segregated schools could be equal in quality.

The Fourteenth Amendment has acquired a broad scope and has provided the foundation for the national government to make changes in the wording and/or the use of state constitutional provisions. In *Gitlow v. New York* (1925), the U.S. Supreme Court used the Fourteenth Amendment to extend First Amendment rights under the U.S. Constitution to states. In the 1960s, under the leadership of Chief Justice Earl Warren, a former governor of California, the U.S. Supreme Court used the Fourteenth Amendment to force states to establish legislative districts to provide equal representation for people[17] and to compel state and local law enforcement to uphold the due process rights of individuals accused of crimes.[18] In 1973, the Court continued to champion individual rights when it placed restrictions on the states' authority to limit a woman's decision regarding whether or not to have an abortion.[19] In 1996, the Court voided an amendment that Colorado voters made to their state's constitution that would have prohibited any state agency or any local government from providing protections against acts of discrimination for gay, lesbian, and/or bisexual individuals.[20] The Fourteenth Amendment is also the basis for the federal court ruling that California's ban on gay marriages violates the U.S. Constitution.

It is important to note that the U.S. Supreme Court intervenes in disputes challenging a state's ability to curtail individual rights by establishing a floor, not a ceiling, for state governments. In other words, the Court generally sets a minimum standard for how the federal Bill of Rights restricts states. States can go further than the U.S. Constitution in protecting individual liberties, but they cannot provide less protection. As will be discussed further in Chapters 13 and 14 on state courts and criminal justice policies, some states have gone further than what is required by U.S. Supreme Court rulings in demanding procedures to protect the rights of those accused of criminal behavior.

State constitutions tend to be more detailed and restrictive than the U.S. Constitution on the relationships allowed between churches and government. In 2002, the U.S. Supreme Court ruled that an Ohio program providing government vouchers to parents in Cleveland that could be used to pay for tuition to religious schools could do so without violating the federal constitution. The prevailing argument in the 5–4 ruling was that parents, not the state, were making the choice to use the vouchers for education in parochial schools.[21] The Court also let stand a similar conclusion of the Wisconsin state supreme court for a voucher program in Milwaukee. The Wisconsin court based its ruling on the U.S. Constitution, not on the state constitution. Just two months after the U.S. Supreme Court ruling in the Ohio case, Florida Judge P. Kevin Davey declared that, the federal constitution notwithstanding, a voucher program allowing public

Tribal Festival of the Onondaga Nation.

funds to be used for religious schools violated Florida's constitution. The fate of voucher programs, in other words, may depend on whether they are judged by state or federal constitutions.

MAJOR FEATURES OF STATE CONSTITUTIONS

States take more words to establish their basic principles, procedures, and institutions than the national government does. State constitutions average 27,000 words in length, whereas the U.S. Constitution is only 8,700 words in length. As shown in Table 4.1, Alabama has the longest constitution (220,000 words) and Vermont has the shortest (6,880).

Sometimes states are more detailed and explicit in their descriptions than is the federal government. The respective clauses on freedom of religion in the U.S. Constitution and the state constitution are an example. Whereas Article I of the U.S. Constitution covers freedom

Table 4.1   State Constitutions

State	Number of Constitutions	Effective Date of Present Constitution	Estimated Length (No. of Words)	Number of Amendments	
				Submitted to Voters	Adopted
Alabama	6	Nov. 28, 1901	220,000	1,024	743
Alaska	1	Jan. 3, 1959	16,000	40	28
Arizona	1	Feb. 14, 1912	28,876	240	133
Arkansas	5	Oct. 30, 1874	40,720	186	89
California	2	July 4, 1879	54,645	846	507
Colorado	1	Aug. 1, 1876	45,679	297	143
Connecticut	4	Dec. 30, 1965	9,564	30	29
Delaware	4	June 10, 1897	19,000	N.A.	136
Florida	6	Jan. 7, 1969	25,100	127	96
Georgia	10	July 1, 1983	25,000	81	61
Hawaii	1	Aug. 21, 1959	20,774	119	100
Idaho	1	July 3, 1890	23,239	204	117
Illinois	4	July 1, 1971	13,700	17	10
Indiana	2	Nov. 1, 1851	10,230	75	43
Iowa	2	Sept. 3, 1857	13,430	57	52
Kansas	1	Jan. 29, 1861	11,900	122	92
Kentucky	4	Sept. 28, 1891	27,234	74	40
Louisiana	11	Jan. 1, 1975	54,112	169	113
Maine	1	March 15, 1820	13,500	201	169
Maryland	4	Oct. 5, 1867	41,349	254	218
Massachusetts	1	Oct. 25, 1780	36,690	148	120
Michigan	4	Jan. 1, 1964	25,246	61	23
Minnesota	1	May 11, 1858	23,700	213	118
Mississippi	4	Nov. 1, 1890	23,508	156	121
Missouri	4	March 30, 1945	42,000	162	103
Montana	2	July 1, 1973	11,866	49	27

Table 4.1 State Constitutions (*continued*)

State	Number of Constitutions	Effective Date of Present Constitution	Estimated Length (No. of Words)	Number of Amendments Submitted to Voters	Adopted
Nebraska	2	Oct. 12, 1975	20,048	330	219
Nevada	1	Oct. 31, 1864	20,770	216	131
New Hampshire	2	June 2, 1784	9,200	284	143
New Jersey	3	Jan. 1, 1848	17,800	67	54
New Mexico	1	Jan. 6, 1912	27,200	275	146
New York	4	Jan. 1, 1895	51,700	288	215
North Carolina	3	July 1, 1971	11,000	39	31
North Dakota	1	Nov. 2, 1889	20,564	257	144
Ohio	2	Sept. 1, 1851	36,900	265	160
Oklahoma	1	Nov. 16, 1907	68,800	329	165
Oregon	1	Feb. 14, 1859	26,090	468	234
Pennsylvania	5	Jan. 1, 1968	21,675	34	28
Rhode Island	2	May 2, 1843	19,026	105	59
South Carolina	7	Jan. 1, 1896	22,500	670	484
South Dakota	1	Nov. 2, 1889	25,000	217	112
Tennessee	3	Feb. 23, 1870	15,300	59	36
Texas	5	Feb. 15, 1876	80,806	583	410
Utah	1	Jan. 4, 1896	11,000	154	103
Vermont	3	July 9, 1793	6,880	211	53
Virginia	6	July 1, 1971	18,500	46	38
Washington	1	Nov. 11, 1889	29,400	167	95
West Virginia	2	April 9, 1872	26,000	119	70
Wisconsin	1	May 29, 1848	15,531	181	133
Wyoming	1	July 10, 1890	31,800	116	91

Note: The constitutions referred to in the table include Civil War documents customarily listed by the individual states.
Source: The Book of the States, 2010 (Lexington, Ky.: Council of State Governments, 2010), 11 and 12. © 2010 Council of State Governments. Reprinted with permission.

of religion, speech, and assembly, the constitutions in states like New York, Massachusetts, and Wisconsin devote four separate articles to establishing these rights. In some states, key sectors of the economy are recognized; for example, farmers and ranchers have clearly embedded their special concerns in state constitutions. Oil and mineral interests have done the same.

Regardless of length or special interest clauses, state constitutions commonly have four major segments:

1. Bill of rights
2. Suffrage and elections
3. Structure and power of governmental institutions
4. Amendment process

Exploring the Web

What should be in a constitution?

■ Examine your state's constitution at *www.findlaw.com*. This is a website with links to laws, constitutions, law journals, and law schools.

What are the main sections and provisions of the Constitution?

How long is your state's Constitution? Is it too detailed?

Do you find any provisions that provide special benefits or protections to a particular group?

In addition, state constitutions sometimes include provisions that are very specific and more properly should be an administrative procedure or a statute. Consider, for example, the following provision in the Arkansas constitution:

> All affidavits of Registration shall be made and executed in quadruplicate, the original and each copy of a distinctively different color. Each form shall be printed at the top thereof with the word "Original", "Duplicate", "Triplicate", or "Quadruplicate" as the case may be. . . . The forms shall be bounded together in books or pads and each set of copies shall be capable of being detached from the book or pad and locked into the Registration Record Files.
>
> —*Arkansas Constitution, Amendment 51*

Some state constitutions have language that regulates dueling, and California has a clause specifying the length of a wrestling match.

Bill of Rights

Individual rights are fundamental to the face-to-face interaction between people and their governments. By virtue of the Fourteenth Amendment to the U.S. Constitution, all states must abide by the provisions of the federal Bill of Rights, but many states have gone beyond those basic liberties. Seventeen states now have constitutional clauses that guarantee equal treatment by gender and prohibit sexual discrimination. Ten states provide an explicit right to privacy. Pennsylvania's constitution states that its citizens have a right to pure water, and New Hampshire's residents have a right to revolt.

The exception to the general pattern of expansion is in the area of criminal justice. Some states have curtailed due process guarantees in an effort to fight crime, fearing that too much emphasis on the individual liberties of someone accused of a crime obstructs investigations and prosecutions that might incarcerate criminals.[22] It is not always clear, however, where to draw the line between freedom and limitation, as you can see in the situation described in Debating the Issues later in this chapter.

Suffrage and Elections

Constitutions specify the offices that are filled by election and the terms of those offices. States vary as to how someone can become a state judge. Some states rely on gubernatorial appointments. Most have some form of election. Likewise, some states have governors appoint agency heads and cabinet members; other states elect their attorney general, treasurer, superintendent of public instruction, and the like. We will cover these patterns in more detail in Chapters 9–13 which describe the various institutions of state governments.

States used to determine who had the right to vote, but the national government has gradually standardized the basic requirements. At one time states had different provisions regarding whether to allow African Americans to vote and whether white males had to own property before they could cast ballots. On their own, all states abolished the property requirement. This is not the case with other qualifications.

The Fifteenth Amendment to the U.S. Constitution, passed in the aftermath of the Civil War, prohibits states from denying suffrage "on account of race, color, or previous condition of servitude." The Nineteenth Amendment enfranchises women, and the Twenty-sixth Amendment makes 18 years the standard minimum age for voting.

Despite the Fifteenth Amendment, Southern states sought to keep African Americans from voting by seeking surrogates for race to define eligibility. One approach was to require a **poll tax**, a fee that had to be paid in order to register to vote. The assumption was that, given the general poverty among African Americans in the South, this requirement would effectively disenfranchise that segment of the population. It would also screen out poor white people, but that was regarded as an acceptable price. The Twenty-fourth Amendment, passed at the height of the Civil Rights movement, prohibited states from requiring a poll tax. Table 4.2 lists the constitutional amendments affecting suffrage.

States remain responsible for administering elections, although Congress has increasingly involved the federal government. The Voting Rights Act, for example, authorizes the federal Department of Justice to monitor voting registration procedures to ensure that African Americans are afforded a meaningful opportunity to vote. In 1993, Congress intervened further in the administrative processes states used to register voters. To get more people to register to vote, the federal government enacted legislation encouraging citizens to register to vote when registering their motor vehicles. After the disputed 2000 presidential

Table 4.2 Amendments to the U.S. Constitution Affecting Suffrage

Number of the Amendment	Year Adopted	Provision
Fifteenth	1870	Prohibits race as qualification
Nineteenth	1920	Prohibits gender as qualification
Twenty-fourth	1964	Prohibits payment of poll tax as qualification
Twenty-sixth	1971	Establishes 18 as the minimum age

poll tax Fee that was charged by most Southern states in order for an individual to register to vote. The purpose of the tax was to discourage the poor, especially African Americans, from voting.

DEBATING THE ISSUES

Should public colleges and universities have a speech code?

Suppose you are at a public college or university and you are a member of an ethnic group that is being subjected to hateful, harassing speech by other students and by some faculty members. You are about to have a face-to-face meeting with the dean about the intimidating atmosphere this creates. What should you be able to expect from this meeting?

You are at school to learn, and the verbal harassment you are getting clearly interferes with the learning process. Institutions of higher education are supposed to be forums for you and others to explore, debate, and discuss freely and openly. When the university does nothing to ensure that you have the same opportunity to learn as students who are not subject to hateful speech, then it discriminates. Universities, especially public ones, should be open to members of all ethnic groups.

On the other hand, public universities, like other government bodies, are subject to state and federal constitutions. Don't those constitutions protect speech—even hateful speech? It may be rude and even harmful when some students and faculty repeat words and phrases that are offensive to an ethnic group, but it is not unlawful. The creation of a speech code, even if well intended, clearly violates the protection of free speech.

What, if anything, can you suggest to the dean that will not violate the requirement to protect freedom of expression? Are the rights of an individual to free speech necessarily going to override an individual's right to study in an environment that is not hostile?

Explore this debate on the web:
www.aclu.org/library/pbp16.html The American Civil Liberties Union is a strong defender of the First Amendment to the U.S. Constitution and has taken a position against speech codes.
www.aaup.org American Association of University Professors is an organization that supports academic freedom and opposes speech codes. See its position papers.

election, Congress passed the Help America Vote Act to get states to adopt voting technologies and procedures that would both avoid voter fraud and ensure that everyone's vote is counted as intended. These requirements are tied to receiving federal funds.

The major areas in which states continue to have some discretion are determining residency requirements and designing registration processes. Some states, through constitutions or statutes, make it easy for individuals to participate in the electoral process. Residency requirements are minimal. Registration is simple and may even include allowing those who register voters to go door to door. Other states require relatively long periods of residence in the state and insist on multiple, complicated documentation. An issue since 2000 has been whether to require voters to have photo identification before they cast their ballots. Most of the laws governing elections are in state statutes rather than in state constitutions. Chapter 8 discusses the details of state laws on how individuals get on the ballot, how campaigns may be financed, and what role parties may play.

Structure and Power of Governmental Institutions

The federal government does not tell states how to organize their governments. In *Prentice v. Atlantic Coast Line Railroad* (1908), a complaint was made that the Pennsylvania state government had created a commission that both made laws and adjudicated disputes concerning those laws. Such a commission is not in accord with the separation of powers doctrine in the U.S. Constitution. Speaking for the U.S. Supreme Court, Justice Oliver Wendell Holmes said:

> We shall assume that when, as here, a state Constitution sees fit to unite legislative and judicial powers in a single hand, there is nothing to hinder so far as the Constitution of the United States is concerned.[23]

The underlying historical philosophy of state governments, based in part on the European parliamentary tradition, is that the legislature is supreme. Because legislatures draw their legitimacy from their role as representatives of the people, legislatures are the most fundamental unit of government.[24] The supreme court of Illinois used this reasoning in *Client Follow-Up Co. v. Hynes* (Ill., 1979):

> Under traditional constitutional theory, the basic sovereign power of the State resides in the legislature. Therefore, there is no need to grant power to the legislature. All that needs to be done is to pass such limitations as are desired on the legislature's otherwise unlimited power.[25]

Although legal theory presents the legislature as the dominant and basic institution, unfettered by any assumption that there must be a separation of powers, in fact state constitutions do limit legislatures. The authors of the first state constitutions were very suspicious of government. They did not trust any government institution. Thus, they were explicit in their efforts to place limits on the legislature and on the governor and the courts. They were also explicit in their desire to have a separation among the branches of government and to balance the powers of government.[26] Given the legal assumptions of legislative supremacy, it was essential to be explicit. Once the pattern was set, other states followed.

All state constitutions now have separate articles specifying the general authority of the legislative, executive, and judicial branches of government. Each of these articles also describes the basic structure of the institution. The articles for legislatures (except for those of Nebraska), for example, indicate that there will be two houses, and describe how legislative districts will be drawn, how members will be elected, what the terms of office will be, what constitutes a quorum for conducting business, and when the legislature will meet. Similar provisions exist for the courts and the executive branch.

The separation of powers, based on legislative, executive, and judicial roles, is deceptively simple. In fact, the discretion available to each institution frequently allows for broad roles. When courts hand down a ruling that clarifies an ambiguity or a contradiction in the law, they make policy and create new law. Governors in states with partial veto authority can alter a bill that passes the legislature and effectively write a new law because it is very difficult for legislatures to override vetoes. Legislatures can be so vigilant in pursuing complaints from constituents or so detailed in their laws that they end up administering as well as passing laws. In the most common example, administrators who exercise discretion in their face-to-face encounters become judges and policymakers as they interpret laws and provide services.

Amendment Process

The authors of a constitution cannot anticipate every challenge or change that lies ahead. Principles of property ownership, for example, have changed with an increasingly complex society and the growth of financial institutions. Our more puritanical ancestors did not forecast—nor was it likely that they would favor—the recent popular support for state-sponsored gambling. The rural, landed gentry that dominated politics in so many states prior to the Civil War had to give way to urban populations and commercial and industrial leaders. The controversy over whether same-sex couples should be able to marry is an issue that clearly was not anticipated by those writing constitutions one or two centuries ago. Constitutions, in short, embody principles and procedures that must be changed from time to time.

The most common and often the least visible way of changing constitutions is simply through interpreting the language differently. Property clearly meant real estate to the authors of the original constitutions. The definition of property now includes copyrights, patents, stocks, bonds, and (in some cases) even a job.[27] The central position of the right to privacy means more now than protections from government officials arbitrarily breaking into someone's home. Privacy rights also apply to use of the Internet and to eavesdropping on telephone conversations. These changes have occurred through an evolution in the meaning of terms rather than through constitutional amendments.

As pointed out in Table 4.1, states have engaged in hundreds of efforts to make formal, explicit changes in their respective constitutions. The constitutions themselves describe how these changes must be made. The existing options are summarized in Table 4.3 and are described here:

1. Constitutional Convention and Referendum. Over 200 state constitutional conventions have been called since Delaware and North Carolina met to write their

Table 4.3 Processes for Amending State Constitutions

State	By Citizen Initiative	By Legislature and Referendum	
		Vote Required*	Number of Sessions
Alabama	No	3/5	1
Alaska	No	2/3	1
Arizona	Yes	Majority	1
Arkansas	Yes	Majority	1
California	Yes	2/3	1
Colorado	Yes	2/3	1
Connecticut	No	3/4 in 1 session	or majority in 2 sessions
Delaware	No	2/3	2
Florida	Yes	3/5	1
Georgia	No	2/3 in 1 session	or majority in 2 sessions
Hawaii	No	2/3	1
Idaho	No	3/5	1

(continued)

State	By Citizen Initiative	By Legislature and Referendum	
		Vote Required[*]	Number of Sessions
Illinois	Yes	Majority	2
Indiana	No	Majority	2
Iowa	No	2/3	1
Kansas	No	3/5	1
Kentucky	No	2/3	1
Louisiana	No	2/3	1
Maine	No	2/3	1
Maryland	No	3/5	1
Massachusetts	Yes	Majority	2
Michigan	Yes	2/3	1
Minnesota	No	Majority	1
Mississippi	No	2/3	1
Missouri	Yes	Majority	1
Montana	Yes	2/3	1
Nebraska	Yes	Majority	1
Nevada	Yes	Majority	1
New Hampshire	No	3/5 in 1 session	or majority in 2 sessions
New Jersey	No	Majority	1
New Mexico	No	Majority	2
New York	No	3/5	1
North Carolina	No	Majority	1
North Dakota	Yes	3/5	1
Ohio	Yes	Majority	1
Oklahoma	Yes	Majority	1
Oregon	Yes	Majority	1
Pennsylvania	No	Majority	2
Rhode Island	No	Majority	1
South Carolina	No	2/3 in first session	and majority in 2nd session
South Dakota	Yes	Majority	1
Tennessee	No	Majority in first session	and 2/3 in 2nd session
Texas	No	2/3	1
Utah	No	2/3	1
Vermont	No	2/3 Senate and majority House in 1st session	majority in the 2nd session in each chamber
Virginia	No	Majority	1
Washington	No	2/3	1
West Virginia	No	2/3	1
Wisconsin	No	Majority	2
Wyoming	No	2/3	1

[*]Vote required in each chamber of the legislature in the number of sessions listed before the proposed amendment can be submitted to voters for ratification in a referendum.

Source: The Book of the States, 2010 (Lexington, Ky.: Council of State Governments, 2010), pp. 13 and 14. © 2010, Council of State Governments. Reprinted with permission.

constitutions in 1776. Delegates to conventions typically are elected and meet to consider, debate, and propose either changes to the existing constitution or a whole new constitution. The most common way of calling a convention is for the state legislature to ask the voters in a referendum whether they want to convene one. Illinois requires that every 20 years the voters must decide whether or not to have a constitutional convention. Whatever changes are agreed to by delegates at a convention must be ratified by a referendum open to all voters in the state before the constitution is actually changed.

2. Legislation and Referendum. Every state constitution allows for the legislature to approve a change, usually by a two-thirds or three-fifths majority, and then submit the proposal to the voters in a referendum. Thirteen states require that the proposed amendment pass the legislature in the same written form in two successive sessions. Hawaii stipulates that either two-thirds of both houses approve a proposed change in one session of the legislature, or that both houses approve the proposal by majority votes in two sessions before a measure is presented to voters in a referendum.

3. Initiative. In 18 states, a proposal for a constitutional amendment can be placed on a ballot without action by the legislature or a convention if enough registered voters sign a petition to do so. This process anticipates the possibility that a proposal that has wide voter support may get bottled up in the legislature and allows the electorate to make the change directly.

4. Commission. To provide for careful consideration by a group of experts, a number of states use commissions in the amending process. Utah is an example of a state that has a permanent commission that reviews proposals for constitutional amendments and then reports with recommendations to the legislature before they take action. Others convene commissions on an ad hoc basis as proposals are made. Florida is unique because its Constitution Revision Commission can submit proposals directly to the voters. All other commissions make reports to the legislature and to the public as an extra deliberative step in the process.

All but 19 states have adopted wholly new constitutions since they were first admitted. Most of the changes to constitutions, however, have been piecemeal, involving rather narrow and specific matters. Sometimes initiatives and referenda to change state constitutions are used as a way of attracting specific groups to the polls and bolstering the support for particular candidates or parties. This was the acknowledged strategy in the 2004 elections when voters in 13 states voted on amendments to ban same-sex marriages. The idea was to activate social conservatives who would presumably vote to reelect President George W. Bush as well as support the ban. While this strategy had some of the desired effect in 2004, results in 2006 were mixed. Arizona voted against the proposal to amend its constitution to ban same-sex marriages. Of the other seven states that included this ban on the 2006 ballot, three elected Republican governors and legislatures and four elected Democrats. Nonetheless, it is safe to anticipate that future referendums to amend state constitutions will include issues designed to mobilize certain voters as well as deal with substantive changes.

LOCAL GOVERNMENT CHARTERS

Philosophically, local governments are the building blocks of our democracy. Alexis de Tocqueville, who is frequently cited as having captured and effectively articulated the spirit and principles of early American democracy, discussed the social contract that formed the basis of the United States. He wrote that individuals, by covenant, formulated the basic terms and conditions of government and that "the township was organized before the county, the county before the state, the state before the union."[28] Legally, however, local governments are not the building blocks of states; they are creatures of state governments. This doctrine, known as **Dillon's rule**, was part of a judgment issued by Judge John F. Dillon in 1868:

> The true view is this: Municipal corporations owe their origins to and derive their power and rights wholly from the (state) legislature. It breathes into them the breath without which they cannot exist. As it creates, so it may destroy. If it may destroy, it may abridge and control.[29]

In 2011 Michigan created a stir when it passed legislation that authorized the governor to appoint an emergency manager to assume control over a local government in the event of a fiscal emergency. It seemed antidemocratic to have gubernatorial appointees nudge local elected officials aside and make decisions about community services and taxation. Nonetheless, state lawmakers have authority over local governments, and state officials in Michigan felt that temporary takeovers are required when local governments are in financial crises.

Local governments are created from the top down and from the bottom up. School districts are examples of top-down creation. State governments draw the boundaries of school districts so that children in every part of the state are under the jurisdiction of some school district. State governments also determine how school districts will be governed and what basic services must be provided. Some states also set teacher salaries or set general guidelines for determining teacher salaries. States provide some of the funds needed to run public schools and determine how individual school districts can raise any remaining revenue that might be needed.

Cities, on the other hand, come into being from the bottom up. As people congregate in a particular area and develop the need for basic urban services, they must petition the state for recognition. An emergent urban community needs legal city status in order to levy taxes, borrow money, provide services, and pass laws. It gets that status and authority from state governments. Thus, even bottom-up governments need state recognition.

The equivalents to a constitution for a local government are state statutes and charters. Statutes, or laws, grant local governments authority to provide certain services, enact regulations, enforce laws, enter into contracts, raise revenue, and the like. They also make demands. Sometimes the statute mandates that certain procedures be followed. Sometimes the requirements are for performance standards. With only a handful of exceptions, school districts are good examples of a local government created by state statute.

Charters are documents that describe the basic government structure for a jurisdiction, specify the role of elections, and outline the scope of authority. Most municipalities have

---

Dillon's rule Principle articulated in a federal court ruling that local governments are creatures of state governments.

a charter. Many counties, which are created by state governments rather than through a bottom-up process, are authorized to adopt a charter. There are five types of charters:[30]

1. Special Charters. These charters are specifically designed for a given jurisdiction. As urban areas emerged, most municipalities had a special charter written for them. In part to avoid inconsistent treatment and meddling, most state constitutions now prohibit the granting of special charters.

2. General Charters. Some states have a standard charter that all jurisdictions, regardless of size or circumstances, must adopt. The problem is that sometimes the general provisions do not fit a particular situation.

3. Classified Charters. Some states have classifications for cities according to population and then provide a standard charter for each classification. The basic assumption is that population size determines the kinds of problems and issues that a community faces. That is not always the case.

4. Optional Charters. This system offers people in a community the opportunity to choose from among several standard, already-approved charters. The idea behind this approach is to have both consistency of forms and citizen approval.

5. Home Rule Charters. Increasingly, states are enabling citizens in a community to draft, adopt, and amend their own charters. State governments must approve the charter, much as the federal government must approve new state constitutions. The 1875 Missouri constitution was the first to authorize home rule charters. Now, all states except for Alabama, Indiana, Illinois, Kentucky, North Carolina, and Virginia allow for locally

Public schools that do not follow general rules and guidelines need to have a special charter that describes how they will teach students. These charter schools provide options within the public school system.

drafted charters. The National Civic League has suggested model charters that municipalities might consider as they draft or amend their own.[31]

In 1992 and 1993, Minnesota, California, and Colorado began an experiment by authorizing charter schools. These are bottom-up public schools that can be organized, depending on the state law, by parents, entrepreneurs, or certified teachers who wish to offer an alternative within a school district. A formal charter describing the administration of the school, its curricula, admission policies, facilities, and general philosophy must be approved by the school board of the district in which it will be located and by a state agency. Approval means the charter school will be eligible for public funding and will be exempt from general state mandates and requirements. The school will have to comply with its own charter, but not with all of the other regulations that apply to other public schools. Charter schools and other approaches to educational reform are discussed more fully in Chapter 15.

TYPES OF LOCAL GOVERNMENTS

There are about 87,000 local governments throughout the United States. As Table 4.4 indicates, most of these are special districts. **Special districts** are confined to specific policy areas or functions. School districts are the most common special district. School districts are consolidating as rural areas lose enough school-age children to support a school. Other special districts are increasing in number, in part as a response to urban sprawl. Some examples are districts established to provide library services, regulate the use of water, maintain sewerage facilities, and offer firefighting services. Illinois has mosquito control districts. What are special districts in some states will be agencies within a city or county government in others.

Most of us think of city, town, or county when we think of local government. These are general-purpose jurisdictions that have responsibility for multiple functions and the overall benefit of the community. When special districts and general-purpose jurisdictions coincide and serve the same people, the special districts maintain authority over their

Table 4.4 Types of Local Governments	
Type of Government	**Number in 2007**
County	3,033
Townships and towns	165,199
Municipalities	19,492
School districts	13,051
Special districts	37,381

Source: Bureau of the Census, 2007 Census of Governments (www.census.gov/govs/cog/GovOrgTab033ss.html).

---

special district A local government created for a narrowly defined purpose and with a restricted source of revenue. Examples of special districts are school districts, water districts, and sewerage districts.

policy sphere, and the city or county is responsible for everything else. This overlap is common. Sometimes, however, it leads to fragmentation and conflict.

Suppose, for example, that you purchase some land and want to build a complex of apartment buildings on it. You will have to get permission from a city or county to use the land for that purpose, and you will have to submit detailed construction plans to get a building permit. In many parts of the country, a separate jurisdiction is responsible for providing water and sewer service to your land. If pipes have not already been extended to your land, you will have to petition for this service. Prospective occupants in your apartments will want to know where their children will go to school. The school district, which is probably separate from the other governments you have contacted, may have to build or expand facilities before you can give prospective tenants a satisfactory answer. You and your insurance company will both want to know who will provide fire protection. Is it the volunteer fire department of a nearby village or the professional force of the neighboring city? What about police protection and library services? What parks will your tenants use? You may want to sell the land, forget the plans, and invest in a coffee house on Main Street!

The mosaic of local governments differs somewhat from one region to another. State governments have pursued different traditions and responded to different needs as they created or recognized jurisdictions within their respective boundaries.

Counties

Counties are created by states and generally have the broadest set of responsibilities. With few exceptions, the boundaries of a county are arbitrary and have no relation to the location of people or natural resources. There are instances where the boundaries of as many as three counties run through parts of a single, medium-size city.

States use counties as basic administrative units for welfare and environmental programs; courts and law enforcement; registering land, births, and deaths; and for holding elections. Rhode Island uses counties for its court system, but not for other administrative purposes. In Louisiana counties are called parishes, and in Alaska they are called boroughs. Counties are most important in Southern states and in the Northeast and Midwest. They are least used in rural areas of Western states.

In some large cities, such as New York, San Francisco, Denver, St. Louis, Nashville, and Honolulu, county governments have been merged with the city. In most cases, however, counties and urban governments overlap and coexist. In Virginia, when the state recognizes a city that crosses county boundaries, it avoids overlap and automatically gives the city the authority and responsibilities of the affected counties.[32]

Townships

In some states and in general lay terms, the term **town** refers to a classification of a midsize city. In New England and in the Midwest, however, this term is used to describe a form of local government in which the community gathers in the town hall once a year and,

---

town A local government with general responsibilities for order and services in a midsize community.

as needed, to elect officers, pass ordinances, adopt budgets, and levy local taxes. Town meetings began in New England, although elected councils and mayors have now replaced many town meetings.

The Northwest Ordinance of 1787 attempted to export the model of the New England town by creating **townships**. Townships are geographic entities, not forms of government. The Northwest Ordinance imposed a grid of 6-mile by 6-mile square blocks over the Midwest states to create townships. As people settled in these townships, many—but not all—used town meetings as their form of government. As urban areas emerged, municipalities tried to annex and assume control over townships. Efforts at annexation are sometimes resisted, however, and when those efforts are successful, they can contribute to fragmentation and confusion in community governance.

Municipalities

State governments provide charters to urban areas as they emerge. Municipal governments—which include towns, villages, and cities—are created in response to the needs and demands of people living together. As communities change, they may petition their state governments for charters that respond to those changes. Some of the most intense and most critical battles in the United States are among local governments and between local governments and state governments over the boundaries, the scope of authority, and the sources of revenue for municipal governments.

Special Districts

Most local governments in the United States are special districts created for specific functions in a specific geographic area. Despite consolidation, school districts are the largest single type of special district. Only five states have public schools operated by agencies or departments of municipal or county governments. A total of 33 use independent school districts, and 12 use a mixture of independent school districts and education departments in other jurisdictions.

The next most common type of special district is the one that regulates some type of natural resource—usually water. Water districts are especially important in Western states where the allocation of water from a single source, like a river, is of fundamental importance to farmers, ranchers, industries, and communities.

Special districts do not follow any single pattern of authority or structure. Depending on state statutes, some have elected district heads, and appointed officials run others. Some may collect certain fees or taxes, and others may depend on allocations in a state or county budget for their revenues. Some have considerable discretion, and others must process license applications or provide permits according to a fairly rigid formula.

The complex and diverse array of local governments has led to both conflict and cooperation. One example is the city of Philadelphia, which has responsibility for

---

township A 6-mile-square geographic area created by the Northwest Ordinance of 1787 to be used for local governance in the affected territories.

resolving serious urban problems of crime, poverty, infrastructure, and basic services, but lacks the resources to address these issues meaningfully. The city of Philadelphia has jurisdiction over only one part of the Philadelphia metropolitan area and has received very little cooperation from other jurisdictions in the area or from the Pennsylvania state government.

Although there is no example at the opposite end of the spectrum, communities like St. Paul and Minneapolis, Minnesota, and Miami and Dade counties in Florida are noted for having made formal and informal arrangements to go beyond the strictures of boundaries and charters to cooperate in solving problems and providing services. Critical environmental, transportation, and social problems, discussed in the last section of this book, cross the geographic and functional boundaries of local governments. Metropolitan areas, especially in the Northeast, cross state and local government lines. Clearly, the legacy of past decisions and current local government structures pose challenges to officials and to citizens facing these issues.

SUMMARY AND CONCLUSIONS

Constitutions legally define what governments may and may not do, how they should do it, and how they are organized. These documents place limits on governments and provide them with the capacity to act. In face-to-face interactions, constitutions help determine the discretion available to government officials. They also define individual liberties and provide a general framework within which individuals participate in the electoral process.

The initial concern as the United States took shape was to limit government and protect individual rights. As states acquired more responsibility for addressing the issues of an increasingly complex society, constitutions had to be rewritten in order to provide a legal and institutional capacity to be effective. At the same time, constitutional amendments limiting the ability of many state governments to generate revenue have been enacted.

The squeeze between fiscal limits and scope of responsibility is the result of political dynamics. Constitutions are political as well as legal documents. This is reflected in the length and detail of state constitutions that go beyond the fundamental framework of government and include policies and procedures that really ought to be laws or administrative rules.[33]

Local governments are legally creatures of state governments. Some, like counties and most school districts, were created by a state law. Others, like cities, exist because communities have successfully petitioned to be recognized and authorized by the state. The latter typically have a charter that, somewhat like a constitution, establishes the basic framework of what the government is empowered to do and how the government is to be organized.

Fundamental changes in a community may prompt the need for alterations in the charters and laws that shape local governments. A major challenge throughout the country concerns the capacity of local governments to solve current and future problems. The sometimes arbitrary geographic and functional limits placed on local governments are often narrower than the issues faced by actual communities. Restrictions on how local governments may raise revenue also may frustrate problem solvers.

In the next section, we turn our focus from an emphasis on government discretion to individual participation. The chapters that follow are written with the general framework of constitutions and charters in mind. We must recognize, however, that these basic documents have been and will continue to be dynamic, not static. As individuals and groups work through and in government to address policy concerns, it is sometimes necessary to change how we define government and alter the rules of how we play the game.

Discussion Questions

1. How are state constitutions relevant to face-to-face interactions between individuals and officials of state, tribal, and local governments?

2. Discuss the difference between constitutional provisions that are meant to empower a government and those that are meant to limit what a government is authorized to do. What are examples of empowering and of limiting provisions?

3. What are the implications of processes that make it relatively easy to amend a constitution?

4. What are the potential implications for the governance of a growing community of having various local governments, some of which are special districts, that have jurisdiction over the place where the community is located?

Glossary

bill of rights 89
Carpetbag Constitution 93
charters 88
confederation 93

constitution 88
Dillon's rule 107
Northwest Ordinance of 1787 90
poll tax 101

Progressive Movement 94
special district 109
town 110
township 111

Endnotes

1. Albert L. Sturm, "The Development of American State Constitutions," *Publius* 12 (Winter 1982), 62–68.

2. Paul G. Reardon, "The Massachusetts Constitution Makes a Milestone," *Publius* 12 (Winter 1982), 45–55.

3. T. Harry Williams, Richard N. Current, and Frank Freidel, *A History of the United States*, Vol. 2 (New York: Alfred A. Knopf, 1959), 167–169.

4. Albert L. Kohlmeier, *The Old Northwest as the Keystone of the Arch of the American Federal Union* (Bloomington, Ind.: Principia Press, 1938), and *Pathways to the Old Northwest* (Indianapolis: Indiana Historical Society, 1988).

5. Sturm, "The Development of American State Constitutions," 57–97, and *State Constitutions in the Federal System* (Washington, D.C.: ACIR, 1989).

6. Theodore Clarke Smith, *Parties and Slavery* (New York: Harper and Brothers, 1906).

7. Jay Monaghan, *Civil War on the Western Border* (Boston, Mass.: Little, Brown, 1955).

8. Arthur Charles Cole, *The Irrepressible Conflict, 1850–1865* (New York: Macmillan, 1934).

9. Diane D. Blair, *Arkansas Politics and Government* (Lincoln: University of Nebraska Press, 1988), 121–124.

10. George E. Mowry, *The Progressive Era 1900–2000* (Washington, D.C.: American Historical Association, 1972), and *The California Progressives* (Berkeley: University of California Press, 1951).

11. John J. Carroll and Arthur English, "Traditions of State Constitution Making," *State and Local Government Review* (Fall 1991), 103–109.

12. Norman Meller, "Policy Control: Institutionalized Centralization in the Fiftieth State," in *Politics and Public Policy in Hawaii*, ed. Zachary A. Smith and Richard C. Pratt (Albany State University of New York Press, 1992), 13.

13. Ibid., 13–17.

14. Meller, "Policy Control," 22–24.

15. Tribal constitutions can be found at www.tribal-institute.org/lists/constitutions.htm, a website maintained by the University of Oklahoma Law School, the National Indian Law Library of the Native American Rights Fund, and the tribes.

16. Sharon O'Brien, *American Indian Tribal Governments* (Norman: University of Oklahoma Press, 1989), 261–275 and 291–297; Eric Lemont, "Developing Effective Processes of American Indian Constitutional and Governmental Reform: Lessons from the Cherokee Nation of Oklahoma, Hualapai Nation, Navajo Nation and Northern Cheyenne Tribe," *American Indian Law Review* 26, no. 2 (2002), 20–39.

17. *Baker v. Carr* (1962).

18. *Mapp v. Ohio* (1961) and *Gideon v. Wainwright* (1963).

19. *Roe v. Wade* (1973).

20. *Romer v. Evans* (1996).

21. *Zelman v. Simons-Harris* (2002).

22. Harry C. Martin and Donna B. Slawson, "The Expanding Role of the State Constitution," *Intergovernmental Perspectives* (Summer 1989), 27–29; Dorothy T. Beasley, "State Bills of Rights: Dead or Alive?" *Intergovernmental Perspectives* (Summer 1989), 13–17.

23. *Prentice v. Atlantic Coast Line Railroad* (1908).

24. Advisory Commission on Intergovernmental Relations, *State Constitutions in the Federal System* (Washington, D.C.: ACIR, 1989), 38–40.

25. *Client Follow-up Co. v. Hynes* (Ill., 1979).

26. Gordon S. Wood, *The Creation of the American Republic, 1776–1787* (Chapel Hill: University of North Carolina Press, 1969), 409.

27. *Roth v. Board of Regents* (1972).

28. Alexis de Tocqueville, *Democracy in America*, ed. Phillips Bradley (New York: Alfred A. Knopf, 1945), 40.

29. *City of Clinton v. Cedar Rapids and Missouri River Railroad Co.* (Iowa, 1868).

30. Joseph F. Zimmerman, "Charter Reform in the 1990s," *National Civic Review* 78, no. 5 (September/October 1989), 329–338.

31. Ibid.

32. Vincent Ostrom, Robert Bish, and Elinor Ostrom, *Local Government in the United States* (San Francisco, Calif.: Institute for Contemporary Studies, 1988), 4, 5.

33. Carroll and English, "Traditions of State Constitution Making," 104–106.

5

Policy-Making Processes: The Framework for Participation

LEARNING OBJECTIVES

- Know how government actions affect the public in many different ways.
- Understand that policies affecting the public are made using several distinct policy-making processes.
- Know the difference between individual and group participation in public policy making.
- Identify the procedural similarities and differences between the substantive bill legislative process and the budgetary process and their associated politics.
- Understand the different origins of legislative initiatives and their relative significance.
- Understand the centrality of budgeting as a policy-making vehicle in the states.

The governor calls in his budget director and chief legislative liaison to discuss what the state senate just did to the governor's recommendations for highway spending. Although the senate stayed within the executive budget's recommended spending level, it changed the construction priorities developed by the state highway department and agreed to by the governor. Passing an amendment from the floor, the chamber substitutes a major construction project, which just happens to be located in the senate president's district, for another that ranked high on the department's priority list. Because the senate has to enumerate the new project in the budget bill, the governor decides to use his line-item veto power to line it out. The state budget director argues that the governor has to send a clear message to legislative leaders that he will stand firmly behind the department's priorities and that he won't allow pork-barrel changes. The legislative liaison reminds the governor, however, that a line-item veto could well cost the governor the senate president's support of the administration's centerpiece initiative to cut state income tax rates. The governor decides to think some more about the prospective veto.

Public policy can be thought of as government actions that affect the lives of citizens. Both state and local governments tax their residents to support numerous and varied programs that provide services to the population at large, others that provide targeted services and even financial assistance to individuals who meet certain eligibility requirements, and still others that regulate the behavior of their residents. Those programs have been authorized by law, and public officials and their employees are charged with administering and implementing them. Yet in implementing programs, government employees may use some discretion as they apply laws and rules to individual cases. In many instances, government agencies promulgate rules and issue guidelines that are aimed at confining or constraining that discretion. Nevertheless, agents of government still make innumerable choices and determinations that affect citizens' relationships with their government. Appeal routes, in turn, often exist for state and local residents to petition for review of those determinations.

City residents, for example, typically have the opportunity to appeal assessments of the value of their real estate if they believe a good case can be made that the city assessor erred in placing a value on their property. To make their case, property owners often contrast their assessment with the assessed values of comparable properties. Yet motorists caught speeding have a hard time convincing a judge that others were really driving faster, and that they just happened to be pulled over. Although that might very well have been the case, the police officer chose to pursue and cite the speeders in question. Sometimes when motorists are stopped for speeding, however, the officer may issue only a warning or simply suggest that they slow down a bit. To guide such exercise of discretion, police agencies commonly issue internal administrative guidelines that suggest when warnings are appropriate and when they are not. It is still the individual officer who interprets the situation and applies or even disregards the guidelines.

PUBLIC POLICY INSTRUMENTS

Recognizing that public policies cannot usually be fashioned so precisely that no room is left for administrative discretion, state and local policymakers have designed institutions and processes that structure the way public policies are created and that guide their implementation. In doing so, they have created several different **instruments of public policy**. These instruments include (1) legislation; (2) budgets; (3) the mechanisms of direct democracy; (4) regulation, including administrative rules; and (5) court decisions and orders.

Majoritarian rule serves as the democratic principle underlying the policy-making processes associated with the first three instruments. Only the first two, however, make use of **representative democracy**, in which popularly elected representatives cast votes on their constituents' behalf. The prevailing decision rule is that a majority of those voting, after a quorum has been reached, pass laws that authorize or modify government programs or that appropriate funds to finance them. Then, where permitted, elected chief executives have the opportunity to veto those acts, subject to provisions for legislative override of the veto. The legislative and budgetary processes will be highlighted later in this chapter.

---

instruments of public policy Authoritative tools used to make public policy.
representative democracy The form of democratic government in which popularly elected representatives cast votes on the constituents' behalf.

The third policy instrument, direct democracy, which is discussed in greater detail in Chapter 6, is based on the principle of plebiscitary democracy, in which voters take the policy reins into their own hands by a majority vote on ballot propositions. Direct democracy is most often identified with the initiative and the referendum. The **direct initiative** allows citizens to make or change laws, or to modify the state constitution, without any involvement from the governor or legislature. A minimum percentage of registered voters' signatures is needed to qualify proposals, commonly called *propositions*, on a statewide general election ballot, to be approved by a majority of those voting. In contrast, the legislature is involved in the indirect initiative and the referendum. The **indirect initiative** requires that the petition, having garnered a specified number of signatures, be submitted to the legislature, which can adopt the proposal as received, place it on the ballot unaltered, or modify the proposal before placing it on the ballot.

The referendum can take one of three forms. In the first, the **general referendum**, the state constitution may require the legislature to submit certain of its acts, such as proposed constitutional amendments or bond issues, to voters for their concurrence or rejection. In the second form, the **advisory referendum**, the legislature may submit proposals to the voters for their counsel on whether the legislature should pass certain legislation. The third form, the **popular referendum**, puts the impetus in the hands of the voters, who can decide within a specified time after the legislature's adjournment whether to reject a law passed in that legislative session. As with the direct initiative, the popular referendum requires the collection of a specified number of signatures for the question to be put on the ballot, with a majority vote required for passage. Chapter 6, on grass-roots policy making, includes a much expanded treatment of the politics of direct democracy, including a discussion of which mechanisms are available in which states.

Regulation, the fourth policy instrument, can be viewed in a broad context to include the actions of executive branch agencies and regulatory commissions that affect the public. Both bodies can issue binding regulations within a process that is largely nonmajoritarian. Both promulgate **administrative rules**, sometimes referred to as secondary legislation, to guide the implementation of laws enacted by the legislature—rules that themselves have the force of law. Although these rules often elaborate on the law, they must be consistent with its provisions.

---

direct initiative The form of direct democracy in the states that allows residents to make or change laws directly, without any involvement of the governor or legislature. A minimum percentage of registered voters' signatures is needed to qualify proposals, called propositions, on a statewide general election ballot, to be approved by a majority of those voting.

indirect initiative The form of direct democracy that requires a successful petition to be submitted to the state legislature, which can adopt the proposition as received, place it on the ballot unaltered, or modify the proposition before placing it on the ballot.

general referendum A vote of the electorate taken on certain actions referred to it by the legislature, such as bond issues and proposed amendments to state constitutions.

advisory referendum A vote of the electorate providing advice to the legislature on whether it should pass certain legislation.

popular referendum A vote of the electorate on whether to reject a law passed by the legislature in the most recent legislative session.

administrative rules Regulations promulgated by state agencies to guide the implementation of laws enacted by the legislature—rules that have the force of law.

A law authorizing the state department of motor vehicles to test and license drivers, for example, could well be followed by rules developed by the department specifying what tests are to be used, how they are to be administered, how performance is to be evaluated, what constitutes a passing score, and what options are available for people who fail the exams. In this paralegal process of rule making, persons or organizations affected by the proposed rules are typically given an opportunity to appear at rule-making hearings to support or oppose rules under consideration.

Although administrative rules fall within the province of executive branch agencies or independent regulatory commissions, many state legislatures have established committees to oversee rule making. If the committee believes that a proposed rule exceeds the bounds of statutory authority, it usually suggests that the issuing body rescind or modify the rule. Eleven state legislatures have given a standing committee the authority to suspend the rule if the agency or commission refuses to go along with the committee's admonition. But in all but one of those states, the entire legislature must pass legislation that sustains the committee's action, thus incorporating a dimension of majoritarian rule into a process that would otherwise hinge on administrative policy making.[1]

In enforcing regulatory legislation and its accompanying rules, government agencies often possess some freedom to exercise discretion in applying sanctions to those who are noncompliant. Bargaining between regulators and the regulated is not uncommon. Regulatory officials may extend timelines for compliance and resort to graduated penalties for noncompliance, if the law allows. The philosophy of "half a loaf is better than no loaf at all" applies to regulatory enforcement in many areas, as agencies seek to avoid administrative or court litigation brought by the regulated interests. The exercise of such discretion varies among the different policy areas regulated. The politics of regulatory policy making will be covered extensively in Chapter 12.

The fifth policy instrument includes court decisions and orders, which emanate from a process that can be either majoritarian or nonmajoritarian. Courts exist to resolve disputes, either between the government and individuals or entities, or between individuals and/or entities themselves. In the former case, a state may prosecute an individual alleged to have committed a felony in violation of the state's criminal code. In the latter, the court may be asked to decide on a lawsuit filed by a person who believes another violated the terms of a contract. In both instances, the judge plays the part of a third, neutral party who knows the law and guides the judicial process in accordance with it. When juries are not appointed, the judge also determines guilt or innocence. When juries are involved, the judge remains the "judge of the law," and the jury renders the verdict.

In courts of original jurisdiction (those that do not hear appeals), the decision-making process is clearly nonmajoritarian. A single judge renders determinations on the law, and a jury, when it is used, arrives at a unanimous decision. Verdicts are not rendered by majority vote. However, appeals courts and state supreme courts use panels of judges to decide questions of the law and the legal process. At those judicial levels, the majority prevails.

Courts can make public policy as they decide cases. It is not always possible for courts to resolve a dispute by simply ascertaining the facts of a case and then fitting those facts to the law. Even if the facts are clear, the governing body of law may be vague or even contradictory. As noted earlier, both framers of constitutions and legislators cannot anticipate every unique situation. When the court clarifies a law during the process of ruling on a case, in a very real sense it creates a new law for that case and establishes a precedent for all future comparable cases. Sometimes the clarifications are minor, having little effect; others can be highly significant, having broad public policy ramifications. For example, decisions about what constitutes equal educational opportunity or about how to define obscenity can widely affect school districts and communities.

In considering cases brought before state courts, judges can issue orders directed at remedying situations that the court believes violate state constitutional or statutory law. State judges, for example, have ordered legislatures to alter the manner in which they distribute state aid to school districts. These decisions came in response to appeals from parents of students enrolled in districts that spend well below the statewide average per pupil. Parents argued that such wide inequality of financial support deprives their children of the equal educational opportunity guaranteed by their state's constitution. Federal courts have intervened in state matters when judges have ruled that state actions deprive individuals of rights and protections guaranteed by the U.S. Constitution. Examples abound of federal courts ordering state policymakers to eliminate heavy overcrowding in prison cells because the condition has been deemed to constitute "cruel and unusual punishment," a practice prohibited by the Constitution. The role of the courts in public policy making will be discussed thoroughly in Chapter 13.

INDIVIDUAL AND GROUP PARTICIPATION IN PUBLIC POLICY MAKING

Individuals can participate in all five policy-making processes, but they commonly do not bother to make the effort. Their participation is not aimed at broadly influencing policy making, but instead it is limited to making contacts with government agencies or their elected representatives to fix a concrete problem that affects them directly. These problems frequently border on the mundane: getting a darkened streetlight fixed or a pothole repaired near their home, accelerating a delay in securing a building permit, increasing police presence in a troubled neighborhood, lodging an equal rights complaint, or appealing a property tax assessment or income tax determination.

Private citizens can also channel their energies into shaping public policies. The policy-making processes afford them opportunities to do so. Their participation in policy making can be either proactive or reactive. *Proactive participation* often involves efforts to set the government's agenda. Individuals can write to executive officials and their legislative representatives, urging them to place certain issues at the top of their agendas and to take positions in concert with the preferences of the writer. They also can speak to government officials or their key staff members. Members of a city council, school board, or state legislature, even when their government positions are not full-time jobs, frequently interact with citizens making complaints and offering suggestions. Alternatively, individuals may confine their participation to *reacting* to policies they oppose or favor, with opposition usually proving the most alluring. Both courses take time and effort—time away from a job, from the family, or from recreational pursuits.

Even if they tried, the efforts of individual citizens would compete with a multitude of other interests vying for the attention of chief executives and their key officials and aides, or for a sympathetic legislative ear. The individual citizen's main handicap, however, is her or his solitary position. A unitary voice sometimes has difficulty being heard in the process of public policy making, except perhaps when that voice is directed at the courts from a position of compelling constitutional interest. Generally, the larger and more diverse the political jurisdiction, the more difficult it is for individual voices to be heard. There is indeed strength in numbers, and that strength is relative to the size of the political community in question.[2] That is precisely why organized interests have a decided advantage in policy making. They represent the collective interests of people. It is not just Ms. Smith's interests as an individual that are at issue, but the collective interests of groups such as gun owners, dairy farmers, public school teachers, retirees, or conservationists. In addition to their large membership, these organized interests have paid staff members who research and analyze policy problems and legislative proposals, along with others who lobby executive officials and legislators to support their members' interests. They also raise funds to finance the electoral campaigns of the very elected officials who act on the legislation or regulations that affect them.

As the in-depth discussion provided in Chapter 7 will illustrate, organized interests are well positioned to influence policy agendas and to mount efforts to advance, amend, or defeat proposals under consideration. Because policy issues are often complex and technical, both the executive and legislative branches at the state level, and to a lesser extent at the local level, have organized and equipped themselves to deal with this reality. The executive branch has been organized along functional policy lines, with one agency, for example, dealing with tax matters, another with health policy, and still another with highways. Similarly, the legislative branch has structured its committees along roughly parallel lines. This has resulted in an institutionalization of **contained specialization**,[3] in which substantive policy specialists in the executive branch interact with their counterparts in the legislative branch, be they committee chairpersons, members, or staff assistants. That very environment provides natural points of access for interest group representatives. Symbiotic relationships frequently develop. Interest group representatives need access to policymakers in order to be effective in their jobs. At the same time, agency officials and legislative committee members and their staffs need current information and data in order to analyze policy issues and to take and defend policy positions.

Consistent patterns of interrelationship emerge. Interest group representatives make themselves most available to executive policymakers during the period preceding legislative sessions because that is when agencies develop their legislative agendas and brief their respective chief executives. Because governors, mayors, county executives, and school superintendents soon thereafter transmit their recommendations to their corresponding legislative bodies, interest groups know that they need to be heard if they want a chance at helping to shape the executive policy agenda. That is also the time when executive branch staff members are looking for assistance from those who know the policy terrain best.

In addition to needing information, executive branch representatives also want to see how interest groups might react to prospective policy changes. For example, state executive officials may want to get a good sense of the likely reactions of physicians, hospital

---

contained specialization   The organization of policymakers and staff members in both the executive and legislative branches along substantive policy lines, enabling them to be recognized and to interact as policy specialists.

administrators, and drug companies to alternatives aimed at strengthening state cost controls in the Medicaid program. It is not surprising, then, that executive branch officials would turn to representatives from the state medical association, the state hospital association, and prominent pharmaceutical groups.

A similar relationship exists between legislative committees and interest group representatives, a relationship that peaks during legislative sessions. Legislators and their assistants also interact with officials and staff members of government departments during this time, often sharing information and testing one another's assumptions. In addition, both commonly deal with the same interest group representatives. They all know each other well, understand each other's needs, and grant each other access. In a real sense, they form a triangular working relationship of interdependence—commonly referred to as an **iron triangle**.[4]

Interest groups are also prominent players in regulatory policy making. Regulatory commissions and executive branch agencies seek their involvement in decision making, and interest groups can be a prominent presence at rule-making and regulatory hearings. This process of public review and comment tests regulations before they take effect, affording organized interests an opportunity to go on record about the likely effects of regulations and to suggest how the regulations might be modified to eliminate or minimize undesirable outcomes while still accomplishing their desired objectives. From the agencies' perspective, that opportunity could prevent bad regulations, regulations that otherwise would have unexpected deleterious outcomes, from being adopted. In addition, agencies hope that involvement of the relevant interest groups in the regulatory process will lead to a better understanding and compliance with the regulations. Voluntary compliance makes the work of the agency much easier. Organized groups, on the other hand, see the process as giving them a method of protecting their interests.

That same regulatory process also gives individuals a chance to go on record and represent their interest. As with the legislative and budgetary processes, their impact is minimized by their solitary voice. Yet when their voice echoes the pleadings of many others, that voice is magnified, as is the impression it makes. Again, such collective strength can come from a number of unorganized individuals making the same or a similar case, or it can come through the unified voice of an interest group. Individuals, however, still can have an impact when they point out flaws in a regulation or identify unanticipated problems that had previously gone unnoticed. In other words, the strength of the case at times can sell itself, even though its proponent lacks the resources typically associated with political influence. But that is probably the exception rather than the rule.

To balance the strength of interest groups in the regulatory process, the legislatures in several states have passed legislation creating so-called **public intervenors**, or proxy advocates, who are charged with representing the interests of consumers in public service

---

iron triangle Triangular working relationships of interdependence formed by executive branch officials and key staff members, legislators and key staff members, and interest group representatives around specific areas of substantive policy.

public intervenors Advocates created by state legislatures to represent the interests of consumers in public service regulatory proceedings, such as hearing on utility rate increases.

regulatory proceedings—for example, those at which utility rate increases are under consideration. Because individual utility users usually do not take the time to get involved, or because they find the arguments and their accompanying analysis too complex to follow, public interveners and their staffs have been given the institutionalized role of analyzing requests for rate increases with an eye toward protecting the interests of consumers.[5]

The influence of interest groups, however, is not restricted to the legislative, budgetary, or regulatory processes. They also can be a force in direct democracy, throwing their organizational and financial strength behind efforts to get propositions on the ballot as well as employing those same resources to secure passage or defeat of measures that successfully make it on the ballot. To qualify propositions on the ballot, interest groups normally have to go beyond their membership to obtain the required number of signatures, even though they might first turn to their own members for support. They may join forces with other groups and financially support advertising campaigns and direct mail appeals to solicit additional signatures. For measures that have already made it onto the ballot, interest groups may throw their financial support behind political advertising that attempts to attract votes in line with their position. At the same time, the individuals whose signatures and votes they seek ultimately will decide the outcome of propositions. Although individuals face great obstacles in getting their own propositions on the ballot, through their signatures and votes, they can contribute to a proposition's approval or rejection. Sovereignty, in this sense, is in their hands.

Neighborhood organizations represent collective interests at the community level. They often take positions on issues of particular importance to the residents living within their boundaries. A proposal to realign school attendance areas might well spark an outpouring of interest from the parents in a given neighborhood, not only because of the prospect that their children might have to be bused to a new school, but also because of the possibility that such a change could make the neighborhood a less attractive place in which to live and could result in reduced property values. This neighborhood association might be opposed, however, by parents in other neighborhoods who would reap benefits from the proposed changes. The association also might find that school district planners and news media support the realignment plan's directions despite the opposition of teachers' unions. Ultimately, the question of school attendance areas probably would come before the local school board for a vote, with the decision reached on majoritarian grounds, unless opposition mounts to a point that prompts the school superintendent to withdraw the plan in the face of an expected defeat. Even if that should happen, a disgruntled parent who supported the plan might file suit in state court, alleging that the existing school districting, based on defined neighborhoods, constitutes de facto racial segregation, thereby depriving children of the equal educational opportunity guaranteed by the state constitution.

This discussion of grass-roots participation will be continued in Chapter 6, but the point that deserves to be underscored here is that individuals seeking to shape policy making can greatly improve their prospects if they aggregate support for their position—either by getting others to join their political efforts or by joining others whose cause they embrace. Their political effectiveness is strengthened further when, in addition to numbers, they have adequate staff assistance and financial resources to mount public relations and lobbying campaigns in support of their objectives. Staff and financial resources amount to the proverbial "time and money," commodities that individuals often lack or are unwilling to devote to political pursuits. That reality contributes to channeling individual participation into tangible, though often limited, directions that hold the promise of immediate return. Thus, a call to the mayor's citizen's assistance line, for example, to ask for help in speeding up the processing of a building permit might seem to offer a better return on investment than would an individual effort to get legislation passed, influence budgetary priorities, get a proposition qualified on the ballot, or secure a significant change in an administrative rule.

Individuals are personally affected by public policy making in significant ways, but those effects are variously distributed across the population: all state residents must pay an increase in the state sales tax; only property owners benefit financially from a statewide rollback of the property tax, although all residents may experience the effects of cutbacks in local government services; welfare recipients lose purchasing power when faced with grant increases that fail to keep pace with inflation; symphony patrons benefit from government subsidies to the arts, but all taxpayers pay for them; mass transit riders have their fares subsidized by state aid, with that support paid for by all taxpayers and justified in part by mass transit's contribution to reducing vehicular congestion and air pollution. These things don't just happen. Policymakers consciously act to bring them about, and they make choices within established policy-making processes—processes that structure not only how authoritative decisions can be made but also how citizens can participate in public policy making. See Exploring the Web for a framework of face-to-face participation in the policy-making process.

THE CENTRALITY OF LAWMAKING IN SHAPING PUBLIC POLICY

The legislative process and its important variant, the budgetary process, have the most pervasive effects on residents of state and local governments across the nation. They are indeed government's main lawmaking processes, whether employed at the state, municipal, county, school district, or national level. The remainder of this chapter describes and analyzes the politics of the state legislative and budgetary processes. (Chapters 9 and 10 cover the institutional features of the governorship and state legislature, respectively.)

What comes out of these two central processes affects not only state residents but local residents as well. State residents pay the taxes and fees that finance the various programs of state government, but both state and local residents benefit from state taxpayers' efforts. Local residents benefit through state financial assistance to local governments—aid that helps to pay for schools, roads, mass transit, general welfare assistance, and other categorical purposes. Most states also share some of their revenues in the form of general revenue sharing or shared taxes, which can be used for almost any local government purpose. In addition to aiding local governments, state policy choices shape what local governments are legally allowed to do and, in some cases, the procedures they must follow while doing it. On the revenue side, local governments can employ only those tax instruments given them by state law. For instance, they cannot use a local income tax unless the legislature has enacted provisions giving local jurisdictions that option. States also may require local governments to do something whether or not state financial aid is provided to pay for it. These mandates have become a sore spot between local governments and their state governments.

Exploring the Web

Process and Action

How can governors and state legislators use the rules and procedures of the legislative and budgetary processes to get what they want?

- To better understand how the general legislative process works, go to the National Conference of State Legislatures' homepage, at www.ncsl.org.
- To learn about how the budgetary process works in your state, take a look at the report, *Budgetary Processes in the States*, found at the National Association of Budget Officers' website *www.nasbo.org.*
- Then turn to these two organizations to find out substantively what state legislatures did in the most recent budgetary session: how they spent taxpayer revenues. Click on the NCSL's *State Budget Actions* and NASBO's *State Expenditure Report.*

To sum up, this policy reach justifies detailed attention being given to the *state* legislative and budgetary processes and their politics. At the same time, an understanding of these state processes and their politics provides an extremely useful backdrop for an appreciation of legislative and budgetary politics in the communities in which we live. The institutional actors and their political interactions bear close resemblance to those at the local level, although significant differences deserve the careful exploration that will be provided in Chapter 11.

THE SUBSTANTIVE BILL STATE LEGISLATIVE PROCESS

The process of lawmaking represents a shared executive–legislative function at the state level. (Plebiscitary democracy will be discussed later in this chapter.) Although only the legislature can pass legislation, that legislation is not enacted into law until the governor approves it or the legislature overrides the governor's veto. Then, on its effective date, the legislation becomes law. The effective date may be specified in the legislation itself, or it may be governed by constitutional provision.

Legislatures also may approve joint **legislative resolutions**, which make a unilateral statement, without gubernatorial approval, but do not have the force of law. Examples might include the expression of the legislature on national affairs, such as its opposition to U.S. involvement in Afghanistan, or a proclamation rendering thanks to a retiring key legislative staff director. Joint resolutions can be used as the means for the legislature to establish referenda, the results of which can be either advisory or binding, depending on the action of the legislature and the constraints stipulated by state constitutions or statutes. Such unilateral actions do not require the governor's approval.

---

legislative resolutions Actions of the legislature that make a unilateral statement not requiring gubernatorial approval and that do not have the force of law.

Legislative Initiatives and Their Origin

Laws are enacted in all states through the proposal of **bills**. A bill can propose a new law or change an existing one through amendment or outright repeal. Although bills may be introduced in the legislative process only by a legislator or legislative committee, they have many different points of origin. A bill can originate from within any one of the three branches of government: the executive, the legislative, or, in very limited instances, the judicial.

Gubernatorial Agenda. Key policy staff in the governor's office, executive planning and budget officers, and top state agency administrators all get involved in policy initiation and its accompanying bill development. Governors and their executive office staffs often think in terms of their administration's broad **policy agenda**. Governors, for example, may commit their administration to property tax relief, welfare reform, new highway construction, and legalized gambling. Although these items provide the general policy outlines to be pursued, specific program proposals still have to be developed for submission to the legislature. Governors and key executive office aides also must decide which policy vehicles should be used to advance the proposals. Relevant considerations include whether initiatives should be floated as several separate bills; collapsed into a few broad-based, functionally related bills; or included within the state budget bill, if this is permitted. Such strategic decisions are geared toward successful attainment of the governor's policy objectives.

Not only do key gubernatorial aides help to set the administration's policy agenda, they also work with other administration officials to formulate the substantive proposals that embody the agenda. Agency heads and their top administrative officials, along with the state budget and planning directors, often assume the leadership for shaping specific proposals. But the real work for proposal design usually falls to program experts who occupy mid-level positions in the state bureaucracy. They have the in-depth program expertise to deal with the nuts-and-bolts issues of proposal development. They do so, however, under the close supervision of top administration officials.

The process differs somewhat for state agencies whose heads are not appointed by the governor and do not serve at the governor's pleasure. For noncabinet agencies, the role of the governor's office becomes one of monitoring the status of bills and, when important enough, of trying to influence their outcome in the legislature. Here, the customary proactive stance of the executive office gives way largely to review and reaction. This should not suggest that governors or their top aides do not occasionally attempt to convince noncabinet officials to withdraw or modify legislative proposals—they certainly do. But with noncabinet agencies, governors possess fewer tools with which to elicit compliance.

Gubernatorially appointed task forces and commissions provide still another vehicle for the initiation of legislation. Task forces and commissions are frequently formed to deal with controversial policy issues, serving as sounding boards for public opinion. As an illustration, the potentially divisive issues of tax or welfare reform could become the

---

bill The medium by which legislatures enact legislation.

policy agenda An expressed comprehensive commitment to pursue a range of policy initiatives.

subject of task force or commission review. In addition to its potential substantive value, such action can be of major symbolic value to an administration. Appointment of a task force or a commission allows governors to separate themselves from the appointed body's recommendations while creating the popular image that chief executives are taking steps to deal with a pressing public problem. If the recommendations engender broad political support, the administration can claim credit. Conversely, if they spell political trouble, governors can ignore or deemphasize them, pursue only selected recommendations, or combine other gubernatorial initiatives with them.

Legislative Agenda. Legislators and their staffs also initiate legislation. Individual legislators come into office with a sense of which policies they wish to advance, and they seek committee assignments that reinforce their policy preferences and help them best serve their constituencies. For example, legislators in heavily agricultural states can be expected to show an interest in farm matters, highway construction and repair (particularly farm-to-market roads), and property tax relief. They hire staff members who have or will develop expertise in these areas. Both legislators and staffs tend to take proactive legislative postures; they usually perceive themselves as voted into office to *do* something, and that most often entails sponsoring or supporting legislation of benefit to their constituents.

Staffs, too, tend to be initiators. They are employed to help accomplish their bosses' objectives. Interacting with other legislative staff and agency officials, they readily get caught up in the heady activity of legislative business while developing program expertise of their own. Along with such subject matter expertise frequently comes insight into how programs can be improved, or at least how they can be of greater political benefit to their legislators.

Unlike the executive and legislative branches, it is relatively unusual for the courts to initiate legislation directly. However, judges—particularly appeals court justices—occasionally suggest in their rulings that a particular contested issue would be most appropriately left to the state legislature for resolution. In addition, existing statutory law might be internally contradictory, requiring corrective amendment. Most states have a judicial council that reviews cases in which statutory remedies appear necessary and endorses bills that accomplish the task.

Initiative from Outside Government. Bills can be initiated from sources outside government. People contact their legislators or legislative staff about policies that they want to see enacted, changed, or eliminated. Legislation may be pursued that relates to one's views about how society could be improved, for example, through tougher penalties for drug trafficking, increased funding for schools, or laws against pornography. Individuals may have a more personal concern, such as pursuing a financial claim against the state through legislation, even though they may have unsuccessfully exhausted available administrative channels for remedy. Legislators, responding to this latter request for assistance, can introduce what is referred to as a private bill—one having very limited, particular interest. Such introduction largely amounts to a symbolic gesture because the vast majority of private bills fail to be enacted; most do not even make it out of the committee.

Groups may develop legislation that advances the collective interests of their members, whether economic or professional. Among the more active groups at the state level are the

Deval Patrick is sworn in as the governor of Massachusetts.

AFL-CIO, representing a large segment of both private- and public-sector organized labor; the American Federation of State, County, and Municipal Employees (AFSCME), representing public-sector employees; associations of manufacturers, representing the larger industries; chambers of commerce, representing local business; coalitions of road builders, representing engineering firms and highway contractors; associations of local government jurisdictions, including cities, counties, and school districts; and a wide range of professional associations, representing most of the major professions—from physicians and lawyers to school teachers and university professors.

These groups often supply like-minded legislators or committees with drafts of proposed legislation, which can then be forwarded to the legislature's bill-drafting department for production in official bill form. Examples of such **special-interest legislation** might include proposals that eliminate a mandatory one-week waiting period before unemployment compensation benefits can be collected (benefiting organized labor), increase the state's share of financing local school costs (benefiting school districts and teachers' unions), include chiropractic services under the state's Medicaid program (benefiting chiropractors, while being adverse to the interests of physicians), and increase funding for new highway construction (benefiting civil engineering firms and highway contractors). As mentioned previously, close relationships often form among interest group representatives, agency officials, and legislative staff in the development of legislation. Interest group representatives are only too

---

special-interest legislation Legislation narrowly designed to benefit specific interests.

happy to share information with agency officials and legislative staff in the hope that they will consider their organizations when developing policy proposals and taking legislative initiatives. Likewise, agency officials and legislative staff solicit information, data, and perspectives from lobbyists on proposed legislation.

The Process of Legislative Consideration and Approval

Following a longstanding tradition that began in England, all bills must be read three times in each legislative chamber. Upon introduction, a bill is read for the first time by the clerk of the chamber of origin and is referred to the standing committee determined to have jurisdiction over its subject matter (i.e., transportation, education, or agriculture). The bill's number, the dates of its introduction and first reading, the committee to which it is assigned, and the date of referral are generally recorded on the bill's cover. Depending on state law, the bill may or may not contain an indication that it was introduced at the request of a specific constituent, public official, or state agency. The introducer's identity is always noted on the bill.

The rules of legislative procedure, adopted by each chamber, require that committees hold public hearings on all bills assigned to them. Committee hearings may be held during the legislative session or during periods when the full legislature is formally in recess. However, most states—either by law or procedural rules of the legislature—prescribe a minimum period of time after a bill's introduction before the committee can act on it. This waiting period is required to give legislators and the public adequate time to consider a bill and determine what action, if any, to take.

A schedule of committee hearings is prepared at the behest of the committee, usually at its chairperson's direction. The schedule is then published and posted, satisfying public notice requirements where mandated by state law. Most states require a three- to five-day advance notice of hearing.

The full committee may conduct the hearing, or the bill may be assigned to a subcommittee for review and hearing. Both subcommittees and committees can recommend amendments to bills. The subcommittee makes its recommendations to the full committee, and the committee, in turn, makes its recommendations to the chamber. Some states make use of joint committees, on which legislators from both chambers serve. Joint committees send their recommendations to both chambers simultaneously. The use of joint committees can increase the efficiency of the legislative process not only because one hearing takes the place of two, but also because representatives from both chambers have an opportunity in committee to begin to work out intrachamber differences on legislation. In most states, a bill can be reported out of committee with either a positive or negative recommendation. In some states, only bills receiving positive recommendations clear the committee; bills that fail to get a favorable vote die in committee.

On clearing the committee, the bill usually is read for a second time and scheduled by the chamber's legislative leadership for debate on the floor. Prior to floor debate, or during recess, legislators of both parties may meet separately, in partisan caucus, to consider possible amendments and the relative support they are likely to receive on the floor. Both committee-endorsed amendments and those offered by individual legislators are considered on the floor. Amendments usually are approved by a majority vote of the chamber;

however, state constitutions or statutory law may require a "super majority" for certain amendments, often 60 percent or two-thirds, for appropriations or revenue bills.

After a bill has been passed by the house of origin, it is engrossed. **Engrossing**, the incorporation of all approved amendments into the bill, is considered the third and final reading. The bill is then sent to the second chamber, where all the previously described steps (see Figure 5.1) are repeated. That chamber can pass, defeat, or amend the bill. If passed in identical form, the bill is returned to the house of origin and from there sent to the governor for signature or veto. If the bill is amended by the second house, it is sent back to the first house for concurrence. If that chamber concurs, it goes to the governor. If concurrence cannot be attained, a **conference committee**, consisting of equal representation from each chamber, may be appointed to come up with a compromise version. State law may permit the full legislature to amend the conference report, or it may require an "up" or "down" vote without amendment. If the conference committee cannot reach agreement, the conferees may be named as replacements. If agreement fails, the bill dies. Conversely, if agreement is reached, rejection of the conference report by either house also results in the bill's death.

After both legislative chambers have passed a bill, it is enrolled with all approved amendments incorporated and sent to the governor. The governor usually has only a limited number of days during which to sign or veto the **enrolled bill**. If not signed within that period, the bill automatically becomes law. If vetoed, the bill is returned to the house of origin, most often with a written statement of the governor's objections. The legislature then has a period of time in which to act on the veto. If no action is taken within the prescribed period, the veto is automatically sustained. If the veto is overridden by both houses of the legislature, usually requiring a two-thirds vote, the legislature-approved version stands. Gubernatorial vetoes are upheld because the governors need the support of only one-third plus one of the members of either house in order to sustain their veto.

Two Variants of the State Legislative Process

Alan Rosenthal, a close observer of the state legislative process, draws a distinction between the legislative "assembly line" and the executive–legislative policy-making process.[6]

Legislative Assembly Line.   The assembly line operates more like a "bill-passing machine" than a deliberative process, according to Rosenthal. Many bills are introduced with little or no expectation that they will ever come to the floor for a vote. Several are introduced at a constituent's request or as a symbolic gesture. They may be introduced, read, and referred to committee, then fail to receive serious attention in the process, typically languishing there.

Other bills can be treated more seriously by their authors, then fail to engender much interest on the part of legislative colleagues. In a crowded legislative docket, such bills may

---

engrossing The process of incorporating all approved amendments into a bill.

conference committee A committee of appointed representatives from both the lower and upper legislative chambers to work out differences in the bills passed by their respective chambers.

enrolled bill The final approved form of a bill sent to the governor for signature.

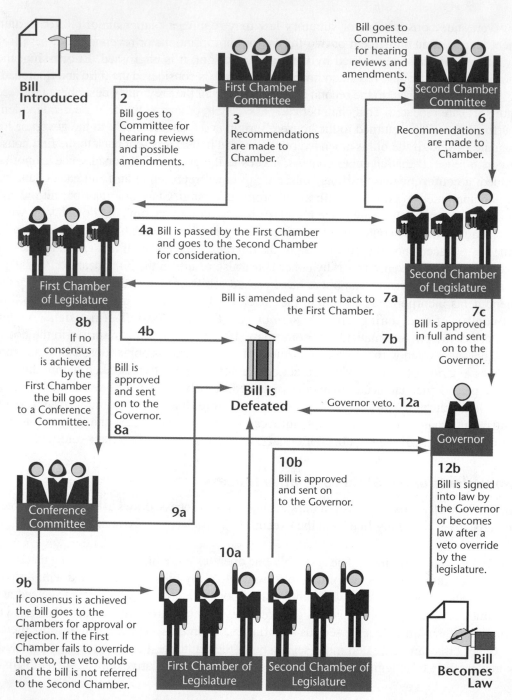

Bill Introduced 1

2 Bill goes to Committee for hearing reviews and possible amendments.

First Chamber Committee

3 Recommendations are made to Chamber.

Bill goes to Committee for hearing reviews and amendments. **5**

Second Chamber Committee

6 Recommendations are made to Chamber.

4a Bill is passed by the First Chamber and goes to the Second Chamber for consideration.

First Chamber of Legislature

Second Chamber of Legislature

Bill is amended and sent back to the First Chamber. **7a**

8b If no consensus is achieved by the First Chamber the bill goes to a Conference Committee.

4b

7b

7c Bill is approved in full and sent on to the Governor.

Bill is Defeated

Governor veto. **12a**

Bill is approved and sent on to the Governor. **8a**

Governor

10b Bill is approved and sent on to the Governor.

12b Bill is signed into law by the Governor or becomes law after a veto override by the legislature.

Conference Committee

9a

10a

9b If consensus is achieved the bill goes to the Chambers for approval or rejection. If the First Chamber fails to override the veto, the veto holds and the bill is not referred to the Second Chamber.

First Chamber of Legislature

Second Chamber of Legislature

Bill Becomes Law

Figure 5.1 The Substantive Single-Bill Legislative Process

fail to make it out of committee. Only so much legislative business can be conducted within the constraints of limited time and staff resources. Yet several bills fitting this description are enacted into law annually without the strong support of the legislative leadership, and often without even gaining much notice. The latter factor could be a significant element in their success. Although these bills do not generate much support, they often attract little or no opposition. The leadership does not tag them for defeat, nor do others coalesce to stop their progress. The press of the docket becomes their greatest enemy. As they compete for consideration, some will successfully make it through the legislative process uncontested. In such cases, the executive branch may not even have become involved other than for the governor's ultimate signature. At that stage, the governor may have no reason not to sign the approved legislation. The governor, like the legislators who earlier considered the bill, might not feel strongly enough to prevent it from becoming law.

Governors choose to use the veto sparingly, saving it for priority cases where it matters. Hence it is fair to say that a good portion of legislation makes it through the screening process because no party, legislative or gubernatorial, cares enough to sidetrack it. Saying no uses up some political capital and can make others less willing to go along with the naysayer's own initiatives.

Executive–Legislative Policy. The process for legislation that really matters is different. First, the executive branch is likely to be more closely involved throughout the legislative process. In fact, the executive branch may even have initiated a number of the major legislative proposals. A state agency may have drafted the bill and sought legislative introduction, often with the intercession of the governor's office. In some states, executive office staffs clear all legislation initiated by cabinet agencies. In others, appointed agency heads are relatively free to work directly with sympathetic legislators. Cabinet agencies may produce a draft bill, providing it to a legislator who requests that state's legislative reference bureau to prepare the official bill for introduction. Noncabinet agencies are free to work directly with supportive legislators. They face no obligation, other than the maintenance of goodwill, to seek the governor's support for introduction. In many cases, the governor may be an intense political rival of the attorney general, state superintendent of public instruction, or another elected public official. With boards or commissions, the current governor cannot appoint, or control, a majority of their members.

For the most important bills, which generate executive and legislative interest, the participants in the lawmaking process are less willing to allow them to roll along unimpeded. Coalitions of support and opposition form around their deliberations—coalitions that often reflect political party lines, business or labor positions, or urban or rural divisions. Such legislation becomes more hotly contested in committee. Gubernatorial aides are more likely to take the trouble to appear in support or opposition at committee hearings. Legislative caucuses—separate meetings of the Democratic and Republican members of each house—flag the bill for discussion. Legislative leaders and other legislative supporters or opponents work to convince the governor and/or executive office staff either to support or, at a minimum, not oppose legislative initiatives. State officials may take the trouble to appear at committee hearings, taking positions for or against legislation. The agency's expert testimony that a bill is technically or substantively flawed can put the brakes on an otherwise fast-track initiative, often causing legislative reviewers to take note and possibly reconsider their support.

Fiscal Notes and Deadline Systems

In most states, agencies or legislative staff offices are legally required by state statutes to review all introduced legislation for their anticipated effect on state revenues and/or expenditures and to prepare **fiscal notes**. These notes, which must be appended upon referral of a bill to committee, provide an estimate of the extent to which the legislative proposal increases or decreases state revenues or expenditures. For example, a bill that stiffens parole eligibility laws, making it more difficult for prisoners to be released from prison before their mandatory release date, would increase the costs of prison operations because inmates would remain in prison longer. Thus, the fiscal note would illustrate the cost implications of what, on face value, appears merely to be a statutory change.

Fiscal notes openly disclose the otherwise hidden costs of legislative initiatives. Like open meetings and public information laws, they are premised on making the public aware of the effects of government's activities. Full disclosure theoretically gives the public the information needed to make informed choices in support of, or in opposition to, proposed legislation.

One institutional effort to change the legislative process to make it more manageable has been for legislatures to institute **deadline systems**. Such systems provide deadlines for the introduction of bills, committee review, and floor consideration. They are aimed at reducing the end-of-session congestion that obligates legislatures to rush some bills through without the customary deliberation or to let other, late-introduced legislation die without adequate time to consider properly their relative merits. In that late-session logjam environment, the usually decentralized legislative process becomes much more centralized, with the top legislative leadership directing traffic. Earlier in the session, a bill will pass unless the leadership singles it out for derailment; at session's end, bills pass because they have the leadership's support. Most bills caught up in the final legislative rush die for lack of attention. Favored bills that have the leadership's support must be rushed through during a session's waning days and hours, perhaps without the deliberation they deserve.

The growing use of deadlines is directed at more evenly distributing the legislature's workload throughout the session. Because a predetermined period of time has been reserved for consideration of those bills meeting the deadline, a bill's failure to be introduced or moved to the next stage in the process can be attributed to its lower priority and not to its getting caught up in the last-minute shuffle. The volume of legislative business is not necessarily eliminated, but it is spread over several periods with different deadlines during a session.

The numerous steps in the legislative process and the requirement that both chambers agree on identical wording favors opponents, rather than advocates, of proposed

---

fiscal notes Estimates of the extent to which a legislative proposal increases or decreases revenues or expenditures.

deadline systems Systems created by legislative leadership to provide deadlines for the introduction of bills, committee reviews, and floor consideration in an effort to reduce end-of-session congestion.

legislation. One must anticipate that some officials and interest groups will regard no legislation as better than a proposed change. Opponents of a bill have many opportunities to kill it.

We have discussed the traditional single-bill legislative process, in which bills embrace distinct subjects and are referred to standing committees that have jurisdiction over a particular area of substantive policy. However, a major caveat needs to be interjected at this point. The state budget, often encapsulating several diverse subjects depending on the latitude granted by a state's constitution or statutes, necessitates a separate discussion. Not only does the budget differ from other bills in form and effect, so does its legislative process. This distinctive process, along with its associated distinctive politics, merits special attention. The significance of the budget bill, in both dollars and policy, ensures that it takes center stage in the policy-making process.

THE STATE BUDGETARY PROCESS

"Put your money where your mouth is" is an oft-heard refrain in everyday discourse. It captures the sense of folk wisdom that "money talks." Social scientists may instead choose to speak about the importance of "programmed resource commitments," yet the gist is the same: dollar commitments cut through rhetoric, clearly disclosing priorities. The **state budget** constitutes such a statement of the state's priorities—backed up by dollars—from one year or biennium to the next.

State legislative sessions are structured to accord the state budget a privileged position. The governor kicks off the budget-year legislative session with a **budget message** delivered to the legislature. This message, presented with considerable fanfare and media attention and often preceded by selective attention-getting leaks of key elements, provides a substantive and highly symbolic statement of the administration's agenda for the coming budget period and beyond. In most states, no bill that makes an appropriation may be approved by the legislature or sent to the governor until the budget bill is enacted into law. From the governor's budget message, through committee hearings, caucus deliberations, and floor debate, the budget process disproportionately focuses the attention of state policymakers and close observers alike. This is not to say that important state policies are not enacted outside the state budget; they surely are. Major matters of state policy, such as the death penalty, high school graduation requirements, abortion restrictions, and binding labor arbitration, are most commonly enacted as separate legislation, apart from the budget. In fact, several state constitutions proscribe the inclusion of statutory authorizations or changes within the budget bill. In other states, the budget bill may include appropriations as well as statutory authorizations and changes. In this type of environment, the **budget bill** can most readily serve as a policy vehicle; major policy initiatives can be included in

---

state budget An annual or biennial plan of expenditures, representing policy proposals, to be financed within
      expected available revenues.
budget message An address to the legislature highlighting the governor's fiscal policy and budgetary priorities.
budget bill The legislative vehicle for enacting the budget.

the budget, whether or not they involve the appropriation of funds or have a fiscal effect. Twenty-seven states permit appropriations bills to be used in this way. Maine, New York, Ohio, Pennsylvania, and Wisconsin give policymakers the greatest flexibility to include substantive policy in appropriations bills. Twenty other states, prominently including California, Maryland, Michigan, Texas, and Washington, permit the inclusion of conditions on spending or expressions of legislative intent. At the other end of the spectrum, the constitutions of Colorado, Illinois, and New Hampshire prohibit substantive language in the appropriations bills.[7]

The practice of including statutory provisions in the budget has many advantages from an executive perspective. First, it permits the governor to use the line-item veto, where that authority exists, to selectively veto policy initiatives that have no associated appropriations because, once they are included in the budget bill, they become subject to the line-item veto. Second, it is easier for the governor to work with the legislative leadership in managing the more contained budgetary process than to manage the more fragmented, substantive bill legislative process. Third, the governor has greater opportunity to offer and entertain compromises when a number of major policy initiatives are considered in the same bill.

The legislature may wish to include policy in the budget for some of the same reasons. The budgetary process may afford the leadership an opportunity to bargain on the various policy items that are incorporated into the budget bill. The budgetary process restricts the number of legislative actors who are in a position to shape the outcome of policy initiatives. The appropriations or fiscal committees exercise decision-making authority over the budget, referring their official version of the budget to their respective legislative chambers. The substantive standing committees play no official decision-making role in the budgetary process, although they may make nonbinding recommendations to the appropriations committees on matters of policy and budget levels affecting agencies and programs falling within their jurisdiction. They may hold committee hearings, but these generally have more of a palliative and symbolic value rather than a substantive one. Where the budget is concerned, the real power at the committee stage rests with the appropriations or fiscal committees—a fact other legislators, the executive branch, and lobbyists are well aware of.

Herein lies a major difference between the state budgetary process and that of the federal government. At the federal level, the authorizing committees review requests and recommendations for changes in statutory authority. The money committees (variously called appropriations and finance) approve the funds to be spent in a given budgetary period. Although this overly simple distinction between statutory authorization and appropriation generally applies at the federal level, the increasing practice in Congress of loading up appropriations bills with riders, restrictions, and expressions of congressional intent has weakened the distinction in practice. Nonetheless, a proposed program must secure congressional approval twice.

States have either an annual or a biennial budgeting period. As Table 5.1 shows, 27 states are on an annual basis, and 21 have a biennial period. In Kansas and Missouri, some agencies are on an annual budget cycle, while others are on a biennial cycle.

Table 5.1 Budgeting Periods

State	Annual	Biennial	Mixed*	Beginning Month of Fiscal Year
Alabama	X			October
Alaska	X			July
Arizona		X		July
Arkansas		X		July
California	X			July
Colorado	X			July
Connecticut		X		July
Delaware	X			July
Florida	X			July
Georgia	X			July
Hawaii		X		July
Idaho	X			July
Illinois	X			July
Indiana		X		July
Iowa	X			July
Kansas			X	July
Kentucky		X		July
Louisiana	X			July
Maine		X		July
Maryland	X			July
Massachusetts	X			July
Michigan	X			October
Minnesota		X		July
Mississippi	X			July
Missouri			X	July
Montana		X		July
Nebraska		X		July
Nevada		X		July
New Hampshire		X		July
New Jersey	X			July
New Mexico	X			July
New York	X			April
North Carolina		X		July
North Dakota		X		July
Ohio		X		July
Oklahoma	X			July
Oregon		X		July
Pennsylvania	X			July
Rhode Island	X			July
South Carolina	X			July
South Dakota	X			July

(continued)

Table 5.1 Budgeting Periods (*continued*)

State	Annual	Biennial	Mixed*	Beginning Month of Fiscal Year
Tennessee	X			July
Texas		X		September
Utah	X			July
Vermont	X			July
Virginia		X		July
Washington		X		July
West Virginia	X			July
Wisconsin		X		July
Wyoming		X		July
Total	27	21	2	

*Some agencies are on an annual budget cycle, while others are on a biennial cycle.

Source: Budget Processes in the States (Washington, D.C.: National Association of State Budget Officers, 2002), p. 4. Reprinted with permission.

Whether a state has an annual or a biennial budget does not materially affect the process leading up to budget enactment. It does, however, influence the character of the legislative sessions because budgeting tends to crowd out other executive and legislative activities. With annual budgeting, no off-year exists to give the governor and the legislature a breather from budgeting, which would allow them to concentrate on other legislative initiatives. Similarly, state agencies tend to devote more of their top-level managers' time to developing budget requests for additional resources as well as preparing defenses against attempts to cut or reduce existing programs and their funding.

Executive Budget Development

The budgetary process usually begins with the governor's state budget office issuing budget instructions in the summer of the year preceding the upcoming budget period. Materials generally include a timetable for budget submission, instructions for formatting and packaging requests, and—most important—a statement of major policy guidelines that agencies should follow in structuring their requests.

Once the state budget receives requests in early fall, the internal pace of analysis and recommendation is brisk. Briefings with the governor generally must begin by November or early December if the budget is to be ready for the printers in time to meet constitutional or statutory deadlines for submission to the legislature, usually timed to the beginning of the legislative session in January or February. Analysts have at most 8 to 10 weeks to prepare recommendations for the governor's consideration. During this time, the state budget office not only reacts to agency requests but also may make recommendations for the governor's consideration if no agency requests are made. To get a head start on the process, meetings with the governor may be held during the summer months to identify the major policy issues that need to be addressed in the budget development process and to get some preliminary policy direction from the governor.

The Involvement of the Legislative Fiscal Committee

Upon completion, the executive budget is transmitted to the legislature. Beyond the narrative material describing the executive budget—its priorities and general outlines—the legislative leadership introduces one or more budget bills on behalf of the administration. Nineteen states consider only one comprehensive budget bill containing all the executive budget-related appropriations.

The number of appropriations bills has implications for legislative decision making as well as for executive–legislative relations. A higher number of appropriations bills will probably fragment the legislative decision-making process. Because action is taken on the bills, at different times, by a wide assortment of subcommittees, the legislative leadership is put in a difficult position, not only to exercise leadership for the process but also simply to know what has occurred at any given time. Thus the existence of many appropriations bills greatly constrains the legislature's ability to produce a comprehensive alternative to the governor's budget, which is drawn together and highlighted in the executive budget book.

The budget is assigned to the legislative fiscal committee of the chamber into which the bill was introduced or to a joint fiscal committee if one exists in that state. Following its review, the committee reports on the amended budget to the legislative house to which the executive budget was first sent and introduced. In the process of the committee's review, committee members are assisted by staff members who frequently prepare issue discussion papers and suggest alternatives or make recommendations for the committee's consideration. When staff members do not make formal recommendations, the way in which issues are framed and alternatives are presented often structures the decision-making process and determines the options that will be considered by the committee.

Committee deliberation can be divided into two phases. The first consists of full formal committee hearings, in which the agency and state budget office representatives participate. The first hearing is generally attended by the committee as a whole. It focuses on the overall budget—its directions, costs, major policy initiatives, and position implications. Much of the hearing is largely of symbolic value, providing a widely publicized forum for a good deal of public and partisan staging.

The second and more important phase involves the subcommittee hearings. Subcommittees are organized most often along functional policy or state agency lines, with subcommittees frequently established for education, transportation, health and human services, natural resources, general government, and the like. Subcommittee staffs, who have developed expertise in these functional policy areas, prepare analyses of the executive budget recommendations in their assigned areas of responsibility and may present them to the subcommittee at the chairperson's or members' request. In addition, representatives of the state budget office often attend and, on invitation by the subcommittee, present the governor's recommendations and respond to questions. Agency representatives are also usually present and may be asked questions about the programmatic nature of the governor's request. They may be put in the difficult position of being invited to express any concerns they may have with the executive budget of their agencies. This dilemma presents a clear problem for cabinet agencies whose heads serve at the governor's pleasure. How far can they go in indicating that their agencies' needs merit increased resources beyond what the governor recommended and, at the same time, remain loyal to the governor and her or his budget directions? For noncabinet agencies, the problem is less direct, and some may welcome the opportunity to take on the governor in the public legislative arena.

After its deliberation, the subcommittee votes on motions to amend the executive budget. Successful motions are referred to the full committee for action. Through subcommittee votes, members get an opportunity to hear the opinions of other members, and thus are able to assess the likely outcome when the full committee votes.

Although the decision-making process can accommodate subcommittee strife, such strife is the exception. Subcommittees try to work out their differences before potentially divisive issues come to the full committee. When this effort is successful, committee members of other subcommittees are more likely to go along with the group's recommendations. **Reciprocity** is an important element underpinning the full committee's decision making. Subcommittee recommendations often carry the entire committee with no or only a few dissenters. Frequently, it is the chairs of other subcommittees who second motions for passage in the full committee. Discipline is maintained largely out of recognition that, if one subcommittee does not support the recommendations of others, it cannot expect to receive their support for its own recommendations.

Exceptions to the norm of reciprocity do occasionally occur, most frequently involving issues of financial aid to local units of government.[8] Each committee member, after all, represents at least one municipality, county, or school district. Committee members, through the aid of computer simulations, know what various changes in formula or funding levels will mean for their district. Thus, decisions governing local units are less easily contained within the subcommittee than are budget items dealing with state agency operations. On completion of subcommittee work, the full committee reconvenes and takes up unresolved items, considers the aggregate spending package that the subcommittees have recommended, makes adjustments depending on revenue availability, and then reports on recommended amendments.

Six states do not use appropriations subcommittees; committee work is done by the committee as a whole.[9] In Wisconsin, for example, the Joint Legislative Finance Committee is divided into what are called discussion groups for the purpose of reviewing the budget. Each group reviews a different portion of the budget and is assisted by staff members who are organized along functionally based discussion group divisions. Although no binding votes are taken at meetings, a sense of the discussion group emerges, giving observers a good indication of how the committee would probably vote on an issue. Just as with subcommittees in other states, the norm of reciprocity among discussion groups is strong.

---

reciprocity The expectation among legislators that they will receive support for their legislative initiatives from those legislators whose legislation they have supported.

DEBATING THE ISSUES

What's a good way to get something into the state budget?

Let's say that you want to get a special provision included in the state budget. Perhaps your organization has been working to get the State Department of Transportation to add three new bike lanes in an urban area. Tired of inaction on the department's part, you and your friends decide to get it done through the policy-making process. How might you proceed?

You know that it will take funds to finance the project, so you decide to work through the state budgetary process. But where should you begin? You might start by contacting your legislator to see if he or she would sponsor an amendment to the budget bill in support of the added lanes. Yet you realize that the money would have to be designated specifically for the new bike lanes in question, and that such designation would send the signal to other legislators that this is a constituent favor, not to be treated all that seriously. You decide to try a different tack. From your state and local government course, you learned that the state budget office reviews agency budget requests and makes recommendations to the governor. You also learned that the governor delegates some of the less significant choices to the state budget director, and that budget analysts make recommendations to the budget director. So you set out to find the analyst who handles the Department of Transportation's budget. You drop by and make your case.

Why might that tactic offer the best chance of getting your proposal included in the budget? Why is it important to have access at this point in the budgetary process?

To explore the role of the state budget office in budget making, check out the National Association of State Budget Officers' website at *www.nasbo.org.*

Discussion groups generally accede to the motions advanced by other groups in votes of the full committee.[10] (See Figures 5.2a and 5.2b.)

Utah offers a distinctive variation because all legislators serve on the joint appropriations committee and are assigned to one of its subcommittees.[11] The committee of the whole, then, is the entire legislative body meeting in the committee forum. To make this arrangement workable, an *executive* appropriations subcommittee, composed of legislative leaders from both parties, is charged with reconciling the other subcommittees' recommendations and making the final fit between expected revenues and expected spending. In carrying out this function, the executive appropriations subcommittee exercises a great deal of power in shaping the legislative version of the budget.

Action Shifting to the Legislative Chambers

After receiving the amended version of the executive budget from its fiscal committee, the first house of the legislature is given one to three weeks to complete its process of amendments from the floor. Then, after clearing the first house, the budget bill is sent to

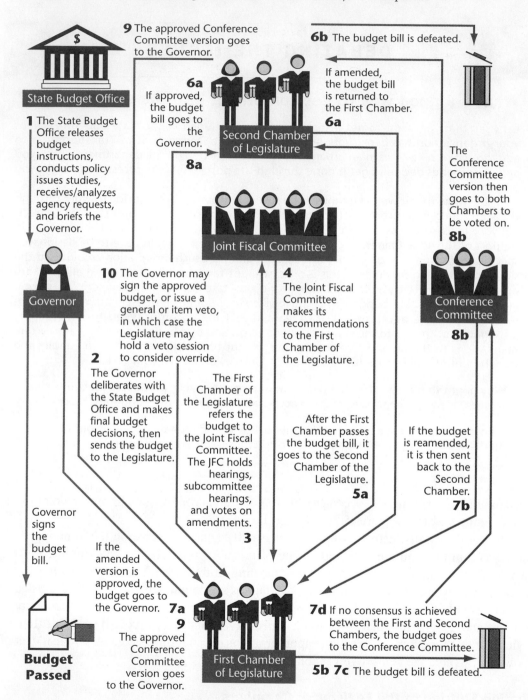

Figure 5.2a   The State Budgetary Process: Option 1—Joint Fiscal Committee

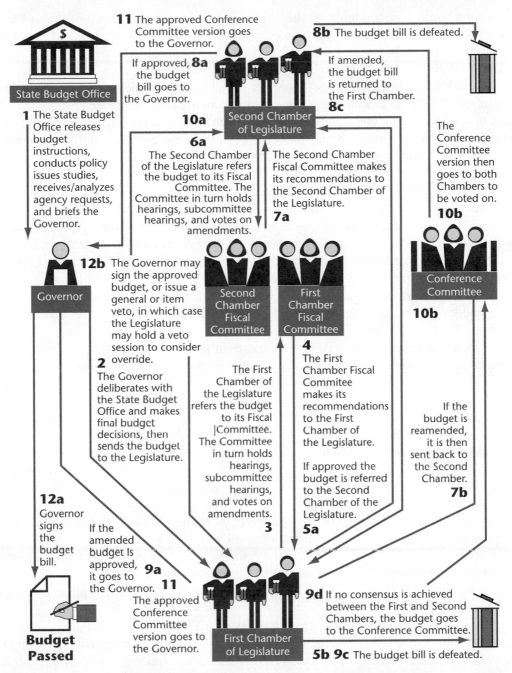

11 The approved Conference Committee version goes to the Governor.

8b The budget bill is defeated.

If approved, **8a** the budget bill goes to the Governor.

If amended, the budget bill is returned to the First Chamber. **8c**

State Budget Office

Second Chamber of Legislature

1 The State Budget Office releases budget instructions, conducts policy issues studies, receives/analyzes agency requests, and briefs the Governor.

10a

6a
The Second Chamber of the Legislature refers the budget to its Fiscal Committee. The Committee in turn holds hearings, subcommittee hearings, and votes on amendments.

The Second Chamber Fiscal Committee makes its recommendations to the Second Chamber of the Legislature.
7a

The Conference Committee version then goes to both Chambers to be voted on.
10b

12b The Governor may sign the approved budget, or issue a general or item veto, in which case the Legislature may hold a veto session to consider override.

Governor

Second Chamber Fiscal Committee

First Chamber Fiscal Committee

Conference Committee

10b

2
The Governor deliberates with the State Budget Office and makes final budget decisions, then sends the budget to the Legislature.

The First Chamber of the Legislature refers the budget to its Fiscal |Committee. The Committee in turn holds hearings, subcommittee hearings, and votes on amendments.
3

4
The First Chamber Fiscal Commitee makes its recommendations to the First Chamber of the Legislature.

If approved the budget is referred to the Second Chamber of the Legislature.
5a

If the budget is reamended, it is then sent back to the Second Chamber.
7b

12a
Governor signs the budget bill.

If the amended budget Is approved, it goes to the Governor. **9a**

11
The approved Conference Committee version goes to the Governor.

First Chamber of Legislature

9d If no consensus is achieved between the First and Second Chambers, the budget goes to the Conference Committee.

5b 9c The budget bill is defeated.

Budget Passed

Figure 5.2b The State Budgetary Process: Option 2—Separate Fiscal Committees

the second house, where (similar to the process just discussed) it is referred to that chamber's fiscal committee. The ensuing process proceeds similarly to that described for the first house. Of course, in those states having a joint fiscal committee, the committee's recommendations are provided to both chambers simultaneously, even though each house deliberates on the executive budget separately, beginning with the house in which it was first introduced. If the second house cannot agree with the first, suggested changes are sent back to the first for its consideration. Modifications may then be made, and the revised version is sent to the second house for review. The process continues until agreement is reached. Obviously, consistent lack of agreement can extend this phase of the process beyond the normal time frame.

If agreement cannot be reached, the legislative leadership may appoint a conference committee. The conference committee is normally allocated no more than two weeks to work out an agreed-upon version, which is then sent to both houses for a vote. Depending on the state, the conference report may or may not be amended by the legislature. In some states, it must be voted up or down without amendment. Very seldom, however, do one or both houses reject the conference report altogether.

Debate on the floor characterizes the *public* arena for budget deliberations at this stage in the budgetary process. Citizens frequently gather in public galleries to observe the debate; however, most citizens already have an opinion about the matter being debated. The more important arena for decision making is the partisan legislative caucus, which tends to be more extensively used for budget deliberation than for the single, substantive bill legislative process. A **partisan caucus** comprises all the legislators from a given party in a particular legislative chamber. Thus, a state senate will have a Republican caucus and a Democratic caucus, as will the other chamber. Legislators advocate amendments and attempt to generate support for them in the caucus. At times, straw votes (unofficial tallies) are taken to gauge support for amendments. Legislative staff directors and key staff members frequently are invited, along with the caucus aides, to participate in discussions. When the governor is of the same political party as the legislature, the state budget director may be invited to attend and respond to questions.

In the caucus, which may or may not be open to the public, members of the fiscal committee coalesce around the recommendations endorsed by the committee. A unified voice gives them considerable influence and contributes to preserving a budget that largely reflects the committee's work. However, the partisan caucus may become the battleground for those legislators who did not prevail during the committee's phase of budget deliberations.

When assessing the relationship of legislative leadership to the fiscal committee's endorsed budget, remember that the institutional role of the committee is to put together a fiscally responsible budget, which cannot exceed revenues and must also include a basic cushion to accommodate unforeseen events. Overall, the leadership supports this strategy, but support may break down on specific items. Coalitions of maverick legislators may form in opposition to the leadership's position. Such coalitions try to gain a stranglehold

---

partisan caucus A meeting of legislators of a given party from each legislative chamber.

on the entire budget by aggregating support for a broadly inclusive package of amendments not supported by the leadership. If they are successful in getting enough support so that a majority no longer exists in the majority party, these subcaucuses can hold the leadership hostage.

For the less broadly significant items that involve little cost and affect few other legislators' interests, a threat by majority party caucus members not to vote for the budget unless their pet items are included may win a concession from the leadership if the final caucus vote looks marginal. On the other hand, for significant issues affecting a large number of caucus members, a much broader supportive coalition is needed to hold the leadership hostage.

Two features characterize this segment of the budgetary process. First, time constraints are the most severe of any phase; thus, legislators must be selective in their deliberations. Second, the agenda is less shaped by staff members at this stage than at any other stage in the process. Legislators bring their own distilled agenda to the caucuses, and the deliberation process is one of determining where consensus lies among the legislators themselves. Fiscal staff members may prepare fiscal notes and discussion papers on the major proposed amendments, but they generally exercise less influence at this stage than during committee deliberations. The emphasis in the caucuses is more on coalition building and less on policy analysis.

At the conclusion of the caucus sessions, the legislative leadership has a good sense of which amendments will receive sufficient support for passage on the floor. To the extent possible, the majority party leadership attempts to mobilize support to reject amendments that have not been approved in caucus.

The Governor's Chance Again: The Veto

After the budget clears the legislature, the governor again gets an opportunity to shape its final form. As discussed in detail in Chapter 9, governors in 44 states possess line-item veto authority for appropriations bills, including the state budget. In addition, governors in 10 states have the power to reduce an appropriation without vetoing it entirely. Line-item veto power allows governors to line out appropriations or expressions of legislative intent over how funds can be used, depending on the specific authority given them by state law. Veto recommendations generally are made by the state budget and may be supported by issue discussion papers. Agencies, interest groups, and individual legislators may also submit veto recommendations. Individual citizens may do so as well, if they know the issues, keep up with the legislation, understand the opportunities and limits of the line-item veto, and have access to communicate their veto recommendations so that their suggestions do not get lost in piles of correspondence in the governor's office.

Although the state budget office normally plays a role in identifying sections of the budget bill for veto, it plays a less direct role during veto deliberation than during the earlier period of executive budget development. The decision-making process for veto deliberation is less self-contained and more subject to influences by forces outside the governor's executive budget agency. Legislative leaders of the governor's political party frequently are brought in to discuss the politics of vetoes. An often discussed question is, Can the vetoes be sustained? In addition, the governor and/or executive office staff members consult with those legislators who will be most affected by prospective vetoes. Their reactions to the vetoes, and how hard they will work for override, are subjects of much conversation. In addition, the governor's aides query interest group representatives to get their reactions to veto candidates.

In summary, then, input is considerably broader for veto consideration than is that for executive budget development. Because vetoes represent a relatively small but controversial part of the budget, the governor personally takes a more focused, active part in the deliberations.

Legislative Review of Gubernatorial Vetoes

Legislative requirements for overriding budget vetoes, in whole or by line item, are the same as for other legislation. When considering attempts to override, legislative leaders once again use the partisan caucus. The leadership submits its recommendations for overrides, and other legislators attempt to generate enough caucus support to add or delete items from that list.

This period in the budgetary process is a time of intense lobbying by the governor's staff, particularly with members of the governor's political party. This so-called political hardball, when needed, is the name of the game. Favors are called in, and promises of future benefits are made in return for cooperation. Gubernatorial vetoes often become highly publicized, and a governor's political reputation can depend on his or her ability to get those vetoes sustained in the legislature. If a governor is unable to win support from his or her own party, that inability sends signals to the opposition party, the media, and the public at large that the governor lacks the political strength required to lead the state effectively.

Legislative committee staffs play a much less direct role in the **veto override session** than in the earlier segments of the budgetary process. They may prepare analyses of the effects of veto overrides, but much of the staff's work at this stage is usually taken over by the partisan legislative caucus staffs. The emphasis becomes coalition building with strongly partisan solidarity.

The Process Recycles

The budget, after veto considerations, becomes the state's fiscal blueprint for the next year or two. Adjustments to the budget can be made through the enactment of legislation in the intervening period before the next budget bill is considered, if the legislature is in session. However, few such changes are made in normal times. When the legislature is not in session, the fiscal committee in some states is empowered to appropriate limited amounts of money

---

veto override session A special session of the legislature in which members decide whether to nullify gubernatorial vetoes.

from a contingency fund to cover emergencies or unforeseen events. The committee may also usually transfer funds from one appropriation to another.

The process then repeats itself. New administrations come into office, yet the essential characteristics of the process generally endure among the states.

SUMMARY AND CONCLUSIONS

The political institutions of state and local governments create public policy in several ways that significantly affect our lives. They do so by using a number of distinct processes, most notably the single-bill legislative process, the budgetary process, the processes of direct democracy, the regulatory process, and the judicial process. The first three processes are based on the democratic principle of majority rule, whereas the regulatory and judicial processes are nonmajoritarian.

Individual citizens can participate in all five policy-making processes, but their participation tends to be scant. Organized interest groups, in contrast, participate actively. They represent the collective strength of their members, and they often employ staff members who research policy issues, prepare position papers and other correspondence, and lobby executive and legislative leaders. Interest groups also commonly raise funds to finance the electoral campaigns of the elected officials who act on legislation or regulations directly affecting them. That expertise and influence gives interest groups access to the process, allowing them to forge close working relationships both with legislators and their key staff members as well as executive branch officials. Individual citizens, in contrast, are not as well positioned to enjoy that same ready access. At the same time, however, individuals appear less interested in shaping public policy than they are in solving problems that affect them personally. Calling to get a darkened streetlight repaired, for example, often takes precedence over efforts to change public policy through legislation.

State policy making commonly affects both state and local residents. States not only prescribe the framework within which local governments can operate, they also provide financial assistance to them. Because of this broad policy reach, the state legislative and budgetary processes merit special attention. Understanding how they work provides a useful context from which to view local policy making, recognizing its inherent similarities, and appreciating its differences as well.

The two lawmaking processes share similarities in their patterns of executive and legislative involvement and interaction, but some significant differences can be noted. The budgetary process generally involves greater gubernatorial initiative and influence, and it also alters patterns of legislative involvement and influence associated with the substantive bill legislative process. The budgetary process narrows the scope of legislative involvement and shifts influence from the substantive standing committees to the appropriations committees and their subcommittees. In addition, the budgetary process tends to crowd out the substantive bill legislative process, given the significance of the state budget as both a resource allocation and a policy vehicle. Because governors and legislatures tend to put more policy into the budget, where permitted by state law, the state budgetary process will become even more central to state policy making.

Discussion Questions

1. Compare and contrast the substantive bill legislative process and the state budgetary process. How does each process represent a shared executive–legislative function?

2. Discuss the various points of origin for legislative initiatives. Do some offer greater prospects for successful passage than others? Provide illustrations to support your answer.

3. What is the significance of Alan Rosenthal's distinction between the legislative "assembly line" and the executive policy-making process? How does it help to make the policy-making process more easily understood?

4. What roles do partisan legislative caucuses play in the policy-making process? Explain their significance.

Glossary

administrative rules 117
advisory referendum 117
bill 125
budget bill 133
budget message 133
conference committee 129
contained specialization 120
deadline systems 132
direct initiative 117

engrossing 129
enrolled bill 129
fiscal notes 132
general referendum 117
indirect initiative 117
instruments of public policy 116
iron triangle 121
legislative resolutions 124
partisan caucus 142

policy agenda 125
popular referendum 117
public intervenors 121
reciprocity 138
representative democracy 116
special-interest legislation 127
state budget 133
veto override session 144

Endnotes

1. *The Book of the States*, 2002 (Lexington, Ky.: Council of State Governments, 2002), 127–128.

2. Paul Peterson, *City Limits* (Chicago, Ill.: University of Chicago Press, 1981).

3. This concept comes from Richard Fenno Jr. in *The Power of the Purse: Appropriations Politics in Congress* (Boston, Mass.: Little, Brown, 1966).

4. A. Grant Jordan, "Iron Triangles, Wooly Corporations, or Elastic Nets: Images of the Policy Process," *Journal of Public Policy* 1, no. 1 (1981), 95–124.

5. William T. Gormley Jr., "Alternative Models of the Regulatory Process: Public Utility Regulation in the States," *Western Political Quarterly* 35, no. 3 (1982), 297–317; Gormley, "The Representation Revolution: Reforming State Regulation Through Public Representation," *Administration and Society* 18, no. 2 (1986), 179–196; Beth Givens, *Citizens' Utility Boards Bear Watching* (San Diego, Calif.: Center for Public Interest Law, University of San Diego Law School, 1991).

6. Alan Rosenthal, *Legislative Life* (New York: Harper & Row, 1981), 256–272.

7. James J. Gosling, *Budgetary Politics in American Governments*, 4th ed. (New York: Routledge, 2006), 157.

8. James J. Gosling, "Patterns of Influence and Choice in the Wisconsin Budgetary Process," *Legislative Studies Quarterly* 10, no. 4 (1985), 457–482.

9. *Legislative Budget Procedures* (Denver, Colo.: National Conference of State Legislatures, 1998), Table 5-4.

10. James J. Gosling, *The Wisconsin Budgetary Process: An Interpretive Description* (Madison, Wis.: The Robert M. La Follette Institute of Public Affairs, 1985), 3–8.

11. F. Ted Hebert, "Utah: Legislative Budgeting in an Executive Budget State," in *Governors, Legislatures, and Budgets: Diversity Across the American States*, eds. Edward T. Clynch and Thomas P. Lauth (Westport, Conn.: Greenwood Press, 1991), 103–114.

CHAPTER 6

Grass-Roots Participation

LEARNING OBJECTIVES

- Identify the characteristics of people who are active in politics.
- Understand the different ways in which people participate in governance.
- Know the forms of direct democracy used in some states and understand the arguments for and against direct democracy.

"This is what democracy looks like," chanted the more than 97,000 people who gathered at the capitol building in Madison, Wisconsin, on February 26, 2011. Protests began on February 14 after Governor Scott Walker proposed eliminating the rights of state and local government employees to form effective unions and bargain contracts establishing compensation, work rules, and working conditions. Exempt from the proposal were police and firefighters, whose unions had supported Walker during his campaign. This proposal seemed especially radical in Wisconsin, which was the first state to authorize collective bargaining and was the birthplace of the American Federation of State, County, and Municipal Employees, a major national public employee union. While the protests—which included police and firefighters—took over the grounds around the capitol, inside the building leaders of the Republican majority in the legislature suspended procedures and tried to limit debate in order to act quickly on the governor's proposal. Democrats in the State Assembly offered 117 amendments to slow the process, and Democratic state senators left the state in order to keep that body from having the quorum necessary to conduct business. Demonstrations continued in Madison and other communities around the state and at one point protestors camped inside the capitol building. While opponents delayed legislative action, the bill was signed into law.

Protestors did not give up, however. They circulated petitions to recall from office Republicans in the state senate. Wisconsin is one of 17 states that allows voters to initiate a special election to remove elected officeholders before their terms expire. In the summer of 2011, nine Republicans and three Democrats faced recall elections. To gain control of the state senate, Democrats had to achieve a net gain of three seats. While they fell just one seat short of that, Democrats actually outpolled Republicans when taking all the recall races as a whole and sent a warning to Governor Walker who worried that he, too, might be recalled. In Ohio, where the governor and legislature also placed severe limits on the collective bargaining rights of public employees, opponents first demonstrated and when that did not work they placed on the statewide ballot a proposal to repeal the new law. Ohio does not provide for recall elections, but the state does allow citizens to place a referendum on the ballot to reject laws passed by the legislature and governor—the reverse of what is possible in Wisconsin. On November 8, 2011, 61 percent of Ohio voters approved the measure to repeal the law and preserved collective bargaining rights for public employees in that state.

The political activity described in this vignette is an example of the variety of ways in which individuals can affect state and local government. There is a long history in the United States of political protests. Demonstrators do not always get what they want, but they are often successful in raising the visibility of issues and prompting other action. In some states, that action can include recall elections. There are states where it is possible to get proposals on a ballot so that voters can enact legislation without any involvement of legislatures or governors. It is also possible to have a popular vote to veto or repeal actions of the legislature. Grass-roots political participation can be very powerful, and each of us enjoys the right to engage in an almost limitless array of political expressions. But very few people do.

In fact, college students and graduates are among the 15 percent of the population that controls the United States of America.[1] Reading this book places you in an elite category. Those who actually participate in politics—other than voting—tend to be those with the most education. The chances are fairly high that you are and will be active in some kind of political activity if:

- you have a college education.
- your family has participated in politics.
- you are employed.

Each category that doesn't apply reduces the probability.

Grass-roots participation is about opportunities for individuals to play a role in shaping government and about who actually seizes those opportunities. We act politically both as individuals and as members of groups. The focus in this chapter is primarily on individuals. Chapter 1 discussed how the face-to-face interaction that is at the core of state and local government involves instances in which individuals are the subjects of governmental action and instances in which individuals are the actors. This chapter is about individuals as actors.

ACCESS TO GOVERNMENT

Fundamental to participatory democracy is the presumption that the records and proceedings of government are open and accessible. If individuals are going to participate meaningfully in government, they must be able to get information and attend meetings. In the United States, everything is open to the public unless the government can demonstrate a need to withhold information.

The federal government has encountered well-publicized battles to withhold records pertaining to the assassination of President Kennedy; President Nixon's Watergate scandal; the Iran-Contra affair involving President Reagan; and the September 11, 2001, attacks and the Iraq War during President George W. Bush's years in office. The justification of federal officials has been that release of relevant records would reveal the identities of some of our spies and endanger national security.

State and local governments usually cannot claim they must act in secret because of national security. Their major justification for withholding documents or having a private meeting is to protect an individual's right to privacy. The federal government also must uphold this right.

Since the 1960s, states have made explicit and specific the commitment to accessibility by passing laws requiring state agencies and local governments to have open meetings and open records, except when necessary to protect the privacy rights of individuals. These laws have been added to traditional provisions for access, such as the use of advisory committees and public hearings. The major instruments used by state and local governments to protect public access include **open meeting laws**, **open record laws**, and hearings.

1. Open Meeting Laws. In 1967, Florida, the so-called Sunshine State, passed what was referred to as a sunshine law. This was not an attempt to mandate blue skies, but rather a statute making it clear that state government meetings were to be open to the public. All the other 49 states followed Florida's lead. Open meeting laws only apply to the legislative and executive branches of state and local government, not to courts.

To make open meeting laws more meaningful, 41 states require advance notice of meetings, 37 states obligated agencies to keep minutes, and 31 states do not recognize any action as official unless it is decided in an open meeting. Officials who meet in secret may be personally fined or otherwise punished in 35 states.[2]

2. Open Record Laws. Shortly after it joined the Union in 1848, Wisconsin enacted a law establishing the right of individuals to see the written records of government. All states now have a freedom of information act or open records law. As governments adopted computer technology, open records laws applied to electronic as well as hard copies. State and local governments may charge for the cost of making copies of the records that are requested.

3. Hearings. A standard part of the operations of state legislatures, school boards, city councils, or county boards is to hold hearings on proposals. In addition, all states require that their administrative agencies hold a hearing and allow for written

---

open meeting laws State requirements that meetings of committees and officials that are part of the policy-making process must be open to the public. Exceptions are allowed for personnel matters and for contract negotiations.
open record laws State laws that require all written and electronic records, except individual personnel files, to be open to the public.

comments on any proposed rule or regulation before it is adopted. Thus, if the agency in a state that certifies teachers wishes to require that all elementary school instructors take a course in educational psychology, the agency must first announce its intent to establish such a requirement and then allow individuals to comment before it takes final action.

The opportunity to secure records, attend meetings, and provide comments is essential for grass-roots participation. Although only a handful of citizens take advantage of these opportunities for face-to-face interaction with public officials, many citizens benefit indirectly.

A major effect of open meetings and open records laws is to enable the press to report on the activities of state and local governments. Rather than going to the meetings or perusing records themselves, many individuals rely on newspapers, radio, television, and blogs for their information about government. This might raise a concern about the influence of the interpretations of reporters and bloggers, but at least there is some dissemination of what government is or might be doing.

News coverage does encourage some people to take advantage of opportunities to participate. Parents who generally are not active on education issues may be prompted to attend a school board meeting when they learn that district officials are considering closing a neighborhood school or cutting some extracurricular activities. Individuals who learn that their community is being considered as a site for a prison or a hazardous waste disposal facility are likely to join their neighbors at a hearing to learn the details and to air their reactions. Access to government is essential for issue-specific, ad hoc grass-roots participation, as well as for more general involvement.

Exploring the Web

All state governments and most local governments have sites on the Web. These sites provide information about meetings, laws, and services and may allow citizens to interact with agencies and officials electronically through e-mail, chat lines, and html forums. You can get the homepage of your state by inserting the two post office initials for your state in the blank in the following address: www.state.__.us.

Critique the website of your state and/or local government.

■ Is the format clear and easy to use?
■ Is the information on the website useful and interesting to you?
■ Are there opportunities for you to request and to send forms for permits, licenses, and so on?
■ Can you send and receive comments electronically?

It makes sense that individuals exercise their right to interact with government officials when the issues are of personal importance and interest. We all know of examples in our own communities of policy proposals and government actions that inspired citizens to take action. Perhaps the more difficult question is, Why don't some people get active, even when there is a matter that affects them personally? Much depends on whether or not you think voicing an opinion makes any difference.

WHO PARTICIPATES?

Studies of who participates in governance invariably are linked to how they participate. The most common measure is voting. As Table 6.1 illustrates, data collected by the U.S. Census Bureau show a common pattern over the past four decades for who votes in presidential elections. Men and women vote at about the same rate, although the percentage of women voting is slightly higher than that for men. Whites vote at higher rates than other racial groups, except for 2008 when Barak Obama ran for president and African Americans voted at a rate slightly higher than did whites. Individuals over the age of 65 and people with a college education are much more likely to vote than those who are younger and/or have less education.

Table 6.1 Voting Rates in Presidential Elections (Percentage Voting of Those Eligible)

Category	1988	1992	1996	2000	2004	2006	2008
Male	56.4	60.2	55.1	53.1	56.3	46.9	61.5
Female	58.3	62.3	57.8	56.2	60.1	48.6	65.9
White	59.1	63.6	59.6	60.4	65.3	49.7	64.4
African American	51.5	54.0	50.9	54.1	60.0	41.0	64.7
Hispanic	28.8	28.9	25.9	27.5	47.1	32.3	49.9
18- to 24-year-olds	36.2	42.8	32.4	32.3	41.9	21.7	47.9
25- to 44-year-olds	54.0	58.3	49.2	49.8	52.2	39.5	59.9
45- to 64-year-olds	67.9	70.0	64.4	64.1	66.6	57.6	69.2
Those over 65	68.8	70.1	67.0	67.6	68.9	62.5	70.3
School years completed							
Less than high school	36.7	35.1	33.3	33.6	40.1	26.8	39.9
High school	54.7	57.5	49.1	49.4	56.2	40.5	54.9
College							
1 to 3 years	64.5	68.7	60.5	60.3	64.4	49.4	98.0
4 years or more	77.6	81.0	72.6	75.5	80.1	63.9	78.9
Employed	58.4	63.6	55.2	54.7	66.3	48.4	65.9
Unemployed	38.6	46.2	37.2	35.1	51.2	31.1	54.7
Total population	57.4	61.3	54.2	54.7	64.0	47.8	63.6

Source: Bureau of the Census, http://www.census.gov/compendia/statab/2011/tables/11s0416.xls accessed 07/09/11.

Figure 6.1 presents the rates of eligible voters, by state, who cast ballots in presidential elections. Note that the patterns are consistent with the political cultures described in Chapter 2. Moralistic states in the Northeast and Midwest have the highest turnout rates, and the traditionalist states in the South have among the lowest. Note also that Western states are affected by time zones. Many eligible voters in those states know the results of the presidential election from news reports after polls have closed in Eastern time zones and do not bother to vote. This is especially noticeable in California and Hawaii.

Other studies, based primarily on public opinion polls, point to additional characteristics of those who vote in presidential elections.[3] Professor James Davis gathered data that showed that income, organizational membership, and party affiliation make a difference. Again, the lesson seems to be that those who have more and do more tend to be the ones who vote more. It is important to remember that the studies we have reported are of presidential elections. Most states hold some elections at the same time as the presidential contests. When voters are prompted to go to the polling booth because of the presidential race, they cast ballots for state and local candidates as well. However, some state and many municipal elections are held in the spring or in years when there is no presidential contest. The turnout for these elections is generally 25 to 35 percent of the eligible voters, about half that of the turnout for presidential elections.[4]

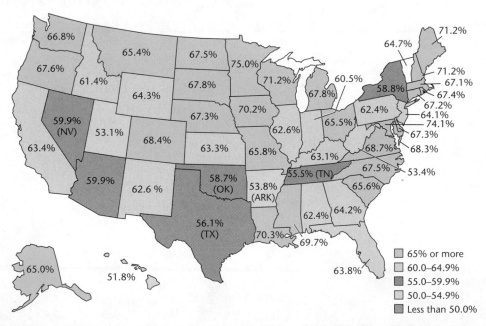

Figure 6.1 Voting Rates by State in the 2008 Presidential Election, Percentage of Voting-Age Population.

Source: U.S. Census Bureau, *Voting and Registration in the Election of November 2008* (Washington, D.C.: U.S. Census Bureau, 2010), 8.

In a major study, political science scholars Sidney Verba and Norman Nie surveyed 3,000 adults about a broad range of political involvement.[5] When Verba and Nie analyzed the responses to their survey, they found that 4 percent of the people contacted public officials about specific problems or concerns, but they did not vote or participate in campaigns. This group, which Verba and Nie refer to as parochial participants, are confident, articulate, and well informed. These are traits of individuals one would expect to vote. However, parochial participants feel they can be much more effective through face-to-face contacts with public officials than they can through voting in general elections.

Verba and Nie identified another group, communalists, who are very active in a variety of groups that work to influence public policies in local communities. Communalists, about 20 percent of the people, seek to improve their cities and neighborhoods through various service organizations and charitable societies. Individuals in this category regularly vote, but they do not engage in any campaign activities and they do not contribute money to political campaigns.

On the other hand, Verba and Nie identify a category of people who are very active in campaigns and elections but they do not belong to or work in community service or charity organizations. Members of this group, about 15 percent of the people surveyed, are called campaigners. It appears that the excitement of competition distinguishes campaigners from communalists.

Other categories developed by Verba and Nie in their analysis are voting specialists, 21 percent of the people, who vote but are not active in any other electoral or community service activities; complete activists, 11 percent, who are engaged in the full range of both electoral and community activities; and inactives, 22 percent, who are not active in any community or political activities. The Verba and Nie study contributed to a more complete and sophisticated understanding of the levels of individual political participation. Sidney Verba has worked with other scholars to continue research on who participates in politics. A major finding of these works is that only a few people take full advantage of the opportunities that exist for being active in governance and that many more are only marginally and sporadically involved or not involved at all.[6]

A sense of **efficacy** is essential if individuals are to invest time and energy in political participation.[7] Efficacy is a belief that one can have an impact and make a difference. People who think that their opinions don't matter or that their vote is not going to make a difference have a low sense of efficacy and are unlikely to be politically active. Members of minority groups tend to have a low sense of efficacy and, as pointed out earlier, have a lower voting rate than do whites. Historically, minority groups have not been allowed or welcomed into the general political, societal, or economic system. As a result, they are now skeptical that they can influence policy.[8] In contrast, those who have enjoyed high status, wealth, and power identify more positively with political institutions and processes. They are more likely to believe that their participation would be efficacious and thus are more likely to get involved in political and community affairs.

---

efficacy Citizen belief that action and participation by the public make a difference in governance and public policies.

Balancing Access and Integrity

While there is a general commitment to encouraging broad participation in governance, there is also a tradition of limiting access to the ballot box and public office to law-abiding citizens. In part, partisan calculations influence the adoption of measures to make it relatively easy for individuals to participate in the electoral process. Based on evidence that the Democratic Party benefits when more people vote, a Democratic Congress and President Clinton in 1993 passed the National Voter Registration Act. This federal law, often referred to as the motor-voter law, requires states to provide the opportunity to register to vote when individuals get their driver's license or get hunting and fishing permits. Democrats were very upset when Republican-controlled states did not comply with the law. President Bill Clinton's attorney general, Janet Reno, sued California, Illinois, and Pennsylvania for not implementing the act. Republicans have since mounted their own get-out-the-vote drives, targeted, of course, to those segments of the population that tend to support the GOP.

In the 2000 presidential election, George W. Bush won the majority of Electoral College votes, although Al Gore won the majority of popular votes. The discrepancy focused in large part on Florida, where flaws in the way votes were cast and counted disenfranchised thousands of Gore supporters, many of whom were African Americans. In response, Congress passed the Help America Vote Act, which provides federal standards and some financial assistance so states will have more reliable technology for recording votes. The act also includes measures to minimize voter fraud, a concern harbored more by Republicans than Democrats. Some states that had Republican-controlled legislatures followed through with requiring voters to have picture identification in order to cast their ballots. Democrats charged that such a requirement puts the poor and the elderly at a disadvantage because they tend not to have driver's licenses. Student also suffer because they tend to have their home address on their driver's license but vote where they go to school, thus creating a discrepancy between the photo ID and the voting address. Democrats sued to void Indiana's law, passed in 2005, requiring voters to show government-issued photo identification. In 2008, in *Indiana Democratic Party v. Rokita,* the U.S. Supreme Court upheld the law, noting that while Democrats might be right in anticipating problems, they did not produce evidence that disenfranchisement in fact occurred.

Voter Fraud.   There has been no evidence, in Indiana or in other states, of widespread voter fraud. Yet there is no requirement that there be evidence of wrongdoing in order for state legislatures to adopt policies restricting access to the polling booth. Some states have policies that provide such easy access as to raise the possibility of voters casting ballots more than once or misrepresenting who they are. In Oregon, all balloting is done through the mail and one can easily imagine the possibilities for fraud with this system. Other states encourage the use of mailed and absentee ballots by not requiring an excuse from the more traditional balloting. Even with such easy access, studies and investigations have not identified any significant fraud.[9]

Convicted Felons and Voting.   States differ over whether convicted felons should be allowed to vote and over how laws disenfranchising felons should be administered. Only Vermont and Maine allow felons to vote. Only Kentucky and Virginia bar them for life. Georgia and

Alabama are among a handful of states that specify that only those guilty of crimes of moral turpitude be disenfranchised. Georgia does not define this term, but in 2003, the Alabama state legislature identified the crimes that should be included as murder, rape, sodomy, sexual abuse, incest, sexual torture, and nine crimes involving pornography and abuses against children. Alabama's attorney general, however, added another dozen, most of them nonviolent.

The more common pattern in the states is to treat all felons alike and to take away the right to vote while someone is in prison or on probation or parole, but to allow them to vote again once they are no longer under the supervision of the state's correctional system. Although this seems straightforward, states have not always culled names from lists in accordance with this policy. In 2000, Florida turned away thousands from the ballot box on the grounds that they were felons. Investigations after the election found numerous errors that disproportionately disadvantaged African Americans and advantaged Hispanics. Although these errors helped Republican candidates, Governor Charlie Crist (a Republican) oversaw a purging of a list that had grown to exceed one million names and included lifetime bans on individuals who had not committed violent crimes.

WAYS OF PARTICIPATING

Citizens participate in governance at the grass-roots level using different methods. Several of these methods are discussed in the following sections.

Engaging in the Electoral Process

The most visible arena in which individuals participate in politics is by electing people to office. Voting is often regarded as almost synonymous with democracy. There is a hierarchy of electoral involvement in addition to voting. These methods include wearing a button or displaying a bumper sticker or yard sign, or volunteering time in campaign activities. Likewise, there are numerous opportunities to contribute money and to help solicit contributions from others. The ultimate form of involvement in the electoral process is to run for office.

Testifying at Hearings and Meetings

State and local legislative and administrative bodies provide opportunities to present written and oral testimony on issues. Parents can appear before a school board and argue for a particular service or policy. Neighbors can go to a city council meeting to express concern about how a proposed project might affect them. Farmers can inform a state environmental protection agency about the impacts of banning a certain pesticide. The testimony presented at these hearings or meetings is not like that presented in a court case. Individuals are not reciting facts or observations in an effort to determine who did what to whom. Instead, information and opinion are provided in order to persuade officials to act in a certain way.

Being on Advisory Committees

Individual public officials and various legislative and administrative bodies form committees of citizens to provide advice on policies and procedures. Membership on these committees is typically on a volunteer basis. Nonetheless, individuals sometimes are very anxious to get appointed to a committee advising a school board on curriculum, or a city council on assistance to the homeless, or a governor on business development. Sometimes the advice of these committees is not taken seriously. However, they can be genuine opportunities for influencing policy, especially if there is media coverage; in that case, politicians must make some response to the recommendations of an advisory committee.

Contacting Public Officials

Public officials receive calls, letters, and e-mail messages from friends and individuals who supported them during an election. They are also contacted by constituents who feel strongly about a particular issue. The substance of the communication is similar to that provided in testimony in a public meeting. The style, however, tends to be more intense. In his study of Birmingham, Alabama, political scientist Philip Coulter found that about one-third of the people he surveyed reported that they had personally contacted one of their local officials to express an opinion.[10] These contacts included complaints, requests, and outright demands. Sometimes authors or callers refused to identify themselves, but the messages were usually clear.

Using the Media and the Internet

When an individual writes a letter to an editor, calls a radio talk-show host, develops a blog, or participates in an online discussion, the intent is generally not to influence the editor or the host but to persuade officials indirectly by shaping public opinion. (Of course, some people call talk shows or write newspaper editors as a form of personal entertainment or catharsis.) A goal, at least implicitly, is to state the argument in a forum that will persuade others to join in pressuring public officials or to vote for or against particular candidates or referenda.

Civic Journalism and Focus Groups

Reform efforts use a combination of select groups of citizens and open forums to draw the attention of government officials to issues. Civic journalism is when the news media sponsors a forum to address concerns in a community and then covers the discussion as part of the news. Some journalists object to this practice and contend that newspapers, television, and radio should report news, not generate it. Others see this as a valuable contribution to policy discourse. Similarly, the reinventing-government movement started in the mid-1990s includes active steps to hold forums, electronic town halls, and surveys to solicit the concerns and views of the public so that governments can know and address the needs of their customers.

Protesting

Another way of using the media to place pressure on government is to engage in a public protest that will get coverage and therefore enable one to convey a message. The protest could be as mild as displaying a sign and as dramatic as disrupting an event. The Civil Rights movement of the 1950s and 1960s used a wide range of protest activities to get local, state,

Exploring the Web

Civic journalism: Should newspapers play an active role in making public policy, or should they just report the news?

Should the press just report the news that others make? Is it appropriate for the media to sponsor forums and discussions among citizens that aim to raise issues for government officials to address? The latter approach is known as civic journalism. The websites of organizations that promote civic journalism provide examples of it:

www.pewcenter.org The Pew Center, which is a foundation sponsoring civic journalism around the country.
www.democracyplace.org A link to a forum explaining and promoting civic journalism.
www.gspa.washington.edu/trust/links/journalism.html A website that provides links to numerous examples of civic journalism.

Alternative examples of websites designed to inform individuals about public policy issues so they might be prepared to participate in public decision making are www.dlcppi.org and www.publicagenda.org. These are addresses for nonpartisan organizations that have information and discussions on a wide variety of public policy issues. The address for the Center for Policy Alternatives, which is particularly concerned about state government issues, is www.cfpa.org.

and federal officials to end racial discrimination. The efforts to restrict the option to get an abortion have included displaying signs and engaging in violence against doctors and facilities. Although protesting is, by definition, unconventional and outside formal political processes and institutions, it has been a common form of participation throughout U.S. history.

DIRECT DEMOCRACY

Some states have established formal ways for individual citizens to take direct action beyond electing officials or trying to influence them once they are in office. Direct democracy is most often identified with the initiative, the recall, and the referendum. Both the initiative and the recall allow citizens to act without any involvement of the governor or the state legislature. With the **direct initiative**, voters can enact a new law or amend the state's constitution by putting it on the ballot. The legislature and governor are not involved.

With the **recall**, citizens can remove an elected official in office before his or her term has expired. A recall need not be based on criminal charges or malfeasance in office and

---

direct initiative A process in which citizens can petition to have a proposed law on a ballot and, if passed, the proposal becomes law without any approval or involvement of the governor or the legislature.
recall A process in which citizens can vote to remove an elected official from office before his or her term expires.

does not require action by the legislative, executive, or judicial branches of government. Legislatures can also remove elected officials from office, but they must use an impeachment process, which requires formal charges of wrongdoings and follows procedures similar to a court trial.

The legislature is involved in the indirect initiative and the referendum. The **indirect initiative** requires that a petition from citizens be submitted to the legislature, which can either adopt the proposal or place it on the ballot. Seventeen states have the direct form of statutory initiative, and six have the indirect. Nevada has both. Three states, Florida, Michigan, and Mississippi, have the direct initiative for constitutional but not statutory change. Table 6.2 summarizes the types of direct democracy. The referendum can take one of three forms:

1. **General Referendum.** A state or local government is required to place items such as a constitutional amendment or a bond for borrowing money on a ballot and get approval from voters.
2. **Advisory Referendum.** Legislators place a question on the ballot to get the sentiment of voters. Legislators are not obliged to enact laws that reflect the way the majority voted.
3. **Popular Referendum.** Voters can veto a bill passed by their state legislature if enough citizens sign a petition to get it on the ballot and then a majority vote to nullify the law.

Direct democracy became an element in state political systems during the Progressive Era at the beginning of the twentieth century, but its roots can be traced back to the New England town meeting, and further back to the Greek city-state. To reduce the influence of political machines, organized interests, and powerful elites, the Progressives initiated a set of devices designed to promote the direct involvement of voters in public policy making. Direct legislation has its historical roots in the Upper Plains states and the West. In 1898, South Dakota was the first state to institute both the initiative and the popular referendum, followed by Utah in 1900. By 1918, a total of 17 other states followed suit and authorized both reforms.

The philosophy behind direct democracy is similar today, although the emphasis on destroying machines and thwarting special interests is not as strong. The motivating concern today appears to focus more on the responsiveness of government institutions. As the popular rhetoric goes, if elected representatives are not going to listen to what the people really want, citizens will take action themselves.

---

indirect initiative A process in which citizens can petition to have a proposed law on a ballot and, if passed, the law goes to the legislature for adoption, modification, or rejection.

general referendum A process in which a proposed law is first passed by the legislature and then placed on a ballot for adoption or rejection by the voters.

advisory referendum A process in which the legislature places a proposed law on a ballot and then acts to accept, modify, or reject the result after it learns the sentiment of the voters.

popular referendum A process in which citizens can petition to accept or reject a law that has been passed by the legislature and signed by the governor.

Table 6.2 Instruments of Direct Democracy

	Initiative		Referendum		Advisory	Recall
	Direct	Indirect	General	Popular		
Purpose	Make new laws, change existing laws, or amend state constitution	Make new laws, change existing laws, or amend state constitution	Certain acts of legislature submitted to voters for concurrence or rejection (e.g., amendments to constitution, bond issues)	Voters decide whether to reject law enacted by legislature	Voters provide advice on whether legislature should pass certain legislation	Remove elected officials from office
How Gets on Ballot	Specified number of signatures of registered voters to qualify proposition for placement on ballot	Specified number of signatures of registered voters to qualify proposition for placement on ballot	Placement on ballot required by law following legislative approval	Required number of signatures within specified period of time to qualify for placement on ballot	Legislature submits proposals to electorate	Required number of signatures of registered voters to qualify for placement on ballot
Requirements for Passage	Majority of those voting required for passage	Majority of those voting required for passage	Majority of those voting required for passage	Majority of those voting required for rejection	Percentage of vote conveys electorate's sympathies	Majority of those voting to recall official from office
Relative Involvement of Governor/Legislature	Citizens act directly, bypassing governor and legislature	Legislature can adopt proposal, place it on the ballot unilaterally, or modify it before placing on ballot	Citizens act only after legislature has acted (with approval of governor or after veto override)	Citizens act only after legislature has acted (with approval of governor or after veto override)	Citizens act only if legislature puts the question to them	Citizens act directly, bypassing governor and legislature to remove elected officials from office

"Occupy Wall Street" demonstrators rallied in cities in 2011 to protest growing income inequality and cuts in public services.

The basic argument against direct democracy is that it lacks the opportunity for the kind of deliberation that is possible in a legislature. The options available on a direct initiative ballot are either for or against a particular proposal. Moreover, skeptics argue, what was intended as a grass-roots process is now artificial turf, sponsored by and paid for by special-interest groups. Voters have a barrage of 30-second television advertisements on which to base their decisions, rather than information on the details and subtleties of a proposal.[11]

The Initiative and Popular Referendum

Table 6.3 presents detailed information regarding the initiative and popular referendum process in individual states. There is a general pattern.

The Petition.   To begin legislation through the initiative or popular referendum, citizens must be able to show that the proposal has a certain minimal level of support among the electorate. The most common requirement for the direct initiative is to get, on a petition, the signatures of voters equal to 8 to 10 percent of the vote cast in the most recent gubernatorial election. The typical requirement for the popular referendum is 5 percent. But the actual percentage requirements vary considerably by state. On the more lenient end of the spectrum lies North Dakota, which requires signatures equal to 2 percent of the voting-age population. In contrast, Wyoming requires 15 percent of the total votes cast in the preceding general election.[12]

Initiators and supporters of initiative and popular referendum measures can seek the required number of signatures in two ways: through either volunteers or paid signature collectors. The obstacles facing a wholly volunteer organization are several: (1) the sheer magnitude of the required number of signatures means that the volunteer organization has to be large and highly active; (2) the time limits placed on the signature drive greatly constrain the volunteer organization, which often has to spend considerable

Table 6.3 Authority for the Initiative and Popular Referendum

State	Direct Initiative	Indirect Initiative	Popular Referendum
Alabama			X
Alaska	X		X
Arizona	X		X
Arkansas	X		X
California	X		X
Colorado	X		
Idaho	X		X
Illinois	X		
Kentucky			X
Maine		X	X
Maryland			X
Massachusetts		X	X
Michigan		X	X
Mississippi		X	X
Missouri	X		X
Montana	X		X
Nebraska	X		X
Nevada	X	X	X
North Dakota	X		X
Oklahoma	X		X
Oregon	X		X
South Dakota	X		X
Utah	X		X
Washington	X		X
Wyoming		X	X

Source: Based on *The Book of the States, 2008* (Lexington, Ky.: Council of State Governments, 2008), 307.

front-end time just getting itself organized. Table 6.4 presents the maximum period of time to qualify a statutory initiative for each state that has the initiative option. With clever ways to target audiences, computers and direct mail solicitation have enabled supporters to get tailored information to prospective signers. Not only is this method effective in yielding signatures, but it has also proven successful in winning financial support that can, in turn, be used to expand initiative efforts. This is basically the way Howard Jarvis and Paul Gann were able to qualify Proposition 13 in California for the ballot and to continue to finance subsequent tax-limiting initiatives. In one direct mail campaign, the Jarvis letter contained the following postscript: "This petition was made possible by a $12 contribution by Ms. Barbara Murphy of Vista. If you fail to return your petition, the Murphy family's contribution will have gone to waste. Mail it *today.*"[13] The clever appeal also invited the reader to become one of the "fighting Murphys" by including a check along with the signature.

Table 6.4 Time Limits to Gather Signatures to Qualify a Statutory Initiative

State	Signature-Gathering Period
Alaska	1 year
Arizona	2 years
Arkansas	Unlimited
California	150 days
Colorado	6 months
Idaho	18 months
Illinois	2 years
Maine	1 year
Massachusetts	3 months
Michigan	180 days
Missouri	20 months
Montana	Unlimited
Nebraska	Unlimited
Nevada	276 days constitutional amendment; 291 days statute
North Dakota	1 year
Ohio	Unlimited
Oklahoma	90 days
Oregon	2 years
South Dakota	2 years constitutional amendment; 18 months statute
Utah	1 year
Washington	6 months
Wyoming	18 months

Note: All initiative petitions are circulated during a single designated time period. As noted in table, there have been a number of recent changes.

Source: Based on *The Book of the States, 2008* (Lexington, Ky.: Council of State Governments, 2008), 314–315.

Paid signature collectors earn between 50 cents and 2 dollars for each signature obtained. For those who collected signatures for cash rather than out of commitment, the incentives are obviously to spend the least possible time per signature. This does not lead to the kind of face-to-face contacts that emphasize voter education. The executive director of California's Common Cause described the signature-gathering process as follows:

> The people out front were salespeople-pitchmen—their commission was a signature, and the fewer words they had to use, the greater their commission.
>
> Once at the table anyone who wished to read the document was ushered to the side and given a copy so as not to block the petition itself. Antagonists were ignored or asked to

Those protesting a law passed in 2011 repealing collective bargaining rights for public employees in Wisconsin initiated an effort to recall Governor Scott Walker and Republican State Senators.

move on. . . . People with questions about the content were given information to read, but not discussion time from the workers. . . . The singular objective was 500,000 signatures in five months. Education on the issues would have to wait until after the measure was qualified.[14]

The Campaign.   Once the petition becomes qualified for the ballot, both supporters and opponents attempt to convince the electorate on how to vote on the proposition. Several forms of advertising can be employed to influence public opinion, among them television and radio spots, billboards, newspaper ads, bumper stickers, and direct mail campaigns. Highly visible public figures and celebrities may provide endorsements in support of or in opposition to ballot propositions.

The costs of these campaigns can be high, particularly when significant or controversial measures are before the voters. A study of California initiatives found that most campaigns spend over $4 million. But the study also showed that the balance of spending bore only a modest relationship to success at the polls. Outspending the other side was shown to be most effective when employed opposing a proposition.[15]

Recent Experience with the Initiative.   Voters in California and Oregon traditionally make the greatest use of the initiative. Successful initiatives have covered a wide range of topics. Voters have used the initiative process to freeze or reduce taxes, approve lotteries, and reform criminal codes or establish victims' bill of rights. Other initiatives have limited the terms of elected officials; regulated lobbying and campaign contributions; designated English as the official state language; rationed medical care; and, in Maine, prohibited the testing of cruise missiles over state air space.

In late 2005, California governor Arnold Schwarzenegger could not get support from the Democratic-controlled legislature for changes he wanted to pursue. Instead, he got the signatures required to have four initiatives and called a special election. He and his supporters spent $72.7 million, mostly on television advertising, to persuade California voters to put more budgetary authority in the governor's office, take redistricting power away

DEBATING THE ISSUES

Is the direct initiative too much democracy?

The direct initiative, which is allowed in 19 states, allows citizens to enact laws without going through the legislature or the governor. The original intent was to avoid the influence that special-interest groups have over elected officials. Proponents of the direct initiative argue that voters are intelligent and savvy enough that they can make laws without interference from the corrupting dynamic between legislators and special interests.

Opponents doubt whether voters have enough information to vote proposals into law. They note that special-interest groups are not absent from the direct initiative process. In fact, they sometimes sponsor these initiatives and they frequently try to influence results with their campaign advertisements. Opponents prefer the deliberative processes of the legislature, where there can be debate and amendments to proposals.

What do you think? Is the direct initiative an indication that we do not trust representative democracy? Is opposition to the direct initiative an indication that we do not trust direct democracy?

You can get information on initiatives by going to the homepage of individual states that have the direct initiative. In addition, you can go to the Public Affairs Web, www.publicaffairsweb.com, for both information and relevant links. The Center for Responsive Politics, www.crp.org, provides information on who is funding campaigns for and against initiatives.

from the legislature, extend probationary periods for public school teachers, and restrict political spending by public employee unions. The governor's opponents spent $148.5 million—again, mostly on television advertising. All of the initiatives promoted by the governor failed.

Voters in 2010 approved direct initiatives in Arizona allowing the medical use of marijuana; in California and Florida revising legislative redistricting to make it nonpartisan; in Oregon establishing tougher minimum sentences for repeat offenders of drunk driving and of sex crimes; and in Missouri regulating large-scale dog breeding. As usual, initiatives restricting taxation found support, although in Massachusetts a measure passed that increased the tax on alcoholic beverages.

The Courts and Direct Democracy

Opponents of initiatives sometimes wage their battles in court. Such litigation may challenge the constitutionality of the initiative and/or the relationship with other laws.[16]

Courts halted enforcement of the 1994 California initiative to deny services to unregistered immigrants (Proposition 187) immediately after it was passed. One suit asked the courts to void the initiative because it contradicted a U.S. Supreme Court ruling that residents, even when not citizens, had protection of liberty and other basic rights under the Constitution. Another suit argued that the proposition had the effect of trespassing on the federal government's jurisdiction over immigration policy. Still another suit contended that federal provisions accompanying aid for many of the services and benefits provided by state and local governments preempted the limitations of the proposition. In 1994, Oregon was the first of 12 states in which voters used the direct initiative to approve laws allowing the medical use of marijuana. These laws run contrary to federal laws, and in 2005, the U.S. Supreme Court, in *Gonzales v. Raich*, ruled that federal authorities could enforce those laws, the initiatives notwithstanding. The federal government has generally deferred to states on medical marijuana, although in 2011 federal agents took action against growers and distributors in California that were considered to be too big to be operations that included other controlled substances.

Courts are also asked to void any initiative that fails to follow the process correctly. When Nebraska voters adopted term limits in 1994, they were acting on an initiative that had passed previously but had been tossed out because the initial petition signatures had not been certified properly.[17] In short, public policies established through state initiatives must be considered in the same context as laws passed through other means.

Recall

Voters in 18 states can recall elected officials from office before their terms have expired. As mentioned above, a recall does not have to be based on any particular grounds. In 2003, for example, state senator Gary George was recalled from a district in Milwaukee, Wisconsin, primarily because of a concern over charges of corrupt behavior. In contrast, that same year, voters in California recalled Governor Gray Davis and replaced him with Arnold Schwarzenegger. Governor Davis was unpopular, not corrupt. Days after he was reelected, wealthy Republicans in California initiated the recall of Governor Davis. It served as an opportunity to rerun the election, not to punish him for what he had done since the votes were counted. The opening vignette presents an example of recall being used to punish legislators for supporting specific policies.

As with the initiative process, a recall begins with a petition. If enough valid signatures are submitted on a petition requesting a recall, a special election is scheduled and voters decide whether or not to retain the official who is the subject of the recall. California and Wisconsin represent two patterns of the recall process. In California, a recall petition can begin at any time after the election. In Wisconsin, a petition cannot be circulated until the official has been in office for at least one year.

California voters cast, at the same time, a vote for retaining or recalling the official and a vote for the candidate they would like to fill the office if the majority of votes are for a recall. There is no party primary. In the 2003 case, 54 percent of the voters marked their ballot to recall Governor Davis from office. On the second part of the ballot, voters could choose from among 134 candidates to replace Davis. Schwarzenegger garnered 46.9 percent of those votes and became the first person elected governor through the recall process in California. In the model followed by Wisconsin, when a valid petition is filed, a recall election is scheduled in about four weeks with the incumbent automatically included on the ballot. The incumbent must specifically ask to have his or her name removed from the ballot if he or she does not want to continue in office. If more than one candidate runs in any political party, a primary is held, and then the general election takes place about 4 weeks after the primary.

SUMMARY AND CONCLUSIONS

A distinctive characteristic of the American political system is the array of opportunities for individuals to learn about what is happening in government and to participate in the shaping of public policies. The opportunities for grass-roots participation are especially evident in state and local governments. The hearings and meetings and the occasions for contacting public officials are numerous. In over half the states, the mechanisms of direct democracy allow citizens to make laws and/or influence policies through initiatives and referenda.

The proportion of people who take advantage of these opportunities, however, is small. Only about one-third of adult citizens participate minimally, by voting and voicing their concerns and opinions in face-to-face ways with public officials. About 15 percent are consistently and meaningfully active. Active citizens tend to be those who enjoy the advantages of higher education, wealth, and political power.

While the limited extent of grass-roots participation runs contrary to the ideology and principles of democracy in the United States, there are some reassurances. The opportunities are genuinely available, even to those who, for whatever reason, have not previously used them. Some would remind us that the nuances and complexities of many issues do not lend themselves to resolution by a public that cannot be expected to develop the ideal level of expertise to make a good decision. Grass-roots involvement may be better at placing issues on the agenda of policymakers and at providing general reactions than at working on the details of policy planning and consensus building. As individuals, we frequently work in groups, and groups play important roles in policy making; thus, we turn our attention to them in Chapter 7.

Discussion Questions

1. Why do some individuals choose to get involved in politics or policy making? What about you?
2. Are there times when the press should be barred from government files or meetings?
3. Under what circumstances would you participate in protest activity? Are there any forms of protest that you would refuse to use? If so, why?
4. Should there be any checks on the use of the initiative, where voters can directly enact laws without the deliberation of legislative analysis or debate or without the consideration of the governor? Should the initiative be available at the national level, or just in states and local communities?

Glossary

advisory referendum 158
direct initiative 157
efficacy 153

general referendum 158
indirect initiative 158
open meeting laws 149

open record laws 149
popular referendum 158
recall 157

Endnotes

1. This is based on the assumption that the readers will earn a college degree, earn a modest to high income, and have some interest in community and political affairs. These assumptions can be matched with findings reported in Sidney Verba and Norman H. Nie, *Participation in America: Social Democracy and Social Equity* (New York: Harper & Row, 1972). See also Louis J. Ayala, "Trained for Democracy: The Differing Effects of Voluntary and Involuntary Organizations on Political Participation," *Political Research Quarterly* 53, no. 1 (March 2000), 99–115.

2. Sarah McCally Morehouse, *State Politics, Parties and Policy* (New York: Holt, Rinehart and Winston, 1981), 79–84.

3. Gerald Pomper, *Elections in America: Control and Influence in Democratic Politics* (New York: Dodd, Mead, 1968); Raymond Wolfinger and Steven J. Rosenstone, *Who Votes?* (New Haven, Conn.: Yale University Press, 1980); Verba and Nie, *Participation in America.*

4. Albert K. Karnig and B. Oliver Walter, "Municipal Voter Turnout during the 1980s: The Case of Continued Decline," in *State and Local Government and Politics*, eds. Harry A. Bailey Jr. and Jay M. Shafritz (Itasca, Ill.: Peacock Publishers, 1993), 26–38.

5. Verba and Nie, *Participation in America.*

6. Sidney Verba, Kay Lehman Schlozman, and Henry Brady, *Voice and Equality: Civic Voluntarism in American Politics* (Cambridge, Mass.: Harvard University Press, 1995) and Nancy Burns, Kay Lehman Schlozman, and Sidney Verba, *Private Roots of Public Action. Gender Equality and Political Participation* (Cambridge, Mass.: Harvard University Press, 2001).

7. Paul R. Abramson and John H. Aldrich, "The Decline of Electoral Participation in America," *American Political Science Review* 76 (September 1982); Richard Brody, "The Puzzle of Political Participation," in *The New American Political System*, ed. Anthony Kind (Washington, D.C.: American Enterprise Institute, 1978); Frances Fox Piven and Richard Cloward, *Why Americans Don't Vote* (New York: Pantheon, 1987).

8. Susan Welch and Philip Secret, "Sex, Race, and Political Participation," *Western Political Quarterly* 34 (March 1981), 5–16.

9. R. Michael Alvarez, "How Widespread Is Voting Fraud?" California Institute of Technology, November 2002, and R. Michael Alvarez and Thad E. Hall, *Point, Click and Vote* (Washington, D.C.: The Brookings Institution, 2004).

10. Philip B. Coulter, *Political Voice: Citizen Demand for Urban Public Services* (Tuscaloosa: University of Alabama Press, 1988), 67–70.

11. Dennis W. Johnson, *No Place for Amateurs* (New York: Rutledge, 2001), 201–236.

12. David B. Magleby, *Direct Legislation* (Baltimore, Md.: Johns Hopkins University Press, 1984), 62.

13. Maureen S. Fitzgerald, "Computer Democracy," in *California Government and Politics Annual 1984–1985*, eds. Thomas R. Hoeber and Charles M. Price (Sacramento: California Journal Press, 1985), 98.

14. Magleby, "Ballot Initiatives and Intergovernmental Relations in the United States," 62.

15. John R. Owens and Larry L. Wade, "Campaign Spending on California Ballot Propositions, 1924–1984: Trends and Voting Effects," *Western Political Quarterly* 39 (December 1986), 681–685.

16. Craig B. Holman and Robert Stern, "Judicial Review of Ballot Initiatives: The Changing Role of State and Federal Courts," *Loyola Law Review* 31 (Summer 1998), 1579–1584.

17. Thomas E. Cronin, *Direct Democracy* (Cambridge, Mass.: Harvard University Press, 1989), 219–220; Magleby, "Ballot Initiatives and Intergovernmental Relations in the United States," 35–58.

Interest Groups

- Know what an interest group is and be able to distinguish different types of interest groups.
- Understand the role of interest groups in politics and policy making.
- Identify the resources that interest groups have.
- Recognize the strategies and tactics of interest groups.
- Understand what lobbyists are and how they try to influence policy.

Mining and chemical companies have invested heavily to influence state government in West Virginia. Like other interest groups, they have contributed to the campaigns of elected officials, and they have provided information and arguments to persuade policymakers to favor the needs of the companies. The focus of these efforts has covered all the major players—legislators, governors, and justices of the state supreme court. At times, the efforts have crossed the line defining what is ethical and appropriate.

Don L. Blankenship, chief executive of the Massey Energy Company, a major coal miner in West Virginia, treated Elliott E. Maynard, who was the chief justice of the state's supreme court, to an expensive vacation on the French Riviera just prior to a court decision on an appeal of a $50 million jury verdict against Massey. Justice Maynard voted with the majority ruling in favor of the coal company. Democratic voters reacted against this apparent conflict of interest and ousted Justice Maynard in the 2006 primary when he made a bid for reelection. Massey then spent $3 million to get Brent Benjamin elected to the state supreme court. In 2009, the U.S. Supreme Court ruled that Justice Benjamin should have recused himself from cases in which he was in the 3–2 majority that decided in Massey's favor. The campaign contributions were so substantial that they created a conflict of interest for the justice.

On May 19, 2011, an independent team of investigators appointed by former Governor Joe Manchin III reported that a pattern of negligence by Massey Energy led to the deaths of 29 miners on April 5, 2010, in the worst American mining disaster in 40 years. The 120 page report documented how Massey had refused to comply with minimal safety standards and had misled government regulators into thinking that it had complied.

Interest groups can make valuable contributions to public policy debates and deliberations. They can also damage the credibility and integrity of governments when they rely more on money and favors than on information and arguments.

Interest groups are organizations that seek to influence public policies and their implementation. Individuals can approach their governments on a one-on-one basis, or they can work through groups. Lobbyists present the face-to-face interaction with government officials on behalf of the groups they represent. The effectiveness of lobbyists depends on their credibility and persuasiveness as individuals and on the political resources of their respective organizations. Interest groups are a common part of the political landscape. Although they do not have formal authority and they are not part of the formal structure, they are key, ubiquitous actors in state, local, and national governments.

In 2010, the U.S. Supreme Court ruled in *Citizens United v. Federal Election Commission* that corporations and labor unions enjoyed the same First Amendment rights as individual persons when acting as interest groups in the political arena. The issue was whether Congress could impose limits on corporate campaign contributions. The Court ruled it could not. Supporters hailed the ruling as a victory for free speech. Opponents worried that corporations would use their money to increase their influence over government decisions to the detriment of the interests of consumers and the general public.

Our founders regarded the formation and activity of interest groups as inevitable. James Madison, in *Federalist Paper* No. 10, not only anticipated the emergence of interest groups but warned of the ill effects that could result.[1] Madison would have understood fully that you would have wanted to have group support as well as a good argument when you visited with the governor and legislators about university tuition. He clearly recognized the wisdom of such a strategy. He also appreciated the contributions that this form of informal representation made to the formal operations of a democratic government. Nonetheless, Madison worried that interest groups might pursue their own interests to the detriment of the common good of society as a whole. He referred to this selfish activity as "the mischiefs of faction."

An organization that seeks its own narrow goals without regard for society is a **special-interest group**. In one sense, a special-interest group is any group that you or I oppose. More seriously, Madison's concerns have continued to worry observers and scholars of U.S. politics.[2] They fear that public policy is little more than an aggregation of responses to well-organized interest groups rather than a coherent direction attentive to the needs of society as a whole. The need that candidates have for raising money for their campaigns fuels a concern that interest groups that have large amounts of cash have an inordinate influence over public policy. Given the difficulty of defining what the needs of society as a whole are, it is impossible to resolve the debate about the extent to which interest groups are facilitating or impeding democracy. We can note some important changes, however, in the existence and the position of interest groups in state and local governments.

---

special-interest group An organization that seeks to influence government policy to serve the needs and/or pursue the beliefs of the members of the organization.

Public school teachers have organized themselves into one of the most visible and active interest groups in state governments.

GENERAL TRENDS

Less than a century ago, many states were clearly under the control of a small number of interest groups. The railroads and banks ran states in the Midwest and West. Oil was king in Louisiana, Oklahoma, and Texas. Missionary families who owned plantations controlled Hawaii. Politicians in these states were the best money could buy.

The region of the country that has been controlled by a handful of interest groups for the longest period is the South. In his classic study of politics in Southern states, V. O. Key described the dominance of white business and agricultural groups who were determined to disenfranchise African Americans and to control poor whites.[3] They kept the institutions and powers of state and local governments weak. Political parties were nonentities. After Reconstruction, the Republican Party was almost extinct, and any competition between individuals or groups took place within the Democratic Party. Stereotypes about Southern politicians pictured them as members of a small and often rural elite who quibbled with one another but did not engage in serious debates or battles with other segments of society. Politics and political participation in the South were confined to a narrow, closed group. These stereotypes constituted reality from the aftermath of the Civil War to the civil rights period. The traditionalist political culture described in Chapter 2 is the legacy of a region that was controlled by a small, white, powerful elite.

The South, like other parts of the country, has been affected by a number of changes that have led to a more sophisticated and open role for interest groups. The legacy of anemic parties and weak government institutions has been so prominent and so pervasive in the South, however, that interest groups there are still more powerful and traditional than one finds elsewhere.[4]

Not surprisingly, as the economies of states have diversified and as urbanization has increased, the number of active interest groups has grown. One is not likely to see industrial labor unions participate in the politics of a state if that state's economy does not include major industries or service activities. Likewise, citizen groups concerned with the services and the issues faced by urban areas emerge with the growth of cities. The representation of urban interests lagged behind urbanization in some states until the U.S. Supreme Court, in *Baker v. Carr* (1962), mandated that the boundaries of legislative districts be drawn so that about the same number of people reside in each district. Prior to this ruling (which will be discussed in greater detail in Chapters 8 and 10 on elections and state legislatures), rural interests were overrepresented. It seemed futile for urban interest groups to form and try to influence policy.

The expanded scope of state government responsibilities, discussed in Chapter 3, also prompted an increase in interest groups operative in state capitols. States have always had responsibility for land use, transportation, education, and occupational licensing policies. Thus, land developers, railroads, financial institutions, and professional associations had a history of efforts to influence state and local governments. Later the federal government, by design and default, withdrew from transportation and environmental regulation and from many areas of consumer protection, health, and safety. States became increasingly important in the eyes of interest groups.

The general expectation is that the more urbanization, professionalization, and socio-economic development there is, the more participation and involvement of interest groups we will see. Virginia Gray and David Lowery documented this pattern among registered interest groups in the states during the last two decades of the twentieth century. They noted that interest groups were especially numerous in large states with diverse economies and competitive political parties. States like Minnesota, with primarily a moralistic political culture, had the highest number of citizen-based interest groups. States like New Jersey, with individualistic cultures, had the highest number of business interest groups.[5]

Interest groups, in short, are part of their environments. Gray and Lowery note that this relationship includes a limit on interest group development in states. They introduce the concept of carrying capacity to explain that interest groups will not emerge in a state that doesn't have the economic activities or political interests to support them.[6] To understand them requires knowledge of the specific state and time in which they exist. Interest groups also have important internal characteristics.

INTERNAL CHARACTERISTICS

Membership

Sometimes the major reason people join an organization is to influence government policies. For some interest groups, however, participation in public policy making is only secondary and perhaps only occasional.

Individual Membership. Students interested in the level of tuition and other higher education policies may join an organization that devotes itself almost entirely to trying to influence government. Common Cause is an organization of individuals concerned about clean and open government. It does little other than work to make state governments and the national government accessible and to report on conflicts of interest. Membership is determined by who pays dues and lists themselves on the roster. The act of becoming a member may involve registering, paying dues, and agreeing to be on certain committees. Those who wish to go beyond just being listed as a member can volunteer for various committee assignments, run for an office within the organization, or apply for paid staff positions. Research shows that, consistent with our discussion in Chapter 6 about who participates in politics, individuals who join interest groups tend to be white, educated, and relatively wealthy.[7]

Organizational Membership.   The student government or some other group on your campus could belong to a state, regional, or national coalition of student groups concerned about higher education policies. In a sense, this removes you one step further from face-to-face interaction. The benefit, however, is that the extended organization presumably has more clout and visibility than the student organization on your campus.

Businesses are typically represented in three types of organizations. One type is an individual firm, such as IBM, Bank of America, or Ameritech, which may have someone on the staff who is responsible for making sure the firm's interests and concerns are communicated to appropriate public officials. The firm may be active in supporting particular candidates, although sometimes campaign finance laws restrict how that support can be given. Prohibitions against a firm directly providing funds can be circumvented by encouraging individual officers and employees to make financial contributions and then bundling the checks together so that the candidate will identify the support with the firm.

Individual businesses are typically members of **trade associations**. These associations exist for specific types of enterprises such as grocers, auto dealers, and florists. It is common for trade associations to alert members to government actions that may affect them as well as to represent them at public hearings.

Finally, businesses—often through their trade associations—belong to **peak associations**. These are umbrella organizations that include a wide variety of businesses. An example would be a chamber of commerce. Industries and manufacturers commonly belong to state associations. Local labor unions also affiliate at the state level. The AFL-CIO is the most prominent example. These state associations are typically further linked at the national level. Peak associations can be even more active and visible in efforts to influence government policies than are trade associations.

Surrogate Agencies.   One concern of critics of interest group politics is that those who are not organized do not get represented in the policy-making process. The general consumer, the poor, and groups who had been disenfranchised (racial minorities and women) are inherently more difficult to organize than individuals who are in the same occupation or business. To respond to this concern, states have established **surrogate** agencies to be sure the interests of certain groups are represented.

Affirmative action and equal opportunity offices in state and local governments are examples of surrogate groups charged with acting as internal watchdogs. These offices are given a certain amount of independence and then told to report on progress and suggest ways

---

trade association An organization of similar businesses or professionals.

peak association An organization of a wide variety of trade associations, businesses, or unions. Examples are state chambers of commerce and the AFL-CIO.

surrogate interest groups Government-sponsored agencies or boards that are supposed to advocate for the needs of unorganized groups, such as the poor, consumers, and minorities.

of achieving diversity goals in hiring and contracting. Federal antipoverty programs initiated in the 1960s and 1970s required the establishment of organizations to represent the poor.

Some in-house advocates are self-appointed. Professionals in administrative agencies and certain legislators assume the role of a resident expert and represent certain groups, even when they have no mandate either from the group itself or from an official body in government. Employees in environmental protection agencies, for example, are sometimes zealous advocates of clean air or clean water. Social workers at times act as spokespersons for the people they serve. These advocacy roles are not part of their formal job descriptions, but individual employees assume them.

Surrogate arrangements for interest group representation lack the accountability links that formal organizations provide. If you represent a formally established student organization on a university committee, the members of that organization can displace you if you fail to represent students well. A parent appointed by a school board to a committee or task force to represent the interests of parents is in a fundamentally different position from someone designated by a parent-teacher association as its representative. Accountability here is to the school board rather than to parents. Individuals who share common concerns are best represented when they have their own organization. Surrogacy is a second-best arrangement.

Resources

Policy making in government involves consideration of what is the best *substantive* decision and what is the best *political* decision. Interest groups have resources that relate to both of these dimensions of policy making. Sometimes public officials take political risks in order to pursue what they think is right. At other times, because of political pressures, one goes with a course of action that is acceptable or satisfactory rather than the best alternative. The information provided by interest groups can relate to likely political risks or benefits or to the substantive advantages and disadvantages of a proposed or existing policy.

Expertise.   Almost all interest groups have specialized knowledge of the substantive policy area that concerns them. Farmers know farming. Utility companies acquire knowledge about energy sources, telecommunications technology, and the costs of producing heat and electricity. Even when there is a debate among experts on a certain issue, specialists have the kind of information that is valuable to those outside the field who must make decisions. State and local government officials who want to make informed decisions value and appreciate the expertise held by interest groups. Public policymakers often invite interest group representatives to comment on proposals and to offer suggestions for change.

Mass Membership.   Some interest groups have many members, which can translate into many votes. Labor unions, the National Organization for Women (NOW), the Sierra Club, Common Cause, the American Legion, the National Rifle Association (NRA), organizations on both sides of the abortion issue, and fundamentalist Christian organizations are examples of interest groups that can help officials estimate the political gains and losses that might accompany certain decisions. Candidates for office can make some calculations about whether they are likely to win an election based on the support they receive from these groups.

The extent to which membership constitutes a resource depends on several other considerations. Members do not always follow their leaders. Nationally, in 1984, the AFL-CIO leadership endorsed Walter Mondale for president only to have union members vote with most other Americans for Ronald Reagan. State leaders are usually close enough to their members to avoid such embarrassments.

Another factor to consider is whether the members of a group are constituents of the officials they are approaching. Support from teachers, police officers, and firefighters is valued by almost all state and local politicians. These professionals are important components of every community. Obviously labor unions and farm groups are constituents in only certain kinds of communities. Likewise, individuals of various religions and cultures tend to be more prevalent in some districts than in others.

Finally, it is important to know whether the members vote. Although people who are joiners tend to be voters as well, not all interest groups have members who actively make a decision to join. In some occupations, becoming a member of a union or professional association is more a result of getting a job than it is of consciously joining. Likewise, church membership is not always the result of a reasoned, meaningful decision.

Public officials value membership in organizations for more than electoral support. Groups can and do play major roles in securing compliance with new laws and procedures. The American Automobile Association (AAA), for example, conveys information about speed limits and safety belt laws to its members and to the general public. This effort has contributed to greater awareness and compliance, thus minimizing the need for punitive actions and for public education programs from state and local agencies. The American Association of Retired Persons (AARP) keeps its many members informed about developments in programs and tax laws that apply to senior citizens. Environmental groups, farmers' groups, and labor unions play similar roles.

Money. Business interest groups are dominant forces in state governments.[8] They are numerous, but they do not have, individually or collectively, many members or voters. Their two most valuable resources are expertise and money. The political clout of the business community is highly related to the cost of campaigning. For candidates to get their message to potential voters, it is necessary to air radio and television advertisements. These and other expenses prompt all but the independently wealthy to solicit campaign funds.

Other interest groups also have money. Organizations that have many members can accumulate considerable sums by getting modest contributions from each. Unions, the NRA, and other mass membership organizations have established large treasuries from many small contributions.

The connections between money and politics are increasingly a subject of investigative journalism and public interest research. Common Cause reports on national and statewide lobbying. Nonpartisan and nonprofit state organizations like Wisconsin Democracy Campaign, California Watch, Ohio Citizen Action, and Democracy Reform Oregon monitor in detail campaign contributions and policy making. The National Institute on Money in State Politics and MAPLight.org provide studies on all 50 states. These organizations

Exploring the Web

What kinds of interest groups are there?

The wide variety of interest groups can be categorized in different ways. Below are different approaches, with some examples. Visit their websites and list others that you think represent your interests or views. What resources (expertise, votes, money, prestige) do each of these interest groups have?

Mass membership organizations that individuals join:

- Sierra Club www.sierraclub.org
- Common Cause www.commoncause.org
- National Rifle Association www.nra.org

Businesses and unions as individual organizations:

- IBM *www.ibm.com*
- Ameritech *www.ameritech.com*
- American Federation of Teachers *www.aft.org*
- United Steelworkers of America *www.uswa.org*

Businesses as members of trade associations:

- Associated Grocers of Florida *www.agfla.com*
- Kentucky Corn Growers Association *http://kycorn.org*
- Wisconsin Paper Council *www.wipapercouncil.org*

Businesses and unions as members of peak associations:

- United States Chamber of Commerce *www.uschamber.org*
- U.S. Hispanic Chamber of Commerce *www.ushcc.com*
- American Federation of Labor and Congress of Industrial Organizations *www.aflcio.org*

Governments:

- National Governors' Association *www.nga.org*
- National League of Cities *www.nlc.org*
- National Association of State Boards of Education *www.nasbe.org*

provide their reports online. Table 7.1 presents the top 10 states in which interest group spending occurred in 2010.

Economic Activity. Businesses can wield influence on public policy making because of the impact they can have on the general economic conditions of a state or community. Business activity means jobs and opportunities. Taxes based on income, sales, and property

Table 7.1 Top 10 Interest Group Contributions to Campaigns for State Offices, 2010

California	$717 million
Florida	$332 million
Texas	$235 million
Illinois	$201 million
New York	$197 million
Ohio	$179 million
Pennsylvania	$155 million
Connecticut	$109 million
Oregon	$99 million
Alabama	$96 million

Source: www.followthemoney.org/database/nationalview. phtml?l=0&f=0&y=2010&abbr=1 accessed 07/10/11.

values vary considerably with the health of a region's economy. When a spokesperson for an industry or for a business association praises or condemns a proposed policy because of its likely effect on the economy, government officials pay attention. If a particular firm indicates that it will stay in a community or that it will relocate depending on the fate of a tax proposal, a transportation plan, or a renovation of local schools, policymakers respond.

Business groups are not the only ones to use their ability to affect jobs and a local economy as a resource for getting what they want from government. Universities and school systems tout their contributions to a quality work force. Labor unions cite the need for stability and productivity among workers. Environmental advocates remind policymakers about the long-term consequences of spoiling natural resources. Because businesses can make immediate and direct decisions on whether to expand or relocate, their arguments about economic impacts are usually taken the most seriously.

Prestige. Prestige is in the eye of the beholder. Money, jobs, votes, and expertise are fairly objective resources, but prestige depends on values and perceptions. If a public official has a high regard for a particular group or members of a particular occupation, then the representative of that group or occupation is going to have an advantage in gaining access and having influence. Government officials are also mindful of those groups that have prestige in the views of their constituents.

In general, interest groups that represent individuals with high status are going to enjoy more prestige and respect when they are taking positions on issues that do not directly affect them. Doctors and lawyers make more use of their prestige when they address social issues than when they seek legislation on health care costs, medical malpractice insurance, and tort reform. Churches have been valuable allies to civil rights groups, but they are treated just like any other interest group when they defend the tax exempt status of church property.

Government Authority. The major resource of surrogates for interest groups is their official government status. In-house advocates for the unrepresented do not provide votes or money. An affirmative action council or an advisory commission on women's issues does, however, have ready access as a government body. Their reports and recommendations, even when they provoke opposition, are government documents. The official status and authority of surrogates are specifically designed to compensate for the lack of organizational and political resources of these groups.

Interests Represented

As previously stated, the scope of interests represented by groups active in state capitols and town halls is broad and has been increasing. Interest groups reflect the variety of issues and concerns that form the agenda of governments in states and communities.

Business.   About 60 percent of interest groups that are registered as lobbyists in the 50 states represent businesses. The range is from 21.9 percent in Arizona to 73.5 percent in Utah.[9] Included in this count are individual firms as well as trade and peak associations. On the whole, businesses are the most visible of all the types of interest groups. Businesses pursue tax and licensing policies that have direct and specific implications for them. In addition, businesses are active on general issues, such as education, transportation, the environment, welfare, and health, which have important indirect effects on the economy and on businesses. They generally want a **business climate**—an approach that a government generally takes toward matters of concern to commercial enterprises—that supports growth and profit for commerce and industry.

Labor and Professional Associations.   State governments license professions, and therefore professional associations have traditionally been active in state governments. These associations get involved in matters beyond licensing issues. State bar associations, for example, are typically key players on court reorganization measures, crime bills, and proposals on property, contract, and inheritance matters. Labor unions weigh in on health care.

Governments.   Given the importance of intergovernmental funding and the mandates that the national and state governments impose on other governments, it is not surprising to see governmental agencies active in lobbying one another. Like businesses, governments are represented not only individually but by trade and peak associations as well. Most states have separate associations for school boards, towns, counties, and other types of local governments.

Citizen and Issue Organizations.   Citizen groups, like the League of Women Voters and Common Cause, include those concerned with good government. There are also single-issue, ad hoc organizations that are established to promote or oppose the expansion of a certain highway or to advocate for or against a particular state or local referendum. Some citizen groups represent particular segments of society. Examples are the various organizations that represent women, racial minorities, or individuals with certain types of physical disabilities or ailments. Other citizen groups are ideological, like those concerned about the environment or those

---

business climate The effects of the efforts and attitude of officials in a government on businesses.

committed to a given religious philosophy, cause, or vision. The major growth in the number of interest groups registering in states has been among citizen and issue organizations.[10]

Neighborhood Associations.   Local governments interact with many of the same interest groups that are active in state governments. In addition, city halls commonly receive demands from **neighborhood associations**. Businesses and residents in various areas of a community define themselves as a neighborhood. That definition may include a religious, racial, or ethnic identity; a certain mix of small shops, parks, and single-family residences; and perhaps a link to a major industry or financial institution. Neighborhood associations can be very active in pursuing or opposing change and in demanding services. Some associations supplement city services with their own efforts at keeping the area clean, providing security, and offering recreational and social activities. Like other interest groups, these associations are important politically and have information that can enhance the substantive quality of decisions.[11]

FUNCTIONS AND ACTIVITIES

To influence public policies, interest groups perform several important functions:

1. Provide information about the policy area. This is the most central and fundamental activity of interest groups.
2. Advocate for the policies that best serve the needs and concerns of interest group members.
3. Mobilize voters and contributors to support the positions advocated by the interest group.
4. Give feedback to interest group members about what government has done and why.

These functions are performed within the electoral process and through lobbying.

Interest Groups and Elections

From the perspective of interest groups, elections present an opportunity to elect individuals who understand and sympathize with their concerns. Candidates see interest groups as important sources of support.

In the early stages of a campaign, interest groups typically distribute questionnaires and seek interviews with candidates. These are get-acquainted activities. Aspirants to office get to know the agenda of an interest group simply by fielding its questions. Some interest groups publish the answers in a newsletter that is distributed to their members. Others consider whether to endorse a candidate, which would mean urging members to vote for him or her and contributing funds to the campaign. Sometimes someone from an interest group drafts speeches and statements for candidates that the group endorses.

---

neighborhood association A volunteer organization that works to preserve or to improve the nature of a particular neighborhood.

DEBATING THE ISSUES

What is the difference between a special interest and a public interest?

It is common for an advocate for an interest group to talk at least as much about how society as a whole will benefit from a particular proposal as about how members of the interest group will benefit. Is there really a public interest? Or are there just a wide variety of special interests? Do special interests have to be compromised or sacrificed in order to pursue the more general welfare of society? How would you define public interest? More specifically:

- Are businesses ever concerned about the impacts of what they do on society, or are they just interested in profits?
- Are "good government" groups, such as Common Cause or the League of Women Voters, interested in quality governance in an abstract way, or do they favor certain groups in power?
- When school boards lobby a state legislature, are they interested in quality education or in getting reelected?
- If you and your fellow students lobbied for lower tuition, are you interested in providing more access and equity in society, or are you concerned about your own bills for getting an education?

States and the national government require interest groups to establish **political action committees (PACs)** if they wish to make contributions to campaigns. The intent of this regulation is to identify which groups are making contributions and to monitor the amounts that are given. As will be discussed in greater detail in Chapter 8, states have differing limits on how much a PAC may give to a candidate.

Some interest groups have been so eager to see certain individuals elected to office that they have found ways of getting around the limits placed on PACs. One tactic is to **bundle** the personal checks of individual members of an interest group or employees of a firm and then send them to a candidate's campaign fund. The contributions are technically from individuals, but when they are sent together from a particular organization, a candidate will make the intended linkages.

Another tactic is to give funds to a **conduit**, which is an organization, usually established by a political party, that is not linked to any particular interest group and therefore is not covered

---

political action committee (PAC) A registered organization that raises funds and makes campaign contributions on behalf of a particular interest group.

bundling The collection of campaign contributions made by individuals who are members of a common interest group or firm in order to make visible to candidates the support they are getting from that group or firm. This practice is a way of avoiding the rules that apply to interest groups that make campaign contributions.

conduit An organization that receives funds from individuals and/or organizations with the understanding that the money is to be contributed to a particular campaign. This is done to avoid some of the rules that apply to interest groups making campaign contributions.

under PAC legislation. In addition to circumventing regulations on the size of campaign contributions, conduits do not have to disclose who is funding the effort. The clear understanding of the conduit, which might be named something like Citizens for Better Government or Families for Progress, is that the contribution is to be passed along to a specific candidate.

The skyrocketing costs of campaigns and the increased importance of state and local government have led interest groups to invest more and more money in efforts to get "the right people" into office and to have access to those who get elected. Interest groups can make strategic soft money contributions and can run issue ads without disclosing their identity or staying within contribution limits. This activity can be critical to the outcome of an election and is regarded as an important role of interest groups.[12]

This kind of spending inevitably raises suspicions about the ties between individual legislators and interest groups. It is almost impossible to distinguish one from the other. Do interest groups buy the sympathies and loyalties of a legislator, or are interest groups and candidates who genuinely share values and concerns doing whatever they think is necessary in order to win?

Issues central to campaigns and elections are the main topic of Chapter 8. The next topic for our discussion of interest groups is what efforts are made to influence policymakers once they are in office, whether they got there through election or appointment.

Interest Groups and Lobbying

A lobbyist may evoke the image of a cigar smoking, overweight guy with money stuffed in his pockets, roaming the halls looking for votes to buy. For the most part, smoking is now out. Health foods and aerobics are in. Doling out cash, credit cards, or gifts is the exception and can be prosecuted. The major currency that lobbyists pedal today is information. Campaign contributions and votes are rarely offered in a crass quid pro quo manner. They serve primarily to gain access or to get someone's attention. Information and expertise are key. The kind of behavior described in the chapter-opening vignette is the exception, not the rule.

In their review of interest groups and lobbying in Western states, Clive S. Thomas and Ronald J. Hrebenar make the following observations:

> The major trend in group tactics is taking place in the nature of lobbying. This transformation is affecting the type of lobbying that is conducted and demanding new skills of those who perform it. This is a consequence of the increasing complexity of issues and the movement towards a more technological society. . . . Gone are the days of the "super lobbyists" like Artie Samish in California and John Mueller in Nevada, who wined, dined and entertained legislators. The new breed is a purveyor of technical information, well informed and less likely to rely on "the old boy network" or directly help a candidate raise funds for his or her election campaign.[13]

These same authors found that the pattern they described in Western states was also replicated in other regions.[14]

An examination of lobbying on almost any bill illustrates the point. For example, when Monsanto developed a bovine growth hormone (BGH) that increased the milk production of a cow by 20 to 40 percent, dairy farmers in California and especially the

Exploring the Web

Lobbying Online

You can inform and try to persuade your state and local officials face to face, on the phone, or by mail. In most cases, you can also communicate information and arguments electronically. Go online and see if your elected officials have home-pages and e-mail addresses. For state governments, you can search the state website. See the directions in the box on page 150. For county governments, the address is www.co.countyname.stateinitials.us; for cities, it is www.ci.cityname.stateinitials.us.

Librarians and supporters of public libraries meet in the office of the New York state legislator to lobby her for continued budgetary support. Implicitly, these lobbyists pledge support during the next elections. Explicitly, the spokespersons provide important information and reasoning.

Midwest felt threatened. More milk from fewer cows translates into fewer farmers. The stereotype of lobbying would have us expect that any legislation to prohibit or to limit the use of BGH would pit the money Monsanto was willing to pledge to legislative and gubernatorial campaigns against the money and the votes of dairy farmers. Instead, lobbyists on both sides commissioned and used studies of what the economic impacts might be and whether there were any harmful side effects to cows or to people from BGH. Lobbyists also articulated somewhat philosophical arguments about accepting technological advances and preserving family farms. In the end, farmers were not able to identify any evidence of harmful side effects, and state governments were persuaded to do no more than require that milk from cows given BGH be labeled so that consumers who felt nervous could select an alternative. Information, not the promise of campaign support or the proffering of personal gifts, made the difference.

Regulation of Lobbying

States require lobbyists to register and to disclose their financing. In some states, lobbyists must report their expenses. In others, they must report both their sources of income and their expenses. As discussed in the section on campaign financing, political action committees of interest groups must also register and report their financing. As a further check, candidates must disclose the sources and amounts of contributions to their campaign treasuries.[15] In most states, lobbyists and legislators are prohibited from offering or soliciting campaign contributions in a state office.

When Wisconsin legislative leaders replaced this rule with a demand that lobbyists "pay to play," watchdog groups and the media cried foul. In a state once known as the model of clean government, felony charges were filed against the speaker of the assembly, the majority leader of the senate, and a co-chair of the legislature's joint committee on finance. Except for the speaker of the assembly, those charged either admitted guilt or were convicted.[16] The assembly speaker was convicted by a jury, but the conviction was set aside because of a technicality.

While there are efforts to regulate where and when a lobbyist might make a financial contribution to a campaign, it should now be understood by all that it is never appropriate for a state official to accept payments from lobbyists that enhance personal wealth. A key concept in the banning of old-style lobbying that benefits legislators personally is the prohibition against lobbyists offering and public officials accepting "anything of value."[17] This is admittedly a vague term and sometimes can be used to outlaw normal social interactions that almost everyone agrees are harmless, such as treating someone to lunch or buying someone coffee.

However, it does seem important to be broadly inclusive when dealing with ethics. The state supreme court in Alabama, for example, used the clause prohibiting the offering of something of value to rule against a telephone company's lobbyist who "reached out and touched someone" by providing "the services of a lady of the evening" (the court's phrase) to an important legislator.[18]

Who Are Lobbyists?

Lobbyists are often former legislators or legislative aides who are familiar with the legislative process and know best how and when to intervene. The lobbyists' staff members are specialists and technicians who have access to the data and information valued highly by today's policymakers. Lobbyists who do not have a political background tend to come from within the company or association that they represent.[19] Their challenge is not to master the subject they are representing but to learn the policy-making process in government.

Professional lobbying has historically been a male occupation. Less than 20 percent of all professional lobbyists are women. Although the records for volunteer lobbyists of various citizen and grass-roots groups are not complete, it appears that about 75 percent of volunteer lobbyists are women.[20]

Types of Lobbyists

Lobbyists can be categorized according to whom they represent and how they are paid. One such category is **contract lobbying**. As the term implies, these are individuals who agree to represent an organization for a particular period of time and for a fee. Some fees are hourly rates, whereas others are specific sums. Contract lobbying is done by individuals, by groups, and increasingly by law firms as part of their services to clients. Hrebenar and Thomas estimate that less than 15 percent of the lobbyists in state capitols work under contracts.[21]

About half the lobbyists are employees of the businesses, unions, or associations they represent; these are **in-house lobbyists**. Some of these individuals spend all their time

---

contract lobbyist An individual or firm that, for an agreed amount, lobbies on behalf of clients.
in-house lobbyist An individual or agency that, within an organization, lobbies on behalf of the organization.

watching the operations of state government, researching issues and proposals, and presenting information and ideas to policymakers. For others, this is only part of their jobs. A common pattern is to combine these responsibilities with community affairs and philanthropy or with public relations.

Organizations like the League of Women Voters, the American Legion, and Gray Panthers rely on volunteer lobbyists. Ad hoc groups concerned about a specific issue often use volunteers as well. Those representing causes or citizen organizations can be expected to be enthusiastic. Often they are very well versed in the policy processes of state and local governments and in the issues of concern to their organizations. Volunteers will sometimes lack the background, time, or energy to be effective lobbyists. About 10 to 20 percent of the state lobbyist community consists of volunteer lobbyists.

A similar proportion of lobbyists are government employees. Government lobbying is now commonplace. Interagency and intergovernmental issues have made it as important for governments to lobby one another as it is for interest groups to lobby government. If you attend a public university, it is almost certain that your university will have a lobbyist—perhaps called a government relations specialist or something even more esoteric.

What Lobbyists Do

Lobbying is usually thought of as talking with legislators in order to convince them to vote a particular way on a pending bill. While that is a major activity of lobbyists, efforts to influence public policy involve more than the legislature and more than talking.

Public policymakers include governors, mayors, administrators, citizen boards, judges, and legislators. The chapter-opening vignette describes justices on a state supreme court as the targets of lobbying. Effective lobbyists approach the full range of policymakers, which can be challenging. Mayors and governors are usually more difficult to see than legislators. Judges are not permitted to have discussions outside the courtroom about cases on which they will have to rule.

Contacts with legislators can be written or verbal, formal or informal. Lobbyists make presentations at hearings, send written material to offices, and arrange face-to-face meetings wherever it is convenient. The content of the messages from lobbyists to legislators and other elected officials is both substantive and political. Information on issues and concerns is critical to the process. In addition, elected officials are understandably interested in securing the support of interest groups for future campaigns.

To link political support to the position that an interest group may be advocating on a particular bill, lobbyists engage in grass-roots mobilization. This may involve getting the members of the organization the lobbyist represents to write individual letters or make phone calls to key officials. E-mail is increasingly being used. Sometimes it is possible to go beyond the membership and get the active support of members of the public.

---

lobby The efforts to attempt to influence decision making by government officials.

Grass-roots strategies have come naturally to labor unions, consumer interest groups, environmental groups, and others with relatively large memberships. Businesses sometimes generate their own grass-roots—or artificial turf—support on specific issues. Anheuser-Busch, maker of Budweiser and Michelob beers, has been particularly successful in mobilizing public support (primarily among beer drinkers) for various issues involving the regulation of taverns, drinking, and the taxation of alcoholic beverages.[22] Texas banks and financial institutions were very clever and convinced the public to voice support for legislation allowing higher interest rates on their credit cards.[23]

Effective lobbyists are good at arranging key contacts with elected officials. This is a targeted approach. An individual known and trusted by a mayor, legislator, or school board member is much more likely to be persuasive than someone who is unknown. Those from a legislator's district will be treated more seriously than those who are not. Some lobbyists make special efforts to identify or to develop one key contact they can use with each elected official.[24]

Judges in most state courts are elected. Interest group support can be provided for these elections just as it is for elected legislative and executive positions. There is a general tradition, however, that judicial elections should be based more on qualifications than on issues. Unlike other elected officials, judges are not considered to have constituencies. A judge who rules on cases involving campaign contributors is considered to have a conflict of interest, whereas this is not an issue for legislators or governors.

Interest groups can and do use the courts to pursue their goals in more accepted ways by strategically suing someone or by asking for an injunction. Environmental groups, for example, have secured injunctions to keep companies from polluting or to prevent government agencies from authorizing a particular development.

Interest groups lobby courts through the filing of an **amicus curiae** (friend of the court) brief, rather than through letters from constituents and discussions with interest group representatives in an office. Someone other than a litigant in a case files an amicus curiae brief. The purpose of such a brief is to present an argument and suggest an application of the law that may not be part of the presentation of one of the litigants. An environmental group may identify itself as an interested party in litigation between a chemical company and a state environmental protection agency (EPA). The environmental group may want to file an amicus curiae brief not so much to show the court it is in a coalition with the state agency but to supplement the arguments presented by that agency. Courts are not interested—or are not supposed to be interested—in coalitions. Judges, however, are concerned about different interpretations of the law.

Administrative agencies are lobbied primarily through formal hearings held by agencies when they are considering rule changes and through informal links between administrators and interest group representatives. A city department considering changes in how

---

amicus curiae Literally, a "friend of the court." This is a process where interest groups and other interested parties can argue orally and in writing in a particular court case that concerns them, even though they are not directly involved in the dispute. In this way interest groups can lobby in the judicial arena.

it will issue building permits will, in most cases, schedule a public hearing. Contractors, lending institutions, and neighborhood associations are likely to voice their opinions at such a hearing. In addition, representatives of these groups may talk one on one with key department officials in their offices to try to explain why a change is or is not necessary. Department administrators, in fact, may have arranged such a meeting even before drafting the proposals.

Administrators are typically not elected and so do not have the same concerns as other officials about interest group support. Nonetheless, career professionals usually prefer to have public support for what they do. A sense that a new program or procedure is likely to generate considerable resistance and perhaps trouble for their elected bosses may prompt administrators to alter their course.

IMPACT OF INTEREST GROUPS

No precise indicators exist for determining the relative power of interest groups and their impact on policy making in state and local governments. Success scores in legislative action mask the complexity of the legislative process and ignore efforts to influence other governmental institutions. Also, circumstances that set the agenda are important in determining whether an interest group is going to be active. The combination of its satisfaction with the status quo and the absence of significant demands for change may make a powerful interest group seem inactive, even though it remains dominant.

To try to gauge the relative power of interest groups in the states, Thomas and Hrebenar asked experts on each state to categorize their state in one of five classifications. The results of this study are presented in Table 7.1. The states in the dominant category are those in which interest groups have an overwhelming influence on public policy. The dominant/complementary group includes states in which interest groups are very strong, but they face some limitations due to the capacities of other political actors. The complementary label characterizes a balance between the power of interest groups and the power of state government institutions, political parties, and individual political participation. States in the complementary/subordinate category have interest groups with some power and influence, but other actors generally are primary. No states have weak, inconsequential interest groups. As we noted at the beginning of this chapter and as the authors of the study summarized in Table 7.2 have found, the general trend is for states to move toward the complementary category, especially as their economies diversify and as their state and local government institutions become more professional and more capable. In another study, Hrebenar and Thomas ranked specific interest groups according to what state policymakers—mainly legislators—said were the most influential. These rankings are presented in Table 7.3. Teachers and peak business associations top the list in all regions of the country. We would expect teachers to be politically powerful. They have all the traits of those individuals who are inclined to participate in politics; they are spread throughout the state in every legislative district; they know that state governments have primary responsibility for education. Likewise, the high ranking of peak business

Table 7.2 Classification of the 50 States According to the Overall Impact of Interest Groups

Dominant (5)	Dominant/ Complementary (26)	Complementary (16)	Complementary/ Subordinate (3)	Subordinate (0)
Alabama	Arizona	Colorado	Minnesota	
Florida	Arkansas	Delaware	Michigan	
Montana	South Carolina	Connecticut		
West Virginia	Utah	Vermont		
Nevada	Alaska	Indiana	South Dakota	
	California	Hawaii		
		Maine		
	Georgia	Massachusetts		
	Idaho			
	Illinois			
	Iowa	New Hampshire		
	Kansas	New Jersey		
	Kentucky	New York		
	Louisiana	North Carolina		
	Maryland	North Dakota		
	Mississippi	Pennsylvania		
	Missouri	Rhode Island		
	Nebraska	Wisconsin		
	New Mexico			
	Ohio			
	Oklahoma			
	Oregon			
	Tennessee			
	Texas			
	Virginia			
	Washington			
	Wyoming			

Source: Adapted from Clive S. Thomas and Ronald J. Hrebenar, "Interest Groups in the States," *Politics in the American States,* 8th ed., eds. Virginia Gray and Russell L. Hanson (Washington, D.C.: CQ Press, 2004), p. 122. Reprinted with permission.

associations is not a surprise. They have the money that can help pay campaign expenses; the actions of businesses can be key to a state's economic growth and stability; businesses have expertise that is valued by policymakers. Note that besides the peak business associations, 19 of the remaining 39 types of interest groups listed in the study are business associations or companies. Financial institutions, manufacturers, and utilities enjoy very high rankings. The general prevalence of business interest groups active in states has been a continuing feature of state politics and was evident again in a 2002 ranking compiled by Hrebenar and Thomas.[25]

Table 7.3   The 25 Most Effective Interests in the States

National Ranking	Number of States In Which Interest Is Very Effective
1 General business organizations (chambers of commerce, etc.)	40
2 School teachers' organizations (NEA and AFT)	37
3 Utility companies and associations (electric, gas, telecommunications, water)	24
4 Insurance companies and associations (general and medical)	21
5 Hospital/nursing home associations	21
6 Lawyers (predominantly trial lawyers, state bar associations)	22
7 Manufacturers (companies and associations)	18
8 General local government organizations	18
9 Physicians/state medical associations	17
10 General farm organizations	16
11 Bankers associations	15
12 Traditional labor associations (predominantly AFL-CIO)	13
13 Universities and colleges	13
14 State and local government employees	11
15 Contractors/builders/developers	13
16 Realtors' associations	13
17 K–12 education interests (other than teachers)	9
18 Individual labor unions (Teamsters, United Auto Workers, etc.)	8
19 Truckers and private transport interests (excluding railroads)	9
20 Sports enthusiasts/hunting and fishing (includes antigun control groups)	9
21 Gaming interests (race tracks/casinos/lotteries)	9
22 Environmentalists	6
23 Agricultural commodity organizations (grain growers, ranchers, etc.)	7
24 Retailers (companies and trade associations)	8
25 Individual banks and financial institutions	6

Source: Clive S. Thomas and Ronald J. Hrebenar, "Interest Groups in the States," in *Politics in the American States: A Comparative Analysis,* 8th ed., eds. Virginia Gray and Russell L. Hanson, (Washington, D.C.: Congressional Quarterly Press, 2004), p. 119. Reprinted with permission.

SUMMARY AND CONCLUSIONS

Individuals participate in state and local government through interest groups, whether they consciously and actively work through a group or just happen to be represented because of the efforts of an association that shares their concerns. Interest groups are credited with fostering democracy and informing policy debates. Interest groups are blamed for government actions that seem merely to respond to one special demand after another without any regard for common interests.

There may be no way of resolving the debate begun by Madison about whether or not interest groups contribute to the democratic process or whether they threaten it. Interest groups clearly exist and are active. Historically, specific groups have controlled some states and some communities. That continues to some extent in a handful of states and in many smaller, single-company towns. The trend, however, is for more balance. Economic development and diversification is accompanied by growth in the number and the activity of interest groups. Increases in urbanization also tend to generate political pluralism.

Another explanation for the emergence of more interest group activity in state and local governments is institutional. State and local governments have greater competence and capacity than they did prior to the *Baker v. Carr* Supreme Court decision mandating one-person, one-vote representation. The enhancement of the abilities of state and local governments has been both tested and furthered by the continued devolution of responsibility from the federal government since the presidency of Jimmy Carter. In short, because state and local governments can do more and are responsible for more, interest groups understand the need to increase their presence and activity in state capitols, city halls, and local government offices. Interest groups want to be where the action is.

Discussion Questions

1. Describe one or two interest groups that you support. What type of membership do they have? What are the purposes of the interest groups, and how are decisions made? What resources do they have? What strategies do they use to influence public policy?

2. How would you measure the strength of an interest group? Would different measurements apply to different types of interest groups?

3. Are there certain types of interest groups that are more or less desirable for democracy in a society?

4. Describe regional differences in the positions and roles of interest groups in state governments. What accounts for these differences?

Glossary

amicus curiae 184
bundling 179
business climate 177
conduit 179
contract lobbyist 182

in-house lobbyist 182
interest group 169
lobby 183
neighborhood association 178
peak association 172

political action committee (PAC) 179
special-interest group 169
surrogate interest group 172
trade association 172

Endnotes

1. James Madison, *Federalist 10*, in *The Federalist Papers*, 2d ed., ed. Roy P. Fairfield (Baltimore, Md.: Johns Hopkins University Press, 1981).

2. See, for example, Theodore Lowi, *The End of Liberalism* (New York: W.W. Norton, 1969), and Dwight D. Eisenhower's farewell speech when he left the presidency.

3. V. O. Key Jr., *Southern Politics in State and Nation* (New York: Alfred A. Knopf, 1949).

4. Clive S. Thomas, "Understanding Interest Group Activity," in *Interest Group Politics in the Southern States*, eds. Ronald J. Hrebenar and Clive S. Thomas (Tuscaloosa: University of Alabama Press, 1992).

5. Virginia Gray and David Lowery, *The Population Ecology of Interest Representation: Lobbying in the American States* (Ann Arbor: University of Michigan Press, 1996).

6. Virginia Gray and David Lowery, "Trends in Lobbying in the States," *The Book of the States*, Vol. 35 (Lexington, Ky.: Council of State Governments, 2003), 258.

7. Kay Lehman Schlozman and John T. Tierney, *Organized Interests and American Democracy* (New York: Harper & Row, 1986), 49.

8. Sarah McCally Moorehouse, *State Politics, Parties and Policy* (New York: CBS College Publishing, 1981); L. Harmon Zeigler, "Interest Groups in the States," in *Politics in the American States*, 4th ed., eds. Virginia Gray, Herbert Jacob, and Kenneth N. Vines (Boston, Mass.: Little, Brown, 1984).

9. Virginia Gray and Peter Eisinger, *American States and Cities* (New York: HarperCollins, 1991), 59, 60.

10. Gray and Eisinger, *American States and Cities*, 61.

11. Matthew A. Crenson, *Neighborhood Politics* (Cambridge, Mass.: Harvard University Press, 1982).

12. David B. Magleby, *Outside Money* (Chanham, Md.: Rowman and Littlefield, 2000).

13. Clive S. Thomas and Ronald J. Hrebenar, "Comparative Interest Group Politics in the American West," *The Journal of State Government* (September/October 1986), 134.

14. Clive S. Thomas and Ronald J. Hrebenar, "Interest Groups in the States," in *Politics in the American States: A Comparative Analysis*, 5th ed., eds. Virginia Gray, Herbert Jacob, and Robert B. Albritton (Glenview, Ill.: HarperCollins, 1990), 123–158. Also, Hrebenar and Thomas, eds., *Interest Group Politics in the Southern States*.

15. Virginia Gray and David Lowery, "State Lobbying Regulations and Their Enforcement: Implications for the Diversity of Interest Communities," *State and Local Government Review* 30, no. 2 (Spring 1998), 78–91.

16. Dennis L. Dresang, "Mr. Clean Gets Dirty: The Demise of Public Ethics in Wisconsin," *Public Integrity* 5, no. 4 (Fall 2003), 319–330.

17. Beth A. Rosenson, *The Shadowlands of Conduct: Ethics and State Politics* (Washington, D.C.: Georgetown University Press, 2005).

18. *Mayberry v. State of Alabama*, 419 So. 2nd 262 (1982). Cited in David L. Martin, "Alabama: Personalities and Factionalism," in *Interest Group Politics in the Southern States*, eds. Hrebenar and Thomas, 261, 262.

19. Alan Rosenthal, *The Third House: Lobbyists and Lobbying in the States* (Washington, D.C.: Congressional Quarterly Press, 1993), 20–38.

20. Thomas and Hrebenar, "Interest Groups in the States," 150–151.

21. Ronald J. Hrebenar and Clive S. Thomas, "Trends in Interest Group Politics in the States," *The Book of the States* (Lexington, Ky.: Council of State Governments, 2003), 265.

22. Rosenthal, *The Third House*, 158.

23. Keith E. Hamm and Charles W. Wiggins, "Texas: The Transformation from Personal to Informational Lobbying," in Hrebenar and Thomas, *Interest Group Politics in the Southern States*, 171.

24. Rosenthal, *The Third House*, 160–164.

25. Ronald J. Hrebenar and Clive S. Thomas, "Trends in Interest Groups," and L. Harmon Zeigler, "Interest Groups in the States," in *Politics in the American States*, 4th ed., eds. Virginia Gray, Herbert Jacob, and Kenneth N. Vines (Boston, Mass.: Little, Brown, 1984).

CHAPTER 8

Political Parties and Elections

LEARNING OBJECTIVES

- Know the primary purpose of political parties in the United States.
- Understand the importance of candidate-centered organizations and informal factions within political parties.
- Appreciate the role that state governments play in defining and regulating campaign financing and administering the electoral process.
- Identify techniques and strategies used in campaigning.
- Know the patterns and trends of party competition in the states.

After the November 2010 elections, Republican governors and legislative leaders quickly moved to enhance the chances of staying in power. Republicans did extraordinarily well in those elections and in 21 states held the office of governor as well as the majority in both houses of the state legislature. Democrats had this kind of dominance in only 11 states, and the rest had split partisan control. Governors John Kasich of Ohio, Scott Walker of Wisconsin, Rick Scott of Florida, and Rick Snyder of Michigan led initiatives to weaken public employee unions, which have been a major source of support for the Democratic Party. Republicans took steps to change election laws in ways that would discourage those who typically vote Democrat. And legislatures drew maps to revise legislative districts to make as many of them as possible safe for Republicans.

Elections matter, and both the characteristics of parties and the rules governing the electoral process are key to the outcome of contests between candidates. States are responsible for determining how individuals get on the ballot and how votes are cast. States also determine the rules that shape political parties. Federal campaign and election laws are general and respect the roles of states. Also, the rulings and legislation of the federal government usually apply only to federal offices.

Political parties and elections have all the trappings of democracy and popular participation in the governance of our society. The media coverage of the struggles within parties to secure a nomination and of the rhetoric and dynamism of campaigns is extensive. Electoral contests spawn blogs and e-mail traffic. Candidates and parties buy airtime on television and radio and establish websites to woo voters. Considerable time and effort are spent raising money to hire consultants and media firms. Most candidates for state and local offices go door-to-door in search of votes in their districts and make themselves visible and available at neighborhood gatherings, shopping areas, sporting events, and other public places. Armies of volunteers work long hours making phone calls and distributing literature with the hope of being on the winning team. Campaigns can get very intense, costly, and even nasty. The results can be dramatic shifts in partisan control.

The rate of participation in elections and campaigns is low, as we saw in Chapter 6. When the ballot includes a contest for president of the United States, only about half of those eligible to vote actually participate in elections. When just state and local government offices are at stake, the figure drops to between 20 and 40 percent. The opportunity to vote is almost universally available, but relatively few take advantage of it.

Nonetheless, elections are of central importance. We elect all legislators, most judges, and many of the top administrators in state and local governments. In about two-thirds of the states, voters can take direct action to enact laws through initiatives and referenda, as explained in Chapter 6. In all states and communities, balloting may include changes to constitutions and charters. The electoral process is not only about deciding who fills certain offices and which referenda will pass, but also about candidates and advocates actively making contact with individual citizens and seeking their support. Elections bring citizens and those who would govern them face to face, either directly or via print and electronic communications.

The way in which elections are conducted is important when determining the kind of support and cooperation public officials can expect. Negative campaigning, in which candidates attack one another as persons and emphasize why constituents should not vote for their opponents, generates disgust and dismay for candidates and for the process. Elected officials in this context cannot legitimately claim they have a mandate from the electorate. The style and strategy of campaigns, in short, have important effects on how individuals identify with government and how cooperative they are likely to be.

The formal processes and the role of political parties in elections also affect face-to-face interaction. Prior to the Progressive reforms at the beginning of the twentieth century, political parties determined, behind closed doors, who would run for office. Now state laws throughout the country provide for a more open process. The more open processes place an emphasis on candidate-centered campaigning. Parties are still relevant and important, but they are not the powerful machines they once were.

THE ROLES OF POLITICAL PARTIES

As we saw in Chapter 7, interest groups are often very active by supporting candidates and causes through votes and dollars. A fear is that interest group involvement in elections is excessive and threatens democracy. Candidates' dependence on the contributions of interest groups may have the effect of excluding individuals without financial resources but nonetheless with important and legitimate concerns.

Political parties come into the equation here. Are political parties coalitions of interest groups, thereby reducing the dependence of candidates on any single interest group? Or are political parties captured by interest groups, thus reinforcing the links between candidates and special interests? Are political parties important in the electoral process? What role do they play?

Responsible Parties

One role of political parties, at all levels of government, is to advocate for certain public policies and to bring together groups and individuals interested in those policies. This perspective of political parties is often referred to as the **responsible party** government or the party democracy school of thought. This role also assumes parties use an ideology or a set of principles to screen new members and to reward and sanction existing members so that everyone conforms to the same strategies and objectives.[1]

The Democratic Party, for example, is characterized as a party that regards government as responsible for ensuring a basic-level quality of life for everyone. That general philosophy has formed the basis for a traditional coalition of workers, ethnic minorities, and service professionals. Democrats generally favor measures to regulate corporations to keep them from exploiting workers and consumers or from spoiling the environment. The party has also supported taxation policies that emphasize the ability to pay, using rates that are higher for the wealthy than the middle class or the poor.

In contrast, the Republican Party is identified with a philosophy that the role of government is primarily to ensure a vibrant and healthy economy, in large part by staying out of the way and letting the market operate. The Republican philosophy is to rely on general economic activity and individual generosity to provide for the welfare of the less fortunate. The Republican Party has been labeled the party of the wealthy and the business community. Since the mid-1990s, Christian fundamentalists have mobilized and been successful in getting Republican candidates to support incorporating their religious doctrines into public policies.

In 2009, a so-called **Tea Party** (it is not really a party, but a faction within the Republican Party) emerged emphasizing libertarian ideals and reducing government expenditures. Libertarians celebrate individual freedom and oppose government involvement in social or economic matters. Unlike the Christian fundamentalists, libertarians do not believe government should regulate private or family life, such as same-sex unions or abortions. Concern over government borrowing and public bailouts of failing banks and auto companies fueled the Tea Party drive to cut government spending. Tea Party candidates ran in Republican primaries in 2010, sometimes winning and sometimes prompting other Republican candidates to support reducing the size and scope of government.[2]

Although the images of the parties are based in part on their respective records and their formal positions, the distinctions are not always clear and predictable. The basic unit of political parties in the United States is the state party. And in most states, the basic building block is the county. The national Democratic and Republican parties are loose confederations of state organizations. State parties are sometimes at odds with the national party on basic policy positions. The most dramatic and longstanding example of this was

---

responsible party A political organization whose major purpose is to pursue a particular philosophy or set of positions. Responsible parties restrict their membership and their sponsorship of electoral candidates to those who adhere to party positions.

Tea Party A segment of the Republican Party that emerged in 2009 to protest high levels of government spending and borrowing and to advocate generally for a reduction in the role of government.

the conflict in the 1950s and 1960s between the national Democratic Party and Democratic Party organizations in Southern states over racial issues.[3]

Although the national parties have a structure and establish platforms that include the positions the party has taken on various issues, no major party has required its members or its candidates to support the platform. The description of political parties as coalitions pursuing a common philosophy or a common set of public policies is imperfect at best. What distinguishes parties from one another is tradition and a general image.[4] The labor orientation of the Democratic Party and the business orientation of the Republican Party are general and imprecise portraits that tend to attract people and groups that favor labor causes on the one hand and that respond to business concerns on the other. Yet some Democratic governors have been particularly kind to business, and some Republican mayors have established especially close ties with labor. Party labels allow us to make some guesses about public policy positions, but we cannot make confident predictions. The polarization of the parties since the mid-1990s has made these predictions easier and safer.

Electoral Parties

When Lee Sherman Dreyfus was elected governor of Wisconsin in 1978, he quipped that he thought it would be a good idea to join the Republican Party before he ran as its candidate.[5] Governor Dreyfus, who himself did not have a clear policy agenda, viewed the role of parties as vehicles that candidates could use to get elected to office, rather than as ideologically committed organizations running candidates to influence the direction of public policy. This perspective considers a party as an **electoral party**. Indeed, parties often provide an organizational shell that gets filled temporarily each electoral period by those eager to get their candidates elected. Campaign workers include some who are active each election on behalf of a particular party and others who are participating because of their interest in specific candidates.

The classic use of parties primarily as vehicles for elections was in evidence during the period from the Civil War until the middle of the twentieth century, when political machines were at their peak.[6] Machines emerged primarily in urban areas, and they had their base of support in ethnic neighborhoods. Immigrants from various parts of Europe formed neighborhoods that had their own restaurants, churches, grocery stores, and social clubs. These neighborhoods coincided with wards and precincts used by urban governments for conducting elections and providing services. Political parties responded to this situation by developing organizations that were based on a quid pro quo; that is, a neighborhood or ward that turned out a sizable vote for a party candidate received services and jobs if the party got into power. Once a party machine established control over a city or state government, it set in motion a cycle of patronage and services for votes that retained control of government for the party in power. Several state and many urban parties were built on these machines.

The Progressive movement, led by Theodore Roosevelt, Woodrow Wilson, Robert M. La Follette Sr., Hiram Johnson, and others, attacked and dealt fatal blows to machine

---

electoral party A political organization whose major purpose is to get its candidates elected. Electoral parties do not have or apply a well-defined ideology or reject members or candidates who do not adhere to a particular philosophy or set of positions.

politics during the first quarter of the twentieth century. Although some machines lingered through the middle of the century, the effects of primary elections, civil service reform, and the direct election of many executive officials in state governments were to deprive machines of the closed operation and control over rewards and punishments.[7]

One of the legacies of the Progressive Era is that some states have laws establishing **nonpartisan elections**. These laws prohibit party identity on the ballot and do not allow any formal party involvement in the nomination process or in campaigns. Even when elections are formally nonpartisan, the party identity of some candidates is generally known and may play a role in influencing voters.

The demise of strong machines did not end the role of parties in elections. State laws define how candidates can get on the ballot, who will be declared a winner, how election results can be challenged, and what rules must be followed for financing and running a campaign. All states have laws assuming the existence of parties that nominate and work for candidates.

About 60 percent of American voters have a tradition of identifying with and voting for a particular party.[8] Candidates therefore regard parties as an important element in their electoral strategies. Because of party loyalties, candidates can count on a certain core of support and a certain core of opposition even before they begin their campaigns. In districts that traditionally vote for a particular party, the strategy of candidates in that party is to emphasize partisan identification. Candidates running in districts that have a history of supporting the party of their opponents will downplay partisanship and emphasize issues and personal traits. The strategy for campaigning in districts where parties have roughly equal strength is obviously more complex.

In short, political parties are integral to the electoral process and are usually an important factor in campaigns. Although there are links between parties and interest groups and, especially now, parties differ from one another on policy preferences, there is not the level of screening and discipline to ensure that all candidates and elected officials in a particular party adhere to the same positions that one would find in parliamentary systems. The electoral model, with its emphases on winning and on individual candidates, is much more applicable to the United States than is the responsible party model.

PARTY ORGANIZATION

Because political parties exist primarily to get candidates elected, formal party organization parallels the geographic boundaries of constituencies. Other organizational structures (discussed later) emerge around the efforts to elect a specific candidate.

Formal Organization

State laws play a major role in defining the formal structures and functions of political parties. These laws can be very detailed, as in the cases of Illinois, Ohio, and Louisiana. They can specify how local and statewide committees are selected, what those committees

---

nonpartisan election   A contest in which candidates appear on a ballot without any party identification.

Voter registration booth.

must do, and even when they must meet. Other states, like Alaska, Delaware, Hawaii, Kentucky, and North Carolina, have nothing other than brief, general statutory provisions for the role of political parties in the nomination of candidates.[9]

In 1986, the U.S. Supreme Court voiced concern about potential conflict between state laws regulating political parties and constitutional provisions protecting freedom of speech and association. California had required that political parties in that state limit their respective chairs to a two-year term, rotate between individuals from southern and northern California for the position of chair, and refrain from endorsing candidates in primary elections. In *Eu v. San Francisco County Democratic Central Committee*,[10] the Court unanimously invalidated this statute as too intrusive on First Amendment rights of freedom to assemble and advocate. This ruling suggests that many state regulations on political parties might be invalid.

Committee Structures

The major components of formal party organization are the geographically based committees, staff resources, and statewide conventions. Figure 8.1 depicts the typical committee structure of a state political party. Party members elect representatives to ward or precinct offices. Those elected at the local level either are automatically on the county committee or elect, among themselves, representatives to the county committee. Congressional district committees can consist of individuals elected by county committees, persons appointed by the member of Congress representing the district, or a combination of elected and appointed individuals. Likewise, state central committees, depending on the state, can consist of elected officials, their appointees, and/or representatives from county committees. State central committees can include positions reserved for representatives from particular groups such as women, ethnic minorities, and college students. This practice is more common among Democrats than among Republicans.[11]

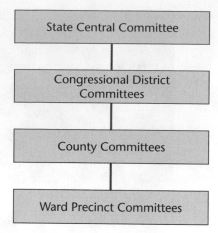

Figure 8.1 Committee Structure of a State Political Party.

Resources

Parties typically have an executive staff, a budget, and a headquarters. These resources are key to providing campaign services to candidates. The Republican Party has been more successful than the Democratic Party at securing financial and staff resources.

Political science scholars Malcolm E. Jewell and David M. Olson point out that state parties only recently have had substantial resources. Republicans began a strong and concerted effort to build their organizational strength after the electoral disaster following the Watergate scandal and the resignation of President Richard M. Nixon. Democrats were prompted to begin rebuilding their organizations in the aftermath of the heavy losses they suffered at the polls in 1980 and again in 1994.[12] Republicans invested three times as much in their state parties as did Democrats. The resource advantages of Republicans contributed to their dramatic successes in the fall 1994 elections; the party made gains in 46 of the 47 states in which there were elections. Republicans gained a total of 472 state legislative seats around the country and increased their control of governorships from 21 to 31. Democrats learned from the Republicans and matched their investment in elections. In the fall 2006 elections, Democrats reversed the 1994 results by winning 364 more state legislative races than did Republicans and gaining a 28 to 22 advantage over the Republican Party in governors.

The year 2008 was generally a good one for Democrats in states as well as the federal government, but 2010 was even better for Republicans. Voters were generally in a sour mood in November 2010. The country had just experienced the worst economic downturn since the Great Depression of the 1920s, and although there were signs of recovery, the jobless rate continued to plague individuals and communities. Despite a general consensus among economists and politicians that the government had to come to the rescue with expensive programs and bailouts, no one liked this level of intervention. As in similar situations in the past, the overwhelming sentiment was to express frustration by throwing incumbent elected officials out of power. Republicans reversed—and then some—the big gains Democrats had made just two years earlier. Besides securing control of the U.S. House of Representatives, Republicans took 11 governorships from Democrats and won control over

21 state legislative chambers in which Democrats had been in charge. Republican gains in 2010 were especially significant because states are obliged to revise the boundaries of their legislative districts after each census, providing Republicans the opportunity to shape districts in ways that advantage them. We discuss legislative districts in Chapter 10.

Conventions

Most state political parties hold annual conventions attended by delegates from various committees and by elected officials. These conventions are typically gala events, and they are perfect for partying, posturing, and strategizing. Before the establishment of primary elections, parties used conventions to select a slate of candidates to run for state and local offices. Those seeking the party's nomination wooed party leaders and delegates. The process was often dramatic, filled with intrigue and sometimes mischief. Party bosses reigned.

Although much of the frenzied drama continues, party conventions no longer determine who will be on the ballot. Connecticut law provides for an exception. Until 1955, the only way for a candidate to get on the ballot in Connecticut as a Republican or a Democrat was by beating other contenders at the respective party conventions. Since 1955, victory at the convention is still sufficient, unless at least one other candidate gets the votes of at least 20 percent of the delegates. If this happens, then a challenge primary is held and voters determine the party nominee. In order to vote in a Connecticut primary, voters must be registered for at least six months as a Republican or Democrat, depending on the party holding the challenge primary.[13]

Primary elections are now the way in which most candidates get their names on the ballot. Some state parties allow endorsements at their conventions, but endorsed candidates must still win in the primary to become their party's nominee. Conventions are for informal networking and face-to-face interactions among candidates, elected officials, and the party faithful. Conventions are also for adopting resolutions on various policy issues and for writing a party platform.

Exploring the Web

How do political parties run?

How do the political parties differ in their organization and their approaches toward attracting voters? What is involved in becoming a member of a political party? Given the information provided by the parties, which are you most inclined to support?

The Republican National Party has a website at *www.rnc.org*, and links to state parties are at *www.fastlane.net/homepages/weide/state.shtml*. The Democratic National Party has a website at *www.democrats.org*, and state parties can be accessed by using the initial of the state followed by "democrats.org."

Two useful general resources on parties and campaigns are *www.msnbc.com/new/politics* and *www.vote-smart.org*.

Those running for a statewide office, such as governor, attorney general, or U.S. senator, usually are eager for the platform to articulate positions consistent with their own campaign themes. Candidates prefer to avoid awkward situations in which they have to justify to the media and to party loyalists why they disagree with planks of the platform. Nonetheless, election is more important than discipline and consistency. It is not unusual for candidates to distance themselves from platforms adopted at conventions.

INFORMAL ORGANIZATIONS

Candidate-Centered Organizations

Regardless of party, candidates for elected offices establish their own campaign organizations. States typically mandate that candidates identify a treasurer so that contributions and expenses can be monitored for their compliance with campaign finance laws. Beyond the office of treasurer, candidates appoint someone as an overall manager and have individuals or task forces for policy development, media relations, fundraising, voter mobilization, and event scheduling. Candidates for statewide offices and in districts where television advertising is important usually hire professional political consultants.[14]

Political scientist Robert Salisbury has suggested that political organizations can secure commitments from campaign volunteers by offering three kinds of incentives or rewards: material, solidary, and purposive.[15] All three are provided in **candidate-centered organizations**.

- **Material incentives** are primarily jobs but sometimes also include the hope for sympathetic treatment if the candidate is elected. The jobs might include positions on the staff of the elected official, or agency appointments if the election is for a governor, mayor, or other executive. Other material incentives include favorable treatment when bidding for a government contract or the establishment or enhancement of a tax benefit or public service.
- **Solidary incentives** are the social benefits that come from the interaction with people. Political campaigns rank with singles' bars, church gatherings, and similar opportunities for meeting people. Volunteers at campaign headquarters include neighbors and old friends.
- **Purposive incentives** refer to the pursuit of a particular cause or ideology. Candidates sometimes are closely identified with a policy objective or a value perspective, and their campaigns represent an opportunity for individuals to work toward a general policy goal that extends beyond the candidate.

---

candidate-centered organizations Informal organizations within political parties that work in support of a particular candidate.

material incentives Jobs, contracts, and other rewards that attract individuals to campaign in support of a candidate or political party.

solidary incentives The opportunities for working with others that attract people to campaigns in support of a candidate or party.

purposive incentives The satisfaction of pursuing certain values or policy objectives that attract individuals to campaign in support of a candidate or party.

Campaign organizations rely heavily on solidary and purposive rewards. As soon as the election—win or lose—is over, however, volunteers and paid consultants move on and very little, if any, of the organization remains.

Factions

Some state political parties comprise very real, but informal **factions**. These factions might be based on ideology, geography, or personalities. Since the early 1980s a number of state Republican parties, like those in Kansas, Indiana, Virginia, Minnesota, Wisconsin, Ohio, Oregon, and California, have experienced a split between regular (old guard) participants and an emergent force of Christian fundamentalists. The Tea Party has been a force in some state Republican parties. Democratic parties in California and New York have been split between reformers and the old guard, with the reformers generally being more liberal.[16]

California, Illinois, and Pennsylvania are states that traditionally have experienced regional conflicts. In California, the conflict has been between the northern and southern parts of the state. The major differences in Illinois have been between Cook County (Chicago area) and "downstate" (southern Illinois). General regional rivalries in these states translate into factions within both major political parties. In Pennsylvania, the division between the urban areas of Philadelphia and Pittsburgh and the rest of the state has affected the Democrats much more than the Republicans.

Democratic parties in Southern states have been known for factions revolving around prominent personalities such as Herman Talmadge in Georgia, George Wallace in Alabama, and Huey Long and Edwin Edwards, both of Louisiana.[17] The increase in African American voter participation since the 1960s and the growth of the Republican Party since the 1990s has reduced, though not entirely eliminated, the importance of personal factions in Southern Democratic parties.[18]

A distinction between the candidate-centered organizations and personality factions is that the latter are continuous, whereas the organizations established to elect a particular candidate last just for the duration of the campaign. Most candidates do not see the party as important enough to try and control it. They recognize the party as a resource for helping to get elected but are not interested in it per se, and thus do not devote the time and energy necessary to establish and manage an ongoing faction within the party.

CONSULTANTS

Consultants have emerged as a major force in campaigns. Some would even say that they are frequently *the* major force.[19] Political consulting firms tend to align themselves with candidates of one party or another, and the consultants, more than the parties, end up influencing how electoral contests are run. Consultants are hired, fired, and paid primarily by candidates.

---

factions Informal and ongoing organizations within political parties that work in support of a particular set of interests or persons.

The business of consultants is to get their client elected. Winning is key to their future. Consultants readily admit that they focus on winning even when they have doubts about the quality or character of candidates that have hired them. Issues and ethics are not fundamental concerns.[20]

One implication of the importance of consultants is that the place and role of volunteers in campaigns has been reduced. While individuals who are willing to spend time getting their favorite candidate elected can be a resource for some of the most routine and menial tasks, the paid consultants make the strategic and tactical decisions. In state and local elections, there is still an emphasis on campaigning door to door. However, in statewide contests and in areas where electronic media are important, candidates spend a considerable amount of time on the phone or at exclusive events raising money to pay consultants, often sacrificing face-to-face work with volunteers and voters.

LEGISLATIVE LEADERS

Legislators seeking to retain or secure leadership positions are replacing political parties as the ones who recruit individuals to run for office. Those legislators then help the new recruits find political consultants and raise funds. The understanding is that winning candidates are then obliged to vote for the aspiring leader when it comes time to choose a speaker or president or majority leader in the state legislature. This phenomenon has led to increased party discipline and cohesion in state legislatures. Leaders are able to command more loyalty when they want their party to take a particular stand on an issue. They are also able to threaten credibly to punish defectors by sponsoring opponents in primary campaigns for reelection.

While this role of aspirant legislative leaders is understandable, it has led to increased polarization of parties, and at times it has led to unethical and illegal behaviors. Scandals that rocked a number of states, including Texas, Florida, Ohio, New Jersey, and Wisconsin, in the first decade of the twenty-first century had to do with legislative leaders using staff on state payrolls and violating campaign financing rules in order to get others in their party elected. These were not the typical corruption cases in which people got richer; instead, they got powerful.

PARTY NOMINATIONS

Between 1902 and 1955, all of the then 48 states adopted some form of primary election for determining who got a party's nomination for the general election. Gone are the days when party bosses determined who got on the ballot. (Eighteen states—like Iowa, Nevada, and Washington—use caucuses and conventions for selecting delegates to national presidential nominating conventions, but rely on primaries for nominating candidates for state and local offices.) New York and Connecticut adopted a challenge primary, in which voters select nominees if delegates to a party convention cannot agree on a candidate. Iowa and South Dakota use a reverse process. In these states, if no candidate receives more than 35 percent of the votes cast in a primary, the party must call a convention to select a nominee. In some states, minor parties must select their nominees in conventions, not primaries. In Kansas, for example, any party that is so small it cannot get more than 5 percent of the votes cast for secretary of state may not participate in primary elections. In New Mexico, a party must get at least 15 percent of the votes cast for governor. In Alabama, Colorado, Georgia, South Carolina, and Virginia, the executive committees of parties can choose to call conventions rather than use primaries. In all other states, primaries alone determine party nominees.

Twenty-eight states have a **closed primary** system in which registered voters identify their party preference and are given a ballot with only the candidates running for nomination from that party. The most recent changes were in 2010 when Idaho joined the ranks of closed primary states and California left to adopt the top-two system used by Louisiana and Washington. Fifteen states require that voters register their party identification before the day of the election. The other 14 keep records of the party affiliation of voters but allow voters to change their party affiliation on Election Day. This system allows candidates to target their campaigns and focus on party members. Two exceptions should be noted: (1) Utah does not report the party primary in which registered Independents vote, and (2) West Virginia allows registered Independents to vote in the Republican primary (but not the Democratic primary).

Three states, Louisiana, Washington, and California, have a **single primary**, or **top-two primary** for their contests. Nebraska uses a top-two primary for elections to its non-partisan, unicameral legislature, but a closed primary for partisan races, such as governor and U.S. congressperson. In the single or top-two system, all candidates, regardless of party identity, run in the same primary. Based on the assumption that Louisiana would always be a single-party (Democratic) state, the legislature passed a law that provides for all candidates to run in the same primary election. If any candidate wins more than 50 percent of the votes, he or she is declared the winner and no general election is held for that office. If no candidate receives a majority of the votes cast, the top two run against one another in the general election. Republicans have been successful since 2000 in running first or second in the primary and forcing a general election. Voters in the state of Washington approved the top-two primary in a direct initiative in 2004, and California did the same in an indirect initiative in 2010. The Republican and Democratic parties in Washington challenged this system in court, and it was not implemented until the U.S. Supreme Court approved it in 2008. California's change was effective in 2011.

The remaining 19 states have an **open primary**, in which voters do not register party affiliation and instead choose which party primary in which to vote when they go to the polling booth. Eleven of these states record which party a voter chooses and makes that information available. The other eight do not keep any record of party preferences. Table 8.1 identifies the type of primary system used in each state.

---

closed primary A party primary system that does not allow voters registered with one party to vote in the primaries of other parties.

single primary or **top-two primary** A primary system in which all candidates, regardless of party affiliation, for the same office appear on the same primary ballot and, unless one candidate receives more than 50 percent of the votes, the top two vote earners run in the general election.

open primary A party primary system that allows anyone, regardless of her or his political affiliation, to vote for candidates running for a particular party's nomination.

Table 8.1 Types of Primary Elections in the States

	Closed		Open	
Prior Registration Required	**May Change on Election Day**	**Record Kept of Party Choice**	**No Record Kept**	**Top-Two**
Connecticut	Alaska	Alabama	Hawaii	Louisiana
Delaware	Arizona	Arkansas	Washington	
Florida		Georgia	Michigan	California
Idaho				
Kentucky	Colorado	Illinois	Minnesota	Nebraska
Maine	Iowa	Indiana	Missouri	
Nebraska	Kansas	Mississippi	Montana	
Nevada	Maryland	Ohio	North Dakota	
New Jersey	Massachusetts	South Carolina	Vermont	
New Mexico	New Hampshire	Tennessee	Wisconsin	
New York	North Carolina	Texas		
Oklahoma	Oregon	Virginia		
Pennsylvania	Rhode Island			
South Dakota	Utah			
Wyoming	West Virginia			

Note: Nebraska uses a closed primary for its partisan contests and a top-two for its nonpartisan unicameral legislature.

Source: National Conference of State Legislatures, http://www.ncsl.org/default.aspx?tabid=20112 Accessed July 11, 2011.

CAMPAIGNS

Campaign Techniques

Formal campaigning begins with an announcement of intent to run for a particular office. The announcement may be preceded by media stories that an individual is considering running. These stories help extend media coverage of the candidacy. Typically, campaigning consists of the following activities:

1. Having the candidate go door to door to meet voters personally and get their support.
2. Speaking before small groups and major organizations to seek their support and perhaps formal endorsement.
3. Establishing websites and blogs to post information about the candidate and his or her positions.
4. Soliciting funds from supporters, including individuals and organizations, through mailings, phone calls, events, and the Internet.
5. Getting media attention through press conferences, interviews, press releases, rallies and other media events, paid advertisements, and debates with other candidates.
6. Securing grass-roots visibility through bumper stickers, pins, brochures, and yard signs.

7. Mailing, to specific groups, letters or brochures that address their particular concerns.
8. Encouraging supporters to vote. This effort includes identifying potential supporters through surveys; helping them register to vote if they are not already registered; reminding them to vote; and, in some cases, giving them rides to and from the polls.
9. Attacking the opponent and trying to generate a negative image of the opponent personally and politically.

Because of uncertainty and anxiety, consultants and campaign managers typically use all the above strategies. They might emphasize some activities more than others simply because of the availability of funds, the resources of the opposition, or the size of the district. Candidates who are behind in the polls often rely heavily on negative campaigning to lower the level of support of their opponents.

For many elections for state legislative seats and for local government offices, the constituencies are small enough that the candidates are personally involved in almost all campaign activities. Candidates have the time to go door to door and can meet with relatively small groups of people. It is realistic to aim at meeting every eligible voter in the district at least once. Advertising on television and radio has become standard.

Media

Media campaigning is a multibillion-dollar and growing business. Production costs of a single television spot typically start at $5,000 and frequently go from three to ten times that amount. Airtime for a 30-second commercial can vary from $3,000 to $75,000. The expansion of cable channels has multiplied the opportunities for candidates to reach voters. Each cable channel and each radio station appeals to specific parts of the population. Sports fans and news buffs have their stations. Age groups that prefer golden oldies, country music, or contemporary rock have their favorite spots on the radio dial. Thus, candidates can target their messages to these groups with some precision and can focus on crime, jobs, farm issues, retirement matters, or any pertinent issue. Likewise, campaigns use major television stations to target different regions of the state where they feel they can and must generate support.

A state senator campaigning at a street festival in his district in Hartford, Connecticut. Even with all the money spent on television and radio ads, face-to-face campaigning is essential in most state and local races.

Although the creation of media advertisements is an art, research on public opinion has led to some standard practices. An individual must see an ad five times before it makes a meaningful impression. Ads must not only be aired repetitively but also at times when persuadable voters are likely to be viewing or listening. Candidates running for U.S. senator, governor, and other offices elected statewide typically produce and run 20 to 30 different radio and television ads.[21]

Campaign commercials selling a candidate usually follow a common sequence:

1. Early ads introduce candidates by describing their lives and accomplishments.
2. Testimonials by both prominent and ordinary people present the candidate's empathy and problem-solving abilities.
3. Short (10-second) spots highlight a policy position.
4. Thirty-second and 10-second ads attack the opponent and make charges that raise doubts about the opponent's competence or character.
5. As the campaign comes to a close, the candidate is identified with good feelings: patriotism, progress, hope, and general satisfaction.

Blogs and Websites

Since the 2004 presidential campaign, use of the Internet has become part of almost every political campaign, including campaigns for state and local offices. The 2008 election saw extensive use of websites and blogs. According to a survey by the Pew Research Center, over 50 million people each day get their daily news from the Internet. People, especially between the ages of 18 and 34, look to websites and blogs for information and opinions about people and issues in politics.[22] Candidates value someone who can design an attractive, accessible website. Blogs, websites, and twitter messages are used for informing supporters, persuading voters who are undecided, raising money, and getting people to vote. The distribution of messages is immediate, and it is inexpensive. Sometimes the communication is direct and other times it is indirect—supporters and news reporters get information and ideas from Internet searches; then they share what they learn with others. In contrast with television and radio, the Internet provides an opportunity for interaction with voters as they respond to e-mails and surveys.

Blogs and websites are sources of misinformation and negative attacks as well as news and positive images. An attempt to obfuscate the author of a negative attack against a candidate raises concerns about accountability, but the message nonetheless gets out.

Negative Campaigning

Hamburgers had a profound effect on political campaigns. Advertisers found that an effective way to sell one kind of fast-food hamburger was to say negative things about the hamburgers sold by the competition. This approach was transferred to political campaigns, into efforts to portray a political opponent as incompetent, untrustworthy, immoral, or otherwise ill-suited for public office. **Negative campaigning** is not pointing out differences on issues. It is attacking—often with exaggerations, lies, or irrelevant statements—the

---

negative campaigning Attacks on the personal traits or behavior of an opponent. Attacks are usually based on exaggerations, lies, or information that is irrelevant.

Christine Gregoire, Democratic candidate for governor of Washington.

personal traits and/or behavior of an individual. Negative ads divert voter attention from the issues and from why they should vote *for* a candidate.

Negative campaigning is not new in U.S. elections, but in the past decade consultants have persuaded candidates to use this approach more frequently and more robustly.[23] Since the 2006 elections, the Internet has also been a medium for attacking candidates with misleading statements and sometimes outrageous accusations.

Karl Struble, a media consultant who helped engineer a number of successful campaigns, expressed the consensus of his profession: "People have become very cynical about positive advertising. People hate negative ads, but they remember them."[24]

Although negative campaigning does not seem to please voters, it can contribute to winning elections. Aggressive attacks by candidates, regardless of their truth value, can attract attention to the election and enhance the passion of supporters. Although almost everyone decries the existence of negative campaigning, it is not going away and is expanding.[25]

A tactic known as a voter suppression phone campaign, or push polling, has become part of political electioneering. The specific purpose of this tactic is to discourage some voters from going to the polls. A campaign worker calls individuals who are likely to support the opposing candidate and asks a question that implies a flaw in that candidate. For example, the question might be: "Would you support (name of opposing candidate) if you knew that four years ago he paid off a judge to avoid being convicted of sexually molesting a 4-year-old girl?" Typically the person making the call says that he or she is working for a polling organization that has a name separate from a political party or a candidate. The question posed technically does not say that the opposing candidate is guilty of the misdeed, but the implication is clear. Like other forms of negative campaigning, voter suppression efforts are cynical and calculating. The goal is more to dissuade than to persuade.

CAMPAIGN FINANCES

Campaigning is expensive, with television advertising costs constituting the bulk of the expenditures. In addition, candidates rent or purchase computers, software, and databases to identify and target likely supporters; generate general and targeted written material; establish websites and blogs; send automated robo-calls urging supporters to vote; manage finances; and schedule activities. The traditional bumper stickers, yard signs, buttons, and other paraphernalia cost money. Phone lines and transportation are essential. These expenses are common to campaigns for school board, city council, county board, and state legislature, as well as for statewide offices. In large-scale campaigns, some staff will have to be compensated, which drives costs up even more. The total cost of all state and local elections reached the $1 billion mark for the first time in 1994. The cost only 10 years earlier was $228.9 million.[26]

Not surprisingly, costs are highest in the most populous states and in states where there is heavy use of electronic media. In 2003, gubernatorial candidates spent a total of $2.2 million in Montana and $238.1 million in California. In the California recall election in 2004, candidates spent $82.4 million in a 77-day period. Even with record-high spending in the 2008 presidential election, campaign expenditures for state offices reached almost $2.5 billion.[27] Spending probably would have been even higher, but there were only 11 states that had gubernatorial contests in 2008. In 2010, with over three times that number of gubernatorial races and no presidential contest, total campaign spending was over $4 billion.

Candidates for most local elections rely on contributions from individuals. State offices, especially those like the governorship, which are statewide, and federal contests attract financial support from the organized interest groups discussed in Chapter 7. The most effective method for a candidate to solicit funds is face to face, whether with an individual, a group, or a corporate donor. The response rate to direct contacts is almost 90 percent. This rate drops to 5 percent when mail and telephone solicitations are made without prior direct personal contact.[28]

Concerns about the need for money and the influence that money might have on elected officials have prompted states and some local governments to place limits on campaign financing. All 50 states begin with a requirement that candidates disclose their sources of funds. Although no systematic research proves that campaign contributions garner influence with elected officials, this link seems reasonable enough to assume. Disclosure may or may not reduce this influence, but at least everyone can be aware of its potential.

States use a variety of approaches to regulate the funding of campaigns.[29] One is to set limits on contributions that can be made to candidates. Frequently, different limits apply to statewide, upper-house, and lower-house offices. States also differ on how they treat contributors, whether they are individuals, organizations, or political action committees (PACs). As we saw in Chapter 7, PACs are usually formed by or associated with interest groups. For the most part, PACs were established as a result of campaign finance regulation. Organizations had to keep records of their campaign finance activity in order to determine their compliance with state laws.

Emphasis in new laws regulating campaign contributions has been on when and where donations can be made. Florida and Wisconsin are among the states that forbid making a contribution in a public building. All states prohibit state employees from soliciting or giving during working hours. The clear intent of these laws is to put as much substantive and symbolic distance as possible between campaign contributions and public decisions.

Another approach is to control spending. The U.S. Supreme Court, in *Buckley v. Valeo* (1976), ruled that, while state legislatures could limit contributions to political campaigns, the First Amendment prohibited limiting spending. The way around this ruling is to provide public funding that carries conditions on spending. In other words, if a candidate accepts public funds, then he or she must agree to the limits on spending. While half of the states have some type of public funding program, most of these programs have little money to offer candidates and there is little incentive to take the money and agree to the limits. Through the direct initiative process, Maine in 1996 and Arizona in 1998 adopted the most effective programs. They are well funded, and there is a provision that if one candidate accepts the public funds and his or her opponent does not, the publicly funded candidate will receive funds to match whatever is spent by the opponent. This provided a strong incentive for all candidates to accept the public funds—and the limits on spending.[30] In 2011, however, the U.S. Supreme Court in *Arizona Free Enterprise Club v. Bennett* ruled that it was unconstitutional to use public funds to match private spending. The 5–4 decision reasoned that this policy had the effect of limiting free speech in campaigns.

Two major loopholes frustrate efforts to regulate campaign financing. One is contained in the federal legislation passed in 2002. While there are limits on what can be contributed to candidates for federal offices and to the national political parties, there are no limits on what can be given to state parties. Since the federal law took effect following the 2002 elections, money has been channeled through state organizations rather than staying within the new limits. State parties then spend to help candidates for federal as well as state offices. Money that is channeled through political parties and is unregulated is referred to as **soft money**. In contrast, **hard money** is money that is regulated, either by contribution limits or by spending limits.

Another loophole is that, while states set limits on what can be contributed to specific candidates, they have no limits on what can be given to campaign committees run by legislative leaders. This allows those in leadership positions to generate huge sums of cash and then to allocate that money to candidates whom they wish to help. As pointed out earlier, this loophole for spending has the effect of enhancing the power of leaders because winning candidates will be beholden to leaders who helped them fund their campaign.

INDEPENDENT EXPENDITURES

One of the most difficult areas to regulate is the way an individual or an organization that is independent of the candidate's campaign spends money. Instead of writing a check to your favorite candidate's campaign committee, for example, you could buy a newspaper ad urging readers to support your candidate. That expenditure would not be counted as a campaign contribution. Your action, it should be clear, would have to be entirely independent of the campaign. Staffers working in the campaign could not help design the ad or even suggest where and when it should appear. Your action would be regarded as an independent expression of your beliefs and therefore protected by the First Amendment of the U.S. Constitution.

Such independent expenditures can subvert the intent of campaign finance regulation. When Senators John McCain and Russ Feingold successfully shepherded a campaign

---

soft money Unregulated funds collected and spent by political parties.
hard money Regulated funds collected and spent by candidates.

finance bill through Congress that would limit the ability of political parties to solicit and spend money on behalf of candidates, the Federal Election Commission allowed, in Section 527 of its rules, for individuals and organizations to continue to act independently of campaigns and express support or opposition to particular candidates. So-called 527 organizations emerged and effectively compromised the intent of the McCain–Feingold legislation. The *Citizens United v. Federal Election Commission* (2010) ruling, discussed in Chapter 7, made it clear that the government cannot place limits on corporate political spending in campaigns when that spending was done independent of campaigns.

The First Amendment also keeps states from tightly regulating spending. In *Buckley v. Valeo* (1976), the U.S. Supreme Court made clear that state governments cannot place limits on how much personal money candidates spend on their own campaigns. This ruling obviously gives independently wealthy candidates an important advantage over people of more modest means.

A state response to independent expenditures in campaigns is to emphasize disclosure of the identity of the individuals and organizations who are attempting to independently influence election outcomes. All states have a disclosure law, although details differ. Forty-two states require electronic filing of campaign contributions to provide easy access to the media and the public.[31] Florida and Iowa specify that those who make independent expenditures notify all affected candidates within 24 hours of obligating the funds. This allows candidates to respond in a timely manner, without abridging rights of free expression.

ISSUE ADS

Another challenge for those who seek to control spending in campaigns and to reduce the importance of money in elections is the problem of **issue ads**. There is a First Amendment protection for those who run issue ads. Issue advertising urges an audience to support or to oppose a particular candidate but does not explicitly ask someone to vote for or against a candidate. Typically, the ads urge people to call or to write to the candidate to express support or opposition for what they have done or what they stand for. Courts have ruled that, despite the obvious message of the ad, as long as there is no explicit plea to vote a certain way, individuals and groups may run issue ads and not have that count toward contribution limits to a campaign.

TERM LIMITS

Advocates of limiting the terms of legislators began a movement in the mid-1980s that had immediate but limited success. Proponents argued an intuitive logic that a regular turnover of elected officials was good for representation and for fresh ideas. Those opposing change had to defend an existing, unpopular institution and the general virtues of continuity and seniority.[32] The specific targets of term limit advocates were primarily Democrats who

---

issue ads Campaign advertisements sponsored by someone other than the candidates that are designed to influence voters but do not explicitly advocate voting for or against anyone. These ads are not covered by campaign finance regulations.

maintained control over the House of Representatives in Washington, D.C. Ironically, the primary impact of term limitations is on state governments, not the federal government. In May 1995, the U.S. Supreme Court ruled that states do not have the authority to limit terms of U.S. Congress members.[33]

As of 2011, a total of 15 states have measures limiting the terms of legislators. Proposals to limit terms have been successful in states that have the direct initiative (discussed in Chapter 6). In four states—Massachusetts, Oregon, Washington, and Wyoming—initiatives enacted term limits, but state supreme courts invalidated the results. California's initiative successfully withstood a challenge in federal courts. Idaho and Utah passed initiatives to limit legislative terms, but the legislatures in these states then repealed these laws. Table 8.2 lists the states that have adopted term limits for their elected officials. In general, states have selected from two alternatives: eight years for all officials, or six years for representatives and eight years for others.

When gubernatorial terms were limited to two years and incumbents were prohibited from succeeding themselves, the intent was clearly to weaken that position. Chapter 10 includes a discussion of whether legislative leaders or the legislature itself is likely to be weakened. Besides the concern about the institutional capacity of the legislature, there is the issue of party control. The fact that incumbents cannot or will not run for reelection does not necessarily determine whether their replacement will be a Republican or a Democrat. If a constituency traditionally votes for a particular party, this voting pattern may continue, term limits notwithstanding. Given the prevalence of candidate-centered campaigns, much may depend on the specific candidates in the race.

Table 8.2   Term Limits for Elected Officials in State Government, in Years

State	Senate	House	Executive
Arizona	8	8	8
Arkansas	8	6	8
California	8	6	8
Colorado	8	8	8
Florida	8	8	8
Louisiana	12	12	8
Maine	8	8	No limits
Michigan	8	6	8
Missouri	8	8	No limits
Montana	8	8	8
Nebraska	8	n/a	8
Nevada	12	12	8
Ohio	8	8	8
Oklahoma	12	12	No limits
South Dakota	8	8	8

Source: National Conference of State Legislatures, www.ncsl.org/Default.aspx?TabId=14844. Accessed July 11, 2011.

THE ELECTION

States regulate the election process, subject to some basic rules in the U.S. Constitution and in federal law. The federal rules, for example, provide the right to vote to all citizens who are at least 18 years old, regardless of gender or ethnicity. States, however, determine how eligible voters register so they can actually cast a ballot. All states have residency requirements, but the mandated period of residency ranges from 10 days to 6 months. In some states, it is necessary for someone to go to city hall or a courthouse to register to vote, while others allow individuals to get a form and then to go door to door in a neighborhood or college dormitory and register voters. The most open states allow people to register to vote at a polling place on Election Day, just prior to casting their ballot. The various patterns of requirements and processes affect the poor, disabled, and transient in different ways. Some states require photo identification to register, and others require voters to provide photo identification when they cast their ballots. Democrats have objected to this practice, fearing that the photo identification requirement would deter some elderly, poor, and minority groups from voting. Republicans counter that they are concerned about ensuring the integrity of the electoral process. The evidence of either voter suppression or voter fraud is negligible. In 2008, the U.S. Supreme Court ruled in *Crawford v. Marion County Election Board*—a challenge to Indiana's law—that, in the absence of evidence of voter suppression linked to the photo identification requirement, state legislatures were free to adopt whatever policy they determined was best for their state. The Missouri Supreme Court, on the other hand, invalidated that state's photo identification law because it was persuaded that certain demographic groups were indeed likely to vote in fewer numbers.

The federal government has set the second Tuesday in November in even-numbered years as Election Day for federal offices. States have free rein in setting the dates for state and local offices and for presidential primaries. A federal law requires that there be at least a two-month period between a state's presidential primary and the general federal Election Day so that ballots can be printed and sent to military personnel stationed abroad.

State and local governments are responsible for how ballots are cast and counted. Studies have demonstrated that state election administration practices are far more serious in disenfranchising voters than fraud or efforts to prevent fraud.[34] The importance of how states design ballots and administer balloting became dramatically evident in the presidential election of 2000. Al Gore won the popular vote nationally, but for six weeks after the election it was unclear whether he or George W. Bush won the Electoral College vote—which, of course, is the vote that determines who is president. The uncertainty was due to problems with the way Florida counted ballots. The two candidates were in a virtual tie in Florida, but thousands of ballots were not counted because of malfunctions with voting machines, confusing formats in the ballots themselves, and controversial challenges to the registration of large numbers of African American voters in the Miami area. (Note that the issue was not fraud; the problems were technical.) Most of the problems occurred in heavily Democratic areas, and so the suspicion was that, if the disqualified ballots and voters had been counted, Al Gore would have won Florida and a majority of the Electoral College votes. The U.S. Supreme Court ruled, however, that the inconsistencies in how the various counties in Florida formatted and counted ballots were such that it was impractical to count the disputed ballots, thus making George W. Bush the winner. Both state and federal lawmakers—including supporters of Gore and Bush—were prompted to consider measures to standardize the balloting process among and within states. In 2002, Congress passed the Help America Vote Act, which provides some funding to states that comply with federal standards for voting procedures and technology.

PARTY COMPETITION

The Democratic Party has continuously had more strength in state and local governments than has the Republican Party. Looking at the country as a whole, Democrats won more than 60 percent of all state legislative seats in every election from 1905 to 1990 except for two (1966 and 1968). In part, this is because of the Democrats' traditional dominance in the South. Dramatic growth of the Republican Party in Southern states in the 1990s and early 2000s is making two-party competition the model throughout most of the country.

Elections since 1994 provide some evidence that the Republican Party might be acquiring significant, long-term strength that will enhance party competition and perhaps lead to stable Republican dominance in some states. Republicans have notched impressive victories throughout the country for federal and state offices. The result was to seize control of the U.S. Senate and House of Representatives; to win gubernatorial contests in populous states like New York, Texas, California, Illinois, Florida, and Pennsylvania; and to secure the majority in more state legislative chambers than ever before captured by the Republican Party.

In 1994, in state assemblies or houses across the country, Republicans won 362 seats away from Democrats. Democrats took seats that were held by Republicans in only eight cases. The pattern was similar in state senate races, where Republicans won 110 seats that had

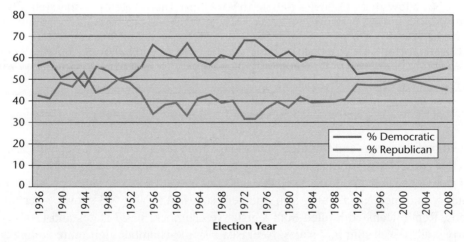

Figure 8.2 Democratic Share of Total State Legislative Seats.

Source: National Conference of State Legislatures, www.ncsl.org/programs/legman/elect/demshare.htm.

DEBATING THE ISSUES

Should we all vote the same way?

George W. Bush won the presidency in 2000 on a technicality. Al Gore won the popular vote nationally and might have won the Electoral College if Florida had not disqualified thousands of votes because of problems with voting machines in heavily Democratic counties. In addition, in West Palm Beach County, many voters argued that they meant to vote for Al Gore but, because of a confusing butterfly ballot format, they think that they voted for Pat Buchanan, the Reform Party candidate. The lingering concerns and charges surrounding the balloting in Florida prompt suggestions about the role of states in determining the way in which voters cast their ballots.

Should states allow counties to determine whether they will use paper ballots, voting machines, computers, or something different? The lesson from the Florida experience would be that there should be consistency throughout the state. The people who work at polling places verifying that someone is eligible to vote and operating the balloting system are volunteers. States should design voting operations so that these people, with a minimum amount of training, can do their job flawlessly and smoothly. The procedures to confirm that someone is eligible to vote should not be cumbersome, and they should not require forms of identification that put at a disadvantage people who don't have or drive cars or don't have other needs for a license with a photo. The process needs to be open.

An argument against single systems for the state might be costs. Machines and technology cost money, and these machines are used only once every two years in most communities. A sophisticated system might be necessary in a location where there are likely to be many voters, but why use such a system in rural areas and small towns where relatively few people will vote? This would be a classic case of waste and overkill.

It is important that procedures are in place to verify that someone is eligible to vote and effectively stop fraud. People who do not have identification should not be allowed to vote. To allow this is to invite people to vote more than once by simply going to different polling places. It is little to ask those who want to vote to plan ahead and meet requirements.

How important is it to reduce or eliminate the error rate in balloting? Is it more important to combat potential voter fraud or to make it easy for everyone to vote? How would you approach these issues?

been held by Democrats and Democrats took only three seats away from Republicans. While Democrats in the 1996 elections recovered some of their losses and had a net gain of control in four state legislative chambers, Republicans continued to show strong support throughout the country and increasing strength in Southern states. As Table 8.3 shows, after the 2010 elections, Republicans controlled both legislative chambers in 27 states and Democrats in 15. Party control was split in 7 states. Nebraska's single-chamber legislature is nonpartisan. Another way of viewing the results of the 2010 elections is that of the 7,382 total seats in state legislatures, Republicans occupy 3,944, Democrats 3,356, and independents or other parties

Table 8.3 Party Control of Gubernatorial Offices and State Legislatures after the November 2010 Elections

	Governor	House	Senate
Alabama	GOP	GOP	GOP
Alaska	GOP	GOP	tie
Arizona	GOP	GOP	GOP
Arkansas	GOP	Dem	Dem
California	Dem	Dem	Dem
Colorado	Dem	GOP	Dem
Connecticut	Dem	Dem	Dem
Delaware	Dem	Dem	Dem
Florida	GOP	GOP	GOP
Georgia	GOP	GOP	GOP
Hawaii	Dem	Dem	Dem
Idaho	GOP	GOP	GOP
Illinois	Dem	Dem	Dem
Indiana	GOP	GOP	GOP
Iowa	GOP	GOP	Dem
Kansas	GOP	GOP	GOP
Kentucky	Dem	Dem	GOP
Louisiana	GOP	GOP	GOP
Maine	GOP	GOP	GOP
Maryland	Dem	Dem	Dem
Massachusetts	Dem	Dem	Dem
Michigan	GOP	GOP	GOP
Minnesota	Dem	GOP	GOP
Mississippi	GOP	GOP	GOP
Missouri	Dem	GOP	GOP
Montana	Dem	GOP	GOP
Nebraska	GOP	Unicameral and nonpartisan	
Nevada	GOP	Dem	Dem
New Hampshire	Dem	GOP	GOP
New Jersey	GOP	Dem	Dem
New Mexico	GOP	Dem	Dem
New York	Dem	Dem	GOP
North Carolina	Dem	GOP	GOP
North Dakota	GOP	GOP	GOP
Ohio	GOP	GOP	GOP
Oklahoma	GOP	GOP	GOP
Oregon	Dem	Tie	Dem
Pennsylvania	GOP	GOP	GOP
Rhode Island	Independent	Dem	Dem
South Carolina	GOP	GOP	GOP
South Dakota	GOP	GOP	GOP

(continued)

Table 8.3	Party Control of Gubernatorial Offices and State Legislatures after the November 2010 Elections (*continued*)		
	Governor	**House**	**Senate**
Tennessee	GOP	GOP	GOP
Texas	GOP	GOP	GOP
Utah	GOP	GOP	GOP
Vermont	Dem	Dem	Dem
Virginia	GOP	GOP	Dem
Washington	Dem	Dem	Dem
West Virginia	Dem	Dem	Dem
Wisconsin	GOP	GOP	GOP
Wyoming	GOP	GOP	GOP

Dem = Democrat; GOP = Republican.

the remaining 82. Also, as of 2011, there are 29 Republican governors and 20 Democrats. Lincoln Chafee, the governor of Rhode Island, is an Independent.

One reason for Republican successes is that voters in the South, who had been voting for conservative Democrats, began voting for conservative Republicans. Southerners have supported Republican presidential candidates since the Democratic Party began asserting leadership for civil rights following World War II. Alignment with Republicans in contests for state and congressional positions, however, has been much slower and more the exception than the rule. Southerners are part of the majority within the Republican Party. The two major parties increasingly represent more polarized ideological differences.

SUMMARY AND CONCLUSIONS

Elections present an obvious opportunity for citizens, individually and in groups, to influence their own governance. Those seeking public office must secure votes. Especially for state and local offices, this means actively meeting and conversing with people face to face. The victorious candidate for the school board, city council, or state legislature is frequently the one who spent the most time and energy going door to door and participating in community events. Voters can converse and question. They can base their decisions on very direct evidence.

Elections are candidate-centered. Political parties in the United States play an important role in the electoral process, but they are not "responsible" parties, shaping and maintaining an ideological stance. The Republican and Democratic parties differ on policies and have different traditional bases of support, but this does not translate into litmus tests for members or candidates. Particularly since the demise of political machines, parties use a fairly open process for nominating candidates. Party support for those nominated consists of the loyalty of a rather small portion of the electorate. Candidates organize and run their own campaigns, determining their own stance on issues and the extent to which they will identify with the party as an organization.

The longevity and stability of the two major parties is due, in part, to the lack of demands made by the parties and the looseness of their structures. State laws defining the nomination process and regulating political parties also contribute to the longevity.

Elections are not fully what we like to think of as democracy. Most people don't vote in state and local elections. Candidates run negative attacks on their opponents and generate disgust among the voters. Campaigns are expensive, prompting concern about the need for and thus the influence of money.

Regardless of the imperfections, elections are important individual and community experiences. Close elections can provide drama. The outcomes can be critical. This is the way we select individuals for important offices and also the way we determine the structure and control of our institutions. The next chapters discuss the major institutions of state and local governments.

Discussion Questions

1. Explain the differences between responsible parties and electoral parties. To what extent does each model apply to political parties in the United States?

2. Compare and contrast three systems for getting party nominees on a ballot. What is the system in your state? Would you suggest any changes?

3. From the perspective of someone running for an elective office, what is the importance of a political party? As a candidate, how would you select a party to join? What might you expect from the party, and what would the party expect from you?

4. Negative campaigning seems to be effective in influencing voter behavior. Does this approach pose any threat to democratic principles or processes? Should anything be done to curb negative campaigning?

5. Describe ways in which eager and wealthy contributors can avoid the restrictions of campaign finance laws. Do these techniques suggest other approaches toward the regulation of campaign finance, or should there be deregulation altogether?

6. What, if any, differences in strategy would you expect among separate campaigns for a nonpartisan city council seat, a partisan state legislative seat, and a governor? What strategies would be used in all three races?

Glossary

candidate-centered organizations 198
closed primary 201
electoral party 193
factions 199
hard money 207

issue ads 208
material incentives 198
negative campaigning 204
nonpartisan election 194
open primary 201
purposive incentives 198

responsible party 192
single primary or **top-two primary** 201
soft money 207
solidary incentives 198
Tea Party 192

Endnotes

1. Austin Ranney, *The Doctrine of Responsible Party Government* (Urbana: University of Illinois Press, 1962), 8–22.

2. Scott Rasmussen and Doug Schoen, *Mad As Hell: How the Tea Party Movement Is Fundamentally Remaking Our Two-Party System* (New York: HarperCollins, 2010); Kate Zernike, *Boiling Mad: Inside the Tea Party* (New York: Henry Holt, 2010).

3. V. O. Key Jr., *Southern Politics in State and Nation* (New York: Alfred A. Knopf, 1949).

4. Sarah McCally Morehouse, *State Politics, Parties and Policy* (New York: Holt, Rinehart and Winston, 1980), 45–94.

5. William M. Kraus, *Let the People Decide* (Aurora, Ill.: Caroline House, 1982), 27.

6. Bruce M. Stave, ed., *Urban Bosses, Machines, and Progressive Reformers* (Lexington, Mass.: D.C. Heath, 1972); Milton L. Rakove, *Don't Make No Waves—Don't Back No Losers: An Insider's Analysis of the Daley Machine* (Bloomington: Indiana University Press, 1975); V. O. Key Jr., *Politics, Parties and Pressure Groups*, 5th ed. (New York: Crowell, 1964).

7. Stave, *Urban Bosses, Machines, and Progressive Reformers*, 115–147.

8. Sidney Verba and Norman H. Nie, *Participation in America: Social Democracy and Social Equity* (New York: Harper & Row, 1972), 69–71.

9. *Eu v. San Francisco County Democratic Central Committee*, et al., 103 L. Ed. 2nd 271 (1989). See also Clifton McCleskey, "Parties at the Bar: Equal Protection, Freedom of Association, and the Rights of Political Organizations," *Journal of Politics* 46 (1984), 346–368.

10. Advisory Commission on Intergovernmental Relations, *The Transformation in American Politics* (Washington, D.C.: ACIR, 1986), 95–162. See also Timothy Conlan, Ann Martino, and Robert Dilger, "State Parties in the 1980s,"*Intergovernmental Perspective* 10 (1984), 6–13.

11. Key, *Politics, Parties and Pressure Groups*, 316.

12. Malcolm E. Jewell and David M. Olson, *Political Parties and Elections in American States*, 3d ed. (Chicago, Ill.: Dorsey Press, 1988), 48.

13. Gary L. Rose, *Connecticut at the Crossroads* (New York: University Press of America, 1992), 8–10.

14. Dennis W. Johnson, Campaigning in the Twenty-First Century. A Whole New Ballgame? (New York: Routledge, 2011); Dennis W. Johnson, *No Place for Amateurs: How Political Consultants Are Reshaping American Democracy* (New York: Routledge, 2001).

15. Robert Salisbury, "An Exchange Theory of Interest Groups," *Midwest Journal of Political Science* 13 (February 1969), 1–32.

16. Jewell and Olson, *Political Parties and Elections in American States*, 82–84.

17. Key, *Southern Politics in State and Nation*.

18. Dewey W. Grantham, *The South in Modern America* (New York: HarperCollins, 1994), 281–331.

19. Johnson, *No Place for Amateurs*.

20. Ibid., 3–86.

21. Advisory Commission on Intergovernmental Relations, *The Transformation in American Politics*, 161–206; Advisory Commission on Intergovernmental Relations, "Comparisons of Campaign Commercials," *National Journal* (November 1, 1986), 2610–2614.

22. http://people-press.org/reports/display.php3?ReportID=248.

23. Johnson, *No Place for Amateurs*, 15–34; Kathleen Hall Jamieson, *Everything You Think You Know about Politics . . . And Why You're Wrong* (New York: Pegasus Books, 2000), 49–54.

24. Cited in Advisory Commission on Intergovernmental Relations, "Comparisons of Campaign Commercials," 2621.

25. Larry Sabato, ed., *Campaigns and Elections: A Reader in Modern American Politics* (Glenview, Ill.: Scott, Foresman, 1989).

26. Keon S. Chi, "Financing State and Local Elections: Trends and Issues," *The Book of the States, 1992–1993* (Lexington, Ky.: Council of State Governments, 1994), 285.

27. The National Institute on Money in State Politics posts contributions by state and by types of contributors on its website: www. followthemoney.org.

28. Ruth Jones and Anne Hopkins, "State Campaign Fund Raising: Targets and Response," *Journal of Politics* 47 (1985), 433–449.

29. For details, go to www.campaignfinance.org and follow the links.

30. Ronald D. Michaelson, "Trends in State Campaign Financing," *The Book of the States 2003* (Lexington, Ky.: The Council of State Governments, 2003), 270–280.

31. University of California at Los Angeles Law School, www.campaigndisclosure.org.

32. Gerald Benjamin and Michael J. Malin, eds., *Limiting Legislative Terms* (Washington, D.C.: Congressional Quarterly Press, 1992).

33. *Thornton v. Arkansas* (1995).

34. R. Michael Alvarez and Thad E. Hall, "Controlling Democracy: The Principal-Agent Problems in Electoral Administration," *Policy Studies Journal* 34, no. 4 (2006); and Richard L. Hasen, "Beyond the Margin of Litigation: Reforming U.S. Election Administration to Avoid Electoral Meltdown," *Washington and Lee Law Review* 26, no. 4 (2005).

CHAPTER 9

Governors

LEARNING OBJECTIVES

- Appreciate the evolution of the office of governor from an institution of weakness to one of strength.
- Identify the formal and informal sources of gubernatorial power.
- Understand the key role a governor plays in establishing the policy agenda for state government.
- Know the interdependence between governors and legislatures, courts, and administrative agencies.

It seemed impossible. South Carolina, the state where the Civil War began and a bulwark of Southern conservative political culture, broke ground in 2010 when voters put Nikki Randhawa Haley in the governor's office. She is the daughter of immigrants from India and is the nation's youngest governor. In 2004, Ms. Haley beat the longest serving state legislator in the Republican Party primary and went on to win in the general election. She quickly became known as a strident and articulate spokesperson for conservative fiscal and social issues. Her gubernatorial race got strong backing from the Tea Party movement.

As governor, Nikki Haley has emerged as a strong critic of President Barak Obama and the federal government generally. Like other governors, she has tried to cut state government spending and to push for economic growth. She was incensed when the National Labor Relations Board sued Boeing for opening an assembly plant in South Carolina in what appeared to be retaliation against union workers in the state of Washington who went on strike in 2008. Although she has won general praise from state legislators, they rejected her leadership in shaping the state's $6 billion general fund budget, overriding most of her vetoes. The state's Supreme Court sided with the legislature to limit her authority when she tried to force the State Senate back into session to act on an administrative reform bill she proposed. Legislators also opposed her appointment of one of her campaign contributors to the University of South Carolina board of trustees. Some have expressed concern about her style, which they refer to as that of a scolding schoolmarm. Despite these setbacks, Governor Haley retains popular support and is frequently mentioned as a potential candidate for vice president.[1]

Consider the following job vacancy announcement:

> WANTED: Chief Executive Officer. Complex organization of 55,000 employees; annual operating budget exceeding $25 billion. Wide diversity of responsibilities, including policy leadership; public relations and negotiations; and managerial direction over programs in education, criminal justice, social welfare, health, corrections, highway construction, occupational licensing, environmental protection and regulation, agriculture, and economic development. Travel and long hours. Job security for four-year term only. Annual salary: $130,000—not negotiable.

No sane person would apply. The complexity and demands of the job are not at all commensurate with either the job security or the salary. Governors like Nikki Haley would add to this job advertisement that the state's chief executive officer has to fulfill the diverse responsibilities with limited authority. The legislature and courts have to be on board with most major changes.

Someone with aspirations to be a chief executive officer would be advised to forget about being governor and instead pursue such a position in, for example, a midsize insurance company. In such an enterprise, the number of employees might be half that listed above, the scope of functions would be singular (insurance), the authority more substantial, and the salary would be two to three times that listed in the announcement. In 2011, the average salary earned by governors declined because of budget problems. The average was $130,595 and ranged from $70,000 a year in Maine to $179,000 in New York.[2]

Despite the high job demands and relatively low pay, individuals and groups spend millions of dollars and hundreds of hours fighting to fill one of the 50 jobs in the country described in the ad. Clearly these efforts do not reflect widespread insanity. Despite the unattractive features of the governorship, people of character and ability have sought the office. Their motivations vary from a sincere commitment to public service to a lust for power and prestige. Whatever the array of intentions, states have, with few exceptions, been fortunate that able men and women usually have been available to occupy gubernatorial offices.[3]

Being the governor of a state is, for some, not just an end in itself but a step toward other offices. Past and current governors include some of our country's most colorful and famous people, many of whom have served—or will serve—as congressional members, ambassadors, and presidents.

Governors and the office of governor are considerably more accessible to individuals than the president of the United States. Nonetheless, few constituents have meaningful conversations with a governor. If an ordinary citizen meets face to face with a governor, the interaction is likely to be little more than a handshake or an exchange of brief greetings. The role of governor includes attending ceremonial responsibilities and campaign or campaign-like activities. Governors do not directly provide services to or enforce regulations. These elected chief executives of state governments, however, have important and direct effects on the capacities and the discretion of public agencies that deal with individuals. Moreover, governors can affect citizens' confidence in government. Individuals who consider their governor to be honest, dedicated, and competent are likely to be more supportive of the government. Governors who are crooks in their personal or public lives feed into the cynicism and negative stereotypes of politicians.

The governor is usually the most visible official in state government and in some ways personifies his or her respective jurisdiction. This chapter will first discuss the institutional aspects of the governorship and then return to the individuals who are and have been governors.

HISTORICAL DEVELOPMENTS

A legacy of America's colonial period is a guarded mistrust of governors. England had structured its empire so that governors not only represented the Crown but also ruled their respective territories with substantial autonomy. The discontent that led colonists to seek independence from England was focused primarily on governors, and governors figured prominently in the struggles that led to independence. Thus, in the aftermath of revolt, few were inclined to endow the office of the governor with much power.

The constitutions of the first states made legislatures the dominant institution. Only four of the thirteen original states directly elected their governors. Legislatures in the other nine states selected the governors. Budgets and personnel appointments were decided by the legislatures. Initially, only South Carolina, New York, and Massachusetts gave their governors the right to veto legislation—and South Carolina revoked that power after a few years. Governors did little other than represent their states in ceremonial roles.

With Jacksonian democracy and the enfranchisement of all white men, states provided for the direct popular election of their governors. This provided governors with their own base of power, independent from state legislators. It did not, however, lead inexorably to a strengthening of the office. Other events and concerns placed important constraints on state chief executives:

- In an attempt to keep Southern political leaders weak after the Civil War, the federal government insisted that postwar constitutions prohibit governors in the states of the former Confederacy from succeeding themselves in office. In addition, gubernatorial terms were limited to two years.
- At the beginning of the twentieth century, the Progressive movement consciously sought to establish weak governors. As part of the effort to destroy political machines, Progressives advocated for the direct election of state agency heads and the establishment of civil service systems rather than risk patronage appointments by governors. They also established part-time citizen boards and commissions to direct state executive and regulatory bodies. The direct democracy instruments, like the initiative and referendum, enabled voters to decide public policy without going through governors and legislatures.
- With the efforts of Progressives to locate more power in the people rather than in the institutions of government or the party machines, the country simultaneously confronted the challenges of rapid urbanization, industrialization, international strife, and westward expansion. These challenges required responses that presupposed effective managerial leadership. The country looked to Washington, not to state capitols, for that leadership.

After the Great Depression, the New Deal, and major wars, state governments were increasingly regarded as irrelevant or even as impediments to effective problem solving. It appeared that governors would simply head federal administrative units rather than direct governments with meaningful discretion and authority.[4] In the 1970s, however, when political sentiment against the size and scope of the federal government emerged, state governments generally, and governors specifically, strengthened in status and power. Remember the general effects of the *Baker v. Carr* (1962) decision, making state governments more representative, more relevant, and more attractive to people who are serious about shaping good public policies. The legacy of distrust of powerful executives is still apparent, but it is tempered by the requirements for effective leadership and management.

FORMAL POWERS

Term of Office

A two-year term almost guarantees a weak chief executive. By the time an individual gets acquainted with the formal and informal rules for getting something done, the term is almost over or it is time to run for reelection. Short terms, especially when combined with a prohibition keeping a governor from running for reelection, is a recipe for a weak office. Common to most of the initial constitutions of the first 13 states was a provision that governors serve for only one year and not be allowed to run for reelection. As mentioned, states of the former Confederacy had to accept two-year terms and a prohibition against reelection. These provisions were conscious attempts to prevent a strong, monarchical executive.

As a way of providing for managerial continuity and allowing a governor to provide effective direction, states moved toward four-year terms and removed some of the limitations on reelections. Table 9.1 shows the changes that have taken place since 1960. New Hampshire and Vermont are the only states that still have two-year terms. Thirty-five states have a limit of two four-year terms. Twelve have four-year terms and no prohibitions on reelection. Virginia has a four-year term, and it is the only state that does not allow

Table 9.1 State Provisions for Gubernatorial Terms of Office

	1960	2008
Four Years		
No limits on reelections	12	12
Two consecutive terms	7	35
No consecutive terms allowed	15	1
Two Years		
No limits on reelections	14	2
One reelection allowed	2	0

Source: Adapted from *The Book of the States, 1959–1960* (Lexington, Ky.: Council of State Governments, 1959 and 2010, pp. 21–22, 183–184.).

a governor to serve consecutive terms. Virginia and sixteen other states with term limits allow an individual to serve again after a one-term hiatus.

Appointment Powers

A corollary to the four-year term is the opportunity for governors to appoint their own people to head major state agencies. It makes little sense to acknowledge the need for chief executives who can exert meaningful managerial leadership and then to keep them from assembling their own team of managers and policymakers. On the other hand, most would agree that if governors have only two-year terms, they should not have full discretion to hire and fire all agency heads. To allow for wholesale changes in top executive leadership every other year would foster too much instability throughout state government. Some of the people most qualified for agency head positions would not be interested in a job with such short tenure. In other words, the combination of a four-year term and the authority to appoint the heads of major agencies is a significant step toward strengthening governors and the executive branch. This reform is often called the establishment of cabinet government.

The term **cabinet government** is used to refer to situations in which agency heads serve at the pleasure of the governor. This usage differs from its original meaning in Europe. There, agency heads are also current legislators from the majority party or the ruling coalition in a parliament. European democracies have a tradition of collective decision making and collective responsibility for running government. Cabinets in state governments, however, rarely make decisions together and often do not meet on a regular basis. When they do meet, it is often done as a media event. Nonetheless, the opportunity for governors to determine who heads state agencies is important for their establishment of policy priorities and managerial styles.

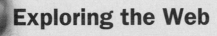

Exploring the Web

What are the resources of a governor's office?

What are the characteristics of the governor's office in your state? What is the term of office? How much is the governor paid? What kind of staff does he or she direct? Do you think the resources available to your governor are adequate?

You can get information on your governor by going to the following websites:

- The website of your state government (see the directions in the box on page 150)
- The National Governors Association at *www.nga.org*
- The Council of State Governments at *www.csg.org*

---

cabinet government As applied to state governments, this term refers to agency heads who are appointed by and serve at the pleasure of the governor.

Executive branch reorganizations since the 1960s have included providing governors with more cabinet positions to fill. These reorganizations also typically consolidate many small agencies into larger departments, thus allowing for more central and coherent executive direction.[5] Still, small independent agencies continue to be part of the organizational landscape, and less than a majority of state agency heads are gubernatorial appointments. Legislative leaders, boards, commissions, and even some lieutenant governors have direct authority to determine leaders of state agencies, and they do not have to involve governors in their decisions.[6]

As shown in Table 9.2, the positions of attorney general, secretary of state, treasurer, and auditor are usually elected. The most significant of these positions is that of attorney general. The attorney general provides legal advice to state government, represents the state in court, and manages an agency that includes prosecuting attorneys and criminal investigators. The 43 states that elect their attorney general allow this official to act independently of the governor. It is not unusual, in fact, for an attorney general to be a candidate running against an incumbent governor. In Illinois, West Virginia, and Wisconsin, attorneys general have even sued governors.

The least significant of the independently elected offices is that of state treasurer. At a time when receiving revenue and sending payments was done by hand, it was important to have someone with integrity and good accounting skills as a treasurer for state government. Now this work is computerized, and state treasurers have little substantive work to do.

The secretary of state position once had a broad range of administrative responsibilities, such as purchasing, contracting, and maintaining state facilities. These functions are now assigned to administrative agencies in state governments. Alaska, Hawaii, and Utah do not have a secretary of state. In 39 of the states, the secretary of state is responsible for running elections—a job that was routine and low-profile until the problems in Florida and Ohio in the 2000 and 2004 presidential contests, respectively. Concerns about electronic voting, voter fraud, and access to the balloting process have enhanced the visibility and importance of this office in those states where duties include election administration.[7]

Gubernatorial appointment powers also extend to the judiciary. State courts are the subject of Chapter 13, and, as we explain there, governors appoint judges in only three states. They play a key but limited role in the selection of judges in 24 states under a hybrid system known as the merit plan or the Missouri plan, which combines appointment and election (see Table 13.4). Even when judges are elected, however, governors have authority to appoint someone when judges leave the bench before their term expires. This is a very consequential role for governors because incumbent judges running for reelection almost always win.

Budget and Fiscal Management

Until the 1920s, the common pattern in state governments was for the legislature to have the responsibility of initiating a budget proposal, passing it, and submitting it to the governor for approval. Governors played only an informal role in establishing the policies and priorities reflected in the budget. Instead, they were in the position of reacting to legislative deliberations.

Table 9.2 Elected State Officials

	Secretary of State	Attorney General	Treasurer	Auditor	Comptroller	Education	Agriculture	Labor	Insurance	Other (Number)
Alabama	X	X	X	X			X			2
Alaska										2
Arizona	X	X	X			X				2
Arkansas	X	X	X	X						1
California	X	X	X		X	X				1
Colorado	X	X	X							2
Connecticut	X	X	X		X					
Delaware				X					X	
Florida		X	X		X	X	X			
Georgia	X	X			X	X	X	X		1
Hawaii										
Idaho	X	X	X	X	X					1
Illinois	X	X	X		X					
Indiana	X	X	X	X		X				
Iowa	X	X	X	X			X			
Kansas	X	X	X						X	1
Kentucky	X	X	X	X		X	X			1
Louisiana	X	X	X				X		X	2
Maine										
Maryland		X			X					
Massachusetts	X	X	X	X						1
Michigan	X	X								2
Minnesota	X	X	X	X						
Mississippi	X	X	X	X			X		X	2
Missouri	X	X	X	X						
Montana	X	X		X		X				1

(continued)

Table 9.2 Elected State Officials (*continued*)

	Secretary of State	Attorney General	Treasurer	Auditor	Comptroller	Education	Agriculture	Labor	Insurance	Other (Number)
Nebraska	X	X	X	X						3
Nevada	X	X	X		X					2
New Hampshire										1
New Jersey										
New Mexico	X	X	X	X						3
New York		X			X					
North Carolina	X	X	X	X		X	X	X	X	
North Dakota	X	X	X	X		X	X	X	X	2
Ohio	X	X	X	X						
Oklahoma		X	X	X		X			X	1
Oregon	X	X	X	X		X		X		1
Pennsylvania		X	X	X						
Rhode Island	X	X	X							
South Carolina	X	X	X	X						1
South Dakota	X	X	X	X						2
Tennessee										1
Texas		X			X		X			2
Utah		X	X	X						1
Vermont	X	X	X	X						
Virginia		X								
Washington	X	X	X	X		X			X	
West Virginia	X	X	X	X			X			1
Wisconsin	X	X	X			X				
Wyoming	X		X	X		X				

Source: Adapted from Council of State Governments, *The Book of States 2011*, 43 (Lexington, Ky.: Council of State Governments, 2011), pp. 179–185.

Since then, all but four states have statutorily defined a central role for the governor in the budget process. Most governors have the upper hand because they formulate and propose a budget to the legislature and then, after legislative approval, can sign or veto what the legislature has done. For those who want funds from the state treasury, the key is getting gubernatorial support.[8] To rely on the legislature is to risk inaction and, even if both houses do agree and do act, to risk gubernatorial veto. The budgetary process was described in Chapter 5. It is important to note the central position of the governor in this essential policy-making process.

Once the legislature and governor pass a budget, it still must be administered. Governors have responsibility for ensuring that funds are spent within established limits and for the purposes outlined in the budget. Governors enjoy important discretion regarding exactly how, where, and when money will be spent. A budget may, for example, include funds for modernizing and expanding state prison facilities. The budget is unlikely to say exactly what modernization involves, however, and may leave it up to the governor to determine which of the state's prisons will be scheduled first. In this situation, a governor might emphasize the construction of training facilities as opposed to solitary confinement cells. Some governors have the flexibility to use the funds to contract with private firms for the care or rehabilitation of prisoners, to send inmates to prisons in other states, or to expand facilities and programs within the state.

Governors are also responsible for federal funds given to states.[9] Although certain rules and regulations must be followed, opportunities exist for creativity and leadership. A governor, sometimes with the assistance of U.S. senators and representatives from his or her state, negotiates with federal agencies to get waivers that allow the state to use federal monies in ways that were not envisioned when federal laws and rules were written. Jobs and projects funded by federal grants are valued resources that can be distributed in ways that support the political and policy agendas of the governor. But federal funds are not always valued. In 2011, newly elected governors in Florida, Ohio, and Wisconsin surprised many by turning back almost $4 billion in federal money for high-speed rail projects. Even though these funds would have provided jobs in a lagging economy, the governors had other priorities and did not want to commit their states to support this mode of transportation after the projects were completed. Similarly, governors opposed to federal health care reforms enacted in 2010 sometimes refused funds to implement the law.

Veto

Like presidents, governors have a **general veto** or **package veto**. A bill passed by the legislature can be rejected in its entirety and thus would not become law. Unlike presidents, most governors also have **line-item veto** authority. This power allows a governor

---

general veto or **package veto** The rejection by a governor of an entire bill that has been passed by the legislature. The bill does not become law unless the veto is overridden by a legislative vote.
line-item veto The rejection by a governor of specific lines, numbers, or words in a bill passed by the legislature. The rejected parts do not become law unless the veto is overridden by a legislative vote.

Governor Jerry Brown of California signs a bill encouraging the use of solar power.

to delete parts of a bill passed by the legislature while signing the rest of the bill into law. Line-item veto authority applies only to bills that contain taxing and spending provisions. The intent is to enable governors to manage state finances so that state budgets are balanced. Governors in all but seven states can use the line-item veto.

The power available in veto authority is substantial. State legislatures can override a veto only with the support of at least two-thirds of the members of each chamber in 40 of the states. Delaware, Illinois, Maryland, North Carolina, and Rhode Island require three-fifths. Alabama, Arkansas, Indiana, Tennessee, and West Virginia require only a majority in each house. Legislatures have overridden only 6 percent of vetoes by governors.[10]

Creative use of the line-item veto can be awe-inspiring. A veto to strike such words as *not* and *whenever* and *with the approval of* from sentences can turn legislative language on its head. Consider the impact of removing any or all of those words and phrases from the following:

> [With the approval of the Board of Regents,] athletic teams of the state university shall [not] participate in postseason competition or tournaments [whenever the graduation rate of student athletes is 10 percent or more lower than the graduation rate of the student-body generally].

A governor's pen could eliminate the role of the Board of Regents from this process. A veto of "not" would establish a policy that penalized student athletes when they did well academically. If the governor vetoed just the "whenever" clause and the provision regarding the Regents, the state would prohibit the university from participating in any postseason athletic competition.

Wisconsin has empowered its governor with a veto that extends beyond the normal use of that term. The state constitutional provision reads:

> Appropriation bills may be approved in whole or in part by the governor, and the part approved shall become law.[11]

Wisconsin governors used this **partial veto** with increasing creativity, including the elimination of letters within words so that the remaining letters made entirely new words. Governor Tommy Thompson (in office from 1987 to 2001) was so creative in using his veto pen that he changed the substance of bills beyond anything ever contemplated by the legislature. Lawmakers cried foul and noted that policies were being enacted without any of the deliberation or public oversight that should be part of the legislative process. In 1993, voters ratified what became known as the Vanna White amendment and added the following to the state constitution:

> In approving an appropriation bill in part, the governor may not create a new word by reject-ing individual letters in the words of the enrolled bill.[12]

Governor Thompson then turned his attention from words to numbers. He vetoed indi-vidual numbers within larger numbers to make new figures, and he actually wrote in num-bers that were not in the document passed by the legislature. He contended that as long as he did not increase spending, he could modify budget allocations by inserting numbers as well as crossing them out. In response to a legal challenge to this interpretation, a majority of justices on the state supreme court supported the governor.

The threat of a veto can be as effective as its actual use. Not surprisingly, there are noticeably more vetoes in states where different political parties control the legislature and the governor's office.[13] Indeed, a detailed study of the use of the partial veto over a 12-year period revealed that governors used this authority more out of concern for partisan conflict and policy choices than for fiscal reasons.[14]

Judicial Powers

To varying degrees, governors have what might be thought of as judicial vetoes. After individuals or corporations are convicted of crimes in court, governors in most states have a wide range of authority in forgiving and forgetting. The most sweeping judicial authority of a governor is the **pardon**, which has the effect of eliminating a conviction and all its penalties. A governor also can **commute** all or part of a sentence. In this case, the convic-tion would still stand, but the individual would not have to serve time in prison.

The distinction between a pardon and a commuted sentence was illustrated in the late 1970s when an individual who wanted a senior government appointment in a Midwestern state misrepresented himself. The state constitution barred convicted felons from senior positions in government. The individual concerned had been convicted of a felony, but at

---

partial veto The rejection by a governor of any part, including parts of specific numbers, in a bill passed by the legislature. The rejected parts do not become law unless the veto is overridden by a legislative vote.

pardon Gubernatorial action to eliminate penalties and convictions applied to individuals by the judicial system.

commute Gubernatorial action that eliminates sentences and penalties but not the record of a conviction.

the time of his conviction the governor took pity and commuted his sentence. This situation was misrepresented as a pardon, and the individual was about to be appointed by a new governor to an agency head position when someone with a good memory spoke up. Although the individual never saw time behind bars because his sentence was commuted, his conviction still stood, and he was ineligible for the appointment.

Governors are also able to grant **paroles**. Individuals who have served part of a sentence can sometimes petition to be released from prison for the remainder. A parole board—usually a three- to five-person committee appointed by the governor—that meets to decide whether to pardon or parole an individual or to commute a sentence, advises governors. Some governors delegate parole authority to these boards and avoid direct involvement. Paroles are granted on the condition that the individual will not engage in certain activities, like associating with specific individuals or carrying a gun. Violation of the conditions of parole typically means a trip back to prison.

For those states that have a death penalty, governors typically have the authority to grant a **reprieve**, which postpones the execution. Reprieves have a time limit, usually 30 days. In dramatic situations that are likely to provide a story for a movie, a reprieve might be granted at the very last minute because of new evidence that the individual did not commit the crime. The reprieve might then be followed by a pardon or a retrial. In 2000, Illinois governor George Ryan imposed a general moratorium on the death penalty after investigations found that 13 death row inmates were wrongfully convicted. In 2011, Illinois abolished capital punishment.

Finally, governors, under the U.S. Constitution, have the authority to **extradite** individuals. This means that a governor determines when someone will be sent, against his or her will, to another state to face charges of committing a crime. While governor of New York, Mario Cuomo was heavily criticized for not exercising his extradition powers when he refused to send someone to a state where the death penalty was in effect. One of the critics was George Pataki, who defeated Governor Cuomo in his bid for reelection in 1994. After he was inaugurated, Governor Pataki ordered the extradition.

The gubernatorial role in the judicial system is very visible and sometimes has generated considerable controversy. Governor John C. Walton of Oklahoma, for example, pardoned 693 prisoners in an 11-month period (November 1922 to October 1923). He was removed from office for doing so and later was convicted for taking bribes from some of those to whom he had given a pardon.[15]

In Texas, Governor James E. Ferguson granted 2,253 pardons between 1915 and 1917. His successor, William P. Hobby, granted 1,518 pardons during his two years in office. Miriam "Ma" Ferguson then took office and outdid her husband by more than 1,500. This prompted Texas to amend its constitution, removing pardoning power from the governor and

---

parole Gubernatorial action—sometimes delegated to a board or agency—to release individuals before they have served full sentences. Paroles are typically conditional upon abiding by certain rules and good behavior while incarcerated.

reprieve Gubernatorial action to temporarily suspend the execution of a sentence, especially the death penalty.

extradition Gubernatorial action to send an individual from the governor's state to another state where the person faces court or correctional action.

placing it in a Board of Pardons and Paroles.[16] The governor, however, was authorized to veto decisions of the board. That worked relatively well until the 1970s, when governors began vetoing paroles at the rate of almost 1,000 per year. A 1983 amendment to the Texas constitution removed the gubernatorial power to veto paroles issued by the board. The Texas case is not typical of other states' parole procedures.

National Governors Association

The National Governors Association (NGA), a supplement to staff resources within a governor's own state, is an organization to which all states belong . It provides the 50 governors with a forum through which to take positions on issues and press the federal government for policies and procedures that the states find advantageous. The NGA also sponsors a series of meetings and symposia in which suggestions are offered for everything from how to manage a smooth transition when assuming office to how to deal with certain policy and political issues. The NGA website is www.nga.org.

Beginning in 1985, under the leadership of Governor Lamar Alexander of Tennessee, who was then the chair of the NGA, the organization adopted a policy of focusing its energies on a different policy issue each year. The initial topic was public education. Governor Alexander directed seven subcommittees and the NGA staff to set goals for policy changes to be adopted by 1991.[17] The substance and the visibility of this concerted effort had considerable impact on education reform throughout the country. Inevitably, governors made modifications to fit their specific state, but they had the NGA model as a common source of ideas and information.

Similarly, when Bill Clinton (as governor of Arkansas) chaired the NGA in 1986–1987, the chief executives of the states focused on economic development and job creation.[18] That report, too, sparked policy initiatives among the states and then served as the basic blueprint of the welfare reform introduced by President Clinton in 1994. The NGA and governors individually use both the substance and the focus of their reports and conferences to lobby federal policymakers. The general move to devolution enhances the significance of this activity. In short, the NGA has become an important resource for governors in their roles as both agenda setters and policymakers.

The governors also associate by party in the National Republican Governors Conference and the National Democratic Governors Conference. While these organizations provide a forum for lobbying and information sharing, they have not had the resources or played the range of roles offered by the NGA.

Lieutenant Governor

The lieutenant governor can be (but rarely is) a resource to a governor. The primary purpose of the position, like that of vice president of the United States, is to provide for orderly succession should governors not be able to complete their term of office. Most of those who have served as a lieutenant governor find it a forgettable experience and a dead-end job. The office tends to be of little significance. The states of Arizona, Maine, New

Hampshire, New Jersey, Oregon, West Virginia, and Wyoming, in fact, do not even have a lieutenant governor. In 25 states, the lieutenant governor presides in the state senate but can vote only to break a tie.

In almost all instances, governors have little, if any, role in the selection of their respective lieutenant governors. Unlike the model in which a presidential candidate selects a vice-presidential running mate, in most states, individuals independently seek a party nomination for lieutenant governor in primaries. In 23 states, voters in the general election must cast their ballot for a governor–lieutenant governor pair on the same party ticket, but 20 states still have separate ballots. Occasionally the governor and lieutenant governor are from different parties. Even when they are of the same party, conflict is not uncommon.

There are, of course, situations in which the governor and lieutenant governor work well together. The governor accepts advice from the lieutenant governor and is comfortable assigning tasks to her or him. Governors can, and sometimes do, appoint the lieutenant governor to head a state agency or to monitor a particular policy issue. Absent this, lieutenant governors usually have little to do and can become politically invisible.

Transition

One indication that states are taking their governors seriously is the conscious provision of personnel, funds, and legal authority for transitions from one gubernatorial adminis-tration to another. Prior to the mid-1970s, the incoming and outgoing administrations worked out issues of transition on their own. It was assumed that if those involved could work out arrangements, they would, and that if they could not work together, it really didn't matter.

Now 34 states no longer regard a change in administration as inconsequential; they have passed legislation that provides policies and resources for gubernatorial transitions. State budgets have become very complex. States recognize that gubernatorial teams should work together at least minimally to avoid unnecessary delays and disruptions in programs and state fiscal management. A newly elected governor, for example, might delay pay-ments of state aid to local school districts in order to use part or all of that money for some other purpose. The implications of the delays and uncertainties that this would cause are enormous. It would be far better, for the orderly establishment of new policies and priori-ties, if the governor-elect could be involved in whatever budget and financial decisions were being made in the months between election and inauguration.

Although structures and resources are provided, transitions still depend heavily on per-sonalities and politics.[19] Probably the best circumstance is when a governor decides not to run for reelection, and inherently the worst is when a governor has been defeated in a bid for another term. Fundamental to smooth transition is communication. An outgoing staff can comply with transition laws and still not communicate fully. Likewise, an incoming administration that is arrogant and haughty can block communication—probably to their own detriment.

ROLES

Agenda Setting

The most important policy-making role that governors play is to establish the agenda for state governments. Agenda setting is a critical first stage in the deliberative process. If an issue is never raised, it will never be addressed.

As the most visible officeholder in state government, a governor is in an ideal position to identify policy priorities and to initiate changes. Governors can use an annual State of the State address to set an agenda for the coming year and to report on how the state has fared most recently. Budget proposals provide another opportunity for leadership initiatives. If a governor calls a press conference to describe a problem or launch a change, the media will cover it and will usually seek responses from other state officials. Behind the scenes, as a party leader, governors can convene meetings of other leaders and map a strategy for change.

How a governor raises an issue is important to how it will be addressed. A proposal to require all able recipients of welfare to get job training or work for their benefits, for example, can be presented as a way of helping those on welfare become self-sufficient and independent. On the other hand, this proposal might be presented as an effort to discourage recipients from remaining on welfare, thereby cutting welfare costs. One perspective on a job requirement emphasizes jobs, and the other stresses the requirement. The former approach conveys the image of an empathetic governor and focuses attention on job-training programs, placement services, and support systems. The latter way of defining the issue pictures the governor as tough on deadbeats and emphasizes compliance with welfare eligibility rules.

The role of the governor in determining which issues will be addressed offsets many of the formal limitations of the office. The agenda-setting role is a leadership role. Governors can let the legislature legislate and then decide whether or not to approve or veto its work. With such a passive approach, a governor will not be able to take credit for policy direction or policy initiatives. In contrast, a governor can work with his or her staff to identify an issue, develop a proposal, and then campaign publicly for that proposal, much as the governor campaigned for office. Such a governor, particularly if he or she is persuasive, will leave a legacy and will be remembered for vision, even by those who might oppose his or her initiatives.

It should be added that state policy making depends heavily on how a governor plays the agenda-setting role. Legislatures are too fragmented to be a major source of policy initiative. If a governor wants to be a passive caretaker of state government, little cohesive change is likely to occur, even in response to external political and economic events. It is very rare that legislative leaders can fill the void and provide a central source of direction. They have more limited constituencies than governors do, and they lack the overall gubernatorial authority and resources.

Legislators recognize these constraints, and most of them expect governors "to define issues and set the process in motion."[20] It is not that legislatures are passive bodies, but rather that they are often best able to contribute to policy making by evaluating and perhaps modifying a proposal. Governors occupy an office that positions them well to make

Exploring the Web

Governors As Agenda Setters

What is your governor's agenda? See the directions in the box on page 150 to get to the website of your state's governor. What is the agenda of the NGA? Its website is www.nga.org. Compare these agendas with those of governors in some of the states that surround yours and/or in those you have visited. The website of the NGA includes the State of the State addresses of each governor. Also compare them with issues highlighted by the Council of State Governments (*www.csg.org*), the National Conference of State Legislators (*www.ncsl.org*), and the U.S. Conference of Mayors (*www.usmayors.org*).

Are these agendas consistent? Which agenda items most concern you?

What are ways in which you might affect a gubernatorial agenda?

proposals and to set statewide priorities. Even when governors are from a different party than the one in control of one or both houses of the legislature, they can have a major impact on the activities of the legislature by setting the agenda.

Governors cannot act in isolation, even when they are setting the agenda. They share lawmaking and policy-making authority with other officials and need to work with these officials in order to be effective. When voters in Minnesota elected Jesse Ventura as governor in 1998, they put in office someone with a rather bold agenda and someone who seemed to relish confrontations with legislators. The first two years of his term proved opposites. The first was a case of effective agenda setting, and the second was unproductive and hostile. The difference was Governor Ventura's willingness to work with legislators when he first took office. Problems became apparent when legislators encountered what they regarded as bullying and disrespectful behavior during the last three years of his term. The governor's popularity with voters declined, and he had minimal effect on setting the state's agenda. As a result, he decided not to run for reelection in 2002.

Ceremonial

The oldest and most enduring role of governors is as the chief representative of the state. Even when the office had few formal powers, the governor was regarded as the most visible, central figure in state government. The governor was called on to represent the state at key functions and to preside at solemn occasions. The challenge to appointment secretaries of contemporary governors is to assign priorities to the myriad requests to be present at opening ceremonies, to hand out awards, and to greet guests. Governors cannot afford to reject all such requests, yet the ceremonial opportunities must not overwhelm a governor's schedule. One strategy is to define this role personally and politically rather than in terms of representing the state. Thus, governors often prefer invitations to appear before large gatherings or important groups of supporters. Also, the gubernatorial staff makes sure that appearances become media events, affording them broader exposure and publicity.

Party Leader

Governors are the most visible, central officials not only in state government but also in their political party. Most state parties defer to their respective governors in naming chairs of the party. At national political conventions, governors are typically the leaders of their party's state delegation.

DEBATING THE ISSUES

Should governors appoint all executive branch officials?

The president of the United States appoints the heads of executive branch agencies, but the common pattern in the states is for positions such as attorney general, treasurer, secretary of state, and the head of the education department to be elected independently. The rationale for the federal model is that, when we elect a president, we need to give him or her the authority to select those who will help run the government. To do otherwise is to select candidates whose policies and leadership we prefer and then to tie their hands when those people get in office by placing other people in charge of government agencies. The same reasoning applies to governors. Elect them based on their campaigns, give them a chance to govern, and then hold them accountable.

The argument in favor of the current structure of state governments is that we need to place checks on governors. Independently electing at least some of the executive branch heads builds in checks on what might become excessive gubernatorial power. Also, this arrangement allows voters to have a direct influence on the policies of the agencies of state government. This is both preferred and practical at the state level where the people are closer to their government than they are to the federal government.

> Should we apply the national model to states and eliminate independently elected executives in favor of gubernatorial appointments, or are there reasons states should be different from the federal government?

> Do we need to check the power of governors? If so, do independently elected executives provide an effective check?

Explore this debate on the Web:
Model State Constitution for Responsible Government: www.geocities.com/~responsegov/stateconst.html
National Governors Association: *www.nga.org*
National Association of Attorneys General: *www.naag.org*
National Association of State Treasurers: *www.nast.net*
National Association of Secretaries of State: *www.nass.org*

Except for some of the machines that once prevailed in several states, however, parties are not strong, monolithic, disciplined organizations in the United States. Governors rarely can eliminate factions within their parties; they must cope with them. Governors do not regard their party as a source of policy guidance, nor do they think of party leadership as their most important role. Lynn Muchmore and Thad L. Beyle interviewed 15 governors who left office between 1976 and 1979 and found a consistent attitude that party platforms were meaningless, parties were not ideological, and patronage appointments to maintain party strength were inappropriate.[21] Governors, in short, appear to agree with the description of parties offered in Chapter 8 that they are somewhat useful in electoral strategies but not as sources for policy guidance.

Manager

An elementary civics lesson is that elected executives—presidents, governors, and mayors—are the chief administrators of their respective jurisdictions. Studies of state administrators have found, however, that governors set in place certain managerial styles and processes, but legislators tend to have more influence over the direction of agencies than do governors.[22] Primarily through their appointments of agency heads and through fiscal management devices, governors can influence whether state governments emphasize centralized control or local discretion and whether specific efficiency goals or a more casual approach prevails. Most state agency administrators, however, reported that governors do not use their appointment, budget, or other powers to establish policies that emphasize mass transit over roads or pollution controls over industrial activity. Those priorities are attributed mostly to legislators.

Governors are increasingly concerned about their role as managers. The NGA has devoted more attention to this subject since the mid-1980s, and governors individually are focusing on how they might provide more effective direction to state agencies.[23] The frustrations arise not so much because governors face hostile agencies but rather because time periods are so different. Administrators have perspectives that are influenced by their careers, whereas governors must operate within two- or four-year terms.

The general pattern of limited influence by governors over administrative agencies should not be interpreted as an indictment of those who have held this office. Given the broad scope of responsibilities and the relatively short time spent in office, even the most effective governors have only a limited impact on what state governments do. In her study of Governor Francis Sargent of Massachusetts, Professor Martha Weinberg found that Governor Sargent began to exert effective policy leadership only when he defined a very short list of goals and then concentrated his personal time and the resources of his office on accomplishing those goals. For Governor Sargent, that meant providing special leadership over the Department of Public Works and the Department of Public Welfare. Meanwhile, other policies and other agencies continued on their existing courses, receiving almost no gubernatorial attention unless a crisis emerged.[24]

Governor Nikki Haley
of South Carolina sets
her agenda with a state
of the state speech.

Similarly, a study of eight governors who led their states in the early 1990s showed the importance of focusing gubernatorial energies.[25] Those governors all faced the dual pressures of limiting the expense of state governments while simultaneously accepting responsibility for new policy areas. Success in managing state resources to meet the challenges in this situation depended in large part on clearly setting priorities. The governor's role as manager overlaps with the governor's role as agenda setter.

Governors with fairly specific agendas and with the willingness to concentrate their personal energy and their political capital can accomplish significant policy change. The kind of governor that someone will be is determined only in part by the formal duties and powers of the office. To understand fully the nature of governors requires an understanding of the personalities of those who are elected. This office is more heavily influenced by those who occupy it than is true for other institutions of state government.

Governors as Individuals

We need not resolve the age-old debate about whether great leaders are products of their times or whether leaders are responsible for great times. As governor, few individuals will have the opportunity to change the course of history—the scope of a governor's influence and authority is simply too limited. The exceptions to this rule—Nelson Rockefeller of New York and some of the Progressive governors in the early decades of this century—are people who had unusual leadership skills and long enough tenures to accomplish major change.

Within the context of a state, governors with vision, governors inclined toward corruption, and governors not willing or able to lead will perceive opportunities and will react differently. The variation in state responses to the emergence of high technology and the decay of traditional industries is explained in part by differences in gubernatorial leadership. Similarly, governors have provided different direction in response to the partial withdrawal of federal support for social welfare and for urban and agricultural conditions.

As a whole, governors look alike. They tend to be male, white, married, Protestant, college educated, lawyers or business leaders, and in their mid-forties.[26] However, women and minority group members made new gains in securing governorships in the 1980s and 1990s. Between 1950 and 1980, only three women, all Democrats, were elected governors: Lurleen Wallace (who succeeded her husband) in Alabama in 1966; Ella Grasso, Connecticut, 1974 and 1978; and Dixie Lee Ray, Washington, 1976. The 1990s began with female governors in six states (Arizona, Kansas, Nebraska, Oregon, Texas, and Vermont). Six states had women as governors in 2011, including Arizona, New Mexico, North Carolina, Oklahoma, South Carolina, and Washington. Massachusetts was led by an African American, New Mexico a Latina, and Louisiana and South Carolina by children of immigrants from India.

Some governors have been prominent and colorful enough to capture the attention of biographers and historians. Huey Long, Orval Faubus, George Wallace, Nelson Rockefeller, Earl Warren, Pat Brown, Robert La Follette, and James Folsom are some who have etched prominent places in U.S. history. Governors have become president, ambassadors, justices of the Supreme Court, and members of Congress.

What emerges from studies of individual governors are qualitative descriptions of individuals with ambition, vision, agendas, fervent supporters and detractors, and a bit of luck. Notable governors usually were not caretakers, as many governors have been. They were—or tried to be—change agents. They used the formal authority of their office and the informal but real influence of their prestige and their respective power bases to pursue specific objectives. In most cases they evoked both intense devotion and intense hatred. The Progressives, like La Follette, were loved by farmers and workers and hated by the old political machine bosses and some business leaders. Segregationists, like Faubus and Wallace (in his first years as governor), were heroes to white conservatives and villains to African Americans and liberals.

Governors are vulnerable, just as chief executive officers are in a private company. Policy initiatives risk failure or the perception that the consequences are not desirable. Circumstances outside the realm of a governor's authority or influence can be to the governor's benefit or detriment. The economic recession in 2001–2002 led to multimillion- and, in some cases, multibillion-dollar budget deficits in all but a handful of states and hurt incumbent governors running for reelection in 2002. Likewise, governors were challenged by the recession, job losses, and home mortgage foreclosures of 2008, even though they were not responsible for these developments. The expectations of a governor's ability to lead and to react are not always matched by the institutional or personal abilities to do so. Whether governors come near, or appear to come near, those expectations affects not only the directions pursued by state governments but also the personal careers pursued by individual governors.

GOVERNORS AND MOBILITY

Slightly more than one-third of the governors who have run for reelection since the mid-1970s have been defeated either in the primary or in the general election. This is a rather high percentage given the usual advantages of incumbents in getting media attention and attracting funds for a reelection bid. Only about 10 percent of the incumbents of other offices fail to win their bids for reelection.[27]

In his study of governors, Larry Sabato found that the single issue most associated with the defeat of governors running for reelection was taxes. This was particularly true between 1960 and 1975, when tax increases were especially common to support the expanding responsibilities of state government.[28] Most gubernatorial elections are not on the same cycle as presidential contests, so local issues and personalities are more important than riding into office on presidential coattails.

Governors leave office, voluntarily or involuntarily, to go to a wide variety of positions. Many resume their professions or their businesses. Some become chief executive officers in private, educational, or nonprofit organizations. Some assume other public service responsibilities. Former governors are judges, cabinet officers, ambassadors, and regulatory commissioners. Former governors make up one-fourth of the U.S. Senate. Of the 44 presidents of the United States, 16 (36 percent) were governors.

A few governors retire in disgrace or obscurity. In Illinois, the governor's office has the dubious distinction of being a step toward a cell in a federal penitentiary. In 2011 Rob Blagojevich became the third governor in a row from that state to be convicted of corruption felonies. Governor Blagojevich was impeached and removed from office by the Illinois legislature in 2009 and faced federal prosecution for conspiracy to commit bribery and mail fraud. His most visible misdeed was an effort to secure campaign contributions and personal benefits for himself and his wife in return for using his power to appoint someone to the U.S. Senate seat vacated by Barack Obama when he was elected president. Governor Eliot Spitzer of New York, who had earned a national reputation fighting white-collar crime and corruption, had to resign in 2008 when it was revealed that he got the services of high-priced prostitutes. Arizona, in 1988, impeached its governor, Evan Mecham, for misusing state funds and trying to block an investigation of a murder threat against someone on his staff. These instances, it should be emphasized, are exceptions. For the most part, governorships have attracted high-quality men and women.

SUMMARY AND CONCLUSIONS

Primarily out of recognition of the need to manage the dramatically increased scope and size of state governments, steps have been taken since the 1960s to provide governors with more resources and power. The length of terms has increased, staff resources have grown, and more agency heads are now appointees of the governor.

Governors can make a difference if they have personal vision and energy and if they use their authority strategically. Their most important role is to shape the agendas of state governments. They can define the issues that need to be addressed, and they can begin the deliberations by offering their own proposals. Governors who want to have any impact on policy must limit their agenda and concentrate their own energies and political capital on a few agencies and a few issues. Governors affect the face-to-face relationship between state officials and the public indirectly. They define the key concerns and issues of government and, through their leadership and examples, generate trust or cynicism, respect or hostility.

Discussion Questions

1. Explain the differences between current perspectives of the office of governor and the perspectives after the Revolutionary War. What accounts for the differences in what has been prescribed for gubernatorial power?

2. In what ways can governors exert control or leadership over administrative agencies? What resources do governors have to monitor agency activity, and what formal and informal powers do governors have that are relevant here?

3. Discuss the role that governors play in the criminal justice system. What is the extent of gubernatorial powers in amending or setting aside convictions and sentences? Do these powers serve as checks or as potential threats to the integrity of the courts?

4. Why would anyone want to be governor? Discuss the demands and rewards of the office, and speculate about probable motives for seeking the job.

5. Based on your understanding of the nature of the office of governor, what advice would you give to newly elected governors eager to leave a legacy of significant policy changes? How might they make a positive mark in history?

Glossary

cabinet government 221	**general** or **package veto** 225	**parole** 228
commute 227	**line-item veto** 225	**partial veto** 227
extradite 228	**pardon** 227	**reprieve** 228

Endnotes

1. Kim Severson, "South Carolina's Young Governor Has a High Profile and Higher Hopes," *New York Times*, July 3, 2011, 11 and 15.

2. Council of State Governments, *The Book of the States, 2011*, Vol. 43 (Lexington, Ky: Council of State Governments, 2011), 199.

3. Lee Sigelman and Roland Smith, "Personal, Office and State Characteristics as Predictors of Gubernatorial Performance," *Journal of Politics* 43 (February 1981), 169–180.

4. Sabato, *Goodbye to Good-Time Charlie*, 9; Ira Sharkansky, *The Maligned States* (New York: McGraw-Hill, 1972).

5. James L. Garnett, *Reorganizing State Government: The Executive Branch* (Boulder, Colo.: Westview, 1980), 8–9; Diane Kincaid Blair, "The Gubernatorial Appointment Power: Too Much of a Good Thing?" *State Government* 55, no. 3 (Summer 1982), 88–91.

6. *The Book of the States 2006* (Lexington, Ky.: Council of State Governments, 2006), 169–180.

7. George A. Munro, "Secretaries of State: Trends and Issues," *The Book of the States 2006* (Lexington, Ky: Council of State Governments, 2006), 189–197.

8. Ira Sharkansky, "Agency Requests, Gubernatorial Support, and Budget Success in State Legislatures," *American Political Science Review* 62 (December 1968), 1220–1231.

9. Deil S. Wright, "Governors, Grants and the Intergovernmental System," in *The American Governor in Behavioral Perspective*, eds. Thad. L. Beyle and J. Oliver Williams (New York: Harper & Row, 1972), 187–193.

10. Coleman Ransone Jr., *The American Governorship* (Westport, Conn.: Greenwood Press, 1982), 140.

11. Wisconsin State Constitution, Article V, Section 10(1)(b).

12. Ibid., Section 10(1)(c).

13. Charles Wiggins, "Executive Vetoes and Legislative Overrides in the American States," *Journal of Politics* 54, no. 1 (November 1980), 42. See also Glenn Abney and Thomas Lauth, "The Line-Item Veto in the States," *Public Administration Review* (Jan./Feb., 1985), 66–79.

14. James J. Gosling, "Wisconsin Item Veto Lessons," *Public Administration Review* (July/Aug. 1986), 292–300.

15. David R. Morgan, Robert E. England, and George C. Humphreys, *Oklahoma Politics and Policies: Governing the Sooner State* (Lincoln: University of Nebraska Press, 1991), 51 and 52.

16. Leon W. Blevins, *Texas Government in National Perspective* (Englewood Cliffs, N.J.: Prentice Hall, 1987), 169.

17. National Governors Association, *Time for Results: The Governors' 1991 Report on Education* (Washington, D.C.: NGA, 1986).

18. National Governors Association, *Making America Work: Productive People, Productive Policies* (Washington, D.C.: NGA, 1987).

19. Thad L. Beyle and J. Oliver Williams, eds., *The American Governor in Behavioral Perspective* (New York: Harper & Row, 1972), 76–104.

20. Thad L. Beyle, ed. *Governors and Hard Times* (Washington, D.C.: Congressional Quarterly Press, 1992), 103.

21. Lynn Muchmore and Thad L. Beyle, "The Governor as Party Leader," *State Government* 53, no. 1 (1980), 13–22.

22. F. Ted Hebert, Jeffrey L. Brudney, and Deil S. Wright, "Gubernatorial Influence and State Bureaucracy," *American Politics Quarterly* 11, no. 2 (April 1983), 243–264; Glenn Abney and Thomas Lauth, "The Governor as Chief Administrator," *Public Administration Quarterly* (January/February 1983), 40–49.

23. See the July/August 1986 issue of *State Government.*

24. Martha Wagner Weinberg, *Managing the State* (Cambridge, Mass.: MIT Press, 1977).

25. Beyle, *Governors and Hard Times.*

26. Thad Beyle, "Gubernatiorial Elections, Campaign Costs and Powers," *The Book of the States 2006* (Lexington, Ky.: Council of State Governments, 2006), 143–164.

27. J. Stephen Turett, "The Vulnerability of American Governors: 1900–1969," *Midwest Journal of Political Science* 15, no. 1 (February 1971).

28. Sabato, *Goodbye to Good-Time Charlie*, 33–42.

State Legislatures

- Understand the concept of legislative representation and its operation, as interpreted by the U.S. Supreme Court.
- Know how state legislatures are organized, including the similarities and differences between the lower chamber and the senate.
- Know who state legislators are—their sex, race, and occupations—and changes in their composition over time.
- Identify the reforms that have taken place in state legislatures and their effects on the legislature as policymaker and administrative overseer.
- Understand term limits, their effects on state legislatures, and legal challenges to term limit laws.
- Understand the changing executive–legislative balance, in which the legislature has challenged the governor in several areas of traditional executive prerogative, including the budgeting of federal funds, administrative rule making, and auditing.

The majority party caucus chair has his work cut out for him. Aware of his party's slim, three-vote margin in the state assembly, today's closed-door meeting of house Republicans will be a gauge of the members' solidarity in support of the leadership's package of spending cuts to balance the state's budget. The caucus chair knows that it won't be easy to get commitments from enough members to be able to win the floor vote without any Democratic votes, but that's the goal because the Democrats have vowed to oppose the Republican package, which has the strong endorsement of the state's Republican governor. The chair also realizes that some caucus members will demand something in return for their pledge to support the leaders' package on the floor. The first caucus vote proves him right. Despite pressure applied by party whips, only 45 of the 51 house Republicans raise their hands in support—five fewer than the number required for passage. Four of the holdouts represent school districts hit hardest by proposed changes to the school aid formula. The other represents an area containing a mental health institute that the governor's budget has targeted for closing. These members find themselves caught between their party's partisan struggle with the Democrats and the interests of their districts. They threaten to withhold their support until the leadership finds other cuts as replacements. It will be a long evening ahead, as the caucus chair entertains proposals that will produce the needed 50 votes.

Whereas the governor is elected on a statewide vote to represent all the people of the state, legislators are elected from subdivisions of the state, called districts, to represent the interests of their constituents. In every state except Nebraska, legislative representatives are organized into two chambers. Each district in each chamber must have about the same population, but one chamber in a state will have more districts than the other. Representatives in the lower chamber, commonly referred to as the house or assembly, usually represent fewer state residents than do their upper-chamber colleagues, who are organized into senates. (The terms *lower* and *upper* date from the British class-based parliament with a House of Lords and a House of Commons. These distinctions do not apply in the U.S. context.) Usually house or assembly districts are subdivisions of the larger senate districts, with three lower-chamber districts comprising a senate district, on average, nationally. The population basis of the respective districts and the number of house or assembly districts encompassed within each senate district vary considerably among the states.

Legislators in highly populous states represent more people than do their counterparts in less populous states. Each state senator in California, for example, represents an average of about 847,000 constituents. In New York, the comparable figure approaches 312,000. On the other end of the spectrum, state senators in Wyoming and North Dakota represent approximately 16,000 and 13,000 constituents, respectively. Lower-chamber districts also vary greatly in represented population among the states. California assembly districts average nearly 423,000 residents; New York house districts average about 127,000. In contrast, Vermont house districts average only 4,100 residents.[1]

Although the principle of representative government had been enunciated centuries earlier in England and continental Europe, its operation was significantly reinterpreted only four decades ago. In 1962, the U.S. Supreme Court found unconstitutional a reapportionment of the Tennessee House of Representatives that failed to modify district lines despite major shifts in population. The Court applied that finding to the lower chamber of all state legislatures. Its decision in *Baker v. Carr*[2] thus affirmed the principle of equal representation and concluded that unequal representation on the basis of population violates the Fourteenth Amendment of the U.S. Constitution, which guarantees equal protection under the law. A subsequent Supreme Court decision in *Reynolds v. Sims*,[3] rendered just two years later, extended the principle of equal representation to state senates. In doing so, it enunciated the **one-man, one-vote** principle—that each person's vote should secure an equal amount of representation in each legislative chamber. Alabama had sought to base representation in its

---

one-man, one-vote The principle that each person's vote should secure an equal amount of representation in each legislative chamber.

lower house on population, but its senate on geographic grounds. It argued that the representation in the U.S. Congress set a precedent for this distinction. The Supreme Court reasoned, however, that representation in the U.S. Senate was not recognized as an analogous case for state senate representation because U.S. senators are elected statewide and represent all residents of the state. In addition, states enjoy a special sovereignty that is recognized in the U.S. Constitution: each state has two senators, regardless of population. State senators, however, are elected from substate electoral districts and represent only their local constituents.

Chief Justice Earl Warren summed up the feelings of the Court by noting, "Legislatures represent people, not trees or acres. Legislators are elected by voters, not farms or cities or economic interests. The right to elect legislators in a free unimpaired fashion is a bedrock of our political system."[4] The Court's decision in *Westbury v. Sanders*,[5] also in 1964, applied the one-man, one-vote principle to districts represented in the U.S. House of Representatives and to local general-purpose districts.

In response to the Supreme Court's rulings, state legislatures across the country have reapportioned their legislative districts and thereby corrected some glaring inequities. Three very different states provide vivid illustrations of the problems addressed. Before Court-induced reapportionment, 18 percent of voters in Florida could elect a majority of legislators in both the Florida house and senate. Voters in Connecticut's five largest cities, containing over one-quarter of the state's population, could elect only 10 of 294 representatives in the lower house. Finally, California's Los Angeles County, with about 40 percent of the state's population, was accorded only one seat in the 40-seat California senate.[6] These examples, although among the most extreme, highlight the monumental task of reapportionment.

Federal courts, in overseeing implementation of the Supreme Court's ruling, have allowed state legislatures only marginal deviation from the one-man, one-vote rule, permitting limited retention of some district lines that coincide with existing municipal boundaries. Legislative districts can be equally apportioned based on population and therefore not violate the law, but be drawn to provide a distinct advantage for one party over another. Two methods can be employed to maximize one party's representative strength over another. The first involves **splintering**, or dividing, the opposition party's areas of electoral strength; the second involves **packing** areas of partisan strength in ways that guarantee high majority votes for winners but that limit the number of victors. The first method distributes votes to create several marginally competitive districts with a clear advantage to one's party. The second sacrifices one or two big losses to retain a majority in numerous other districts.

Figure 10.1 provides an illustration of **gerrymandering**, drawing district lines to gain a partisan advantage in legislative representation or to minimize or maximize the electoral representation of minority populations. The dark solid lines in the figure divide three legislative districts. Districts 2 and 3 are competitive districts, with the Republicans holding a slight advantage in District 3. District 1, however, is solidly in Republican hands. With redistricting, represented by the heavy dotted line, District 1 becomes even more dominated

---

splintering A form of gerrymandering that divides the opposition party's electoral strength.

packing A form of gerrymandering that consolidates the opposition party's electoral strength in ways that guarantee high majority votes for winners but that limit the number of winners.

gerrymandering Drawing electoral district lines to gain a partisan advantage in legislative representation.

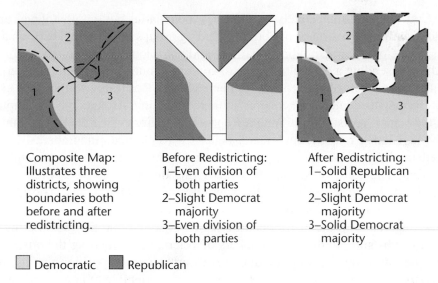

Composite Map: Illustrates three districts, showing boundaries both before and after redistricting.	Before Redistricting: 1–Even division of both parties 2–Slight Democrat majority 3–Even division of both parties	After Redistricting: 1–Solid Republican majority 2–Slight Democrat majority 3–Solid Democrat majority

☐ Democratic ■ Republican

Figure 10.1 Gerrymandering

by Republicans. District 3 swings to a decided Democratic advantage, and District 2 picks up enough Democratic support to provide the Democrats with a moderate advantage.

The redrawing of District 1's lines serves as an example of packing. An already large Republican majority is made even larger. But such an expansion of electoral support comes at the expense of the Republicans' relative strength in District 3. Whereas District 3 had a marginal Republican advantage prior to redistricting, it picked up enough Democratic support from a slice of the old District 1 that it has assumed a decided Democratic advantage. Similarly, the new District 2 picked up sufficient Democratic support from the redrawing of District 3 so that it has gone from a slightly competitive district to a moderate Democratic advantage. Splintering is at work in slicing Democratic strength from District 1 to District 3, and from District 1 to District 2. The net result is to go from a Republican advantage in two districts and close competition in a third to a Democratic advantage in two districts and a solid Republican majority in a third. Obviously, in this example, such gerrymandering would be promoted by a Democratic legislative majority.

Despite its partisan implications, legislatures have not redistricted themselves every time majorities change; they typically reapportioned after the completion of a new census at the beginning of each decade, unless they were directed by the court to do so at other times. However, a 2006 U.S. Supreme Court decision, *League of United Latin American Citizens et al. v. Perry, Governor of Texas, et al.* (discussed in greater detail later in the context of gerrymandering), allows reapportionment to occur at any time within the decade.

The Supreme Court has expressed concern about gerrymandering for partisan purposes, but it has not issued a definitive ruling on this subject. In *Davis v. Bandemer* (1986), the Court considered a complaint from the Democratic Party in Indiana. In 1981, the Republican-controlled legislature drew boundaries to maintain control despite growing Democratic Party strength in the state. As a result, in the 1982 elections, the Democrats garnered 51.9 percent statewide of all votes cast for state legislative seats. However, that translated into only 43 Democratic victories out of the 100 contests for House seats. The

Supreme Court did not immediately mandate new boundaries but said that it was unconstitutional to disenfranchise groups of voters, including groups of party loyalists, on a consistent basis. The Court warned Indiana that it would not tolerate a continuation of the 1982 pattern, thereby sending a general message of concern about partisan gerrymandering.[7]

Another case involved redistricting in Pennsylvania that followed the 2000 elections. Although the dispute centered on congressional redistricting, its outcome had implications for state legislative redistricting. With a Republican majority in the Pennsylvania legislature, the legislative redistricting clearly benefited Republican incumbents. Democrats sued in federal district court, arguing that the redistricting denied Democratic voters equal representation. The court ruled that the redistricting did not deny voters representation; they would still be represented, but by Republicans, not Democrats. The Democratic Party appealed again, this time to the U.S. Supreme Court. The Supreme Court, in *Vieth v. Jubeliver*, agreed with the district court's logic but found that the redistricting created districts with substantially different numbers of voters, thus violating the one-man, one-vote principle. In ruling as it did, the Supreme Court stated the position that it would not deal with partisan gerrymandering *unless* it violates the principle of equal representation.[8]

Gerrymandering for the purpose of *minimizing* the electoral representation of racial minorities has been expressly forbidden. In a 1977 U.S. Supreme Court ruling, *United Jewish Organization of Williamsburg, Inc. v. Hugh L. Carey*,[9] such racially motivated districting was deemed in violation of the **Equal Protection Clause** of the Fourteenth Amendment and the federal Voting Rights Act. However, that same decision also provided the leeway for state legislatures to draw boundaries that preserve the viability of minority representation. In the 1990s, several cases tested the line between preserving minority representation and packing minority electoral strength. The most publicized case involved North Carolina's creation of the so-called I–85 congressional district, which cut a 160-mile swath across the state, following the freeway and adding pockets of African American voters along the way. In *Shaw v. Reno*,[10] decided in 1993, the Court held that white voters had standing to challenge North Carolina's Twelfth District as racially gerrymandered, and it remanded the case to the district court to determine whether any constitutional violation had occurred. Although the case dealt with federal districting, the Court also extended its reasoning to state legislative districting. Justice Sandra Day O'Connor advanced the Court's logic in writing the majority opinion:

> A reapportionment plan that includes in one district individuals who belong to the same race, but who are otherwise widely separated by geographical and political boundaries, and who may have little in common with one another but the color of their skin, bears an uncomfortable resemblance to political apartheid. It reinforces the perception that members of the same group—regardless of their age, education, economic status, or the community in which they live—think alike, share the same political interests, and will prefer the same candidates at the polls. . . . By perpetuating such notions, a racial gerrymander may exacerbate the very patterns of racial bloc voting that majority-minority districting is sometimes said to counteract.[11]

The Supreme Court got the case back on appeal after the district court found that district lines met constitutional tests. In 1996, in *Shaw v. Hunt,* the Court ruled the plan to be in violation of the Equal Protection Clause of the Fourteenth Amendment.[12]

Equal Protection Clause A clause to the Fourteenth Amendment to the U.S. Constitution that guarantees all U.S. citizens equal protection under the law.

Two other cases,[13] in Georgia and Texas, reinforced the judicial logic first spelled out in *Shaw v. Reno.* Both dealt with racial gerrymandering of congressional districts, and in both instances the Supreme Court found the product to be constitutionally objectionable. In both cases, the Court reiterated that race couldn't be employed as a predominant factor in shaping legislative districts, whether for congressional or state legislative races.

A highly visible Supreme Court decision in 2006 selectively struck down reapportionment in one Texas congressional district on racial grounds, while sustaining reapportionment in another. In *League of United Latin American Citizens et al. v. Perry, Governor of Texas, et al.*, the Court ruled that reapportionment of District 23 in the San Antonio area violated the Voting Rights Act by purposefully *diluting the Hispanic vote* in an effort to put the Democratic incumbent at a disadvantage. The Court ordered the district to be redrawn. However, the Court found no substantial weakening of African American voting strength in District 24 in the Fort Worth area. Considering the two decisions, the Court seemed to be saying that partisan gerrymandering in itself does not violate the Constitution. It becomes unconstitutional when it purposefully and substantially minimizes minority voting clout.[14]

In its decision, the Court also sustained the ability of state legislatures to reapportion legislative districts at any time within a decade following the decennial census. That later ruling clears the legal way for state legislatures to reapportion whenever the legislative majority changes party hands, creating the potential for marked instability in legislative district lines.

What difference does state reapportionment really make? One study of 38 state legislatures found that the effects on partisan representation were not all that staggering. Democrats increased their legislative strength by less than 3 percent of the seats contested, and given the Democrats' disproportionate control of state legislative chambers, that percentage appears to be marginal at best.[15] Reapportionments did result, however, in an increase in the number of state representatives and senators from urban and suburban areas, at the expense of rural representation. But such was expected, given the dramatic post–World War II population growth that occurred in urban and suburban areas.

What Legislatures Do

Legislatures exist to perform several important functions, and the most significant among them is making the laws of the state, approving state budgets, serving constituents, and overseeing the executive branch of state government. Each is now discussed in turn.

1. **Make Laws.** Legislatures pass legislation, which becomes state law if approved by the governor or if the legislature overrides a governor's veto. Such legislation can set the maximum penalties for sentencing convicted felons for different crimes, establish eligibility standards for state-financed college scholarship aid, create the legal framework governing assistance to workers disabled on the job, authorize the construction of a new public university, and establish formulas for sharing state revenues with local units of government. In carrying out this legislative function, however, state legislatures typically react to gubernatorial agendas. Given their fragmentation and plural bases of power, legislatures are

not well structured to set policy agendas for their states. Instead they tend to respond to gubernatorial initiatives—approving, modifying, or rejecting them. That is not to suggest that legislatures do not pursue their collective policy preferences, but only that those preferences often emerge as a product of legislative deliberation, a product that represents compromise and accommodation.

2. **Approve Budgets.** Legislatures possess the power of the purse. They determine what is to be taxed; set tax rates; approve tax breaks, if any; and appropriate funds for different spending purposes. In so doing, legislatures establish priorities, determining who pays for and who benefits from state programs. In carrying out this function, legislatures look to the governor for leadership because it is the governor who sets the state's budgetary agenda. The executive budget in most states becomes the focal point of public debate over taxing and spending. Even in those states in which the legislature considers an alternative budget developed by legislative staff, the governor's budget remains the point of departure. The legislature may make significant changes to the governor's budget—the final legislatively approved product usually constitutes an aggregation of unchanged, modified, and added items. But the final version enacted into law usually bears significant vestiges of the governor's original handiwork. For a comprehensive analysis of the legislature's role and influence in state budgeting, see Chapter 5.

3. **Serve Constituents.** Individual legislators provide services to the residents of their districts. Through service-based casework, they obtain information for constituents about government programs and may intercede with state agencies on constituents' behalf. A legislator might assist a constituent by inquiring about a missing unemployment compensation check; another might complain to the state highway department about a planned highway project that would result in the loss of some of a constituent's rich farmland; a third might question why a constituent's request to appeal a driver's license suspension was denied by the state motor vehicle department. Increases in legislative staff have enabled legislators' offices to give greater attention to constituent service.

4. **Oversee the Executive Branch.** Legislatures oversee the operations of executive branch agencies. The primary purpose of this oversight is to ensure that executive agencies are efficiently implementing programs consistent with legislative intent. After all, legislatures enact legislation and approve appropriations with the expectation that the executive branch will implement them according to the legislature's designs. If they do not, the legitimacy of the very lawmaking and budget-making processes would be compromised. Thus, legislatures have established mechanisms to assess executive compliance with legislative intent. One prominent mechanism has been the use of legislative committees to exercise oversight on behalf of the entire legislature. Committees have been created to approve executive requests for certain budget transfers after the state budget has taken effect, review the administrative rules of executive agencies, and consider the implications of performance audits conducted by legislative staff. More will be said about these subjects later in this chapter.

Legislative Organization

With the exception of Nebraska, which is unicameral, legislative representatives are organized into lower and upper chambers. The size of each chamber bears no relationship to a state's population or geographical size. The lower house varies among the states from a high of 400 representatives in New Hampshire to a low of 40 in Alaska. Senates range from 67 members in Minnesota to 20 in Alaska. Nebraska's unicameral legislature has 49 members, called senators. (See Table 10.1 for a listing of legislative membership in each of the states.)

Table 10.1 Number of State Legislators by Chamber

State	Senate	House	Total
Alabama	35	105	140
Alaska	20	40	60
Arizona	30	60	90
Arkansas	35	100	135
California	40	80	120
Colorado	35	65	100
Connecticut	36	151	187
Delaware	21	41	62
Florida	40	120	160
Georgia	56	180	236
Hawaii	25	51	76
Idaho	35	70	105
Illinois	59	118	177
Indiana	50	100	150
Iowa	50	100	150
Kansas	40	125	165
Kentucky	38	100	138
Louisiana	39	105	144
Maine	35	151	186
Maryland	47	141	188
Massachusetts	40	160	200
Michigan	38	110	148
Minnesota	67	134	201
Mississippi	52	122	174
Missouri	34	163	197
Montana	50	100	150
Nebraska	Unicameral		49
Nevada	21	42	63
New Hampshire	24	400	424
New Jersey	40	80	120
New Mexico	42	70	112

(continued)

Table 10.1   Number of State Legislators by Chamber (*continued*)

State	Senate	House	Total
New York	61	150	211
North Carolina	50	120	170
North Dakota	49	98	147
Ohio	33	99	132
Oklahoma	48	101	149
Oregon	30	60	90
Pennsylvania	50	203	253
Rhode Island	50	100	150
South Carolina	46	124	170
South Dakota	35	70	105
Tennessee	33	99	132
Texas	31	150	181
Utah	29	75	104
Vermont	30	150	180
Virginia	40	100	140
Washington	49	98	147
West Virginia	34	100	134
Wisconsin	33	99	132
Wyoming	30	60	90
Mean	40	112	152

State senates can be distinguished from the lower houses on several dimensions. First, as was previously noted, senate districts encompass several house or assembly districts and are therefore larger in size than the individual districts that comprise them. Thus, within the same state, senates are smaller than their lower-house counterparts—most commonly by a 1:3 ratio. Fourteen states have an exact 1:2 ratio, whereas the ratio approaches 1:5 in Texas and Vermont and reaches a high of 1:16 in New Hampshire.

A second distinction is that the terms of state senators are usually longer than those of state representatives. Such is the case in 34 states, where senators serve four years compared to representatives, who serve two. In four other states, senators and representatives alike serve four-year terms, as do members of Nebraska's unicameral legislature. The remaining 11 states have two-year terms for both upper-house and lower-house legislators.[16]

Both a chamber's size and the length of its members' terms can affect its character. Larger bodies tend to be more unwieldy and bound by greater organizational rules and procedures. They also tend to have more pronounced and rigid leadership hierarchies. Because of their larger size and the corresponding greater volume of legislative business before them, houses and assemblies appear to be less collegial than are senates. Lower-house representatives will be the first to suggest that the senate debating club is not where the bulk of the legislature's work gets done. Representatives usually are quick to point to the "roll up the sleeves and get the job done" mentality of the house, in contrast to the senate's decorous sartorial splendor.

The difference in length of terms between the two chambers can influence the nature of politics in each. Shorter terms may prompt incumbents to pay closer attention to the electoral implications of their legislative choices. They may weigh their actions more in terms of their immediate political ramifications than their longer-term policy implications. Yet such a pragmatic orientation can carry with it greater responsiveness to one's constituency. Knowing that you are going to be judged by the voters within a time frame that allows them to remember prominent instances of disregard may prompt more responsive representation.

LEGISLATIVE LEADERSHIP

Political parties compete in elections in order to win and take control of the government. A party hopes to win the governorship and thus be in a position, through gubernatorial appointments, to oversee the operations of the executive branch. It also strives to win majorities in both chambers in order to control the legislative process. We know, however, that political parties are not monoliths. Members of the same party do not always act in concert. They may be pulled simultaneously in several directions as they individually respond to competing influences and problems. Despite the forces that work to divide would-be solidarity, party affiliation plays an important role in the legislature's organization.

As Figure 10.2 illustrates, after the 2010 elections, the Democrats controlled the legislatures in 15 states, the Republicans controlled the legislatures in 27 states, and the control

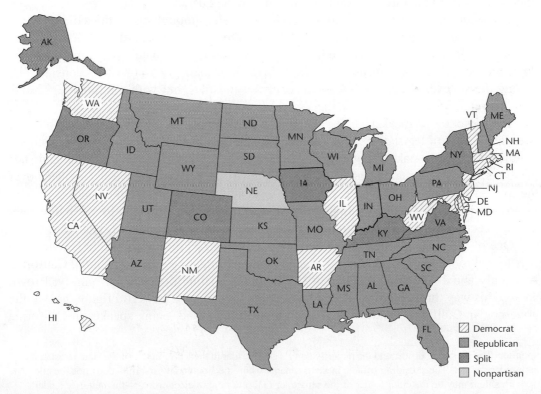

Figure 10.2 Partisan Control of State Legislatures, 2011

was split in 7 states. (Nebraska's legislature is unicameral and elected on a nonpartisan basis.) This distribution has its roots in the major electoral gains the Republicans made in the 1994 legislative elections, which resembled the electoral tidal wave that gave the Republican Party control of both chambers of Congress. This control was modified by the inroads made by Democrats in 2006, which similarly paralleled the Democrats' resurgence in Congress. The Democrats expanded their advantage as a result of the 2008 elections, picking up control of four legislatures. The 2010 election saw Republicans regain their strength to take control of 27 legislatures, the most since 1952.

The majority party in each legislative chamber is in an excellent position to hold all the key legislative leadership positions, although in some states minority party members hold committee chairs. All the majority party needs to do is to hold together its members' votes when the state legislature elects its leadership at the beginning of the legislative session. Would-be party leaders vie for leadership positions within their respective partisan caucus. Candidates compete for specific leadership positions, but, as in general elections, incumbents have a decided advantage unless they have alienated their supporters. During their tenure, incumbents have incurred debts from their legislative colleagues and have established a track record. Often, however, leadership positions become vacant as a result of retirement, election to a higher political office, appointment to administrative positions, or the rare defeat of an incumbent within that incumbent's own district election. Where vacancies occur, competition for leadership positions resembles a free-for-all, although apparent "heirs to the throne" stand prominently in the queue.

The leadership structure is similar in both chambers, although office titles differ. In the lower house the presiding officer is called the **speaker**. In the senate, the presiding officer is usually called the **president**. The lieutenant governor is the senate's presiding officer in 26 states, but the legislative authority vested in the lieutenant governor varies considerably among the states.[17] When the lieutenant governor presides, but with a limited legislative role, the majority leader exercises the real power.

The power of the speaker and the president has essentially three bases: (1) great influence over the process of legislative agenda setting and the flow of legislation within the chamber; (2) the authority to make appointments to key legislative leadership, committee, and staff positions; and (3) the many debts owed by legislative colleagues that have accumulated over the speaker's or president's tenure. Of the two legislative leaders, the speaker tends to possess the greater power, reflecting the higher degree of centralization generally found in the lower house—centralization necessary to bring order to the larger, more unwieldy chamber.

One of the more powerful speakers in the nation was California's Willie Brown, who was forced to leave office in 1996—a victim of term limits after 32 years in the California Assembly and 16 years as speaker. A self-made man from a poor Texas family, Brown worked his way through law school to become the second most powerful figure, next to the governor, in California politics. As Brown himself once said, being speaker in California

---

speaker   The presiding officer and the majority party's chief leader in the lower house of the state legislature.

senate president   The presiding officer in state senates when the lieutenant governor does not preside. The president may be the chief leader of the senate, or that role might be accorded to the majority leader.

The dome of the Wisconsin state capitol building dominates the Madison skyline. State government is a major presence in most of the capital cities.

is the "closest thing you will ever know in the world to the Ayatollah."[18] Brown used his power as speaker adeptly, whether by guiding his legislative agenda through the assembly, making key committee appointments, employing assembly staff, assigning office space, or even deciding whose offices got carpeting. An African American representative from liberal San Francisco, Brown knew how to mix accommodation with hardball partisan politics.

Speaker Brown allowed the Republicans to author and, with endorsed Democratic help, pass some major legislation that traditionally would have been allowed to pass only under the majority party's authorship.[19] But Brown, with a sizable majority in the assembly, knew that he could pass almost any legislation he wanted just by retaining the support of his own party, an ability he often demonstrated. Toward that end, not only did he skillfully employ the traditional prerogatives of the speaker's office, but he also used his powerful legislative position to raise sizable amounts of money—approaching $2 million in an election year—in support of assembly candidates. As one Democratic assemblyman put it, "When you get that kind of money, you get grateful."[20]

The next most powerful leadership position in both chambers is that of the **majority leader**, who can be viewed as the party's chief lieutenant, the "right-hand man" of the speaker or president. Although the positions of deputy speaker and president pro tempore exist, the

---

majority leader Usually the second most powerful member of each state's legislative chamber. However, in some states, in which the senate president is largely a ceremonial position, the majority leader possesses the greatest power.

majority leader really functions as second in command, usually assuming the role of chief legislative floor leader. In contentious floor debate, the majority leader gains the recognition of the presiding officer to enunciate the official party position on a bill. When majority leaders speak in their official roles, the membership is expected to heed the message. The majority leader also plays a key role in caucus deliberations, working continually, both inside the formal caucus and outside in the halls, to shape a clear majority position on legislation—one that will marshal a sizable majority of votes on the floor. Although a caucus chairperson presides at caucus sessions, the majority leader generally plays the dominant role in amassing support. The speaker or president may engage in the caucus debate, but such involvement is usually reserved for particularly difficult or divisive issues.

In a few states, such as New York and Wisconsin, the majority leader exercises the real leadership in the senate. The president presides over the chamber, but the majority leader sets the legislative agenda and shepherds it through the legislative process. In New York, for example, the majority leader makes committee appointments, including naming the chairpersons; controls the legislative staff payroll and dispenses individual staff allowances; establishes the majority party's legislative agenda; and refers bills to committees. But an effective majority leader has to use these substantive and procedural resources judiciously. Senators are frequently wooed and cajoled into compliance. As a perceptive observer of the New York State Senate, John Pitney Jr., has noted:

> In a tough floor vote, the majority leader uses his knowledge of the senators' needs and beliefs to choose who will be let off the hook. If their objections are rooted in principle, he and his staff can muster facts to change their minds. Persuasion conserves his resources: the more he can convince them that they are doing the right thing, the less they think of their vote as a favor to be repaid. And even if he fails to win their hearts, he can at least provide them with a defense against those who attack their vote.[21]

Organized under the majority leader come the deputy majority leader and floor whip positions, held by senior party members who are responsible for garnering the support of the rank and file. These agents of the top leadership try to persuade party members to follow the party line. Yet there may not be a party line on every bill passing through the chamber. Often, when a bill is not of importance to the legislative party leadership, members are free to vote their own choice. It should be understood, however, that when official party positions are taken on legislation, it is the speaker, president, or majority leader who exercises the greatest leadership in setting legislative priorities. Such is particularly the case in the waning days of the session, when huge backlogs of unfinished legislative business accumulate. In those cases the support of the chamber's top leadership is an essential requirement for that legislation to receive consideration on the floor. Without such singling out from among the mass of legislation awaiting action, a bill will probably die for lack of attention.

The minority party in the legislature is similarly organized, the major exception being that minority party members generally hold none of the top leadership positions in the chamber. Rare situations occur in which a **minority party leader** may be elected speaker

---

minority party leader The chief leader of the minority party in the legislature.

or president by a combined majority of both parties' members, but such an anomaly normally occurs only in closely divided chambers when a heated battle for majority party leadership positions has badly divided the majority party.

The minority party elects its own leaders as well as its floor whips. They play similar roles to their majority counterparts in floor debate and caucus deliberations, and their importance is very much a function of the relative competitiveness of their party in the state. Where legislative membership is more evenly divided, minority party strategy becomes important because, with a few defectors from the other side, the minority might be able to forge a majority position on any given piece of legislation. In such instances minority solidarity becomes essential as a core building block of a winning coalition.

The committee chairperson represents another key leadership position in the legislature. Just as the majority party generally controls the speaker's and president's office, committee chairpersons are usually drawn from among majority party members. Among lower houses, the speaker appoints committee chairs in four-fifths of the states.[22] In the others, the caucus as a whole may elect committee chairs, or appointments are made by a committee on committees made up of the majority party's top legislative leadership. The senate often presents a different picture. In several states a committee on committees (or a rules committee) makes the appointments. This is the case in Arkansas, Georgia, Illinois, Kentucky, Michigan, Montana, Nebraska, New Mexico, North Dakota, Ohio, Oklahoma, and Vermont. The full senate elects committee chairpersons in Virginia.[23] This difference in appointments between the lower house and the senate is another reason why the speaker tends to be more influential than the senate president.

Beyond the selection of committee chairpersons, the majority party is in a position to determine both the number of committees and their jurisdictions. The majority party also can establish the relative ratio of majority-to-minority members that each committee will have. The partisan ratio need not be the same for every committee. However, the majority party may give itself a higher percentage of seats on the most important committees, such as appropriations or budget. For the less significant committees, the margin of majority may be much narrower. But the majority party runs some major risks if it goes too far in skewing party representation. Not only may the majority party selectively need cooperation from the minority party on key legislation when some defection occurs, but also majorities can become minorities in the coming election. One's party might well be treated as it treated its competitor. There is often a line that, if crossed, undermines the prospects for interparty cooperation and creates a climate of partisan antagonism.

LEGISLATIVE COMMITTEES

Committees represent the frontline of a legislature in its role as lawmaker. Committees develop subject-matter expertise and get the first substantive crack at introduced legislation. In most states they can hold bills indefinitely (short of the full legislature's action to discharge them), or they can report legislation with or without amendment. The committee phase of the legislative process gives members of the public an opportunity to be heard on legislative proposals because all bills assigned to committee must be scheduled for public hearing before they can be acted on by the full legislature.

Although committees exist in every state legislative body and perform similar functions in the legislative process, marked differences do exist among states. Most states have separate **standing committees** in each chamber of the legislature. For example, both the house and senate may have an education committee made up of members appointed from their own respective chamber and chaired by one of their own. In contrast, three states—Connecticut, Maine, and Massachusetts—make exclusive use of joint committees, that is, committees made up of and co-chaired by representatives from both chambers. California, New York, and Utah make heavy, although not exclusive, use of joint committees. Other states, such as Wisconsin, rely on standing committees for the most part but employ joint committees selectively, usually for the most demanding, technical, and substantive areas such as finance and audit.

Joint committees tend to give the leadership more control over the legislative process, more readily accommodating earlier in the process the sometimes divisive rivalries that exist between the chambers. The recommendations that go to the first house for consideration already have been the subject of interchamber negotiation in the joint committee. To facilitate such negotiations, joint committee members frequently are selected to create a committee closely representative of the legislature as a whole. The legislative leadership makes a clear effort to ensure that not only are constituent and geographic differences reflected in the committee's membership but also that the appointees have demonstrated a willingness to represent the corporate partisan good. The use of joint committees can make it more efficient for citizens to attend hearings and make their feelings known, thus advancing the prospects of face-to-face governance.

Beyond standing committees, state legislatures frequently create **special legislative committees**, which are formed to examine a particular issue or problem, and which are dissolved after issuing their report. Special committees may examine problems such as how to improve a state's business climate or whether and how to revamp the state budgetary process.

A pecking order exists among committees. Some are clearly more prized than others—in the members' eyes and among close observers of a state's policy-making process. The money committees generally hold the greatest prestige. In most states the appropriations, budget, or finance committees make the major recommendations most broadly affecting state residents. Within these money committees, the levels of aid for local units of government are first set by the legislature. In those states in which the executive budget serves as the major policy-making vehicle, a seat on the appropriations or budget committee gains added importance, not just for setting appropriations but also for shaping program initiatives.

In seeking particular committee assignments, legislators are motivated by several factors. Beyond being in a position to influence the most important state policy decisions, other key factors relate to how the assignment positions legislators to be of greatest service to their constituents (and thus improve prospects for reelection) and to pursue personal or political ambitions.

---

standing committees of the legislature Legislative committees that have some permanence, typically existing across legislative sessions.

special legislative committees Legislative committees typically formed to examine a particular issue or problem and then dissolved after issuing their report.

MEMBERS

Although the typical state legislator continues to be a white male, significant changes have occurred in state legislative membership. Two decades ago, most legislators listed their occupation as attorney or business owner, but today most are full-time legislators. Between 1970 and 2010, the percentage of women serving in state legislatures rose from 4 to 24 percent.[24] Women comprise 30 percent or more of the membership of legislatures in seven states: Arizona, Colorado, Hawaii, Maryland, Minnesota, Vermont, and Washington. The percentage of African American state legislators also has increased significantly, rising from 2 to 9 percent over the same period.[25] Figure 10.3 shows the percentage of state legislators who are women or African Americans.

The occupational mix of those serving in state legislatures also has changed. The ranks of attorneys, farmers, and business owners have thinned, and the relative percentage of full-time legislators has grown. A survey conducted by the National Conference of State Legislatures finds that full-time legislators are most commonly found in California, New York, Michigan, Illinois, Pennsylvania, Ohio, Massachusetts, Wisconsin, and Arizona. Legislators who spend the least amount of time on their legislative duties can be found in Montana, Wyoming, Utah, North Dakota, South Dakota, New Mexico, Kansas, New Hampshire, Vermont, and Mississippi.[26]

The rise of the **full-time legislator** is a phenomenon that has both supporters and detractors. Supporters argue that full-time legislators are in a better position than part-timers to spend the rapidly growing time necessary to discharge their legislative duties professionally. They contend that the legislative business has significantly changed over the past decade or two. The demands now placed on legislators greatly exceed those of earlier years. State legislatures today face more numerous and complex policy issues, have become more involved in state budgeting, and have become much more active on many fronts in exercising oversight of the executive branch. Such demands, supporters argue, require full-time legislative attention.

Detractors take a different perspective. For them, full-time legislators can too easily become detached from the real world and can too easily get caught up in the artificial

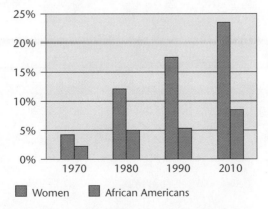

Figure 10.3 Women and African Americans in State Legislatures

---

full-time legislator Legislator whose primary employment is serving in the legislature.

capital-city mentality of the politicians and bureaucrats who make and administer state laws. In contrast, legislators who actively pursue their outside professions and occupations may better understand the problems and needs of working people, and they have a more realistic knowledge of how government affects people's lives. Detractors also often take issue with the career paths of full-time legislators, who increasingly have worked as legislative aides after graduation from college before running for office themselves. Figure 10.4 shows those legislatures that can still be considered populated by part-time citizen legislators, have comparatively short sessions, and provide low compensation, thus requiring members to have other, full-time employment to earn a living.

Despite the different perspectives on the full-time legislator, it is clear that the legislative environment has changed in most states. The exclusiveness of the "good ol' boy" legislative club has broken down. The growth in the number of women, minority group members, and full-time legislators, together with the reduction in the number of attorneys, business owners, and farmers, has changed the makeup of many state legislatures. However, the political culture of state legislatures has also changed. The closer social camaraderie of earlier years has given way to a more autonomous, and perhaps more competitive, professionalization

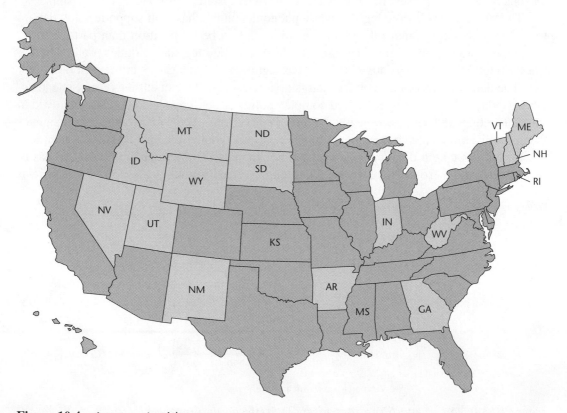

Figure 10.4   Amateur Legislatures

Source: National Conference of State Legislatures, Full and Part-Time Legislatures 2009, http://www.ncsl.org/Default.aspx?TabId=16701.

of independent legislative pursuits. In some states, however, part-time legislators have remained amateurs by choice, and the legislative culture has remained largely unaltered. On the whole the position of legislator is taking on the characteristics of a profession in its own right, and the position does not grant just a membership in an exclusive club.

LEGISLATIVE REFORM

State legislatures have undergone considerable change over the past couple of decades. Not only have the personal characteristics of the individual members changed, but the legislative institution has changed as well. One phrase might sum up the change that has occurred: **professionalization of the legislative institution**.

The need for reform was well documented by an exhaustive study of state legislatures conducted by the Citizens' Conference on State Legislatures in the late 1960s. Although the conference study found considerable variation in the institutional strength and professionalism of state legislatures, many were identified as being in need of major reform. Too many state legislators were popularly characterized as part-time dabblers in the business of legislating, constituency service, and administrative oversight. Legislatures were criticized for being too large and unwieldy, meeting too infrequently, possessing inadequate authority to initiate special sessions, being inadequately staffed to meet the rising demands placed on the legislative institution, providing inadequate office facilities for members, providing insufficient compensation to attract better-quality legislators, and not reducing the inordinate influence of interest groups through more effective regulation of lobbying.

In the course of its work, the conference established a number of factors by which each state might be rated on its relative capability. The principles underlying them were identified as follows:

1. Each chamber should be manageable in size to encourage full participation by its members.
2. Committees should be manageable in number and reasonable in member assignments.
3. Legislatures should not be limited by restrictions on frequency, length, or flexibility of sessions.
4. The legislative process should ensure the fair and effective consideration of bills by all legislators and should be comprehensible to the public.
5. Competent professional and clerical staff should be available to legislative leaders and members as well as to legislative service agencies.
6. Legislative salaries should reflect the demands and importance of the job. Reimbursement should be provided for necessary expenses.
7. The powers, methods of election, and length of terms for legislative leaders should be fair and should effectively distribute power and authority.

---

professionalization of legislatures The process of equipping legislatures institutionally to meet the increasing legislative demands placed upon them. This process includes lengthening the legislative session, providing adequate facilities and staff support, and improving computer support.

8. Adequate office space and other facilities should be provided.
9. Provision should be made for regulating lobbyists and conflicts of interest.[27]

These nine principles were then incorporated into five criteria—functional, accountable, informed, independent, and representative—which were then used to rate the 50 state legislatures. A brief description of each follows:

1. **Functionality.** Getting the job of legislating done and carrying out administrative oversight (a legislature's workability). The functional legislature has the ability to devote adequate time and to organize itself in such a way that it can handle the growing volume of legislative business in a competent, professional manner.

2. **Accountability.** Being responsive to the public it represents. The accountable legislature provides for public understanding of and involvement in its deliberative decision making. Members of the public have access to key documents used in the process of legislative deliberation, and the legislative process is open to public observation and input so that constituents can make judgments on how well their elected representatives are doing.

3. **Informed.** Having the information necessary to make knowledgeable public choices. The informed legislature is not dependent on the executive branch or organized interests for the information it uses to assess issues and analyze problems.

4. **Independence.** Exercising legislative decision making apart from undue executive influence. The independent legislature is not merely a servant of the governor or administrative agencies. It is capable of criticizing executive initiatives and of initiating viable policy alternatives as well as overseeing the activities of executive branch agencies. The independent legislature is free from executive dominance, and it is not beholden to organized interest groups.

5. **Representative.** Reflecting the diversity of the electorate who gave legislators the privilege of representing constituents' interests. The representative legislature is based on the one-man, one-vote principle. It also is responsive to its constituency's interests, such as legislating, overseeing executive branch activities, or providing services for constituents.

Over the past 40 years since the study's release, states have implemented many of the recommended reforms in areas such as session length, compensation, facilities, staff, and information. Examples of these reforms are given in the sections that follow.

Length of Session

Given the significant increase in the workload of state legislatures, pressures on the capacities of legislative bodies to meet the challenge have prompted state legislatures to expand their time in working sessions. In 1960, only 18 legislatures met annually and 32 met biennially. Today, 43 have annual sessions and just 7 meet every other year. In addition, sessions are now longer, and more legislatures are using the interim between sessions to do committee business and carry out special studies.[28]

DEBATING THE ISSUES

Do we really want professional legislators?

More legislators than ever now define their occupation as "legislator." Service as a state legislator has largely become a full-time job in the most populous states. This trend had its roots in the 1970s, the reformist period for state legislatures. Reformers wanted state legislatures to become better equipped to deal with the growing, complex policy issues that increasingly confronted legislative representatives. They saw the full-time legislator, aided by growing numbers of staff assistants, as best able to accumulate the expertise and to devote the attention needed to address pressing policy problems.

Do you agree with that assessment? Are there any trade-offs that should be considered? For instance, are career legislators more susceptible to capture by special interests than are part-time amateur legislators? Are part-timers who hold full-time employment outside the legislature more in touch with the real-world problems that people face in their daily lives? Or are they less able to invest the time necessary to understand policy problems and carefully evaluate alternative solutions? Where do you stand on this matter?

Go to the National Conference of State Legislatures' homepage at www.ncsl.org for a discussion of legislators' occupations and full-time versus part-time legislatures.

Compensation

With legislating becoming more of a full-time business, state legislatures turned their attention to their levels of pay and the facilities available. In 1970, the average salary for legislators from states holding annual sessions was $7,248.[29] By 2005, that figure exceeded $25,000.[30] In 2010, seven states paid their legislators at least $50,000 a year, and legislative pay ranged all the way from $200 for a two-year term in New Hampshire to a generous $95,291 a year in California.[31] In addition, most states provide per diem payments each day the legislature is in session.

Facilities

Office facilities for legislators have greatly improved. Instead of working out of their desks on the chamber floor, legislators have private offices. In many states, this meant the construction of new legislative office buildings; in others, it resulted in nonlegislative occupants of state capitols being ousted from their capitol offices. In Wisconsin, for example, the state treasurer and secretary of state were relocated to state executive office facilities.

Staff

Staffing state legislatures has been a growth industry over the past two decades or so; the greatest increase has come in the area of professional employment. During the six years from 1968 to 1974, immediately following the recommended reforms, the number of professional legislative staff members increased by nearly 130 percent across the states.[32] The actual numbers of professional staff vary considerably among the states, though all states have had considerable growth. The legislatures of Pennsylvania, New York, Texas, California, and Florida, in that order, employ the greatest number of professional workers, and those of Wyoming, North Dakota, South Dakota, Vermont, and Delaware employ the fewest.[33]

The number of staff members has grown in all areas of legislative support—bill drafting; committee assistance; leadership and individual member assistance; partisan caucus support; and other specialized areas such as information systems, reference services, and auditing and evaluation activities. One area of particularly notable growth has been legislative fiscal and audit staff support.

Who constitutes the ranks of recently hired professional staff members? Although a systematic study of legislative staff members has not been undertaken, observation of state legislatures at work, and of staff participation at national meetings, suggests that newer staff members tend to be young, having come to their new positions either directly out of college or after only a few years of work experience. Most often, prior employment was with other agencies of state government. Those who have established favorable reputations in state agencies, frequently while working in support areas such as budgeting, planning, program evaluation, and audit, often are lured away by the appeal of greater personal exposure and firsthand participation in the excitement of legislative politics and policy making.

Information

As legislative workloads grow, and as more legislators become full time, the need for better information storage and processing capabilities has become apparent. In response, most legislatures established or greatly expanded their information systems, including the acquisition and upgrading of computer hardware and applications software. Through networking, legislative computer systems have been connected with executive agency systems, thus providing legislatures with real-time information and enabling legislative staff to run simulations of the consequences of proposed changes in state aid formulas. Laptop computers can be found in legislative chambers and committee rooms in nearly all state capitols. The expanded use of computer technology has enabled legislative service agencies to draft bills and build budgets with greatly increased efficiency, and has enabled the public in a growing number of states to gain access to legislative information through the Internet.

CALLS FOR TERM LIMITS

Ironically, just as state legislatures have become more professional, the electorate in several states has voted to limit the terms of their state legislators, as was discussed in Chapter 8. Advocates of **term limits** include those who seek partisan gain by turning incumbents out of office. They align with individuals who see legislators as entrenched in their positions and more concerned with reelection and the privileges of office than with addressing

---

term limits Laws limiting the terms that legislators and governors may serve.

pressing public problems. Supporters of term limits associate long legislative tenure with detachment from the real concerns of ordinary citizens because professional legislators move within a capital-city crowd of government officials, lobbyists, and other political elites. Detractors, on the other hand, contend that voters already have the means at their disposal to remove unwanted legislators from office, by simply voting them out. The fact that they are returned to office signifies satisfaction with their performance. Critics also view term limits as undermining the legislative expertise that comes with experience and familiarity with programs and issues. Others, including the late journalist David Broder,[34] fear that term limits will invite more, rather than less, influence on the part of unelected political participants because inexperienced legislators can readily turn to legislative staff members, state agency officials, and lobbyists for information and assistance.

The irony is that supporters of term limits rate their own state representative as doing an acceptable job, but somehow they see the institution in need of fixing. These calls for reform are different from those of a few decades ago. Legislatures have indeed become more professional over the past couple of decades, causing a growing number of observers to yearn for a return to the days of the less insulated citizen-legislator. A growing number of national organizations are more than willing to assist them in that quest. Most prominent among them is a group called Americans Back in Charge (ABIC), which evolved from Coloradans Back in Charge, the organizing force behind Colorado's successful effort in 1990 to limit legislators' terms. ABIC provides legal research and advice to state groups on how to work term-limiting measures and get them on state ballots. It also offers guidance on campaign strategies and media promotion.[35]

Eighteen states had term-limit legislation on the books at the beginning of the twenty-first century. The Idaho legislature, however, repealed its statutory term limits in 2002, as did the Utah legislature in 2003. In 2004, the Wyoming State Supreme Court ruled its state's term limits unconstitutional. Thus, the number of states with term limits was reduced to 15.

Exploring the Web

Learning about State Legislatures

Do you want to learn more about your state legislature? Click on your state's link, found on the National Conference of State Legislatures' website, at *www.ncsl.org*.

■ The NCSL homepage also offers a wealth of comparative information about state legislatures across the nation and about the people who serve in them. Find out who serves in state legislatures. Learn about their education and occupations, and discover how many women and racial minority members have joined the ranks of state legislators.

■ Explore the many different policy issues facing state legislatures across the country.

■ Get online access to the NCSL public policy monthly, *State Legislatures*.

California's and Maine's were the first to take effect, in 1996. In California, 22 of the assembly's members were ineligible to run for reelection in that year. All 80 members serving in 1990 were gone in the 1997 session. In Maine, 26 of 151 members of the house and 4 of the 35 members of the senate could not run for reelection. By the 2006 elections, term limits had taken effect in 13 states. By 2010, term limits will take effect in all 15 states, that is, unless the courts or state legislatures take action to reverse them.[36]

As discussed in Chapter 8, term limits have been overturned by court action in Nebraska, Massachusetts, Oregon, Washington, and Wyoming. The Nebraska Supreme Court's action came in 1994, preventing term limits from taking effect. However, the voters passed a ballot measure in the 2000 election that reinstated term limits. Term-limit laws survived legal challenges in California and Michigan.

If limits stand and are implemented, they will decimate legislative tenure and the experience that goes with it. Most legislative leaders will assume their roles with less than four years of experience. Lessened experience may increase the influence of unelected legislative staff members, who will represent continuity in legislative operations. But it is still too early to assess the impact of term limits on lawmaking.

THE CHANGING EXECUTIVE–LEGISLATIVE BALANCE

With greater professionalization has come an increased desire on the part of legislators to challenge the traditional prerogatives of the governor and the executive branch. Critical observers of state politics traditionally have pointed to the governor as being best able to set the state's policy agenda.[37] After all, scholars traditionally view the governor as possessing most of the resources necessary for successful political competition. Beyond drawing on executive office staff, the governor can tap the vast staff resources available in the many cabinet agencies of the state bureaucracy. In addition, the governor is in a position to create task forces and commissions to consider issues and offer recommendations for gubernatorial and legislative action.

In contrast, academic observers in the 1960s and early 1970s characterized state legislatures as institutionally weak and reactive to the chief executive's initiatives.[38] Legislatures were understaffed, and the severe constraints on legislative activity, associated with limited sessions and part-time legislators, yielded a marked advantage to the governor and the executive branch. However, not only have state legislatures become far better staffed, they also have challenged the governor in areas of traditional executive prerogative. The following discussion covers several areas of legislative penetration.

Legislative Budgeting

Legislative fiscal bureaus and budget offices have been created and well staffed in order to add coherence to legislative budgeting—to bring some central order to an otherwise fragmented and disjointed legislative appropriations process. In addition to summarizing executive budget recommendations, legislative budget staffs develop and present alternatives to gubernatorial recommendations and, in some states, present recommendations to legislative fiscal committees and their respective chambers. A prominent example of the latter can be found in California, where the Legislative Analyst's Office presents a comprehensive package of alternatives to the governor's executive budget recommendations, complete with an analysis of their collective fiscal effect.[39] In other states, such as Wisconsin, fiscal staff members may offer alternatives but not make recommendations. The way in which the alternatives are presented often suggests fiscal staffs' preferences. Staff members also play an important role in keeping score of how legislative budget decisions modify the executive budget and affect the fiscal bottom line.

State legislatures have gotten more involved in the review of federal funds, an area of longstanding executive prerogative. Under the separation of powers doctrine, and being closely tied to the governor's role of chief state administrator, the receipt and use of federal funds traditionally has been viewed as a matter of executive discretion. As recently as 1979, most state legislatures chose not to appropriate federal funds. Instead they merely estimated in the state budget the amounts of federal funding that the state could expect to receive.

This picture changed dramatically by the early 1980s. In the 1981 legislative session alone, almost half the state legislatures enacted statutes increasing their oversight of federal funds and placing controls on the administration and expenditure of federal block grants.[40] Thirty-six state legislatures have acquired the authority to make sum-certain appropriations of federal funds. State legislatures have inserted themselves in the traditionally executive prerogative of controlling the receipt of federal funds outside the regular appropriations process. Today that power over interim federal funds resides with the legislature in 12 states. In another 7 states the legislature plays a strong advisory role.[41]

Legislative Review of Administration Rules

State agencies promulgate administrative rules that have the force of law. Such rules cover everything from the criteria to be used by a state highway department when ranking highway construction projects to safety requirements for commercial buildings that provide public access. Although administrative agencies have the authority to make rules following a statutorily prescribed process that involves public notice and hearing requirements, the rule-making process in most states provides a role for legislative supervision. By structuring that supervision, state legislatures assume various degrees of authority. Whereas legislatures in 41 states have adopted some form of legislative oversight, whether as a review of proposed or existing rules, 25 have assumed the authority to veto, suspend, or modify agency rules.[42] Eleven state legislatures give a legislative standing committee the authority to suspend rules. In all but one of those states (North Dakota), however, the entire legislature must sustain the committee's action if the suspension is to become a permanent decision.[43]

Sunset Laws

Another mechanism for legislative oversight of the executive branch is the sunset law. **Sunset laws** mandate the termination of designated agencies after prescribed periods, unless the legislature acts to continue them. Sunset laws, which were in greatest favor

---

sunset laws Laws mandating the termination of designated agencies after prescribed periods unless the legislature acts to continue them.

during the late 1970s and early 1980s, are based on the premise that state agencies should be forced periodically to justify their existence, to demonstrate that they are accomplishing what they are statutorily charged to do and that they are doing it efficiently. Agencies judged to have outlived their usefulness can be allowed to disappear. In addition, discrete laws can have sunset provisions attached, which wipe a specific law off the books unless the legislature acts to extend it.

Although sunset laws are still on the books in nearly half the states, they have accomplished little of substance.[44] Instead, they primarily serve a symbolic function, creating a perception that legislators are cracking down on unbridled government growth or pruning ineffective government activities. Rather than resulting in termination of major state agencies, sunset laws have been used as the basis for "beating up on the cosmetology inspectors." A few of the smaller regulatory agencies, most often those involving the licensing of some occupations, have been eliminated in a few states. As Alan Rosenthal, a close observer of state government, has noted, "Often what is removed is merely a nominal organizational structure, and not much else."[45] For that reason, sunset legislation has been repealed in 14 states.

What sunset laws have accomplished in several states, apart from their sparse record of bureaucratic reduction, is reinforcement of the legislature's role in oversight or administration. Through the review process associated with planned termination, legislative committees have come to learn much more about agency programs and operations. Even though it is not very realistic to expect that a highway or welfare department will be allowed to go out of business, the process of legislative review might turn up a number of issues or problems that could receive further attention in budget reviews or legislative audits.

The Legislative Audit

Whereas the legislature appoints auditors in most states, the people directly elect them in 19 states. An **audit** is a careful and systematic review used to determine whether resources have been spent in the way that was intended. Audits can uncover mistakes and wrongdoing. When popularly elected, state auditors tend to work more independently of the legislature. Six states have both an elected state auditor and a legislative auditor. In four other states, the state auditor is an executive branch official, appointed by the governor, the secretary of state, or the head of the state's chief administrative agency.[46]

Legislative audit agencies across the states have recently been turning away from financial audits to program or performance audits. Instead of exclusively examining whether the state's books balance, auditors have turned their attention toward assessing the degree to which programs are achieving their intended objectives. Such a review might assess, for example, the extent to which halfway house work-release programs have contributed to reduced recidivism. Another example might be a legislative assessment of the degree to which state universities have complied with statutory requirements

---

audit A review to determine whether resources have been spent the way they were intended or whether programs have accomplished their intended purposes.

governing the award of state-funded student financial aid. These new priorities have meant that legislative audit agencies in several states have refused to perform customary end-of-year financial audits of agencies or grants, arguing that they simply do not have sufficient staff members to continue business as usual with the added program auditing responsibilities. The resulting void in several states has been filled through the increased use of private audit firms under contract to state agencies.

Legislative auditors do not function autonomously; legislative committees approve the auditors' agenda, oversee the audit process, accept or reject audit reports, and propose legislation that takes corrective action. Although the committees may vote on which audits should be undertaken and in what order, the legislative auditor (referred to as the state auditor in some states) can greatly influence audit agenda setting—in terms not only of which audits are undertaken but also what is actually examined. The auditor is in a position to suggest how aggressively an audit committee should air its findings in public hearings and how doggedly it should hold agencies accountable for complying with audit recommendations.

Program or performance audits generally result in recommended administrative or managerial changes that state agencies are charged with implementing. In the course of the audit process, agencies are given the opportunity to comment on audit findings and proposed recommendations in draft form. After reviewing the agencies' responses, the audit bureau may make changes in what will become the final report. However, once a determination is made about the content of the final report, the agencies may be given a last opportunity to submit written comments, which most often are transmitted to the audit committee along with the report. Upon receiving the audit report, the committee schedules a public hearing at which the affected agencies are invited to appear. The committee will then vote to accept or reject the report's recommendations and may endorse legislative proposals offered to the full legislature for consideration.

An eight-year study of legislative program audits, involving nearly 500 reports from 31 states, reviewed the nature of their recommendations. Almost 90 percent recommended that agencies adopt administrative and managerial improvements on their own. About one-half proposed statutory changes, and about one-quarter recommended that the legislature pursue budgetary adjustments—providing a significant source of legislative initiatives.[47]

The Clash of Gubernatorial–Legislative Perspectives

Competition between the legislature and the governor has its roots in the very different perspectives that each brings to public policy making and implementation. As Alan Rosenthal has argued, the increased capacities of state legislatures have given them the tools required to pursue their interests through heightened competition with the governor. These interests have their origins in clashing gubernatorial–legislative perspectives.[48] For Rosenthal, the most notable differences include the following:

1. **The District/State Difference.** Legislators represent the interests of their districts, although they have to balance them with other factors such as their own values, policy preferences, and partisan pressures. Those interests can

be generalized across a district, for example, one characterized largely as populated by generally conservative, working-class constituents, or they can be more special interest, for instance, in a district where a large number of the constituents work for a dominant industry within that district's borders. District interests promote fragmentation and a politics of parochialism over what might be considered the broader statewide public good. Legislators may see their own district's fortunes as synonymous with the public good. However, conceptually and often practically, the two can be distinguished in a legislator's mind. Focusing on their district's fortunes, legislators often seek to form coalitions of colleagues whose districts also benefit from legislation, hoping to find enough support to prevail in the legislative process. Conversely, governors who have been elected by voters residing throughout the state, have no specific district interests to represent. Instead, governors pursue their view of what policy course is best for the state as a whole. That, however, does not mean that governors do not have their own policy preferences or special sympathies for certain interests. A governor might be predisposed to support the interests of business, for example, when they conflict with environmental protection, but such a preference cuts across district lines.

2. **The Piecemeal/Comprehensive Difference.** Legislators tend to approach legislation on a piecemeal basis, focusing on particular bills of interest. Targeted bills often affect district interests or fall within the province of a legislator's committee assignment. Governors tend to pay attention to their broader legislative agenda. They are interested in how the budget or other bills advance the thematic thrusts of the administration. The whole becomes most significant, not a discrete part or two.

3. **The Compromise/Coherence Difference.** Legislators thrive on compromise and accommodation, trading support for discrete legislation. Reciprocity is an important legislative norm. Although they engage in compromise, governors are more concerned with preserving the coherence of their legislative agendas. In this light, compromise often becomes a means toward preserving the coherence of the whole.

4. **The Short-Range/Long-Range Difference.** The legislative perspective is immediate, wrapped around getting legislation passed within the confines of the legislative session. The governor tends to take a longer-term view, being more concerned than the legislature with the implications of that legislation once enacted. The executive branch has to implement the legislation and make it work. Executive agencies must deal with unforeseen problems and worry about what comes next. As chief executive officer of the state, the governor has the responsibility to consider and deal with the interagency effects of legislation over time.

5. **The Collective Responsibility/Individual Responsibility Difference.** Legislators share responsibility; no individual legislator or legislative leader bears it fully. The public finds it hard to hold the entire legislature accountable. In fact, although they might grumble about what the legislature does,

they typically support the actions of their own legislative representatives. The governor, in contrast, does not have that luxury. The public associates the governor with the state and with its public policy. It is the governor who accrues favor or blame according to the state's fortunes. The public has one readily identifiable leader to hold accountable.

LEGISLATIVE DECISION MAKING

Given the clash of executive–legislative perspectives, on what basis do legislators make their decisions? Studies of legislative decision making consistently point to seven factors that appear to influence legislative choice most consistently: (1) partisanship, party positions, or stances taken by party leaders; (2) the individual legislator's ideology; (3) committee recommendations; (4) staff recommendations; (5) organized interest group positions; (6) the governor's recommendations and wishes; and (7) constituent interests. Of these factors, research most consistently supports political parties as exercising the most consistent and enduring influence on the policy choices made by state legislators. Yet this finding is in need of qualification because the relevance of party as a major factor in legislative decision making varies among the states, depending on the relative strength and competitiveness of parties in a given state and, to a lesser extent, on the nature of the issues being debated. Partisanship appears to be of stronger influence in urbanized and industrial states, which have greater electoral competitiveness, reflecting urban, suburban, and rural divisions. In competitive industrial states, Democrats tend to represent the urban residents, whereas Republicans generally represent suburban and rural interests.

Ideology appears to exert an influence on legislative decision making that is independent of partisanship. In the context of legislative decision making, ideology can be defined as "a set of general attitudes about the proper role of government in the allocation of values in society, containing a general evaluation of the status quo of wealth and power, and a general orientation toward the extent and nature of any changes that government should pursue."[49]

SUMMARY AND CONCLUSIONS

State legislatures have come into their own as formidable competitors in state policy making. Legislatures perform several important functions, including making state laws, approving state budgets, and overseeing the executive branch of state government. In addition, individual legislators provide services to their constituents. This is not to suggest that governors or the executive branch have lost the resources that have made them highly influential institutional participants in state policy making; they certainly have not. What it does suggest is that the legislature, as an institution, has been greatly strengthened. Legislatures have lengthened their sessions, increased the pay of their members, improved office facilities, added automated information services, and greatly increased staff support. Today, in most states, strong legislatures confront strong governors on matters of policy, reflecting the overall strengthening of the state in domestic policy making. Not only are legislatures exerting themselves in the legislative function, but they also are challenging the governor and executive branch in matters of traditional executive prerogative. They are dealing not from a position of structural weakness but from one of growing strength, and they are pressing their challenge on several fronts.

Discussion Questions

1. Is it legal for legislative districts to be equally apportioned on the basis of population but still be drawn to give one political party a decided electoral advantage over another? Compare and contrast the two methods employed to gerrymander legislative districts. What restrictions, if any, have the courts placed on gerrymandering?

2. In what ways does party affiliation play an important role in legislative organization?

3. Identify the leadership positions in state legislatures, noting the roles they play and the political resources they have at their disposal.

4. Discuss the functions that committees perform in the legislative process, and comment on the source and extent of their influence.

5. Has the executive–legislative balance changed since the 1960s? If so, provide substantive illustrations of any observed changes and discuss the factors promoting change.

Glossary

audit 264
Equal Protection Clause 244
full-time legislator 255
gerrymandering 242
majority leader 251
minority party leader 252

one-man, one-vote 241
packing 242
professionalization of the legislative institution 257
senate president 250
speaker 250

special legislative committees 254
splintering 242
standing committees of the legislature 254
sunset laws 263
term limits 260

Endnotes

1. National Conference of State Legislatures, Constituents per State Legislative District www.ncsl.org/programs/legman/elect/cnstprst.htm, 2004 update.

2. 369 U.S. 186 (1962).

3. 377 U.S. 533 (1964).

4. Ibid.

5. 376 U.S. 1 (1964).

6. 430 U.S. 144 (1977).

7. Peter S. Wattson, "Maps That Will Stand Up in Court," *State Legislatures* 16, no. 10 (September 1990), 15–19.

8. *Vieth v.* Jubelirer, 541 U.S. 267 (2004), www.oyex.org/oyez/resource/case/1648.

9. Sarah McCally Morehouse, *State Politics, Parties and Policy* (New York: Holt, Rinehart and Winston, 1981), 262.

10. *Shaw v. Reno,* 509 U.S. 630 (1993).

11. Quoted in Peter S. Wattson, "1990s Supreme Court Redistricting Decisions," *Treatise* (Minneapolis, Minn.: Senate Counsel and Research, 1997), 9.

12. *Shaw v. Hunt,* 116 S. Ct. 1894 (1994).

13. *Miller v. Johnson,* 115 S. Ct. 2475, 2504 (1995); *Bush v. Vera,* 116 S. Ct. 1941 (1996).

14. *League of United Latin American Citizens et al. v. Perry, Governor of Texas, et al.,* 05-204 (2006).

15. Robert S. Erikson, "The Partisan Impact of State Legislative Reapportionment," *Midwest Journal of Political Science* 15, no. 1 (February 1971), 70.

16. *The Book of the States,* 2005 ed. (Lexington, Ky.: Council of State Governments, 2005), 126–127.

17. Ibid., 136–137.

18. Daniel J. Blackburn, "How Willie Brown Solidified His Speakership," in *California Government Politics Annual 1984–1985,* eds. Thomas R. Hoeber and Charles M. Price (Sacramento: California Journal Press, 1984), 46.

19. Richard Zeiger, "The Odd Couple," in *California Government and Politics Annual 1986–1987*, eds. Thomas R. Hoeber and Charles M. Price (Sacramento: California Journal Press, 1986).

20. Alan Rosenthal, "If the Party's Over, Where's All That Noise Coming From?" *State Government* 57, no. 2 (1984), 53.

21. John J. Pitney Jr., "Leaders and Rules in the New York State Senate," *Legislative Studies Quarterly 7,* no. 4 (November 1982), 502.

22. *The Book of the States*, 2005, 176–177.

23. Ibid.

24. National Conference of State Legislatures, Percentages of Women in State Legislatures (as of May 9, 2011), http://www.ncsl.org/Default.aspx?TabId=21606.

25. National Conference of State Legislatures, Number of African American Legislators 2009, http://www.ncsl.org/Default.aspx?TabId=14781.

26. National Conference of State Legislatures, Legislator Demographics 2007, http://www.ncsl.org/default.aspx?tabid=14850.

27. *The Sometimes Governments: A Critical Study of the 50 American Legislatures,* 2d ed. (Kansas City, Mo.: Citizen's Conference of State Legislatures, 1973), 41–42.

28. National Conference of State Legislatures, www.ncsl.org/programs/fiscal/lbptabls/lbpc2t2.htm.

29. Ann O'M. Bowman and Richard C. Kearney, *The Resurgence of the States* (Englewood Cliffs, N.J.: Prentice Hall, 1986), 82.

30. National Conference of State Legislatures, *Legislator Compensation 2005*, www.ncsl.org/programs/legman/about/05salary.htm.

31. National Conference of State Legislatures, "2010 Legislator Compensation Data," http://www.ncsl.org/default.aspx?tabid=20117.

32. Gary T. Clarke and Charles R. Grezlak, "Legislative Staffs Show Improvement," *National Civic Review* 65, no. 6 (June 1976), 292.

33. National Conference of State Legislatures, *Size of State Legislative Staff 2009,* http://www.ncsl.org/default.aspx?tabid=14843.

34. David S. Broder, "Worse Than the Disease," *The Washington Post National Weekly Edition*, September 24–30, 1990, 4.

35. Stuart Rothenberg, "How Term Limits Became a National Phenomenon," *State Legislatures* 18, no. 1 (January 1992), 37.

36. National Conference of State Legislatures, *Term Limit States: By Year Enacted and Year of Impact,* www.ncsl.org/programs/legman/about/states.htm; Karen Hansen, "The Third Revolution," *State Legislatures* 23, no. 8 (September 1997), 20–26; Drew Leatherby, *State Government News* 40, no. 10 (December 1997), 14–18.

37. Sarah McCally Morehouse, "The Governor as Political Leader," in *Politics in the American States,* 3d ed., eds. Hubert Jacob et al. (Boston, Mass.: Little, Brown, 1976), 196–241; Coleman Ransone Jr., *The American Governorship* (Westport, CT: Greenwood Press, 1982); Larry Sabato, *Goodbye to Goodtime Charlie*, 2d ed. (Washington, D.C.: Congressional Quarterly Press, 1983); Alan Rosenthal, *Governors and Legislatures: Contending Powers* (Washington, D.C.: Congressional Quarterly, Inc., 1990); James J. Gosling, "Patterns of Stability and Change in Gubernatorial Policy Agendas," *State and Local Government Review* 23, no. 1 (Winter 1991), 2–12.

38. J. D. Barber, *The Lawmakers* (New Haven, Conn.: Yale University Press, 1965); Malcolm E. Jewell and Samuel C. Patterson, *The Legislative Process in the United States* (New York: Random House, 1966); Alan Rosenthal, *Legislative Performance in the States* (New York: Free Press, 1974).

39. Report of the Legislative Analyst for Fiscal Year 1996–1997 (Sacramento, Calif.: Legislative Analyst, 1997).

40. William Pound, "The State Legislatures," *The Book of the States*, *1982–1983* (Lexington, Ky.: Council of State Governments, 1982), 184.

41. *Legislative Oversight of Federal Funds* (Denver, Colo.: National Conference of State Legislatures, April 12, 1999), 5–6.

42. *The Book of the States*, 2002, 127–128.

43. Ibid.

44. *The Book of the States*, 2002, 129–131.

45. Alan Rosenthal, *Legislative Life* (New York: Harper & Row, 1981), 51.

46. Information provided by National Association of State Auditors, Comptrollers, and Treasurers.

47. Rosenthal, *Legislative Life,* 326–328.

48. Rosenthal, *Governors and Legislatures,* 52–55.

49. Robert M. Entman, "The Impact of Ideology on Legislative Behavior and Public Policy in the States," *Journal of Politics* 45, no. 1 (February 1983), 165–166.

11

Local Government Executives and Legislatures

LEARNING OBJECTIVES

- Identify the different major patterns of institutional arrangements for the governance of communities.
- Understand the nature of political power in communities, both formally and informally.
- Know the legacies of political machines and Progressive reforms for local governance.
- Appreciate the nature of face-to-face interactions in a setting where most elected government officials are neighbors who fulfill their responsibilities on a part-time basis.

When Richard Howorth moved back to Oxford, Mississippi, in 1979 to open a bookstore, he was returning to the small town where he grew up. He felt fortunate to acquire a lot for his store on a prime corner of Oxford's courthouse square. This was not only an ideal business location, it also put him right in the center of the social and political activity in his community. Howorth looked forward to interacting with people who were not only customers, but friends and neighbors.

In June 2009, Howorth was elected mayor of Oxford by a margin of 119 votes. Running for office was a last-minute decision. He filed his nomination papers just minutes before the deadline. In part, his decision was impulsive. In part, it was the result of conversations he had with individuals in the community who shared his concern over the pressures of growth in the community: inflated housing prices, plans for changing the town square, and big retail development on the town's periphery. The incumbent mayor's plan to cut down a lot of trees to make way for a Wal-Mart superstore was the last straw. Howorth was a leader of a group petitioning to stop that development, and members of that group were his core supporters for his mayoral bid.

In campaigning for election, Howorth went door to door to talk with the residents of Oxford. He found that his face-to-face interactions informed him of the concerns and hopes of his neighbors and also provided an opportunity to educate them about the implications of the kind of growth that had been planned for the community. Like most mayoral jobs, the one in Oxford is part-time. Richard Howorth will continue to run his bookstore while he governs his community.

Local governments are both more diverse and more homogeneous than state governments. The formal structures of cities, counties, townships, school boards, and special districts vary considerably. The informal dynamics among those who rule within communities range from a few families preserving traditional order to a large number of groups struggling to seize the upper hand. Yet at the center of all local governments, more than at the state or federal level, is the face-to-face interaction between an individual with authority and a person who is being served or regulated.

State, and especially federal, agencies deal indirectly with members of the public. Most of what federal officials do is establish policies and procedures to be followed by state and local governments. The Postal Service, the Internal Revenue Service, and the Forest Service, which work directly with the public, are exceptions. More common are the programs of welfare assistance, environmental and safety regulation, and transportation planning, in which federal officials work primarily with and through state and local governments.

Although states do much of their work directly (law enforcement, assistance to farmers, highway development and maintenance, higher education, corrections), governors, legislators, and administrators also address public policy problems by issuing mandates and providing assistance to local governments. As stated in Chapter 4, on state constitutions and local government charters, local governments are creatures of the state. Local government officials struggle constantly to balance the responsibility to administer state and federal programs and the need to make independent policy decisions for the community.

The buck stops at the local level. There is no one left to delegate responsibility to. The enforcement of laws, the application of regulations, and the provision of services by local units of government may be the direct result of a city ordinance or a school board action. What local governments do also might be the indirect result of a federal or state policy. Whether direct or indirect, almost everything local governments do involves face-to-face interactions.

This chapter describes the executive and legislative components of all types of local governments: cities, counties, towns, townships, schools, and special districts. (Remember the discussion on the legal foundations of the different types of local governments in Chapter 4 as you read this chapter.) The major reason for combining executive and legislative is that these two functions are not always separate in local governments. The separation of powers doctrine that is a key element of the federal constitution is not a common element of local government charters and enabling statutes.

The conceptual approach of this book has obvious applications when the locus of government is the community. When friends and neighbors govern one another, the interactions are visibly face to face. (Consider the Debating the Issues box on page 272.) Yet the factors that apply when strangers are face to face in governance are also relevant. It is important to know whether local government officials have competence and discretion and whether members of the public are supportive or cynical.

The intergovernmental setting affects the options available to local government personnel and sometimes challenges effective problem solving. Consider how officials might

DEBATING THE ISSUES

Can local government be too chummy?

An advantage of local government is that it is truly face to face. In most cases, officials are friends and neighbors who are doing civic duty part-time.

But can this kind of governance be too chummy? Suppose you want to appeal the decision of the city assessor about the value of your property. In your view, the assessor places the property at too high a value, and thus your property taxes are too high. Two of the three members of the appeals board are good friends of yours.

- Is this friendship going to give you an unfair advantage over others making an appeal?
- Does your friendship place the two members of the board in an awkward position?
- What should your friends do?
- What should you do?
- What should others making an appeal do?
- Can local government be too chummy?

deal with a case of child abuse. A social worker associated with a county welfare agency has access to various programs and funds that can be used for therapy and care, but he or she would have to get a city police officer to arrest and remove a parent who is responsible for the abuse. We often rely on schools for detecting signs of abuse, but school districts do not have the resources or authority to perform the roles of either the county welfare agency or city police department. In this case, as in many similar situations, problem solving requires the cooperation and coordination of several separate governments.

In small to midsize communities, key officials typically are part-time. Nonetheless, their responsibilities make them available to the public on a full-time basis. When school board members go shopping, city council members visit the park, and appeals board commissioners bowl, they inevitably meet with people who want to talk about pending issues. Home telephones ring throughout the evening. Friendships are sometimes tested.

Face-to-face governance certainly provides an opportunity for making decisions with a sound understanding of the unique character of a community. Voters really know the candidates in a local election. The potential also exists, however, for enforcing regulations, providing services, and electing someone based on friendships and rivalries. When that happens, even those who benefit are likely to view government cynically.

COMMUNITY POWER

We cannot always get an accurate picture of how government works by looking at government officials. It is important to know if power in a community is held by certain individuals or by certain groups or organizations.

Elite Theory

One view of power in American communities is that a single elite class, who has wealth and prestige, is in control. An example of elite power was portrayed in a study of Muncie, Indiana, completed in the 1930s.[1] A single family dominated the town. Anyone seeking job opportunities, political office, loans, or entrance into social circles required the support and assistance of this family.

Political science scholar Floyd Hunter provided another example in his study of Atlanta, Georgia, in the early 1950s. He found that Atlanta was run by a cohesive group of about 40 business owners. These individuals dominated social and civic affairs as well as economic activity. They determined what kinds of development occurred and what public policies were acceptable. Political institutions, according to Hunter, were subservient to an economic elite.

Some scholars criticized both the findings and the methods of elite theory studies.[2] They pointed out that Hunter based his study on an analysis of reputations. He was studying whether people were perceived to be powerful rather than more directly whether they *were* powerful. Although Hunter may have identified an elite, he did not prove that they controlled Atlanta government. Skeptics wondered if any midsize to large city could really be run by an elite group.

Pluralist Theory

Robert Dahl, in his classic study of New Haven, Connecticut, analyzed decision making rather than reputations and found that his own community had a variety of power centers rather than one ruling elite.[3] Each of these power centers (banks, labor unions, manufacturers, churches, political parties, schools, etc.) was dominant in a particular policy area, but not in all. Dahl did not find a core of people who were leaders in their respective groups that then came together as a central elite for the entire city.

Dahl consciously sought to test Floyd Hunter's theory. His finding of plurality of interest groups rather than an elite that governed the city could be interpreted as disproof of the elite theory. It could also simply be that communities in Atlanta and New Haven differ. Small, single-industry towns with ethnically homogeneous populations tend to have a single, dominant elite. Larger communities that have diverse economic activities and different ethnic groups better fit Dahl's pluralist model.[4]

And communities change. Studies of Atlanta following Hunter's acknowledge that there is evidence that a business elite did control Atlanta in the 1950s. However, the emergence of an African American majority in the city and the growth and diversification of Atlanta's economy since the mid-1960s have transformed the city. Racial politics are salient. There are urban, suburban, and edge-city differences. A variety of power centers have emerged, and Atlanta now is more like Dahl's pluralist model.[5]

The Disenfranchised

In Atlanta, as in other major metropolitan areas, a segment of the population is poor and undereducated. As pointed out in Chapter 6, these people tend not to participate in politics. They are alienated and have a low sense of efficacy.

The pluralist model does not address the issue of nonparticipants. The focus is on power centers, and the poor and disenfranchised are not part of power centers. As nonparticipants, these people do not force issues on the agenda of policymakers.[6] Nonetheless, while those in poverty have little effect on agenda setting, they are still governed. Police officers, welfare workers, and educators have face-to-face dealings with them, although they are not members of a power center.

Regardless of how community power is configured, formal authority resides in government. It is important to understand both who has informal social and economic power in a community and how local governments structure formal authority.

EXECUTIVE AND LEGISLATIVE INSTITUTIONS IN MUNICIPAL GOVERNMENT

Except for the traditional New England town meetings, in which anyone who is eligible to vote and shows up has the authority to help make decisions, municipal governments have one or more of the following institutions: mayor, manager, and city council. In addition, they all have employees who do the work of repairing streets, maintaining parks, disposing trash, policing neighborhoods, licensing bars and restaurants, and collecting taxes. These employees, often referred to as bureaucrats, are the subject of Chapter 12. Here we focus on legislative and executive offices.

Elected Executives

Mayors are elected, either from among the members of the city council or by the voters directly. A mayor is the chief elected executive in the city, just as the governor is the chief officer of the state. Elected chief executives in those villages or counties that have such an office are usually called a president or simply executive rather than mayor. The formal authority of elected chief executives varies considerably, even among cities or among counties. Regardless of the powers of the office, incumbents are the most visible figures in their respective governments. Like governors, these executives are in a position to shape the agenda.

Mayors of large cities work full-time and have a work force and scope of responsibilities similar to many governors. Most elected local government executives, however, hold their office part-time (20 hours or less per week). Average mayoral salaries average slightly below $10,000 per year. The jobs mayors have in addition to their government positions may create conflicts of interest. Mayors may be able to affect a decision on zoning or on a contract that benefits their own private property or business. The potential for conflict of interest is present for almost all officials, but especially for those who hold office part-time.

Since the 1960s, African Americans have made breakthroughs and won elections as mayors in some of the country's largest cities—Detroit, Philadelphia, Chicago, Los Angeles, New York, Atlanta, Baltimore, Seattle, New Orleans, and Memphis. Latinos have been

Los Angeles Mayor Antonio Villaraigosa interacts with politically active city residents.

successful in big cities such as Los Angeles, San Antonio, Miami, and Denver. Women have been in charge of city halls in San Francisco, San Diego, Houston, Atlanta, and Dallas.

Managers

Managers are full-time professionals who are hired to provide executive leadership to a community. Some managers are hired from among existing administrators who run departments in the jurisdiction. Others pursue a career in which they move from one community to another, often seeking appointment in a more desirable or larger community. In this category are people who got degrees in political science or public administration with the idea of becoming a city manager. There are also individuals who have been in private organizations or a public or not-for-profit agency and then move into local government management.[7]

Increasingly, individuals consciously pursue careers as local government managers. City managers have traditionally been white males. Women and minorities are increasingly entering the profession but still make up less than 5 percent of the total nationwide.[8]

As professionals, local government managers are supposed to avoid the fray of electoral politics. City managers who become identified as Democrats or Republicans or who are closely associated with a particular group in a community jeopardize their future if a leadership change occurs in a city council. A politically tainted manager does not fare well in the profession as a whole.

It is not easy to maintain isolation from political forces. City managers are expected to engage in agenda setting and policy analysis as well as to manage fiscal and human resources. City council members invariably rely on city managers for information and evaluation. When city managers assist one group, opponents of that group may identify them as part of the opposition rather than as a neutral resource.[9]

manager A professional hired by a government to direct daily operations and services and to make recommendations for policy changes.

Councils

A wide variety of local governments, including cities, villages, counties, and some towns, have elected **councils** or, as they are sometimes called, boards. In 60 percent of municipalities, the members of their councils are elected in **at-large elections**, which means that candidates compete in the city or town as a whole. There are two major types of at-large elections. In pure at-large elections, voters cast ballots for as many seats as there are being filled, and those candidates with the most votes are elected. In other words, if there are five vacancies on the council, each voter could vote for five candidates. The five candidates with the most votes are the winners. Another type of at-large system is position-oriented. In this system, each open seat on the council is given a number and candidates must announce which numbered seat they are seeking. Then voters cast a ballot for one candidate for each of the contested seats. This system allows groups and individuals to strategize in a way that avoids having candidates with similar views run against one another. Again, if there are five vacancies, a group might recruit and endorse one candidate for seat number 1, one for seat number 2, and so on, hoping to get what the group regards as five good candidates

DEBATING THE ISSUES

Do you think the local government in your hometown works well?

First, what kind of local government do you have in the city or town where you live? You might have one or more of the following:

- Mayor (or president)
- Manager
- City or town council

Or are you one of the few remaining communities governed by a commission?

What about the informal power in your community? Is there a particularly influential family or set of families? Are there businesses or churches that determine what happens? Do the most powerful actor or actors change depending on the issue?

Now, what are the criteria you would use in judging how well your local government works? Does it identify and solve the problems of the community? Are all groups in the community represented? Is the government run efficiently or is there a lot of waste? Is there corruption?

What, if any, changes would you make in your local government?

---

council An elected body that has the responsibility of running a local government. Local government councils may have both legislative and executive authority.

at-large election A process in which the entire jurisdiction serves as the constituency for an elected position.

elected. Under the pure at-large system, this group risks losing some or all candidates if others form effective coalitions supporting other individuals. Although strategies change, any at-large system emphasizes communitywide campaigning.

Thirteen percent of communities elect their members from **wards** or districts; the remaining 27 percent have a mixture of ward and at-large seats. Those elected from a ward or district focus on the concerns of specific neighborhoods.[10]

The problem with at-large elections in some communities is that ethnic minorities have a very difficult time getting their representatives elected. In 1982, Congress amended the 1965 Voting Rights Act to prohibit electoral systems that result in a dilution of the voting power of minorities. In *Derrickson v. City of Danville* (1987), a federal court ordered Danville, Illinois, to change from an at-large to a district election system because the city council historically underrepresented African Americans. In the next election, two African Americans gained seats on the city council. From 1982 to 1987, 10 percent of the cities with at-large systems changed to districts or mixed ones.[11]

Although local government councils are becoming more diversified, the last time the U.S. Census Bureau reported on the demographic traits of elected local government officials was 1992. It found that the typical member of a local government body is a white male between 40 and 49 years old. Women are on over one-third of all councils, but constitute only one-fourth of all council members. African Americans hold only 3 percent of local government council seats, and Hispanics hold only 1.5 percent.

Except for the largest cities, councils are only part-time bodies. They vary in size from 50 members in Chicago to 9 in Pittsburgh. California and many of the other Western states have statutes that provide for councils of five members unless the local community takes special steps to have more.

Although it was common in the nineteenth century for city councils to be bicameral, almost all are currently unicameral. To some extent, the committee responsible for budget issues—sometimes known as the board of estimates—creates a process similar to a bicameral legislature. Almost all city ordinances must get the approval of both the budget committee and the city council as a whole.

The procedures used by local government councils differ in a number of ways from those of state legislatures. Councils meet on a regular basis throughout the year rather than in a session that lasts two or three months. In large cities, the meetings are one or more times per week, whereas small municipalities might schedule sessions once a month. It is common for council sessions to begin with a public hearing in which citizens may speak for a limited time on topics of concern to them. Senior administrators usually are expected to be present to provide background information and to answer questions.

Professional administrators can sometimes co-opt members of a part-time city council. The head of a street department, for example, is bound to know much more about constructing and repairing city streets than a city council member. A detailed response filled

---

ward A geographic district within a jurisdiction. Wards can be electoral districts and/or administrative areas for the provision of services.

with cost estimates, asphalt qualities, and five-year plans is likely to overwhelm anyone who asks a question about a pothole. While expertise must be appreciated, a city council that is intimidated and becomes reluctant to ask questions and set priorities is not serving effectively.[12]

Patterns of Executive and Legislative Relations in Municipal Government

Historical Developments

In previous chapters, we noted the legacies of machine politics and of the Progressive Era on state constitutions, political parties, elections, governors, and state legislatures. These eras had profound effects on local government institutions as well. Political machines were founded and thrived in urban areas. The ethnic neighborhoods in Northern and Midwestern cities provided the building blocks for political machines. The efforts of Progressives to destroy these machines left lasting imprints on municipal institutions.

Urban Political Machines. Although the term *political machine* generally has a negative connotation, the history of this organization includes positive contributions. A major reason for the emergence of machines was to help new immigrants get settled. A family from Poland, for example, could enter a city in the United States; settle in a neighborhood in which other Polish immigrants lived; and get assistance with finding a job, house, church, school, and grocery store. Key to some of the assistance was the political machine. Electoral support from the Polish neighborhood helped the machine gain control of city government; in return, the machine gave the neighborhood good schools, streets, services, and jobs.[13]

What Progressive reformers found objectionable about political machines was their exclusiveness.[14] In part, they fought the emergence of political power that was at the expense of those who had already established residence and citizenship. In part, they argued against the provision of favors and opportunities in return for votes rather than on the basis of merit or open competition.

Urban political machines are almost, but not entirely, things of the past. The oldest and most celebrated political machine was Tammany Hall in New York City. This machine began as a social club in 1789 and became a well-oiled mechanism for Irish bloc voting and for patronage and services to those in Irish neighborhoods. Tammany Hall's most famous leader was William Marcy "Boss" Tweed, who controlled city hiring, contracts, franchises, construction activity, and licensing in the late 1800s. Boss Tweed stole millions from the city for his personal wealth, eventually was arrested, and died behind bars.[15] Tammany Hall ceased to function in the middle of the twentieth century.

The last major city machine was in Chicago. Mayor Richard J. Daley led this machine during its peak years, 1955 to 1976. He worked through local leaders in each of the city's 50 wards and in many of the suburban municipalities, dispensing favors and collecting votes. In his book on the Chicago machine, Milton Rakove detailed the links to ethnic groups as follows:

> The mayor's job has been an Irish job since 1933. The city clerk's job belongs to the Poles. The city treasurer can be a Jew, a Bohemian, or a black. On the county ticket, the county assessor, the state's attorney, and the county clerk must usually be Irish, but the county treasurer, the county superintendent of public schools, or the sheriff can be a member of one of the other ethnic or racial groups. A judicial slate is made up of three or four Irishmen, two or three Poles, several blacks, a Lithuanian, a German, a Scandinavian, several Bohemians, and several Italians.[16]

Daley died in office in 1976. His successors, including his son, Richard Jr., were unable to keep the machine cohesive and effective, and a federal investigation in 2006 brought indictments to a number of Chicago officials for patronage hiring.

The heyday of political machines seems over, but some of the patterns associated with this era continue. Ethnic bloc voting persists in many neighborhoods. Ethnicity is one of the informal but very real community power centers. Although no single boss or committee wields control from the center, patronage and favors are still available from individual candidates and specific ward bosses. Due largely to the establishment of civil service (discussed in Chapter 12), the opportunities for trading votes for jobs have diminished considerably, but they are still there.[17]

Progressive Reforms. The major goal of Progressives was to destroy political machines.[18] As covered in Chapter 8, some of the reforms aimed at opening the nomination and election process beyond the smoke-filled offices of party machine bosses.

Electoral reform for local governments included the removal of party identification of candidates on the ballot and the abolition of neighborhoods as constituencies. The first reform is known as **nonpartisan elections**; the second is known as at-large. Seventy-seven percent of all cities elect their officials in nonpartisan elections.[19] Both, especially when combined, almost eliminated the importance of ward or district leaders in a party machine. Nonpartisan elections make contests candidate-centered because party identification is at least formally irrelevant. When candidates are elected at-large, the links between neighborhoods and city officials are indirect and perhaps even nonexistent.

Progressives further sought to weaken machine influence by placing city jobs and services under the direction of professional managers instead of elected officials. The most common reform used for this purpose was the establishment of a city manager. The first community to establish a city manager form of government was Staunton, Virginia, in 1908. Elected representatives under this model make general policy, and the city manager implements that policy and provides information and advice for improving it. Some argue that the agenda-setting and policy evaluation roles of the city manager tend to make the manager a political leader in the community as well as a professional manager at city

---

nonpartisan election The ballot used in this kind of contest does not include any political party affiliations for the candidates. All candidates essentially run as independents.

government.[20] The model works best when both the elected council and the appointed manager are strong and assertive.

Intergovernmental Changes.   Chapter 3 discussed the legal and political relationships between local governments and the federal and state governments. The dramatic increase that was noted in federal government programs aimed at eliminating urban poverty had a major impact on the formal roles and structures of municipal governments. The War on Poverty during the presidency of Lyndon Johnson shaped the agendas of cities throughout the country. The availability of funds for housing and community development projects had the intended effect of focusing local attention on these issues. Cities often hired people and established agencies to develop a capacity for applying for federal grants. Thus, some city employees became in-house advocates for working with the federal government on these programs.[21]

A common feature of the War on Poverty programs was the requirement for "maximum feasible participation" by those most affected. Federal funds were used to encourage the formation of community groups. Funds generally went directly to community groups, bypassing state and local governments. This had the effect of isolating these groups from local politics and causing resentment and hostility.

Diversity among city governments continued to exist, but the mandates that accompanied federal programs forced a certain amount of homogenization of structures and processes.[22] Mandates continued to flow from Washington, even after Presidents Carter and Reagan reduced federal funds going to municipalities to a trickle.[23] Not surprisingly, mandates and requirements coming out of Washington typically set a single set of standards and follow a one-size-fits-all model.

Devolution, as pursued by President Clinton, worked primarily through state governments and prompted more diversity in how federally funded and federally mandated programs were implemented. Federal agencies identified a set of best practices and gave state and local governments fairly wide discretion in choosing among those practices when exercising delegated authority or using federal funds. Presidents Bill Clinton, George W. Bush, and Barak Obama also invited state and local governments to petition for waivers from federal rules they found did not apply well to a local situation.

The National League of Cities, the National Civic League, the National Association of Counties, the International City Management Association, and the U.S. Conference of Mayors also act to standardize local governments. They provide common sources of information and suggestions that lead to similar changes in the policies and procedures of municipalities.

Types of Municipal Governments

Table 11.1 shows the major forms of government. The size of the population in a city is to some extent associated with the different types. Cities over 25,000 do not have town meetings, and cities over 500,000 usually have a mayor–council organization.

Table 11.1 Major Forms of Municipal Government	
Mayor–council	39%
Council–manager	54
Commission	1
Town meeting	6

Source: The 2006 Municipal Year Book (Washington, D.C.:
  International City/County Management Association, 2006), 6.

Town Meeting.   This form of governance is found in small communities in New England and the Midwest. Town meetings are an almost pure form of democracy. Everyone in the community is invited to the meeting and may vote for officers and for policies. In practice, few take advantage of the opportunity, and grass-roots participation is minimal, as we noted in Chapter 6.

Mayor–Council.   The traditional American distrust of strong executives led some states and communities to provide mayors with very limited authority, which is reflected in one subset of the mayor–council form of government, the weak mayor system.

Weak Mayor: Usually the mayor in this subset is picked by the city council from among its own members. Weak mayors usually have a two-year term and can make only a few appointments to top city jobs. Department heads are in career positions and serve regardless of who is mayor. Weak mayors cannot veto legislation and have only a small role in the budget process. State laws or city charters endow city councils with both executive and legislative authorities, relegating mayors to little more than a ceremonial role.

Strong Mayor: A strong mayor variation has emerged as a common form in large municipalities. In this model, voters in the city directly elect the mayor, and the mayor usually serves a four-year term. He or she has the authority to hire and fire most or all department heads and is responsible for introducing a budget. The strong mayor may veto legislation passed by the city council, and some have a line-item veto. In short, strong mayors are similar to governors.

The mayor–council system is used most frequently by very large and by very small towns and villages, where the term *president* may be used instead of mayor. Newer, mid-size jurisdictions have opted for a type of government that is inherently less political and more professional: the council–manager form.[24]

---

weak mayor A governance system in which the elected chief executive has little formal authority over appointments, no or limited veto authority, and a minor formal role in the budget process.

strong mayor A governance system in which the elected chief executive has significant formal authority over appointments, veto authority over council actions, and a formal central role in the budget process.

Council–Manager. This form of government is a major legacy of the Progressive Era. Sometimes the **council–manager** form is referred to as reformed government, acknowledging the link to the Progressive reforms. As mentioned, the major intent was to remove the allocation of city jobs and services from politics and place the city under professional management. Some cities that have a manager also have a mayor, who possesses very limited formal authority.

The council–manager form of government is most often used by midsize cities. A majority of cities with populations between 25,000 and 250,000 employ this type of organization.

Commission. The **commission** form of government evolved from the response of Galveston, Texas, to a hurricane in 1900 that killed almost 10,000 people—a hurricane even more devastating than the one that hit Galveston in 2008. A group of prominent people in the business community formed a task force in the aftermath of the 1900 hurricane, with each member of the task force assuming responsibility for a specific functional area, such as housing, public safety, and finance. Task-force members took on the roles of both legislators making policy and managers implementing policy. The citizens of Galveston were so impressed with how well this task force or commission worked that they changed

Exploring the Web

Information from Local Government Associations

Several associations represent and serve various forms of local governments. These are good sources of information about local governments and about the issues of concern that officials at this level share. A general site is www.localgov.org. Sites for specific organizations are as follows:

- U.S. Conference of Mayors, *www.usmayors.org*
- National League of Cities, *www.nlc.org*
- National Association of Counties, *www.naco.org*
- National Civic League, *www.ncl.org*
- International City Management Association, *www.icma.org*
- International Institute of Municipal Clerks, *www.financenet.gov*

What issues are of concern to these associations? Is there a consensus among the associations?

---

council–manager A governance system that features an elected council that then hires a manager to run agencies and recommend policies.

commission A governance system in which individuals elected to the commission assume administrative responsibility for a specific dimension of government as well as legislative obligations for the jurisdiction as a whole.

their city charter to replace the mayor and city council with a commission, elected at large and on nonpartisan ballots. As with the task force, each commissioner had legislative and executive authority, and each specialized in one function area.

Shortly after Galveston established its commission, this form of government spread rapidly. Progressive reformers promoted the commission as an alternative to machine politics. By 1917, almost 500 cities had commissions. However, the inherent problems with having each commissioner responsible for a different area of government soon became evident. Commissioners tended to advocate their own policies and programs rather than unite to address the needs of the city. No one filled the role of a leader who set overall priorities or who initiated changes that went beyond existing budgets, programs, and agencies.

Cities, including Galveston, started abandoning commissions and adopting either the council–manager or mayor–council forms. As of 2011, slightly less than 3 percent of all cities still had commissions. Portland, Oregon, is the largest city with this form of government.

Hybrids. Increasingly, communities are adopting forms of government that include elements from more than one of the major types already described. A common pattern is to have a mayor and a manager, plus a city council. The mayor might be elected directly by voters, as in the case of the strong mayor system, or from among the members of the city council, as in the case of the weak mayor system. In 2000, 65 percent of the communities with council–manager forms of government also had a directly elected mayor.[25] An advantage of this hybrid, especially when the mayor is part-time, is that the community has the services of a full-time, professional manager and also has a visible, chief elected official who can set the agenda and represent the city.

Formal Structures and Informal Power

The initial attractions and then widespread abandonment of commissions illustrate the significance of formal structures. The locus of authority and the specialized roles of institutions within a government have a significant impact on decision making. A commissioner of parks may favor pleasant gardens in which to stroll and may oppose the construction of playgrounds, ball fields, and other facilities that might attract noisy crowds. If so, new neighborhoods developed in a community are not going to have city-sponsored green spaces that meet the needs of families with children. A change in park policy will require either a change of commissioner or a restructuring so that the authority to determine what kind of parks a city will have is held by officials who have a more comprehensive perspective on city needs. A mayor or city manager is more likely to be concerned about how parks fit in with community needs and with plans for growth than is someone who is just looking at parks.

Although formal structures matter, the dynamics of community power and informal relationships are also important. Floyd Hunter's analysis of Atlanta in the 1950s presented a case in which a fairly limited elite ruled Atlanta, regardless of precisely who was mayor or who was on the city council. Similarly, in some small towns, a family or small group of families may dominate behind the scenes. Newspapers can wield great influence by running stories that set the public agenda and by covering leaders in a favorable or an unflattering way. In the past, urban political machines were major sources of behind-the-scenes power.

Sometimes personalities play a role. An assertive member of the city council may have more influence on certain major decisions than the mayor. In governments that include both a mayor and a city manager, the latter often exercises more formal authority than does the mayor. Yet a popular mayor with a strong personality may turn those assets into formidable informal power.[26]

When Pete Wilson was the mayor of San Diego in the 1970s, for example, he held office in a council–manager government. At the time, San Diego had just experienced almost two decades of rapid but smooth growth. Much of the credit for this achievement went to the city manager, who had sound strategies and who provided effective leadership. Once the population reached about 700,000, the community debated whether further growth should be encouraged. Mayor Wilson, not the city manager, emerged as the one most effective in responding to the progrowth and antigrowth factions. In the process, he strengthened the mayor's office and weakened the city manager's.[27] Pete Wilson went on to become a U.S. senator and then governor of California.

Another important factor when considering the actual, not just the formal, roles of offices and institutions in municipal governments is the perception of the public. Most Americans assume that mayors are central political leaders and policymakers in their communities. Few are aware of the distinctions between strong and weak mayoral systems. Few understand the formal role and authority of a city manager.[28] The perception that mayors are strong and influential is a resource that can be used by mayors to turn perception into reality. They can claim to have the support of the community and assert both political and managerial leadership.

COUNTY GOVERNMENTS

As pointed out in Chapter 4, counties have been established as administrative divisions of the state. They do not exist because people have congregated together and need some form of governance in their communities, as is the case with cities. Originally, states appointed county officers. Counties have arbitrary borders set by the state. County lines can cut through a metropolitan area or become engulfed by a growing city. There are cities in which as many as three different counties have adjoining boundaries. This poses obvious problems when states make counties responsible for 911 services or welfare administration.

As administrative regions or districts for the state, counties have major responsibility for land registration and land use, local roads and highways, and law enforcement. More recently, states have given counties the responsibility for implementing public policies in other areas such as environmental protection and social welfare. In urban areas, counties sometimes operate regional facilities like airports, zoos, sports facilities, and convention centers.

County boards do not legislate general ordinances, as does a city council. The agenda of county board meetings is filled primarily with zoning issues and building regulations. The debates are usually over growth and environmental issues.

Table 11.2 Chief Executives and Counties	
System	**Number of Counties**
No executive	1,841
Elect administrator or executive	388
Hire administrator or executive	786
Merge with other jurisdictions	27

Source: Bureau of the Census, *Statistical Abstract of the United States, 2002* (Washington, D.C.: Government Printing Office, 2002), 292.

In large part because county law enforcement officers are directly elected and are charged with applying state laws to individuals, county boards rarely consider criminal justice issues. County sheriffs, coroners, and district (prosecuting) attorneys enjoy considerable autonomy, although the county board may have to approve their budgets and thus influence what they can do. County facilities such as airports, parks, zoos, and convention centers are usually set up to operate independently. County boards usually only deal with them when there is a crisis or major change.

The budget and personnel management responsibilities for the county lie with the county board. Decisions in these areas inevitably mean the county board gets involved even in the most independent operation. Members of the county board must allocate money in the budget to the various programs and departments. The board must authorize borrowing through the issuance of bonds to finance long-term projects such as buildings, bridges, and highways. Usually a committee of the board authorizes the hiring and firing of employees and, where unionization occurs, the approval of a collective bargaining agreement.

County board members can become involved in a broad range of policy and management issues. In some counties, in fact, the scope and complexity of county responsibilities have grown beyond the capacity of part-time board members. In response, states have allowed counties to elect or hire an executive, similar to a mayor or a city manager. As Table 11.2 shows, most counties have an elected board or a commission that performs administrative as well as legislative roles. Only 1.22 percent elect a county executive or administrator, and 27.8 percent hire one.

TOWNSHIPS

Townships share many of the characteristics of counties. Like counties, townships are administrative districts with arbitrary boundaries (usually 6-mile by 6-mile squares) that relate neither to where people live nor to where natural geographic features such as rivers exist. Voters in a township elect a board to govern the area. Again, like most counties, townships do not have a chief executive or manager; they rely on the boards to handle administrative and legislative issues.

Townships should not be confused with New England towns. The latter govern communities rather than predetermined 6-mile-square geographic areas. The New England towns

Table 11.3 Growth and Decline of Local Governments

Type of Government	1962	1972	1982	1992	2002
County	3,043	3,044	3,041	3,043	3,043
Municipal	18,000	18,517	19,076	19,296	19,437
Township and town	17,142	16,991	16,734	16,666	16,589
School district	34,678	15,781	14,851	14,556	14,226
Special district	18,323	23,885	28,078	33,131	35,472
Total	91,186	78,218	81,780	86,692	88,767

Source: Bureau of the Census, *Statistical Abstract of the United States, 2002* (Washington, D.C.: Government Printing Office, 2002), 291.

are governed by the almost romanticized town meeting, in which resident voters participate directly in passing ordinances and conducting other business. Town meetings consider budgets and make decisions about hiring employees, renewing contracts, and the like.

Only states in the Midwest and East have townships. Cities sometimes annex some or all of the land in a township in order to tax and provide services more efficiently to everyone in the area. States use townships to administer land laws, provide police service, and maintain roads. In urban areas it is often much more efficient to have the city perform all these functions by itself and to eliminate the townships. State laws specify how townships can be annexed or eliminated. Usually such actions are accompanied by emotional controversies. Table 11.3 reflects the growth and decline of the various types of local governments over a 30-year period. The number of townships, towns, and school districts has decreased; municipal and special districts have increased; and counties have held steady.

SCHOOL DISTRICTS

Public schools, kindergarten through grade 12, generally follow the council–manager model of governance. This represents a major change. Prior to the Progressive Era, schools were run by cities, and political machines regarded schools as an important part of patronage. The machines located schools in supportive neighborhoods and hired school employees from the pool of party workers. Reformers removed public schools from city governments and created special districts with their own governing structure and their own authority to levy taxes and borrow money.[29]

Some of the largest cities in the Northeast continue to run their public schools. The norm throughout the country, however, is governance by an independent, separate board, which usually has five to seven members but in large cities may have as many as fifteen. Typically, members are elected on a nonpartisan ballot. Campaigns are usually very low key, unless there is a scandal or major controversy. Since the mid-1980s, the religious right has targeted school board elections in certain communities in order to shape curricula to fit with fundamentalist Christian doctrine. This challenge has increased attention paid to school board elections. In some other communities, racial minorities concerned about the quality of education for their children have sought representation on school boards.[30] Most school board elections are at-large. In the Southern states, it is common for city or county officials to appoint school board members.

Women comprise a larger percentage of school board members than they do for any other elective office, although men dominate here, too. Over 34 percent of school board members are women, whereas only 19 percent of other local elective offices are held by women. African Americans constitute 1.6 percent of all school board members, and Hispanics 1.1 percent.[31]

School board members serve on a part-time basis, with no or very little compensation. A few run for school board as a steppingstone to some other office or to gain visibility for their business, but most are prompted by a genuine interest in educational policy issues, school financing, and the quality of educational opportunities.[32] The concern for education may be general in nature or may be specific. Someone may run for the school board to advocate keeping a neighborhood elementary school open, despite a recent decline in school-age children in the area.

As in the council–manager model, school boards hire a professional manager to administer the schools in the district. This manager, usually holding the title of superintendent, is not only in charge of operating the schools on a daily basis, but also is responsible for presenting the board with budget and policy recommendations. Although board members typically respect the superintendents they hire, they might also suspect them of being too defensive about current operations and too resistant to new ideas. On the other hand, superintendents understand the need for the school board to provide authorization and guidance for general policies, but they often resent interference and detailed scrutiny in matters that require educational and managerial expertise.[33] The tension involved in balancing the need for electoral representation with professional expertise is very visible in school districts, but this tension is endemic to almost all institutions of government in the United States. We will discuss this issue in Chapter 12.

Parents, teachers, and sometimes students are also involved in the governance of public schools. Parents, individually and collectively through structures like the parent–teacher organization, identify concerns and suggest improvements.[34] Parents present their issues to school board members, teachers, principals, and the superintendent.

Teachers likewise assert themselves individually as well as collectively. On an individual basis, teachers interact with school administrators. Collectively, teachers have formed unions and bargained contracts that include policy as well as compensation issues.[35] Policy may get into a union contract as provisions determining the size of classes, methods of teaching, teacher discretion in curriculum, and evaluation techniques. Teacher unions traditionally support Democratic candidates, and so Republicans have initiated moves to weaken these unions.

Students are more the recipients than the participants in the governance of school districts. Especially before high school, students are not in a position to interact meaningfully in the educational policy process. Although many high school students are more concerned with getting through school than they are with improving school, individuals at this age have the ability and sometimes the interest to offer evaluations and suggestions. Some students even make demands. In some school districts, boards include student representation or have an official link with student councils and organizations. In almost all districts, high school students can take advantage of the opportunity to address the school board through written petitions or during the public hearing parts of board meetings. Student concerns that are also voiced by parents or by some other actors are especially likely to have an impact. (Educational policy and its policies are discussed more fully in Chapter 15.)

OTHER SPECIAL DISTRICTS

As pointed out in Chapter 4, special districts have proliferated. In part, the explosion fits into a strategy by local governments to avoid taxation or bonding limits placed on them by governors and state legislatures. By establishing a special housing district, for example, a municipality can develop or redevelop living units in a particular area and pay for it with bonds or user fees that will not appear on the city's financial books.

The usual governing arrangement for a special district is a board of three to five persons appointed by city or county officials. In the housing example, the mayor would probably appoint the board. The mayor would want to appoint members who are supportive of the city's plans and priorities. Members of special district boards (also referred to as a corporation or **authority**) typically serve four-year terms and are paid very little, if anything. The terms are fixed, and it is nearly impossible to remove board members once they begin serving. Thus, although a mayor, city council, or county board may appoint individuals supportive of a given policy, the members of these special district boards have considerable independence. The independence allows these authorities and special districts to take unpopular actions such as raising fares for a mass transit system or using public bonds for a new facility to benefit a sports franchise.[36]

Most special district boards hire a manager and follow the council–manager model, much like school districts do.[37] Water and sewerage districts employ as many as 200 to

Kansas is one of the few states that has an elected state board of education. Most states have local boards. Here the Kansas Board discusses how to deal with evolution in textbooks.

---

authority   A local government that has a very specific responsibility and authority for services in a community. The most common authorities are those operating mass transit systems, airports, harbors, and sewerage systems.

300 workers. The Chicago Transit Authority has over 12,000 employees and a budget over $250 million. Clearly a full-time, professional manager is necessary to run these operations.

Special districts, other than school districts, are an invisible part of government, but not because there is an attempt to hide these districts or because they do not matter. They are covered by the open meeting and open records laws discussed in Chapter 6, and they are responsible for vital services in our society, such as fire protection, water and sewerage, urban transit, and public hospitals. The invisibility of special districts stems simply from a lack of general awareness about them.

In March and April 1993, over 403,000 people in Milwaukee became ill from an outbreak of cryptosporidiosis, which is caused by contaminated drinking water. Over 100 residents died. Individuals complained to the mayor's office instead of to the managers of the special district actually responsible for water. Even state and federal agencies dealing with environmental protection got more calls and letters than did the special district, which has low visibility.

Although the mayor's office, members of the city council, and officials in state and federal agencies can respond to questions and complaints by pointing citizens to special districts and by conveying the concerns to the proper authorities, such indirect communication is not preferred. An irate member of the public, having expressed anger and concern, may not make another phone call. Something important is lost when someone in the mayor's office reports to the manager of a special district how desperate and frustrated people are. A face-to-face communication is more effective in conveying the individual emotion that is part of the message. Special districts were not established to remove the leaders from the view of those they serve, but the effects are there nonetheless.

REGIONAL GOVERNANCE

The complex mosaic of local governments often cries out for cooperation and even consolidation of jurisdictions. When a community grows because of the location of new businesses and homes, one can have the emergence of a metropolitan area that includes several cities and villages; more than one school district; and multiple special districts providing water, sewerage, and transportation services. This is almost inevitable when governmental changes do not keep pace with demographic developments. This is also inevitable when we have some jurisdictions, like counties and school districts, that are created top-down by the state, and other jurisdictions that emerge bottom-up, like cities and villages. Unfortunately, existing local governments sometimes resist change and engage in conflict with one another, complicating growth and fragmenting communities.

To varying degrees, there have been voluntary agreements among local government units in some communities, and in others there have been formal moves consolidating jurisdictions in a region. The emergency 911 systems, for example, have forged coordinated responses in communities that include a number of police and fire departments. The process of establishing these systems has not always been easy. There are also examples of regional planning commissions, interlibrary loan systems, and joint recreation programs for young people. Counties have merged with cities and sometimes even with another county. The consolidations between Nashville and Davidson County, Jacksonville and Duvall County, and Indianapolis and Marion County are frequently cited as mergers that were well designed and effective.[38] Likewise, school districts have merged to serve growing needs in metropolitan areas and sometimes in rural areas where school-age populations have declined.

Cooperation is necessarily required when the governments in a metropolitan area or region include a tribe. As pointed out in Chapter 3, Native American nations have a sovereign status that is dependent on the federal government. Therefore, they are beyond state or local government taxation or regulation. Regional agreements that include reservation or trust land must be negotiated with the tribes, who typically agree to pay fees in lieu of taxes as part of a negotiated agreement.

State governments have exercised their authority over local governments, to encourage as well as to mandate regional pacts and consolidation. For example, legislatures have redrawn the boundaries of school districts to reflect population shifts in their respective states. Processes are spelled out in statutes that allow one jurisdiction to annex all or part of another and that describe how jurisdictions can merge specific agencies and still be eligible for state financial assistance. These processes are not always effective in avoiding conflict or in resolving problems. Sometimes they exacerbate the problems. Nonetheless, they do establish rules of the game.

It is easier, and thus more common, to consolidate services than to consolidate jurisdictions. Local governments can contract with one another to provide joint public health services or fire protection without having to re-draw boundaries or disband a town government. There might, of course, be contract disputes or stalemates in negotiations that would not be issues if one government clearly controlled an area. Nonetheless, having different governments design agreements for joint services is the more realistic approach and still results in savings and efficiencies.

SUMMARY AND CONCLUSIONS

Face-to-face governance is the direct and prevalent experience of local governments. Ironically, local government institutions and officials are often less visible than those of state and national governments. Individuals are much more likely to know who their senators and representative in Congress are than who is on their school board or city council. Yet local officials are readily available by phone; they live and work just down the street. They are our friends and neighbors.

The landscape of local government is a mosaic of overlapping jurisdictions and variations in form. Formal structures and informal power distribution do not always coincide. And the scenery is constantly changing. Townships are abolished. School districts consolidate. Special districts keep multiplying. Local governments in a region contract for joint services. Traditional community elites give way to professionals.

The complexity of local governments can be confusing. Nonetheless, local government employees are still accessible, especially for those who take the time and have the interest to get involved.

Discussion Questions

1. How would you describe the distribution of power in your hometown? Is there an elite group of families? Are there major businesses that seem to wield the most influence? Is the distribution of power fairly stable? On what is power based?

2. Relate community power in your hometown to the formal institutions of government. Are those who hold office the same as those you would describe as having informal power and prestige? Is there a group that is perceived to control what happens in government from behind the scenes? Do the concepts and processes of democracy seem relevant?

3. Are there disenfranchised people in your hometown? If so, can you explain why? What might realistically be done about it?

4. What are the pressures on a part-time elected official in local government? Why do you think individuals take on these responsibilities in addition to their family and job commitments?

5. When several jurisdictions, like a county, city, school board, and water and sewerage district, try to govern and serve the same community, one might expect chaos. Are there examples of chaos in your community that result from the multiplicity of rulers? In what ways might this actual or potential chaos be resolved?

Glossary

at-large election 276
authority 288
commission 282
council 276

council–manager 282
manager 275
nonpartisan election 279
strong mayor 281

ward 277
weak mayor 281

Endnotes

1. Robert S. Lynd and Helen M. Lynd, *Middletown in Transition* (New York: Harcourt, Brace, 1937).

2. Raymond Wolfinger, "Reputation and Reality in the Study of Community Power," *American Sociological Review* 25 (October 1960), 636–644; Robert A. Dahl, "A Critique of the Ruling Elite Model," *American Political Science Review* 52 (June 1958), 463–469; Nelson Polsby, *Community Power and Political Theory* (New Haven, Conn.: Yale University Press, 1963).

3. Robert Dahl, *Who Governs? Democracy and Power in an American City* (New Haven, Conn.: Yale University Press, 1996).

4. Robert E. Agger, Daniel Goldrich, and Bert Swanson, *The Rulers and the Ruled: Political Power and Impotence in American Communities* (New York: Wiley, 1964); Linton C. Freeman, *Patterns of Local Community Leadership* (Indianapolis, Ind.: Bobbs Merrill, 1968); and Aaron Wildavsky, *Leadership in a Small Town* (Totowa, N.J.: Bedminster Press, 1964).

5. M. Kent Jennings, *Community Influentials: The Elites of Atlanta* (New York: The Free Press, 1964); Edward C. Banfield, *Big City Politics* (New York: Random House, 1965).

6. See Peter Bachrach and Morton S. Baratz, "The Two Faces of Power," *American Political Science Review* 56 (December 1962), 945–953; Clarence N. Stone, "Systemic Power in Community Decision Making: A Restatement of Stratification Theory," *American Political Science Review* 74 (December 1980), 978–990.

7. Richard J. Stillman II, *The Rise of the City Manager: A Public Professional in Local Government* (Albuquerque: University of New Mexico Press, 1974).

8. Richard J. Stillman, "Local Public Management in Transition," *Public Management* (May 1982), 2–9.

9. James H. Svara, "Dichotomy and Duality: Reconceptualizing the Relationship between Policy and Administration in Council-Manager Cities," *Public Administration Review* (January/February 1985), 225–232.

10. James Clingermayer and Richard Feiock, "Constituencies, Campaign Support and Council Member Intervention in City Development Policy," *Social Science Quarterly* 74 (March 1993), 199–215.

11. Tari Renner, "Municipal Election Processes: The Impact of Minority Representation," *Baseline Data Report* 19 (November/December 1987), 4. See also Peggy Heilig and Robert J. Mundt, *Your Voice at City Hall* (Albany: State University of New York Press, 1984); Richard L. Engstrom and Michael D. McDonald, "The Election of Blacks to City Councils: Clarifying the Impact of Electoral Arrangements on the Seats/Population Relationship," *American Political Science Review* 75 (June 1981), 344–354.

12. Judith E. Gruber, *Controlling Bureaucracies: Dilemmas in Democratic Governance* (Berkeley: University of California Press, 1987). See also Cortus T. Koehler, "Policy Development and Legislative Oversight in Council Manager Cities: An Information and Communication Analysis," *Public Administration Review* 33 (September/October 1973), 433–441.

13. Steven P. Erie, *Rainbow's End: Irish-Americans and the Dilemmas of Urban Machine Politics, 1840–1985* (Berkeley: University of California Press, 1988); Alfred Steinberg, *The Bosses* (New York: New American Library, 1972).

14. Raymond E. Wolfinger, *The Politics of Progress* (Englewood Cliffs, N.J.: Prentice-Hall, 1964).

15. Seymour Mandelbaum, *Boss Tweed's New York* (New York: Wiley, 1955).

16. Milton Rakove, *Don't Make No Waves—Don't Back No Losers: An Insider's Analysis of the Daley Machine* (Bloomington: Indiana University Press, 1975), 96.

17. Raymond Wolfinger, "Why Machines Have Not Withered Away and Other Revisionist Thoughts," *Journal of Politics* 34 (May 1972), 365–398.

18. Samuel P. Hays, "The Politics of Reform in Municipal Government in the Progressive Era," *Pacific Northwest Quarterly* 55 (October 1964), 157–166.

19. Census Bureau, *Popularly Elected Officials, 1992*, 17.

20. See the debate in *Public Management* 34 (February 1962) between H. G. Pope, "Is the Manager a Political Leader? No." and Gladys Kammerer, "Is the Manager a Political Leader? Yes." See also Roy E. Green, *The Profession of Local Government Management: Management Expertise and the American Community* (New York: Prater, 1989).

21. Mark Gelfand, *A Nation of Cities: The Federal Government and Urban America* (New York: Oxford University Press, 1975).

22. James L. Sundquist, *Making Federalism Work: A Study of Program Coordination at the Local Level* (Washington, D.C.: Brookings Institution, 1969).

23. Martha A. Fabricius, "The 102nd's Multiplying Mandates," *State Legislatures* 18 (January 1992), 17–18; Martha A. Fabricius, "More Dictates from the Feds," *State Legislatures* 17 (February 1991), 28–31.

24. *The 2004 Municipal Year Book* (Washington, D.C.: International City/County Management Association, 2004), Table 2, xi.

25. Susan A. MacManus and Charles S. Bullock III, "The Form, Structure, and Composition of America's Municipalities in the New Millennium," *The 2003 Municipal Year Book* (Washington, D.C.: International City/County Management Association, 2003), 3–18.

26. Robert Paul Boynton and Deil S. Wright, "Mayor-Manager Relations in Large Council-Manager Cities: A Reinterpretation," *Public Administration Review* 31 (January/February 1971), 28–35.

27. Glen Sparrow, "The Emerging Chief Executive: The San Diego Experience," *National Civic Review* 74 (December 1985), 538–547.

28. David R. Berman and Bruce D. Merrill, "Citizen Attitudes toward Municipal Reform Institutions: A Testing of Some Assumptions," *Western Political Quarterly* 29 (June 1976), 274–283.

29. Mario Fantini, Marilyn Gittle, and Richard Magat, *Community Control and the Urban School* (New York: Praeger, 1970); Robert Bendiner, *The Politics of Schools* (New York: New American Library, 1969).

30. Kenneth J. Meier and Robert E. England, "Black Representation and Educational Policy: Are They Related?" *American Political Science Review* 35 (June 1984), 392–403; Ted P. Robinson, Robert E. England, and Kenneth J. Meier, "Black Resources and Black School Board Representation: Does Political Structure Matter?" *Social Science Quarterly* 66 (December 1985), 976–982.

31. Census Bureau, *Popularly Elected Local Officials, 1992*, 35 and 36.

32. Donald T. Alvery and Kenneth E. Underwood, "School Boards and Superintendents: How They Perceive Each Other," *Education Digest* 51 (February 1986); J. B. Hayden, "Superintendent-School Board Conflict: Working It Out," *Education Digest* 52 (April 1987), 11–13.

33. On school reform issues and processes, see John Chubb, *The Dilemma of Public School Improvement* (Washington, D.C.: Brookings Institution 1987), and John Chubb and Terry Moe, *Politics, Markets and School Performance* (Washington, D.C.: Brookings Institution, 1987).

34. Alan Rosenthal, *Pedagogues and Power: Teacher Groups and School Politics* (Syracuse, N.Y.: Syracuse University Press, 1969); Stephen Cole, *The Unionization of Teachers: A Case Study of the UFT* (New York: Praeger, 1969).

35. Nancy Burns, *The Formation of American Local Governments: Private Values in Public Institutions* (New York: Oxford University Press, 1994).

36. Robert G. Smith, *Public Authorities, Special Districts and Local Government* (Washington, D.C.: National Association of Counties, 1964).

37. Committee for Economic Development, *Reshaping Governments in Metropolitan Areas* (New York: Committee for Economic Development, 1970); Daniel R. Grant, "Urban and Suburban Nashville: A Case Study in Metropolitanism," *Journal of Politics* 17 (February 1955), 82–99; Brett W. Hawkins, *Nashville Metro: The Politics of City-County Consolidation* (Nashville, Tenn.: Vanderbilt University Press, 1966).

38. Burns, *The Formation of American Local Governments*.

CHAPTER 12

Bureaucracies

LEARNING OBJECTIVES

- Recognize the characteristics of bureaucracies.
- Appreciate the efforts to reform government bureaucracies and thus keep them efficient and focused on customers.
- Understand how governments hire and manage employees.
- Know how and why state agencies became regulators and know the process used for promulgating and implementing regulations.

Jane looked across her work desk. She saw that Sally clearly needed help and certainly seemed eager to get herself and her two small children into a stable and safe situation. Sally had been on welfare for five months and needed to use the remaining seven months of eligibility she had for benefits. She had enrolled in a training program to learn how to be a dental assistant. She was doing well. The salary for this job would allow her to be on her own and provide for her children, but the program lasted for 10 more months.

Jane was a caseworker for the state of Pennsylvania, and she was charged with administering the state's welfare program. She was concerned about the rule that would stop benefits from going to Sally three months before she completed her training program. Sally would have to halt her training and probably get two minimum-wage jobs to make ends meet. She would have to work extra hours. That would have serious negative side effects: less time with her children and additional child care expenses. Jane doubted that her superior would waive the rule limiting Sally's eligibility; however, Jane was determined to be a problem solver, not a rule-oriented bureaucrat.

Jane talked further with Sally. She learned Sally had a learning disability that had limited her ability to do well in high school and to seek certain job opportunities. This information provided the key that Jane needed. She could take Sally off the welfare program and place her on a six-month program that the state designed to help disabled individuals learn a job skill. The benefits of this program could be supplemented with food stamps and some child care assistance. At the end of that six-month period, Sally could return to the welfare program and have the support she needed to finish the dental assistant training and get a good job.

Sally is now a dental assistant. She sends Jane a message of thanks and best wishes every holiday season.

*B*ureaucracy is a four-letter word: one way to insult someone is to call him or her a bureaucrat. To do so is to describe an individual as insensitive, uncaring, and unthinking. The common image of bureaucrats is that of administrators so caught up with rules and procedures they have lost any interest in or ability to address the needs of people. Bureaucrats are aloof and arrogant. They are dull and unimaginative. Bureaucracies are organizations that are so big and so complex they are unable to get anything constructive done. They are impersonal. But as the chapter-opening vignette indicates, this stereotype is not always an accurate description.

In a more formal sense, the term *public bureaucracy* refers to institutions of government that carry out the wishes of the people as expressed by their elected representatives. When a state legislature and governor enact a law providing service to elderly citizens, a **bureaucracy** is charged with determining who is eligible, deciding how often and in what manner assistance will be delivered, and then making sure that quality work is completed. A city council that authorizes a particular plan for traffic flow relies on the street department to erect and maintain the necessary signal lights and street signs, and relies on the police department to enforce speed limits. (See the Debating the Issues box in this chapter for some of the agencies found in the bureaucratic structure of state and local governments.)

When the governor and legislative leaders in Minnesota could not agree on a budget in 2011, it was necessary to shut down most of the state's administrative agencies and send government workers home. Exempt were those essential for public safety, like prisons and the State Patrol. The results of suspending the state bureaucracy were complex and far-ranging. Barges could not go down the Mississippi River because state officials were not available to help dredge the shifting sand bars. A couple who had come from Texas to finalize adoption papers and get their baby were stuck in a motel room because the agency with which they needed to work was closed. Campers were turned away from state parks. State lottery sales halted, losing the state $1.25 million per day. The state lost even more money as they paid unemployment benefits to the 22,000 employees who were laid off.

Government institutions are necessary to implement the public policies made by governors, mayors, state legislatures, city councils, and school boards. Are public agencies necessary evils? As state and local government employees do their work, they can act like impersonal cogs in a bureaucratic machine. They can also be empathetic and discretionary as they do their jobs. What circumstances lead to service and problem solving as opposed to arrogance and insensitivity?

THE NATURE OF BUREAUCRACY

The negative image of bureaucracies comes primarily from the rules and routines—often referred to as red tape—established by organizations. Ironically, the creation of bureaucracies was intended to establish rules and routines that would ensure fairness, effectiveness, and efficiency.[1] The emphasis was on order, not insensitive treatment.

---

bureaucracy A large, complex organization; the administrative agencies that implement the public policies and provide the services of governments.

DEBATING THE ISSUES

Examples of administrative agencies

State Governments

- *Department of Public Instruction.* Provides financial aid and program assistance to public elementary and high schools and monitors compliance with regulations regarding compulsory school attendance, basic curriculum, and programs for children with special needs.
- *Department of Transportation.* Constructs and maintains highways throughout the state and implements federal interstate highway programs; also is responsible for highway safety and licensing drivers.
- *Department of Corrections.* Operates the state's prison system and directs parole programs.
- *Department of Justice.* Defends the government in legal actions brought against the state, investigates and prosecutes certain crimes, and assists local law enforcement and prosecution agencies.
- *Department of Health and Social Services.* Administers the variety of institutions and programs for the poor, the elderly, the mentally ill, the disabled, and other groups with special needs; monitors compliance of private and nonprofit providers of these services with state regulations.
- *Licensing and Regulatory Boards and Commissions.* Enforces compliance with state laws licensing occupations, regulates insurance and public utility companies, mandates equal employment opportunities, specifies health and safety standards for buildings and industries, and provides for labor relations agreements.
- *State University and Vocational-Technical Education.* Operates public colleges and universities and, in some states, administers programs for vocational and technical education.
- *Budget, Purchasing, and Personnel Departments.* Provides administrative services to other state agencies and ensures compliance with purchasing, personnel, and other policies and procedures that state government has set for itself.

Local Governments

- *School System.* Operates public elementary and high schools.
- *Park Department.* Constructs and maintains parks in the jurisdiction.
- *Police and Fire Departments.* Provide emergency services and public safety education; enforce laws.
- *Health and Human Services Department.* Determines individual and family eligibility for government programs for the poor, disabled, and elderly; provides services directly or through contracts with private and not-for-profit organizations.
- *Sanitation Department.* Collects refuse from homes and businesses on a regular schedule and cleans debris after storms and various emergencies.
- *Library System.* Maintains a collection of multimedia material for individuals to borrow and answers requests for a wide variety of information.
- *Budget, Purchasing, and Personnel Departments.* Provide administrative services to other local government agencies and ensure compliance with purchasing, personnel, and other policies and procedures that local government has set for itself.

The idea was to design organizations so that general policies would be made at the very top and then would be translated into operational decision rules and routines that could be followed consistently and easily by workers at even the lowest level of the organization.

A simple illustration of a bureaucratic organization that follows this model is the state government agency that issues driver's licenses. Why do we have to have a driver's license? Presumably, the fundamental concern is safety.

When your grandparents got their license to drive, it was probably a fairly casual and informal process. They went to the local police station and asked for a license. Depending on the officer or the town, they might have had to drive the family car a little or answer a few questions. There was nothing very formal or standard, and they went to the local police rather than to a state agency for licensing drivers.

As the incidence of auto accidents increased and as research was completed on what led to accidents, licensing got more complicated and more standardized. Agencies were established in state governments. Lawmakers and senior agency officials were persuaded that it was important for drivers to know basic laws and to have good eyesight. Road tests to be sure drivers knew how to operate vehicles seemed like a good idea. A minimum age also seemed reasonable.

These general principles and policies were then translated into rules and standardized routines. If you want to drive, you have to be at least 16 years old, pass an eye test (with glasses, if necessary), score well on a written test, and successfully run through a set of maneuvers with the vehicle. Since 2001, three-fourths of the states have adopted some form of a graduated driver's licensing program that restricts how many passengers new drivers may carry and what hours they can drive. Organizationally, senior officials decided what the general routines and requirements would be; middle-level officials then would be sure the lower-level staff administering the exams knew what to test for, and supervised them to be sure they were following directions.

Over time, more and more individuals wanted a driver's license. Agencies developed procedures for handling all the applicants, scheduled appointments, and kept regular office hours. Researchers and policymakers added more requirements that had to be passed down the organization. Individuals with a history of seizures had to be identified. Point systems were developed to suspend someone's license after a certain number of driving violations. All this meant more forms, more record keeping, and more bureaucrats.

Then society started using driver's licenses for purposes other than road safety. Businesses found it convenient to use them for identification purposes and pressured government to place photos on the licenses. Birthdates on the licenses allowed for determining who met age requirements for purchasing alcohol. Government agencies also relied on driver's licenses to identify individuals for security purposes. Again, implementation required new standards, procedures, and routines that were developed by middle management and performed by employees in their face-to-face interactions with the driving public.

DEBATING THE ISSUES

Should private companies do what public bureaucracies are now doing?

We could, it is argued, reduce the size of government and rely on private businesses to do much of what government agencies are doing. Private companies can (and in some communities do) take care of parks, pick up garbage, plow snow, and operate parking lots. Do local governments need to have their own agencies and employees provide these services? There are enterprises that take care of prisoners, and there are firms that collect debts that might also be able to collect taxes.

Proponents of government contracting with private companies argue that the competitive, profit-motive dynamic central to private enterprise leads to more efficient services and functions at less cost than is possible with government agencies. If we are not satisfied with the operations of one vendor, it is a lot easier to contract with another than it is to change the behaviors of a public bureaucracy.

Those who oppose using private companies point out that competition among vendors doesn't always exist in a given community, and they note the historic and contemporary cases of corruption that have accompanied government contracts. Businesses desperate for the contracts have used bribes and kickbacks. Public employee unions argue that one reason costs are sometimes lower is that some of these private companies do not pay their employees well.

Are private companies inevitably more efficient than public agencies? Are there functions such as operating prisons and collecting taxes that should not be contracted to profit-making firms? Why or why not?

This example of bureaucracy and organizational decision making is illustrated in Figure 12.1. The basic structure and levels of responsibility for policy making and implementation can be applied to many organizations, including your university—whether public or private.

Efficiency, not democracy, is the primary, traditional goal of administration. Bureaucracies, as traditionally defined, share four basic characteristics:

1. Job Specialization. An organizational innovation, key to the Industrial Revolution, was the establishment of assembly lines. Rather than expecting each worker to master all the skills needed to build a car or a radio, the producer of goods used many individuals, each of whom specialized in a particular task. The work of these specialists was orchestrated so that they made the contribution in the proper sequence and so that they would be kept constantly busy.

2. Hierarchy of Authority. The specialized skills that go into providing a service or making a product must be coordinated. That is typically done through control and direction from a central source and exercised through a chain of command from the top to the bottom of an organization.

3. System of Rules. Coordination depends not only on supervision but also on an understanding by everyone about what must be done and how it should be done. Rather than

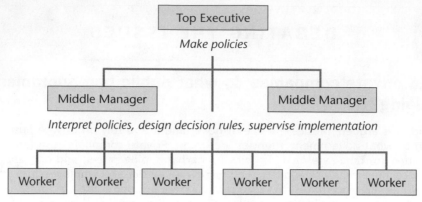

Figure 12.1 Bureaucratic Organization

considering anew what response should be made every time a common situation occurs, a rule provides guidance for quick, efficient action and for fair, consistent treatment.

4. Impersonality of Operation. If the administrative operations of any large organization are to proceed efficiently, employees must not let their personal feelings affect their decisions. Fairness and efficiency demand that rules be applied without regard for subjective concerns or personal stereotypes. Agencies that collect taxes, provide welfare, or educate students, for example, devise a set of rules so that all individuals who fit a certain category are treated the same.

One concern expressed by critics of bureaucracy is that each of these four traits can take on a life of its own.[2]

Some of the behavior of administrative agencies, as they wrestle with themselves as institutions and with what they were established to accomplish, can be understood by recognizing that agencies pursue two general types of goals: (1) those that are intended to have an impact on individuals or on society, and (2) those that concern the internal health and character of the agency itself.[3] Examples of the first type are the desire to improve the quality of water in a river or to aid farmers faced with the effects of a drought. Examples of the second include the need for an adequate budget and for qualified personnel.

Administrators must pursue both types of goals. A prison without adequate resources risks riots. A tax department with few auditors cannot identify many of the mistakes made on returns. Sometimes agencies are so successful in achieving their housekeeping goals that they acquire more employees and/or money than they need to do their job. This is the "fat" that budget cutters and efficiency experts try to identify.

What prompts an attack on a bureaucracy is not always clear. An accusation that an agency is too big can be a comment on how many employees and how much money it takes to get something done. It can also be a comment on how many people are on welfare; on the harassment of taxpayers over small, inadvertent errors; on the quality of students allowed to enroll in a university. Given the favorite refrain of politicians to cut government spending, public agencies are perennial targets. Thus, there is an ongoing cycle of suspicion and tension in which politicians assume waste and inefficiency and try to cut, whereas administrators assume they do not have all they need or could use and try to expand.[4]

PROFILE OF PUBLIC EMPLOYEES

The most common face-to-face interaction between individuals and government is with the employees of government agencies. Public school teachers, police officers, driver's license examiners, and park attendants are all public employees.

Public employees bring authority and expertise to the face-to-face interaction. The authority comes from the law that establishes the agency for whom the employee works. A state statute, for example, indicates that insurance companies will be regulated by an insurance commissioner and then specifies the general criteria for licensing insurance companies to operate in the state. Employees who work for the office of the insurance commissioner do their jobs under the authority of that statute. Laws also empower agencies to provide services such as education and to operate facilities like prisons and hospitals.

Librarians, police officers, firefighters, safety inspectors, teachers, and social workers all have expertise. Like other employers, governments usually have several applicants competing for an available job, and they choose the one who seems best prepared. When someone needs a service or is being regulated by a public agency, the employee with whom one deals has the authority and the expertise necessary to implement the agency's policies. A social worker has the authority to determine eligibility for various welfare and treatment programs and has the training to help solve individual and family problems by matching needs with available programs.

Members of the public approach face-to-face interaction in ways that depend on why the interaction is occurring and on what expectations might exist. An individual who is being arrested is likely to be hostile, whereas someone who is being rescued is likely to be grateful. Police officers know that part of their job involves hostile encounters and that part of it involves service. Teachers accept that they have to discipline students at times, but they also look forward to helping individuals learn and develop. As mentioned before, certain segments of society approach government from a history of poverty, neglect, and discrimination. They understandably tend to have low, negative expectations of both law enforcers and service providers.

A survey of public attitudes toward public employees found that, generally, individuals have low regard for bureaucrats as a group but positive views about the specific ones with whom they have dealt. As Table 12.1 shows, those surveyed did not think bureaucrats in general were competent, fair, or considerate. But when asked about specific, actual encounters with government employees, respondents reported a high level of satisfaction with the competence, fairness, and consideration that they experienced. In other words, like racial, religious, and gender stereotypes, it is common to hold a general negative image about bureaucrats even though this may not be confirmed by personal interactions.

State and local governments employ over 19 million people. Most (about 85 percent) work full-time (see Figure 12.2). School districts have the largest number of these

Table 12.1 Citizens' Opinions of Bureaucrats in General Versus Those with Whom They Have Dealt Personally (Percentage Satisfied or Highly Satisfied)

	General Evaluation	Own Experience
Overall satisfaction	65	74
Competence	31	72
Fairness	43	82
Consideration	38	77

Source: Robert I. Kahn, Barbara A. Gutek, Eugenia Barton, and Daniel Katz, "Americans Love Their Bureaucrats," *Psychology Today* (February, 1975), 22–29. Reprinted with permission.

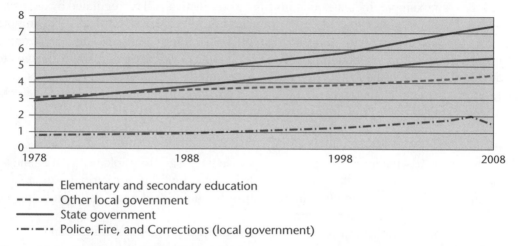

——— Elementary and secondary education
----- Other local government
——— State government
·—·—·· Police, Fire, and Corrections (local government)

Figure 12.2 Employment Growth in State and Local Government (in Millions of Employees)
Source: Calculated from *The Book of the States, 2006* (Lexington, Ky.: Council of State Governments, 2006), 444.

employees (32 percent of the total). State governments employ about 29 percent, counties 18 percent, and municipalities 16 percent. The remaining employees are hired by townships and special districts other than school systems. In contrast, the total number of federal government workers is about 3 million, or one-fifth the number of state and local employees. (These totals do not include employees who are working for private firms under contracts with governments.)

Organizations in the United States face the challenges of a major exodus of employees, particularly in senior positions, that has been sparked mainly by the retirement of baby boomers that began in 2011. This has been felt in state and local government agencies as well as most other sectors of society. It is common to have annual turnover rates of 6 to 8 percent. Depending on the agency and the occupation, vacancy rates beginning in the next decade will be 28 to 55 percent. Although some of the effects have been buffered by the recession that began in 2008, turnover due to retirements means more opportunities for college graduates. Inevitably, some jobs and routines will have to change because there simply will not be enough people to fill all the expected vacancies.[5]

Like other employers in our society, state and local governments have a history of segregating their jobs. Women traditionally have been hired as elementary school teachers, librarians, clericals, and nurses. Men are predominant in blue-collar jobs and as police officers, prison guards, firefighters, engineers, and managers.[6] In the South and Southwest, certain jobs, like those in trash collection and park maintenance, have been filled with minorities. Although it has been illegal since 1972 for state and local governments to screen job applicants on the basis of gender or race, the effects of past practices are still evident.[7]

PERSONNEL MANAGEMENT

Government is a labor-intensive enterprise. The ways in which state and local governments hire, promote, compensate, and treat their employees is crucial. The term **personnel management** refers to the full range of activities involved in securing and utilizing employees, including hiring, promoting, training, compensating, disciplining, and retiring workers. Much of personnel management applies to all organizations, public and private. Unique to the public sector are the issues related to democracy and the election of some key officials. Concerns about the possible effects of politics on personnel management have led to some important prohibitions.

Antimachines: The Merit System

The current approach to personnel management in state and local governments is the legacy of the battle against political machines. The assassination of President James Garfield provided reform advocates with a dramatic opportunity. On July 2, 1881, Charles J. Guiteau shot Garfield in the head because the president refused to reward Guiteau for his work in the campaign with a federal appointment. Guiteau was angry and hoped he would have better luck with Vice President Chester A. Arthur, a noted practitioner of patronage. After two months of painful lingering, Garfield died on September 19, 1881. In the public's mind, patronage was now visibly linked with evil. Something had to be done. Republicans, who had been the major beneficiaries of patronage opportunities, suffered severe losses in the 1882 elections, and civil service reform was enacted with the federal Pendleton Act of 1883.[8]

The essential features of a **civil service** or **merit system** are as follows:

1. Prohibition against using political party identity as a criterion for appointment to or retention in a government job.
2. Use of open, competitive examinations to rank qualified applicants for a job.
3. Establishment of a bipartisan, independent commission to act as a watchdog, thus ensuring the avoidance of patronage.

---

personnel management The actions taken to recruit, hire, supervise, train, discipline, compensate, and dismiss employees.

civil service A governmental personnel management that tries to insulate government employment from the partisan political process.

merit system Process for employing and retaining government employees that prohibits the consideration of partisan political ties. The term should *not* be used to refer to processes designed to hire and reward the most competent and productive employees.

The most important feature of a civil service or merit system is the prohibition against patronage. *Merit* seems a misnomer. The examination was designed to put at a disadvantage all the non-English-speaking immigrant groups that provided the building blocks of the political machines.[9] The examinations that were used did not test the ability of applicants to do the job they were seeking. Instead, a standard examination was administered to all applicants, regardless of which job they sought, and that examination was primarily an instrument that tested an individual's use of white, middle-class English in the United States.

The Pendleton Act applied just to the federal government, but in the immediate aftermath of this federal action, New York and Massachusetts passed laws outlawing patronage as a basis for state government jobs. So did Albany, New York, the first city to adopt a civil service system, and Cook County, Illinois, the first county to do so. As the Progressives won victories in Midwestern and Western states in the early twentieth century, civil service spread to those jurisdictions.

The federal government forced state and local governments to adopt so-called merit systems as a requirement for receiving funds from Washington. This string was first attached to the 1940 Social Security Act and then became a common requirement in federal programs. By 1949, a total of 23 states had adopted civil service laws. The number gradually grew to include all states and almost all local governments by 1972.[10]

Laws prescribe; they do not necessarily describe. Ironically, many of the first jurisdictions to adopt a merit system, like Massachusetts, Albany (New York), and Cook County (Illinois), continued to be notorious for patronage and machine politics. One way around the law was to appoint people on a temporary basis, even though *temporary* sometimes meant over 20 years. States like Nebraska and Indiana adopted civil service laws to cover only employees who were involved in administering federal programs, leaving others vulnerable to patronage politics.

In a series of cases, the U.S. Supreme Court has ruled that hiring and firing government employees on the basis of their partisan identity is a violation of First Amendment rights. Thus, the major objective of civil service legislation has now been accomplished in a more sweeping form: the establishment of constitutional protection. In *Elrod v. Burns* (1976) and *Branti v. Finkel* (1978), the Court ruled that governments firing employees because of their political party allegiances violated their rights of freedom of expression and association. The Court also ruled that dismissal on political grounds was justified only when the job involved an activity that was inherently political in nature, like speech writing. In *Cynthia Rutan et al. v. Republican Party of Illinois* (1990), the Court likewise said that hiring, promoting, or transferring individuals on the basis of party identity violated First Amendment rights. These particular Court rulings do not specify how individuals should be hired or fired, and they do not require the establishment of civil service commissions or personnel boards, but they do raise the general prohibition of patronage to a constitutional level.

Antidiscrimination: Job-Related Personnel Management

In 1964, the federal government enacted the Civil Rights Act. Title VII of that act prohibits discrimination in employment on the basis of race, gender, ethnicity, religion, or national origin. Originally, the act applied only to private-sector employers with more than

25 employees. In 1972, the act was amended to cover state and local governments and all employers with 15 or more employees.

Appointments and Dismissals.   In response to the Civil Rights Act and the court decisions that followed, state and local governments made major revisions in the way they advertised job opportunities and in the examinations they used to rank applicants.[11] The key legal defense if someone charged an employer with discrimination, and the key concern of public personnel managers, was to use only job-related criteria.[12] No longer could there be a standard civil service examination that was used for all jobs and that was biased against those who did not use white, middle-class English. No longer could physical strength tests be used to screen out women from firefighter or game warden jobs unless the jobs actually required certain physical attributes. The emphasis on job-related recruitment and examinations puts merit into the merit system.

There is a myth that the 1964 Civil Rights Act promotes and sanctions **quota systems** and **reverse discrimination**.[13] Employers who believe this myth may be engaging in a self-fulfilling prophecy. If, however, employers exclude white males from serious consideration for a job or a promotional opportunity, they are actually violating the law, not implementing it. U.S. Supreme Court decisions have made it clear that quota systems that exclude whites or men from certain opportunities are as unconstitutional as quota systems that exclude minorities or women.[14]

Less clear is the status of **affirmative action**, that is, conscious steps taken to remedy the effects of past discrimination. To varying degrees, employers have made efforts to diversify their work forces. Some say that preferences for diversification have been so strong that they lead to reverse discrimination. Others worry that efforts to abandon discrimination have not been serious enough. Facts can be used to support either side. The work forces of state and local governments are considerably more diversified today than they were in 1972, when the federal mandate for equal employment opportunities was put into effect. Just as clearly, white men continue to dominate, especially in the higher ranks of agencies and in the traditionally male jobs.

Compensation.   The federal Equal Pay Act of 1963 makes it illegal for employers, including state and local governments, to pay men and women differently if they are doing the same job. The allowable exceptions are differences in seniority or in productivity. The general language of the 1964 Civil Rights Act may prohibit differences in pay between job categories traditionally filled by men and those traditionally filled by women if the levels of responsibility and difficulty are the same.

---

quota system A requirement that a certain percentage or number of positions is available only to members of a particular gender and/or ethnic (or similar) groups.

reverse discrimination A process or set of criteria that puts men and/or whites at a disadvantage.

affirmative action Conscious efforts to remedy the effects of past discrimination. This term is distinct from and broader than the term *quota system*; *see* quota system.

In other words, the Equal Pay Act establishes the principle of **equal pay for equal work**. A beginning male police officer and a beginning female police officer, both working for the city of Boston, must be paid the same. The Civil Rights Act establishes the principle of equal pay for jobs of **comparable worth**. If librarians (traditionally female) and civil engineers (traditionally male) have jobs that are of similar complexity and responsibility, then these two job categories should be paid the same.

Comparable worth, or **pay equity**, is about making an adjustment in compensation to remedy the effects of past practices when women were allowed into only a few occupations (clerical, food service, teaching, nursing, and library work), and those jobs were paid on the assumption that women needed less because they were either supplementing their husband's salary or supporting just themselves.[15]

State and local governments, especially during the 1970s and 1980s, led employers in utilizing rather sophisticated methodologies to evaluate job categories and to determine the extent of gender-based pay disparities. This activity occurred amid controversy in the courts and among legal scholars about whether the 1964 Civil Rights Act requires pay equity. Another debate has been over whether, regardless of legal requirements, pay adjustments should be made. Proponents argue that the issue is justice, that the effects of past discrimination must be removed.[16] Opponents express concern about paying higher salaries than might be required by market forces. Although the issues remained unresolved, state and local governments continued to conduct studies and to make pay equity adjustments through the 1990s.[17]

Work Environment.   Sexual and racial harassment is the major form of discrimination found in the work environment. **Sexual harassment** includes both quid pro quo (in the form of employment opportunities for sexual favors) and hostile treatment that is gender-related. Racial harassment is hostility based on race. Harassment includes everything from rape and unwanted touching to inappropriate jokes and posters. The settings for sexual and racial harassment seem to increase as women and minorities enter occupations that once were closed to them.[18]

The U.S. Supreme Court affirmed in *Miller v. Bank of America* (1979) that the general language of the 1964 Civil Rights Act includes prohibiting sexual harassment. The Equal Employment Opportunity Commission (EEOC), which was established by Congress to oversee implementation of the 1964 Civil Rights Act, promulgated guidelines for state and local governments, as well as other employers, to ensure that their work environments are free of sexual harassment. These include informing all employees that sexual harassment

---

equal pay for equal work   Principle that individuals, regardless of race or gender, who are doing the same job should be paid the same wage.

comparable worth   *See* pay equity.

pay equity   Policy that adjusts the pay scales of jobs traditionally filled by women to the market value of male-dominated jobs of similar complexity and responsibility.

sexual harassment   Includes both efforts to require sexual favors for employment or favorable conditions of employment and activities that create a hostile work environment for someone because of his or her gender.

is not allowed and providing them with an opportunity to report instances of harassment to a central source in case the harasser is an employee's supervisor.

Besides the issue of fairness, sexual and racial harassment causes a loss of productivity. Some individuals are so affected by this hostile treatment that they become ill. Workers may quit their jobs rather than continue to endure harassment.[19] At a minimum, workers are distracted when there is harassment. A workplace that is hospitable for everyone is not only good for employees, it is also good for business.

State Immunity.   As employers, state and local governments are immune from lawsuits charging them with discrimination based on age or disabilities. The U.S. Supreme Court in *Kimel et al. v. Florida Board of Regents* (2000) ruled that the Eleventh Amendment to the U.S. Constitution protected states from being sued for violating the federal Age Discrimination Act of 1974. Similarly, in *University of Alabama v. Garrett* (2001), the Court said that states were protected from suits based on the 1990 Americans with Disabilities Act. In both instances, states might be guilty of discrimination, but the victims have no legal remedy under federal law. The Court did make it clear, however, that Eleventh Amendment immunity does not apply to the 1964 Civil Rights Act. The justices made a distinction between discrimination based on race or gender on the one hand, and age and disability on the other.

Employee Participation

State and local governments have sometimes been harsh employers. Public employees have experienced job insecurity, poverty-level salaries, and arbitrary management. One of the most infamous cases of ill treatment of employees was in the Boston Police Department in the early 1900s. Police officers worked an average of 87 hours per week. Stations were unsanitary and were infested with rats. The annual salary range was at the poverty level: $1,100 to $1,600 per year.

Conditions became so desperate that Boston police officers organized in 1919 and went on strike. Thieves and hoodlums had a field day. There was mayhem. The response, however, was not to listen to the officers and respond to their grievances, but to dismiss them and call out the State Guard to restore order. Calvin Coolidge, as governor of Massachusetts, acted swiftly and firmly. In doing so, he gained national popularity and catapulted himself into the White House.

Since before the Civil War, employees in the private business sector had formed unions to discuss issues with management and to bargain for work rules and compensation. It wasn't until 1959, however, that state and local government employees could negotiate a contract. In that year, Wisconsin passed a law requiring local governments to bargain if their employees formed a union. The major national public employee union, the American Federation of State, County, and Municipal Employees (AFSCME), started organizing in Madison, Wisconsin, in 1932.

During the 1960s and 1970s, the fastest growing unions in the United States represented state and local government employees. By 1992, a total of 41 states provided the right of public employees to organize and to bargain contracts. As of 2002, about 40 percent of all state employees belonged to unions, as did 50 percent of local government employees. Teachers, 70 percent of whom are union members, are the most unionized group of public employees.[20]

Unlike their private-sector counterparts, unionized public employees have severe restrictions on what they can include in their contracts. No state or local government allows bargaining on hiring. Union hiring halls, such as those that exist for workers in trades and crafts, do not exist in the public sector. No government allows bargaining on the mission of an agency. That is a legislative function. Only 31 states permit bargaining on compensation, and only two will bargain about retirement payments or benefits. All jurisdictions that allow any bargaining include work rules and processes for settling disputes and grievances.

In other words, public employee unions present a way for employees to participate in decisions about working conditions and sometimes about compensation. The foundation of every contract with state and local governments is a way of resolving disputes between managers and workers. Not all disputes, of course, are easily resolved. Sometimes there are high levels of frustration and bitterness that can lead to a strike, although strikes by public employees, with few exceptions, are illegal.

Unions, public and private, have functions other than representing members at the bargaining table. As pointed out in Chapter 7, unions are interest groups. They lobby and they help candidates get elected. As mentioned in the opening vignette to Chapter 6 and in the discussion of parties in Chapter 8, public employee unions have tended to support Democrats, and Republicans in some states have drastically repealed bargaining rights as a way of weakening unions and the Democratic Party.

Since the mid-1980s, state and local governments have been adopting a new approach to how agencies are run. That approach is called **total quality management (TQM) or continuous improvement**, or some variant of these titles.[21] A major component of TQM is employee participation in the analysis of how an agency is functioning and in designing improvements. The primary focus is on identifying and serving the customers of government (or the citizens served by government). Although unions have often resisted TQM, this approach is not necessarily contradictory to union collective bargaining.

Although some object that the term *customer* does not accurately describe voters and clients, TQM can be credited with changing the orientation and attitudes of many public employees to be more conscious of providing a service and of satisfying legitimate needs. This contribution of TQM is one of style, and it helps define the problems and agendas of public agencies. The emphasis on the customer promises more sensitive and service-oriented face-to-face interactions.

---

total quality management (TQM) An approach to management that emphasizes focus on customers, participation of workers, and ongoing analyses to improve productivity.

continuous improvement *See* total quality management (TQM).

An owner of a new vehicle registers it and gets a license at a community office of the Texas Motor Vehicle Bureau. Citizens appreciate convenience and courtesy in their face-to-face dealings with state and local administrations.

Exploring the Web

State and Local Agencies on the Web

Critique the website of a state or local government agency. Search for an agency in your community or state. Then evaluate the information and the format of the website.

- What information is on the website? Are there rules and regulations? Is there a description of services?
- Can you complete applications on the Web? If not, is there a need for face-to-face application?
- Is there an invitation to provide feedback on how the agency is doing?
- Can you ask for specific information?
- In general, does this website give you the image of an agency that is customer friendly?

State and local governments joined with the federal government in the 1990s to **reinvent government**. The term is taken from a book, by David Osborne and Ted Gaebler, that describes success stories primarily of various state and local agencies and then draws general lessons from them.[22] The proverbs of reinventing government reinforce the prescriptions of TQM, especially those on maintaining a focus on the customer and avoiding waste and irrelevancies.

The reinventing government lessons also reinforced the perspective that public officials should use private firms as partners or vendors wherever possible. Governments have always contracted with businesses. The renewed emphasis on **privatization** since the 1980s has been out of a concern that government bureaucracies were growing too large and doing more than they could handle effectively. The push for using the private sector is also due both to a belief in the virtues of competition and to political pressure to direct taxpayer dollars to businesses. The pressure is especially strong when those businesses strategically make substantial contributions to campaigns.

President Bill Clinton made the reinvention of government a visible plank in the platform of his presidential campaign in 1992. In part, he preferred the more positive and optimistic approach of drawing from the successes of state and local governments to the negative, pessimistic tone of bureaucrat bashing. Governors, mayors, school superintendents, and other leaders throughout the country then initiated task forces to consider how they might reinvent their governments. For some, the agenda was primarily to cut the size of government or to privatize certain public agency activities. However, the focus in general has been on customers and on what is essential to serve the needs of customers.

The twenty-first century began with most state and local governments having adopted TQM in some form. The new emphasis in improving public bureaucracies was to identify **best practices**. Agencies that have figured out a way of delivering services or administering regulations in a more efficient and effective way use websites and professional conferences to share their approaches. In a way, this approach is a sophisticated show-and-tell that uses well-documented success stories as models to be adopted.

AGENCY DISCRETION AND ACCOUNTABILITY

Another theme emphasized at the turn of this century has been accountability. Elected officials have renewed a search for ways of measuring how well public agencies are doing and then rewarding or punishing them accordingly. This approach often uses a form of contract that specifies performance objectives and budgetary consequences for reaching,

---

reinventing government A reform movement that focuses on the needs of government's customers and the most efficient way of providing for those needs. The reforms include cutting government activities that are not serving customer needs and using private firms whenever appropriate and possible.

privatization Steps to use private firms to accomplish the goals and missions of public agencies.

best practices An approach toward administrative improvement in which an agency identifies and documents a way that it has improved performance and then shares that with others.

exceeding, or failing to meet those objectives. Accountability reflects a concern about how public agencies perform and how they use their discretion.

Discretion used by individual administrators is, to a large extent, dependent on the discretion available to their respective agencies. Chapter 5 describes the general policy-making process that provides authorization to the bureaucracies of state and local governments. Authorization comes with some limits. Police departments are authorized to arrest individuals suspected of committing a crime. Police officers are limited in making arrests to those actions that have been identified as crimes, and they must proceed in ways that do not violate the constitutional rights of individuals. A public university is authorized to provide educational opportunities. Unless it secures enabling legislation, it may not make toothpaste or start a commercial airline. Private companies, however, have the option of changing their product line or expanding their scope of activities without securing legislative authorization.

The link between public bureaucracies and voters is primarily through elected officials. A source of frustration for many public administrators is that this means they have several bosses and that sometimes their multiple bosses are in conflict with one another. Governors and legislators share responsibility for directing the activities of state agencies. Governors and legislatures are frequently in conflict with one another. The pattern is the same for mayors and city councils. A superintendent who is hired and fired by a school board is obviously affected by the level of cooperation and conflict among school board members.

Accountability to Chief Executives

The traditional view is that governors and mayors are the heads of their respective executive branches and they direct their administrative agencies. Perhaps the most visible evidence of gubernatorial and mayoral concern with managerial control is the flurry of reorganizations common at the beginning of a chief executive's term of office.[23] The major purpose of reorganization sometimes is not to reflect new policies but rather to run government more efficiently.[24] Agencies are combined to eliminate redundancy and to provide better coordination. Agencies are created to reduce complexity and to provide better managerial control. Governors, mayors, county executives, and school boards typically launch reorganizations with promises of cutting costs and improving services.

Chief elected executives can use budgets to exercise policy control over administrative agencies. Budgets allocate resources to emphasize those items of most importance to a mayor or governor. Budgets have policy content, implicitly and explicitly, in the way they authorize spending. A transportation department that has funds for road construction or street repair, but little for mass transit, knows the priorities of elected officials. In a survey of top public administrators, the budget was cited as more important than the appointment of department heads for setting policy direction for an agency.[25]

It seems natural to regard mayors and governors as heads of the executive branch, but administrators perceive them as important primarily for management, not for policy direction. Chief elected officials, according to this survey, have more of an impact on how things get done rather than what gets done.[26] Legislators seem to be of prime importance for policy direction.

Accountability to Legislatures

A key concept in determining agency accountability is **legislative intent**, which refers to the objectives of the legislators when they pass a bill. Where the intent is clear, the mandate to agencies is also clear. Affirmative votes on proposed legislation, however, do not always reflect the same motive or intent. Legislative compromises sometimes consciously produce ambiguous and contradictory language. In these instances, administrative agencies may have an opportunity to exercise some freedom in interpreting the law and what it authorizes. Disputes over legislative intent can be resolved through subsequent clarifying of legislation or through litigation in court.

Agencies are rarely passive while legislatures deliberate over agency missions and resources. In fact, the origin of legislative intent sometimes is the agency itself. Agencies work with concerned legislators and with relevant interest groups in initiating new laws and revising old ones. Agencies lobby to affect legislative behavior. Like other lobbyists, agencies have information important to legislative deliberations, and they mobilize support from the governor or mayor, from interest groups, and from the media. The relationship among an agency, relevant interest groups, and key legislators is referred to as an **iron triangle**. The three can become so dependent on one another and so cozy that it is difficult to penetrate the relationship and exert accountability to a larger set of interests.

Agencies elaborate on the law through the promulgation of **administrative rules**. These rules, which usually can be implemented only if they are written in a process that allows for public comment, have the effect of law. A state statute authorizing the department of transportation to license drivers might be followed, for example, by rules specifying what the tests must include, who may administer them, where and when they may be administered, and what appeals may be made by those who fail them. State legislatures typically establish one or more committees to review administrative rules to be sure they conform to legislative intent. These committees can even suspend administrative rules for a limited period of time to allow the legislature to pass a clarifying law. If the legislature fails to act, the rules take effect.

The ongoing work of administrative agencies usually gets only limited legislative scrutiny, except when they come back before the legislature, city council, or county board at budget time. Further legislative involvement is either through casework for constituents or in response to a problem. City council members are approached by a neighbor, and state legislators are approached by a constituent, to get information or to pursue a complaint. Invariably this leads them to administrative agencies. A common response from agency personnel is to be annoyed with these inquiries, but also to recognize that a serious and prompt response is important to maintaining good relations with legislative officials.[27]

---

legislative intent The goals and mission of an administrative agency as defined by the purposes legislators had in mind when they passed a bill.

iron triangle An analytical perspective that focuses on relationships among the administrative agency, a legislative committee, and interest groups that are concerned about a particular policy.

administrative rules Legally binding regulations and procedures issued by an administrative agency as it interprets and implements a particular statute.

Governors and legislators understandably get upset when they think laws they helped enact are implemented by agencies in ways that disregard or are even contrary to their major intent. Public officials also are concerned that administrators act as efficiently as possible, reaching objectives while using the least amount of time, money, and human resources. The challenge to administrators is simultaneously to act in accordance with professional norms, to be responsive to the intent of policies, to communicate effectively with the public and public officials, and to develop routines that are fair and simple.

INDEPENDENT REGULATORY AGENCIES

Governments have created some agencies that are removed from the usual budgetary and appointment mechanisms for direction and oversight. The purpose is not to remove them entirely from accountability to elected officials, but to place more emphasis on professional discretion and responsibility. These agencies are purposely distanced from the potential pressures and discontinuities of electoral politics. In most cases, these agencies are located in state or federal rather than local governments and they are charged with regulating private enterprises.

Development of State Governments as Regulators

State-level actions defining standards of fairness in the marketplace began during the colonial period.[28] For the first century of the Republic's existence, states were the primary actors in regulation. States passed laws and established agencies to incorporate businesses; license certain occupations; and regulate banking, transportation, insurance, and utilities. Industrial states adopted regulations ensuring the safety and health of workers in factories. In 1874, Illinois led the way in regulating food and drugs.

The construction of an interstate railroad system prompted a major change in the role of the federal government in regulation and, concurrently, in the role of states. Railway transportation became a major feature of the economy. Railroad companies were in an enviable position. They also were suspect. Customers, sometimes with good reason, questioned price structures and service schedules. Community leaders raised concerns about what they regarded as the public interest.

State governments responded with investigations and regulations. States in the Northeast created advisory commissions to consider the many and conflicting interests associated with railroad development. In the 1870s, states in the Midwest created regulatory commissions that set rates and prohibited prices that would discriminate against any particular region or economic group.

Not surprisingly, the railroad companies feared continued state action. They could imagine high administrative and financial costs as they sought to comply with the variety of regulations coming out of each state. To avoid this situation, the railroad companies advocated regulation by the federal government. Their efforts led to passage of the Interstate Commerce Act in 1887, which established the first major federal regulatory agency, the Interstate Commerce Commission (ICC).[29]

This action by the federal government did not mean the demise of regulation by state governments. Some states recognized that the ICC preempted them, but they promulgated additional rules to apply to the railroads when they thought the ICC did not fully address certain issues. States continued to be active in other policy areas.

The regulation of public utilities by state governments took form during the turn of the last century and followed a pattern parallel to that of the railways. Electric companies were initially dependent on municipal governments for franchises and licenses. For some companies, this meant cooperating with the bosses of political machines. Executives of utility companies considered their options. They did not relish continuing to work with municipalities because they feared another option: public ownership by city governments. They rejected federal government regulation primarily because utilities, unlike railways, were more regionally based, and national standards were not likely to be sensitive to the unique needs and circumstances of local areas. State governments appeared the most feasible level of government. Governors Robert M. La Follette of Wisconsin, Charles Evans Hughes of New York, Woodrow Wilson of New Jersey, and Hiram Johnson of California, consistent with their Progressive philosophies and their desire to destroy political machines, were eager to assert a state role in utility regulation. The convergence of political and business objectives first led to laws establishing public utility commissions in Wisconsin and New York (1907). Within six years, two-thirds of the states followed suit.[30]

Regulatory policies, both in state governments and in the federal government, focused primarily on economic activities until the 1960s. The scope has since broadened to include concerns about the environment, general health hazards, and social issues such as discrimination.

Reasons for Regulation

Any single regulation can usually be based on several justifications. It is important to understand the various reasons why regulations exist.

Surrogate for Market Forces.   A traditional concern that has prompted government regulations is the need to prevent monopolies from charging exorbitant fees for essential services. An electric power company in a particular region, for example, could charge very high fees to businesses and private residences or provide inadequate service. The company could have a very short-term perspective and might not plan or research for the future. To avoid these problems, government regulations can set prices based on giving owners a reasonable but not exorbitant return on their investment. In addition, government agencies can require certain standards of services. Public service commissions can also demand that plans exist for future development. In effect, government regulations force businesses in this situation to behave as if there were competitive market forces in operation.

Technological developments have reduced the need to regulate some industries. Telecommunications, for example, now use satellites and dishes, not just wires. Electricity need not be conveyed by a single supplier to a given community. In response to these situations, state governments are withdrawing from some of their regulatory roles and allowing market forces to keep prices down and service up.

Protection. It is natural to think of the need for government regulations as a way to protect consumers from unscrupulous businesses. Consumers are not the only ones, however, who seek protection. Businesses themselves find some government regulations useful. The antitrust laws, both state and federal, were in large part a response to the concerns of some firms that they might be put out of business by the ruthlessness and unfair practices of a major competitor.

Government regulations can also be used as protection against bad public relations. Next time you fly on a commercial airline, listen to the standard speech about smoking and about putting carry-on baggage under the seat in front of you. Why are these restrictions in place? The speech cites federal regulations. In fact, the Federal Aviation Agency (FAA) promulgated these rules at the encouragement of the airline industry. Nonetheless, should a passenger object, the cabin attendant can conveniently blame the government. Similarly, state regulations are blamed when customers complain about the specifications of building design and materials, even though builders and architects usually play a major role in drafting those regulations.

Professions and occupations protect themselves through the use of state licensing boards. Investigations in 1986 suggested that as many as 10,000 people were practicing medicine as physicians or hospital residents with fraudulent degrees and licenses.[31] Individuals appointed to state licensing boards, with few exceptions, are members of the occupation that is being regulated. The requirements set by these boards make it illegal for someone to practice medicine, cut hair, sell real estate, or embalm a body unless the person meets the standards of that profession or occupation.

Likewise, the revocation of a license or some other sanction is done by state boards. This is another way for the profession to use government authority to police and protect itself. It also offers reassurance and protections to those who must rely on licensed practitioners but who are not in a position to judge personal qualifications. The public's protection is a critical part of justification for almost any government regulation.[32]

Externalities. A chemical company that dumps its waste into a nearby stream, thus polluting it, illustrates the need for government regulation because of an externality. The fundamental transaction for a chemical company is producing and selling a product to a customer. The waste produced is external to this transaction, and the issue created by the waste is called an externality. In this example, the waste becomes a central concern for the community and thus prompts government action. The federal government and state governments have established regulations to deal with externalities in order to foster and preserve a healthy environment.

Safety. State governments traditionally have regulated for safety reasons. Public health rules, for example, determine what must be done when someone has a contagious disease. Public health concerns are the impetus for state rules on the production, storage, transportation, processing, and serving of food. The federal government and some states regulate tools, machinery, and general working environments to ensure safety for workers. Safety is not always a value around which a consensus readily forms. Proposals to require motorcyclists to wear a helmet have been met with impassioned pleas to uphold the principle that individuals may choose their own risks and fate.

Equity.   Although the most visible example of a regulatory agency promoting equity is the federal EEOC, states are also active in this area. Some state regulations overlap federal ones. Others provide more protection than what is offered by the federal government. In the 1960s, states were generally considered laggards in the fight against discrimination. In the 1980s, states—particularly on both coasts and in the upper Midwest—pioneered efforts to prohibit discrimination based on sexual orientation and to ensure adherence to the principles of pay equity.

Regulation and Federalism

Several points have already been made about the relationships between federalism and regulation. Over the years of the Republic, distinct patterns of state and federal involvement in regulation have emerged.

Sole Responsibility: State Governments.   The regulation and licensure of occupations is an example of states acting without the involvement of the federal government. Another example is the regulation of the insurance industry. Interestingly, shortly after the U.S. Supreme Court ruled that the federal government had the constitutional authority to regulate insurance, Congress passed the McCarran Act of 1945, which provided for state government jurisdiction over this industry.

Sole Responsibility: Federal Government.   The Securities and Exchange Commission (SEC), which regulates the stock market, and the Federal Communications Commission (FCC), which regulates radio and television broadcasting, are the only regulatory agencies that have oversight of these industries. States do not have a role.

Parallel: Federal Preemption.   States and the federal government each have established regulations in some areas. Railway transportation and environmental protection are two examples. Wherever federal and state regulations conflict, the federal rules prevail. State regulations can supplement those of the federal government, but they do not contradict them.

Parallel: Federal Partial Preemption.   Federal partial preemption has become the most common pattern of state and federal involvement in regulation.[33] The federal government assumes responsibility in a particular policy area, thus potentially displacing conflicting regulations issued by states. However, the federal government can, on a compulsory or voluntary basis, hand responsibility to state governments. The Clean Air Act of 1970 is an example of a mandatory program of partial preemption. States must submit their own air pollution regulations to the federal government for review. Minimum standards must be met. More commonly, the pattern is voluntary, as with the Occupational Safety and Health Act (OSHA) of 1970. The federal government encourages state participation through the provision of authority and financial support. If states do not promulgate their own regulations, then federal rules apply. State governments do not always take advantage of a federal offer to assume responsibility. Some states appeared to take advantage of the OSHA partial preemption by enforcing their regulations less seriously than was done by the federal government.[34]

State Veto.   In a few instances, the federal government allows individual states to veto the application of regulations issued by Washington. Two examples of this are the Coastal Zone Management Act of 1972, which regulates drilling for oil in outer continental shelf areas, and the Nuclear Waste Policy Act of 1982, which governs the location of permanent depositories of high-level radioactive waste and spent nuclear fuel. In both of these acts, the U.S. Congress could override the vetoes of states, but because the process is so complicated, it will probably never be used.[35]

States retain considerable authority and autonomy in issuing regulations, even when the federal government is active. States do not necessarily celebrate this independence. When states are competing with one another for the location of economic enterprises, they do not enjoy being unique in promulgating new regulations. Although sound policy objectives may support the new regulations, states tend to want to avoid the image of having an overbearing, overregulating government. It is sometimes preferable, from this standpoint, for the federal government to mandate that everyone follow the same (hopefully beneficial) policy.

The Regulatory Process

The formal process of government regulation (see Figure 12.3) starts with passage of a law that authorizes an agency to regulate a certain activity. Let us suppose that a state legislature is concerned about the sale of dangerous firecrackers. The legislature knows that new firecrackers are being developed each year and that it would not be effective to pass a law banning those that are currently deemed dangerous because that presumably would not cover those that are still being developed. The legislature, however, does not want to pass a law banning all firecrackers. Instead, it passes a law establishing a Firecracker Control Commission to regulate the sale of firecrackers, with the specific intent to prohibit the sale of those regarded as dangerous. The law stipulates that the governor will appoint five persons to the commission, and they will serve five-year, staggered terms. The state senate must approve the appointments. The commission is given funds and authorization to hire a staff to provide legal, expert, and clerical support.

The commission is empowered to promulgate rules that specify criteria for banning a type of firecracker, penalties for violating regulations, requirements for dealers to report what they are selling, and so on. The process begins with writing a draft of proposed regulations. The commission must schedule public hearings to allow comment from interested parties.

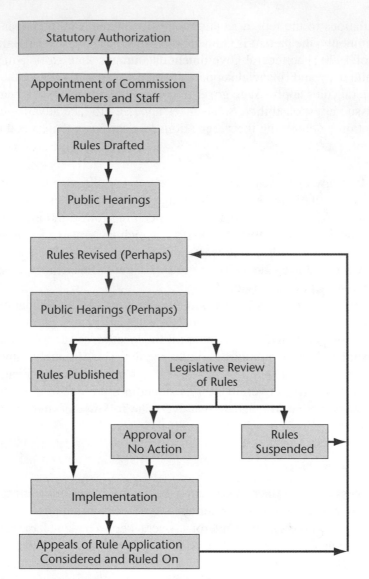

Figure 12.3 The Regulatory Process

These hearings are open to the public, and anyone may make a presentation or ask questions. (Typically, few individual consumers or citizens take advantage of this opportunity for participation.) After the hearing, the draft may be revised and more hearings may be held.

The commission then sends the regulations to a legislative committee that, in most states, may object to the rules, suspend them for a limited time, and try to persuade the commission to submit different regulations. The committee cannot revise the rules. Because statutes supersede rules, however, the full legislature and the governor can enact a law that changes an unpopular regulation.

Once the regulations have passed this limited legislative review, the commission then acts as both an administrative and a judicial body. It is responsible for educating the public to secure compliance and for enforcing the regulations when there is a violation.

Those penalized for not conforming to the regulations may appeal to the commission. In addition to ensuring that a penalty is justified, appeals provide another opportunity for reaction to what the commission is doing. One result of an appeal may be the revision of some of the existing regulations. Reevaluations and revisions are sometimes prompted by information gathered through the face-to-face interactions that are part of the application of decision rules.

PRIVATIZATION

In part as a response to what some perceived as high taxes and excessive government regulation, a push began in the 1980s to replace government bureaucracy with private efforts. Another motive for this effort—known as privatization—is the desire to help businesses by giving them government work. Included are two rather distinct approaches to privatization: deregulation and contracting.

Deregulation

Deregulation changes the scope of government responsibility and authority. Advocates of this form of privatization argue that government should not have laws that govern certain business, social, or private behaviors. Perhaps they feel government should never have had regulations in that area or that something has changed so that governmental restrictions are no longer necessary or appropriate. An example of the latter is the need for controls over prices and supplies of electricity. When technology allowed only one company to provide electricity over a line, monopolies were necessary and restrictions on the behavior of these monopolies also became necessary. Now, however, several companies can simultaneously send electricity over the same line, thus allowing competition. The assumption is that competition will keep prices low and service high.

Deregulation may mean more choices rather than no rules at all. In the environmental area, for example, companies may have several different ways to reduce pollution, rather than having to adhere to one approach. In accordance with the ideas of reinventing government, an agency can identify the end result that is required but then may be flexible in how that result is achieved.

Within federalism, a form of deregulation is devolution. In some policy areas—like the environment and public health—the federal government has chosen to maintain general standards that must be met, but then relies on states to conduct day-to-day monitoring and to exercise discretion in how to apply the rules to specific situations. In some sense, devolution is deregulating state governments and is an acknowledgment of the capacities of the professionals and agencies in the states.

Waivers by federal agencies are a type of devolution. As described in earlier chapters, when a federal agency waives or exempts a state from a particular regulation, it does so only for a limited amount of time, and the waiver cannot cost the federal government more money.

DEBATING THE ISSUES

Views on government regulation

One debate on government regulation has to do with what, if anything, should be regulated. Should government regulate businesses or should it let market forces determine what businesses should and shouldn't do? Are there perhaps only some aspects of business operations that should be regulated—such as pollution, prices, labor practices, advertising, or driving out competition? What are the public needs, if any, that should supersede market forces—safety? Fair prices? Environment? Labor conditions?

What about personal and social behavior and government regulation? Should the government pass laws mandating the use of seatbelts or motorcycle/bike helmets? Should the government restrict sexual behavior? Marriage? Abortion? With the consideration of business regulation, what are the general principles of public interest or needs that should override private behavior?

Another set of concerns about government regulation is whether the public is served or whether special interests are served. For example, are state regulations licensing doctors, lawyers, and other professionals a way of keeping some people from doing the work, or are they protecting the public? Are building codes ensuring sound and safe structures, or are they really a way of favoring professional builders, plumbers, and electricians?

Contracting

Privatization frequently refers to contracting by a government agency with a company or a not-for-profit organization. This is also referred to as outsourcing. The public sector in the United States has always been relatively limited, and governments have always contracted with private vendors. Contracts traditionally have included a wide variety of services, such as road construction and repair, waste collection, managerial evaluations, and job training. More recently, the scope and frequency of contracting have expanded considerably. States are now contracting with private companies to incarcerate criminals, and with both profit and not-for-profit organizations to administer welfare programs and school systems. There are no apparent limits to what might be included in contracting.

Both philosophical and empirical concerns drive the use of contractors rather than public agencies and employees. Advocates of expanded contracting include those who believe that government bureaucracies are inherently inefficient and wasteful, whereas private firms provide more benefits and fewer costs. Proponents of contracting tout the advantages of competition between service providers and also point to situations where a private company can complete a two- or three-year project or a very specific task and there is no need to establish a more permanent bureaucracy. Arguments against contracting include a view that government is the most appropriate provider of law and order, security, and common goods. Sometimes contracts with private vendors cost more than if done by public agencies. Public employees point out that when there are savings, these are often achieved by paying lower wages or fewer benefits to the workers of the private business or nonprofit organization.

Not surprisingly, there are instances when contracted services are not delivered and when the money provided to a contractor is not used appropriately. Contracts might also be linked to campaign contributions given by those seeking business from a state or local government. These cases cause scandals. Contract monitoring is the responsibility of both the agency and the legislatures.

SUMMARY AND CONCLUSIONS

Most face-to-face interactions with state and local government officials are with the non-elected employees of public agencies. Although we generally hold a negative stereotype of bureaucrats and bureaucracy in our minds, actual experiences with individuals are usually empathetic and service-oriented. Current management reforms, such as TQM and reinventing government, place a major emphasis on service and problem solving.

Nonetheless, organizations rely on rules and on impersonality. Ideally, this provides for fairness but sometimes leads to rudeness and arbitrary treatment. The decision rules that were originally meant to ensure that a policy is implemented can take on lives of their own and divert employees from problem solving.

The discretion that public employees may exercise in the substance of their decisions and the style of their behavior is framed in part by the laws that authorize actions by an agency. Those laws limit as well as enable. The organizational hierarchy within which government workers operate also provides both limits and discretion. Supervisors who trust their employees will give them more discretion than those who do not and thus closely monitor employee behavior. Organizations that have service-oriented cultures do more individual problem solving than those with rigid approaches.

How discretion is exercised is also a function of who the employee is. The stereotypes that individual public employees might have are likely to have an impact on how they treat members of various groups. The personal expertise and confidence of a professional enable him or her to be useful.

Finally, elected officials and government institutions affect the behavior of government workers. Political officials are responsible for ensuring that agencies follow legislative intent and serve the public interest. These officials can use their authority inappropriately, however, by pressuring for favoritism and patronage. Public watchdogs can pursue private goals or partisan objectives. In these instances, it is critical for public employees to protect their discretion and to act as professionals.

Discussion Questions

1. Describe the basic characteristics of bureaucracies. Select an example of a state or municipal agency and discuss the extent to which the general definition of *bureaucracy* applies to that agency. What might explain deviations, if there are any?

2. To what extent do you agree with the following statements? Unlike other institutions of state and local governments, administrative agencies are based on rules and regulations rather than on democratic principles and processes. By their very nature, these agencies pose a threat to democracy.

3. Describe the interaction between legislatures and administrative agencies. Identify and discuss the tools available to legislatures to provide direction to the bureaucracy.

4. Discuss the differences between the activities regulated at the beginning of the twentieth century and those for which regulations have been established since the 1960s. Has government simply expanded its scope of regulation, or have different issues emerged that have prompted new regulations?

5. The reinventing government and TQM prescriptions emphasize the importance of focus on customer needs. Select a state or local government agency and identify who the customer is and how you would know what customer needs are. Might others disagree and identify someone else as the primary customer? What are the implications of different definitions of the customer for the administrative agency?

Glossary

administrative rules 310
affirmative action 303
best practices 308
bureaucracy 294
civil service 301
comparable worth 304
continuous improvement 306

equal pay for equal work 304
iron triangle 310
legislative intent 310
merit system 301
pay equity 304
personnel management 301
privatization 308

quota system 303
reinventing government 308
reverse discrimination 303
sexual harassment 304
total quality management
   (TQM) 306

Endnotes

1. Max Weber, "Bureaucracy," in *Max Weber Essays in Sociology,* eds. H. H. Gerth and C. Wright Mills (New York: Oxford University Press, 1971), 196–244; Peter M. Blau and Marshall W. Meyer, *Bureaucracy in Modern Society,* 2d ed. (New York: Random House, 1971).

2. Robert K. Merton, "Bureaucratic Structure and Personality," *Social Forces* (September 1940), 560–568; Michael M. Harmon and Richard T. Mayer, *Organization Theory for Public Administration* (Boston, Mass.: Little, Brown, 1986).

3. Lawrence Mohr, "The Concept of Organizational Goals," *American Political Science Review* (June 1973), 470–481.

4. See Hugh Heclo, *A Government of Strangers* (Washington, D.C.: Brookings Institution, 1977), for a lucid description of the tensions between administrators and politicians in the federal government that is similar to the picture in state and local governments.

5. William J. Rothwell, *Effective Succession Planning,* 2d ed. (New York: American Management Association, 2001).

6. Donald J. Treiman and Heidi I. Hartmann, *Women, Work and Wages* (Washington, D.C.: National Academy Press, 1981).

7. Nelson C. Dometrius and Lee Sigelman, "Assessing Progress toward Affirmative Action Goals in State and Local Government: A New Benchmark," *Public Administration Review* (May/June 1984), 241–246; and Peter K. Eisinger, "Black Employment in Municipal Jobs: The Impact of Black Political Power," *American Political Science Review* (June 1982), 380–390.

8. Paul P. Van Riper, *History of the United States Civil Service* (Evanston, Ill.: Row, Peterson, 1968); Carl R. Fish, *The Civil Service and the Patronage* (New York: Longmans, Green, 1935).

9. Ari Hoogenboom, *Outlawing the Spoils: A History of the Civil Service Reform Movement, 1865–1883* (Urbana: University of Illinois Press, 1961), 197; Dennis L. Dresang, *Public Personnel Management and Public Policy,* 2d ed. (New York: Longman, 1991), 28–31.

10. Dennis L. Dresang, "Public Personnel Reform: A Summary of State Government Activity," *Public Personnel Management* (September/October 1978), 287–294.

11. Dresang, "Public Personnel Reform," 287–294.

12. *Griggs et al. v. Duke Power Company* (1971).

13. Nathan Glazer, *Affirmative Discrimination: Ethnic Inequality and Public Policy* (New York: Basic Books, 1975).

14. *University of California v. Bakke* (1978); *Cleveland Firefighters Local Union No. 1784 v. Stotts* (1984); *Wygant v. Jackson (Michigan) Board of Education* (1986).

15. Dresang, *Public Personnel Management,* 77 and 78; Treinan and Hartmann, *Women, Work and Wages,* 44–68.

16. Michael W. McCann, *Rights at Work: Pay Equity Reform and the Politics of Legal Mobilization* (Chicago, Ill.: University of Chicago Press, 1994).

17. Alice H. Cook, "Pay Equity: Theory and Implementation," in *Public Personnel Management: Current Concerns—Future Challenges,* eds. Carolyn Ban and Norma M. Riccucci (New York: Longman, 1991), 100–113.

18. Dennis L. Dresang and Paul J. Stuiber, "Sexual Harassment: Challenges for the Future," in *Public Personnel Management: Current Concern—Future Challenges,* eds. Carolyn Ban and Norma M. Riccucci (New York: Longman, 1991), 114–125.

19. Helene L. Gosselin, "Sexual Harassment on the Job: Psychological, Social, and Economic Repercussions," *Canada's Mental Health* (September 1984), 21–24; Catherine A. MacKinnon, *Sexual Harassment of Working Women: A Case of Sex Discrimination* (New Haven, Conn.: Yale University Press, 1979).

20. U.S. Bureau of the Census, *Labor–Management Relations,* Vol. 13, *Public Employment* (Washington, D.C.: Government Printing Office, 1987).

21. W. E. Deming, *Quality, Productivity, and Competitive Position* (Cambridge, Mass.: Cambridge University Press, 1982); W. E. Deming, *Out of Crisis* (Cambridge, Mass.: Cambridge University Press, 1986); Steven Cohen and Ronald Brand, *Total Quality Management in Government* (San Francisco, Calif.: Jossey Bass, 1993).

22. David Osborne and Ted Gaebler, *Reinventing Government: How the Entrepreneurial Spirit Is Transforming the Public Sector* (New York: Addison-Wesley, 1992).

23. James L. Garnett, "Strategies for Governors Who Want to Reorganize," *State Government* (Spring 1979), 135–143.

24. Kenneth J. Meier, "Executive Reorganization of Government: Impact on Employment and Expenditures," *American Journal of Political Science* (August 1980), 396–412.

25. Glenn Abney and Thomas P. Lauth, *The Politics of State and City Administrators* (Albany: State University of New York Press, 1986), 47–60.

26. Ibid., 45.

27. Ibid., 79.

28. Jonathan R. Hughes, *Social Control in the Colonial Economy* (Charlottesville: University of Virginia Press, 1976).

29. Gabriel Kolko, *Railroads and Regulation, 1877–1916* (Princeton, N.J.: Princeton University Press, 1965), 217–221.

30. Douglas D. Anderson, "State Regulation of Electric Utilities," in *The Politics of Regulation,* ed. James Q. Wilson (New York: Basic Books, 1980), 5–16.

31. Council of State Governments, *The Book of the States, 1986–1987* (Lexington, Ky.: Council of State Governments, 1987), 30.

32. Michael D. Reagan, *Regulation: The Politics of Policy* (Boston, Mass.: Little, Brown, 1987), 20–22.

33. Ibid., 91.

34. Frank J. Thompson and Michael J. Scicchitano, "State Implementation Effort and Federal Regulatory Policy: The Case of Occupational Safety and Health," *Journal of Politics* (December 1985), 689.

35. Reagan, *Regulation,* 191–192.

CHAPTER 13

Courts

LEARNING OBJECTIVES

- Understand the relationships among state, tribal, and federal court systems.
- Know the fundamental principles and procedures of litigation.
- Appreciate law enforcement, dispute resolution, and policy-making roles of state courts.
- Know the role and character of juries.
- Identify how judges in state courts are selected and removed from the bench.

The judge explained the essentials of the case to 25 individuals brought into the courtroom as potential jurors. Of the 25 individuals, 12 would be selected. The state's attorney had charged a man with battery and assault for beating his son. His son, 17 years old, was in the courtroom, with his leg in a cast and his face still swollen. The judge asked if any of the potential jurors knew either the man or his son. No one responded. The judge asked if anyone had a reason why she or he should not serve on the jury. One man asked to be excused because this was a critical time for him to be planting on his farm. The judge excused him. Another explained that he was in the midst of doing inventory at his business. The judge did not grant his request to be dismissed.

Lawyers defending the man and the state's attorney (or district attorney) then posed questions to the remaining 24 potential jurors. Who believed that parents had a right to discipline their children and, if necessary, use physical punishment? Who had been spanked hard or beaten by their parents? Did anyone believe that a 17-year-old son was to be treated as an adult, not as a child?

Based on the responses, the lawyers asked the judge to excuse another six individuals. The judge then gave each side the right to select two potential jurors, without giving any reason. The defense chose two young men; the prosecution chose one man who looked like he was about the age of the accused father and a woman who had looked stern and concerned throughout the proceedings. Both sides wanted jurors who would be open to—if not predisposed to—the arguments they would be making. The judge randomly dismissed another two individuals and declared that the court now had a jury.

Almost every one of us will end up in court at some point in our lives. Crime is likely to bring us into a courtroom, whether we are the victim, the accused, a witness, a member of a jury, a lawyer, or a judge. We may also go to court if we have a dispute with someone over a contract, a family relationship, or property ownership. We might even get involved in a political movement and use the court to further our cause.

Courts exist to resolve disputes. They play the role of a third, neutral party who knows the law and will apply it fairly. Courts also play administrative and legislative roles. The judicial branch of state government certifies adoptions and name changes, processes wills, and licenses lawyers. These functions are not substantively different from those of administrative agencies that register births and deaths, process tax returns, and license workers in various occupations.

Courts make public policy as they decide cases.[1] This has led groups who disagree with a judicial ruling to make speeches deriding so-called activist judges and to insist that those who wear black robes stick to applying the law as it is written. Both conservatives and liberals are guilty of engaging in this political rhetoric. Legislators and framers of constitutions cannot anticipate every unique instance. Sometimes laws are vague or contradictory because they are the result of a political compromise. When the court clarifies the law while ruling on a case, a new law is created, both for that case and for similar situations. Sometimes the clarifications are minor and not controversial. In other instances, such as determining circumstances that meet the definition of obscenity or disturbing the peace, or deciding whether constitutional guarantees of equal rights prohibit the enactment of statutes restricting the application of marriage laws to heterosexual couples, the court makes a major contribution to public policy making and can be at the center of debate and dispute.

Public policy advocates use courts strategically. If a judge or panel of judges is likely to support a particular interpretation of the law, advocates will present a **test case**. The objective of a test case is not so much to resolve a particular dispute as it is to get a court ruling that can be used to support general policy. As Michael W. McCann showed in his study of pay equity legislation in state governments, advocates can use the *threat* of court action to further their cause.[2] A test case in which a preliminary ruling made the state of Washington liable for almost $100 million because it refused to correct gender-based pay inequities in salaries for state jobs prompted governors and legislatures in other states to reform their pay scales. Even though the initial ruling in the Washington case was overturned, the combination of legal ambiguities that remained and the inherent value of the changes, regardless of legal liabilities, kept the pay equity reform movement alive and successful.

Although courts share the authority and discretion of other policy-making institutions, they are distinct from the bureaucracy, elected executives, and legislative bodies in one major way: the courts may not set their own agenda. Legislators, governors, and administrators can initiate new policies. Judges cannot initiate litigation. The policies made by judges are limited to the issues that exist in the cases they adjudicate. The conflicts resolved by the courts are only those that are brought before the bench.

---

test case A specific dispute strategically litigated in order to get a court ruling establishing precedent and principles that would apply to others in a similar situation.

A court scene.

Each of us has an interest in the nature of face-to-face interactions in courts. Courts are about fairness. Anyone who is a direct participant in a court proceeding has the right to expect fair treatment. A key role for judges and jurors is to draw a conclusion about the credibility of witnesses and litigants. They do this, in part, from the facts and arguments presented, but credibility is also determined through interpreting the face-to-face interaction. The chapter-opening vignette addresses this from the standpoint of jury selection. A witness who appears confident is much more valuable to a case than one who is nervous and appears shifty. Likewise, litigants are much more likely to feel comfortable about a decision, even if they lose, if the lawyers, judge, and jurors seemed attentive than if jurors dozed off or the judge seemed distracted.

STATE AND FEDERAL COURTS

Almost everyone is bound to have some interaction with state courts. State courts, which include those at the municipal and county levels, have jurisdiction over traffic violations, divorces, wills, most contracts, crimes against persons and property, and the decisions and processes of state and local governmental institutions. Litigation in state courts includes, in other words, the areas that affect the daily lives of most people. The jurisdiction of federal courts is limited to disputes involving federal constitutional rights, federal laws, and the activities of federal agencies and institutions.

A common misunderstanding is that the courts in the United States are all part of a single system, with the U.S. Supreme Court at the head. Instead, state and federal courts have their own systems, with their own types of cases and their own routes for appeals. These two systems overlap only when a case involves both state and federal laws or constitutions.

If you were arrested for a traffic violation, for example, you could contest the charge in a state court because state and local governments enact traffic laws. You could not have the case tried in a federal court, and you could not appeal the verdict to a federal court unless you went beyond the traffic violation and involved some federal law or constitutional provision. To secure access to a federal court, you would have to allege, for example, that in making the arrest the local police officer violated your right to due process. The Fifth Amendment of the U.S. Constitution provides the right to know what crime one supposedly committed, the right to have a lawyer, and the right to avoid self-incrimination. The Fourteenth Amendment requires state and local governments to abide by the first 10 amendments—the Bill of Rights.

The famous 1990 case involving Rodney King and the Los Angeles Police Department provides an example of the relationship between state and federal court jurisdictions. Rodney King was arrested on a Los Angeles freeway for a traffic violation. When Los Angeles police officers pulled him over to arrest him, they beat him severely and were videotaped by an amateur photographer who witnessed the event. The police officers were first tried in a California state court on charges of using excessive force when they arrested King. The police officers persuaded the jury that King was resisting, and therefore the use of force was justified. Because the videotape, which was shown extensively on local and national television, seemed to indicate to the contrary, the public reaction to the verdict of not guilty was outrage. The local reaction in Los Angeles was a destructive riot.

Federal prosecutors then stepped in and charged the officers with violating Rodney King's civil rights, a federal crime. The federal government argued that the police officers, who were white, denied Rodney King equal protection under the laws—as guaranteed under the Fourteenth Amendment—because he was African American. The prosecution used as evidence racial slurs and comments, some of which were captured on a police department audiotape. The jury in the federal court convicted the officers.

The reverse sequence can also occur. In separate trials in 1997, Timothy McVeigh and Terry Nichols were convicted in federal court for their roles in the April 19, 1995, bombing of a federal office building in Oklahoma City. McVeigh, who planted the bomb, received the death penalty. Nichols was convicted of the federal crimes of conspiracy to commit an act of terror and, because he did not accompany McVeigh and actually plant the bomb, of involuntary manslaughter in the deaths of the eight federal law enforcement officers who were in the building. He was not sentenced to death. Unhappy with the sentence, the state district attorney for the Oklahoma City area proceeded in 2004 to prosecute Nichols under state law and in state courts for participating in the murder of all 168 people who died in the bomb blast. A conviction in an Oklahoma court could have meant execution. The jury in the state court found Nichols guilty of 161 counts of first-degree murder, but spared his life and sentenced him to life in prison without parole. As in the Rodney King case, when the same incident involves breaking two different sets of laws, there is dual jurisdiction and prosecutions can proceed through both state and federal courts. Figure 13.1 illustrates the state–federal court relationship.

When federal and state laws conflict, the general rule is that the federal law prevails. If a state said that employers may discriminate on the basis of race when they hire people, that state policy would directly contradict the Fourteenth Amendment to the U.S. Constitution and Title VII of the federal 1964 Civil Rights Act. The federal law

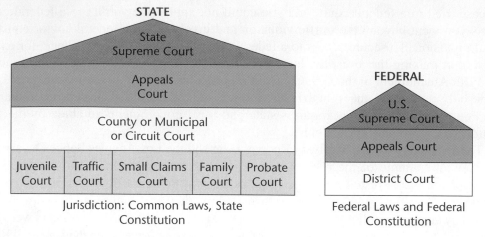

Figure 13.1   State and Federal Courts

supersedes the state law and would be the one followed. Not only would federal courts so rule, but state courts, through a process known as inclusion, would abandon on their own the state law in favor of the federal. Federal courts and federal law are in this way regarded as supreme.[3]

Some issues are not either-or but instead raise questions of more or less. For example, states can add to the Fifth Amendment due process rights of the U.S. Constitution, but they cannot subtract from them. The federal government, in other words, provides a floor, and states can determine ceilings. In states that supplement federally guaranteed rights, state courts are the arena for litigation regarding the added protections.[4]

Since the mid-1970s, state courts have taken the lead in elaborating individual rights. Table 13.1 shows the dramatic increase in the number of times during the 1970s and 1980s that state courts granted greater rights to individuals than those guaranteed under U.S. Supreme Court interpretations of the U.S. Constitution. Note that Table 13.1 includes only part of the decade of the 1980s and yet still shows the dramatic increase.

Table 13.1 State Supreme Court Decisions Extending Constitutional Rights		
Years	Number	Percentage of Total
1950–1959	3	1.0
1960–1969	7	2.2
1970–1979	124	39.9
1980–1986	177	56.9
Total	311	100.0

Source: Ronald K. L. Collins and Peter J. Galie, "State Constitutional Rights Decisions," *National Law Journal* (August 11, 1986), 29.

This activity by state courts has been encouraged and monitored by the U.S. Supreme Court. Justice William J. Brennan wrote an essay in the *Harvard Law Review* in 1977 urging state courts to look to their own constitutions to enhance the rights of individuals.[5] Former Chief Justice Warren Burger celebrated the decrease in rulings by the U.S. Supreme Court and the increase in state courts as the judicial version of "new federalism."[6]

It is easy to imagine widely different laws and court rulings on the same issues or crimes as one goes from state to state. The exercise of discretion by the 50 state court systems, however, has not engendered wide disparities in courtrooms around the country. Several traditions and principles work to provide cohesiveness in our judicial system across state boundaries:

1. The *inclusion* of U.S. Supreme Court rulings into the framework within which state judges make decisions provides a common set of standards for state courts. Legal reasoning, by lawyers and by judges, applies the precedents set by previous rulings in similar cases to the dispute at hand. This practice is reinforced by the desire of judges to avoid having their decisions overturned by courts hearing cases on appeal.

2. Certain states have established reputations as *leaders* in developing and clarifying legal principles through the decisions of their courts. Judges and lawyers around the country look to these states and cite their rulings when presenting their own arguments, much as they watch and cite the actions of the U.S. Supreme Court.[7] The state supreme courts of New York and Massachusetts were cited by courts in other states most frequently in the first half of the twentieth century. California has been the most frequently cited court since World War II.[8]

3. Central to state courts is the *common law* tradition, which comes from the British jurisprudence system and is part of our colonial legacy. Common law originated as an aggregation of the decisions made by judges in England in the thirteenth century. Today's law is now a combination of those historic decisions and contemporary customs. Although common law is not always in written form, courts nonetheless apply it as they decide issues regarding family disputes, charges of indecency and disorderly conduct, and allegations of criminal behavior. Even with its rich ethnic and regional diversity, the United States generally subscribes to the basic edicts of Anglo-American culture and common law. Louisiana used to be an exception. It followed the Napoleonic Code of French tradition. Today, however, even Louisiana subscribes to common law principles.

STATE, TRIBAL, AND FEDERAL COURTS

In contrast to the states, tribal courts do not share a common legal tradition. Cultural differences between Indian nations are significant. The rule of inclusion does not apply to tribal courts. The federal push to get Indian nations to adopt a written constitution has led to common formal structures with appeals courts, but these structures mask continued differences in substance.

There are some commonalities, however, in the relationships between tribal courts and their counterparts in state and federal governments. The sovereignty of the individual tribes and their status within the United States, as described in Chapters 3 and 4, translates to **dual jurisdiction** for tribal and federal courts, parallel to that for state and federal courts. The jurisdiction applies to tribal members and to tribal land.[9]

Thus, tribal courts rule when tribal laws are broken on tribal land, regardless of whether or not those who violated the laws are American Indian. Tribal courts also apply tribal laws to their members, even if they do not reside on tribal lands. The federal courts enforce federal laws and guarantee constitutional rights in all parts of the United States, including Indian reservations, and to all individuals, including American Indians. A native person who committed an act of violence against a federal law enforcement officer could be prosecuted in federal courts. If that action also involved breaking a tribal law, that person could be prosecuted in a tribal court as well.

State courts have jurisdiction over tribal land or tribal members only if specified in a particular agreement or if granted authority by the federal government. As mentioned in Chapter 3, Public Law 280 gives most of the states that have reservations the authority to extend the enforcement and the adjudication of their criminal codes to American Indians, whether on or off tribal land. Some tribes, particularly those in urban areas, have voluntarily made agreements with state and local governments for cooperation that extends court jurisdiction. Issues of family, probate, land use, and contract law tend to remain solely within tribal courts.

With these relationships among court systems in mind, we now turn to a discussion of the traits and challenges common to courts in the 50 states.

STRUCTURES

For a case to be brought to court, someone who has been injured or is in danger of being injured must bring a charge against someone else. The party bringing the charge is referred to as the **plaintiff**. The accused party is the **defendant**. Our legal system is based on an adversarial process in which two (or more) sides argue facts and principles and rely on the court to act as referee.

Upon receiving a plea for action, the court first determines whether the plaintiff has standing and whether the complaint involves a violation of the law. **Standing** is a legal determination that the plaintiff has indeed suffered some kind of damage or injury or is about to suffer damage or injury. With very few exceptions, courts in the United States do

---

dual jurisdiction   When two different courts (state, tribal, federal) have the authority to try someone for crimes committed in the same incident.

plaintiff   The party that initiates a legal dispute.

defendant   The party in a legal dispute that responds to charges brought by the plaintiff.

standing   Determination by the court that a party has sufficient tangible interest in a dispute to allow him or her to pursue these rights in a lawsuit. Standing is based on actual or imminent damages, not hypothetical instances.

not provide **advisory opinions**. They decide cases where something is at stake. People who think that government should be stricter about false advertising by businesses, for example, do not have a standing in court, but someone who has been lured into buying an appliance that cannot do all that was promised can proceed. Standing is not enough, however.

The court must have **jurisdiction** over the matter. In other words, the plaintiff must identify the law or laws that have allegedly been broken and demonstrate that the court has the power to rule in disputes based on that law. A state court, for example, can only accept cases involving the laws of the state in which the court is located. The laws of a state include the ordinances and rules of that state's local governments, as well as the constitution, laws, and administrative rules of the state itself. In addition, state laws sometimes limit which laws are subject to action by the courts when there are disputes. State laws also describe the general role and procedural jurisdiction of the various types of courts. See Exploring the Web for an example of the considerations to be made when deciding whether or not to initiate a court case.

Specialized and Lower Courts

With few exceptions, cases must begin at the most local level possible. The lowest traditional level of state courts has been the **justice of the peace**. This judicial office, which vanished in court reorganizations that many states adopted in the 1970s,[10] handled marriages, traffic violations, and local ordinances such as curfew laws and some land-use restrictions in small towns and villages. Justices of the peace have been a favorite subject of humor and ridicule in American theater. Typical scenes depict an unscrupulous and sometimes pompous person of minimal intelligence enjoying the power he or she wields over a stranger passing through town. The justice of the peace decided cases without a jury. Often, the position was part-time, and remuneration depended at least in part on the fines collected. All the ingredients for injustice existed, especially when the justice of the peace also doubled as local sheriff.

Figure 13.2 illustrates the court structure currently common to states. Many cases begin in various courts that specialize in small claims (disputes involving less than $1,000 or $500, depending on the state), traffic violations, family issues, juvenile cases, and wills. In addition, courts that have general jurisdiction are at the lowest level. General jurisdictional courts can be found in both rural and urban areas. Specialized courts tend to exist only in urban areas. Most specialized courts have a single judge or commissioner presiding and no jury. If specialized courts exist within a district or municipal court, the case can be appealed to the general jurisdiction court. If this happens, the case is presented and argued in its entirety as if it were the first time the case was being tried.

The lowest level of general jurisdiction courts is most commonly called district, circuit, municipal, or county courts. Over 1,500 of these courts exist in the United States, and

---

advisory opinion A ruling by an attorney general about a law or proposed law regarding whether it is constitutional or may conflict with other laws. This is not a binding ruling.

jurisdiction Determination by the court that it has the authority, under statute or constitution, to hear and rule on a dispute.

justice of the peace The lowest level of a court system, often filled by someone in a community on a part-time basis. Few contemporary state court systems continue to include this office.

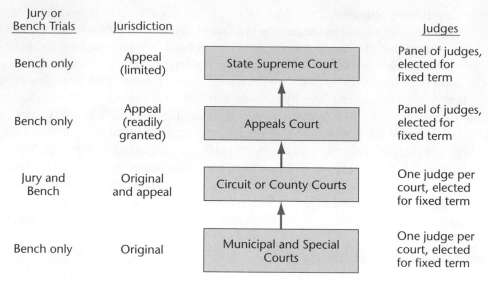

Jury or Bench Trials	Jurisdiction		Judges
Bench only	Appeal (limited)	State Supreme Court	Panel of judges, elected for fixed term
Bench only	Appeal (readily granted)	Appeals Court	Panel of judges, elected for fixed term
Jury and Bench	Original and appeal	Circuit or County Courts	One judge per court, elected for fixed term
Bench only	Original	Municipal and Special Courts	One judge per court, elected for fixed term

Figure 13.2 State Court Structure

most of them have either a city or a county as their geographic area of jurisdiction. These courts also have one judge presiding, but litigants can request a jury trial. Juries are used only in the lower-level courts. The defendant usually has the option of choosing a jury trial or a **bench trial**, one tried before a judge only. Once a case reaches the appellate levels, there are no juries. Only judges hear the case.

An important role of judges and juries in district, circuit, municipal, and county courts is to assess the credibility of the litigants and witnesses. Only at this level do all the witnesses appear face to face with a judge and jury. Especially when both sides have a reasonable case to present, the one who seems most sincere and honest (even if it is just good acting) is likely to prevail.

Appeals Courts

Those unhappy with the decisions of district or municipal courts may appeal their cases. Depending on the state, appeals courts consist of either a panel of judges or a single judge. Appellate judges review cases as they have already been presented and then consider the arguments of lawyers about whether the original court used a flawed process or whether the judge or jury made an error in reasoning. Appeals courts do not include juries, and they do not try the case over from the start. Judges in appellate courts do not see and hear testimony from witnesses. They defer to the conclusions of lower courts regarding the credibility of witnesses. Appeals in 15 states are made directly to a state supreme court. The other 35 states have an intermediate appeals court that hears cases, and the state supreme court considers cases appealed beyond the intermediate level.[11]

---

bench trial Trial conducted by a judge without a jury.

Table 13.2 Judicial Standards and Processes for Civil and Criminal Cases

	Civil Case	Criminal Case
Litigants	Private individuals or organizations; public agencies	District/state attorney versus individual(s) accused of crime
Settlement before verdict	Out-of-court settlement	Plea bargain or drop charges
Pretrial discovery	Both sides must disclose all witnesses, exhibits, and evidence	Prosecutor must disclose enough to show probability; defense has no obligation to disclose anything
Standard of proof for plaintiff to meet	Preponderance of evidence	Preponderance of evidence; beyond reasonable doubt for punishment
Consequence of guilty verdict	Award of cash and remedies to plaintiff	Fine, imprisonment, probation, court-ordered punishment and/or rehabilitation

Supreme Courts

State supreme courts are the last step in litigation, unless the issue falls under the jurisdiction of the federal courts. In some states, this court is known as the Court of Last Resort. Oklahoma and Texas each have two supreme courts, one for **civil law** and one for **criminal law**. State supreme courts usually have seven members, although some states have as few as three and others as many as nine.

Prior to the court reforms of the 1960s and 1970s, most state supreme courts had to rule on all cases presented to them. Unlike the U.S. Supreme Court, they did not have the option of refusing to hear a case, thereby letting the judgment of the lower courts stand. This caused a backlog of cases before the state supreme courts, sometimes as long as 10 years; the reforms included providing state supreme courts with the discretion to decide whether or not to hear cases. Table 13.2 outlines judicial standards and processes for civil and criminal cases.

ROLE OF STATE'S ATTORNEY OR ATTORNEY GENERAL

In cases involving criminal law, when the victim or alleged victim has been killed, physically injured, or suffered loss or damage to property, then society generally—not the victim—is considered the plaintiff. Local district attorneys will initiate and pursue the necessary legal action once they have evidence indicating who committed the crime. The state attorney general provides consultation, training, and investigatory assistance to district attorneys.

It is easy to understand the philosophical position that it is society and not just an individual victim that is hurt by criminal activity. It is also nice to know that the victims

---

civil law Crimes that relate to contractual and liability relationships between organizations, between individuals, and between individuals and organizations.

criminal law Crimes against persons and property that deal with fundamental law and order in a society.

of assault or robbery are not going to have to pay their own investigatory and legal fees to bring the criminal to justice. Nonetheless, reliance on a district attorney can be frustrating. Suppose that your roommate assaulted you. You might report this to the police, but then the district attorney might decide that the evidence was not solid enough to warrant prosecution. You are likely to feel angry and frustrated. In addition, you might fear another assault because you went to the police.

Victims sometimes frustrate district attorneys. If a victim refuses to cooperate with an investigation and prosecution, the district attorney is likely to be left with a very weak case. Key witnesses to a murder or an assault may fear the attacker so much that they will not help authorities. Domestic violence often continues because a battered spouse fears revenge due to reporting incidents and cooperating with law enforcement officials. Also, domestic violence victims frequently blame themselves for provoking their partner rather than recognizing the real problem and the need for safety. Programs exist to protect witnesses, but they too have risks.

When governmental jurisdictions are involved in legal disputes other than criminal cases, they get legal advice and representation from a law firm with whom they have a contract; from a full-time attorney hired by the city, school board, or other local government; or from the state attorney general. In larger jurisdictions and in state governments, agencies sometimes have their own legal staff. The attorney general is available to all these units for advice and assistance.

Most attorneys general and district attorneys (or state's attorneys, as they are called in some states) are elected to office. Governors appoint the attorney general in Alaska, Hawaii, Wyoming, Tennessee, New Jersey, and New Hampshire. In Maine, both houses of the legislature meet every other year to elect the attorney general. Invariably, attorneys general are lawyers, although only 27 states require this credential. For those who must run for office, the keys to electoral success are image, policy positions, party identity, and name recognition, which are instrumental in getting any candidate into office. With election comes independence. In contrast, the attorney general of the United States does not enjoy independence because she or he is appointed by and serves at the discretion of the president.

One role of attorneys general that can have considerable policy and political impact is the issuance of **legal opinions**. As indicated in Table 13.3, all attorneys general provide formal legal opinions to other state officials. Unlike courts, a state's attorney general can conduct a legal analysis and then formally give an opinion on whether an action or contemplated action is legal or constitutional. These opinions are not legally binding but can thwart or prompt legislative and administrative behavior in state governments. Participants in the policy-making process will seek an attorney general's opinion as a way of getting support for their own position or as a way of combating a charge that a proposal is unconstitutional. The substance and the timing of an opinion can be critical to the success or failure of a policy initiative.

Some states have given their attorneys general responsibility beyond acting as lawyers for government. Table 13.3 presents those roles. The most common function is

---

legal opinion The interpretation of the law rendered by an attorney general. It is not binding but carries considerable weight.

Table 13.3   Roles of the State Attorney General, by State

	Serves as Counsel for State	Appears for State in Criminal Appeals	Litigates for State Agencies	Litigates Against State Agencies	Reviews Administrative Rules	Issues Advisory Opinions	Reviews Legislation Before Passage	Reviews Legislation Before Signing	Investigates Antitrust Activities	Administers Consumer Protection Agencies	Represents State Before Regulatory Agencies	May Intervene in Local Prosecutions	May Supersede Local Prosecutor
Alabama	X	X	X	X	X	X	X		X	X		X	X
Alaska	X	X	X	X	X	X	X	X	X	X	X	X	X
Arizona	X	X	X	X	X	X	X		X	X		X	X
Arkansas	X	X	X		X	X	X	X	X	X	X		X
California	X	X	X	X	X	X	X	X	X			X	X
Colorado	X	X	X	X	X	X	X	X	X	X	X	X	X
Connecticut	X		X		X	X	X	X	X	X	X	X	
Delaware	X	X	X	X	X	X	X	X	X	X	X	X	
Florida	X	X	X		X	X	X	X	X	X	X		X
Georgia	X	X	X	X	X	X	X	X	X		X	X	X
Hawaii	X	X	X	X	X	X	X	X	X		X	X	X
Idaho	X	X	X	X	X	X	X	X	X	X	X	X	X
Illinois	X	X	X	X		X			X	X	X	X	X
Indiana	X	X	X			X		X	X	X			X
Iowa	X	X	X	X	X	X	X	X	X	X	X	X	
Kansas	X	X	X	X	X	X	X	X	X	X	X	X	X
Kentucky	X	X	X	X	X	X	X		X	X	X	X	X
Louisiana	X	X	X	X	X	X	X	X	X		X	X	X
Maine	X	X	X		X	X	X	X	X	X	X	X	
Maryland	X	X	X		X	X	X	X	X	X	X	X	X
Massachusetts	X	X	X	X	X	X	X	X	X	X	X	X	X
Michigan	X		X		X	X	X		X	X	X	X	X
Minnesota		X	X	X	X	X	X		X	X	X	X	X
Mississippi	X		X		X	X			X	X	X		
Missouri	X	X	X		X	X	X	X	X				
Montana	X	X	X		X	X			X			X	X
Nebraska	X	X	X	X	X	X			X	X	X	X	X
Nevada	X	X	X		X	X			X			X	X
New Hampshire	X	X	X	X	X	X	X	X	X		X	X	X
New Jersey	X	X	X	X	X	X	X	X	X	X	X	X	X
New Mexico	X	X	X	X	X	X	X	X	X	X	X	X	X
New York		X	X	X	X			X		X	X		X
North Carolina			X	X	X		X		X	X	X	X	
North Dakota	X	X	X		X	X			X	X		X	X
Ohio	X		X	X		X			X	X	X	X	X
Oklahoma		X	X	X	X	X	X	X	X	X	X	X	
Oregon	X	X	X		X	X			X	X		X	X
Pennsylvania	X	X	X	X	X	X	X	X	X	X	X	X	X
Rhode Island	X	X	X		X	X			X	X	X	X	
South Carolina	X	X	X		X	X	X	X	X		X		X
South Dakota	X	X	X		X	X	X	X	X	X			X
Tennessee	X	X	X		X	X			X	X	X	X	X
Texas	X	X	X	X	X	X	X	X	X	X	X		
Utah	X	X	X	X	X	X			X		X	X	X

(continued)

Table 13.3   Roles of the State Attorney General, by State (*continued*)

	Serves as Counsel for State	Appears for State in Criminal Appeals	Litigates for State Agencies	Litigates Against State Agencies	Reviews Administrative Rules	Issues Advisory Opinions	Reviews Legislation Before Passage	Reviews Legislation Before Signing	Investigates Antitrust Activities	Administers Consumer Protection Agencies	Represents State Before Regulatory Agencies	May Intervene in Local Prosecutions	May Supersede Local Prosecutor
Vermont	X	X	X	X	X	X	X	X	X	X	X	X	X
Virginia	X	X	X	X	X	X	X	X	X	X	X	X	X
Washington	X	X	X	X	X	X	X	X	X	X	X	X	X
West Virginia	X	X	X			X			X	X	X		
Wisconsin	X	X	X	X		X			X	X	X	X	X
Wyoming	X	X	X			X	X	X	X		X		X

Source: Adapted from *The Book of the States 2011* (Lexington, Ky.: Council of State Governments, 2011), 207–212.

providing protection to consumers from reckless and unscrupulous businesses. In a sense, this is an extension of the role of monitoring businesses for unfair competitive practices and thus avoiding the establishment of monopolies. The antitrust responsibilities assumed by attorneys general at the beginning of the twentieth century were supplemented with consumer protection authority in the middle of that century. The focus on individual consumer protection has led to action against mail-order fraud, misleading advertising, and other schemes. Attorneys general from 36 states collaborated to sue major tobacco companies for misleading the public on the effects of smoking on health. The attorneys general reached a settlement with the tobacco companies that resulted in payments totaling $206 billion.

PROCESS

One of the adages that applies to the judicial system is "Justice delayed is justice denied." The principal beneficiaries of a contested will may themselves die before the case is settled. That is certainly an example of injustice because of a slow judicial process. Likewise, someone who seeks damages because of an injury should have the matter resolved as soon as possible so that person may make rehabilitation plans. Individuals accused of rape or murder should either begin a prison term or be declared not guilty rather than be held in jail or restricted by bail provisions for a long time while awaiting trial.

   To avoid delays due to a backlog of cases, states have appointed court administrators to assign cases to judges so that caseloads are distributed evenly or to accommodate a judge who tends to be slow. In addition, to provide for a fair and expeditious court process, participants in a case pursue a number of practices, including submitting the case to a grand jury, plea bargaining, pursuing out-of-court settlements, sharing evidence, exchanging lists of witnesses and taking depositions, and submitting amicus curiae briefs.

Grand Jury

Submitting a case to a **grand jury** before filing a case in court is the least effective of the practices for providing either fairness or expediency. In accordance with British judicial traditions, some states require public prosecutors to seek an **indictment** (a formal accusation of a crime) from a grand jury before going to court. A grand jury is made up of 12 to 25 citizens and is established to determine whether enough evidence exists to accuse someone of a crime. Grand juries operate in secret. They do not determine guilt or innocence but instead review the evidence and arguments of a district attorney and then decide whether the district attorney should proceed to trial.

The intent behind a grand jury process is to be certain that district attorneys are not accusing people without evidence and are not going to court with weak cases. Individuals suffer in personal, financial, and professional terms just by being accused of a crime, even when they are innocent. Grand juries, however, are rarely effective in providing protection against frivolous or unwarranted cases. Grand juries tend to rubber-stamp the plans of public prosecutors and thus can become a costly and needless step in the process. Typically a grand jury spends five to ten minutes on each case and then votes unanimously to follow the recommendations of the district attorney.[12]

Because grand juries seem to be valuable in concept but unnecessary in practice, most states now allow district attorneys to file cases directly with the court, without first securing a grand jury indictment.[13] The hearings and motions preliminary to a trial serve many of the purposes of a grand jury. As described in the sections that follow, each side has an opportunity to discover and challenge each other's evidence and witnesses, and the defense can seek dismissal if the prosecutor seems to have a weak case.

Plea Bargaining and Out-of-Court Settlements

Many disputes are resolved outside courtrooms. Law schools, in fact, offer courses that train students to negotiate as well as to litigate. Of those cases that are filed in courts, only about 10 percent actually go to trial.[14] Cases are dropped usually because the parties have negotiated a settlement, although sometimes legal action is stopped when one of the parties concludes her or his case is too weak to pursue.

Parties in a civil case can reach an **out-of-court settlement** any time prior to a decision announced by a judge or a jury. Typically the attorneys for the two sides calculate that each side risks losing and that each party gains by agreeing to a partial award or payment. The judge assigned to the case must—and usually does—accept the settlement. The authority of the court is then invoked in making sure both parties abide by the terms of the settlement.

---

grand jury   A panel assembled to consider whether enough evidence exists to issue an indictment.
indictment   A formal charge accusing someone of committing a crime.
out-of-court settlement   When the parties in a civil suit agree on how to resolve a dispute after formal complaints are filed but before a judge or jury announces a decision.

Exploring the Web

Want to sue someone?

So you want to sue someone—for breaking a contract, selling you a defective appliance, discriminating against you, dumping garbage in a lake, vandalizing your car, or being disruptive when you are trying to study. Here are some questions you need to answer before taking legal action:

- What law was broken?
- Is the law that was broken a state, local, tribal, or federal law, or some combination of these?
- Is this a criminal case that a district or state attorney has to prosecute or a civil case that you can file?
- With which court(s) can you file the case?
- What evidence do you have to support your case?
- What is the accused party's likely arguments and evidence?
- Can you afford a lawyer? If not, is there an organization or advocacy group that might take this on?

Here are some possibilities: Sierra Club (www.sierraclub.org); National Association for the Advancement of Colored People (www.naacp.org); American Civil Liberties Union (www.aclu.org); National Immigration Law Center (www.nilc.org); and a women's law center, Equal Rights Advocates (www.equalright.org).

In criminal cases, the parallel to an out-of-court settlement is a **plea bargain**. Individuals charged with a crime can reduce potential fines or sentences and avoid the need for a court trial if they plead guilty to only some of the charges or to crimes that are less serious than those in the initial complaint. For example, someone charged with assault, burglary, and trespass may agree, after discussions with a district attorney, to plead guilty to the burglary and trespass charges. In return, the district attorney will drop the assault charge and suggest to the judge some leniency in sentencing. Someone charged with first-degree murder (intent to kill) may agree to plead guilty if the charge is reduced to homicide due to reckless behavior. The individual charged receives a less severe penalty, and the district attorney and courts have a reduced workload. Plea bargains are negotiated between the district attorney and those accused of a crime, but a judge must approve the agreements.

Ideally, out-of-court settlements and plea bargaining achieve justice in an efficient and fair manner. The fear is that there may be instances in which criminals are not punished fully or in which innocent people without the necessary will or resources to fight plead guilty under

---

plea bargain   Admitting to a crime or crimes in order to avoid being charged or tried for a crime or crimes that carry more severe penalties.

pressure from aggressive prosecutors. In civil cases, in which one party is suing another for a breach of contract, malpractice, or the like, out-of-court settlements may not always be ideal. Attorneys in these cases are often paid on a contingency basis and receive 25 to 40 percent of the award. One may suspect that the lawyers have too strong an incentive to settle in order to get payment without having to go through the risk or expense of going to trial.

Despite the potential for mischief and misfortune, plea bargains and out-of-court settlements characterize much of what happens in litigation. Given the limited resources of courts and state attorneys, this action outside courtrooms is essential for the timeliness of justice achieved through trials.

Sharing Evidence

For purposes of efficiency and fairness, judicial procedures require parties in a dispute to exchange information, evidence, and expert opinions before arguing their cases in court. Under court rules in most states, this is more true for civil than for criminal cases. Part of the drama of the 1994 proceedings in which former football star O. J. Simpson was charged with killing his former wife and her friend was over what evidence was and was not appropriately shared. Under California rules, the prosecution had to present enough preliminary evidence to convince the court that there was a good chance that O. J. Simpson was guilty. The prosecution, however, did not have to share all the evidence that it intended to use in the trial itself. The strategy of the defense was to discredit as much of the initial evidence as possible and to get the prosecution to reveal nearly all the evidence it planned on using. That way, even if the court ruled that the prosecution's case was strong enough to proceed to trial (in this case, the court so ruled), then the defense could plan its approach at trial with a fairly complete understanding of what the prosecution would present. In criminal cases, the defense does not have to reveal what evidence it plans to use before trial.

In a civil case, each side files **motions of discovery** with a court in order to secure needed information from the other. A contractor who alleges that a state government violated the law in the way it received and considered bids for building a new prison, for example, will almost certainly need information in the files of the state agency responsible for the bidding process in order to proceed with a legal challenge. A motion of discovery will secure those files. Once a judge approves these (or similar) motions, they become legally binding, and failure to comply fully and candidly can lead to contempt of court or perjury charges.

Similarly, the two parties may need to clarify issues and facts through **interrogatories**—that is, a series of questions that each side poses to the other and that must be answered under oath and in writing. The contractor may need to know when certain decisions were made and who was at certain meetings. The agency may need to get more details about why the contractor feels he or she was placed at a disadvantage. Interrogatories generate the information needed.

---

motions of discovery Formal requests made to a court for evidence or information that the opposing side in a legal dispute has in its possession.

interrogatories Questions posed through the court by one party to another party in a legal dispute. The answers must be answered truthfully, under penalty of perjury.

The two parties must also exchange the **exhibits** (documents, physical evidence, and visual aids) they intend to use during the trial. If one of the parties objects to the use of an exhibit, she or he must make the objection before the trial, and the judge will rule on whether to allow the exhibit. Usually, new exhibits or new objections are not allowed during trial in a civil case.

The role of the judge receiving these motions and issuing orders underscores the importance of enabling both parties to have the information they need to argue their cases fairly and efficiently, and of doing so before the actual trail. Imagine the delays and frustrations if, in the middle of a trial, each side demanded documents from the other.

Exchanging Lists of Witnesses and Taking Depositions

As with the sharing of documentary evidence, litigants must exchange the names and identities of witnesses they intend to call. In civil cases the information exchanged must be complete, whereas in criminal cases the objective is to require the prosecution to show there is enough evidence to justify a trial.

Witnesses, including both those involved in the dispute and outside experts called to comment on specific aspects of the case, must be available to the opposing side before the trial to answer questions under oath. The answers are transcribed into written form and are called **depositions**. Written statements, also made under oath, secured from a witness or expert are called **affidavits**. In some instances, the deposition or affidavit is the only contribution made by a witness. In other instances, the written statements are supplemented by oral testimony at the trial itself.

Although exchanging lists of witnesses and securing testimony from them before trial takes something away from the surprise and drama that television and movie scripts associate with trials, it does allow the two parties to come to the court better prepared. Lawyers can focus their presentations to make them more effective, and they can anticipate the approach of their opponents. Surprise and drama occasionally still occur in criminal cases because the pretrial revelation of evidence is only partial. When the preliminary exchange of evidence, exhibits, and testimony reveals vulnerabilities, a settlement or plea bargain is likely.

Amicus Curiae

As we saw in Chapter 7, interest groups can participate in court proceedings under limited circumstances. A group or individual who is not directly involved in a case may ask permission from a judge to present relevant arguments or evidence. This is a petition to be recognized as amicus curiae, or "friend of the court."

Environmental protection advocates, for example, may not have standing in a particular dispute over plans to build in a wetland area or to dump waste near a stream, but they

---

exhibit   Physical evidence used in a court proceeding.

deposition   A statement, made under oath and prior to a trial, in response to questions posed orally by the attorney of one side to a witness or party on the other side of a legal dispute.

affidavit   A sworn written statement that may be used in a court proceeding.

might have a relevant legal argument that they would like the court to consider in rendering its decision. Civil rights groups and business associations file amicus curiae briefs in some cases if a ruling on whether or not someone was the victim of discrimination may have far-reaching implications for employment practices.

JUDICIAL ACTIONS

Judges and juries must decide more than guilt or innocence. They must also determine remedies. In criminal cases, the consequence of a guilty verdict is generally a **sentence**, a fine, or a set of requirements involving rehabilitation for the criminal and restitution for the victim. As will be discussed in more detail in Chapter 14, sentencing is tied to theories about rehabilitating and punishing criminals and about what it takes to deter crime. State laws determine the range, if any, of sentences that may be imposed with given crimes. Judges usually decide on sentences, but in 2002 the U.S. Supreme Court insisted in *Ring v. Arizona* that juries participate in decisions applying the death penalty. Jury participation does not always mean that juries decide. In Alabama, for example, judges are allowed to overrule juries in cases where the death penalty may be applied. From 1976 through 2010, Alabama judges rejected jury decisions 107 times and 92 percent of the time imposed execution after juries called for life sentences. Judges in Florida and Delaware also can override juries, but when exercising this authority they have always chosen life sentences instead of death.[15]

In civil cases, the judges and often juries must determine what **award** will be granted to the winning side. In a medical malpractice suit, for example, the judge or jury first decides whether or not there was malpractice. If the answer is yes, the judge or jury determines how much the patient or the patient's family must be paid. This determination may include the cost of remedial treatment, the cost of long-term care if the malpractice caused a permanent disability, the earnings lost because of a disability, and perhaps a punitive assessment. If the malpractice was a joint mishap, shared by a doctor, nurse, and hospital, for example, the court will also decide the percentage of responsibility each had. (The law in some states provides that if one codefendant cannot pay all of his or her share, then the wealthier codefendants must make up the difference.)

Awards in civil cases usually involve money but may include other benefits. Employment cases often include someone getting a job or a promotion. Contract cases may require someone to perform a given task or provide a specified service. Only criminal cases may mete out jail time or fines as punishment because only the government can issue these penalties.

Judicial action may result in prohibitions or restrictions as well as awards and sentences. In criminal cases, for example, courts may issue a **restraining order**, which prohibits an individual from having contact with certain people or from going to certain

---

sentence   The punishment given by a court to someone found guilty in a criminal law case.

award   The payment that the court directs one party to make to another in a civil law case.

restraining order   A court directive prohibiting one party from being in certain places or engaging in certain behaviors, usually issued while a dispute is being resolved.

places. Universities occasionally secure a restraining order to keep off campus those individuals who have harassed and threatened students and faculty. Sometimes when a marriage or love affair goes sour, one party threatens or stalks the other, prompting him or her to get a restraining order. These orders can be controversial. To restrict someone's movement is a serious infringement on liberty and must have sufficient justification. However, these orders are difficult to enforce, and threatened individuals can take little comfort from them. A number of well-publicized tragedies have occurred in which someone has been severely beaten or killed by an individual violating a restraining order.

The parallel to a restraining order in civil law is an **injunction**, in which the court orders a person or organization to cease doing something. Often an injunction is temporary and serves to give the court time to consider a dispute in a more orderly way. Thus, a company may receive an injunction to keep it from firing an employee who has alleged discrimination, or a city agency may be enjoined from issuing any further building permits while the court determines the validity of a charge that proper procedures and criteria are not being followed. Injunctions, like restraining orders, are not given unless the court is convinced that irreparable harm might otherwise occur.

Courts, like other government institutions, have rules and procedures to guide their deliberations and to determine, at least formally, how decisions are made. These procedures provide predictability of judicial behavior. But courts are more than institutions and rules. They are made up of people, with their own personalities and preferences. These people include plaintiffs, defendants, attorneys, witnesses, and interest groups. The central actors who make authoritative decisions are judges and juries.

SELECTION OF JUDGES

In contrast to the appointment process for a judge in the federal government, most state governments rely on some method of election for selecting judges. Federal judges are appointed by the president and confirmed by the Senate, and they serve indefinitely. As shown in Table 13.4, a total of 48 states elect some or all of their judges, with governors in half of these states selecting someone to be a judge and then voters in a sense ratifying that choice. In Maine and New Jersey, governors appoint all the judges, and in California some judges are gubernatorial appointments and some are elected.

Electing judges seems contrary to the role of the court. The judicial system is supposed to provide a neutral, wise, and objective arbiter of disputes. Electoral success, however, depends on relative popularity and not necessarily on evidence of competence and neutrality.

An important distinction between the election of judges and the election of legislators, governors, and other officials is that judges are not supposed to have constituencies that they represent or special-interest groups that they might favor. Again, judges are to be neutral and unbiased. Contests in Ohio, Wisconsin, and West Virginia (as we saw in the chapter-opening vignette in Chapter 7) have appeared to be dominated by spending by business

---

injunction   A court directive that an individual or organization either do or not do a particular act.

Table 13.4   Judicial Selection Patterns

Partisan Election	Nonpartisan Election	Election by Legislature	Appointment by Governor	Missouri or Merit Plan
Alabama	Arkansas	South Carolina	California	Alaska
Illinois	California	Virginia	Maine	Arizona
Indiana	Florida		New Jersey	Colorado
Kansas	Georgia			Connecticut
Louisiana	Idaho			Delaware
Missouri	Indiana			Florida
New York	Kentucky			Hawaii
Ohio	Michigan			Indiana
Pennsylvania	Minnesota			Iowa
Tennessee	Mississippi			Kansas
Texas	Montana			Maryland
West Virginia	Nevada			Massachusetts
	North Carolina			Missouri
	North Dakota			Nebraska
	Oregon			New Hampshire
	South Dakota			New Mexico
	Utah			New York
	Washington			Oklahoma
	Wisconsin			Rhode Island
				South Dakota
				Tennessee
				Utah
				Vermont
				Wyoming

Note: Some states use different selection systems for different courts.
Source: Adapted from *The Book of the States 2011* (Lexington, Ky.: Council of State Governments, 2011), 307–309.

groups concerned about litigation that affects them. Spending by interest groups in a judicial campaign raises concern about a conflict of interest for the judges benefiting from this support. This threatens the trust that courts need in order to operate fairly and effectively.

In discussions about campaign finance reform, judicial elections form a distinct category. Generally, there is significantly more support for public funding of campaigns for the bench than there is for a legislative seat or gubernatorial office. The logic is that it is critical that judges and justices have the appearance of being a neutral third party rather than being partial to a particular interest group or ideological movement.[16] Public funds, instead of campaign contributions from special interests, are therefore a way of avoiding ties that might compromise the credibility of the judiciary. Judicial elections are not always arenas for combative politics. The election of a judge is often a bore, attracting few voters. Candidates traditionally do not discuss specific cases or run on issue-based platforms. Candidates seek to create images of being tough, reasonable, compassionate,

Exploring the Web

How is the court in your state organized?

While all state courts follow a general model, each state has its own unique features. Use the websites discussed below to understand more about the courts in your state.

The National Center for State Courts (www.ncsc.dni.us) is a useful source for information and for links to other sites. Included are links to the website for each state.

The U.S. Department of Justice has a Bureau of Statistics that keeps descriptions and information on each of the state courts (www.ojp.usdoj.gov/bjs/abstract/sco98.htm).

Other information, including the texts of decisions made in court cases, is available from Find Law (www.findlaw.com?11stategov/index.html).

When you visit these websites, you should try to find the answers to the following questions:

- How are judges selected?
- How long do they serve?
- Does your state have justices of the peace?
- Does your state have specialty courts that focus on probate, family issues, small claims, and the like?
- How does a citizen in your state appeal a case?

and experienced. However, in 2002, in *Republican Party of Minnesota v. White*, the U.S. Supreme Court ruled that Minnesota's law prohibiting judicial candidates from discussing substantive issues or telling voters how they would handle certain types of cases was unconstitutional. The ruling did not, however, set aside the principle that candidates should not make promises of how they would handle specific, pending cases. The Court said that Minnesota's broad restrictions violated the First Amendment protection of free expression. This ruling may change the character of judicial elections in states other than Minnesota.

Reforms of state court systems since the 1960s have been modeled after the **Missouri Plan**, an approach that combines appointive and elective processes. According to this system, when a vacancy on a bench occurs, a select committee of judges, attorneys, and citizens nominates individuals they regard as highly qualified. The governor must then select someone from this list of nominees. After the person selected has served as a judge for a year, the following question is placed on the ballot during a regularly scheduled election: "Shall Judge [name of judge selected] of the [name of court] be retained in office?" Voters

---

Missouri Plan   A process for selecting state judges, in which a judge is appointed initially for a term of office and then continues in office by receiving support from voters on a yes–no ballot (rather than a ballot with opponents).

DEBATING THE ISSUES

Should judges be elected or appointed?

One might argue that we are more likely to have qualified, impartial judges if they are chosen by governors, with confirmation by the state senate, than if they are elected via general election. On the other hand, governors are political people, and perhaps they provide no guarantee of a judicial system through which we can be certain of impartial justice.

Is the Missouri Plan a reasonable compromise of these competing approaches to judicial selection, or does it also provide a system rife with politics?

If we elect judges, should we make these nonpartisan elections?

Would it be more useful to provide public funding of the campaigns in order to avoid the influence of special-interest campaign contributions?

Do you believe that it doesn't matter how judges are selected?

register a yes or no. If the majority of votes cast are yes, the judge serves a full term. If the majority of votes are no, the governor must select someone else from the original list of nominees, and he or she in turn must be confirmed by a yes vote in a general election.[17]

Although the Missouri Plan (also known as the Merit Plan) may be conceptually appealing, studies do not show that judges selected in this manner differ from judges selected through straight gubernatorial appointments, partisan elections, or nonpartisan elections. All selection methods appear to provide judges with similar educational, experiential, and social backgrounds.[18] How an individual becomes a judge does not appear to influence whether she or he will tend to rule in favor of or against criminal defendants, corporations, government agencies, or poor people.[19] The way judges are selected, in other words, may be more significant for determining how comfortable the public is with the process than for determining how the courts will actually operate.

DISCIPLINE AND REMOVAL OF JUDGES

As already presented, a crucial resource of courts is the image of judges as fair, impartial, honest, and intelligent arbiters. Courts rely primarily on this image for compliance with their decisions. They do not control armies or police forces that might enforce compliance, nor do they have financial resources to provide or withhold and thus affect behavior. Despite the importance of image to the court, it would be unreasonable to expect all judges to maintain an aura of objectivity and integrity.

Judges have, at times, made statements or issued rulings on procedures that may have prejudiced the outcome of a trial. This can provide grounds for the losing side to appeal the case. Inappropriate behavior by judges sometimes extends beyond what happens in the courtroom. Judges have been convicted of accepting bribes, not paying their income taxes, engaging in sexual misbehavior, and driving while drunk.

Because most state judges are elected for fixed terms, they can be removed from the bench by suffering defeat in a bid for reelection. Sometimes the mere publicity—apart from the facts—about an indiscreet or potentially criminal act is enough to thwart a bid for reelection. States that allow for the recall of elected officials typically include judges among those subject to recall.

Thirty-two states rely heavily on impeachment by the legislature to remove judges from office. This process, which also applies to governors, legislators, and other major officials, necessitates hearings and investigations by the legislature, a vote by the lower chamber to indict, and a trial and vote in the upper chamber to convict. This process is rarely used.[20]

In 2000, New Hampshire impeached a judge for the first time since 1790. By a vote of 253–95, the New Hampshire House of Representatives voted to have David Brock, chief justice of the state's supreme court, stand trial in the state senate. He was charged with talking to lower court judges with the purpose of influencing their decisions on his own divorce case. He did the same for another politically connected lawsuit. The House was also concerned that the chief justice allowed judges who were disqualified from hearing cases in which they had conflicts of interest to comment on pending rulings. Finally, he was accused of lying under oath during the investigation. The New Hampshire Senate, acting as a panel of judges, found Justice Brock guilty and removed him from office.

Led by California, 30 states have established judicial review commissions to receive and investigate complaints of misbehavior by judges and, when necessary, to prosecute the case—usually before the state supreme court.[21] Judicial review commissions typically include lawyers, judges, and citizens. The discipline meted out to convicted judges can range from reprimands to suspensions to dismissal. Contemporary court reformers prefer judicial review commissions to other ways of disciplining judges. One advantage of the commissions is that they have a wide range of punishments, which allows for sanctions appropriate to the indiscretion. Also, commissions are more efficient and less expensive than impeachment or recall.[22]

JURIES

A hallowed principle of justice in the American and British jurisprudence systems is the opportunity to be tried by one's peers. The original implementation of this principle is quite different from contemporary practices. Initially, a "jury of one's peers" was interpreted to mean those in the community who knew the litigants and the circumstances of the dispute intimately.

Today, jury selection emphasizes the identification of individuals who will enter the courtroom without any previous knowledge of the people involved in the case and, ideally, the case itself. Due to the amount of publicity about the murders of O. J. Simpson's former wife and her friend and to the arrest of Simpson, it took 11 weeks to find a jury that seemed removed and would be impartial. Lawyers and the judge gave up on impaneling a jury of hermits; they satisfied themselves with evidence that jurors had not prejudged the case. When a case has been publicized or discussed so much in one community that it would be almost impossible to get an impartial jury there, judges will grant a motion for a **change of venue** and move the trial to another community.

While a case is being tried, jurors are instructed not to discuss it with anyone or read newspaper accounts of the trial. In sensational cases or in cases being discussed extensively in the community, jurors may be **sequestered**—kept in a hotel and prevented from going home during the trial and from using electronic social media—to limit the influences on their decisions to the presentations made in the courtroom.

Over 150,000 juries are impaneled each year. States differ somewhat in the number of jurors that constitute a jury. In most states, the number is between eight and fifteen. Jurors are selected randomly from a list of registered voters, taxpayers, or driver's license holders. Judges may excuse people from jury duty if they are convinced that serving would cause a serious hardship. Lawyers on either side can ask that specific individuals be excused because they suspect that, based on answers to preliminary questions or on some other information, the individuals are likely to be prejudiced when considering the case. Lawyers try to predict that certain demographics, like women, older people, or college-educated individuals, are apt to be sympathetic to their side and then try to use objections to other potential jurors so the resulting jury is likely to be persuaded by that lawyer's arguments.

Jurors must consider the evidence and the arguments presented at the trial, the credibility of the witnesses, and the law that applies, and then render a verdict of guilt or innocence. The judge in a jury trial makes certain that the litigants and their lawyers follow proper procedure in presenting their cases, and that the jury receives proper instruction about applicable law and the standards that must be used to determine guilt or innocence. State laws specify whether the jurors must consider the defendant guilty only if the evidence meets the test of **beyond reasonable doubt**, as for first-degree murder and other major felonies, or a different standard, like **preponderance of evidence** for the lesser offenses. The latter requires weighing the evidence on each side to determine which is most convincing. States generally apply the preponderance of evidence standard to contract law.

A certain amount of subjectivity in jury decisions is inevitable. But this is also true for decisions made by judges. Support for our system of jurisprudence depends in part on ignoring or downplaying this subjectivity. Appeals are always an option when the subjectivity is considered excessive or somehow in error.

---

change of venue   A decision to conduct a trial in a different community than the one in which the crime was committed, usually on the grounds that a fair trial is not possible unless the trial is moved.

sequester   To keep members of a jury from going to their respective homes in order to isolate them from inappropriate influences on their decision in a court case.

beyond reasonable doubt   A standard of proof that must be met in order to find someone guilty. This standard is reserved for the most serious crimes with the most severe penalties.

preponderance of evidence   A standard of proof that must be met to find someone guilty of almost all but the most serious crimes. This standard essentially requires a determination of whether the plaintiff has a more persuasive case than the defendant.

SUMMARY AND CONCLUSIONS

Courts have tried to maintain a position above politics. The image of judges as fair and impartial is essential to the dispute settlement role that they must play. The selection process—even when electoral—and the provisions for discipline and removal have fostered the image of judges as being objective and professional. Attorneys general and district attorneys are more explicitly involved in partisan politics, but the aura of impartiality of the law and the courts tends to help these officers appear more like objective enforcers of the law than political hacks.

In addition to resolving disputes and enforcing the law, the judicial system is centrally involved in policy making. Attorneys general and district attorneys are politicians, by definition, and win in partisan and sometimes issue-oriented campaigns. Attorneys general increasingly provide services and pursue policies that are outside the strict boundaries of legal work. The application and interpretation of laws by judges and by prosecuting attorneys invariably involves the exercise of discretion.

Policies that affect more than the specific litigants in a lawsuit are made when judgments clarify ambiguities in statutes. Citizens and the legal community take note of these rulings. Administrators, police officers, legislators, governors, and mayors are also attentive to court rulings because they exercise discretion and make and implement policy in their respective positions. These officials are compelled to operate within the boundaries of the law, as interpreted by the courts and the state's attorneys. In short, although courts and prosecutors maintain a certain distance from other governmental institutions and other actors in the political arena, they play a central role in the functions of state and local governments.

Perhaps even more than is the case for legislative and executive institutions, the most dynamic aspect of court proceedings is face-to-face interaction. Judges and juries ascertain the credibility of witnesses. Lawyers spar with one another and sometimes with witnesses, with an eye on the impressions they are making on the judge and on jury members. Plaintiffs and defendants nervously watch and interpret the actions of everyone in the courtroom. While the outcome of the proceedings may have general policy implications, for the primary litigants what is at stake is immediate, personal, and often very serious.

Discussion Questions

1. What is meant by the phrase *judicial version of new federalism*? Explain the relationships among state, tribal, and federal courts.

2. What are the various roles that state courts play? How would you compare the limits and opportunities that courts have in policy making with those of the legislature or the governor?

3. Explain the differences between criminal law and civil law. If you were a victim of some injustice, what are the advantages and disadvantages of pursuing remedies under each type of law?

4. What criteria and concerns might affect a decision to request a jury trial rather than a bench trial? Do options that invite strategies for pursuing a case in one versus the other suggest that the judicial system is not objective?

5. Describe the general structure of most state court systems. In your description, pay particular attention to appeals. Who hears appeals? How do appeals cases differ from original court cases?

Glossary

advisory opinion 329

affidavit 338

award 339

bench trial 330

beyond reasonable doubt 345

change of venue 345

civil law 331

criminal law 331

defendant 328

deposition 338

dual jurisdiction 328

exhibit 338

grand jury 335

indictment 335

injunction 340

interrogatories 337

jurisdiction 329

justice of the peace 329

legal opinion 332

Missouri Plan 342

motions of discovery 337

out-of-court settlement 335

plaintiff 328

plea bargain 336

preponderance of evidence 345

restraining order 339

sentence 339

sequester 345

standing 328

test case 323

Endnotes

   1. David Rottman, "The State Courts in 2005: A Year of Living Dangerously," *The Book of the States 2006* (Lexington, Ky.: Council of State Governments, 2006), 237–241.

   2. Michael W. McCann, *Rights at Work: Pay Equity Reform and the Politics of Legal Mobilization* (Chicago, Ill.: University of Chicago Press, 1994).

   3. Earl M. Maltz, "Federalism and State Court Activism," *Intergovernmental Perspective* (Spring 1987), 23–26.

   4. Ronald K. L. Collins and Peter J. Galie, "Models of Post-Incorporation Judicial Review: 1985 Survey of Constitutional Individual Rights Decisions," *Publius* (Summer 1986), 117–118.

   5. William J. Brennan Jr., "State Constitutions and the Protection of Individual Rights," *Harvard Law Review* (January 1977), 489–504.

   6. Douglas Robs, "Safeguarding Our Federalism: Lessons for the States from the Supreme Court," *Public Administration Review* (November 1985), 723.

   7. Gregory A. Caldeira, "The Transmission of Legal Precedent: A Study of State Supreme Courts," *American Political Science Review* (June 1985), 178–193.

   8. Ibid., 187; P. Harris, "Some Predictors of the Interstate Diffusion of State Common Law, 1870–1970," paper presented at the Annual Meeting of the Law and Society Association, San Francisco, Calif., April 1979.

   9. Richard A. Monette, "A New Federalism for Indian Tribes: The Relationship between the United States and Tribes in Light of Our Federalism and Republican Democracy," *University of Toledo Law Review 25* (1996), 1–50.

   10. Herbert Jacob, "State Courts and Public Policy," in *Politics in the American States. A Comparative Analysis*, 3d ed., eds. Herbert Jacob and Kenneth N. Vines (Boston, Mass.: Little, Brown, 1976), 247.

   11. *The Book of the States, 1996–1997* (Lexington, Ky.: Council of State Governments, 1996), 129–130.

   12. Robert A. Carp, "The Behavior of Grand Juries: Acquiescence of Justice," *Social Science Quarterly* (March 1975), 853–870.

   13. David C. Saffell, *State and Local Government*, 3d ed. (New York: Random House, 1987), 173.

   14. Henry Robert Glick and Kenneth N. Vines, *State Court Systems* (Englewood Cliffs, N.J.: Prentice-Hall, 1971), 179.

   15. Adam Liptak, "Overriding the Jury in Capital Cases," *The New York Times*, July 12, 2011, A13.

   16. James C. Foster, "Rethinking Politics and Judicial Selections during Contentious Times," Kevin B. Smith, ed., *State and Local Government 2005–2006* (Washington, D.C.: Congressional Quarterly Press, 2006), 129–133.

   17. Richard A. Watson and Ronald G. Downing, *The Politics of the Bench and Bar: Judicial Selection under the Missouri Nonpartisan Court Plan* (New York: Wiley, 1969).

   18. Bradley Cannon, "The Impact of Formal Selection Processes on Characteristics of Judges—Reconsidered," *Law and Society Review* (May 1972), 570–593.

   19. Stuart Nagel, "Unequal Party Representation in State Supreme Courts," *Journal of the American Judicature Society* (1961), 62–65.

   20. *The Book of the States, 1996–1997*, 136.

   21. *State Court Systems* (Lexington, Ky.: Council of State Governments, 1979), 57.

   22. Herbert Jacob, *Justice in America*, 4th ed. (Boston, Mass.: Little, Brown, 1984), Chapter 3.

14

Crime and Corrections

LEARNING OBJECTIVES

- Identify the types of crimes that are committed and the trends of crime rates.
- Know the characteristics of those convicted of crimes.
- Understand how state governments have approached the prevention of crime and the rehabilitation and punishment of criminals.
- Appreciate the issues raised when women and children are incarcerated.
- Understand the relationships between constitutional protections of individual rights and societal efforts to provide safety and justice.

The judge sentenced James to nine years of imprisonment for dealing drugs. James came from a family and a neighborhood where drugs and crime were commonplace. His father, a brother, two uncles, and four cousins had already served time. Now it was his turn. Yet James vowed that he was going to make the most of this and when he got out, he would pursue a more responsible and safer lifestyle. While in prison, he would finish his high school diploma or get a Graduate Equivalency Diploma (GED) and learn some kind of trade.

Prison, however, was anything but a boarding school. In fact, he got no schooling at all. He got on waiting lists for courses but never got any further than that. Instead, he spent three years simply watching television, playing some basketball, and hanging out with other inmates. He was then released on parole. His parole officer had a caseload of 118 individuals and provided neither help nor supervision. James tried to find a job, but after being turned down four times he went back to dealing drugs to make a living. He moved in with a woman and took out his frustrations on her, beating her severely almost every week. She never reported him; instead, she blamed herself for his behavior. His parole officer was supposed to know where he was living, but James gave him a fictional address that was never checked. He also lied to his parole officer about having a legitimate job, and the parole officer was too busy to confirm the information.

James's drug dealing prompted him to travel to a neighboring state—another violation of his parole. On the fifth visit to that state, police making a drug bust caught him. When they did a background check on him, they discovered he was on parole and returned him to his home state. James is back in prison. Authorities still do not know he was beating his girlfriend. James still does not have a GED or any job skills.

Crime evokes outrage and frustration. When we hear that someone has been robbed, raped, or murdered, we empathize with the victim and demand that the perpetrator be punished. When a scam wipes out a family's hard-earned savings, we think of the con artist as cruel and callous, not as cunning and clever. Our emotions show. We feel sympathy for the victims, hate for the criminals, and concern for ourselves and those close to us. We want government to act decisively to prevent crime and to catch and punish criminals. Specifically, we look to police officers, courts, and correctional institutions to keep us safe.

Indirectly, all of us are affected by face-to-face interactions in the criminal justice system. We seek safety. This requires at least temporarily removing dangerous individuals from our communities. We need police officers, prosecutors, and judges who are competent but do not violate the constitutional rights of those accused of crimes. Nothing is more frustrating than to see someone who appears guilty of a crime let free because eager or abusive officials trampled constitutional protections. On the other hand, no one feels secure in a community where the police are criminals and cannot be trusted. Mayor Mitch Landrieu and his new police chief, Ronal Serpas, vowed sweeping changes in the New Orleans police force following the 2010 federal indictments of officers for corruption and, especially, for their behavior during Hurricane Katrina. For decades New Orleans police have been busted for drug trafficking, bribes, rapes, and murders.

Ideally, the face-to-face interactions between criminals and the courtroom and prison officials should have the effect of stopping and preventing criminal behavior. Despite considerable debate and research, we are still not sure what prevents crime and what rehabilitates criminals. Although courts and prisons may not be very effective arenas for our efforts to curtail crime, they are essential for justice, especially when applying the principle that those who do wrong should be punished. (See the Debating the Issues box on page 355.)

THE NATURE AND INCIDENCE OF CRIME

Crime is a perennial concern. Understandably, we always want reassurance that we are safe. We become especially upset and fearful in response to a specific incident, such as a woman being stalked, terrorized, and gruesomely murdered by a jilted lover; the life of a promising and energetic young adult getting snuffed out by a random shooting; or a frail old man getting beaten to death for pocket change.

Although violent crimes, especially rape and murder, are the most publicized, over 90 percent of the crimes committed in the United States do not involve violence. As Figure 14.1 shows, slightly less than 1 percent of all crimes reported in 2008 were murders and rapes. Over 77 percent, on the other hand, were robberies, larcenies, and thefts, including car thefts. Figures 14.2 and 14.3 show that the trends for both violent crimes and property crimes, respectively, have been declining since reaching a peak in 1973.

Your likelihood of becoming a victim of crime depends in part on where you live. The South and the West have the highest property and violent crime rates, if we compare the incidence of crime to the population numbers. As Figure 14.4 shows, the Midwest and Northeast are safest with respect to violent crime, and the Northeast is the safest with respect to property crime. Crime rates are over twice as high in urban areas than in rural

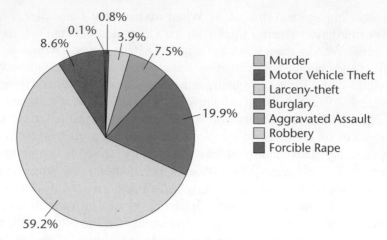

Figure 14.1 Distribution of Crimes Committed, 2008

Source: Federal Bureau of Investigation, U.S. Department of Justice, *Uniform Crime Rates,* www.fbi.gov/ucr/cius 2007/data/table_0.1.html.

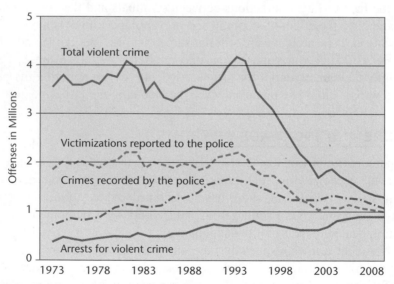

Figure 14.2 Four Measures of Serious Violent Crime

Source: Bureau of Justice Statistics, *National Crime Victimization Survey* 2009, http://www.ojp.usdoj. gov/bjs/glance/viort.htm.

areas.[1] Figure 14.5 provides information about the age of victims of violent crimes. Clearly, those between 12 and 19 are most likely to be victims. Men and African Americans continue to be victimized at higher and higher rates.

Available statistics indicate some change in who commits crimes. The number of adult arrests has dropped, but the number of juvenile arrests has increased. Between 1988 and 1998,

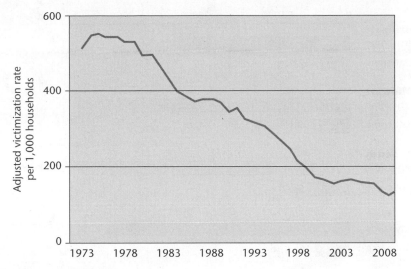

Figure 14.3   Property Crime Rates
   Note: Property crimes include burglary, theft, and motor vehicle theft.
   Source: Bureau of Justice Statistics, *National Crime Victimization Survey* 2007, http://www.ojp.usdoj
.gov/bjs/glance/house2.htm.

juvenile arrests increased 13 percent. Almost all of that increase was associated with violent crimes.[2] In 1998, 53 percent of all those arrested were under the age of 25. Of those arrested for all crimes—violent and property—in 2009, one-third were between the ages of 18 and 24. Another 13 percent were between the ages of 25 and 29. In contrast, only 6 percent of those arrested were over 50, and 15 percent were between the ages of 40 and 49.

Those arrested for crimes other than drunk driving are disproportionately African American men who are under the age of 25 and have less than a high school education. In contrast, very few women are arrested, particularly for crimes of violence. Table 14.1 provides a profile by gender and race of those arrested in 2007. It should be noted that there is a concern about **racial profiling** by police officers that may contribute to the disproportionate number of African Americans who are arrested.

Our capacity to understand crime and criminals is limited to some extent by the available data. Federal Bureau of Investigation (FBI) statistics include only *reported* crime. Despite efforts to encourage victims to notify authorities, the common assumption is that assaults and rapes are not always reported. More broadly, many individuals who are victims of theft and fraud fail to file reports. They simply do not want to bother, or they blame themselves for being careless. According to annual surveys conducted by the U.S. Department of Justice, the rates at which victims report crimes to the police vary from about 30 percent for petty theft to 55 percent for rape to 75 percent for auto theft.[3]

---

racial profiling   The practice of treating someone as a suspect or criminal because of his or her race or
   appearance.

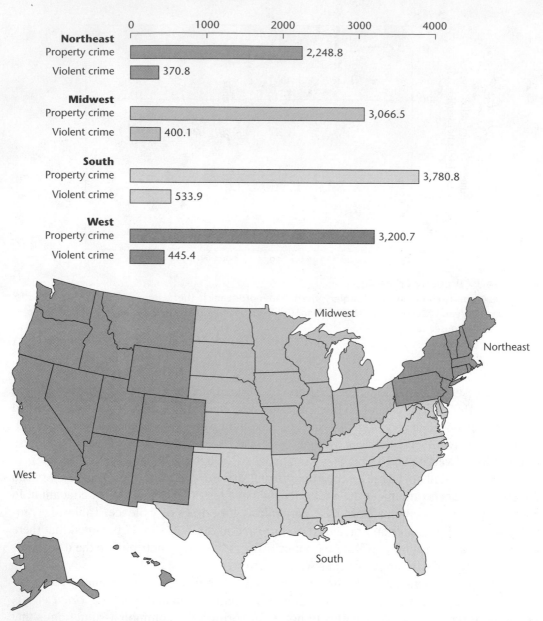

Figure 14.4 Regional Crime Patterns

Source: Federal Bureau of Investigation, *Uniform Crime Report 2008*, http://www.fbi.gov/ucr/
cius2007/offenses/standard_links/regional_estimates.html.

Another limitation of the FBI reports is that they do not include so-called white-
collar crimes, such as cheating on income taxes, filing fraudulent claims to insurance companies, violating copyright laws, or misleading investors or home buyers in schemes like
those that contributed to the financial crisis in 2008. The twenty-first century began with
shocking scandals of corporate executives and accountants who used a variety of tricks and

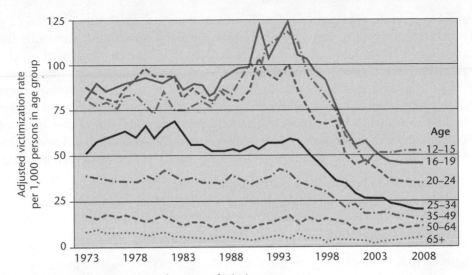

Figure 14.5 Violent Crime Rates by Age of Victim

    Source: Bureau of Justice Statistics, *National Crime Victimization Survey* 2008, http://www.ojp.usdoj .gov/bjs/glance/vage.htm.

Table 14.1 Demographic Characteristics of Persons Arrested, 2007

| | Percentage of Arrests | | | | | |
| | Sex | | Race | | | |
	Male	Female	White	Black	American Indian	Asian
All offenses	75.8%	24.2%	69.7%	28.2%	1.3%	0.8%
Runaways	43.9	56.1	69.3	27.2	2.1	1.4
Violent						
Murder[a]	89.8	10.2	49.6	50.4	1.0	1.0
Rape	98.9	1.1	64.4	33.5	1.2	0.9
Robbery	88.4	11.6	42.2	56.7	0.6	0.7
Aggravated assault[b]	78.7	21.3	64.0	33.7	1.3	1.0
Property						
Burglary	85.5	14.5	68.5	29.8	1.0	0.7
Larceny	60.0	40.0	68.3	29.3	1.3	1.1
Fraud	55.9	44.1	69.1	29.6	0.5	1.0
Other						
Drug offenses	81.2	18.8	63.7	35.1	0.6	0.6
Driving under the influence	79.2	20.8	88.5	9.2	1.4	0.9
Disorderly conduct	73.7	26.3	63.6	34.2	1.6	0.6

[a]Includes nonnegligent manslaughter.

[b]Includes offenses such as negligent manslaughter, sexual assault, and kidnapping.

Source: Federal Bureau of Investigation, U.S. Department of Justice, *Crime in the United States, 2007*,   Tables 35 and 43.

maneuvers to get rich at the expense of stockholders, company employees, and retired workers. Technological advances have provided new opportunities for crime. Computer hackers can extract funds from someone else's bank account, amateur electricians can tap into a cable television line, and college students can make copies of their roommates' music CDs or download copyrighted material without paying fees or royalties to authors and performers.

Public policy agendas are shaped by anecdotes, scandals, and impressions, as well as statistical patterns. Although the crime rate generally has been going down, polls indicate that crime continues to be a major concern of the American public. As the data in Table 14.2 show, the public has an image of crime and danger that is not based on fact. Most do not realize that:

1. The incidence of crime has steadily declined since 1973.
2. It is more dangerous to be a farmer than a police officer.
3. Corporate crime costs more than street crime.
4. Pollution is responsible for more deaths than handguns.

These facts notwithstanding, when there is a tragic case of violent crime in the community, politicians are not going to argue for placing the incident into a broader, more comforting perspective.

Table 14.2 Opinions and Realities Regarding Crime

	Opinion		Reality
Trend 1973–1993			
Rapes	Increase	91%	Increase from 10 to 19
	Decrease	3	per 10,000 people
	Same	6	
Robberies	Increase	92	Decrease from 70 to 58
	Decrease	4	per 10,000 people
	Same	4	
Police officers killed	Increase	78	Decrease from 125 to 62
in the line of duty	Decrease	11	per year
	Same	11	
Rates for 1993			
Who is more likely to	Police	77	Police 15.4
be killed on the job?	Farmer	16	Farmer 26.9
	Uncertain	7	per 10,000 workers
Which costs the	Street crime	53	Street crime, $19 billion
average American	Corporate crime	39	Corporate crime,
more money?	Uncertain	8	$130 billion
Which causes more	Handguns	81	Handguns, 34,000
deaths every year?	Air pollution	8	Pollution, 140,000
	Uncertain	11	

Source: Bureau of Justice Statistics, U.S. Department of Justice, *National Crime Victimization Surveys 1993* (Washington, D.C.: U.S. Government Printing Office, 1994); Federal Bureau of Investigation, *Uniform Crime Reports 1993* (Washington, D.C.: U.S. Government Printing Office, 1994); Gallup Poll, 1993; Bureau of Labor Statistics, *Injury Fact Book 1993* (Washington, D.C.: U.S. Government Printing Office, 1994).

DEBATING THE ISSUES

Face to Face with Crime

Crime and punishment is a series of face-to-face interactions.

- Criminal and victim when the crime is committed
- Criminal and police officer(s) during investigation and arrest
- Criminal and defense attorney during trial and/or plea bargaining
- Criminal and jury during trial and sentencing
- Criminal and judge during trial and sentencing
- Criminal and victim when making impact statement after trial
- Criminal and prison guards
- Criminal and parole board
- Criminal and probation/parole officer

Each of these interactions has its own dynamics and is critical in a process that has many steps. Why are there so many steps in the process?

APPROACHES TO CRIME

Crimes involve three key elements:

1. Criminals
2. Victims
3. Locations

State governments have devoted considerably more attention to criminals than to victims or location.

Criminals

Four policy approaches are applied to individuals who have been convicted of a crime:

1. Punishment. A general sentiment is that a crime should incur punishment and that the punishment should fit the crime. For some, this extends to supporting the death penalty for those convicted of the worst crimes.

2. Deterrence. Some believe that the courts can help prevent crime by making it clear, through consistent sentencing, what consequences follow a given crime. The reasoning is that potential criminals will not commit certain acts if they know that the penalties will outweigh the possible benefits. Although evidence does not support this theory, many remain inclined to increase penalties in order to deter criminal activity.[4]

3. Rehabilitation. Another approach is to turn criminals into law-abiding citizens by treating whatever emotional, psychological, or economic problems caused them to commit a crime. A major study completed by Robert Martinson in 1974 discouraged continued

Exploring the Web

Targeting Crime

We can use our money and resources to reduce crime if we look for important, fundamental information. Where would you target efforts?

Criminal

The U.S. Department of Justice's Bureau of Statistics (www.ojp.usdoj.gov/bjs) provides profiles of those convicted of crimes. For information that might work to deter individuals from committing crimes, see www.thejusticeproject.org.

Victim

The Bureau of Statistics also gives information about the types of crimes that are committed. Who are the victims? Do we need more information?

Location

Does your police department keep a record of where crimes are committed? What about records of the times (days and hours) of the frequency of crime?

---

efforts to emphasize rehabilitation, although all states continue to provide rehabilitation programs.[5] Efforts are still made to design new, more effective programs.

4. Confinement. Prisons may not deter. They may not rehabilitate. But they can keep those with criminal records from further endangering society.

A reform that was popular nationally in 1994 and 1996 was to direct courts to confine indefinitely individuals convicted of a third crime. This is known as **three strikes and you're out**. The federal government joined the trend and included this provision in the anticrime bill it passed in 1996. In part, this application of a baseball rule was a reaction to several widely publicized cases in which individuals who had been released from prison committed gruesome, violent crimes.

California's version of the three strikes rule is so arbitrary that it has become both expensive and controversial. The state includes all infractions, regardless of their severity, as a strike. In March 2003, the U.S. Supreme Court reviewed two applications of California's three strikes policy. In one, Gary Ewing, who had previous convictions for robbery and burglary, was sentenced to life imprisonment when he was found guilty of stealing three clubs from a golf pro shop—his third strike. The other case involved Leandro Andrade, who was convicted of two "third strikes" when he stole videotapes worth $153.54 from two Kmart stores. Under California law, the crimes counting as third strikes in both cases would normally carry up to one year in prison. But Ewing and Andrade were sentenced to

---

three strikes and you're out   A policy requiring that after individuals have been convicted of three felonies, they must serve a life sentence without the possibility of parole.

life behind bars. Almost all of the justices on the U.S. Supreme Court indicated that they thought California's law was bad public policy, but in a 5–4 decision, they said that it did not violate the Eighth Amendment prohibition against cruel and unusual punishment.

States with a three strikes rule have found it expensive. Individuals accused of committing a second and especially a third crime have no incentive to enter a plea bargain for a lesser offense because conviction of any offense counts as a strike. The admission of guilt to a third crime may be tantamount to acceptance of a life sentence. Thus, more cases are going to trial in California, consuming the time and resources of the judicial system. Also, more individuals are being sentenced for life than had been anticipated, and prison costs have more than tripled since the law was passed as a direct initiative in 1994.

Death Penalty. Execution is the ultimate act for removing someone from society. All but 15 states (Alaska, Hawaii, Illinois, Iowa, Maine, Massachusetts, Michigan, Minnesota, New Jersey, New York, North Dakota, Rhode Island, Vermont, West Virginia, and Wisconsin) have a death penalty. See Figure 14.6 for the number of executions per state between 1976 and 2009.

Popular support for the death penalty is based on a desire to punish, not on empirical evidence that executions deter crime.[6] Virginia, for example, uses the death penalty, yet it has a higher homicide rate than Maine and West Virginia, which do not execute criminals. The South uses the death penalty more than any other region in the nation, yet it has an annual homicide rate almost twice as high as that of the Northeast and Midwest, where the death penalty is used the least[7] (see Figure 14.7).

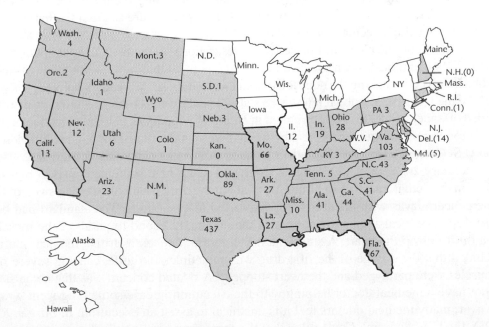

Figure 14.6 Executions by State, 1976–2009
Source: Death Penalty Information Center. *Facts about the Death Penalty.* www.deathpenaltyinfo.org.

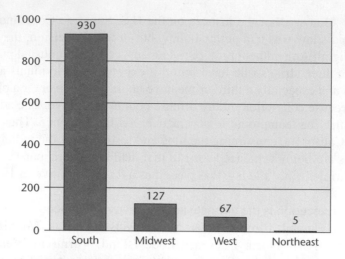

Figure 14.7   Executions by Region, 1976–2009
Source: Death Penalty Information Center. *Facts about the Death Penalty.* www.deathpenaltyinfo.org.

Few would argue that an issue as grave as taking someone's life should be settled according to the calculations of a cost–benefit analysis, but the relative costs of incarceration and execution are important secondary considerations. Contrary to expectations, the cost of executing people is about the same as imprisoning them for life.[8] The major expenses are the legal fees and court costs necessary to be as sure as possible that innocent people are not being executed by mistake.

The U.S. Supreme Court has placed some restrictions on the use of capital punishment by states. As mentioned in Chapter 13, the Court has ruled that juries—not judges alone—must be involved in making the decision of whether to impose the death penalty. In *Atkins v. Virginia*, the Court struck down laws in 18 states that allowed for the execution of mentally retarded offenders. In 2005, the Court ruled in *Stanford v. Kentucky* that the execution of individuals for crimes committed before they were 18 years old violated the Eighth Amendment to the U.S. Constitution. This affected 19 states and 72 young people on death row.

In January 2006, the U.S. Supreme Court joined 12 state supreme courts in blocking executions by lethal injection until questions about the drug protocols were answered. One of the concerns was with the drugs that were used in executions. The standard had been to use three chemicals—one to anesthetize the inmate, a second to paralyze the muscles, and a third to stop the heart. A study published in *The Lancet*, a British medical journal, concluded that the dosage of the first drug was sometimes too little, causing severe pain as muscles were paralyzed and the heart stopped.[9] A related concern was that some states did not have a medical doctor helping with the execution in case something went wrong. However, many medical doctors feel it is unethical to assist an execution. In *Baze v. Rees* (2008), the U.S. Supreme Court ruled that the three-drug protocol for lethal injection did not violate the Constitution, thus freeing the 36 states to resume executions.

DEBATING THE ISSUES

Should the punishment fit the crime, or should the treatment fit the criminal?

Correction policy can focus on crimes or on criminals. One approach can be to make it clear that no matter who you are or what your background, you will have to suffer a particular consequence if you commit a crime. A predictable, stable link between crimes and punishments will send a clear message and deter criminal activity.

Another approach is to consider carefully the person who committed a crime and then design a program of punishment and incentives to keep him or her from becoming a repeat offender. This is perhaps more complicated and cumbersome than using a predetermined formula that metes out punishment dependent on *what* was done, but it gets to the important issue of *why* it was done. Criminals need more than punishment. They need rehabilitation.

Where would you place the emphasis? If you would mix the two approaches, how would you do that?

Concerned about the number of mistakes that have been made in sentencing innocent people to death, Illinois suspended executions in 1999, and in 2002 a commission suggested that the state consider abandoning its death penalty. As Governor George Ryan left office in December 2002, he pardoned four inmates on death row because of faulty evidence, and he commuted the death sentences of all others to life in prison. In 2007, New Jersey repealed its death penalty law, and Illinois did the same in 2011.

Incarceration. Facilities incarcerating those convicted of serious crimes go by a number of names. **Jail** is the term used when a local government runs the facility. Although **prison** is a common term used by the federal and state governments, other labels have conveyed particular philosophies in the purpose of incarceration. **Penitentiary** was used when the assumption was that a criminal needed to be punished. **Correctional institution** became a common term when the objective was rehabilitation. Many states continue to use this term, even though there is general disenchantment with the prospects for rehabilitation. As the 2004 prisoner abuse scandal during the U.S. occupation of Iraq dramatically reminded everyone, jailers must respect the basic human rights of prisoners, no matter what the purpose of incarceration.

States typically classify their prisons according to the overall prospects for rehabilitation and according to the risks that convicted felons present to society and to themselves.

---

jail County or city facility for incarcerating individuals who are waiting for trial or are serving relatively short sentences.

prison State or federal facility for incarcerating individuals convicted of major crimes.

penitentiary Term used for *prison* when the major explicit purpose of incarceration is punishment.

correctional institution Term used for *prison* when a rehabilitation approach toward inmates is emphasized.

States have separate prison facilities for convicted criminals who are regarded as minimum, medium, and maximum security risks.

- A minimum security facility usually assumes that inmates are not likely to try to escape and would probably not commit major felonies even if they did escape.
- Maximum security prisons make the opposite assumptions. They are populated with individuals who have been convicted of the most serious crimes against persons and property. In states with death penalties, the chambers used for executions are included in a maximum security prison.
- Medium security facilities are between the extremes. Escape would be difficult. Rehabilitation programs are provided with some hope that they will have a constructive effect.

States also have facilities for those judged to be criminals because of severe mental and emotional problems. Sometimes the facility is located within a prison complex, and sometimes it is separate. The inmates of these facilities are incarcerated, just like others convicted of serious crimes. The major difference is that they might be released if it can be documented that they have been cured of the illness that prompted the criminal behavior. In 2008, for the first time in history, over one out of every 100 adults in the United States were in jail or prison. North Dakota had the fewest (1,440) and Texas the most (171,790).

Characteristics of Prisoners.   The profiles of inmates in jails and prisons are generally similar. The typical prisoner is a relatively young male with little education. Over half the prisoners have never been married, and although African Americans constitute about 12 percent of the general population, they constitute about 45 percent of those behind bars. Ironically, Wisconsin and Iowa—two states with relatively few African Americans—rank highest among the states in their incarceration rate of members of this minority group.

The major differences between prisoners in local jails and those in state facilities are that the latter are somewhat older and more likely to have a high school education. Local jails are primarily for those serving short sentences and those incarcerated for the first time. State prisons house those who must spend longer periods behind bars because they have been convicted of more serious crimes or are repeat offenders.

Women in Prison.   Not surprisingly, the profile of those who are incarcerated is similar to those who have been arrested (Table 14.1). Women are a notable exception. They constitute about 14 percent of those arrested, but only 5 percent of those imprisoned. Judges may be concerned about the implications of incarceration for dependent children. In addition, there may be more of an inclination to believe that women can be rehabilitated or that they represent less of a threat to society than male criminals. Most of the serious crimes that prompt the arrest of women are property- and drug-related rather than crimes of violence.

Despite their fewer numbers, concerns arise about the treatment of women in prison.[10] Wisconsin was successfully sued when inmates were injured severely because they were shackled while giving birth. Men work as guards in state prisons for women. This raises issues of personal privacy because inmates have to be observed—or are subject to observation—at all times, and security practices include body searches. In many states, facilities for female prisoners are located in rural areas that are even more remote than is the case for men. Women's prisons tend to consist of smaller cells and fewer support facilities for treatment, recreation, education, or skill training.

Youth in Prison. The increase in gang activity and juvenile crime since 1980 has been frustrating and alarming. The response has been consistent with the general "get tough" inclination of the electorate and public officials. We can see this most dramatically in the laws that give judges the discretion to treat young people as if they were adults. In many states, this involves moving young people out of a court system designed for juveniles. The statutory framework for juvenile justice systems tends to assume that rehabilitation is likely. Juveniles convicted of crimes go into facilities and programs that emphasize treatment and that provide opportunities for the inmates to complete their high school education.

The fear about transferring juveniles into adult court and sentencing them to adult prisons is that their schooling will be in crime, and their primary instructors will be other inmates. The concern, in short, is that treating young people as if they are incorrigible adults may become a self-fulfilling prophecy. The dilemma is that we are not confident in diagnosing who is incorrigible and who might benefit from the kinds of programs typically associated with juvenile correction facilities.

Costs of Imprisonment. It costs more per year to keep people in prison than it does to send them to college. In 2008, for example, the average annual operational prison costs were almost $36,000 per prisoner. It cost $245,000 per inmate to construct prisons. In a study on prison spending, the Pew Center on the States found that state and local governments spent over $48 billion in 2007 on incarcerating prisoners, and on average, states spend almost 8 percent of their budgets on prisons.

Since the mid-1970s, with the emphasis on putting more people behind bars and for longer periods of time, the costs of incarceration have risen faster than in any other area of state and local government spending.[11] State and local government spending on corrections grew over twice as fast as overall state spending from 1985 to 2005.

One-third of the growth in prison populations reflects increases in the general population, more reported crime, and stronger law enforcement. About one-fourth can be attributed to tougher sentencing laws, and the remainder is due to a dramatic increase in the incarceration of drug offenders. According to the U.S. Department of Justice, there were 25 commitments to state prisons for every 1,000 drug offense arrests in 1981. In 1992, the rate increased fourfold, to 104 for every 1,000.[12] That ratio has held steady since 1992.

Overcrowded Cells. One of the implications of the explosion in the prison population has been overcrowded facilities. Corrections officials in some states had to put as many as four prisoners in a cell built for one. Despite the risks involved, prisoners were bedded in a barracks arrangement in hallways and open rooms. They took turns using the cells.

The Eighth Amendment to the U.S. Constitution protects us from cruel and inhumane punishment by the federal government. The Fourteenth Amendment extends this prohibition to state and local governments. In the 1970s, prisoners and their advocates succeeded in getting federal courts to find that the states of Alabama and Arkansas were subjecting their prisoners to overcrowded, unsanitary, and unsafe conditions, in violation of the Eighth and Fourteenth Amendments.[13] In 1980, in the case of *Ruiz v. Estelle*, a federal court ordered the Texas Department of Corrections to halt putting three and four people in one cell, reduce the use of force by prison guards, hire more guards, and provide healthier and safer conditions. California's prison system became so overcrowded and conditions for inmates got so bad that in 2005 federal courts ordered the state government to address the issue and appointed a receiver to manage the prisons until California came up with a satisfactory solution. Unhappy with the lack of progress, on May 23, 2011, the U.S. Supreme Court ordered the state to remove 30,000 inmates from its prison rolls within two years. Only the states of Maine, Minnesota, Montana, Nebraska, New Jersey, New York, North Dakota, Oregon, and Vermont have thus far avoided litigation over prison conditions.

An obvious response to overcrowding and to the court cases demanding humane treatment is to spend millions of dollars to build more prison facilities, hire more guards, and improve existing prisons. States are contracting with private companies to take some of their prisoners. This has become a major industry.[14] Some counties are making money by housing in their own jail cells prisoners from states that have run out of room in their own prisons. Another response is to consider alternatives to incarceration. Despite the political rhetoric of getting tough on criminals, state and local officials have pursued a number of approaches to dealing with criminals outside prison walls.

Alternatives to Prison.   Concerns about prison overcrowding and the skyrocketing costs of incarceration have prompted judges, governors, policy analysts, social workers, and others to consider alternative ways of dealing with those convicted of crimes. Among the most active professional groups studying and proposing alternatives are the American Bar Association and the National Association of Criminal Justice Planners.[15]

Alternatives are important not only for financial reasons (the more expensive options cost about $5,000 per person, per year, compared with $36,000 for incarceration), but also because not all criminals are alike. A young person, from an abusive family, who is a burglar and is a first-time offender is not the same as a middle-aged man who has been in and out of jail for 25 years because he continually assaults people. States vary in how they treat people convicted of nonviolent offenses. Some incarcerate them; others find other punishments. To deal with the diversity and complexity of specific individual cases, courts and correctional officials need alternatives and discretion.

1. Parole. A common and obvious response to overcrowded prisons is to release some inmates and place them on parole. A person on **parole** is allowed to live and work in a community, but under certain restrictions. These restrictions usually include reporting to a parole officer on a regular basis, either face to face or by telephone. In addition, the

---

parole   The release of someone from incarceration before a full sentence has been served. Parole is typically granted with certain conditions that, if not met, can result in a resumption of incarceration.

conditions of parole may include prohibitions against drinking alcoholic beverages, driving a car, changing jobs, logging onto the Internet, moving, or marrying. A violation of parole may mean a return to prison.

In most states, prisoners can apply for parole after they serve one-third of their sentence. Parole boards, usually consisting of five to seven individuals appointed by the governor, hear the petitions for parole and make decisions based on the behavior of the prisoner while he or she was incarcerated, the nature of the crime that was committed, and the risk of danger to society if the prisoner is released.[16]

One of the "get tough" reforms of the 1990s was to limit the discretion of parole boards by requiring that a higher percentage of the sentence be served before someone is eligible for parole. An even tougher version, known as **truth-in-sentencing**, eliminates parole. North Carolina pioneered this approach in which prisoners do not get time off as an incentive for good behavior. Instead they get time added for bad behavior. A companion reform to truth-in-sentencing is to reduce the sentences attached to various crimes. The old policies assumed inmates would be paroled after serving only part of their sentences.

In response to some tragic instances in which a sex offender released from prison has sexually assaulted a child, states have passed laws specifying that neighborhoods must be notified when a convicted offender moves into the community. A concern here is balancing public safety with providing a chance for an offender to reintegrate into society.

2. Probation. Probation, like parole, allows those convicted of crimes to live in the community as long as they abide by certain restrictions and conditions. Probation is in lieu of incarceration, whereas parole occurs after time in prison. If someone violates the conditions of her or his probation, then imprisonment is possible. A pattern of multiple violations almost certainly results in time behind bars.

A judge has the discretion to place someone on probation instead of sending him or her to prison. Almost two-thirds of those who are convicted of crimes are placed on probation. Juveniles, first offenders, and those who plea bargain are most likely to get probation. The judge specifies the time for probationary status and the restrictions that apply. Implicit in probation is the hope that individuals will change their lifestyles and will not engage in future criminal activities. The conditions of probation, therefore, often include treatment programs, community service, and other constructive projects.

3. Work Release. In most states, if a judge determines that a convicted criminal is not likely to be a continued danger to society, the judge may allow the individual to work regular hours at a job and then to spend the rest of the time, including evenings and weekends, in jail.

4. Electronic House Detention. Technology allows use of the convict's home or apartment as a type of prison. A judge may order an individual to wear an electronic bracelet or anklet that emits signals to a receiver in the home. Should the receiver fail to receive the signals, it automatically dials a central computer and notifies law enforcement officials.

---

truth-in-sentencing A policy of not allowing individuals sentenced for a period of incarceration to be paroled before the full completion of that sentence.

probation A sentence that allows an individual to avoid incarceration as long as he or she fulfills certain conditions.

Inmates doing calisthenics in a Florida prison. Ideally prisoners learn discipline and are rehabilitated as well as punished while behind bars.

The receiver can be programmed to allow the individual to keep a work schedule, go to classes, or participate in a treatment program.

Florida, New Jersey, New Mexico, and Oklahoma have used electronic monitoring since the mid-1980s. Some jurisdictions not only avoid prison costs through this approach, but they also recover the expenses of the monitoring by requiring the individuals using the equipment to rent it.

5. Boot Camps. Almost half the states operate **boot camps**, primarily for juvenile offenders. These programs are modeled on the classic initiation camp for military recruits. Correctional boot camps are designed to teach discipline. The schedule is intense and rigorous, and includes demanding physical activity as well as psychological, drug, and alcohol counseling. The hope is that the camp will provide training in self-discipline and will generate better compliance with rules and regulations. Judges allow appropriate individuals to opt for a three- to six-month boot camp, usually followed by a period of probation, instead of a longer prison term.[17]

6. Intensive Sanctions. The usual caseload for a probation officer is over 60 juvenile offenders or 100 adults.[18] That does not allow for very close supervision. **Intensive sanctions** or intensive supervision programs limit the workloads to about one-tenth of that level so that individuals are seen almost daily. Not only do they feel the presence of their probation officer more closely, but they also have a heavier set of requirements than traditionally has been associated with probation or parole. Participants typically have to work full-time, pay restitution to the victims of their crimes, be in treatment or vocational training programs, and provide community service. The general goal is to get tough, but to have rehabilitation and punishment programs within the community.[19]

---

boot camp A sentence that involves an intensive period of incarceration in a program in which rules are detailed and strictly enforced. A boot camp is intended to rehabilitate inmates in part by emphasizing the need to adhere to rules and schedules.

intensive sanctions A sentence in which an individual is not incarcerated but instead is closely monitored and must adhere to a highly structured schedule, usually involving work and/or treatment programs.

7. Crime Prevention. Some clues to effective crime prevention can be found in the profile of criminals. Approximately 60 percent of prison inmates are high school dropouts. About the same percentage earned less than $10,000 in the year before their arrest. Over half the prisoners report they were under the influence of alcohol or other drugs when committing crimes. Many inmates were victims of child abuse.[20]

Victims

Most of the public policies that focus on victims are concerned with what might be done *after* a crime has been committed. For example, states require criminals to make payments to victims to help pay for the damage that has been done.

Less attention has been paid to keeping people from becoming victims. Three groups considered vulnerable have received attention:

1. Children are told in school that they should not talk with or accept rides or candy from strangers.
2. The elderly are warned about scams designed to get their money.
3. Programs train women to avoid circumstances that make them vulnerable to sexual assault.

In addition, many police departments give advice on how to get locks and security devices to keep burglars out and to prevent auto thefts. Many of these and similar programs depend on someone asking questions. More active and aggressive efforts might have a significant impact on the incidence of crime.

Location

Cities of over 1 million people reported 80 percent more crime and 300 percent more violent crime than the national average.[21] Location is an important issue in crime policy.

Police departments in major metropolitan areas record the location of crimes on a map. Invariably, these maps show clusters rather than random dots. This information allows police, city planners, park departments, and others to redesign neighborhoods to make them safer. Successful responses have included increasing the number of street lights; simplifying intersections; providing more open space in parks; and, in some Florida communities, erecting walls around a block and establishing a central square or commons, as is done in some European and South American countries. These efforts are intended to provide a *sense* of safety and community, as well as to eliminate the structures that allow criminals to prey on people.

The identification of where crimes are frequently committed has at times led to intensive policing, sometimes known as a **blanket**. Police can deploy their resources to increase surveillance in an unsafe area.

---

blanket Intensive efforts and a heavy presence by police in a specified area, designed to stop criminal activity in that location.

Community policing is another way of providing safety and service. Under this approach, each neighborhood has a police station and a core of police officers assigned to patrol the area and to get to know the residents. In addition, citizens are encouraged to help police with programs such as Neighborhood Watch (individuals pledge to report any suspicious people or events to the police) and Crime Stoppers (people call the police with clues they have about who might have committed a crime).[22] Police and community groups work to inform people about steps they can take to minimize the probability that their property might be stolen or that they might be robbed or raped.

Simply hiring more police officers and having them visible on the streets has some effect on reducing crime.[23] One provision of the federal Anticrime Bill of 1994 was to provide five-year matching grants to help and to encourage local governments to hire more officers.

CRIME AND THE CONSTITUTION

Government officials, including police officers and prison guards, must do their job in ways that do not threaten individual rights and liberties protected by the U.S. Constitution. U.S. citizens want to be tough on criminals, but there is no support for creating a police state in which everyone's activities and behavior are tightly monitored and controlled. Americans prize safety and freedom; the challenge to the courts and to the law enforcement officials of state and local governments is to ensure both.

Gun Control

Whether or not to regulate private use and ownership of guns is one of the most controversial issues in crime prevention. The Second Amendment to the U.S. Constitution reads:

> A well regulated Militia, being necessary to the security of a free State, the right of the people to keep and bear Arms, shall not be infringed.

A long-standing debate has been over whether the focus of the Second Amendment is on a militia or on individuals. In 2008 the U.S. Supreme Court ruled in *District of Columbia v. Heller* that the nation's capitol had violated individual rights with its comprehensive and restrictive ban on guns. In *McDonald v. City of Chicago* (2010) the Court extended its ruling beyond Washington, D.C., to states and local governments.

The concern is how to uphold this provision of the Bill of Rights and at the same time curtail the death and violence that result from crimes associated with guns. The rise in juvenile crime seems inevitable when readily available, short-barreled handguns are taken to school along with lunch and homework assignments. The availability of guns makes crimes such as robberies and assaults more dangerous and deadly. Domestic disputes can escalate beyond control when there are guns in dresser drawers and on closet shelves. However, guns do not cause crimes.

---

community policing A policy of assigning police officers to work in a particular neighborhood so that they can get to know the people in the community and work with other service providers.

Those concerned about the abuse of the Second Amendment argue that easy access to guns goes beyond the purpose of making it possible to have a "well regulated Militia." It can be argued that the availability of guns threatens, rather than protects, "the security of a free State." Proposals for gun control do not advocate a total ban, but instead include registering guns, requiring safety and security devices, prohibiting the sale of guns to convicted felons and to minors, and banning certain weapons that have extraordinary firepower and ones that are easily concealed. Police officers tend to favor limits, in part to make their jobs less dangerous. Police departments have joined with business, medical, and philanthropic organizations in many communities to trade guns for shoes or jackets. These efforts to get guns off the street include a promise of immunity from prosecution for any violations of existing gun control laws.

Opponents of gun control want to ensure the preservation of sports and recreational activities that involve guns. They also express concern about the ability to protect themselves and their families from criminals. Some take the position that the right to bear arms under the Second Amendment ought to be treated as an absolute right. They argue that any limit threatens the integrity and effectiveness of the amendment as a whole.

The National Rifle Association (NRA, www.nra.org) has led the fight against gun control efforts at all levels of government. In 1997, it outspent proponents of an initiative in the state of Washington to require safety devices on guns by four to one. The NRA won. At times, the NRA has waged single-issue campaigns, urging its supporters to vote for or against a candidate solely because of his or her position on gun control.

Like other interest groups, the NRA combines activity in elections with the dissemination of information and arguments to support its positions. One of the approaches of the NRA has been to respond to the concern about deaths and injuries due to accidents with guns by emphasizing the need for education programs that promote safety.

Health care professionals in many communities have waged campaigns for gun safety. They have linked their campaigns primarily to concerns about the use of guns in juvenile crime, domestic disputes, and suicide. Local physicians in midsize and large cities have offered, free of charge, trigger locks as a way of reducing gun-inflicted death and injuries.

Rights of the Accused

The Fourth through Eighth Amendments to the U.S. Constitution, which provide rights to individuals accused of crimes, are sometimes faulted for thwarting efforts to fight crime. These amendments are philosophically grounded in the principle that an accused person is innocent until proven guilty. They provide specific protections against the arbitrary and abusive actions of a police state, including the following:

1. Protections against searches and invasions of privacy unless there are sufficient grounds to suspect criminal activity.
2. Prohibition against double jeopardy, in which a person is tried more than once by the same jurisdiction for the same crime.
3. Requirements for due process, enabling the accused to know what he or she is accused of doing, to confront the accuser, and to present a defense. Also, individuals are protected from incriminating themselves.

4. Guarantees for a trial by jury.
5. Protections from cruel and inhuman punishment.

The Fourteenth Amendment makes clear that each of these rights must be upheld by state and local governments as well as by the federal government.

The U.S. Supreme Court, under Chief Justice Earl Warren, applied these provisions in ways that favored individual rights. In 1961, the Court established the **exclusionary rule** in *Mapp v. Ohio.* According to this principle, evidence could not be used if it was secured by police without a search warrant that specified the person or place to be searched and what was being hunted. This clearly constrained investigators operating on less than complete and detailed information.

- In *Gideon v. Wainwright* (1963), the Court ruled that state and/or local governments must provide attorneys to individuals who were accused of crimes but could not afford to pay for their own defense.
- *Escobedo v. Illinois* (1964) required police officers to inform people about to be arrested that they have the right to remain silent.
- The Court elaborated on these rulings in *Miranda v. Arizona* (1966) and said that when police officers are about to arrest individuals, it is necessary to remind them that they have the right to remain silent; that anything they say might be used against them in legal proceedings; and that they have the right to an attorney, even if the government must pay. Failure to read people their rights might jeopardize the prosecution's case.

While the basic rights upheld in these cases still apply, subsequent Court rulings have removed some of the limitations on police officers and district attorneys. In *Maryland v. Garrison* (1987), the Court ruled that evidence not specified or anticipated in a search warrant may still be used. In this case, police had a warrant to raid an apartment for illegal drugs. They accidentally went to the wrong apartment, found heroin and drug paraphernalia nonetheless, and successfully used this evidence to convict the unlucky neighbor of the apartment they were supposed to raid. Similarly, in *Colorado v. Connelly* (1986), the Court was prompted to ease application of the *Miranda* ruling by allowing the conviction in this case to stand even though the confession was coerced. The Court ruled that there was sufficient evidence to convict even when the confession was disallowed.

In both conscious and implicit ways, some police forces have engaged in racial profiling. They have used statistics of those convicted of crimes, like those presented in this chapter, to construct a general image of individuals most likely to have run afoul of the law. Then the police identify people who fit the profile and treat them as if they were suspects in some crime. The end result is that African Americans and Hispanic Americans are much more likely to be pulled over, questioned, and searched than are members of any other ethnic group. This is particularly true for minorities who are male and between the

---

exclusionary rule   The principle that evidence that is acquired in a manner that violates an individual's constitutional rights may not be used by prosecutors in legal proceedings.

We rely on the police to enforce laws and uphold the Constitution. This includes the obligation to respect the constitutional rights of the individuals who are arrested.

ages of 15 and 30. The problem is the general presumption that people might be guilty not because of what they have done but because of how they look. State and local officials need to protect communities from the actions of criminals, but they must do so without abusing their powers and denying individuals their rights.

SUMMARY AND CONCLUSIONS

Providing safety is a fundamental role of governments, and crime is a major concern of citizens. Although crime is an old and perennial problem, what to do with criminals and how to prevent crime are still matters of some bewilderment, dispute, and frustration. The temptation is to keep it simple. Yet the costs of locking criminals up and throwing away the key are high, in financial and human terms. Some who commit crimes need treatment, not indefinite confinement. Some are first offenders who are generally penitent and can be rehabilitated. Others clearly seem beyond our ability to change and represent continued threats to society.

Criminal justice is similar to other public policy issues. The problems are often complex and defy easy answers. The public mood has been to simplify the issues involving crime and to be tough on all criminals, but state and local professionals and officials have continued to recognize that executions and prison terms are not the only answers. Innovative, creative approaches toward crime prevention and toward the treatment of criminals have emerged. Increased attention is being paid to issues of victims and location. It is unlikely that all of these will be successful. Citizens and public officials will undoubtedly continue to wrestle with the politics and the policies concerned with crime.

Discussion Questions

1. How do you reconcile the evidence that the public concern with crime has been increasing with the decreasing rate of violent crimes?

2. Describe the communities that are the safest and the ones that are the most dangerous. What do those descriptions suggest about strategies for keeping the crime rate low?

3. Describe the population that is committing various types of crime. What do these descriptions suggest about strategies for keeping the crime rate low?

4. Discuss the major approaches that have been used to deal with those convicted of crimes. For each approach, identify the major assumptions about why individuals may or may not commit crimes and the societal values that are emphasized.

5. Debate the issues surrounding capital punishment. When, if ever, should it be used? How? Why?

6. Given the intuitive appeal of "get tough" approaches toward criminals, do you think more sophisticated and complex approaches are doomed to be rejected? What options do candidates and elected officials have on the crime issue?

Glossary

blanket 365	**intensive sanctions** 364	**probation** 363
boot camp 364	**jail** 359	**racial profiling** 351
community policing 366	**parole** 362	**three strikes and you're out** 356
correctional institution 359	**penitentiary** 359	**truth-in-sentencing** 363
exclusionary rule 368	**prison** 359	

Endnotes

1. Federal Bureau of Investigation, U.S. Department of Justice, *Uniform Crime Rates 2008,* www.fbi.gov/ucr/cius_08/offenses_reported/violent_crime/index.html.

2. Federal Bureau of Investigation, U.S. Department of Justice, *Uniform Crime Rates 2008,* www.fbi.gov/ucr/ucr08prs.htm.

3. Bureau of Justice Statistics, U.S. Department of Justice, *Crime Victimization in the United States 1998* (Washington, D.C.: U.S. Government Printing Office, 1999), 8.

4. Sandra Shane-Dubow, Alice P. Brown, and Erik Olsen, *Sentencing Reform in the United States: History, Content and Effect* (Washington, D.C.: U.S. Department of Justice, Office of Development, Testing and Dissemination, 1985); Edward L. Ayers, *Vengeance and Justice: Crime and Punishment in the 19th-Century American South* (New York: Oxford University Press, 1984), 37–40.

5. Robert Martinson, "What Works? Questions and Answers about Prison Reform," *Public Interest* (Spring 1974), 22–54.

6. Thorsten Sellin, *The Penalty of Death* (Beverly Hills, Calif.: Sage Publications, 1980).

7. Federal Bureau of Investigation, *Uniform Crime Reports for the United States, 2006* (Washington, D.C.: U.S. Government Printing Office, 2007).

8. John Roman, Aaron Chalfin, Aaron Sundquist, Carly Knight, and Askar Darmenov, *The Cost of the Death Penalty in Maryland* (Washington, D.C.: Urban Institute, 2009); Ian Urbina, "Citing Costs, States Consider End to Death Penalty," *The New York Times*, February 25, 2009; and Sue Lindgren, *Justice Expenditure and Employment, 1985* (Washington, D.C.: Bureau of Justice Statistics, 1988), 6.

9. M. J. Heath, D. R. Stanski, and D. J. Pounder, "Inadequate Anaesthesia in Lethal Injection for Execution," *The Lancet*, 366, 9491 (September 2005), 1073–1074.

10. Lee H. Bowker, "Females in Corrections," in *Women, Crime, and the Criminal Justice System*, ed. Lee H. Bowker (Lexington, Mass.: Lexington Books, 1978), 225–259.

11. Joan A. Casey and Pamela L. Reynolds, "The Criminal Justice Challenge: An Overview," *Intergovernmental Perspective* (Spring 1993), 7.

12. Bureau of Justice Statistics, U.S. Department of Justice, *Prisoners in 1993* (Washington, D.C.: U.S. Government Printing Office, 1994), 27.

13. Tinsley Yarbrough, "The Alabama Prison Litigation," *Justice System Journal* (1984), 276.

14. U.S. General Accounting Office, *Private and Public Prisons: Studies Comparing Operational Costs and/or Quality of Service* (Washington, D.C.: General Accounting Office, 1996), 19.

15. Warren I. Cikins, "The Community Corrections Response to Crime," *Intergovernmental Perspective* (Spring 1993), 29.

16. Donald M. Gottfredson, "Correctional Decision-Making," in *Decision-Making in the Criminal Justice System,* ed. Donald M. Gottfredson (Rockville, Md.: National Institute of Mental Health, 1975), 82–91.

17. Charles Mathesian, "The March of Boot Camps," *Governing* (June 1991), 21–22.

18. *Reducing Crime and Assuring Justice* (New York: Committee for Economic Development, 1972), 42–43.

19. Warren I. Cikins, "The Community Corrections Response to Crime," *Intergovernmental Perspective* (Spring 1993), 29–31.

20. Casey and Reynolds, "The Criminal Justice Challenge: An Overview," 10.

21. Ibid.

22. Patrick V. Murphy, "Policing and Effective Law Enforcement," *Intergovernmental Perspective* (Spring 1993), 26–28; Dennis Rosenbaum, Arthur L. Lurigo, and Paul J. Lavrakas, *Crime Stoppers: A National Evaluation of Program Operations and Effects* (Washington, D.C.: U.S. Government Printing Office, 1987); James Garofals and Maureen McLeod, *Improving the Use and Effectiveness of Neighborhood Watch Programs* (Washington, D.C.: Department of Justice, National Institute of Justice, 1988).

23. Jerome H. Skolnick and David Bayley, *The New Blue Line: Police Innovation in Six American Cities* (New York: The Free Press, 1986).

CHAPTER 15

Educational Policy

LEARNING OBJECTIVES

- Understand the changing popular orientations toward educational policy and their implications for policy initiatives.
- Appreciate the tension that exists between reforms aimed at improving educational quality and concerns over resources, equity, and educational opportunity.
- Know the form that K–12 educational reforms have taken, including charter schools, school choice, and privatization.
- Be aware that college and university governing boards and administrators have registered objections over what they view as growing undue politicization of higher education policy making.

In April 2011, New York City's chancellor of schools Cathleen Black left office under a cloud of controversy. It was only three months earlier that Mayor Michael Bloomberg appointed the former president of Hearst Magazines to the post to bring business principles to the governance of New York's struggling schools. Yet under opposition by teacher unions and parent groups, her approval rating fell to just 17 percent in that short period.

This brief episode raises the question of not only on what basis educational leaders are to be held accountable, but also the question of who should be held accountable for educational performance. Should it be the school district's top executive official? Or perhaps the focus should be placed differently. Most efforts to reform schools, such as the federal No Child Left Behind reform, put the onus on the schools. The so-called failing schools typically face sanctions for not meeting established standards or for failing to make adequate progress toward meeting them. Rather than holding the school, as an institution, accountable, perhaps accountability should be put on the students themselves (for example, denying them promotion from grade to grade, or keeping them from graduating, for unacceptable performance). Perhaps, teachers should be the object of accountability, whether the key measures are the achievement and relative improvement of their students, or testing teachers on the very subject matter they teach. Or should the burden of accountability be placed on parents? Before education can be reformed, the locus of accountability must be determined.

Educational reform has been at the top of state policy agendas. Its effects have been felt not only at the elementary and secondary levels but at the level of higher education as well. State policymakers have been calling for a restored emphasis on quality and demonstrated achievement. Government boards, administrators, teachers, and students themselves have all voiced criticism, and all have been challenged to play their part in stopping what has been broadly perceived as an erosion of educational quality nationwide.

The reports of several prominent national commissions have shaped and reinforced this negative perception. One report issued by an 18-member commission appointed by former federal education secretary T. H. Bell, entitled *A Nation at Risk*, received the most exposure; it was cited by President Ronald Reagan in his call for educational improvements. Over 700 newspaper articles covered the report's findings and recommendations.[1] Other key reports—most notably *Making the Grade*, a report of a Twentieth Century Fund task force; *Action for Excellence*, a report of an Education Commission of the States task force; and the *National Education Goals Report*, a product of the National Education Goals Panel appointed by President George H. W. Bush and supported by President Bill Clinton—were highly critical of educational practices and recommended a number of measures designed to improve learning, instruction, curriculum content, and assessment standards. The panel called on state leaders to establish educational goals for students and to systematically assess their progress toward meeting them. Although work began in all 50 states on educational standards and the means to assess attainment, progress has been checkered across the states. In response, during his second term in office, President Clinton called for the adoption of national standards against which student achievement in core subjects such as mathematics, history, English, and the basic sciences could be assessed. Despite the president's active and highly publicized support, state and local policymakers were guarded and slow to champion the cause of national standards.

Both candidates for the presidency in 2000 had educational policy high on their campaign agenda. Both saw student achievement as falling short of the mark. Yet their definition of the problem and their proposed solutions, though bearing some similarities, differed in marked ways. Albert Gore, the Democratic nominee, appeared more willing to work within the present system, calling for increased federal investment in the public schools in return for states adopting a number of accountability measures. His proposals called for hiring additional teachers, improving teacher pay, rebuilding old schools, and expanding support for programs aimed at closing the achievement gap between disadvantaged students and their peers.

In comparison, George W. Bush, the Republican nominee, showed a greater willingness to challenge the present system by proposing that low-income parents have the option of using federally funded vouchers to send their children to private schools if the public schools fell short of their expectations. For Bush, accountability and competition constituted a key ingredient of educational reform.

Within five months of assuming the presidency, Bush called upon Congress to pass legislation requiring the states to test every child in grades 3 through 8 on his or her proficiency in reading and math, and to issue annual report cards on school performance and progress. He also asked Congress to make federally funded vouchers available to parents of students attending failing schools. Parents could use these vouchers to send their children to private schools.

Congress rejected the voucher option but still approved mandatory testing and reporting. Congress also authorized the use of federal funds to pay the cost of tutors for children attending schools that fail to bring student performance up to acceptable levels. As a political compromise, Congress agreed to allow parents to use the funds to purchase tutoring from private-sector providers—a concession that supporters of the administration's original proposal saw as a step toward subsequent congressional approval of vouchers.

Several similarities can be found in the policy debate over reform in primary, secondary, and postsecondary educational circles. Most important, educational reforms have come largely from outside the organized educational establishment; governors and state legislatures have pressed educational professionals to pursue reform. Educational policy has become politicized, and the politics are played out in the state capitols of America because it is the states, not the federal government, that most significantly shape substantive educational policy at all levels in this country, even though presidents, national commissions, and task forces play a prominent role in highlighting problems and approaches to address them. Nevertheless, because of some significant differences, it is probably best to treat each level of education separately.

PRIMARY AND SECONDARY EDUCATION

Historically, a strong tradition of local control is inherent in American educational policy. The local school district evolved as the central policy-making and administrative unit for primary and secondary education. Before the twentieth century, community control of education was almost absolute. Although state governments have had the authority to create school districts, state legislatures traditionally have followed the wishes of local communities in granting new district charters. Not until the post–World War II reformist period did the states exercise any meaningful discretion over the composition of local districts. Thus, local districts tended to be small in size and numerous. At the turn of the twentieth century, over 100,000 districts existed, but greater state interest and involvement prompted a move to consolidate adjacent districts, creating fewer but larger districts, and thereby expanding the core educational resources that each district could make available to students. Only about 13,809 districts remain today.[2] Consolidation also had the effect of increasing the operating efficiency of local districts by greatly improving economies of scale. Politically, consolidation reduced the number of local school boards and, in turn, the number of local residents who serve on these policy-making bodies. Although the principle of local control over educational policy remained intact, the schools became both more physically and more psychologically distant from their local communities.

Local school districts are at the center of educational policy making. District administrators, under policies developed by local governing boards, develop budgets

---

local school districts Government organizations organized at the local level and responsible for the administration of primary and secondary education under policies set by the state.

and staffing plans, hire teachers, set school calendars and attendance requirements, select the curriculum to be used, and allocate resources among district schools. Governing boards determine tax levies for school purposes, approve operating budgets and capital construction projects, and establish compensation policies for district staff members.

However, local school districts do not function autonomously. School districts are legally creatures of the state, with their authority both prescribed and proscribed by state constitutions and statutory law. Laws, enacted among states, constrain local districts' ability to tax, spend, or incur debt. State laws establish minimal requirements to be met by all local districts in the areas of curriculum, school calendar and attendance, teacher certification, collective bargaining (often prescribing the use of binding arbitration of labor disputes in certain situations), and graduation. State control tends to be most pronounced in the Southern states, where course curriculum and required texts are commonly mandated at the state level. In contrast, schools in New England enjoy the greatest local autonomy. Beyond the states, the federal government dictates policy requirements in the areas of desegregation, education of the disabled, school discipline, and the equalization of state financial aid to local districts.

Changing Financial Arrangements

Both the states and the federal government have helped finance the costs of elementary and secondary education. Of the two, the states have been the major contributor by far. Today the states pay 48 percent of the costs of public elementary and secondary education in the United States, compared to only about 17 percent at the turn of the twentieth century. Local revenues cover another 44 percent. The federal government provides the remaining 8 percent—a pittance compared to the federal contribution to social welfare and transportation.

As Figure 15.1 shows, the states' share of financing elementary and secondary education increased dramatically from the Great Depression era through the Korean War period, directly displacing local tax support. But post–Korean War enrollment growth kept the pressure on local and state funding because the costs of public elementary and secondary schools rose by 450 percent between 1952 and 1970.[3] Both local school districts and the states greatly increased their financial support of education during that period, with the state share remaining at about 40 percent. It was not until the FY 1978–1979 that the state share exceeded the local contribution. After continued growth throughout most of the decade, the state share fell relative to the local share toward the decade's end and into the 1990s, and state and local taxpayers became nearly equal financial partners.

The post–Korean War baby boom had much to do with the increase in state support. As pressures on property tax revenues mounted, local school officials, supported by state superintendents of public instruction, increasingly called on state governments for assistance. By the early 1970s, however, the rationale for increased state support became less based on responding to an enrollment boom because primary enrollments began to fall and

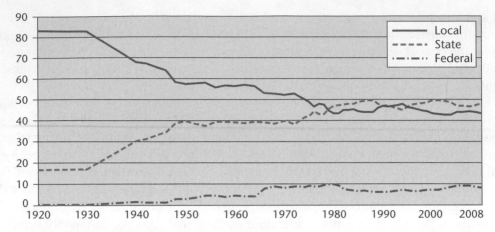

Figure 15.1 Revenue Sources for Public Elementary and Secondary Schools, 1920–2008 Academic Years

Source: National Center for Education Statistics, *Digest of Education Statistics, 2010*, Table 180, http://nces.ed.gov/programs/digest/d10/tables/dt10_180.asp?referrer=list.

decreases in secondary enrollments were expected to follow (see Figure 15.2). Instead, supporters of continued increases in state financial aid emphasized the contribution that school aid makes toward local property tax relief. From the 1980s and into the decade of the 2000s, supporters increasingly tied the need for additional state aid to improvements in educational quality.

Changing Orientations toward Educational Policy

Orientations toward elementary and secondary education changed during the twentieth century. Before World War II, education was not a priority on either the federal or state policy agendas but was largely a local concern. Community efforts involved raising adequate funds to finance the necessary capital construction and operating budget requirements to accommodate the population growth that had occurred during the 1900s. At that time, the growth curve of school-age children allowed for manageable planning and revenue raising. That all changed with the mushrooming population growth following World War II that greatly accelerated during the post–Korean War years. Even beyond the enrollment growth and its associated challenges, other issues emerged to capture the public's attention over the decades following World War II. There have been distinct patterns to their emergence.

1946–1964: An Era of Capacity Building. From the close of World War II to the beginning of the Great Society, the emphasis in education had been placed on *expanding the capacity* of school districts to accommodate the large increases in enrollments because of postwar demographic changes. Faced with steadily rising enrollments, local districts

Enrollment, in millions

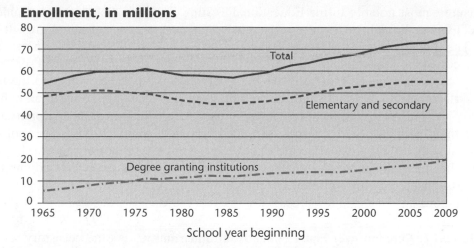

Expenditures, in billions of constant 2006–07 dollars

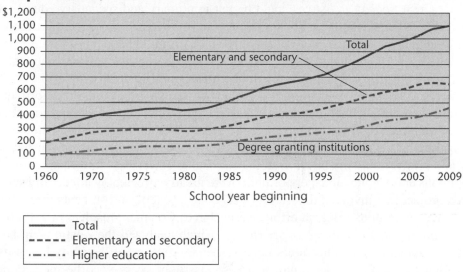

Figure 15.2 Enrollment and Expenditure per Pupil in Constant Dollars for Education, 1965–2009.

Source: National Center for Education Statistics, *Digest of Education Statistics,* Figure 2, http://nces.ed.gov/programs/digest/d10/figures/fig_02.asp?referrer=figures.

turned to bond issues to pay for the new wave of school construction, and to increases in property taxes to finance operating budgets. With the rapid expansion came a concern that quality should not be sacrificed for the sake of growth. The strong push for additional financial resources, beyond supporting capacity building, was also justified as necessary to maintain prized elements of the existing educational system, such as low student-to-teacher ratios and well-equipped facilities. In retrospect, the continuous increases in performance measures, most notably in the Educational Testing Service's Scholastic Aptitude Test (SAT) scores through 1965, suggest that quality did not suffer as a result of growth.

The Soviet Union's successful launch of the *Sputnik* satellite in 1957, in the face of unsuccessful U.S. attempts to beat the Soviets into space, shocked American society. For many, the Soviet success represented an American failure: the Soviets had the technical skill to get the job done, and we did not. Congressional supporters of an expanded role of the federal government in education used the development as an opportunity to press their case. The Soviet success provided a prime symbol. In this context of public concern heightened by extensive media coverage, Congress authorized federal funding to strengthen programs in science, mathematics, and foreign languages. The fledging federal role, associated with the **National Defense Education Act of 1958**, was still greatly limited in scope and financial resources.

1965–1977: Concern over Equal Educational Opportunity.

As the necessary resources were assembled to educate increasing numbers of children, the influence of President Lyndon Johnson's Great Society initiatives could be felt in primary and secondary education. The Great Society's emphasis on attacking the "cycle of poverty" accorded education a key role in breaking the vicious cycle of poverty and welfare dependence, which entrapped the so-called permanent underclass in society. To help break the cycle, educational policy turned toward ensuring all children an **equal education opportunity**.

The value of equal educational opportunity struck a responsive chord in most Americans. Our classic liberal heritage prizes individual choice and action. Individuals are to be free to pursue their own interests, to the best of their abilities, unhampered by artificial constraints. Thus, Americans could readily agree that barriers beyond differences in ability and effort should not be allowed to obstruct the otherwise enterprising individual.

Opinions about educational opportunity were greatly affected by a federally supported research project that involved thousands of schools, teachers, and students throughout the country. This ambitious research effort, led by James Coleman, resulted in a 1966 report entitled *Equality of Educational Opportunity*, which analyzed the relationship between student achievement and educational inputs. The significance of the study lay in its conclusion that the family background of one's classroom peers was the most important element in predicting student achievement—a conclusion that flew in the face of conventional wisdom. The study's findings contradicted the widely accepted belief that resources such as per pupil expenditures, classroom size, available facilities, and teachers' salaries were most closely associated with student success. A reanalysis of the Coleman data by Thomas F. Pettigrew and others for the U.S. Civil Rights Commission found that educational achievement scores were significantly higher (up to two grade levels) for African

---

National Defense Education Act of 1958 In response to the Soviet Union's successful launch of the *Sputnik* satellite in 1957, Congress authorized federal funding to strengthen programs in science, mathematics, and foreign languages.

equal educational opportunity The value that all children should have an equal opportunity to pursue education.

American students attending predominantly white schools than for those attending predominantly African American schools.[4] The policy implications were readily apparent, and the Civil Rights Commission used the findings to advocate desegregation policies. The Coleman report was also used in the courts in support of forced busing to achieve school integration.

Despite the landmark U.S. Supreme Court decision in *Brown v. Board of Education* (1954)—which ruled that the Fourteenth Amendment's guarantees of equal opportunity were being abridged by policies based on race, and that racially separate education was inherently unequal and therefore illegal—little of significance was done through 1964 to change the entrenched patterns of racial segregation in the schools. Although some progress in desegregation was made in some border states (especially Delaware, Kentucky, Maryland, Missouri, Oklahoma, and West Virginia—states bordering the Confederacy during the Civil War era)—the states of the Deep South elected a policy of resistance to the Supreme Court's ruling. A "legislate and litigate" strategy was employed, a strategy involving the enactment of state anti-integration laws, the accompanying long and costly process of litigation, and the passage of new legislation when the former state laws were ruled unconstitutional by the federal courts.

The **Civil Rights Act of 1964** gave some teeth to the federal government's desegregation policies by providing that any school districts that were recipients of federal financial assistance and that practiced racial discrimination would have their federal funding terminated. Concomitantly, the **Elementary and Secondary Education Act of 1965** greatly raised the costs of noncompliance through significant increases in federal funding for elementary and secondary public education. The act also gave the Department of Health, Education, and Welfare (HEW) regulatory authority that required it to develop desegregation plans in cooperation with noncompliant districts.[5] By 1967, HEW had terminated funds to 34 school districts and was in the process of cutting off funds to 157 more. In addition, a federal district court ordered the state of Alabama to begin desegregation by the fall of 1967—the first time an entire state had been so ordered—based on the court's finding that state education officials had thwarted previous selected efforts at the local district level. Alabama was also ordered to establish remedial programs for African American students in the newly integrated schools to make up for past discrimination.[6] But by the late 1960s, it became evident that school segregation had actually increased in many parts of the United States because of the emigration of whites from central-city school districts and their displacement by African Americans from rural areas.

Civil Rights Act of 1964 Authorized the U.S. attorney general to initiate lawsuits to force desegregation of public schools and barred discrimination in any program or activity receiving public funds, including schools and higher education institutions.

Elementary and Secondary Education Act of 1965 Provided significantly increased funding for elementary and secondary education and gave the Department of Health, Education, and Welfare regulatory authority requiring development of desegregation plans in cooperation with districts whose students were segregated by race.

The traditional beliefs about the factors related to student achievement continued to influence educational policy, nevertheless. Professional educators had little interest in agreeing with the proposition that per pupil spending, the level of teachers' salaries, or the quality of facilities bore a weak relationship to learning. Administrators and teachers generally backed the call for equality of educational opportunity, but put it within the traditional context. Expanded public financial support and greater equity in its allocation became their preferred means toward the desired end of higher student achievement.

State financial aid to primary and secondary education increased by over 380 percent from 1964 to 1977.[7] Attentive to the growing national debate over educational opportunity during the mid- to late 1960s, educational policymakers in several states began to pay far greater attention to how these mushrooming state funds were being allocated among school districts. Most commonly, state aid was shared with school districts on a per student basis. On that basis, the more students a district had, the more aid it received. Thus, both poor and wealthy districts benefited. The wealthier districts were already able to provide a higher level of financial resources underlying each student's education. Districts with high property values could set their tax rate at a level well below that of poor districts and still yield considerably more tax revenue in support of their educational programs. Per student state aid tends to perpetuate the inequalities. Even with state aid, poorer districts had comparatively fewer resources to finance their students' educations than did the wealthier districts. Students in poorer districts can be said to be at a clear disadvantage; they are not accorded an equal opportunity for high-quality education. Traditional per student state-aid formulas did little to close the gap between the relatively wealthy and poor districts.

In the context of the growing national debate over equality of educational opportunity, both the governing boards of disadvantaged schools and parents of children attending them increasingly directed their concerns about inequitable treatment to the courts. In a landmark 1973 U.S. Supreme Court case, *San Antonio Independent School District v. Rodriguez*, the Court refused to equate inequities in property values and the resulting differences in per pupil expenditures with a violation of the Equal Protection Clause of the Fourteenth Amendment to the U.S. Constitution. Nevertheless, the airing of the debate, which began years before the Court's decision, set off a national discussion among state educational policymakers. The state courts became the avenue for challenge because most state constitutions guarantee state residents the right to a high-quality, free education.

The first and most significant state court challenge resulted in the California Supreme Court's decision in *Serrano v. Priest*. In that case, the Court ruled that quality education is a fundamental right guaranteed by California's constitution that "cannot be a condition of the wealth of a child's parents or neighbors."[8] Following the *Serrano* decision, 52 lawsuits were filed in 31 states in attempts to elicit similar rulings.[9] In only two instances, that of New Jersey and Connecticut, was a state court's decision in favor of the plaintiff viewed as a mandate that the state legislature enact reform legislation. That very debate, occasioned by the litigation in the other states, and what appeared to be the likelihood of court direction prompted governors and legislatures to take up the call for reform. During the period from 1971 (the year of the *Serrano* decision) through 1977, 25 states reformed their systems of school finance.[10]

Beyond court action, or its likelihood, school finance reforms spread as do reforms in other policy areas. State policymakers, through national associations, become readily aware of reforms that have taken place in other states. National associations of state superintendents of public instruction, school boards, governors, and legislatures provide forums for communicating issues of emerging concern, court litigation, gubernatorial initiatives, and legislative enactments. Although policy learning is strongest among states of the same region, there are a few bellwether states to which others consistently look for innovations. As reforms spread, a nationwide agenda emerges. Such was the case with school finance reform.

School finance reform focused on the **equalization of state school aid**. Legislation enacted in 24 states required that state financial assistance to school districts be based on need and ability to pay. Based on this principle, allocation formulas were changed so that districts with relatively lower property wealth would receive disproportionately more state aid than would those with higher property value. Operationally, state legislation most often set a guaranteed level of property value behind each student in the state. Those school districts falling furthest from the guarantee would receive the greatest amount of aid to make up the difference. Conversely, those districts having a per student property value in excess of the guarantee would receive no state aid because they were deemed to have resources adequate to ensure a base-level financial equity.

Other elements of reform have differentially adjusted state aid to address the unusually higher costs of some disadvantaged big city school districts, with their higher-than-average special educational needs. To meet such problems, California, Florida, Michigan, and Washington have established formula adjustments to benefit urban school districts.[11]

1978 to the Present: Ensuring Educational Accountability. The late 1960s through most of the 1970s saw school costs rising faster than real estate valuations, creating a growing burden on the local property tax. With the spotlight on spending, governors and state legislators, along with taxpayers and parents of school-age children, began to ask what they were getting educationally for their growing financial investment. They believed that they were getting less rather than more, and a 1975 College Board report that test scores had been in a steady decline for a decade reinforced their more intuitive impressions. As the report showed, the mean verbal and mathematical scores of high school seniors taking the SAT had fallen each year since 1965. The College Board's blue ribbon panel, charged with investigating the drop, reported in 1977 that educational standards had declined in most areas nationally as the school curriculum lost required courses in math, science, and language. The authors also noted that "less thoughtful and critical writing is now being demanded and done, and that careful writing has apparently gone out of style."[12]

---

equalization of state school aid The distribution of state financial assistance to local school districts based on the districts' financial need and their ability to pay. Under this principle, poorer districts receive higher aid per pupil than do richer districts.

Several national-level commissions were established in the early 1980s to assess the state of elementary and secondary education in this country. The popular perception was that educational performance was not improving and that it was probably worsening. Gallup polls consistently showed that the general public gave the public schools only a C+ grade for performance (a grade that dropped to C by 2009).[13] Not only were the commissions charged with evaluating student learning and identifying apparent trends, they were also given the more difficult task of accounting for any observed change. Counts vary, but at least a dozen reports and books that were national in scope could be identified by 1983. They all pointed out significant problems meriting attention. The educational system was portrayed as failing in its essential task of grounding students in the basics. Measures of student performance in the classroom and on nationally normed objective tests suggested a further erosion of competencies. The reports, in turn, called for strengthening of the curriculum. *A Nation at Risk*, the most nationally prominent report, identified five new basics that had to be shored up in high schools across the country: four years of English, three years of mathematics, three years of science, three years of social studies, and at least one course in computer science. This core curriculum was intended for all high school students, not just for those intending to go to college. In addition, two years of a foreign language were recommended for students planning to attend college. The other reports also offered similar formulations aimed at strengthening the core high school curriculum. Expanded homework was presented as an important corollary in the prescription for improvement in the basics.

Beyond focusing on the curriculum, the reports also dealt with the educational profession itself. The quality of teacher education programs and of the teaching candidates themselves came in for recurrent criticism. The reports commonly exhorted schools of education to raise their admission standards and strengthen their curriculum. Two highly influential reports, *A Nation at Risk* and *Educating Students for the 21st Century* (which focused on science and math education), criticized the lack of qualifications of newly certified teachers in those fields. They also projected serious shortages of science and math teachers in the near future. The National Science Board, reflecting these concerns, recommended that the states assign top priority to improving teacher education in science and math and to providing special incentives for top students to enter teacher-training programs in these disciplines.[14]

All the reports and books on educational reform that emerged in the early 1980s had one bottom-line concern in common: the need for a commitment to quality. *Quality* also became the watchword of legislative debate in the state capitols. The stubborn decline in quality, sensed by parents and educators alike, had to be reversed. State policymakers readily took up the banner of reform. They felt that, with the states' greatly increased financial commitment to education, they had the right to take the kinds of initiatives necessary to turn the educational record around. States acted quickly, and initiatives soon spread across state borders.

Two categories of reform initiatives could be found among the states by the late 1980s: those directed at student achievement and those aimed at teacher quality. Major state initiatives directed at the students included (1) the establishment of formal statewide course and credit requirements for high school graduation, (2) the imposition of statewide exit tests requiring successful completion as a condition of graduation, (3) the requirement of academic performance assessment tests conducted in selected elementary and secondary grades as a means of monitoring student performance over time, (4) the addition of core course hours to the curriculum, and (5) the institution of mandatory kindergarten. On the teacher side, state initiatives included (1) higher salary scales and entry-level pay, (2) required provisions for merit pay, (3) tests of subject matter competence, (4) higher educational school requirements, and (5) financial aid for teachers entering high-priority academic disciplines.

The subject of testing teachers' competency has been especially controversial. Supporters, including President Clinton, argued that such testing provided a needed element of quality control. They asked how students can be expected to make strides in an academic discipline when their teachers had not mastered the basic knowledge of that discipline. The only reliable way for the public to know whether or not their children's teachers were academically competent, they argued, was to test regularly for that competence, even though more than 30 states test prospective teachers before granting certification. Supporters of teacher testing expressed doubt that supervisory evaluation or peer review alone, where it existed, would identify incompetent teachers. Even where it did, they argued, administrators traditionally had a difficult time assembling a case for dismissal, especially in unionized environments. Armed with consistent unsatisfactory test results, however, administrators and school boards could press their case for dismissal with more tangible evidence. Where passage of minimal competency tests was required for recertification, teachers who failed could not retain certification. Thus, as the argument goes, quality can be better protected with testing.

In 1985, under then-governor Bill Clinton's active urging, Arkansas became the first state to require existing teachers to pass a basic competency test measuring reading, grammar, and elementary math. To pass, teachers need only demonstrate competence at eighth-grade levels. Nevertheless, about 10 percent of the teachers taking it failed. Even with the possibility of retakes and the availability of compensatory continuing education for teachers who failed to achieve required scores, 3.5 percent of Arkansas teachers have had to leave teaching because they could not pass the test.[15]

Opponents of teacher testing, particularly the politically powerful teachers' unions, argued that some teachers may be expert in their subject matter but be poor teachers. Other teachers may not fare as well on subject-based examinations but still be extremely effective instructors, able to communicate well and effectively motivate students. Opponents of testing suggested that such qualities are not readily testable. But beyond the feasibility of testing for teachers' competence, detractors asked who was to decide what teachers in a given academic discipline should know. They wanted to know how substantively and procedurally this basic knowledge was to be identified.

Learning Outcomes as a Measure of Accountability. Attention in the 1990s and beyond centered more on student learning outcomes than on inputs to the educational process. The focus has commonly included three dimensions: (1) the need to identify what students should know and be able to do at different stages in their education, (2) ways of assessing their achievements and progress, and (3) the development of tailored educational plans for each student that are responsive to the diverse needs of different students.

A significant element of the contemporary debate deals with the issue of whether there should be national standards governing what students should know and how that knowledge should be assessed. President Clinton threw his support behind the setting of national standards as well as a national examination system to measure students' and schools' progress in meeting them. He also proposed requiring all eighth graders to pass an exam to go on to high school.[16]

President Bush, Clinton's successor, placed accountability at the center of his **No Child Left Behind** educational reform package. Through mandatory testing of every child in grades 3 through 8 and public reporting of student performance, by schools, Bush believed that parents would have the information they need to hold schools accountable for student performance. But because accountability without consequence is empty, Congress also approved Bush's proposal to require states to allow parents to transfer students out of failing schools and to give students access to publicly funded tutors. With parents "voting with their feet," failing schools would soon lack the numbers to continue in operation, or so the theory went.

Several states had already enacted accountability-based reforms prior to the federal government's national reform initiative. At the beginning of the new century, 44 states had adopted statewide standards for English, math, science, and social studies. Every state, except Iowa, administered at least one form of a statewide assessment test. Eighteen states required students to pass an exit exam in order to graduate from high school.[17]

Pennsylvania became the first state in the nation to base high school graduation on a student's achieving competencies in numerous academic areas instead of accumulating passing grades in required courses. New regulations approved by the Pennsylvania State Board of Education require students to master some 60 outcomes in place of satisfying the old course-based graduation requirement. School districts, in turn, must develop six-year plans for ensuring that students achieve the outcomes. As the board's statement of principles reads, "The basis of the regulations should be student achievement, not the amount of time spent in school. Some students will achieve more quickly than others. Some will achieve in different ways than others. Schools must be given the flexibility to meet the diverse needs of their diverse learners."[18] The policy document goes on to state, "While there are some things all students must know and be able to accomplish, the schools must be free to design programs to meet the individual needs of their specific students."[19]

In 2000, California began to rank schools based on statewide test scores, and the state will eventually expand its assessment to include high school graduation rates, dropout

---

No Child Left Behind A program initiative of President George W. Bush that requires states to test every child in grades 3–8 in reading and math, and to grade all schools on the performance of their students. The 2001 legislation also requires states to allow parents to transfer students out of failing schools and enroll them in better-performing public schools, with school districts providing transportation.

rates, and school attendance rates, creating an academic performance index (API). Florida grades schools based on students' scores on statewide proficiency tests, and it makes publicly funded vouchers available to parents whose children have spent at least two years in a school given a failing grade. Parents can use these vouchers to send their children to private schools as an alternative. Missouri requires that students meet assessment standards in order to be promoted from grade to grade.

Utah is another state that has instituted its own educational reform. It places importance on giving schools increased freedom to determine how higher levels of student learning can best be achieved. It also is built upon the principle that, for schools to exercise that discretion, they must be freed from the many rules and regulations that proscribe or constrain innovation. The Utah legislation authorized the creation of so-called centennial schools, which were given increased latitude and flexibility to define what students should know and be able to do as they progress through their schooling. Each selected school is responsible for developing individualized educational plans for each of its students. For these selected schools, the decisions on curriculum and forms of performance assessment lie not with administrators alone, but with school-specific boards of directors, comprising principals, teacher representatives, and parents. Along with the enabling authority, the Utah legislature appropriated funding in support of the changes.[20] In 1998, the state replaced the Centennial Schools program with Schools for the 21st Century, which incorporated most of the Centennial Schools features. In keeping with Utah's belief that it is in the best position to determine students' achievement, then governor and later 2012 presidential candidate Jon Huntsman made national news when he signed legislation in 2005 that promotes state guidelines over federal No Child Left Behind standards.[21]

EDUCATIONAL ALTERNATIVES

The desire to improve student learning has prompted several states to give public schools even greater freedom from traditional legal and regulatory requirements. Some states have provided their residents with financial assistance to enroll their children in private schools. A few states have even gone so far as to allow school districts to abandon public education altogether and contract with private, for-profit vendors to run their schools. Other states and cities have taken over the administration of failing urban schools. The following sections discuss these controversial departures from tradition.

Charter Schools

Charter schools are autonomous educational institutions within the public school system that operate through charters or contracts that give them far greater flexibility than that enjoyed by traditional public schools. Charter schools can be brand-new schools, created

---

charter schools Autonomous educational institutions within the public school system that operate through charters, or contracts, which give them far greater flexibility than that enjoyed by traditional public schools.

expressly to carry out the terms of a charter, or they can be existing schools converted to charter form. It is even possible to have a charter school formed within an existing school, essentially creating a school within a school.

Although the specific provisions governing charter schools vary among the states that have authorized them, they share common features:

1. They are exempt from most state statutes and administrative rules governing public schools.
2. They must not charge tuition; they must be nonsectarian; and they must abide by the same health, safety, and nondiscrimination laws that apply to traditional public schools.
3. A public authority or sponsor, such as a local school district or the state board of education, grants a charter to a group of individuals (typically composed of teachers and/or parents) to operate a school under the broad terms and goals specified in the charter. Charter provisions address the school's administrative structure, goals, curriculum, and the measures to be used to assess performance.
4. The school may be fiscally autonomous from the school district, receiving property tax support and state aid on the same basis as a school district.[22]

Charter schools focus on accountability through outcomes, fostered by decentralization and flexibility as to how those outcomes can best be attained. Proponents of charter schools argue that they foster experimentation and innovation, operating free of many of the obstacles that traditional public schools confront—obstacles such as a standardized curriculum employing standardized educational materials, constraints on the use of teachers arising from collective bargaining agreements, and limitations on contracting for services. It is also important to emphasize that, although charter schools possess considerable autonomy, they remain part of the public school system.

Minnesota's and California's legislatures were the first to enact laws authorizing the creation of charter schools. The Minnesota legislation, passed in 1991, put the initiative for charter schools in teachers' hands, allowing one or more teachers to petition to create and operate them. The charter describes the governance structure of the school and specifies the pupil outcomes to be sought and how they will be measured. California's program, created a year later, shares many similarities with Minnesota's. Unlike Minnesota's program, any person in California can petition to create a charter school; however, the petition must be signed by not less than 50 percent of the teachers employed in the school, or by not less than 10 percent of the teachers employed in the entire school district. The district governing board reviews proposals and has the authority to approve or reject them; an appeal route exists for reconsideration of denials. The local board then submits approvals to the state board of education, which ensures that the required signatures have been obtained and that the charter contains all the components required by law.

The California law, like Minnesota's, exempts approved charter schools from most state laws and regulations applying to public schools, but neither state's law exempts them from constitutional requirements or federal laws or regulations. California law requires

Table 15.1 States Enacting Charter School Laws

State	Date Law Enacted	State	Date Law Enacted
Minnesota	1991	Illinois	1996
California	1992	New Jersey	1996
Colorado	1993	North Carolina	1996
Georgia	1993	South Carolina	1996
Massachusetts	1993	Mississippi	1997
Michigan	1993	Nevada	1997
New Mexico	1993	Ohio	1997
Wisconsin	1993	Pennsylvania	1997
Arizona	1994	Idaho	1998
Hawaii	1994	Missouri	1998
Kansas	1994	New York	1998
Alaska	1995	Utah	1998
Arkansas	1995	Oklahoma	1999
Delaware	1995	Oregon	1999
Louisiana	1995	Indiana	2001
New Hampshire	1995	Iowa	2002
Rhode Island	1995	Tennessee	2002
Texas	1995	Maryland	2003
Wyoming	1995	Washington	2004
Connecticut	1996	Illinois	2009
District of Columbia	1996	Maine	2011
Florida	1996		

Source: The Center for Education Reform, http://edreform.com. Reprinted with permission.

charter schools to participate in a statewide pupil testing program.[23] As of the summer of 2011 when Governor Paul LePage signed Maine's charter school legislation,[24] 43 states and the District of Columbia had enacted charter school laws (see Table 15.1). As with earlier educational reforms, leadership for charter school legislation has typically come from governors and legislative leaders, not from educational administrators. The laws differ with regard to the number of charter schools they allow to be created and in the degree of autonomy they permit. One study done in 2008 classifies Arizona, California, Delaware, Florida, Indiana, Michigan, and Minnesota as having the strongest laws that give charter schools the greatest relative autonomy, while identifying Alaska, Hawaii, Iowa, Kansas, Mississippi, Rhode Island, Virginia, and Wyoming as imposing the most restrictive conditions.[25]

Voucher Programs

Unlike charter schools, which are part of the public school system, **voucher programs** provide taxpayer-supported financial assistance to low-income parents who wish to

---

voucher programs Provide taxpayer-supported financial assistance to low-income parents who wish to send their children to private schools.

send their children to private schools. In 1990, Milwaukee became the site of the first publicly funded voucher program. Supported by an African American central-city state representative—a Democrat—and the state's Republican governor, the program began on a small scale. As part of the compromise that won approval, the Wisconsin legislature stipulated that vouchers could not be used at parochial (religious) schools, a restriction that the legislature later lifted. In its first year, the 1990–1991 school year, only 341 low-income students attended private schools on vouchers. Twenty years later, about 21,000 students took advantage of the program annually, receiving vouchers worth up to $6,442 per pupil, per year.[26] Students participating in the Milwaukee program come from low-income, single-parent families. Most are minorities, with African Americans constituting almost two-thirds of total enrollees.[27] Approximately 84 percent of students receiving vouchers attend religious schools.[28] In 2011, Wisconsin Governor Scott Walker signed legislation removing the cap, which had been set at 22,500, on the number of youth who can participate in Milwaukee's Parental Choice Program. The bill also expands the program into Racine County.[29]

Borrowing from the Milwaukee experience, the Ohio legislature in 1996 approved a similar needs-based program for Cleveland. From an initial enrollment of 1,996 students in the 1996–1997 school year, enrollment exceeded 13,062 by the 2010–2011 school year. The demographic characteristics of Cleveland's participants mirror those of Milwaukee. However, 99 percent of participating students in Cleveland attend parochial schools.[30] The Ohio legislature approved expanding the voucher program statewide, beginning with the 2006–2007 school year. In the summer of 2011, Governor John Kasich approved a two-year state budget that more than doubles the number of vouchers available from 14,000 to 30,000 for the 2011–2012 school year and then doubles the number again to 60,000 vouchers for 2012–2013.[31]

Opponents of both the Milwaukee and Cleveland programs have challenged them in the courts. In 1998, the Wisconsin Supreme Court ruled that the recent inclusion of parochial schools in the Milwaukee voucher program was constitutional because the money went to parents, not directly to schools. Upon further appeal, the U.S. Supreme Court refused to hear the case. The Ohio Supreme Court found no fault with the constitutionality of devoting state funds to vouchers for use in religious schools, but a federal court in Ohio ruled that it violated the U.S. constitutional requirement of separation of church and state. The Ohio attorney general appealed, and the U.S. Supreme Court heard the appeal, reversing the district court's earlier ruling in a 5–4 decision and thus finding Cleveland's program constitutional.[32] The Florida Supreme Court ruled that the voucher program enacted by the legislature violated that state's constitution.

In 1999, the Florida legislature, at the strong urging of Republican governor Jeb Bush, passed the first statewide voucher program. Instead of basing eligibility on family income, as in Milwaukee and Cleveland, the Florida program uses school performance as its eligibility screen. Students in especially low-performing public schools—schools getting an F grade for two years in a four-year period—can use state-funded vouchers to attend any private school, including religious ones. Started as a demonstration project in the Pensacola School District, up to 60,000 students in the state's other districts could have ultimately qualified for vouchers worth $3,500 each. But the Florida program, like the Milwaukee and

Cleveland programs before it, failed to escape court challenge. In March 2000, a Florida circuit court found the voucher program unconstitutional, yet allowed it to continue pending the resolution of the state's appeal. With no resolution of the appeal, another circuit court found two years later that the voucher program continued to operate in violation of the state constitution. The case finally came to the Florida Supreme Court which, in January 2006, ruled the program unconstitutional, thus preventing its spread statewide and forcing termination of the demonstration project.[33]

The Colorado legislature passed a voucher program in 2003, despite voters' rejection of previous efforts to authorize vouchers through the direct initiative process. The program was never implemented because the Colorado Supreme Court declared the legislation unconstitutional one year later, finding that it violated the state constitution's local control requirement. In 2011, however, the Douglas County School Board approved a pilot program for the 2011–2012 school year that gives parents the option of using up to $4,500 to send their children to private schools.[34] Several groups are challenging the plan in court, arguing that it violates the state's constitutional ban on the use of public funds for religious purposes.

The policy rationale underlying voucher programs is to empower people who would otherwise not be able to exercise choice because of their personal circumstances. It gives low-income families the financial means to opt out of underperforming schools—an option held by those who already have the resources to choose a better-performing private school. However, supporters see a wider benefit beyond individual empowerment and improved educational opportunity. They believe that the entire educational system will ultimately benefit as well from the increased competition for students generated by voucher programs. For them, competition is the spur that will prompt public schools to improve.

Opponents of voucher programs view them as a threat to public education. They see them as draining scarce public resources away from the public schools, and they worry that an exodus to a diverse array of private schools will balkanize American education and thus weaken the unifying forces of public education that foster democratic values. Opponents also worry about those left behind in public schools. Will the private schools draw the better, more motivated students away from public schools, leaving public school teachers with an even more difficult group of students to educate?

Privatization

In 1993, Baltimore's school district took its quest for accountable educational performance a dramatic step beyond convention. Tired of student performance that lagged behind state averages, the Baltimore school board privatized nine of the district's schools by contracting with Educational Alternatives, Inc., a Minnesota-based company, to run the schools. Under the contract, the for-profit enterprise carried out the day-to-day administration of the schools, working with the school superintendent, who serves at the discretion of the school board. Together they set performance outcomes for students. As an incentive for success, if student performance exceeds the standards, the five-year contract provided for financial bonuses to be shared with the instructional staff (most of whom taught under the old system). Two years later, the same firm landed another five-year contract with Connecticut's Hartford school district, but this contract covered all of the district's schools.

Privatization, placing public schools under the direction of private, for-profit enterprises, appeared to be gaining a strong foothold. But only a few months after the Hartford contract had been signed, the school board scaled the company back, from thirty-two to just six schools, over differences in interpretations of the contract's terms. The school board later canceled the contract altogether. The Baltimore district followed suit shortly thereafter.[35]

Despite this experience, the privatization movement has continued to gain strength, with the for-profit Edison Learning, Inc., formerly Edison Schools, emerging as the major player in the twenty-first century. As of 2011, the company had partnered with 391 schools to serve 450,000 students in 25 states, the United Kingdom, and the Middle East. In the 2010–2011 school year, Edison Learning's largest state-driven partnership was with 40 schools in Hawaii.[36]

THE EQUITY OR EXCELLENCE DEBATE

More than half the states have changed their school aid allocation formulas since 1970 in order to achieve greater equity in the districts' ability to provide equal educational opportunity to their students. As discussed, recent reforms have focused primarily on promoting excellence in education. One educational expert, observing the changing contours of the national debate, predicts that it will be very difficult for local school districts, even with increased state financial help, to promote both ideals. Because the newer quality improvement funds have largely been appropriated separately from existing equalization-based appropriations, the two have necessarily been placed in competition with each other for scarce educational dollars.[37] Furthermore, as governors and state legislatures continue to turn their attention toward issues of quality in higher education (to be discussed in this chapter), those pursuits will add a further element of competition with support for elementary and secondary education.

Some advocates of the excellence reform argue that America's preoccupation with equity in the 1960s and 1970s stifled educational quality, leading to a leveling of performance to the lowest common denominator. Contemporary critics such as Theodore Black[38] advocate additional local district spending aimed at strengthening the core curriculum, adding advanced-level courses, and generally expanding opportunities for talented and gifted students, despite the fact that such increases in those districts best able to afford them will likely further enlarge the spending gaps between wealthy and poor districts. For the advocates of excellence, however, relative deprivation is not a sufficient reason to hold back districts that elect to excel.

Advocates of quality reform also argue that educational policymakers have to look beyond interdistrict comparisons and begin to be more concerned about international

---

privatization The practice of turning school administration over to for-profit, private enterprises.

Exploring the Web

Confronting Change

Pressures for change in education are coming from both within and outside the education establishment. Governors and legislatures are pressing for changes ranging from assessment of outcomes to charter schools and voucher programs that provide state funding for students to attend private schools. Faced with these currents of change, how are forces aligning to advance their interests? How can you find out more about the various positions for and against major change?

■ For the more radical reformist side, go to the Center for Education Reform at www.edreform.com. There you will find policy positions supporting school choice and education vouchers, along with charter schools. Access the *Parent Power* newsletter and *The School Reform Handbook*.

■ For the arguments against voucher programs and the infusion of greater state-supported competition in education, check out the webpage of an organization that represents the interests of large central-city public school systems, the Council of the Great City Schools (www.cgcs.org). Look at its *Urban Educator* newsletter and its report, *Critical Trends in Urban Education*.

■ Get the position of the nation's two main teacher unions at the homepages of the National Education Association (www.nea.org) and the American Federation of Teachers (www.aft.org).

■ Find the policy positions of state and local public school administrators at the following websites: chief state school officers (www.ccsso.org), state boards of education (www.nasbe.org), and local school district superintendents and school principals (www.aasa.com).

■ For a reasonably objective analysis of the issues surrounding educational change, visit the Educational Commission of the States' homepage at www.ecs.org. There you can find the commission's policy analysis and research reports and a link to its weekly publication, *ECS e-connection*—a bulletin of education policy news. You can also access state and nationally focused reports from its information clearinghouse.

comparisons. Such advocates see the United States increasingly falling behind in international economic competition, and comparative tests support that contention (see Table 15.2). One contributing factor they identify is the inadequate academic preparation provided to graduates of American high schools, particularly in math and science. In their view, local districts and the states have no choice but to pay additional attention to quality. The price of inaction is a worsened national competitive position.

With the growing concern about the quality gap, some observers fear that tougher core curriculum and graduation requirements will create undue pressure on the marginal students, possibly prompting more to drop out. Others worry that the new reforms

Table 15.2 Mathematics and Science Proficiency of 15-Year Olds: An International Comparison, Selected Nations, 2009

Mathematics		Science	
Nation	**Average Score**	**Nation**	**Average Score**
Hong Kong	555	Finland	554
Korea	546	Hong Kong	549
Finland	541	Japan	539
Switzerland	534	Korea	538
Japan	529	New Zealand	532
Canada	527	Canada	529
Netherlands	526	Australia	527
New Zealand	519	Netherlands	522
Australia	514	Germany	520
Germany	513	Switzerland	517
France	497	United Kingdom	514
Slovak Republic	497	Hungary	503
Austria	496	United States	502
Sweden	494	Czech Republic	500
Czech Republic	493	France	498
United Kingdom	492	Sweden	495
Hungary	490	Austria	494
United States	487	Slovak Republic	490
Italy	483	Italy	489
Spain	483	Spain	488
Russian Fed.	468	Russian Fed.	478

Source: Digest of Education Statistics, 2010, Table 408.

will squeeze out money for programs aimed at addressing the problems of at-risk students—problems such as the nearly twofold dropout rate for African Americans, the limited resources available for non-English-speaking students, and the need for compensatory programs for the socially disadvantaged. In addition, academic professionals have voiced concerns that increased use of empirical assessment devices for measuring quality could have a number of negative educational side effects, including teaching to tests, overuse of workbooks, memorization rather than reflection, and reduced creativity.[39]

Ernest Boyer, president of the Carnegie Foundation for the Advancement of Teaching, views educational reform aimed at improving quality as a positive step, but he argues that substantial improvement in student learning across the social spectrum will occur only when children come to school ready to learn. For Boyer, considerations of both equity and improved learning dictate that a broad commitment be made toward ensuring that a good foundation for learning is laid in all homes and communities across the nation. That means parents need to improve the home environment, providing the love, attention, and parental support for a positive learning environment. Society, in turn, needs to support programs that provide health care, nutrition, and preschool opportunities for children who would otherwise go without. The prescription for Boyer is twofold: get children ready for school, and get schools ready for children.[40]

THE COURTS' RENEWED INTEREST IN FISCAL EQUITY

The concerns about improving educational quality and closing the performance gap between American students and those of other leading industrial nations lured attention away from concerns about interdistrict fiscal equity. That had been the preoccupation of most of the 1970s, or so it appeared. School expenditures continued to rise throughout the 1980s, and the equalized school aid formulas put in place in the 1970s guided their distribution, although a number of states added new programs outside equalized funding, notably those fostering quality improvement and educational assessment. Toward the end of the 1980s, however, activists in several states resurrected the issue of inequitable public financing of primary and secondary education. Once again, they questioned why the public education of a student living in a poorer neighborhood should be financed at only a fraction of that provided to a student residing in a more affluent area. Advocates of renewed fiscal reform argued once again that major differences in per pupil spending across districts in the same state violated the equal protection guarantees of state constitutions or conflicted with provisions of state constitutions requiring "substantially uniform" schools or "efficient" systems of education.

By the end of the 1980s, courts in 25 states were considering similar legislation. Between 1989 and 1996 alone, courts in Kentucky, Montana, Texas, New Jersey, Missouri, Alabama, Tennessee, Arizona, Wyoming—in that order—ruled in favor of the litigants.[41] Several cases deserve special attention. The Kentucky Supreme Court found the Kentucky system of educational finance violated the state constitution, citing that per pupil state aid was about the same for wealthy and poor districts even though Kentucky's two largest metropolitan districts provided 15 times as much local funding per pupil as did its five poorest districts. The court ordered the legislature to remedy the situation.

In response, the Kentucky legislature appropriated $600 million in new budget authority over the 1989–1991 biennium, which increased funding for primary and secondary education by nearly one-fourth. Most of that increase went to equalized aid. To finance that package, the legislature raised the sales tax by 1 cent and increased individual and corporate income taxes as well.

The Montana Supreme Court acted similarly, finding that Montana's school financing practices violated the state constitution's guarantee of "equality of educational opportunity," and it ordered the legislature to rectify the situation. The legislature then increased state school aid by $100 million a year and equalized its distribution, using a 5 percent income tax surcharge to pay the bill.

The Texas Supreme Court pointed to "glaring disparities" in funding, noting that the 100 wealthiest districts in the state spent almost 2.5 times more per student than did the poorest. The court concluded that a remedy was long overdue, calling on the legislature to take immediate action. It did, at an annual cost of $518 million, which was far less than the state's education commissioner estimated would be required to secure equity. In response, the plaintiffs said that the money did not go far enough to remedy the inequities. The Texas Supreme Court agreed. The legislature then developed a plan to reconfigure the state's school districts. It required the state's wealthiest school districts to share their wealth with poorer districts.

New Jersey's solution to disparate local educational finance centered not only on increasing the funds devoted to poorer districts, but also included the imposition of caps on the amount per pupil that any district in the state can spend, in an effort to narrow further relative gaps in spending. That approach drew heated reaction from parents and representatives of the better-off districts, who challenged whether the state has the right to limit what local taxpayers are willing to pay for their children's education. But politically, former Governor Jim Florio won sufficient support in the legislature because over three-fourths of New Jersey's school districts benefited from the legislation.[42]

Missouri unsuccessfully appealed a circuit court judge's ruling that Missouri's method of school finance perpetuates disparities not issuing from different student needs, but from different local property values. The presiding judge noted that "the amount of money available for schools can and does make a difference in the educational opportunities that can be provided to Missouri children."[43] The legislature, in response, changed the aid formula to take into account the amount of tax effort a district is putting into its schools. Districts with high need and high effort (with effort falling far short of meeting need) now receive the largest boost in state funding. The change cost the state more than an additional $500 million a year.

In 1997, the supreme courts of three states—Ohio, New Hampshire, and Vermont—found that their respective state's method of distributing education funding violated the state constitution. The Ohio Supreme Court ordered the legislature to reform the state's system of educational finance by shifting its reliance on property taxes to a more equitable system that narrowed spending gaps between wealthy and poor districts. It also required the legislature to increase state funding to what the court called a more adequate level of support. In response, the legislature changed its funding formula and increased per student aid by about 18 percent between the FY 1998 and 2000, thus imposing a significant burden on the state's budget. The court challenge in New Hampshire focused on increasing the adequacy of state funding, whereas that in Vermont centered on improving the equity of distribution. As the focal point of its reform, New Hampshire radically shifted the obligation for education funding from the local property tax to state aid. Following the governor's lead, the legislature established a new utility property tax and increased the business profits and real estate transfer taxes to finance the higher state contribution, bringing in an additional $800 million a year to pay for the financial reforms. The Vermont law set a uniform amount of state support behind each student and allowed school districts to spend more if they wished. The trick is that Vermont's new law required that a portion of the increased amount raised by wealthy districts be returned to the state and redistributed to poor districts. The richer a district is, the more it must surrender for reallocation—a feature that created considerable political backlash in many areas of the state.[44]

Under the pressure of a state supreme court order directed at the legislature, Arizona voters took it upon themselves in 2000 to approve a ballot proposition that increased educational funding by $800 million a year to provide greater equity in state funding for school facilities throughout the state. A year later, a circuit court in New Mexico found the state's funding formula for capital construction unconstitutional and called on the legislature to fix the problem.[45]

Litigation over educational finance continued to occupy the courts in the 2000s. State courts in Arkansas, Iowa, Kansas, Louisiana, Maryland, Massachusetts, Missouri, Montana, Nebraska, New Hampshire, North Dakota, and West Virginia considered lawsuits over the equity or adequacy of public funding for primary and secondary education. Courts in Louisiana, Massachusetts, Nebraska, and West Virginia ruled in favor of the states, rejecting the plaintiffs' case. In Missouri and North Dakota, the plaintiffs and the state agreed to stay lawsuits pending anticipated action by the legislature. Courts in Arkansas, Maryland, Montana, and New Hampshire found their respective states' system of educational finance unconstitutional. Maryland felt the biggest impact because its legislature added $1.3 billion annually in state school aid for districts with low property value and high-risk students. Kansas supplemented its state aid by $148 million annually.[46]

HIGHER EDUCATION

Growth in higher education demographically followed the growth patterns seen in high schools. It follows logically: as more school-age children progress through elementary and secondary schools, increased enrollment pressure is felt on the educational institutions next in line. That would clearly be the case even if the percentage of high school graduates going on to higher education remained constant. But what happened was that, in addition to the increased size of the postsecondary age group associated with the demographic

Students on the campus of the University of Wisconsin—Madison. Every state has made major investments in a public university or university system, whose mission is in part to provide special access to higher education for state residents.

changes of the mid-1960s through the 1970s, a higher percentage of college-age youths elected to continue their education. This double effect of increased enrollment and self-selection caused college enrollments to skyrocket during the 1960s and 1970s.

Policymakers in the early 1960s faced an imposing challenge: not only did they have to accommodate the growing numbers of postsecondary students who were already at their doors, but they also had to plan for the period of certain accelerated growth that lay ahead. They had to expand existing colleges and universities by erecting new buildings, equipping them, and adding faculty to instruct the growing student population. In addition, new institutions had to be built from scratch. The combination of expansion and new construction placed a tremendous demand on existing universities to turn out students with advanced degrees who could join the ranks of new faculty members.

The job market for graduates with a Ph.D. was excellent. It was not uncommon at all in the mid-1960s for doctoral graduates from top universities in almost any field to receive multiple job offers. Accordingly, graduate programs were expanded at doctoral-granting institutions, and prospective postgraduate students swelled the ranks of applicants. Here, again, demographic factors were at work: an increased number of college graduates were coming out of the higher education pipeline. Beyond the important demographic factor, America's expanding involvement in the Vietnam War represented a salient contributing social factor underlying the growth in graduate student enrollment. For male students, graduate education held out the promise of an education deferment that postponed military service. But for students of both sexes, the Vietnam experience prompted many to pursue professions that involved independence, self-expression, and helping others. In this light, the life of a professor looked appealing.

The growth of higher education was staggering. Between 1960 and 1980, 1,144 institutions of higher education were added.[47] Faculties grew by about 294,500 members, a 77 percent increase, and enrollment grew by 7.9 million students, a 218 percent increase.[48] Although significant growth occurred in both public and private institutions, public institutions experienced the greatest enrollment pressures. As Table 15.3 illustrates, expenditures for public higher education rose by an astonishing 1,160 percent during the 1960s and 1970s. Major increases in state appropriations and student tuition and fees largely paid the bill: state financial support rose by 1,700 percent, and tuition and fees increased by 1,467 percent.

Revenues and expenditures continued to rise well above inflation during the 1980s, even though the rate of enrollment growth dropped off sharply. Although state support continued to outpace inflation, its relative share declined in relation to tuition and fees. Higher education governing boards and state legislatures increasingly called on students to bear a larger share of rising college costs. That trend continued throughout the 1990s.

The Growing Politicization of Higher Education Policy Making

Governors and state legislators are taking a renewed interest in public higher education policy making in their states. Some observers attribute their heightened interest to the increase in state appropriations financing public higher education. However, that explanation alone

Table 15.3 Enrollment, Revenues, and Expenditures for Public Higher Education Institutions

Enrollment			Expenditures (in $ Billions)		
Year	Size	Percentage Change	Year	Amount	Percentage Change
1959–1960	2,180,982		1959–1960	3.0	
1969–1970	5,896,668	170	1969–1970	13.2	340
1979–1980	9,063,822	54	1979–1980	37.8	186
1989–1990	10,844,717	20	1989–1990	85.7	127
1999–2000	11,309,399	4	1999–2000	126.0	47

Note: includes fall semester or quarter enrollments.

Revenues (in $ Billions)						
Year	Total	Percentage Change	State Support	Percentage Change	Tuition and Fees	Percentage Change
1959–1960	3.1		1.0		.3	
1969–1970	13.8	345	5.7	470	1.7	467
1979–1980	38.8	181	18.2	219	4.7	235
1989–1990	88.9	140	37.1	104	13.8	194
1999–2000	130.0	46	46.3	25	24.7	79

Source: Digest of Education Statistics, 1999 and 2002 (Washington, D.C.: National Center for Education Statistics, U.S. Department of Education).

is not very satisfying because state financial support has grown steadily over the past four decades, although the rate of growth has slowed in the 1990s. Something more is at issue. Two factors help to account for the growing government interest.

Governors and legislators historically have recommended and voted for increased state appropriations for higher education. They were, of necessity, in the business of expanding resources to meet a burgeoning popular demand for access. More students needed to be educated, providing a ready rationale for increased state financial support for public higher education. However, the demographic curve also led experts to project enrollment declines in the 1980s—declines that never materialized. Instead, enrollment growth continued despite the relative downturn in the college-age cohort. College costs correspondingly continued to rise, as noted earlier. The expected respite remained elusive.

Considering that nearly one-third of high school graduates now go on to higher education, up from less than one-fourth in 1960, state policymakers began asking if public higher education had been trying to do too much. They are inquiring whether or not all who chose to go to college really belonged there. They worry about declining quality in the face of enrollment growth, yet they also express concern about the ability of state treasuries to meet the growing financial demands and still be able to accommodate public demands for tax cuts, property tax relief, and increased public spending in other policy areas. If they were to continue supporting increased appropriations for higher education after they had already met the demographically based demands for access, they wanted assurance that public colleges and universities were not compromising their standards of quality in pursuit of continued growth—in essence, spreading state support thinner and thinner.

The Rising Call for Accountability.   The debate over quality in elementary and secondary education influenced policymakers' thinking about higher education. Many reasoned that, if it made sense to assess students' and teachers' competence in elementary and secondary schools, why not apply a similar approach to higher education? More theoretically, they asked how anyone—they or general members of the public—could know if higher education was doing its job. For example, the nation's governors, at their annual meeting in 1986, went on record that they "wanted to hold institutions accountable for the performance of their students."[49] Yet most American colleges and universities have continued to utilize the traditional method of student assessment—individual evaluation of the student's performance by faculty members, based on exams, papers, and laboratory projects. Interest in alternative forms of performance evaluation is increasing, evidenced by the growing number of national workshops held on the subject. Among them, one concept, **value-added assessment**, has received the greatest attention, although only a few institutions of higher education have adopted it. With this approach, students are assessed in terms of their general knowledge and skill level upon matriculation, and then again upon graduation. Students also may be tested in a given discipline when they declare their major and during their last semester or quarter of study. The measured difference in knowledge and skill level represents the value that has theoretically been added as a result of their higher education experience.

Beyond academic programs themselves, state policymakers have recently turned their attention to issues of faculty workload and productivity. Tight budgets, constrained by the recessionary economy of the early 1990s, forced governors and legislatures to prioritize public spending. Revenues in many states proved inadequate even to cover mandatory spending increases from one year to the next. In that environment of scarcity, higher education failed to compete effectively with the more immediate claims of Medicaid, primary and secondary education, and corrections. In fact, several states were forced to reduce their budgets for higher education. Those reductions contributed to increased class size and course bottlenecks (making it more difficult for students to obtain required courses for graduation) and prompted university administrations in several states to limit enrollments. Those actions, in turn, elicited the interest of governors and legislators, whose constituents were not shy about sharing their unhappiness over these developments. Without the near-term prospect of significant budget increases to finance marked course expansion,

---

value-added assessment   The practice of measuring knowledge and skill before students begin an education program and again after they finish it, to assess the value that has been added as a result of that education program.

governors and legislative committees began asking tough questions about the workload of existing faculty members. If the faculty were required to teach more classes, so the reasoning goes, more students could get access to the courses they need without an attendant increase in state funding.

That prescription was precisely what contemporary critics of higher education have called for. Two popular books carried that message: Charles Sykes's *Profscam*[50] and Martin Anderson's *Imposters in the Temple*[51] paint unflattering pictures of American professors, characterizing them as self-serving academicians who place their own research and consulting above teaching. Those at the larger universities are accused of having turned over the bulk of undergraduate teaching to unqualified teaching assistants and part-time instructors. As Martin Anderson puts it,

> The critical problem today is not so much that many professors don't teach very well, but that so few of them teach at all, that a significant part of the crucial teaching responsibilities of our universities has been handed over to the people who are unqualified. It is the shame of academic intellectuals, a shabby secret they are loathe to discuss publicly.[52]

This picture has reinforced images held by some legislators that regular faculty, particularly those at research institutions, are underworked, at least in their teaching. For critics, the objective then is to get members of the regular faculty back into the classroom. That interest has led to calls for legislative audits of faculty workload, state appropriations increases contingent upon the achievement of educational performance measures, and faculty salaries tied to the amount of time professors spend teaching.

Tennessee, South Carolina, and Wisconsin were early leaders in performance-based funding efforts. Tennessee developed the first system and has been a leader ever since. Approximately 5 percent of funding for higher education is tied to student improvement and performance, and the state collects data such as the percentage of students taking remedial courses who go on to complete their college course within a year.[53] South Carolina attempted to tie all higher education funding to measurable criteria such as graduation rates, faculty teaching loads, and student/instructor ratios[54] but abandoned the effort due to the complexity of implementing the system.[55] In 2011, however, Governor Nikki Haley announced plans to revitalize the effort and added underrepresented populations as a criterion.[56] Wisconsin divided performance measures into seven categories: quality, effectiveness, efficiency, access, diversity, stewardship of assets, and meeting compelling state needs. Among the key categories, quality measures include student and alumni satisfaction and the amount of teaching done by regular faculty members; effectiveness indicators include performance on sophomore competency tests and graduation rates; and efficiency indicators include credits to degree.[57] Decreasing college graduation rates[58] and pressures on state budgets to do more with less have increased policymakers' interest in performance-based funding.[59]

State policymakers increasingly question the efficiency of higher education operations. They are becoming more concerned about questions of program array and undue duplication among public institutions in the same state. These concerns have made them more interested in the different missions of a state's various public universities and colleges.

The elected representatives' message to state college and university governing boards and administrators is clear: be sure you know what your institution is all about and do it well, but do not try to be everything to everybody.

Higher Education as a Resource for Economic Development.   Policymakers have become more pragmatic about higher education, expressing growing interest in the relationship between higher education and economic development. Their focus is not just on economic development as a concept; it is more on the edge that strong institutions of higher education give a state in competition with other states, regionally and nationally, for development. As former Colorado governor Richard Lamm put it, "The state that is second best educationally will be second best economically."[60] Spurred by the popular association of university education with economic development, state policymakers have provided funding to establish university–industry consortia at major state universities, strengthening and formalizing the university's role in applied research. In addition, entrepreneurship centers have recently sprung up at several universities, with the goal of assisting would-be entrepreneurs in the creation of new business ventures and product lines. Although such developments probably provide solace to deans of engineering and business schools, with their applied orientations, they engender fear in the hearts of administrators and faculty in several liberal arts disciplines. A growing emphasis on the university's role in economic development sets up increased competition for the scarce state dollar between the major universities' research and instruction functions.

Challenges to Faculty Governance.   Increased government scrutiny flies in the face of the well-established tradition of university autonomy and faculty governance. Legislatures historically have acted to insulate state universities and colleges from undue political interference in academic operational matters. In place of cabinet government, in which state agency heads serve at the discretion of the governor and are expected to pursue the chief executive's policy agenda, state university and college presidents are traditionally appointed by citizen boards and serve at their discretion. Members of these distinguished governing bodies are generally appointed by the governor for staggered, fixed terms. With staggered terms, most often set between six and ten years, a first-term governor does not have an opportunity, under normal circumstances, to appoint a majority of the board. In any event, board members are expected to act foremost as trustees who represent the best interests of the institutions that they have been appointed to oversee.

Governing boards exercise responsibility for policy and administrative oversight, having the formal authority to approve legislative budget requests and annual operating budgets as well as the academic degree programs offered at each campus. This does not mean that the regents approve every course that is required as part of an academic major, but it does mean that the regents have to approve the addition of a new major or the creation of a new graduate-level degree program such as a master's of business administration (MBA) at a given campus. In most instances, however, the regents approve the university administration's recommendations, which have their origins in the respective academic departments of the university.

DEBATING THE ISSUES

How should states fund public colleges and universities?

States have traditionally funded public colleges and universities using cost-based enrollment models. In the simplest terms, the level of state support rises as enrollments rise. To complicate matters, the cost-based feature recognizes that different education programs have different costs. For example, it costs more to educate doctoral students than undergraduates, and it costs more to provide scientific and engineering education than it does to educate students in the humanities and social sciences. Thus, state aid to higher education varies according to enrollment growth and students' education level and their program of study.

Critics have increasingly taken issue with this method of funding. They argue that it rewards input at the expense of output, and that it rewards growing enrollments and recognizes their associated costs, but it fails to account for how well or efficiently students are educated. More students may be passing through higher education institutions, but with what results? Critics of the traditional approach want to focus on results. The better the results, the greater the funding. This redirection, however, raises the thorny issue of how to measure performance (beyond the grades given in individual classes). Should universities be rewarded financially for graduating students more quickly (for instance, getting them through a bachelor's degree in an average of four years, down, for example, from 4.6 years)—a so-called measure of efficiency? Should assessments, such as standardized comprehensive examinations, be used to measure students' academic performance in their undergraduate majors, perhaps even comparatively measuring the performance of students at different campuses within the same state system? Following this approach, the performance of graduating political science students at the University of California—Berkeley would be compared to that of students at the University of California—Los Angeles and the other campuses of the University of California system.

Even if you accept this approach, you still must confront the issue of how performance should be measured and how it should be rewarded. Should absolute performance be rewarded or should relative performance (that is, improvement from one year to the next)?

> Which approach do you believe states should follow? If you like the idea of moving to a more performance-based model, how do you believe your performance as a student and the performance of your faculty members should be measured? What do you see as the major problems that would accompany a change to performance-based funding?

Turn to the following webpages for help in considering these issues:
American Association of University Professors, *http://www.aaup.org/aaup*
Education Commission of the States, *www.ecs.org*
Association of Public and Land-Grant Universities, *www.naulgc.org*
American Association of State Colleges and Universities, *http://www.aascu.org/policy*
National Conference of States Legislatures, *http://www.ncsl.org/documents/fiscal/ HigherEdFundingFINAL.pdf, and www.ncsl.org*

Aside from these matters of overall university direction, day-to-day operational governance is shared between the campus's chief executive officer and the faculty, under the broad policy guidance and budget allocations of the governing board. **Faculty governance** is an oft-evoked refrain on university and college campuses. In fact, faculties exercise significant collective decision making. Faculties, organized by departments and schools (also often called colleges), establish the institution's curriculum within policies set by the board, evaluate scholarship, recommend faculty members to be hired or terminated during probationary periods, and advise the campus administration on policies ranging from the assignment of space and parking to the criteria governing sabbaticals. Faculty governance tends to be stronger on the more prestigious, research-oriented, flagship campuses across the states. In California, for example, with two separate university systems, faculty governance is much more pronounced on the campuses of the University of California, particularly at Berkeley and Los Angeles, than at the state university campuses. In fact, faculty unionization at the latter institutions has eroded the role of faculty in university governance.

Despite the long traditions of university autonomy and faculty governance among the states, public college and university governing boards, administrators, and faculty have all expressed a growing concern about what they believe to be an unwelcome intrusion on the part of governors and legislators into their institutions' internal affairs—one they fear may threaten their special status among state agencies.

SUMMARY AND CONCLUSIONS

The public spotlight is currently on education across the states. With the enrollment pressures associated with the post–World War II baby boom behind us, and with public financial support for education reaching record heights, governors and state legislators are turning their attention to the educational product. They appear no longer willing to increase state aid without greater assurance that students are learning. The key concept has become educational quality at both the lower and higher educational levels. State policymakers appear to be less preoccupied today with concerns such as ensuring educational opportunity for the less advantaged than they were in previous decades. Instead, the watchwords of today have become *competence* and *competitiveness*. A growing policy consensus has emerged that students' achievement must be raised if states are to be competitive in the growing interstate competition for economic development and if the United States is to remain competitive internationally. In this pursuit for competitive quality, state policymakers have become less willing than in the past to leave the job of quality assurance largely to educational governing boards, administrators, or teachers. Governors and legislators increasingly support and enact legislation that toughens educational requirements and assessment of educational performance. The federal government has also demonstrated an increased

---

faculty governance   The practice by which faculty in colleges and universities establish the academic curriculum, evaluate scholarship, recommend the hiring and termination of faculty members, and advise the campus administration on policy.

willingness to levy accountability requirements on the states, as evidenced by Congress's passage of President Bush's No Child Left Behind legislative proposal. In addition, education governing boards are embarking on reforms of their own, in anticipation of additional heightened government involvement. The education establishment is under more scrutiny today than at any time in the past.

Discussion Questions

1. Discuss the strong tradition of local control of primary and secondary education in the United States. Does that tradition show signs of breaking down? If so, how is it breaking down?

2. In what ways, if any, is the current concern about improving educational quality at odds with earlier state commitments to equity education aimed at addressing the needs of at-risk students? What are the attendant policy and political implications?

3. Compare and contrast the following contemporary reforms in K–12 education: charter schools, school choice, and privatization.

4. What accounts for the increasing unwillingness of governors and legislators to leave the job of quality assurance in public higher education to regent or trustee governing bodies, and thus incur the charge of unduly politicizing higher education policy making? What initiatives are state political leaders advancing?

5. Compare and contrast the contemporary debate over higher education policy with that over primary and secondary education.

Glossary

charter schools 385
Civil Rights Act of 1964 379
Elementary and Secondary Education Act of 1965 379
equal educational opportunity 378

equalization of state school aid 381
faculty governance 402
local school districts 374
National Defense Education Act of 1958 378

No Child Left Behind 384
privatization 390
value-added assessment 398
voucher programs 387

Endnotes

1. Lorraine M. McDonnell and Susan Fuhrman, "The Political Context of School Reform," paper presented at the Annual Meeting of the Midwest Political Science Association, Chicago, April 1986, 19.

2. National Center for Education Statistics, *Digest of Education Statistics*, 2010, Table 90, http://nces.ed.gov/programs/digest/d10/tables/dt10_090.asp?referrer=list.

3. *Digest of Education Statistics*, 1997, 35.

4. James S. Coleman, *Public and Private Schools* (Chicago: National Opinion Research Center, 1981).

5. Jennifer L. Hochschild, *The New American Dilemma Liberal Democracy and School Desegregation* (New Haven, Conn.: Yale University Press, 1984), 27.

6. Harral R. Rodgers and Charles S. Bullock, *Law and Social Change: Civil Rights Laws and Their Consequences* (New York: McGraw-Hill, 1972), 81–88.

7. *Significant Features of Fiscal Federalism*, 1993 (Washington, D.C.: Advisory Commission on Intergovernmental Relations, 1993), 41.

8. Clarke E. Cochran, Lawrence C. Mayer, T.R. Carr, and N. Joseph Cayer, *American Public Policy*, 9th ed (Boston: Wadsworth Cengage Learning, 2009), 315–316.

9. Ibid., 315.

10. Leanna Stiefel and Robert Berne, "The Equity Effects of State School Finance Reforms: A Methodological Critique and New Evidence," *Policy Sciences* 13 (1981), 92.

11. Michael W. Krist, *The States' Role in Education Policy Innovation* (Palo Alto, Calif.: Institute for Research on Educational Finance and Governance, Stanford University, 1981), 305.

12. William Chance, *The Best of Educations: Reforming America's Public Schools in the 1980s* (Chicago, Ill.: MacArthur Foundation, 1986), 17–18.

13. National Center for Education Statistics, *Digest of Education Statistics, 2009*, Table 22, http://nces.ed.gov/programs/digest/d09/tables/dt09_022.asp?referrer=list.

14. Chance, *The Best of Educations*, 179–187.

15. David Osborne, "Turning Around Arkansas' Schools," in *News and Views* 11, no. 11 (November 1992), 67–74.

16. Remarks by the President of the National Governors Association Education Summit, Office of the Press Secretary, The White House, March 27, 1996.

17. National Conference of State Legislatures, www.ncsl.org/programs/educ/StandAcc.htm.

18. Pennsylvania Board of Education, Principles Guiding the Development of Regulations on Curriculum, Vocational Education, and Student Assessment, 1992, 4.

19. Ibid, 5.

20. *Utah Budget Recommendations, Fiscal Year 1994* (Salt Lake City, Utah: State Office of Planning and Budget, 1993), I–1, IV–21.

21. Associated Press, "Utah Snubs Federal No Child Left Behind Act," May 2, 2005, http://www.msnbc.msn.com/id/7713931/ns/us_news-education/t/utah-snubs-federal-no-child-left-behind-act/#.Tk11ZqjzV2A.

22. Ruth Ellen Hardy, *Charter Schools* (Madison: Wisconsin Legislative Fiscal Bureau, 1997); Michael Mintrom and Sandra Vergari, "Charter Schools as a State Policy Innovation: Assessing Recent Developments," *State and Local Government Review* 29, no. 1 (Winter 1997), 43–49.

23. California State Board of Education, California Senate Bill No. 4, Enrolled as Chapter 781, Statutes of 1992.

24. Christopher Cousins, "LePage Signs Bill Allowing Charter Schools in Maine, *Bangor Daily News*, June 29, 2011, http://bangordailynews.com/2011/06/29/politics/lepage-signs-bill-allowing-charter-schools-in-maine.

25. Center for Educational Reform, *Ranking Scorecard*, www.edreform.com/_upload/ranking_chart.pdf.

26. Research Brief, *Public Policy Forum* 99, no. 2, February 2011, www.publicpolicyforum.org.

27. Barbara Miner, "A Brief History of Milwaukee's Voucher Program," *Rethinking Schools Online* 20, no. 3 (Spring 2006), www.rethinkingschools.org; Howard Fuller, *The Continuing Struggle of African Americans for the Power to Make Real Educational Choice* (Washington, D.C.: The Center for Education Reform, March 2000).

28. Research Brief, *Public Policy Forum* 99.

29. "Voucher Victory in Wisconsin," *PR Newswire*, June 26, 2011, http://www.breitbart.com/article.php?id=xprnw.20110626.DC26236&show_article=1.

30. Kate McGreevey, "Ohio Creates One of the Nation's Largest Voucher Programs," *School Reform News*, September 2005, www.heartland.org/publications; "Cleveland's Voucher System," *Legislative Policy Brief* 1, no. 5 (January 28, 1999).

31. "More Ohio School Vouchers Available in Budget," *WOSU Public Media*, July 2, 2011, http://www.publicbroadcasting.net/wosu/news.newsmain?action=article&ARTICLE_ID=1823040.

32. Zelman, *Superintendent of Public Instruction of Ohio et al. v. Simmons-Harris et al.*, June 27, 2001.

33. Supreme Court of Florida, Case No. SC04-2323, www.floridasupremecourt.org/pub_info/summaries.briefs/04/04-2323/filed01-05-2006.

34. "Douglas County Approves School Voucher Program," *CBS News*, March 15, 2011, http://denver.cbslocal.com/2011/03/15/douglas-county-approves-school-voucher-program.

35. M. William Salganik, "Privatization Suffers Blow with EAI Loss Baltimore School Board Cancels a Pact the Firm Uses as a Selling Point," *The Baltimore Sun*, December 2, 1995, http://articles.baltimoresun.com/1995-12-02/business/1995336075_1_eai-baltimore-school-baltimore-contract. "The Lessions of Hartford's Privatized Schools," *SunSentinel.com,* February 18, 1996, http://articles.sun-sentinel.com/1996-02-18/news/9602150220_1_hartford-schools-education-alternatives-public-schools.

36. EdisonLearning, http://www.edisonlearning.com/about-edisonlearning.

37. John Augenblick, "The Current Status of School Financing Reform in the States," in *The Fiscal, Legal, and Political Aspect of State Reform of Elementary and Secondary Education*, ed. Van D. Mueller and Mary McKeown (Cambridge, Mass.: Ballinger 1985), 12–16.

38. Theodore M. Black, *Straight Talk about American Education* (New York: Harcourt Brace, Jovanovich, 1982).

39. H. Howe, "Giving Equity a Chance in the Excellence Game," *NASSP Bulletin* (September 1984), 74–85.

40. Ernest L. Boyer, *Ready to Learn: A Mandate for the Nation* (Princeton, N.J.: Carnegie Foundation for the Advancement of Learning, 1991).

41. Bill Zuckerman, "The Next Education Crisis: Equalizing Schools Funds," *Congressional Quarterly Weekly Report* 51, no. 13 (March 27, 1993), 749–754; "Texas Meets Deadline for School Finance Plan," *State Legislatures* 19, no. 8 (August 1993), 6; Howard Rothstein, "When States Spend More," *The American Prospect*, no. 36 (January–February 1998), 72–79; *School Finance Litigation: Final Decisions by State Supreme Courts* (Denver, Colo.: Education Commission of the States, 1997).

42. John Augenblick, Steven D. Gold, and Kent McGuire, *Education Finance in the 1990s* (Denver, Colo.: Education Commission of the States, 1990).

43. Zuckerman, "The Next Education Crisis," 751.

44. Ohio Legislative Budget Office, *School Funding in Ohio*, June 20, 2000, 9; Alan Ehrenhalt, "School + Taxes + Politics = Chaos," *Governing*, 12, no. 4 (January 1999), 27–31.

45. National Center for Education Finance, http://204.131.235.671/programs/educ/NcEFupdate.htm.

46. Access Network, www.schoolfunding.info/news/lit_news.php3.

47. *Digest of Education Statistics, 1997*, 258.

48. *Digest of Education Statistics, 1992*, 171.

49. Quoted in Ernest L. Boyer, *College: The Undergraduate Experience in America* (New York: Harper & Row, 1987), 252.

50. Charles J. Sykes, *Profscam* (Washington, D.C.: Regnery Gateway, 1988).

51. Martin Anderson, *Imposters in the Temple* (New York: Simon and Schuster, 1992).

52. Ibid., 49.

53. Midwestern Higher Education Compact, *Completion-based Funding for Higher Education*, February 2009, http://www.mhec.org/Resources.

54. Stephanie Plaisance, "High Performance Higher Education," *State Government News* 40, no. 7 (September 1997), 7–8.

55. Midwestern Higher Education Compact, *Completion-based Funding for Higher Education*, February 2009, http://www.mhec.org/Resources.

56. Harriet McLeod, "South Carolina Moves to Define Performance-based Funding Formula for Higher Education," *Diverse Issues in Higher Education*, April 11, 2011, http://diverseeducation.com/article/15010.

57. Courtney R. White, *Performance Based Budgeting in Higher Education: A Multi-State Comparative Study*, unpublished MPA Thesis, University of Utah, July 6, 2000, 12–28.

58. Jeffrey Brainard and Andrea Fuller, "Graduation Rates Fall at One-Third of 4-Year Colleges," *The Chronicle of Higher Education,* December 5, 2010, http://chronicle.com/article/Graduation-Rates-Fall-at/125614.

59. Thomas L. Harnisch, "Performance-based Funding: A Re-Emerging Strategy in Public Higher Education Financing," American Association of State College and Universities, June 2011, http://www.congressweb.com/aascu/docfiles/Performance_Funding_AASCU_June2011.pdf.

60. Quoted in Frank Newman, *Choosing Quality: Reducing Conflict between the State and the University* (Denver, Colo.: Education Commission of the States, 1987), 3.

CHAPTER 16

Social Welfare and Health Policy

LEARNING OBJECTIVES

- Understand the differences between social insurance and public assistance programs, including their eligibility provisions, clientele, sources of financial support, administration, and the public perceptions of them.
- Identify the poor.
- Debate the two contrasting views of poverty and welfare in the United States and how they influence the public policy debate over public assistance programs and calls for reform.
- Know the history of welfare reform leading to Congress's elimination of public assistance to low-income families with dependent children as a federal entitlement.
- Understand the range and significance of state experimentation with welfare reform.
- Identify the fiscal pressures that rising Medicaid costs place on state budgets and efforts at cost containment.
- Know the state health care reform initiatives in relation to the national debate over health care reform.

A single mother and her three children struggle to get by on her $7.50 an hour job as a receptionist in a downtown office building. She has mixed feelings about how her life differs from what it was just six months ago, when she was on welfare. Since her state's welfare agency found her employment, she has worked 40 hours a week. That has meant getting the oldest child off to school in the morning, and the other two children to subsidized child care. She misses not having her little ones at home with her, but she sees the new job as an opportunity to become independent of public support. Now part of the working poor and considered a success story of welfare reform, she and her children have a monthly income of $1,250 and continue to qualify for food stamps and Medicaid. In addition, her low income and family size entitle her to receive an income tax credit from the federal government of $4,140 a year, bringing her gross annual income up to $19,140. After paying Social Security and Medicare taxes, she is left with an annual cash income of $18,069, putting her family income just below the official poverty line.

Food stamps add a cash value of another $400 or so a month. Without the Earned Income Tax Credit and the transitional support of food stamps, she and her children would face the daunting task of getting by on the income from her $7.50 an hour job alone. Although she still must watch what she spends just to get by, government assistance has improved her standard of living. She knows, however, that economic hard times could add her to the ranks of the unemployed and return her to the welfare rolls.

I t makes sense to look at social welfare and health policy in the same chapter because they are closely related in several ways. As we shall see later in detail, the greatest share of state health expenditures goes to provide medical care for recipients of major public welfare programs. As the state welfare rolls increase, so do public health care costs. Furthermore, states depend heavily on federal funding to help pay for the financial assistance and health care they provide to low-income residents. In return for that financial support, states find themselves subject to detailed federal regulations in both policy areas. For all of these reasons, policymakers tend to view social welfare and medical assistance programs in tandem.

This chapter first examines social welfare policy—its substance, value base, intergovernmental relations, and politics. Special attention will be given to welfare reform. Then the focus turns to health policy, covering similar terrain but also highlighting the connection between the two policy areas.

SOCIAL WELFARE POLICY

Government programs of social welfare at all levels can be grouped into five general categories:

1. Income maintenance, including Temporary Assistance to Needy Families (TANF), General Assistance, Social Security, Supplemental Security Income (SSI), and unemployment compensation.
2. Nutrition, including food stamps, school breakfasts, and school lunches.
3. Social services, including but not limited to community mental health, legal services, and supportive social services such as child day care, adoption, homemaker guidance and counseling, and family planning.
4. Housing assistance.
5. Health, including Medicaid, Medicare, and various public health programs (to be discussed under Health Policy).

These programs serve different clientele and have different bases of funding. Some are organized as insurance programs, in which the recipients of financial support or services, and/or their employers, pay into a segregated fund from which monies are drawn to cover program costs. General taxpayer support is not involved. Conversely, others can be grouped as public assistance programs, for which taxpayers largely foot the bill, although recipients may be required to pay some limited fees. The distinctions between social insurance and public assistance programs, however, are deeper than the differences in their sources of financial support and fund organization. Social differences are significant. Whereas public assistance programs are considered to be welfare, social insurance programs are viewed as debits on a prepaid account. Such different perceptions carry with them important social connotations that influence program content, conditions, and levels of financial and political support.

Social Insurance Programs

Social insurance programs are based on contributions by employers and employees into a revolving account trust fund. Only individuals who have paid, or on whose behalf employers have paid, are eligible for benefits. Contributions support benefits; present contributors, in many instances, are paying for the benefits received by current recipients. Yet current contributions are commingled with carried-forward balances, and today's contributions will become part of future balances.

Social insurance benefits go to workers—those who have regularly been employed in the labor force and are retired, disabled, injured, or temporarily unemployed—*regardless of financial need.* No income or asset requirements need to be met for eligibility.

Social Security. The major social insurance program in the country is Old Age Survivors Disability and Health Insurance (OASDHI), established in 1935, and most commonly referred to as **Social Security**. An exclusively federal program, and therefore one that will be dealt with only in passing, it covers about 90 percent of the working population. The primary exceptions are most federal employees and some state employees, who are covered by their own separate retirement systems. Those who qualify for cash payments also qualify for **Medicare** health insurance benefits, although the monies supporting each are kept in separate trust funds, and each component is expected to be independently solvent. Both employers and their employees contribute to funds; self-employed persons pay a single tax. Over the years, and especially since 1984, Congress has increased both the salary base to be taxed and the tax rate. But given the demographic trends, future draws on the funds are expected to deplete accumulated balances. Not only will baby boomers be retiring in large numbers beginning in 2012, but the ratio of workers to recipients will continue to fall. As an illustration of the problem, in 2005, 3.3 workers contributed to Social Security for every person drawing benefits. Analysts expect that ratio to drop to 2.2:1 by 2030. The program's trustees project that, by 2017, tax revenues will fall short of benefit costs under current law.[1]

Social Security benefits are paid out as legal entitlements; that is, those who qualify are entitled to receive benefits. At the end of 2009, 53 million people received cash payments, including 36 million retired workers and their dependents, 6 million survivors of deceased workers, and 10 million disabled workers and their dependents.[2] Social Security has come to serve foremost as a retirement program, providing financial support and medical care to all who

---

Social Security An exclusively federal social insurance program into which both employees and employers contribute to provide retirement benefits for covered workers.

Medicare An exclusively federal social insurance program into which both employers and employees contribute to provide health care benefits for covered workers during their retirement years.

qualify, regardless of financial condition or social class. Although not considered a welfare program, its benefits to retirees may be the only financial resource keeping some out of poverty. On the other hand, the Social Security check for the well-to-do represents only a modest supplement to their retirement income. For most Americans, Social Security is only one form of retirement income, which is accompanied by employer-provided retirement plans. Yet some employers, in designing retirement plans for their employees, look at these plans as supplements to Social Security, using projected Social Security benefits as the core retirement reserve.

Unemployment Compensation.   A second major social insurance program, **unemployment compensation (UC)**, is administered by both the federal government and the states. The first UC law in the United States was established by the Wisconsin legislature in 1932, and it served as the model for the current federal–state program. In the present partnership, the federal government sets program standards, but state legislatures determine their own tax and benefit levels. The regular program is financed solely from contributions made by employers into state accounts held by the federal government. Employers also pay a federal tax that finances program administration at both the federal and state levels. However, federal law allows employers to credit up to 90 percent of the state tax against the federal tax. The noncredited portion becomes available to fund administration and the limited special programs. As an inducement for states to enact UC programs that meet federal standards, the tax offset is available only to participating states—a good reason that all 50 states have established such programs.

As with Social Security, UC operates using a revolving fund, with contributions supporting benefit claims. In addition to collecting the taxes that support benefits, states also maintain wage records, take claims, determine recipients' eligibility, and pay benefits. Unlike Social Security, individual states can draw down their accounts to a negative balance, requiring them to borrow from the federal trust fund, with interest, to meet unfunded benefit claims. The states, in turn, are expected to enact legislation that will bring errant accounts into balance by increasing the UC tax on employers, reducing benefit levels, or a combination of the two. Failure to do so can result in the federal government directly increasing its administrative tax on employers, without offset, thus recouping sufficient revenues to balance the account over a prescribed period.

In periods of especially high unemployment, Congress can approve the use of federal general revenues to supplement UC funds. Extended benefits kick in after individuals exhaust their benefit entitlement, usually after 26 weeks, but Congress can extend that duration. Federal general funds support extended benefits based on the philosophy that when exceptional levels of unemployment are reached, state accounts are not equipped to finance longer-term benefits. In addition, extended benefits recognize that very high, sustained unemployment must be viewed as a product of the national economy and, consequently, of direct national concern.

---

unemployment compensation (UC)   A program co-administered by the federal government and the states, providing cash benefits to laid-off workers. Employers contribute to the program to pay for benefits and finance the program's administration.

Like Social Security, the UC program carries no means-test requirements. Unemployment benefits are available as a matter of entitlement to unemployed workers who have met minimum requirements for previous work time and earnings. Unemployed workers receiving benefits must also be "ready, able, and willing to work" and be registered with a state job service office.

Worker's Compensation.   Another social insurance program found in all 50 states is **worker's compensation (WC)**, which provides income support and medical services to workers who have been injured or disabled on the job, regardless of their personal financial condition. States administer the program in one of two ways. In the first, states operate their own insurance funds. Twenty-two states have funds into which employers contribute and from which benefits are drawn. The second requires employers to provide proof of privately carried insurance to the state WC agency or to be qualified by that state agency as financially able to be self-insured. In both cases, the state sets program standards and prescribes minimum levels of coverage depending on the employers' size and type of enterprise. With the private insurance approach, the WC agency works with insurance carriers to ensure that they honor all appropriate claims. Where contention exists, the agency, in most states, conducts administrative hearings and makes binding determinations that are subject only to appeals to the courts. The same process applies to claims against self-insurers.

In eight states, however, commercial insurance is not allowed. Employers must insure with an exclusive state insurance fund or be qualified as self-insured. In another 14 states, the state fund competes with commercial insurers. With this second variant, employers pay into a revolving fund held and administered by the state. As with UC, claims are paid from the fund's available balance. Most states that use this method tax employers on an experience-rated basis; that is, employers that have fewer claims pay less than their similar-size counterparts that have more claims.

Regardless of the method used, private employer coverage is mandatory in 47 states, except New Jersey, South Carolina, and Texas, where participation is elective. Employers who reject coverage waive their customary common law defenses against suits by injured employees.[3]

PUBLIC ASSISTANCE PROGRAMS

Public assistance programs, generally labeled as welfare, are aimed at low- or no-income citizens in society. To be eligible for benefits, prospective recipients must meet a means test, based on income and assets.

Two kinds of public assistance programs exist: cash and in-kind assistance. Cash assistance programs put money in recipients' pockets. They provide the income necessary

---

worker's compensation A state-administered program that provides income support and medical care to workers who have been injured or disabled on the job.

public assistance programs Government-financed programs that serve low-income people and consist of cash assistance and in-kind support, including medical care, food stamps, and housing assistance. Recipients must meet means tests, based on income and assets, to be eligible to receive benefits.

to bring the recipients out of poverty. In-kind programs, though not including cash, still provide something of tangible value to recipients that, if not provided, would entail still one more drain on an already tight budget or would not be afforded at all. Examples of in-kind assistance include medical care, food stamps, and public housing. Three major cash assistance programs are available to the poor: Supplemental Security Income (SSI), directed at the aged, blind, and disabled—independent of Social Security; Temporary Assistance to Needy Families (TANF), the largest in terms of recipients and cost; and General Assistance, primarily a local program, providing aid to those who are poor but not eligible for any other form of government cash assistance.

The earliest cash assistance programs provided aid to low-income elderly. Even before the federal government got into the act, the states established their own forms of assistance. Arizona created the first program in 1914, and by the time the federal government adopted the Social Security Act in 1935, a total of 30 states had already established old-age assistance programs.[4]

Prior to passage of the Social Security Act, assistance to the non-elderly poor was largely confined to private charity. Church-related organizations led the way. Local governments, most often in response to state laws passed during the first quarter of the twentieth century, established modest cash assistance programs to aid children whose fathers had died and left them without support. A few states extended coverage to children whose fathers had become disabled or had deserted the family.

The Great Depression placed unprecedented burdens on both the private and the meager public assistance programs. With mounting unemployment, private welfare programs could not meet the cascading demand for assistance. Individuals and families had exhausted their personal resources and found no place to turn for help. State general relief programs were formed to assist those who had pursued all other avenues. But the states, faced with severely declining tax resources, soon became unable to finance the required levels of assistance. In response, Congress passed the 1932 Emergency Relief and Construction Act, which provided funds for public works projects and included $300 million in loans to the states for welfare purposes (none of which was repaid). However, unemployment continued to rise, and 14 million Americans were out of work by the beginning of 1933. The federal government acted again by creating the Federal Emergency Relief Act of 1933, which authorized $500 million in relief grants to the states.[5] By 1935, with passage of the Social Security Act, the federal government's role in public assistance became institutionalized, and programs were created to assist low-income elderly, the blind, and dependent children. In 1950, Congress broadened eligibility to include permanently and totally disabled needy adults. These programs still exist in modified form. General relief became the responsibility of local governments, aided by state financial assistance in some states. The major public assistance programs, discussed next, are financed by the federal government and the states.

Supplemental Security Income.   In 1972, in response to the Nixon administration's recommendation, Congress replaced the various categorical programs for the low-income elderly, blind, and disabled—each of which had its own earmarked funding—with a

State worker dispenses food stamps to eligible recipient.

unified program entitled the **Supplemental Security Income (SSI)** program. Under the change, eligibility requirements and federal benefit payments were made uniform. Recipients, therefore, are now guaranteed the same minimum amount regardless of where they live. In addition, states may choose to supplement by recipient category, by living arrangement, or by geographical area (recognizing different costs of living). Although the basic SSI program is administered by the federal government, states may elect to administer the supplementation component. Most rely on federal administration.

Temporary Assistance to Needy Families. In August 1996, after 61 years of providing cash benefits to low-income families with dependent children, Congress replaced the Aid to Families with Dependent Children (AFDC) program with the new **Temporary Assistance to Needy Families (TANF)** program. The TANF program represents a marked departure from AFDC's guarantee of federally funded cash support to all applicants who meet eligibility requirements. In place of AFDC's entitlement status, the TANF program provides block grants to support state programs aimed at moving participants from welfare dependence to work. Within broad guidelines and reduced federal requirements, states

Supplemental Security Income (SSI) A federally financed program that provides cash assistance to low-income elderly, blind, and disabled people. States may elect to provide supplements to the uniform federal benefit payments.

Temporary Assistance to Needy Families (TANF) A program of federal block grants to the states that provides financial assistance to low-income families with dependent children, replacing the Aid to Families with Dependent Children (AFDC) program.

have a great deal of flexibility to design the specific features of their welfare-to-work programs. The central organizing principle of the highly decentralized TANF program is that participants are expected to work for their public assistance benefits—whether it takes the form of employment in unsubsidized jobs, subsidized jobs, community service, or on-the-job training. Although participants may first be placed in educational or training programs, the expectation is that those programs will provide the needed tools that lead to work.

The TANF program is the most recent and the most comprehensive of a series of efforts that began in the 1980s to reform welfare in the United States. These reforms, culminating in the landmark 1996 legislation, took a system that largely had the states determining welfare eligibility and passing out checks, and transformed their role into one of administering and coordinating a massive job-training and placement operation for many of the nation's poorest and least-skilled citizens.

The 1996 law gives states almost complete discretion to determine eligibility requirements and benefit levels. It places welfare-to-work performance requirements on the states, and it allows states to place more restrictive work requirements on recipients than the federal government minimally mandates. The federal legislation lets states decide how best to design programs that meet the federally imposed performance standards. More will be said about welfare reform later in this chapter, but first let's learn who are the poor in need of public assistance.

WHO ARE THE POOR?

Poverty is clearly not an isolated phenomenon in the United States. Approximately one in eight Americans lives in poverty, as measured by the U.S. Census Bureau. Considering children alone, the proportion rises to about one in five. Children are twice as likely to be poor than the elderly. In addition to age, race and ethnicity correlate with poverty. Although more whites are poor than either African Americans or Hispanic Americans, African Americans and Hispanic Americans are almost three times more likely to be poor than whites.

Regardless of race or ethnicity, female-headed households with children are over five times more likely to be poor than married-couple families, illustrating what has become the **feminization of poverty**.[6] In 2009, there were 43.6 million poor people in the United States (see Figure 16.1). Since 1959, the first year for which poverty estimates are available from the U.S. Census Bureau, the poverty rate (the *percentage* of persons in poverty) has dropped by 8.1 percentage points. Although the rate fell for all age groups, the elderly enjoyed the steepest decline, from 35 to 8.9 percent.[7]

Two Contrasting Views of Poverty and Welfare

The More Conservative Critique.   America's intellectual and cultural inheritance has preconditioned us to look at social phenomena and public problems in certain ways. We believe in the value of the individual: each person should be free to pursue what he or she believes to be in his

---

feminization of poverty   The reality that female-headed households with children are five times more likely to be poor than are married-couple families.

Numbers in millions, rates in percent

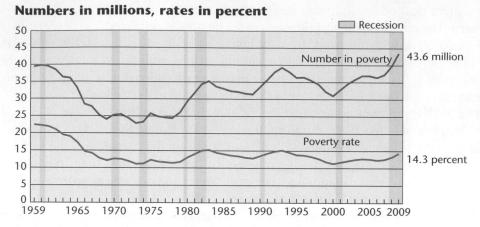

Figure 16.1 Numbers in Poverty and Poverty Rate, 1959 to 2009

Note: The data points represent the midpoints of the respective years.

Source: U.S. Census Bureau, *Current Population Survey*, 1960–2010. Annual Social and Economic Supplements, http://www.census.gov/hhes/www/poverty/data/incpovhlth/2009/pov09fig04.pdf.

or her best self-interest, as long as that pursuit does not unduly infringe on the rights of others. Out of this belief in the individual comes a sense of rugged individualism, which suggests that individuals are best left to their own devices in pursuit of their self-interest. Individuals should not be discriminated against or otherwise artificially held back in those efforts, but neither should they be given unfair advantages. In this view, government's role is, at best, a limited one. Our belief in the value of the marketplace and in the Protestant work ethic provides an economic corollary to our emphasis on the individual. We believe that capitalism provides an environment in which we can better ourselves economically through hard work. We judge ourselves and others in terms of this kind of success. Work is an integral element in individual advancement. But even beyond success, work itself becomes bound up with human dignity.

This world-view looks at poverty as an aberration and as a failure. The poor are unable to succeed in an environment encouraging unlimited individual potential, and because they have become dependent on others, they have lost an essential element of human dignity that is associated with work. Within an intellectual and cultural inheritance that prizes self-help, those who have become dependent on government assistance do not fully measure up. The poor themselves become suspect. They become branded as the "losers" in life, who may have become comfortable relying on the support of others. Some believe that public assistance engenders such dependency, suppressing the "natural" drive to compete in the survival of the fittest. For welfare critic George Gilder, public assistance programs are problematic because they "break the psychological link between effort and reward."[8]

The contemporary conservative criticism of welfare includes concerns about its rising costs and potential for fraud, but the most basic criticism is that public assistance may be helping to maintain or even expand poverty by undermining the natural incentive for the poor to seek jobs. Here the criticism is leveled not so much at the poor as at the structure of the welfare system itself. Critics see the benefit structure of public assistance as rewarding

DEBATING THE ISSUES

Whose responsibility is it to help the poor?

This question evokes strong feelings and an array of responses. Some people place the responsibility on government, arguing that only government has the resources to meet the broad needs of the poor for cash assistance, health care, and financial help for housing. Others look to charitable organizations first, with government stepping in only when religious and other nonprofit organizations have made their best effort to lend a hand. Still others place the ultimate responsibility on the poor to do more to help themselves. From this perspective, individual responsibility is the key: the poor should pull themselves out of poverty in a lasting way, and any assistance should be premised on helping the poor to help themselves, and not undermining personal initiative.

> Where do you think the responsibility lies? What issues must be addressed in coming to a decision? Do these different points of responsibility interrelate? If so, how should they be combined in improving the condition of the poor?

Explore these questions on the Web:
The Welfare Rights Organizing Coalition, *www.wroc.org*
Catholic Charities, *www.catholiccharitiesusa.org*
The Salvation Army, *www.salvationarmyusa.org*
National Association of Social Workers, *www.naswdc.org*

greater dependency. Benefit payments typically rise if additional dependent children are added to a family's size. A part-time job or the income of an older child often results in reduced public assistance benefits. Conservative criticism points to these elements of the system to argue that welfare discourages people from working.

Another criticism of welfare is that it contributes to the breakup of traditional families. Fathers may live apart from their families in order to maintain their family's eligibility for benefits. Critics also argue that public assistance provides an incentive for single mothers not to marry at all. Although this perception persists, research suggests that welfare programs, in themselves, have little or no effect on family instability beyond those problems generated by tight family budgets.[9]

Finally, critics view welfare as creating a **cycle of dependence** that encourages children who grow up on welfare to raise their own children on it. About 20 percent of girls whose families are highly dependent on welfare replicate that dependence in their own lives.[10]

Conservatives make a distinction between the deserving and the not-so-deserving poor. Those who become poor because of something beyond their control, such as becoming

---

cycle of dependence   A perception that welfare creates a dependency that crosses generations. However, only about 20 percent of girls whose families are highly dependent on welfare replicate that dependence in their own lives.

blind or disabled, tend to be viewed differently from welfare mothers. Society does not generally begrudge public financial support of the blind or disabled; they are viewed as being forced into dependency against their will. The aged are the subject of similar public sympathy, but a qualitative difference between the two can be detected. The elderly poor who do not have adequate Social Security benefits might be willingly accorded government aid because they are indeed old and unable to be gainfully employed. At the same time, however, they are not accorded the same degree of benevolence extended to the blind or disabled because the noninsured elderly poor can be suspect for not preparing for their future. When they had the chance, so the argument goes, they were not attached to the labor force sufficiently to qualify for Social Security benefits. In that way, they may be viewed as irresponsible. Nevertheless, they are old and poor and not now able to help themselves. Conversely, the welfare mother may be viewed as young and able-bodied, capable of providing for herself and her family if only she had the drive.

The More Liberal Critique. The more liberal perspective sees welfare as meeting a real need. Families with dependent children do not choose to be on welfare; they are on welfare because of their need. If given the opportunity, welfare recipients would choose to work, deeply appreciating the association between employment and a sense of human dignity. People become unemployed and without income (which may last beyond the expiration of UC benefits) most often through no fault of their own. During these temporary setbacks, they have a right to public assistance. Others just seem to fall through the crack of economic prosperity. They are often the poorly educated and unskilled who have difficulty finding a job even during periods of relatively low unemployment. They appear to be caught in the **cycle of poverty**, without any means of escape. Young, single mothers with infants and toddlers at home have difficulty leaving their children while working or seeking work.

Liberals are quick to debunk what they believe are myths about those on public assistance. In response to the commonly held stereotype of large welfare families, they point out that families on welfare are about the same size as the typical American family—the former has 1.9 children on average, compared with the national average of 1.8. A study of the former AFDC program showed that only one-tenth of recipient families had more than three children, and less than 1 percent had more than five.[11] Furthermore, liberals point out that about half of all women who received benefits from the program remained on the rolls for two years or less—far from long-term dependence.[12] Finally, just as critics of welfare use the fact that about 20 percent of girls raised in welfare families become dependent on public assistance, other observers question whether factors such as low educational attainment and poor job skills, or the absence of parental support and discipline, might be the real contributors to reliance on public assistance.

Liberals argue that the welfare system has worked, that it has kept needy people, mostly children, out of poverty. Welfare is meeting a need, helping to provide necessities to those who would have to go without them in the absence of public support. Yet the

---

cycle of poverty The thesis that poor people have difficulty breaking out of the reinforcing elements of poverty.

contemporary welfare system fails to escape criticism. For liberals, the state–federal partnership breeds inequality. Benefit levels are viewed as inequitable among the states and not related to actual need. For many liberals, however, the real problem is not welfare; it is the broader social system, which tolerates an underclass in society. From the liberals' perspective, changes in the educational system have to come first because education holds the greatest promise of breaking the cycle of poverty.

WELFARE REFORM

Whether coming from a conservative or liberal perspective, almost every major study of public assistance programs has called for significant reform of the welfare system. Reform proposals tend to fall into one of two categories, either incremental or comprehensive.

Incrementalists have accepted the basic structure of the old AFDC program, looking to improve it, fill in the gaps, and make it more administratively efficient. Reform initiatives were often recommended as solutions to specific problems. Examples abounded in the AFDC program. One proposal that was often promoted was greater benefit equality among the states, calling for the federal government to require states to meet certain benefit standards in order to receive matching support. As variations on this basic proposal, other recommendations supported increases in the federal government's matching share. Other proposals have called on the federal government to fully finance the minimum benefit level, with the states left to supplement it as they see fit. Congress has not gone along, however, choosing instead to pursue reforms aimed at getting people off welfare altogether, a pattern of reform that culminated in the landmark 1996 legislation that is discussed in the following section.

The Work Incentive Program

Some earlier congressional reformers, who viewed employment as the surest way to break dependence on welfare, argued that federal programs should focus on finding work for employable welfare recipients and on providing basic education and training to improve the employability of those least prepared to enter the labor force. But for either approach to be successful, reformers recognized that provisions in the AFDC law, which served as disincentives to work, would have to be modified. In an effort to minimize disincentives against work, Congress passed the Work Incentive (WIN) program in 1967. The WIN program (now defunct) included the reformist "30 plus one-third" provision, whereby the first $30 of earned income each month, plus one-third of the remainder, would not be counted as offsets against AFDC benefits, thus making remunerative work more financially attractive. (That provision was later eliminated by Congress during the Reagan administration.) In addition, state welfare agencies were awarded federal funds to provide working AFDC mothers with day care and selected job-training services. All AFDC mothers whose youngest child was age 6 or older were required to participate. These recipients were also required to register for employment referral with state job-service offices, and they often received special help with finding jobs.

Several evaluations of the WIN program suggest that it failed to realize its promise. A U.S. Congress Joint Economic Committee report noted that only 138,000 persons were claimed to have obtained employment as a result of the WIN program during its first six years in existence. The report goes on to suggest that this figure might be inflated by as much as 40 percent.[13] Henry Levin challenges the efficacy of WIN job placements by suggesting that the program "creamed" off the best employment prospects, those with better education and work records, who were already more likely to find a job.[14] Irene Laurice adds that the cost involved in marketing poorly trained and educated AFDC mothers in a highly competitive labor market far exceeded the benefits, whether benefits are measured as reduced AFDC benefit costs or increased family earnings.[15] In explaining the program's lackluster performance, critics generally agree that, even with job training and placement services, welfare recipients are at a distinct disadvantage in the job market. With only so many jobs available, employers are drawn not only to the best-prepared prospective workers but also to those who have a stable track record of work.

Workfare

The Reagan administration, in rejecting the WIN program, did not give up on the concept of work. The orientation changed. Rather than attempting to place those few AFDC recipients who were the most employable, with or without additional job training or other supportive services, the Reagan administration called for Congress to adopt a national **workfare** program requiring all able-bodied recipients to work for their benefits. Under workfare, welfare recipients would be required to work a specified number of hours at a calculated minimum wage to earn the value of their benefits. That work could involve tasks such as snow shoveling, trash cleanup, and routine clerical tasks. The emphasis was not so much on employability as on the value of the work ethic itself. Critics, in response, labeled the proposed program slavefare.

Although Congress rejected President Reagan's proposal for a mandatory workfare program in 1981, it enacted the Tax Equity and Fiscal Responsibility Act of 1982 (TEFRA), which provided incentives for the states to enact workfare programs. In response, more than half the states passed legislation requiring able-bodied welfare recipients to work for their benefits. Yet several states, most notably California and Massachusetts, resorted to forced public service work only after welfare recipients underwent an initial, intensive period of employability preparation and job search—in part, reminiscent of the WIN program.

The California program, known as GAIN (Greater Avenues to Independence) and started in 1985, required two-parent welfare households (permitted under California's AFDC-UP program) and single-parent households with no children under age 6 to meet with a social worker and develop an individualized employment plan. That plan could include language training for non-English speakers, coaching on job search and interviewing techniques for those already possessing marketable job skills and a recent employment record, or job training for those

---

workfare   The label applying broadly to public assistance programs that require recipients to work for their benefits.

lacking such skills. In addition, child care services were provided to mothers during their periods of job search or job training. Welfare recipients who remained unemployed after having been through job training or a "job club" work search were then required to work for the state, for no more than a year, to earn their welfare benefits. The state jobs were valued at the same hourly rate as the lowest paid classified state employee. The concept was that meaningful work gets done and, in the process, welfare recipients get needed employment experience.

An evaluation of the workfare program in San Diego County showed mixed results. Local officials boasted that almost half the workfare participants found jobs; this was a seemingly impressive result that the state legislature used as justification for statewide workfare. In comparison, however, nearly four-fifths as many non-enrolled AFDC recipients were able to find jobs on their own. Supporters of the program claimed a savings of $2.50 for every dollar spent, but detractors questioned the value of the work product. As David Kirp noted, "It is the recipients, not the taxpayers, who are better off. Only by placing a fairly high value on the product of workfare, the better-swept streets and better-organized government files, can society be regarded as benefiting, on the basis of the evidence at hand."[16] A subsequent evaluation conducted in 1994 found that slightly more than half of all GAIN participants in the six-county study area remained on welfare three years after they enrolled in the program. On the positive side, the program cut welfare payments an average of 6 percent and increased participants' income an average of 22 percent.[17]

The Family Support Act

The workfare approach continued to find favor among those attempting to combine the following values: offering the personal benefits of work, paying back society for its financial assistance, and providing the previously unemployable with the training needed to become employable. Policymakers hoped that, in this mix, some individuals would gain the skills necessary for lasting employment; that others would learn the work habits required to keep a job, even if it were a low-skill job; and that still others would make a contribution to their community in a public service job in exchange for their benefits. It was this hope that led Congress to enact the 1988 **Family Support Act**, which required that each state operate a **Job Opportunities and Basic Skills (JOBS) program**. Passed by a Congress controlled by Democrats and signed by a conservative Republican president, that legislation had enough in it to appeal to elected representatives across party lines and ideologies. It honored the conservative ideal that welfare recipients should work in return for their AFDC check, but it also upheld the liberal faith that people can improve themselves if given the tools to get ahead.

The Family Support Act made the receipt of benefits for certain long-term recipients contingent on their participation in educational and employment programs, and it also

---

Family Support Act Legislation passed by Congress in 1988 that required each state to operate a Job Opportunities and Basic Skills (JOBS) program.

Job Opportunities and Basic Skills (JOBS) program A subset of the AFDC program that made the receipt of AFDC benefits for certain long-term recipients contingent on their participation in educational and employment programs.

provided transitional health benefits and child care for up to 12 months after recipients found a job and lost AFDC cash benefits because job-related income made them ineligible for financial aid. The legislation directed states to give special attention to never-married mothers who did not finish high school and who had their first child at a young age—those at the greatest risk of prolonged dependence.

Unlike the earlier WIN program, the amount of federal funding each state received for the JOBS program was flexible: it depended on the number of recipients it enrolled and the amount of matching funds it contributed. The Family Support Act required states to start phasing in education and training programs by October 1, 1990, but the programs were not required to be operational until 1995. States were required to enroll at least 20 percent of their AFDC heads of household in a JOBS program by the 1995 fiscal year or face a one-half reduction in federal funds. Targeted recipients had to participate in the JOBS program unless they had a child age 3 years or younger. If they did not participate, they risked reductions in their benefit checks. A certain mutual obligation existed: welfare recipients were expected to take steps toward self-sufficiency, and government was expected to support recipients' efforts by providing the incentives and services to help them find and keep employment.[18]

The Family Support Act gave the states considerable flexibility to experiment within the framework of the legislation. State welfare departments, if they conformed to the basic terms of the act, could seek waivers from among the various regulatory requirements of the AFDC program. Many states availed themselves of the opportunity. In a very real sense, experiments in welfare reform became the province of the states.

1996 Welfare Reform: The End of an Entitlement

The provisions of the Family Support Act, allowing requests for waivers, gave states the opportunity for experimentation and shifted substantial policy-making discretion from the federal government to the states. By the act's demise in August 1996, 43 states had secured waivers, creating a vast laboratory of reform and laying the foundation for the even greater state administrative and program discretion to come.[19] Supporters of expanded reform readily pointed to the large reduction of welfare caseloads that seemed to accompany state experimentation. Between January 1993 and January 1997, the average monthly number of persons receiving welfare fell by 20 percent, totaling 2.75 million recipients (see Figure 16.2). A report by the president's Council of Economic Advisors later attributed about one-third of that decrease to state policy changes. The council determined that the largest share, over 40 percent, was the product of economic growth, which created 12 million new jobs over the period.[20] Buoyed by what they saw as the fruits of state experimentation, reformers pressed for giving the states broad flexibility in using federal welfare funds without the necessity of seeking waivers—essentially devolving administrative and program authority to the states. The states, in turn, would be expected to comply with overarching federal requirements.

Republican congressional leaders led the campaign for devolution. Having gained control of both chambers of Congress in the 1994 election, and drawing on the support of Republican governors whose states led the way in welfare reform, Republican leaders successfully ushered in a series of welfare reform bills through Congress. President Clinton vetoed the first two, objecting to the first because it included eliminating Medicaid as an

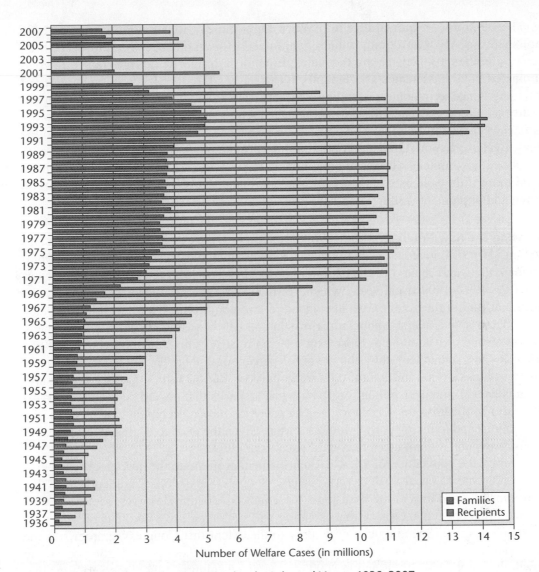

Figure 16.2 Changing Welfare Caseloads: Selected Years, 1936–2007
Source: Administration for Children and Families, U.S. Department of Health and Human Services.

entitlement program, and to the second because it would have forced states to deny cash assistance to children born to welfare recipients and would have reduced benefits to some disabled children who received SSI. But with those provisions removed in the Republican Party's third attempt, and with the 1994 election shortly approaching, President Clinton, who promised as early as the 1992 presidential campaign to end welfare as we know it, finally signed the reform legislation. Clinton called the occasion a historic opportunity to make welfare what it was meant to be: a second chance, not a way of life.[21] It also gave the president an opportunity to get out in front of what opinion polls suggested was a popular preelection legislative initiative.

The **Personal Responsibility and Work Opportunity Reconciliation Act of 1996** abolished the AFDC program, which guaranteed cash assistance to children in low-income families at levels set by the states. In abolishing the AFDC program, Congress eliminated public assistance as a federal entitlement, ending its 61-year-old guarantee of providing whatever amount of funding was necessary to pay benefits to all who met eligibility requirements. The program was replaced with a new program labeled Temporary Assistance to Needy Families (TANF), which provides fixed-amount block grants to the states. Because a sum-certain appropriation finances the block grants, the legislation caps the federal government's financial commitment to public assistance, leaving the states to spend more if they choose. In exchange, the states receive greatly increased flexibility to design and implement welfare programs.

Financing the New Program.   The 1996 legislation provides for block grants to the states totaling $16.4 billion annually, with the aid to be distributed based on states' federal funding for AFDC and related programs in either the 1994 or 1995 fiscal year, or the average of the 1992–1994 fiscal years, whichever is higher. Other provisions of the act make additional funding available to states under certain conditions. The first provision aids states facing above-average population growth and below-average benefits per recipient, and the second provision helps those experiencing relatively high unemployment, defined minimally as a state unemployment rate of 6.5 percent or higher. The act contains separate appropriations of $800 million for the former purpose, and $2 billion for the latter. It also contains an additional $1 billion for performance bonuses that reward states that are most successful in meeting the legislation's goals, such as moving recipients of public assistance to jobs and reducing out-of-wedlock births. Given the need to evaluate performance, the last provision did not take effect until fiscal year 1999.

Overall, the conversion of the AFDC entitlement program to the new block grant program represented a fiscal wash of sorts because Congress set the block grant at a level that approximated spending in the base years used for conversion. However, removing welfare's entitlement status ensures that spending will no longer grow automatically as welfare caseloads rise. Spending can grow only to the extent that Congress appropriates the additional funds to pay for it. Yet this looks to have been a moot point. Strong economic growth during the late 1990s and in 2000 sent caseloads plummeting at the very time that states had been allocated grant amounts based on past spending, which served the needs of higher caseloads. And that decline continued through 2007, even though the U.S. economy fell into recession in 2001. Reduced caseloads meant that states found themselves with more aid per recipient than they had prior to the program's conversion.

Welfare reform not only limited the federal government's financial exposure, it also allowed state officials to reallocate state funds once spent on public assistance to other needs. Under the 1996 legislation, states are no longer required to come up with a financial

---

Personal Responsibility and Work Opportunity Reconciliation Act of 1996   The legislation that abolished the AFDC program, eliminated welfare as a federal entitlement, and substituted the TANF program of block grants to the states.

match to federal funds. The act requires only that they spend at least 75 percent of the funds they spent in fiscal year 1994 on AFDC and related programs. To the extent that states elect to reduce their financial commitments to welfare, any savings can be applied to other pressing state needs. The overhaul legislation for welfare also gives states the flexibility to transfer up to 30 percent of the new federal block grant funds to the already existing child care block grant, and up to 10 percent to the social services block grant, depending on how state policymakers weigh their priorities. By 2000, 33 states spent more on child care than on cash assistance, supplementing existing funds with unused funds reallocated from the TANF program.[22]

Requirements Placed on the States and on Recipients. Federal welfare reform is based on a central premise: states should be in the driver's seat when it comes to designing the specifics of programs that meet the objectives of the reform legislation. The new legislation puts the focus on results, not on means. States must meet requirements to receive federal grants without penalty, but state policymakers have a great deal of freedom to determine how the requirements can best be met. Key requirements center on the states' ability to move welfare recipients into jobs. The act requires states to have at least half their welfare caseload working. For states to be in compliance, single parents must work a minimum of 30 hours per week. The primary wage earner in a two-parent family must work at least 35 hours per week, and both parents must work at least that amount if the family receives federally funded child care. Adults receiving welfare benefits must begin working within two years of receiving aid. States can exempt parents who have a child under 1 year of age from this requirement, but the act limits this exemption to a total of 12 months cumulatively.

Although the reform legislation places work requirements on the states, the use of the term *work*, compared to its traditional usage, is a bit of a misnomer. States can satisfy the work requirements of the law by placing recipients in educational, training, and work experience programs. Actual work can include both subsidized and unsubsidized private-sector and public-sector employment, on-the-job training, and community service. States face having their block grant reduced by 5 percent in the first year they fail to meet the law's work requirements. Escalating penalties can increase the reduction to 21 percent of the block grant's value by the fourth year of noncompliance.

Along with the states, recipients themselves face penalties for not meeting the law's work requirements. Individual recipients who fail to meet the work requirements placed on them face grant reductions commensurate with the amount of work or equivalent activity missed. For example, a recipient who is absent from work or the equivalent 50 percent of the time in a given period receives a 50 percent reduction in aid for that period. The law gives states the right to terminate the benefits of adults who refuse to work at all, although states cannot rescind Medicaid coverage for their children. It also requires states to reduce recipients' benefits by at least 25 percent if they fail to cooperate with authorities in establishing the paternity of dependent children covered under the act. States can choose to withdraw their benefits altogether. Finally, the law requires unmarried parents under the age of 18 to attend school or a training program and to live with a parent or legal guardian in order to qualify for federal block grant funding.

Restrictions on the Duration of Benefits.   The law also limits the time that recipients can receive benefits financed by federal funds. States are prohibited from using block grant funds to assist recipients who have received welfare for more than five years. Previously, no such limit existed in federal law; however, nearly half the states had already imposed time limits through the waiver route.[23] The new legislation provides some flexibility in applying time limits to individual recipients, giving state administrators the prerogative to exempt up to 20 percent of their caseload from the time limit. It also allows states to impose a shorter time limit. About half of the states impose the five-year federal time limit.

For the congressional architects of the law, the time limit feature lies at the heart of welfare reform. As the new program's title suggests, they view welfare as temporary assistance, available to assist people through periods of need on their way to employment. They see the work requirements, discussed earlier, as the tools necessary to speed up that transition.

The Debate over Reauthorization.   The original authorizations included in the Personal Responsibility and Work Opportunity Reconciliation Act expired on September 30, 2002, but Congress has extended them. President Bush supported reauthorization legislation that would continue the program through 2007, but at the 2002 funding level. He also proposed strengthening the act's work requirements by mandating that 70 percent of families receiving welfare must work 40 hours per week. Training could count toward the requirement, up to 24 hours per week, for no more than three months in a two-year period.

President Bush's recommendations drew strong reactions from welfare advocates, who argued that the administration's proposal called for a return to Reagan's workfare. Many state officials saw the proposal as tying their hands, giving them less latitude to offer recipients programs that upgraded their job skills and improved their employability.

After approving a series of continuing resolutions to fund the program, the Republican majority was able to secure sufficient support to include reauthorization within the Deficit Reduction Act of 2005, which President George W. Bush signed into law on February 6, 2006. The legislation reauthorized the TANF program through 2010 but capped the basic block grant at $16 billion, a ceiling demanded by Republican negotiators. The reauthorization also increased the work participation rate required of states, progressively increasing it from 50 percent in 2006 to 70 percent in 2010, meaning that 70 percent of TANF recipients would have to be working or participating in work preparation programs by 2010, which ultimately gave the Bush administration what it wanted. Congress did not work on legislation to reauthorize the program in 2010; rather, it extended the TANF block.

Questions about the Future.   The most central question about the future is, How will families with dependent children fare without their entitlement to benefits? Funding can run out with discretionary spending programs. Eligible recipients can go without benefits if funds are lacking to meet their collective needs. This will not be a problem as long as recipients consistently move from welfare to work in numbers that allow available welfare funds to cover the benefit costs of those still reliant on public assistance. A strong, growing economy can provide the jobs to make that happen. Yet there will always be some individuals who will have great difficulty finding employment, even in the best of economic times. What will happen to them? Perhaps the only realistic option they will have, if they wish to receive public aid, is to satisfy the new law's work requirement by performing various forms of community service. Others will get discouraged and no longer seek public support. Still others, faced with the requirement to work, will elect not to apply in the first place. Despite this dilemma, supporters of reform have hoped that a combination of incentives to work and a growing economy will move an increasing number of Americans from economic dependence to independence. But the strengthening recession that gripped the economy toward the end of the decade dashed that optimism.

It is difficult nonetheless to assess what is happening to those who leave the welfare rolls. One thing is clear: caseloads have fallen dramatically, from a monthly average peak of 5,046,263 families on welfare in 1994 to 1,669,076 in 2007—a dramatic two-thirds reduction. Figure 16.3 shows the drop, by state, from 1993 to 2000, the period of sharpest decline in the rolls. What is less clear is the extent to which welfare recipients have found their way into the jobs created by economic growth. They have come off welfare caseloads in surprising numbers; beyond that fact, we know little more.[24]

Few studies address whether recipients are better off after leaving TANF than while on TANF, and a recent Urban Institute staff report notes that the limited research shows "at most modest average gains in income for those leaving welfare." It goes on to show that "individual families that leave welfare and remain off for a year experience growth in income."[25] Without doubt, however, the Great Recession that began in 2007 complicated life for many of those living on the edges of poverty and will impact assessments of welfare reform.

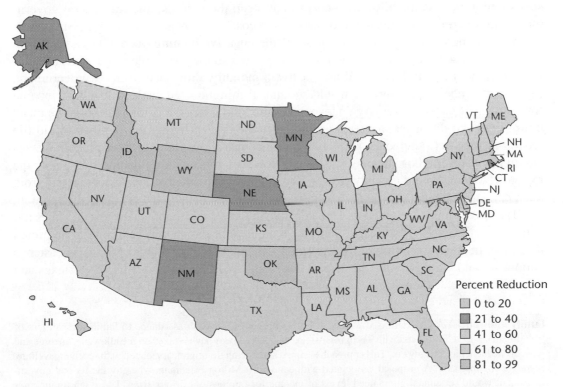

Figure 16.3 Drop in Welfare Rolls, by State, 1993–2000
Source: U.S. Department of Health and Human Services, Administration for Children and Families.

Other Options for Reform

Other options for reform depart dramatically from the present system of welfare in the United States. None has received serious consideration in this country, and the passage of the Personal Responsibility and Work Opportunity Reconciliation Act of 1996 renders the prospect of future consideration unlikely.

The first option is the so-called **family allowance**. With this approach, used widely in western European nations, all families are given a monthly benefit check from the government. It is generally employed in conjunction with a steep progressive income tax. The poor pay no tax on the allowance income, whereas the affluent pay a heavy tax. But every family of comparable size receives the same level of benefit regardless of income. Thus, the stigma associated with welfare is removed. The allowance level is set at a bare minimum level of support, encouraging families to find other income supplements. The family allowance system therefore carries with it little disincentive for the unemployed poor to seek work.

If adopted in the United States, such a system would probably be fully federalized, with the federal government picking up the costs and using the Internal Revenue Service to administer the program. The allowance amounts could be the same for comparably sized families across the nation, or the allowance could be tied to cost-of-living differences among the states or even within states. Another approach would find the federal government and the states sharing both the costs and administration of a family allowance program. The states could process the allowance checks and keep the records, and the federal government, through reimbursement, could share in the costs of allowances and administration.

The second option, commonly known as the **negative income tax** and associated with conservative economist Milton Friedman, works on a similar principle of guaranteed minimum income, but families would not receive a monthly allowance from the government. Instead, the federal government would set annual minimum guaranteed levels of income for families of various sizes. Again, as with family allowances, the amounts could be made uniform among the states or varied according to the cost of living. All families would file federal income tax statements, and those with incomes above the guaranteed income levels would pay taxes on those amounts, as usual. However, those whose incomes fell below the recognized floors would not only pay no tax at all but would receive a check in the mail from the federal government at an amount necessary to bring them up to the guaranteed minimum.

The underlying concept behind the negative income tax is that those whose incomes fall below the guarantees would have unused exemptions or deductions available to be turned into cash. In comparison to family allowances, the negative income tax would be easier to administer and would involve far less money than would have to be collected as taxes and then disbursed as expenditures.

---

family allowance A program used widely in Europe that provides cash assistance to families regardless of financial need. Employed with a progressive tax system, the poor pay no taxes on the allowance income and the affluent pay a heavy tax. This approach is aimed at reducing the stigma associated with receiving welfare.

negative income tax A proposal, associated with economist Milton Friedman, whereby the federal government would set annual guaranteed levels of income for families of various sizes. Those whose incomes fell below the guaranteed levels would receive a check from the federal government for the difference.

Exploring the Web

Promoting Social Welfare

Whose responsibility is it to help improve the social welfare of low-income families across the United States, and how best should that be done? What role should government play, and what is the respective responsibility of the federal government, the states, and local governments? To get different perspectives on these issues, explore the following websites:

■ The homepages of two organizations suggest that government should play less of a role as a distributor of welfare checks, and more of a role as an agent that transforms dependence on public assistance into gainful employment. Both the Manhattan Institute (*www.manhattan-institute.org*) and the American Enterprise Institute (*www.aei.org*) see the roots of improved social well-being as grounded in individual responsibility and economic choice. For them, government has a role to play, but it is to pursue public policies that nurture these values while aiding individuals in making the transition from dependence to independence, and providing more sustained assistance to those whose situations render that transition extremely difficult. In addition, both organizations show a preference for greater state leadership in welfare policy and a decreasing federal role. Find out more about their policy positions and related research.

■ A number of organizations act as advocates for public assistance recipients. The Welfare Rights Organizing Coalition (*www.wroc.org*) brings together welfare recipients to protect their rights to public assistance and fair treatment through activism, including lobbying of state legislators and welfare officials. Similarly, Families USA on Medicaid (*http://familiesusa.org/issues/medicaid*) joins forces with Medicaid recipients and their advocates to influence the direction of Medicaid policy and its administration. Check out their websites and learn about their public information campaigns.

■ To get the perspective of top officials who administer state public assistance programs, go to *www.aphsa.org*, the homepage of the American Public Human Services Association. There you will find information on policy development and analysis, along with electronic access to several publications, including *Policy & Practice* and *This Week in Washington*.

■ Go to the National Association of Social Workers website (*www.naswdc.org*) to see how social workers, who deliver many of the services that welfare recipients receive, look at public assistance policy and welfare reform. Examine how they view their professional interests to be at stake.

Beyond getting money into needy people's pockets, both options are viewed by their proponents as agents for dismantling the present welfare system and its "social welfare–poverty complex." In their view, the government welfare bureaucracy has become an unnecessary appendage, and either of these proposals would greatly decimate both the government bureaucracy and the vast network of social service suppliers. Under a guaranteed income program, the poor would spend their money, including decisions about what social services they might want to purchase. Social workers would have no role to play in those essentially private decisions.

Although a dismantling of the contemporary welfare system is attractive to political conservatives, some conservatives oppose the idea of a guaranteed minimum income, seeing it as a violation of the self-help principle. To put it baldly, the commonly voiced objection is that people would be paid to do nothing to improve their less-than-desirable lifestyles. Others take the position that, although some beneficiaries will rely only on their minimum income, the vast majority will pursue additional earned income, as long as tax rates do not remove such a natural inclination to do so. This school of thought is premised on the belief that people want to work—to get ahead—and will seek to rise above that very minimum standard of living for their family's benefit.

This variety of welfare reform received serious consideration in response to a proposal offered by the Nixon administration in 1969. It was defeated in the Senate by a coalition of liberals and conservatives. Liberal senators argued that the benefits were too low, and the conservatives objected ideologically to the concept of a guaranteed family income, viewing it as too radical a departure from America's traditional work ethic. Although the concept of minimum income support for all Americans still gets some attention in the public debate over welfare reform, it is not likely to receive serious consideration in the modern political environment.

HEALTH POLICY

Americans spent almost $2.5 trillion on health care in 2009, an average of about $8,099 per person, constituting a 9.7-fold increase over what was spent in 1980.[26] Not only are we, as individuals, paying more for health care, but so are our employers and the government. According to the latest estimates,[27] health care expenditures from all sources rose from about 9.2 percent of the U.S. gross national product (GNP) in 1980 to 17.6 percent of the GNP by 2009, the highest in the world.[28]

Most Americans rely on health insurance provided by their employers to meet the rising costs of medical care. About two-thirds of those under age 65 benefit from health care provided by their employer. Retirees on Social Security draw on federal Medicare insurance benefits. Military veterans with service-related disabilities can receive medical care at hospitals operated by the federal Veterans' Administration. Low-income individuals are eligible for the federal–state Medicaid program. Another program, the State Children's Health Insurance Program (SCHIP), finances health insurance coverage for children in families with modest income who lack health insurance but earn too much to qualify for Medicaid. Still, about 47 million people have no health insurance and are ineligible for any of these programs. Those lacking insurance either have to pay the bills out of their own financial resources or receive medical attention from hospitals or clinics designated to provide charity care—usually crowded and underfunded county hospitals or public health clinics.

Within this mix, the vast majority of Americans of all ages pay relatively little out of their own financial resources for the medial care they receive. In comparison, the federal government pays 33 percent, state and local governments pay 13 percent, and private insurance pays the remainder.[29] The reality of health care financing in America is that third parties—employers, insurance carriers, or the government—disproportionately pay for the health care that we use. It is true that health care benefits provided by employers have a monetary value and entail some trade-off with salary and wage compensation, but that trade-off has not been all that obvious. Most working Americans take their fringe benefits for granted, largely measuring their financial fortunes by changes in their income.

This chapter's primary interest in health care policy focuses on government, particularly state government, as a third-party payer. Government's financial obligation has risen greatly during the past several decades and is projected to grow three times as fast as general inflation. Medicaid consumed only 4 percent of state spending in 1970. In 1985, Medicaid took 10 percent of state general-fund expenditures; by 2010, its share had more than doubled to 22 percent.[30] Because of its sizable and growing claim on public resources, Medicaid receives significant attention in this chapter, but it will be examined in the context of America's broader health care system.

Public Health Care in America

Health care in the United States is still largely in the private domain. Outside the United States, government involvement in health care usually takes one of two forms. In the first, government itself operates a national health service. Hospitals are run by the national government, and health care providers, including physicians and nurses, are public employees. Countries in this category include Great Britain, Israel, and New Zealand. In the second form, the government mandates universal insurance coverage by employers, and government policies are available to cover the costs of care for the unemployed or retired. Health care providers remain in the private sector, and most hospitals are either owned by the government or are nonprofit. Government sets the costs of hospitalization and provider fees, and may place limits on drug prices. Countries following this approach include Canada, Germany, and Japan. In the United States, government subsidies for health care are available only to the poor, the elderly, or the disabled, in addition to care provided to certain military veterans at federal hospitals around the country. The two major health care programs administered by the government in the United States are Medicare, a strictly federal program, and Medicaid, a joint federal–state program.

Medicare. Medicare is not a health care program for the poor. Instead, it is a federally administered social insurance program, as is Social Security, financed by contributions from employers and employees alike, along with some general federal revenues. Medicare provides benefits only to those who have qualified for Social Security or Railroad Retirement benefits by working for a certain period and making minimally required contributions into the fund. Others who have reached age 65 but do not qualify can get hospitalization coverage but must pay a high monthly premium for federal insurance.

The Social Security Amendments of 1965, part of President Lyndon Johnson's Great Society initiatives, established two related contributory health insurance plans: a basic compulsory program of hospital insurance (HI), frequently referred to as Part A, and a voluntary program of supplementary medical insurance (SMI), commonly labeled as Part B. The hospital insurance program covers in-patient care after beneficiaries meet a prescribed deductible. The program also covers short-term nursing care as well as home health services and hospice care for the terminally ill. Medicare Part A is financed by a 1.45 percent federal payroll tax. The SMI program helps individuals pay doctors' bills and pay for out-patient diagnostic tests, physical therapy, and prosthetic devices prescribed by physicians. It covers 80 percent of the costs after recipients meet a $100 deductible. Medicare Part B is financed by patient contributions and general federal revenues. General tax revenues support approximately three-fourths of the program's costs.

Although Medicare greatly limits the costs that the elderly or disabled would otherwise have to pay for hospitalization and medical services, its medical insurance protection is far from free, as the previous discussion illustrates. Then again, Medicare was not designed as a program for the needy; it was developed as an insurance program for all working Americans. In adding deductibles and copayments, Congress has operated on the assumption that the vast majority of Americans have the financial resources to pay the added charges.

Over 46 million Americans were covered by Medicare in 2009. Of that total, 38.5 million were retired, meeting age requirements, and 8.1 million qualified as disabled.[31]

Medicaid.   **Medicaid** was enacted along with Medicare in 1965. Unlike Medicare, Medicaid is limited to low-income citizens. Medicaid is jointly administered and financed by the federal government and the states. Although state participation is optional, all states participate. In 21 states, however, only TANF and SSI recipients are eligible for Medicaid. The remaining states open the program to other low-income individuals in need of medical services. To participate in the latter category, individuals, by federal law, cannot have income in excess of one-third above the TANF cash payment for a similar size family, with only marginal exceptions made for those with low income and extraordinary high medical bills.

The Medicaid program complements the Medicare program. Medicaid can be used to pay the premiums for SMI (Part B) and the deductible and coinsurance costs for poor Social Security recipients who lack the means to pay the required patient contribution or deductible.

Over 58 million people received Medicaid benefits as of December 31, 2008.[32] The federal government pays the majority of the costs of benefits and administration, about 57 percent. The states pay the other 43 percent, averaging about 20 percent of state budgets. Based on their per capita income, individual states receive federal financial aid that ranges between 50 and 83 percent of their actual program expenditures.

To receive federal funds, states must provide the following basic medical services to patients: physicians' and nurses' services; in-patient and out-patient hospital services; laboratory and x-ray services; skilled nursing care; home health services; and screening, diagnostic, and treatment services for children. In addition to these mandatory services, the states, at their option, may provide other services or devices and still receive federal reimbursement for the costs. Such services or devices might include chiropractic care, dental care, eyeglasses, hearing aids, and prescription medicines.

Some states provide almost all 32 services or devices permitted by federal law, whereas others provide only a few beyond the required core. Given this state discretion, Medicaid recipients are at a comparative advantage or disadvantage, depending on where they live.

Medicaid   A joint federal–state program that provides health care to the needy.

Although TANF families constitute two-thirds of Medicaid beneficiaries, their medical bills account for only about one-fifth of all Medicaid benefits paid. SSI recipients make up about one-third of Medicaid recipients but represent nearly two-thirds of Medicaid costs, and their share of costs has been growing the fastest of all, with the rising costs of long-term care (such as that provided in nursing homes) leading the way. The remaining claims come from the non-TANF medically needy in states that have elected to extend Medicaid benefits to them.

Many states have also requested waivers from federal regulations governing the Medicaid program. Waiver requests approved by the federal Department of Health and Human Services (DHHS) have taken different forms. One approach has been to expand eligibility to include more families considered to be part of the working poor while, at the same time, reducing the services available to recipients under the traditional program or requiring them to pay more out of their own pockets for care. To make ends meet fiscally, a number of states have offered slimmed-down programs to the new pool of eligible recipients—an initiative that would not be possible without the states securing so-called Section 1115 waivers.

Utah is a notable example: it was the first state to reduce benefits and increase cost sharing for existing Medicaid recipients. Utah secured its waiver in 2002 while Mike Leavitt was governor, before President Bush appointed him secretary of the DHHS. Under the waiver, Utah extended health care services to workers with incomes below 150 percent of the official poverty line, but who were not eligible under the traditional Medicaid program. However, benefits under the expanded program are restricted to primary care. Coverage does not include hospitalization, specialty care, or mental health services.

As a trade-off, the Utah waiver reduces eligible services to recipients under the traditional Medicaid program, including the loss of non-emergency transportation and most dental services, together with restrictions placed on mental health care, vision care, physical and occupational therapy, and prescription drugs. The waiver also requires participants within the expanded program, aptly named Primary Care Network (PCN), to pay a modest annual enrollment fee, small copayments for services, and up to 10 percent coinsurance for some services.[33]

Wisconsin provides another salient example, but with a twist. It successfully attained its waiver under the leadership of Governor Tommy Thompson, who preceded Leavitt as secretary of DHSS. Under its waiver, Wisconsin expanded eligibility for Medicaid to include workers with incomes up to 185 percent of the federal poverty level. Once eligible, recipients under BadgerCare, as the new program was labeled, could increase their income to 200 percent of the poverty line and continue to be eligible for services. Like Utah, the Wisconsin waiver requires the new recipients to defray the costs of services they receive, requiring them to pay a percentage of their income as a monthly premium (currently set at up to 3.5 percent). Unlike Utah, however, beneficiaries of Wisconsin's expanded program are eligible for the same benefits as are enrollees in the traditional program.[34]

State Children's Health Insurance Program.   Congress approved legislation creating the State Children's Health Insurance Program (SCHIP) in August 1997, as part of the omnibus Balanced Budget Act of 1997. The program provides federal matching funds to help states extend health insurance coverage to children living in families whose income exceeds levels that would make them eligible for Medicaid. In 2007, SCHIP added nearly 7 million recipients to the ranks of the insured. Like Medicaid, the program represents a federal–state partnership, with the federal government covering most of the costs and the states administering program operations. States have the option of offering SCHIP benefits within an expanded Medicaid program, or they can operate a separate SCHIP program. Under either option, the federal government contributes a 30 percent higher part of the funding for SCHIP than for Medicaid, up to a maximum federal share of 85 percent.

As discussed in Chapter 3, the program had been steeped in controversy. In 2007, President George W. Bush vetoed two congressional attempts to more than double federal funding for the program, from $5 billion to up to $12 billion annually, and to further enlarge the pool of eligible recipients.

The Centers for Medicare and Medicaid Services (CMS), the federal agency that oversees SCHIP, then issued a directive to state program heads mandating that, before states can cover children in families earning more than 250 percent above the poverty line, they must ensure that the program enrolls at least 95 percent of uninsured children living in families with incomes below 200 percent of the poverty line. As a rationale for the regulatory tightening, the Bush administration argued that the program must adhere to the intent of the authorizing legislation: the program must limit extended insurance coverage to those who can least afford health insurance.[35]

In response, the states of New Jersey, New York, Maryland, Illinois, and Washington sued the CMS, arguing that its directive exceeded the agency's authority under the law. To complicate matters, the federal Government Accountability Office (GAO) issued a report in April 2008, finding that the federal agency exceeded its authority under the SCHIP legislation in restricting state discretion to set eligibility and allocate the program's funding accordingly. After initially threatening to withhold federal funding from states not complying with the regulations, the CMS, in light of the GAO's report, agreed not to impose sanctions on noncomplying states, at least in the near term. In 2009, Congress passed and President Obama signed legislation reauthorizing the program through 2013 and increasing coverage to include 4 million more children.

Measures to Contain Rising Health Care Costs

Recent attempts to contain the rapid growth of health care costs have tried to modify the incentives that have prompted both patients and providers to behave in ways that accelerate the costs of health care. This country's reliance on third-party payers has removed much of the incentives for health care users to conserve on the medical care they use. When all or a sizable majority of costs are covered by the government or by insurance provided by employers, patients tend to err on the side of having their medical needs met, as they see them. They may believe that they are just getting what they have a right to receive. Requirements for deductibles and copayments in Medicare and in many private medical insurance plans provide some disincentive to seek unnecessary or marginally needed medical services; if they are capped, however, such requirements can actually promote usage. Once a deductible is paid, patients may feel free to get as much done as they can, in a sense to recoup their upfront investment. Similarly, when copayments are no longer required after an insured party exceeds an out-of-pocket limit for a given year, that party has a financial incentive to get other ailments tended to before the next year begins and the deductible or copayment provisions for that year apply anew.

Health care providers may have little incentive to restrain costs. If hospitals and physicians are reimbursed for the services they render, they improve their financial positions by performing more services. This does not mean that providers will order unnecessary procedures and tests, although some evidence suggests that this has been a problem. Instead, providers are more likely to tip the balance toward doing diagnostic tests and suggesting services than they might be if they were compensated on a different basis. Under a third-party payer/fee-for-service system, both the providers' and patients' incentives are mutually reinforcing. Patients value comprehensive, responsive medical services, and providers have an economic incentive to meet patient needs.

Congress passed legislation in the 1980s aimed at changing the incentives of health care providers who participate in the Medicaid and Medicare programs. It was directed at both hospitals and physicians.

Prospective Hospital Reimbursement.   To address the fastest growing component of health care costs—hospital charges—in 1981, at the Reagan administration's behest, Congress created a prospective payment system for the hospitalization of Medicare patients. Using a reimbursement approach called **diagnostic-related groups (DRGs)**, the federal government began reimbursing hospitals on a fixed scale for treating each of 467 specified ailments, instead of the customary costs of each separate service provided, as was the previous practice. With DRGs, payments are predetermined based on the patient's illness, age, sex, and medical history, as well as the physician's diagnosis and procedures required to treat the malady. Many states follow the federal government's lead and reimburse hospitals in a similar way for care given to Medicaid patients. Selective contracting allows state Medicaid offices to negotiate DRG-like reimbursement rates with hospitals, adding an element of competition.

With this change, hospitals have a financial incentive to reduce lengths of stays and to cut back on marginal services, lowering costs in relation to predetermined revenues. It is in the hospital's interest to keep the actual costs of services below the prepayment level. Conversely, if the actual costs of services should exceed the DRG payment, the hospital loses. This might lead hospitals to look for possible hedges against revenue shortfalls. One study of prospective hospital reimbursement found that the introduction of DRGs tended to be followed by a rise in the severity of diagnosis, with its attendant increase of reimbursement rate.[36]

Managed Health Care: HMOs.   As part of the same legislation that authorized prospective hospital reimbursement for Medicare patients, Congress also authorized the federal DHHS to contract with **health maintenance organizations (HMOs)** to serve Medicaid patients.

---

diagnostic-related groups (DRGs) A tool of health care cost control that provides reimbursement to hospitals on a fixed scale for treating certain medical conditions instead of on the traditional basis of reimbursing for customary costs.

health maintenance organizations (HMOs) A tool of health care cost control that uses primary care physicians working within a group practice to manage the health care of enrollees, for which payers—typically government or insurance carriers—pay a set monthly or annual fee.

States soon negotiated reimbursement rates with HMOs to care for Medicaid patients. With HMOs, physicians—both primary care doctors and specialists—form a prepaid group practice. Subscribers pay a monthly or annual fee for medical care, and all services, including hospitalization, are covered by that fee. Primary care physicians (in family medicine, internal medicine, and pediatrics) manage patients' health care, deciding when to offer treatment themselves and when to refer patients to specialists within the HMO. Patients normally must use the HMO's doctors, but some plans allow them to see other physicians for a supplementary fee.

The growth in HMOs serving Medicaid recipients has been astounding. In 1991, HMOs enrolled 2.7 million Medicaid recipients. By 2004, the number had risen to 27 million. By that year, 60 percent of Medicaid recipients received health care services through HMOs.[37]

HMOs are required to provide all the mandatory out-patient services covered in the conventional fee-for-service system, and they can offer supplemental services and benefits to attract patients. But for them to do so, they must control the costs of the basic services they provide. That need to keep costs down has led some HMOs to shy away from enrolling Medicaid patients because Medicaid beneficiaries, especially SSI recipients, tend to need more medical care than does the population at large.[38]

Advocates of HMOs argue that they foster greater preventive health care and more continuity of care. Critics counter that, because HMOs are operated for profit, financial incentives exist for affiliated physicians to underserve patients. The evidence that service and quality have, indeed, taken a backseat to economy is mixed. The evidence is clearer, however, that managed care resulted in significant savings in the 1990s compared with standard fee-for-service care.[39]

Despite the introduction of DRGs and HMOs, Medicare and especially Medicaid costs have continued to rise well in excess of the general rate of inflation. Although we do not know how much higher they might have gone without these innovations, most observers see a need for further action to contain the costs of these public programs.

Mandating Improved Corporate Spending on Employee Health Insurance: "The Wal-Mart Legislation." In January 2006, Maryland became the first state to require very large private employers, those with 10,000 or more workers in the state, to expand and improve health insurance coverage for their employees. The legislation required them to devote an amount equal to at least 8 percent of payroll to employee health insurance benefits. Wal-Mart was the only employer at the time with such a large work force in the state.

Maryland's legislature was one of thirty-three that considered similar fair-share legislation. Supporters of such legislation argued that big employers like Wal-Mart, which pay low wages and offer limited or no health insurance benefits to many of their employees, are offloading their cost savings to state and federal taxpayers because the income of many Wal-Mart employees is low enough for them to qualify for Medicaid.[40] The road to legislative enactment in Maryland was not smooth. Governor Robert Ehrlich Jr. vetoed the legislation, and the state legislature subsequently overrode his veto. No other state legislature passed fair-share legislation in 2006.

Wal-Mart joined forces with the Retail Industry Leaders Association (RILA), of which it is a member, in challenging the Maryland legislation. On July 19, 2006, a federal judge of the U.S. district court in Baltimore ruled that the Maryland law violated the federal Employment Retirement Income Security Law (ERISA), which bars state preemption of federal employer benefits provisions.[41] It is unclear whether Maryland will appeal the ruling. Because Maryland's governor vetoed the original legislation, however, it appears unlikely that he would pursue an appeal short of legislative direction.

The general concern about the practices of Wal-Mart and similar businesses getting government subsidies, in essence, through their low wages and limited health benefits has prompted governors and legislators in other states to experiment with the Maryland approach. Cities, too, have taken action. In July 2006, the Chicago city council voted to require so-called big-box stores to pay, by 2010, a minimum wage of $10 per hour and at least $3 an hour in benefits. Although the vote was 35 to 14, the debate was intense. The conundrum is to balance the low prices to customers, the jobs provided by the big discount stores, the low levels of compensation to employees, the government programs for which employees are eligible, and what some regard as the high profit margins of these stores.

Rationing Medical Care: The Case of Oregon

In August 1993, the federal DHHS approved Oregon's request for a waiver from the federal regulations governing the Medicaid program. Oregon requested the waiver following passage of state legislation that approved sweeping changes in its state Medicaid program. That legislation authorized two major departures from existing Medicaid policy. First, it broadened eligibility requirements to include everyone below the poverty line, including single men and childless couples. Second, and most controversial, it identified a number of medical services that would no longer be covered under the Oregon Medicaid program. The Oregon legislature created a trade-off: more needy people would have access to publicly supported health care, particularly preventive care; however, the state would prioritize services, funding only some of the existing services but not others. One observer sums up the Oregon message in this way:

> What Oregon is saying is that it is working in a world of finite resources. It can no longer pay for all the medical procedures that science has to offer. A line has to be drawn somewhere.[42]

Policymakers in Oregon turned to the recommendations of a statewide committee of doctors, businesspeople, labor leaders, consumers, and social services representatives. Committee members held 47 town meetings around the state, followed by a sampling of 1,000 residents drawn at random. As a result of this public input and months of analysis and deliberations, the committee produced a report that prioritized 709 medical conditions, rating them on their seriousness, the costs of treating them, and the likely benefits of that treatment. Given available resources and the state's desire to broaden recipient eligibility, the committee drew the line at rank 587. Thus, if the legislature approved their recommendations, the state would no longer provide Medicaid funding to pay for medical services and procedures for conditions ranked 588 through 709, essentially rationing care. Table 16.1 shows selective examples of ailments covered and those no longer covered.

The uncovered items can be grouped into several categories: those conditions that usually heal slowly on their own, such as viral sore throats and colds; conditions that respond to home treatment, such as diaper rash and athlete's foot; and treatments that are widely judged

Table 16.1 Oregon Health Plan: Examples of Services Covered and Not Covered

Medical Services Covered

Primary and Preventive Services

Routine physical exams
Preventive dental care
Well-child exams
Immunizations
Maternity care
Newborn care
Comfort care (for terminal illness)
Medical exams to determine diagnosis

Treatment for Medical Conditions Ranked 1–587

Appendicitis
Asthma
AZT and treatment for opportunistic infections associated with HIV
Broken bones
Diabetes
Ear infection
Epilepsy
Glaucoma
Heart bypass
Kidney stone
Pneumonia
Severe/moderate head injury
Severe recurrent depression
Spinal deformities
Treatable cancers
Ulcers

Medical Services Not Covered (Ranked 588–709)

Conditions That Improve on Their Own

Common cold
Measles
Noninfectious diarrhea
Tendinitis
Viral hepatitis
Viral sore throat
Conditions for Which a Home Remedy Is Effective
Allergic rhinitis
Canker sores
Food poisoning
Nonfungal diaper rash
Sprains
Sties

Conditions for Which Treatment Is Not Generally Effective or Is Futile

Chronic sinusitis
Extremely low birth weight (under 1.1 pounds)
Surgery for soft-tissue low-back pain
Aggressive medical treatment for end-stage AIDS
Aggressive medical treatment for widely spread cancers
Numerous cysts on the lungs of a newborn

Source: The Oregon Health Plan: Integrated List of Health Services (Salem: Oregon Department of Human Resources, 1993).

to be either largely ineffective or not cost effective, such as treatment for severe brain injury, care for very premature babies, and treatment for advanced cases of AIDS and certain terminal cancers.[43] However, comfort care in these cases will continue to be funded.

THE NATIONAL DEBATE OVER HEALTH CARE REFORM

President Clinton put health care reform at the top of his national policy agenda and broadened the debate well beyond controlling the costs of public medical assistance programs. Although cost containment remains an important element of reform, in the fall of 1993 the Clinton administration pushed for a reform that provides access to health care for all Americans, regardless of their employment status, ability to pay, or previous medical history. Reform for Clinton had to address the irony that, despite the fact that the United States spends more per capita on health care than any other nation in the world, about 14 percent of all Americans lack health insurance and are ineligible for government-supported medical services. Moreover, those who presently have health insurance may be unable to keep it—for example, because they lose their jobs or find their rates greatly increased due to a significant change in their health status. At the same time, they may not be eligible for any program or government-assisted health care. Comprehensive health care reform aims to fill in these cracks through which people figuratively fall.

President Clinton put the problem this way:

> Millions of Americans are just a pink slip away from losing their health insurance and one serious illness away from losing all their savings. Millions more are locked into jobs they have now just because they or someone in their family has once been sick and they have what is called a pre-existing condition. And on any given day, over 37 million [in 1993, but 43 million by 2002] Americans, most of them working people and their little children, have no health insurance at all. And in spite of all this, our medical bills are growing at over twice the rate of inflation, and the United States spends over a third more of its income on health care than any other nation on Earth and the gap is growing, causing many of our companies in global competition severe disadvantage.[44]

President Clinton wanted national health care reform to be based on six principles:

1. Security. Everyone should have health insurance with adequate coverage and be able to keep it, even if they develop serious illness, change jobs, become self-employed, or join the ranks of the unemployed.

2. Simplicity. Bureaucratic mandates and accompanying paperwork required by both government and private insurers must be reduced, freeing physicians and other providers to devote more of their time to patient care and less to filling out forms.

3. Savings. Any reform plans must reduce the amount that government and the private sector spend on health care. Even if cost is held to the present 14 percent claim on personal income, the United States will remain well out in front of other industrial nations in the resources it devotes to health care. The implications of an enlarging share are clear. If health care expenditures are not contained in the public sector, they will continue to consume a rising share of federal, state, and local budgets, squeezing out competing public purposes. For the private sector, rising health care costs mean higher fringe benefit expenses and a likely combination of lower profit margins or increased costs passed on to the consumer.

4. Choice. Not only should Americans have a choice of physicians within a given health care plan, they should also be able to choose among competing plans. Doctors, too, should be able to choose the plans in which they practice.

5. Quality. Any reform must at least maintain, if not improve, the quality of medical care. Quality cannot be sacrificed for more efficient delivery of health care services.

6. Responsibility. Both users and providers must do their part to solve the current problems with health care in the United States. Responsibility entails changing behavior that consumes and provides unnecessary medical services and drives up costs.

President Clinton wanted any plan approved by Congress to meet these six criteria. The debate over whether they will or not was—and will continue to be—intense. The most divisive issues will remain those touching on the appropriate role of government in health care regulation. Who determines the appropriateness of treatment and care, the degree of choice individuals can exercise in selecting health care plans and physicians, and the cost of health insurance, and who should pay for it? Central to the debate on financing will be the relative obligation of employers to pay the costs of insurance for their employees.

President George W. Bush championed **health savings accounts** as a way to control rising health care costs. At Bush's urging, Congress passed legislation in December 2003 authorizing individuals to establish tax-advantageous health savings accounts. To participate, individuals must first be covered by a high-deductible insurance policy to protect them from catastrophic medical costs. To cover the costs of more routine care, resources can be drawn from health savings accounts, to which the law allows annual contributions of up to $5,250 for individuals and up to $10,500 for families. As an incentive to set aside funds, the law makes contributions tax-deductible, and it exempts earnings from the federal income tax. Moreover, distributions themselves are exempt from federal taxation as long as they are used to cover approved medical expenditures.

The legislation rests on the theory that people will be more discriminating in spending their own money on health care. The funds in the account stay with their owners unless they are spent, and the funds can be rolled over from year to year.

On the state front, Governor Mitt Romney led a successful bipartisan campaign to pass legislation requiring all Massachusetts residents to have health insurance coverage by July 1, 2007. Signed into law on April 12, 2006, the gubernatorial initiative overwhelmingly passed the legislature, by votes of 154–2 in the Massachusetts House of Representatives, and 37–0 in the Massachusetts Senate. Under the legislation, those lowest-income earners eligible for Medicaid would continue to participate in the Medicaid program. Individuals earning less than 300 percent of the federal poverty level, whose employers do not provide them with health insurance, would get state financial help, based on a sliding scale, with paying the cost of premiums. Individuals with income totaling or exceeding 300 percent of

---

health savings accounts Tax-advantageous accounts into which individuals and families can deposit funds to finance the costs of health care. Contributions are tax-deductible, and earnings are tax-exempt. Distributions are also exempt from taxation as long as they are used to pay for approved health care costs.

the federal poverty level would be responsible for acquiring their own insurance coverage if it is not provided by their employer. Supporters of this legislative approach expect, however, that increased competition to provide coverage will drive down the cost of premiums.

The legislation also assesses a per-employee fee on employers of 11 or more employees who fail to provide their workers with health insurance. This requirement not only generates revenue to support state subsidies to low-income participants, it also creates an incentive for employers to offer their workers health insurance as a fringe benefit. Although Romney used his line-item veto to eliminate the fee on employers, both legislative chambers overrode the veto.[45]

Health care reform figured prominently in the 2008 presidential election and became a high priority for Obama after taking office in January 2009. President Obama laid out basic principles to guide the debate on national health care reform; prominent among these principles are the following:

> Reduce the long-term growth of health care costs.
> Guarantee choice of doctors and health plans.
> Invest in prevention and wellness.
> Assure affordable, quality health care for all Americans.
> Allow workers to maintain coverage when they change jobs.
> End barriers to coverage for people with pre-existing medical conditions.[46]

After a year of intense debate, Congress passed the Patient Protection and Affordable Care Act. A central and controversial provision requires that all citizens and legal residents have health insurance. To assure access to affordable coverage, the act expands Medicaid to include more lower-income individuals. Businesses with fewer than 50 employees get tax credits covering up to 50 percent of employee health insurance premiums. Employers with more than 200 employees must provide coverage. Individuals and companies with fewer than 200 employees are given several options. The act creates state-based health benefit exchanges through which insurance can be purchased by individuals and businesses that do not have access to affordable coverage. At the federal level, a high-risk insurance pool is created to provide coverage to individuals who are unable to purchase coverage or who are considered difficult to insure. Individuals who fail to have qualifying coverage are penalized through the tax system based on a phased-in schedule starting in 2014, and non-insuring firms with more than 50 employees are also penalized. Exemptions from the penalty are granted for reasons that include financial hardship and religious beliefs.

In addition to increasing the number of individuals covered, the Patient Protection and Affordable Care Act includes the following provisions aimed at reforming the insurance market and Medicare payment practices: health insurers cannot deny children insurance because of preexisting conditions, with the inclusion of adults in 2014. Young adults, up to age 27, can continue to be covered by their parents' health insurance. Insurance companies can no longer deny coverage to someone who becomes sick, nor can they limit a person's lifetime benefit or impose unreasonable annual limits on benefits. Insurers must report how much money is spent on overhead, and the legislation caps non-medical administrative expenses. Medicare payment protections are extended to small rural hospitals and other health care providers that have a small number of Medicare patients.

IMPLICATIONS FOR THE STATES

The massive nature of the Patient Protection and Affordable Care Act prompted strong responses from a number of states. As of July 2011, 17 states passed binding resolutions opposing elements of the reform act, while 30 states debated but failed to enact similar resolutions in opposition to reform. The debate will continue as a number of states have proposed some action to challenge the act, with their efforts being spurred on by national organizations, including the American Legislative Exchange Council, coordinating the opposition.[47]

Nevertheless, the Patient Protection and Affordable Care Act has a number of significant economic implications for the states. It will increase state spending on Medicaid because more low-income individuals who qualify but who have not signed up will do so because of the requirement that everyone be insured. The act also sets the income requirement for all states at 133 percent of the federal poverty level, which will increase the numbers eligible. Estimates of the increased costs to states vary, but a Rand Corporation study of five states shows strong variability in how states will be impacted. For example, the Rand study calculates an increase of $333 for a newly insured individual in California, $540 in Illinois, $120 in Texas, $83 in Montana, but no increase in Connecticut. The differences are due to the differing proportions of individuals who are eligible under the new Medicaid requirement compared to those who qualified previously under differing state rules.[48]

Despite the increase in the number of individuals covered and the administrative costs incurred, some analysts expect the states to experience an overall decline in their health care costs as a result of several factors.[49] First, the federal matching percentage for the Children's Health Insurance Program (CHIP) will increase by 23 percentage points. Second, the federal matching percentage for Medicaid will be increased to 90 percent for the newly eligible adults. And third, state spending on safety-net programs, such as public hospitals and free health clinics, will decline as will the number of uninsured. Without reform, state spending on uncompensated care has been substantial and rising significantly each year. For example, one report estimated that state spending on the uninsured in 2008 came to $17.2 billion.[50]

SUMMARY AND CONCLUSIONS

Social welfare and health policies are closely linked because welfare recipients are eligible for publicly funded medical assistance. Cash assistance programs, primarily TANF and SSI, provide income support to the poor. TANF aids poor adults and their dependent children; SSI provides financial assistance to the elderly and disabled poor. The Medicaid program pays for their health care. Both the federal government and the states provide funds to meet the costs of TANF and Medicaid. The federal government alone picks up the costs of SSI benefits. As TANF and SSI rolls increase, so do the costs of Medicaid. The states pay twice: for TANF benefits and for medical assistance benefits.

Policymakers at both the federal and state levels have called for reforms in both welfare and health care. Welfare reform has had two objectives: to get recipients off welfare and into gainful employment, and to reduce the rate of growth in welfare expenditures. Health care reform has centered on controlling the surging costs of Medicaid. Recent attempts have been made to contain state and federal Medicaid expenditures by introducing incentives for physicians and hospitals to provide only necessary medical services. Two prominent mechanisms intended to contain rising health care costs have been DRGs and managed health care. The former reimburses hospitals on a fixed scale for treating each of 467 ailments, instead of on the basis of customary costs for each separate service. The latter encourages physicians to form prepaid group practices and compete to serve Medicare and Medicaid patients. HMOs, the most common form of managed health care, receive a monthly or an annual fee from state and federal governments to provide medical care for enrolled patients. The prepaid fee covers physician services, required diagnostic services, and hospitalization. Primary care physicians manage patients' health care, deciding when to offer treatment themselves and when to refer patients to the more expensive specialists within the HMO. Because of the prepayment feature, physicians have an incentive to keep costs down and provide only necessary services and procedures.

These attempts at reform have not contained costs as their proponents had hoped. In fact, Medicaid expenditures have grown faster than any other state program since 1985, today comprising 22 percent of state general-fund spending.

The contemporary focus of health care reform as enacted in the Patient Protection and Affordable Care Act, however, is not solely on containing the costs of publicly financed medical services for the poor. It also centers on how best to meet the health care needs of the 47 million Americans who lack adequate health insurance but do not qualify for publicly supported health care—those persons who fall through the cracks of America's health care system. As the Affordable Care Act is implemented and elements continue to be debated, it remains to be seen how successful it will be in achieving the goal of reforming the health care insurance system. Still to be realized is the goal of improving the actual care delivered to all Americans while lowering costs.

Discussion Questions

1. Why should social welfare and health issues be dealt with together?

2. Compare and contrast public assistance and social insurance programs, focusing on their sources of funding, clientele, symbols, and politics.

3. Who are the poor in the United States?

4. Compare and contrast the conservative and liberal views of poverty and welfare in the United States. What are the policy implications of each?

5. Discuss the implications of Congress's action to eliminate public assistance to low-income families with dependent children as a federal entitlement, replacing it with an appropriations-capped block grant to the states.

6. Discuss the implications for the states in the national debate over health care reform. Are there implications for federalism?

Glossary

cycle of dependence 415

cycle of poverty 416

diagnostic-related groups
(DRGs) 433

family allowance 426

Family Support Act 419

feminization of poverty 413

health maintenance
organizations (HMOs) 433

health savings accounts 438

Job Opportunities and Basic
Skills (JOBS) program 419

Medicaid 430

Medicare 408

negative income tax 426

**Personal Responsibility and Work
Opportunity Reconciliation
Act of 1996** 422

Endnotes

1. 2006 *OASDI Trustees Report* (Washington, D.C.: Social Security Administration, 2006), 2, 9.
2. United States Social Security Administration, 2010 OASDI Trustee Report, http://www.ssa.gov/OACT/TR/2010/II_highlights.html#76460 .
3. William J. Nelson Jr., "Workers Compensation: Coverage, Benefits, and Costs, 1990–1991," *Social Security Bulletin* 56, no. 3 (Fall 1993), 69–74.
4. Diana M. DiNitto and Thomas R. Dye, *Social Welfare: Politics and Public Policy* (Englewood Cliffs, N.J.: Prentice Hall, 1987), 89.
5. *Social Security Bulletin* 50, no. 4 (April 1987), 3139.
6. *Poverty 2001* (Washington, D.C.: Bureau of the Census, U.S. Department of Commerce, 2003), Table 2.
7. DeNavas-Walt, Carmen, Bernadette D. Proctor, and Jessica C. Smith, *Income, Poverty, and Health Insurance Coverage in the United States: 2009*, U.S. Census Bureau, Current Population Reports, P60-238, U.S. Government Printing Office, Washington, D.C., 2010.
8. George Gilder, *Wealth and Poverty* (New York: Bantam Books, 1981).
9. Robert Moffit, "Welfare Reform in the 1990s: The Research View," *Intergovernmental Perspective* 17, no. 2 (Spring 1991), 32.
10. Eugene Smolensky, Eirik Evenhouse, and Siobhan Reilly, *Welfare Reform in California* (Berkeley, Calif.: Institute of Governmental Studies, 1992), 27.
11. Ibid., 25.
12. Frances Fox Piren and Richard Cloward, "The Contemporary Relief Debate," in *The Mean Season: The Attack on the Welfare State,* eds. Fred Block et al. (New York: Pantheon Books, 1987), 63.
13. Joint Economic Committee, U.S. Congress, *Handbook of Public Income Transfer Payments,* Paper 20, 1974.
14. Henry M. Levin, "A Decade of Policy Developments in Improving Education and Training for Low Income Populations," in *A Decade of Federal Antipoverty Programs,* ed. Robert H. Haveman (New York: Academic Press, 1977).
15. Irene Laurice, "Work Requirements in Income-Conditional Transfer Programs," *Social Security Review* 52 (December 1978), 551–566.
16. David L. Kirp, "The California Work/Welfare Scheme," *The Public Interest,* no. 83 (Spring 1986), 44.
17. *State Legislatures* 20, no. 10 (October 1994), 8.
18. JoAnne B. Barnhart, "The Family Support Act: Public Assistance in the 1990s," *Intergovernmental Perspective* 17, no. 2 (Spring 1991), 13–14.
19. Jeffrey L. Katz, "Long-Term Challenges Temper Cheers for Welfare Successes," *Congressional Quarterly Weekly Report* 55, no. 42 (October 25, 1997), 2605.
20. Council of Economic Advisors, Office of the President, *Explaining the Decline in Welfare Receipt, 1993–1996,* May 9, 1997.
21. Office of the Press Secretary, *Statement by the President,* August 22, 1996.
22. "Special Supplement on Reforming Welfare Reform," *American Prospect* (Summer 2002), A3.
23. Christopher R. Conte, "Will Workfare Work?" *Governing* 9, no. 7 (April 1996), 20.
24. Rebecca M. Blank, "Was Welfare Reform Successful?" *Economists' Voice*, March 2006, www.bepress.com/ev.
25. Gregory Acs and Pamela Loprest, *TANF Caseload Composition and Leavers Synthesis Report* (Washington, D.C.: The Urban Institute, March 28, 2007), 102–103.
26. United States Department of Health and Human Services, National Health Expenditure Data, http://www.cms.gov/NationalHealthExpendData/downloads/nhe2009.zip.
27. Centers for Medicare & Medicaid Services, Office of the Actuary, National Health Statistics Group; U.S. Department of Commerce, Bureau of Economic Analysis; and U.S. Bureau of the Census, http://www.cms.gov/NationalHealthExpendData/downloads/nhegdp09.zip.
28. The Commonwealth Fund, 2010 Update—How the Performance of the U.S. Health Care System Compares Internationally, http://www.commonwealthfund.org/~/media/Files/Publications/Fund%20Report/2010/Jun/1400_Davis_Mirror_Mirror_on_the_wall_2010.pdf.

29. *Health, United States, 2007* (Hyattsville, MD: National Center for Health Statistics, U.S. Department of Health and Human Services, 2007), 375.

30. National Association of State Budget Officers, Fiscal Survey of the States, Spring 2011, http://nasbo.org/LinkClick .aspx?fileticket=yNV8Jv3X7Is%3d&tabid=38.

31. Center for Medicare and Medicaid Services, U.S. Department of Health and Human Services, http://www.cms.gov/ MedicareEnRpts/Downloads/HISMI2009.pdf.

32. Center for Medicare and Medicaid Services, U.S. Department of Health and Human Services, http://www.cms.gov/ MedicareMedicaidStatSupp//2010Medicaid.

33. Samantha Artiga et al., "Can States Stretch the Medicaid Dollar Without Passing the Buck?" *Health Affairs* 25 (2006): 532–540.

34. Wisconsin Legislative Reference Bureau, *Budget Brief 00-2*, January 2000, 1–2.

35. Jeffrey Young, "Bush's SCHIP Policy Violates Law, Report Says," *The Hill*, August 28, 2008, http://thehill.com/ leading-the-news/bushs-schip-policy-violates-law-report-says-2008-04-18.html.

36. Bruce Steinwald and Laura A. Dummit, "Hospital Case Mix Changes: Sicken Patients or DRG Creep," *Health Affairs* 8, no. 2 (Summer 1989), 35–47.

37. Center for Medicare and Medicaid Services, U.S. Department of Health and Human Services, www.cms.hhs.gov/ MedicaidManagCare.

38. Martin de Alteris, "Medicaid's Role in Moves Toward Universal Health Care," *Policy Studies Review* 11, no. 3/4, 203.

39. Adriel Bettelheim, "Managed Care: The Issues," *Congressional Quarterly Outlook*, May 1, 1999, 9.

40. Kris Hudson, "Maryland Votes to Override Veto of Wal-Mart Bill," *Wall Street Journal*, January 13, 2006, A2.

41. *Retail Industry Leaders Association v. James D. Fielder, Jr.*, Civil No. JFM-06-316 (2006).

42. Penelope Lemor, "Climbing Out of the Medicaid Trap," *Governing* 5, no. 1 (November 1993), 50.

43. Ibid., 19–53.

44. President Bill Clinton's Address to Congress on September 22, 1993, *Congressional Quarterly Weekly Report* 51, no. 38 (September 25, 1993), 2582.

45. Kate Schuler, "Mandatory Insurance Is Romney's Big Pitch," *CQ Weekly* 64, no. 23 (June 5, 2006), 1538–1539; *Medical News Today*, April 15, 2006, www.medicalnewstoday.com/medicalnews.php?newsid−41695.

46. The Whitehouse Briefing Room, *Health Care*, February 24, 2009, www.whitehouse.gov/issues/health_care.

47. Monica Davey, "Health Care Overhaul and Mandatory Coverage Stir States' Rights Claims," *New York Times*, September 28, 2009.

48. Rand Corporation, *How Will Health Care Reform Affect Costs and Coverage: Examples from Five States,* 2011, http://www.rand.org/content/dam/rand/pubs/research briefs/2011/RAND_RB9589.pdf.

49. Council of Economic Advisors, *The Impact of Insurance Reform on State and Local Governments,* September 2009, http://www.whitehouse.gov/assets/documents/cea-statelocal-sept15-final.pdf. Robert Wood Johnson Foundation & Urban Institute, *What is the Impact of the Patient Protection and Affordable Care Act (PPAFCA) on the States,* June 2010, http:// www.rwjf.org/files/research/65049.pdf. The Lewin Group, *Patient Protection and Affordable Care Act (PPACA): Long Term Costs for Governments, Employers, Families, and Providers,* Staff Working Paper #11, June 8, 2010, http://www.lewin .com/content/publications/LewinGroupAnalysis-PatientProtectionandAffordableCareAct2010.pdf. The Urban Institute, *Net Effects of the Affordable Care Act on State Budgets,* December 2010, http://www.urban.org/UploadedPDF/1001480- Affordable-Care-Act.pdf.

50. Hadley, J., J. Holahan, T. Coughlin, and D. Miller. 2008. "Covering the Uninsured In 2008: Current Costs, Sources of Payment, And Incremental Costs." *Health Affairs* 27(5), w399–w415.

17

Environmental Policy and Economic Development

- Define the respective roles of the federal government, states, and local governments in environmental policy making and regulation.
- Know the major national policy initiatives taken by Congress to improve environmental quality.
- Understand the tension that exists between economic development and environmental protection.
- Identify state and local governments' roles and resources in fostering economic development within their borders.

Jane has grown accustomed to taking her car in for its annual emissions test. Her state requires the test because the area in which she lives fails to meet the federal Environmental Protection Agency (EPA) clean air standards. Recently, however, she was informed that her neighborhood service station can no longer perform the emissions test because it does not have the newly required equipment to do the job. With ozone levels worsening, the EPA reclassified her area from marginal to serious nonattainment, bringing with it the requirement that her automobile be tested using an enhanced test—one that requires new, high-tech equipment. The new equipment puts her vehicle through a four-minute driving cycle on a chassis dynamometer, analyzing emissions during both acceleration and deceleration. Although she complains about the inconvenience of having to drive farther to get her car tested, she understands that the tougher test is part of an ongoing effort to clean up the air where she lives. For the service station owner, the more stringent requirement means either investing in new equipment or losing business to a competitor who has. Here, environmental protection runs up against economic development.

I f you live in one of the 124 smoggy areas around the country that violate the federal Environmental Protection Agency (EPA) air quality standards, you may have trouble appreciating the fact that America's air is much cleaner today than it was in 1970. Ground-level ozone and carbon monoxide concentrations fell by about 50 percent between 1970 and 2005, and PM10 (microscopic particles, 10 microns or less in size, that can become lodged in the respiratory tract) readings declined by a staggering 84 percent over that same period. These reductions occurred at the same time the U.S. population grew by 42 percent, and vehicle miles of travel rose by 178 percent.[1] Major strides have been made in reducing industrial pollutants, particularly those released by electric power utilities, chemical manufacturers, mineral smelters, and factories. Automobile emissions have fallen despite increased vehicle use—a result of emissions control devices and gains in fuel efficiency. Nonetheless, over 126 million Americans still live in urban areas whose air fails to meet federal standards.[2] Figure 17.1 shows the most polluted areas in the United States, by major pollutant.

This juxtaposition of improvement and remaining noncompliance prompts the question, Why are so many of us still breathing polluted air even though significant improvement has been made? A following question might be, What will it take to ensure that all Americans breathe healthy air? Perhaps the latter is not practically attainable. Maybe the costs and personal sacrifices needed to clean our nation's urban air are too great to bear. Even though we know that smog and high concentrations of particulate matter (PM) pose health risks, we can take some solace in the fact that our nation's urban air is cleaner than that in most of the world's highly populated metropolitan areas. A trip to Moscow, Beijing, Paris, and the industrial areas of eastern Europe readily bears this out: the smarting eyes and heavy breathing of American tourists provide symptomatic evidence of a deteriorated environment.

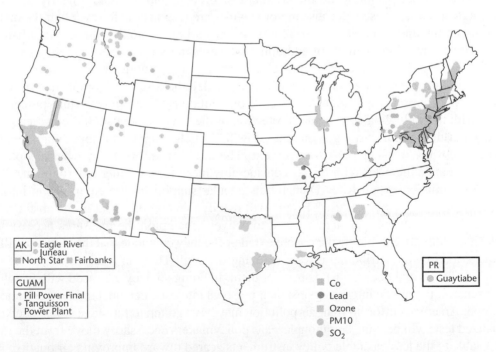

Note: Incomplete data, not classified, and Section 185(A) areas are not shown.
*Ozone nonattainment areas on map are based on the 1-hour ozone standard.
**PM10 nonattainment areas on map are based on the existing PM10 standards.

Figure 17.1   Nonattainment Areas for Air Quality
Source: U.S. Environmental Protection Agency, 2011.

Although progress has been made to clean up America's air, continued industrial expansion and population growth threaten to overtake the gains. Add to this the reality that the so-called easier reductions in air pollution have already been accomplished. Much more difficult challenges lie ahead. Motorists have hardly felt the effects of the toughened tailpipe emissions standards placed on automobile manufacturers. Those living in polluted areas have had to bring their cars in for emissions inspections, but that inconvenience has been limited to once a year. For industrial pollution, environmental regulators have identified those sources exceeding allowable emissions and have taken steps to bring them into compliance. Further gains can be made by strengthening existing standards, toughening enforcement, and extending regulation to previously unregulated smaller enterprises.

Economic development brings with it industrial and population growth. New industrial plants or the expansion of existing ones leads to additional jobs and people looking to fill them. With that growth also come increased air pollution, added industrial and household wastes, and heightened pressure on public water systems.

The effects of growth on air quality are most readily apparent. Each new or expanded industrial plant adds to the total pollution load, even if it complies with all federal and state environmental laws. New workers add motor vehicles to the daily commute, continuing a post–World War II trend of rapidly increasing use. Americans already drive almost twice as many miles per person as do the Germans or French, and we hold a nearly threefold margin over the Japanese.[3] Because motor vehicles are responsible for over half the ozone-forming compounds and close to 90 percent of the carbon monoxide present in urban air, the environmental implications of additional increases in their numbers are obvious.

Citizens and their elected representatives face a conundrum: how to reconcile Americans' penchant for automobiles with their widely held support for cleaner air. Eight out of ten Americans call themselves environmentalists.[4] An almost equal percentage agree with the following statement: "Protection of the environment should be given priority even at the risk of curbing economic growth."[5] Such support is astounding when one thinks about the implications of agreement. The test comes, however, when people are asked to change their behavior or pay considerably more for a cleaner environment.

Public opinion expert Riley Dunlap puts popular support for the environment into the category of "passive consensus."[6] People will readily agree with a goal in the abstract, but they do not feel strongly enough about it to actively champion the measures necessary to make it a reality. In examining the concrete trade-offs, they conclude that they are not willing to make their own contribution toward realizing the goal. They do a personal cost–benefit analysis of sorts and decide what is best for them. In doing so, they are faced with weighing their sense of the public interest against their personal interests. Personal interests commonly triumph. America's effort to fight air pollution may have gotten to the stage where such personalized tests will become commonplace, as policymakers necessarily move from the more acceptable to the less palatable policy instruments geared toward improving air quality.

This generalized support for a cleaner environment conflicts with America's growth ethic. Americans have a deep-seated faith in progress, an infatuation with "onward and upward." We believe that it is still possible to realize the "American dream," and we see economic development as the engine that makes prosperity and personal betterment possible.

The city of Los Angeles engulfed in smog. An ongoing challenge is to reconcile the effects of urban and economic development with the requirements for a clean and healthy environment.

Economic development means jobs—for us and our children. It means the promise of economic mobility and of moving up the social ladder. Its converse, economic decline, holds out the prospect of lost jobs, stagnant careers, and falling real estate values.

Both state and local government policymakers prize economic development. Its associated prosperity makes them look good in the eyes of voters. Economic development also expands a government's tax base, making it possible for it to collect additional revenues without increasing tax rates. New job creation expands personal income, not only providing a bigger wage base to tax (for state and local governments that collect a personal income tax), but also giving consumers increased purchasing power, which puts more money in retailers' pockets. With increased commerce, state and local governments collecting a sales tax see their revenues rise as well. New or expanded businesses increase the value of commercial property subject to local taxation. Where job growth is significant, local governments benefit further from increased housing starts, which add taxable real estate to the property tax rolls. As we shall see later, however, economic development has its share of costs. Yet in weighing the costs and benefits of economic development, our elected representatives typically opt for growth, accepting the costs as a necessary consequence of economic development. In that milieu, who is responsible for ensuring that the attendant environmental costs are held within acceptable limits? Who establishes those limits?

FEDERALISM AND ENVIRONMENTAL POLICY MAKING

The regulatory role of government in environmental protection is a relatively recent one. The U.S. Constitution makes no reference to the federal government's or the states' responsibility for protecting America's environmental resources. In reality, the vast expanse of the western frontier held the promise of unbounded resources that settlers could put to their use. The sheer quantity of land and unspoiled natural resources accommodated the needs of the limited numbers of early settlers without adverse effects on those resources. But the Industrial Revolution of the nineteenth century and rising urban population offered early evidence of a tension between growth and environmental quality. By the early twentieth century, extensive coal burning blackened the skies of many industrial cities. Contaminated drinking water prompted cities to regulate water systems. In rural areas, avaricious loggers cleared large areas of virgin timber from both private and public lands, spurring Congress to create national forests and a national park system for protection. State legislatures, urged on by early twentieth-century Progressives and Populists, enacted parallel legislation creating state forests and wildlife preserves. Despite these actions, government's role in environmental protection remained limited.

As late as the early 1960s, government took a hands-off approach to growing environmental problems. Prior to that time, the little environmental regulation that existed fell to the states. The federal government got involved in the mid-1960s, and its initial role expanded greatly in the 1970s, the so-called environmental decade.

Rachel Carson's book *Silent Spring*, published in 1962, provided dramatic testimony to how agricultural pesticides find their way into the air, water, crops, animals, and humans. She further suggested that science did not know or appreciate the harmful effects these pesticides can have. Most disturbing, however, was her insistence that both scientists and government did not seem to care much about the consequences of environmental pollution to public health. The resulting counterattack from the chemical industry sparked a national debate, which some argue gave birth to this nation's environmental movement—a movement that soon drew strength from the discontent with the status quo generated by the growing national protest over America's involvement in Vietnam.

Other substantive and highly symbolic events also focused the public's attention on the environment. The Cuyahoga River, running through Cleveland, Ohio, became so polluted with combustible wastes that it caught fire in 1969, creating a spectacular image on prime-time national television and on the front pages of major metropolitan newspapers. Accounts of polluted rivers and lakes, hazardous dump sites, and worsening air pollution in metropolitan areas increasingly captured the attention of the media and the public at large. Americans came to realize that environmental quality could no longer be taken for granted; benign neglect would not solve what had popularly come to be seen as a real and growing problem. The throngs who turned out across the nation for the first Earth Day, in 1970, gave testimony to the fact that the environment had taken its place on the nation's policy agenda.

FEDERAL INITIATIVES IN THE ENVIRONMENTAL DECADE

In 1970, at the urging of President Richard Nixon, Congress passed the historic **National Environmental Policy Act**. That legislation created the EPA, headed by a presidential appointee, and gave it the authority to regulate the nation's air and water pollution. Prior to the EPA's formation, the federal government's fledgling responsibility for environmental protection was spread among executive branch agencies, including the departments of Health, Education, and Welfare; the Interior; and Agriculture.

The act requires federal agencies or governments receiving federal funds to prepare an analysis of the effects on the environment of any development project they plan to

---

National Environmental Policy Act Legislation, enacted in 1970, that created the EPA and gave it authority to regulate America's air and water pollution.

undertake. This requirement for an **environmental impact statement (EIS)** applies to all capital projects such as highways, dams, and facilities financed by federal funds. The act also mandates that the public be given an opportunity to comment on those projects affecting them. This provision is frequently used by environmental groups to make their positions on development projects part of the public record. Environmental activists also use the EIS process to delay projects, challenging the adequacy of statements for projects that they consider harmful to the environment.

Although the Environmental Protection Act created an important infrastructure for national environmental regulation, the EPA lacked the policy tools it needed to protect the quality of our nation's air and water. Without additional enabling legislation, the federal government's role would continue to be one of monitoring pollution; assisting the states in defining their own policies, priorities, and standards; and providing limited financial assistance to support state efforts.

Early Federal Leadership in Cleaning the Air

The Clear Air Act of 1970 was the first of a series of successful initiatives that give the EPA the authority it needs to do its job of environmental regulation. The 1970 act clearly established the federal government's leadership in cleaning the nation's air, and it served as the legal foundation for the national government's partial preemption (a concept discussed in Chapter 3) of what had largely been a role left to the states. It contained four major provisions:

1. Congress charged the EPA with setting air quality standards that would apply nationwide. No longer would the states be allowed to determine what constitutes acceptable levels of air pollution within their borders. After all, polluted air can be blown across state lines, theoretically from states possessing lax standards to adjoining states having much tougher ones. In addition, given interstate competition over economic development, some states might elect to gain a competitive advantage over others by greatly limiting their environmental regulations. Under the federal legislation, however, states could only elect to establish tougher standards for major pollutants but could not loosen the minimum federal standards.

2. The act required the states to prepare implementation plans for the EPA's approval, showing what efforts would be made to bring a state's air quality into compliance.

3. It required automobile manufacturers to reduce emissions by 90 percent for all 1975 models or face a $10,000 per vehicle fine, although the technology to do so was not in place at the time.

4. The act charged the EPA with establishing emissions standards for power plants. Procedurally, the act also gave citizens the right to sue polluters for not complying with the standards, and the EPA for not enforcing them.

---

environmental impact statement (EIS) A written assessment of the environmental effects of development projects such as highways, dams, and facilities. Required to be done on projects financed with federal funds.

Under the federal government's oversight, this landmark legislation delegated to the states the responsibility to monitor compliance and enforce it. The states, in turn, can carry out those functions directly or delegate the day-to-day tasks to local government agencies. In the latter case, that responsibility frequently resides at the county level or with metropolitan air quality districts that cut across county lines. But as a fallback, if the states or local governments fail to carry out their delegated responsibilities properly, EPA personnel can step in directly and take over the job of monitoring and enforcing compliance.

In 1977, Congress amended the Clean Air Act, ironically both to expand the EPA's authority and to extend compliance deadlines. Under the 1977 amendments, states were required to submit plans for controlling industrial pollution, including illustrations of how emissions from new industrial sources in noncomplying areas would be offset by corresponding reductions from existing sources. The legislation also required states to use permits to control the addition of new fixed pollution sources, and it mandated that smokestack scrubbers be installed on all coal-burning power plants. The amendments also required states to establish vehicle emissions testing programs in counties whose air failed to meet federal air quality standards. For states not in compliance, the federal law authorized the EPA to withhold federal grants-in-aid for highways and sewage treatment, as well as to prohibit states from issuing permits that would increase aggregate air pollution from industrial sources. At the same time, the amendments extended the heretofore unmet deadline for automakers to comply with the strict, federally mandated auto emissions standards, in recognition that significant progress had been made, even though the mandated 90 percent reduction had not been fully attained on schedule.

The government's strengthened regulatory role over air pollution during the 1970s made a difference in improving America's air quality. Despite economic growth and an expanding population, the President's Council on Environmental Quality found that the five major air pollution emissions (particulates, sulfur oxides, nitrogen oxides, hydrocarbons, and carbon monoxide) declined by 21 percent between 1970 and 1980.[7] Days in which the air was determined to be unhealthful declined by about one-third in 40 metropolitan areas between 1974 and 1980. Nonetheless, air pollution remained a serious national problem: seven major cities still averaged over 100 unhealthful days a year from 1978 to 1980.[8]

Early Federal Leadership in Improving Water Quality

Before 1972, at least 18,000 communities regularly dumped their untreated raw sewage into nearby rivers and lakes. Chemical, metal, paper, food, and other industries discharged about 25 trillion gallons of wastewater each year. A Minnesota industry dumped an average of 67,000 tons of iron ore tailings into Lake Superior each day.[9] Nevertheless, the federal government played only a marginal role in water quality assurance before the mid-1960s, as it did with air quality. Its role had been largely restricted to aiding local governments in building sewage treatment plants. In 1965, Congress increased federal funds for sewage treatment plants but, at the same time, required the states to establish water quality standards and to draft plans to implement and enforce them. The standards were left to state policymakers to determine, and the states were slow to respond. Without minimum national standards, some states were hesitant to take any action that might give nonresponsive states a competitive advantage in keeping and attracting economic development—a dilemma reminiscent of the early debates over air pollution management.

Faced with slow and scattered compliance, Congress in 1972 again followed President Nixon's lead, as it had in enacting the Clean Air Act of 1970, and set minimum national standards, industry by industry, for the release of point-source pollution, that is, pollution that can be traced to a fixed point of discharge. The **Water Pollution Control Act of 1972** (commonly referred to as the Clean Water Act) also required local governments to install secondary sewage treatment facilities by 1977 and authorized 3:1 federal aid to help pay for them. As with air quality protection, the EPA issues the regulations but relies on states and local governments to monitor water quality, issue permits, and take enforcement actions. Again, if they fail to do the job, EPA employees have the authority to come in and do it themselves.

The act addressed the problem of non-point-source pollution, such as that caused by fertilizer or agricultural waste runoff into groundwater, rivers, lakes, and other waterways, although it stopped short of setting national standards. Instead, it authorized funds for state and local planning bodies to analyze the extent of non-point-source pollution regionally and to develop plans to address the identified problems. Without any accompanying federal mandate, little came of the effort.

Subsequent national quality water legislation extended the federal government's reach. The **Safe Drinking Water Act of 1974** directed the EPA to promulgate maximum allowable levels for different chemicals and bacteriological pollutants in local water systems. Subsequently, 1977 amendments to the Clean Water Act authorized additional federal aid for sewage treatment plant construction and, as we have seen with air quality policy, extended deadlines for industries to comply with the point-source standards set in 1972.

Compared with the documented improvement found in air quality, the picture appears to be less clear for water quality. The over $30 billion in federal sewage treatment grants helped to give communities the resources necessary to treat raw sewage before it is discharged into public waterways, but most U.S. cities still did not have adequate secondary sewage treatment facilities by 1980.[10] Despite that large investment, a 1980 EPA survey identified $120 billion in remaining sewage treatment construction needs.[11]

Adequate data do not exist to allow any definitive conclusion to be drawn about whether America's rivers, streams, and lakes were any cleaner in 1980 than in 1970, although lakes Erie and Ontario showed well-publicized signs of rejuvenation. However, the conventional wisdom is that water quality at least did not deteriorate during the 1970s, despite population growth, and that it probably improved somewhat.

Water Pollution Control Act of 1972 Also known as the Clean Water Act, legislation that set national minimum standards for the release of point-source pollution, that is, pollution that can be traced to a fixed point of discharge. The act also required local governments to install secondary sewage treatment facilities by 1977 and authorized federal aid to help pay for them.

Safe Drinking Water Act of 1974 Legislation that directed the Environmental Protection Agency to promulgate allowable levels of different chemicals and bacteriological pollutants in local water systems.

REAGAN'S REDIRECTION OF ENVIRONMENTAL REGULATION

Toward the end of his administration and prior to his defeat in November 1980, President Jimmy Carter vowed to continue to move forward in protecting the environment, extending the progress that had already been made—progress, he noted, "for which we are being repaid many times over."[12] His successor, Ronald Reagan, failed to share these sentiments. Instead, he questioned whether America's investment in environmental regulation and pollution control could meet the scrutiny of cost–benefit analysis. He challenged the EPA's record on ideological grounds, seeing it as an example of overextended big government. Holding up the ideal of private enterprise and the free market, President Reagan focused on the costs of the private sector to comply with what he viewed as the burgeoning environmental regulation of the 1970s. Reagan interpreted his landslide electoral victory as a popular mandate to reverse the course of governmental policy taken since President Lyndon Johnson's Great Society programs. To reach that goal, he pledged to reduce the growth in discretionary domestic spending, return responsibilities appropriately to the states, cut federal grants-in-aid, and scale back federal regulation. Environmental regulation appeared toward the top of the list of what he saw as the national government's misguided priorities and overregulation.[13]

Symbolizing his administration's altered policy course, President Reagan appointed Anne Gorsuch (later Burford) as administrator of the EPA. Gorsuch, a corporate attorney whose clients included many industries hostile to EPA's expanded environmental role, came into office clearly sympathetic toward industry's perspective on regulation. Several other top appointees came from the very industries that EPA regulates. Kathleen Bennett, a lobbyist for the American Paper Institute, became assistant administrator for air, noise, and radiation; Robert Perry, a ranking attorney with Exxon Corporation, became general counsel; and Rita Lavelle, a public relations officer for Aerojet-General, became assistant administrator for hazardous and toxic wastes.[14]

Gorsuch kept many agency positions vacant and used budget cuts initiated by Reagan to eliminate still others. Total employment at EPA dropped from 14,269 at the beginning of 1981 to 11,474 by November 1982. The headquarters' staff in Washington dropped from 4,700 to 2,500.[15] These reductions took a significant bite out of the agency's ability to monitor and enforce compliance with environmental protection legislation. In Gorsuch's first year in office, the number of lawsuits filed by the EPA against the biggest polluters fell from 250 to 78.[16]

Mounting congressional opposition, particularly among Democrats, spurred on by highly mobilized environmental interest groups, forced Gorsuch to resign in 1984, but not until Congress took the extraordinary step of citing her for contempt. The resignations of other initial Reagan appointees soon followed. Gorsuch's replacement, the highly regarded William Ruckelshaus, who enjoyed bipartisan support in Congress, ushered in a period of restored stability to the EPA and renewed enforcement activity.

During Gorsuch's administration, President Reagan made good on his promise to champion budgetary reductions for environmental programs, a direction that Congress supported in an economic environment of severe recession and fast-rising budget deficits. Within two years of Reagan's inauguration, the EPA's budget was cut by nearly 30 percent.[17] Expenditures for environmental programs and natural resources, which had risen from

1.5 percent of the federal budget in 1970 to 2.4 percent in 1980, dropped to 1.2 percent by the end of his first term—lower than at the beginning of the environmental decade.

In the aftermath of rocky relations with Congress during his first term, and faced with rising popular support for environmental protection, Reagan and his Office of Management and Budget eased their hostile forays against environmental regulation. Yet in 1986, that softened stance did not keep President Reagan from vetoing a congressionally approved revision of the Clean Water Act. In response, Congress overrode his veto, drawing upon the support of Republicans in both chambers.

The 1986 amendments added the requirement that states develop EPA-approved plans for controlling pollution from nonpoint sources. Toward that end, Congress required municipalities to regulate stormwater runoff in the same way they regulate the discharge of polluted water from industrial plants. In addition, the amendments required communities whose sanitary and stormwater sewers are combined to develop plans aimed at keeping stormwater surges from overwhelming sewage treatment capacity and causing the release of raw sewage into waterways.[18]

BUSH AND CLINTON: MORE ENVIRONMENTALLY FRIENDLY ADMINISTRATIONS

The Clean Air Act Amendments of 1990

George H. W. Bush campaigned in support of cleaning up the environment. Once elected, he proclaimed himself to be the environmental president, separating himself and his administration from the policy stance of his predecessor. As a gesture of his commitment, Bush appointed William Reilly, a former president of a major environmental interest group, the Conservation Foundation, to head the EPA. The real test of Bush's commitment to the environment would come over deliberations with Congress over amending the Clean Air Act, which had last been modified in 1977—a task put off during the Reagan years.

The product of presidential–congressional negotiations, the **Clean Air Act Amendments of 1990** attempted to create a balanced approach aimed at making continued progress in cleaning the air. Nonattainment areas and mobile-source pollution were singled out for attention. The amendments gave states time limits within which to bring the areas into compliance with federal standards. These time limits ranged from three to twenty years for ozone and from five to ten years for carbon monoxide. The amendments also placed new controls on a wider range of emission sources than ever before, including gas stations, body shops, paint manufacturers, industrial-size bakeries, and many other smaller enterprises. The amendments made states responsible for attaining compliance. What a state must do to bring about compliance depended on the severity of an area's air quality problem.

Clean Air Act Amendments of 1990   Legislation that singled out air quality nonattainment areas and mobile-source pollution for attention. The amendments gave states time limits within which to bring areas into compliance and, at the same time, placed new controls on a wider range of emission sources than ever before, including gas stations, body shops, paint manufacturers, industrial-size bakeries, and many other small enterprises. The amendments also toughened automobile inspection and maintenance requirements.

Enhanced controls on mobile sources of pollution required conversion to oxygenated fuels in 41 areas not complying with carbon monoxide standards, affecting areas in which one-third of the nation's population resides. A higher oxygen content promotes more complete combustion of gasoline and is typically achieved through the blending of ethanol or methanol with gasoline. The EPA expected the introduction of oxygenated fuels to cut carbon monoxide emissions by 15 to 20 percent, while costing motorists only a few cents more per gallon.[19]

The 1990 amendments also toughened the automobile inspection and maintenance requirements included in the 1977 Clean Air Act Amendments. In addition to the mandated basic checks, the 1990 amendments added enhanced test requirements for those metropolitan areas most out of compliance with federal standards for ozone emissions. The enhanced test uses a high-technology testing procedure that measures auto emissions during both acceleration and deceleration, and that tests the effectiveness of the governing electronic sensors and computers found in newer model cars. When the inspection shows that repairs are necessary to correct deficiencies, owners are required to have the work done as long as the costs do not exceed $450 per auto—over three times greater than waiver limits for the existing basic program. EPA estimates that the new tests cut ozone emissions by 28 percent and save 15 million barrels of oil a year.[20]

Reflecting the Bush administration's initiative and its influence at the apex of President Bush's popularity, the 1990 legislation is notable for departing from the traditional approach to regulation. Earlier congressional acts relied exclusively on a "command and control" approach to regulation, built on the concepts of standards and enforcement. Congress established the goals, the EPA developed standards, and the states developed plans to apply and enforce them. Threatened sanctions or legal action by the EPA often won compliance from the states, but they also kicked off what was commonly a protracted series of negotiations, moves, and countermoves that resulted in compromise, frequently culminating in the EPA's conditional approval of state plans. Attention then moved to the steps that state and local governments might take to remove the EPA's conditions, often precipitating another round of negotiations.[21] Because the enforcement of provisions included in state plans falls to state environmental agencies and local governments acting as their agents, the EPA has monitored that enforcement effort, reserving the right to step in and enforce federal regulations directly. It is not surprising, then, that a certain tension has pervaded the relationship between federal and state environmental regulators, even though they share the goal of protecting the environment. They often differ, however, over how best and how quickly to get that job done.

The Introduction of Market-Based Incentives

The traditional regulatory approach relied on **technology-forcing standards** tied to permit granting, which prompted industries to install smokestack scrubbers, filters, and other equipment to reduce emissions. The new approach, in comparison, introduces

---

technology-forcing standards The traditional approach to regulating air pollution, which prompted industries to adopt improved technology to limit pollution through the installation of devices such as smokestack scrubbers and filters.

DEBATING THE ISSUES

What would you do if you suspected pollution?

If you saw or smelled a foul, hazy-looking discharge pouring from a smokestack not far from your home, what would you do, if anything, about it? You might ask someone what is happening. If you failed to get an answer that satisfied you, you might pursue the matter further. To whom would you turn? Whose job is it to regulate such a thing? Is this a problem for local, state, or federal officials?

You might have heard of the federal EPA, and thus you may attempt to call someone at the agency. If you reached one of its regional offices, a representative would likely refer you to the state office, or even to the local environmental regulatory agency, because local agencies typically handle investigations and take enforcement actions on behalf of the state environmental protection agency.

If you still don't get a satisfactory answer, or you believe that corrective action has not been taken, what would you do then? That's when you probably would want to get back to the state and file a formal complaint that becomes part of the permanent record. In response, a state investigator assigned to the case might suggest that the incident had been handled properly and that nothing further needs to be done.

What's your recourse now?

The U.S. Environmental Protection Agency's homepage provides Internet links to and phone numbers for each state's environmental protection department. Find the information at www.epa.gov/epahome/whereyoulive.htm.

market-based incentives into air pollution regulation, aimed at reducing components of urban smog and sulfur dioxide emissions that create acid rain. Although the EPA continues to set overall emissions caps, states can develop plans that would allow regulated industries to buy and sell emissions credits. The system works as follows. As long as the aggregate emissions ceiling is not penetrated, a firm could increase its emissions beyond what it would be allowed if other industries in a nonattainment area reduced their emissions below target levels, in effect leaving room for the first firm to pollute more than it would otherwise be allowed. Why would an industry elect to spend more money than necessary in order to go that step beyond, to make an even bigger reduction than required in its release of pollutants? Altruism, or acting in the public interest, might be one conceivable answer, but the added cost is just one more debit against the bottom line. In practice, few economic enterprises choose to incur added costs out of a sense of altruism.

---

market-based incentives   This new approach to regulating air pollution allows regulated industries to buy and sell so-called emissions credits. It provides the incentive for industries to adopt technological improvements that reduce emissions below required levels, creating emissions credits that can be sold to firms that fail to meet standards. Thus, firms can make the choice to forego technology improvements and purchase credits representing the excess emissions reductions attained by others. This approach can work as long as aggregate admissions in an area comply with federal standards.

Based on the market principle of self-interested behavior, the 1990 act provides an incentive for firms to do more than is required, and that incentive is economic return. If a company is faced with choosing among a number of alternatives to bring its emissions under compliance, it might make the good business decision of selecting the most effective technology to do the job, even though that technology costs more than another option. Because of its effectiveness, it reduces emissions well below what would have been possible by employing the cheaper, less costly methods. The technology generates excess emission credits that can be sold to other industries facing their own need to reduce emissions. Rather than incurring the capital expense required to come into compliance, these other industries can elect to buy some or all of the excess credits—a proposition that might appear to be a good short-run business deal for the company doing the buying. Thus, the rationale goes, the overall ceiling on emissions is not broken, and the individual organizations doing the trading are acting in what they believe to be their corporate self-interest.

California has become a leader in using such market incentives to reduce both aggregate air pollution emissions and the attendant compliance costs. California's highly innovative Regional Clean Air Incentives Market (RECLAIM) program consists of separate markets for nitrogen oxides and sulfur oxides covering the counties of Los Angeles, Orange, Riverside, and San Bernardino, an area including almost half of California's population. Analysts estimate that the operation of these markets could reduce the compliance costs to southern California businesses by up to 40 percent.[22]

Electric utilities, which emit about 70 percent of the sulfur dioxide pollution in the United States, will likely be the major players in interstate emissions credit trading. Confronted with emissions-reduction targets equating to the Clean Air Act's goal of cutting sulfur dioxide emissions in half by the year 2000, coal-burning power plants have faced difficult choices about how to comply. For many, the purchase of credits proved more attractive than investing in scrubbers or switching to more expensive low-sulfur coal.[23]

During the first two years of operation since the program's inception in 1994, industries in the Los Angeles area have traded more than 100,000 tons of nitrous oxide and sulfur dioxide emissions. To participate, facilities must emit at least four tons of pollutants into the atmosphere annually, and some 300 companies are doing so.[24] Eyeing southern California's active market, the Northeastern states are working on a nitrous oxide trading program modeled on RECLAIM.

On taking office, the Clinton administration vowed to enforce the provisions of the 1990 Clean Air Act, and the leadership for that effort was passed to Carol Browner, Clinton's appointee, to administer the EPA. Browner, a longtime aide of then-senator Albert Gore, previously served as head of Florida's environmental agency. Her first initiative was to place added emphasis on prevention of environmental pollution, working with industry to reduce the use of polluting materials in the first place. Examples include reducing the use of toxic raw materials, eliminating excess packaging, and using biodegradable materials.[25]

Several signs suggest that this approach holds promise. The private sector appears to be responding to consumers' growing interest in preventing pollution. McDonald's accomplished its goals to phase out polystyrene packaging materials, reduce the size of its napkins, replace bleached paper bags with brown ones, and introduce reusable coffee mugs.

The 3M Corporation has started a program that rewards employees for devising more environmentally sound ways of reformulating products and packaging them.[26] It has become commonplace for companies to label their products "recycled," "recyclable," "compostable," "biodegradable," or even "environmentally friendly," whether or not they can document the claims. For marketing executives, "green" labeling sells.[27]

Reflecting Vice President Gore's efforts to examine ways in which the Clinton administration could "reinvent government," Administrator Browner pursued efforts to reduce the often overlapping bureaucratic red tape that industries must wade through, and to apply federal regulations in a more targeted fashion, treating different cases appropriately. For example, the requirement that all landfills install double liners has been waived for sparsely populated desert sites but retained for populated Midwestern and Northeastern locations.[28]

The Clinton Administration Toughens Compliance Standards

The 1990 Clean Air Act Amendments require the EPA to review air quality standards every five years to ensure that they adequately protect public health. In a long-anticipated announcement in November 1996, the EPA proposed new, tougher standards for ozone and PM. After a series of public hearings, the EPA announced the final version of the new standards on July 16, 1997, amidst opponents' efforts to get Congress to pass a bill blocking their implementation. Industry officials, aligned with the National League of Cities and the National Association of Counties, led the opposition. Facing a certain presidential veto, Congress demurred.

Under the new regulations, the ozone standard changed from 0.12 parts per million measured over one hour to 0.08 parts per million measured over eight hours. For PM, particles as small as 2.5 microns in diameter would be regulated, compared to the previous 10-micron standard. To get a sense of the minuteness of these finer particles that are most commonly found in soot, about 30 can fit in the width of a human hair. Once breathed in, they can find their way into the lower respiratory tract, decreasing lung function, promoting asthma attacks, and possibly resulting in death. Opponents question whether the health benefits justify business's costs of compliance with the new standards, and both opponents and supporters of the toughened standards have debated not only the assumptions underlying projections of costs and benefits, but the quality of the supporting science as well.

The regulations give metropolitan areas time to meet the new standards. The EPA would not cite areas for noncompliance until 2004 for ozone and 2005 for PM; however, the local governments in each area, working with their state environmental protection department, must develop plans that indicate how compliance will be attained. Market-based emissions trading could be part of these plans. And as a concession to congressional interests concerned with the justification for the tightened standards, the EPA committed to complete another full scientific review of the health effects of fine particles before it would designate any area out of compliance and impose pollution controls. Nonetheless, communities and businesses in targeted areas are expected to begin taking steps toward compliance with both the toughened ozone and PM standards.[29]

In a second wave of initiatives to reduce air pollution, President Clinton announced new regulations on May 1, 1999, subjecting light trucks and the rapidly growing number of sport utility vehicles (SUVs) to the same tailpipe emissions standards that apply to cars. These standards, commonly referred to as Tier 2, took effect beginning in 2004; they are expected to reduce motor vehicle emissions significantly because light trucks and SUVs emit as much as three to five times more air pollution than do cars. In a companion action, the Clinton administration also announced regulations to reduce the sulfur content of gasoline by an average of 90 percent. Also taking effect in 2004, the new regulations set a national low-sulfur standard of 30 parts per million, a significant decrease considering that gasoline averages over 300 parts per million.[30]

On May 17, 2000, President Clinton announced his administration's third major regulatory initiative to reduce air pollution even further, this time reducing the sulfur content of diesel fuel by 97 percent. The EPA projected that the new regulations would reduce smog-causing nitrogen oxides from buses and heavy trucks by 95 percent a decade later. It also projected a reduction of bus- and truck-emitted PM by 90 percent over the same period. Such a dramatic reduction would also produce a tandem benefit, allowing buses and heavy trucks to use pollution-control devices for the first time—devices that would not have worked without a major reduction in the sulfur content of diesel fuel.[31]

GEORGE W. BUSH AND EXPANDED MARKET-BASED INCENTIVES

The Bush administration proposed new legislation in July 2002 that would greatly expand the system of market-based pollution credits introduced in 1990 during his father's administration. The legislative initiative, called **Clear Skies**, would place higher caps on nitrogen oxides, starting in 2008, and on sulfur dioxide, starting in 2010. It would also place a new cap, for the first time, on mercury emissions, also starting in 2010. Under the proposal, industries could buy or trade credits involving all three pollutants. For example, an industry able to reduce its emissions below the cap for sulfur dioxide could sell its excess emissions credits to another firm that fails to bring its nitrogen oxides emissions under the allowable level. The EPA projects that the legislation would cut sulfur dioxide emissions by 73 percent, from 11 million tons in 2002 to 4.5 million tons in 2010. The EPA also projects reductions of 67 percent for nitrogen oxides and 69 percent for mercury over the same period.[32]

The Bush initiative faced considerable opposition in Congress, with Republicans failing to elicit sufficient support from Democrats to secure its passage. Opponents included enough Republicans to bottle up the Clear Skies bill in the Senate Environment and Public Works Committee. Critics argued for tighter caps and complained that the Bush administration's initiative put deadlines for compliance too far into the future. They also objected to a companion provision in the legislation that rolls back a Clean Air Act mandate about the upgrade of older plants. Older plants that upgrade or add equipment to increase output must also modernize their pollution controls. The Bush administration countered that their recommended caps and credit trading would effectively reduce aggregate emissions alone.[33]

Clear Skies Legislative proposal of the George W. Bush administration that would expand the system of market-based pollution credits to include trading of credits earned by reducing levels of nitrogen oxides, sulfur dioxide, and mercury emissions. The proposal would also roll back a clean air mandate that older plants that upgrade or add equipment to increase output must use the most effective technology in that expansion.

Critics of the Bush administration's environmental record were quick to lend their opposition to the Clear Skies initiatives, portraying the proposed legislation as part of a pattern of efforts to weaken environmental protection that favor the interests of industry. Using EPA data, the National Resources Defense Council (NRDC) was quick to point out that, during the first three years of Bush's presidency, the EPA's citations for pollution violations were down by 57 percent compared to the last three years of the Clinton administration, and lawsuits filed by the EPA against companies violating federal environmental laws declined by 75 percent over the same years.[34]

In a move that pleased environmentalists, the EPA, in December 2005, promulgated regulations to strengthen the existing 2.5-micron standard for PM by cutting almost in half the allowable concentration in the air, averaged over 24-hour periods. The EPA estimates that the tougher standard will increase the number of noncomplying counties from 208 to at least 283.[35]

Late in his second term, President Bush signed into law the bipartisan **Energy Independence Act of 2007**. As one of its major provisions, the act required motor vehicle manufacturers to increase the fuel efficiency of autos, light trucks, and SUVs to an average of 35 miles per gallon by 2020. If this goal is attained, it would increase fuel efficiency by 40 percent over those years. As discussed in the following section, however, Bush's signature came partly in response to a series of state actions to limit greenhouse gas emissions.

THE STATES' PROMINENCE IN ENVIRONMENTAL PROTECTION

Although the EPA has exercised policy leadership nationally for environmental protection, the states have played a highly significant role in administering federal policies—a role for the states that Congress intended. Congressional legislation provides for administrative delegation to the states. The EPA has delegated direct administrative oversight to state environmental protection agencies for about three-fourths of its programs. That makes states the primary enforcers of federal environmental laws for delegated programs. In practice, states assume most of the day-to-day responsibility for ensuring that federal environmental standards are met. State agencies issue 90 percent of pollution permits and take about 75 percent of enforcement actions. The states also play the dominant role in information gathering, collecting over 90 percent of all available data on air and water.[36]

In addition to enforcing federal standards for environmental protection, the states often impose standards that are tougher than the federal government's minimum standards. According to the Council of State Governments, about 80 percent of the states impose air pollution control standards that exceed federal minimum standards for at least one form of air pollution.[37] California provides the prime example of state leadership on tougher standards.

California's emissions standards for gasoline and diesel fuel exceed those imposed by the federal EPA. California's stricter standards for both gasoline and diesel fuel reduce the components of ozone by 300 tons a day, compared to federal standards.[38]

Energy Independence Act of 2007 Legislation signed into law by President George W. Bush in December 2007 that, among other provisions, mandated that automobiles, light trucks, and SUVs average 35 miles per gallon by 2020, achieving a 40 percent increase in fuel efficiency by that year.

Beyond requiring cleaner burning fuel and the less-polluting exhaust it produces, California's policymakers have used their regulatory powers to mandate that automakers increase their production of both zero-emission vehicles (electric- or fuel cell–powered) and low-emission vehicles for sale in the state. In addition, California was the first state to require automobile and light truck manufacturers to reduce carbon dioxide emissions for vehicles sold in the state. Legislation signed into law by Governor Gray Davis on January 22, 2002, directed the California Air Resources Board (CARB) to develop and adopt rules that "achieve the maximum feasible and cost-effective reduction of greenhouse gas emissions from passenger cars, light trucks, and SUVs sold in California." Rules promulgated by CARB in September 2004 required new 2009 model-year vehicles sold in California to emit 22 percent less carbon dioxide (CO_2) by 2012, compared to vehicles sold in 2000. That requirement rises to 30 percent by 2016.[39]

By mid-2008, 12 more states—Oregon and Washington in the West, and Connecticut, Delaware, Florida, Massachusetts, Maine, New Jersey, New York, Pennsylvania, Rhode Island, and Vermont in the East—had adopted California's requirements for CO_2 reduction as their own. In addition, the governors of four other Western states—Arizona, Colorado, New Mexico, and Utah—had announced their intention to take steps toward adopting the tougher standards.[40]

In response, automobile manufacturers raised the issue of having to meet potentially disparate standards among the states for vehicular emissions. Policymakers in some states are making their states' requirements stricter than those in effect in other states, and automobile manufacturers see disparate rules as unworkable and a restraint on interstate commerce.

Representing the automobile industry, the Alliance of Automobile Manufacturers launched a series of lawsuits against the states' actions, beginning in California. To date, the California suit remains unresolved; however, a circuit court judge in Oregon ruled in the state's favor. Suits in the other states have yet to yield decisions. Before any of the states' regulatory standards for carbon dioxide emissions can take effect, the EPA must issue a waiver. And the EPA has been unwilling to approve such waiver requests, arguing that it does not have the authority under the Clean Air Act to regulate CO_2 emissions from motor vehicles. Yet the EPA's receptivity to state waiver requests may change as a result of the U.S. Supreme Court's ruling in April 2007 that the EPA does indeed possess that authority under the Clean Air Act.[41] Whether the EPA will choose to grant waivers in light of the Court's decision is unclear at this time, especially following Congress's passage of the Energy Independence Act of 2007 in December 2007 (discussed earlier), which toughened existing federal motor vehicle fuel efficiency standards, and which President Bush characterized as a nationwide solution for reducing vehicular emissions through greater fuel efficiency, a solution that would be preferable compared to a myriad of state-by-state actions.[42]

The 2008 elections could render the White House and Congress more amenable to even tougher state initiatives for reducing greenhouse gas emissions, but both parties in the federal government may stand pat on the Energy Independence Act of 2007. The question of how strongly the states will push their waiver requests, in light of the national legislation, remains to be seen.

In another initiative to reduce greenhouse gas emissions, nine Northeastern and Mid-Atlantic states have joined forces to create the Northeastern States Regional Greenhouse Gas Initiative (RGGI). The effort, when implemented, would create a regional cap on CO_2 emissions, combined with a regional emissions trading program similar to existing programs already in effect and applied to sulfur dioxide and nitrous oxide emissions.[43] In summer 2008, RGGI announced its formal release of auction application materials in preparation for launching its trading program.

Several states have also taken the lead in reducing point-source air pollution. Oregon requires that carbon dioxide emissions from new electric power plants fall at least 17 percent below those of the most efficient natural gas-fired plants now in operation, pushing the industry to develop even cleaner burning technologies. Massachusetts has issued regulations that require the state's largest electric power facilities to reduce their carbon dioxide emissions by 10 percent, prompting the electric industry to make further technological improvements or change fuel. Connecticut, Illinois, New York, and North Carolina have taken action to decrease sulfur dioxide and nitrogen dioxide emissions below the federal government's compliance requirements for power plants.[44] In addition, as of 2007, a total of 21 states had approved stricter regulatory restrictions on industrial plants' mercury emissions compared to those of the federal EPA.[45]

States also provide policy leadership for solid-waste disposal. The federal Solid Waste Disposal Act of 1976 requires states to adopt solid-waste management plans, but day-to-day management and operations remain largely the responsibility of local governments. The federal EPA gets involved when local disposal of solid wastes threatens air or water quality.

Four types of solid waste exist: municipal, industrial, construction, and sewage. We tend to refer to municipal waste as garbage, and we are producing more and more of it. Americans produced 88 million tons of municipal waste in 1960, and that amount grew to 225 million tons in 2000, a dramatic increase of 156 percent. The average American produces 4.4 pounds of solid waste per day.[46] Once produced, garbage must be disposed of. It can be buried in landfills, burned in incinerators, or recycled into new products. The majority, 55 percent, goes to landfills; 28 percent is recycled; and 17 percent is incinerated. About 12 percent of our nation's solid waste crosses state lines: it is generated in one state and disposed of in another. New York and New Jersey lead the nation in exporting their waste to other states, while Pennsylvania and Virginia are the biggest importers of other states' waste.[47]

Although we all produce waste as a by-product of daily living, the burden of waste disposal is not shared equally among the population. The poor, particularly racial minorities, bear a disproportionate share of the environmental hazards associated with waste disposal. For example, a study conducted by the General Accounting Office found that three of four off-site commercial hazardous waste landfills in the Southeast are located in predominantly African American neighborhoods.[48] This reality has led policy advocates to call for greater equity, or **environmental justice**, in sharing the negative consequences of solid-waste disposal.

---

environmental justice A value placed on attaining greater equity in sharing the increased environmental risks associated with having solid-waste disposal facilities located in one's neighborhood.

THE ENVIRONMENTAL CHALLENGES LYING AHEAD

Expected population growth and expansion of the economy will continue to put pressures on the environment. Continued progress will have to be made just to maintain the status quo, to prevent pollution from getting any worse. Extra efforts will be required to make strides toward cleaning up the environment. America's heavy dependence on gasoline-powered automobiles presents a serious constraint on our nation's ability to clean up its air. Reformulating gasoline so that it burns more cleanly has its limits. For marked progress to be made in reducing air pollution, alternative sources of power must be employed. That means introducing significant numbers of vehicles powered by electricity and natural gas. Municipalities and school districts around the nation have selectively converted trucks and buses to natural gas, but they represent only a tiny percentage of vehicles on the road today. Detroit automakers are just starting to build a few models with natural gas engines, but a shortened driving range and limited retail fuel availability present obstacles to rapidly expanding use.

Mounting garbage generated by a growing populace will require additional disposal sites. Expanded recycling efforts could cut into that need, but the current economics of recycling offers only marginal or no incentives to foster marked expansion. Yet its contribution to waste reduction has been unmistakable.[49]

The United States has made progress toward improving its environment. In many ways we are ahead of the rest of the world, but contemporary environmental problems have become increasingly global in their reach. The chemical components of acid rain can drift across national borders, and hydrocarbon emissions from around the globe have contributed to a growing depletion of the earth's protective atmospheric ozone layer. Heightened environmental protection efforts within the United States can improve our air and water quality, but this country alone cannot solve the global problems of atmospheric ozone depletion or global warming.

Americans are indeed concerned about environmental issues and support protection measures. They also want to see a strong and growing American economy. The trick, then, is for policymakers to find ways to protect the environment without significantly retarding economic performance. That balance can be found if Americans are willing to change their behavior somewhat, perhaps trading some personal convenience for a cleaner environment. Government, too, needs to continue implementing policies that bias the options of businesses toward taking the steps to reduce the pollution they put into the air and water. Strengthening industry's incentives to operate in more environmentally friendly ways may be the key to a cleaner environment. Yet government's regulatory role, with credible sanctions, represents its trump card. Regulatory zeal must be balanced with the costs it entails, costs that can retard economic development. To appreciate the tension in that relationship, we must turn toward an examination of economic development's allure.

THE ALLURE OF ECONOMIC DEVELOPMENT

It is a truism that both government officials and the public at large welcome economic prosperity. Economic growth means added jobs, rising real incomes, the prospect of career advancement, sound commercial activity, and business profits, as well as healthy

I. The Private Benefit Model

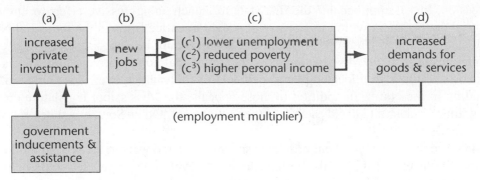

(employment multiplier)

II. The Public Benefit Model

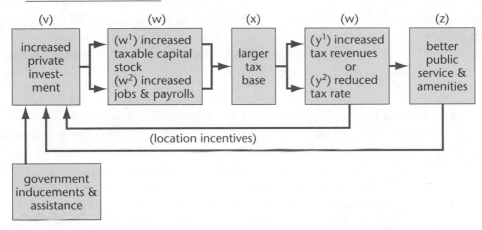

(location incentives)

Figure 17.2 Economic Development Benefit Models
Source: Peter K. Eisinger, *The Rise of the Entrepreneurial State* (Madison: University of Wisconsin Press, 1988), 35. Reprinted with permission of the publisher.

government treasuries. Figure 17.2 shows the benefits of economic development, to both individuals and government. A strong, growing national economy is the key to such prosperity. Fast, widespread national economic growth creates an environment in which all share in the prosperity, although some parts of the country may do somewhat better than others. Broad-based growth mitigates the chance that some parts of the nation will do well at the expense of others. The reality of the past couple of decades, however, shows that the national economy has not soared, and when sustained moderate economic growth has occurred, it has been far from even, as the discussion in Chapter 2 illustrated. In that context, a certain competition has existed among states and local governments over economic development. That competition has taken various forms: regions with regions; states with states within the same region; and local governments with local governments within the same state, even within the same metropolitan area.

Government efforts to entice and nurture economic development have taken several forms over time. The first form, commonly known as smokestack chasing, focused on attracting new industrial development within a state's borders. During the Great Depression, Mississippi became the first state to launch an aggressive effort to lure new industrial development within its borders. It sought to entice firms in the industrial North to relocate or expand plant operations in the South, basing its appeal on the lower costs of doing business there. Mississippi recruiters argued that comparatively lower taxes and labor costs would give relocated plants a competitive advantage over those remaining or expanding in the North. In addition to those appeals, the Mississippi legislature created a program of industrial subsidies as a further enticement. Other Southern states followed Mississippi's lead.

State economic development programs spread north and west in the second half of the century. By the end of the 1960s, formal economic development agencies could be found in most states. By the next decade's close, similar offices had sprung up in many major cities around the nation. Interjurisdictional competition fueled their creation and expansion.

State and local government policymakers turned to a common set of policy tools to advance themselves in that competition and to make them more attractive to would-be development. These earliest employed tools, which have been labeled **supply-side incentives**, commonly include the following:

1. Recruitment. Recruitment consists of active promotional campaigns to attract new industry to locate within a given state or local government jurisdiction. Instruments of recruitment typically include advertising and marketing; personal visits paid by state and local officials; supportive contacts made by friendly businesses on a government's behalf; and orientation visits for executives of recruited firms, complete with wining and dining. The idea is to get businesses interested enough to take the next step of closely examining the advantages of the relocation or expansion. Then, after a firm has established its interest, governments may turn to any one or more of the following incentives to help close the deal.

2. Tax Abatements. States and local governments frequently offer interested businesses temporary or long-term tax breaks to increase their after-tax profits. They can consist of reduced tax rates, deferrals of tax liability, or outright exemptions from taxation.

3. Loans. In addition to their license to raise tax revenues for approved public purposes, states and local governments have the ability to borrow money that is not always available to businesses. They can use these resources to make no-interest or low-interest loans to development prospects. As an alternative, state and local governments can make loans directly or guarantee loans made by private banks.

4. Physical Infrastructure. States and local governments can help pay for or provide the physical infrastructure needed by a major industrial operation. That can include highway access ramps, curbs and gutters, street lighting, power sources, and extensions of sewerage lines.

---

supply-side incentives Policy tools used to attract economic development within a governmental jurisdiction's boundaries or to entice industries to expand within those boundaries. Such tools include tax abatements, loans, the provision of physical infrastructure, and the relaxation of regulations.

5. Relaxed Regulations. Where they possess the authority, governments can relax regulations as a means of attracting new development. Compliance with government regulations takes time and entails costs. Consequently, if requirements are relaxed, businesses save the respective costs of compliance, thereby increasing profits on their bottom line. Regulations regarding land-use restrictions and pollution controls are the prime candidates for selective relaxation. Yet in areas such as environmental protection, federal laws and regulations often place constraints on the liberties that state and local governments can take.

State and local officials also try to promote their jurisdiction's business climate and general quality of life. Business climate includes the types of taxes a government employs and the associated tax effort it makes, prevailing wage rates, the availability of job-training programs, the relative preparedness and cost of labor, and a government's regulatory climate. Quality of life relates to the quality of schools, crime rate, climate, price of housing, availability of recreational opportunities, and quality of air and water.

In making choices about location, business executives also consider other factors traditionally bearing on business decisions, such as the ready availability of raw materials and energy resources, proximity to suppliers and transportation facilities, and access to key markets. Despite all the efforts that state and local policymakers have put into creating supply-side incentives, research over three decades suggests that these traditional criteria of business decision making continue to influence choices about location the most.[50] This does not mean that supply-side incentives fail to make a difference, but that difference appears to be only marginal.[51] This research raises the issue about whether state and local government investments in tax abatements, favorable loans, highway and street improvements, and the like, are really worth it. In a highly competitive environment, however, many states and local governments have not been willing to take the chance of losing ground because they fail to match or exceed the concessions offered by their competitors. At the same time, concern about the return on their investment has prompted state and local policymakers to turn to other policy instruments to spur economic development.

Faced with so-called attempted raiding by other states, governors and state legislators increasingly came to appreciate that their state's economic development efforts could reap bigger returns if they were concentrated on keeping industry and encouraging its expansion within their state's borders. This does not mean that recruitment efforts stopped altogether; they often continued selectively alongside the new initiatives. The emphasis did shift, however, from the former to the latter. By the early 1980s, about two-thirds of the states were spending more on bolstering in-state firms than on efforts to lure out-of-state companies.[52]

In a competitive interstate environment, governors and state legislatures have continued to support selective incentive packages to attract out-of-state firms, retain existing ones, and entice still others to expand within the state. These inducements come into play only after a business or an investor identifies an economic opportunity.[53] Entrepreneurs first arrive at a set of options that represent potentially sound business decisions. In the process of analyzing alternatives and weighing their relative advantages and disadvantages, firms and prospective investors look for concessions and incentives that might swing their decision one way or the other. The point is, however, that such inducements become relevant only after an entrepreneur has made the preliminary judgment that a business move looks attractive enough to pursue further. For that to happen, the basic elements of a sound business decision must first be satisfied.

At the local level, government leaders have continued to devote most of their economic development efforts to attracting new businesses to locate within their community's boundaries. More of a zero-sum game, therefore, exists at the local level: a local government's success often comes at the expense of other jurisdictions.

State policymakers, in contrast, increasingly turned their attention in the 1980s to expanding the size of the economic pie, rather than just enlarging their slice at another state's expense. This departure shifted the emphasis to state initiatives aimed at encouraging private interests to undertake new ventures that develop new products and services in response to emerging needs—moving to **demand-side policies**. As Peter Eisinger reminded us, the idea behind this shift from supply-side to demand-side policies is to "discover or point out opportunities and to assist investors to capitalize on them."[54]

Toward this end, state economic development officials have focused a significant part of their efforts on small businesses that hold the promise of strong growth. States have provided fledgling enterprises with loans for venture capital, financial assistance for product development (often with provisions giving the state an equity share of profits), managerial and technical assistance, work force training, and even help in finding new markets.

This nurturing of new entrepreneurial activity through public–private partnerships, accompanied by a widespread desire to foster industrial growth that does not contribute significantly to environmental pollution, has prompted state policymakers to go after high-technology growth. High-technology industries, whether in the computer field or in biotechnology, lend themselves to partnerships directed at new business incubation and new product development. They also provide a hospitable environment for cooperative research and development efforts between state universities and industry. Breakthroughs created by basic and applied research can lead to the development of new products and new applications. For that very reason, governors and legislatures in the 1980s supported increased funding for applied research and technology transfer programs.

In contrast to supply-side policies, demand-side economic development policies look less to short-term gains and more toward making investments and creating partnerships that hold the promise of expanding capital and creating jobs over the long term. Table 17.1 provides a systematic comparison of the two approaches.

The lingering economic recession of the early 1990s squeezed financial support for state economic development programs. In contrast to previous experience, in which states commonly increased their spending on economic development programs during economic downturns, many states cut financial support for those programs. Economic development programs found themselves in tough competition with other pressing claims on state tax revenues that frequently fell short of projected expenditures. The greatest competition

---

demand-side policies   Initiatives aimed at encouraging private interests to undertake ventures that develop new products and services in response to emerging needs, that, in a sense, expand the size of the economic development pie.

Table 17.1 Supply-Side Policy versus Demand-Side Entrepreneurial Policy

Supply Side	Demand Side
Growth is promoted by lowering production factor costs through government subsidies of capital and land, and through low taxes.	Growth is promoted by discovering, expanding, developing, or creating new markets for local goods and services.
Main focus is on established, potentially mobile capital.	Main focus is on new capital.
Strategies focus on stimulating capital formation relocation or capital retention.	Strategies focus on new business and small business expansion.
Development involves competition with other jurisdictions for the same investment.	Development proceeds by nurturing indigenous resources.
Government supports low-risk undertakings.	Government becomes involved in high-risk enterprises and activities.
Any employer is a suitable target for development assistance.	Development assistance is offered selectively according to strategic criteria.
Government's role is to follow and support private-sector decisions about where to invest, what businesses will be profitable, and what products will sell.	Government's role is to help identify investment opportunities that the private sector may either have overlooked or be reluctant to pursue, including opportunities in new markets, new products, and new industries.

Source: Peter K. Eisinger, *The Rise of the Entrepreneurial State.* © 1989 by the Board of Regents of the University of Wisconsin System. Reprinted by permission of The University of Wisconsin Press.

came from Medicaid, adult and juvenile corrections, and public education. In that competitive arena, state operations programs such as economic development promotion became prime candidates for budget reductions. Growing questions about the payoff of state economic development investments rendered them susceptible to cuts. Governors and legislatures increasingly came to wonder whether demand-side policy instruments, like the supply-side tools that preceded them, were cost effective. Their growing skepticism was reinforced by academic observers' suggestions that their contribution to economic growth has been modest at best.[55]

State policymakers have come to appreciate that the condition of a state's economy, its physical and social infrastructure, and its general quality of life are what attract business development and prospective residents. Business leaders look for places that offer strong, sustained economic performance; good highways, roads, and airport facilities; successful schools; proximity to research universities and technical education centers; low crime; hospitable weather; and a clean environment. A favorable tax and regulatory climate enhances their allure, but the former factors now appear to be more compelling than the latter, in balance. With expanding telecommunications capabilities, the less-populated, more remote areas of the nation that measure high on quality of life considerations have recently attracted firms and residents from states whose quality of life has been in decline. It is not uncommon today to find state legislatures appropriating funds for fiber-optic communication highways that crisscross states and make it possible to transmit video, voice, and data to and from areas that had previously been isolated both commercially and socially. That strategy is also aimed at spreading out development and encouraging firms to locate outside metropolitan areas to minimize the environmental impact on heavily populated areas.

Despite budget reductions in state economic development programs, governors and legislatures are likely to continue their financial support for industrial recruitment and capacity-building programs, albeit at reduced levels. They also are likely to justify increased spending on infrastructure—both physical and social—in terms of their contribution to economic development. Economic development will probably become much more synonymous with quality of life and new ways of connecting people, businesses, and their customers. At the same time, however, the traditional spirit of competitiveness will likely prompt both state and local policymakers to continue to offer inducements and concessions as the icing on the cake to attract development within their borders. The signs now suggest that they must have something more to offer in exchange for the hoped-for added tax base—a place in which to live and raise a family: a place with good schools, safe streets, recreational and social amenities, and a clean environment. Communities that can offer these features, and which otherwise have the ingredients to satisfy the traditional tests of a good business decision, are the ones that will attract economic development.

ENVIRONMENTAL PROTECTION AND ECONOMIC DEVELOPMENT: A STRAINED RELATIONSHIP?

Few question that the addition of industries and the expansion of existing ones place a greater pollution load on the environment, everything else being equal. That is why existing air pollution regulatory policy has not only toughened its compliance standards and extended their application, but also required states to show how added emissions from new industrial sources in noncomplying areas will be offset by corresponding reductions from existing sources. Through the use of market-based incentives, federal and state law has given firms the incentive to install pollution abatement technology that can reduce emissions below mandated levels, thus allowing corporations to sell the excess credits in the marketplace (as discussed earlier). Nevertheless, the following question remains: do toughened regulations, even with the recent mix of incentives and constraints, retard economic development? A related question also deserves an answer: will the potential economic consequences of heightened environmental regulation lead state officials to relax their enforcement of those standards?

Recall that one of the reasons Congress gave the federal government partial preemption authority over air pollution regulation was to create uniform minimum standards for noncompliance that apply to all states, thus reducing incentives for pollution-generating industries to shop around for lenient policies. In an environment of competition for economic development, however, perhaps some states might relax their delegated enforcement of the federal standards, readily agreeing to good faith compromises that accept progress toward meeting the standards in place of actual compliance.

This very inquiry assumes that the relative stringency of environmental regulation is a significant element in a company's decision about location. However, a U.S. General

Exploring the Web

Forces in the Trade-off

Policymakers have come to recognize that there are trade-offs between environmental protection and economic development. Cleaner air and water come at a price. Businesses bear the costs of meeting increasingly tougher pollution abatement requirements, and environmental controls can constrain industrial expansion and cost prospective jobs. Conversely, industrial expansion, and the employment and population growth associated with it, can increase pollution emissions that foul our nation's air and water. Interests on both sides of the balance organize to tilt the trade-off in their favor.

■ On the environmentalist side of the balance, take a look at the activist agendas of the Environmental Defense Fund (*www.edf.org*), the Wilderness Society (*www.wilderness.org*), and the Sierra Club (*www.sierraclub.org*).

■ On the economic development side of the balance, browse the websites of the Commercial Real Estate Development Association (*www.naiop.org*), the Society of Industrial and Office Realtors (*www.sior.com*), and the National Association of Home Builders (*www.nahb.com*).

■ For government agencies charged with regulating environmental pollution, check out the following websites: at the national level, the U.S. Environmental Protection Agency (*www.epa.gov*); at the state and local levels, the National Association of Clean Air Agencies (*www.4cleanerair.org*).

■ To find out about government associations that promote economic development, turn to the U.S. Economic Development Administration (*www.eda. gov/Resources*) and the Council of State Community Development Agencies (*www.coscda.org*).

Accounting Office analysis of interstate differences in toxic air pollution regulation[56] concluded that the relative strictness of regulatory controls was not associated with the location decisions of industry. Instead, qualified labor, markets, and raw materials were found to be the major factors driving decisions to stay put or move—consistent with the findings reported earlier.

SUMMARY AND CONCLUSIONS

America's air and water are cleaner today than they were four decades ago. Major improvements have been made in reducing pollutants from industry and motor vehicles. Nevertheless, over 133 million Americans live in metropolitan areas whose air quality fails to meet federal standards. Although progress has been made toward cleaning the nation's environment, much more remains to be done. At the same time, continued expansion and population growth threaten to eat into or overtake the gains that have been made.

Americans support environmental protection, but they also benefit from economic growth and the mobility that the automobile offers. Policymakers at both the state and local levels overwhelmingly support economic development. It expands government tax bases and increases their popularity. Yet economic development has its costs, among them environmental degradation. The responsibility for setting the balance between economic development and environmental quality falls to policymakers at the federal, state, and local government levels. Federalism provides the framework for those choices.

The federal government has taken the lead in environmental protection. Important legislation passed by Congress during the past three decades has charged the EPA with setting national standards for both air and water quality—standards that are enforced by the states. If the states fail to carry out their delegated responsibilities properly, the EPA can step in and exercise that authority directly.

Federal legislation requires states to use permits to control the addition of new industrial pollution sources as well as reduce emissions from motor vehicle use. It also requires automobile manufacturers to take continued steps to reduce auto emissions. In addition, federal legislation provides federal aid to assist local governments to upgrade sewage treatment plants.

Congress enacted most of its key environmental legislation during the 1970s, the so-called environmental decade, although the 1990 amendments to the Clean Air Act extend pollution controls and introduce significant new approaches to environmental regulation, including market-based incentives for reducing air pollution emissions. The 1990 amendments also toughen the automobile inspection and maintenance requirements included in the Clean Air Act Amendments of 1977.

The Clinton administration used the EPA's authority under the 1990 amendments to promulgate tougher standards for ozone and PM pollution. Although industry officials and national associations of county and municipal governments opposed the new regulations, and despite the threat of congressional action to block their implementation, the Clinton administration persisted. Metropolitan areas had until 2004 to comply with the toughened ozone standard and until 2005 to meet the new fine PM standard. With President Clinton's strong support, the EPA also promulgated regulations aimed at reducing tailpipe emissions from SUVs and light trucks, as well as other regulations that would drastically lower the sulfur content of gasoline and diesel fuel. Both sets of regulations are scheduled to take full effect by 2010.

The George W. Bush administration proposed tougher caps on sulfur dioxide, nitrogen oxides, and mercury emissions. It also called for the trading of excess emissions credits to include nitrogen oxide and mercury emissions, creating a broadened system that would allow trading credits applied to all three pollutants.

Heightened environmental regulation does have economic costs of compliance. Not only does industry pay for the improvements necessary to meet higher air and water quality standards, but state and local government officials worry that enforcement of toughened requirements may help to drive industrial growth outside the borders of their jurisdictions.

State and local governments have put a great deal of effort into recruiting business development and encouraging existing enterprises to expand locally. They traditionally have employed supply-side policies such as tax abatements, loans, infrastructure improvements, and the relaxation of regulations. States have added demand-side policies aimed at encouraging firms to undertake new ventures and to develop new products. Here, useful instruments have been loans for venture capital, financial assistance for product development, managerial and technical assistance, work force training, and help in finding new markets.

Dogged about concerns over the cost effectiveness of these initiatives and squeezed by budget cuts for economic development agencies occasioned by the early 1990s recession, governors and legislators have turned their attention less to government-financed incentives for economic development and given increased emphasis to making investments that improve their state's physical and social infrastructure and their residents' quality of life. Good roads and airport facilities, successful schools, low crime, and a clean environment have been accorded increased importance in attracting and keeping development. They have come to be viewed as the icing on the cake after entrepreneurs first conclude that the traditional elements of a good business decision have been met— access to qualified labor, markets, and raw materials. These infrastructure investments have costs that cannot be met with existing tax resources. These efforts, which make significant improvements in infrastructure and quality of life, will require tax increases— increases that will likely encounter widespread political opposition and be viewed as constraints on economic expansion. That is a dilemma that policymakers at all levels of government will continue to face.

Discussion Questions

1. Discuss the sources of strain that exist between economic development and environmental protection. How have they been manifested politically?

2. Environmental protection measures cost business and industry money. How can the market economy, with its objective of increasing profit, be employed to create incentives for industry to make further efforts to clean the environment? Discuss recent attempts to introduce market incentives to meet that goal.

3. Discuss the different forms that state and local government efforts to entice and nurture economic development have taken over time.

4. Compare and contrast the supply-side and demand-side incentives used by state and local governments in their efforts to foster economic development within their borders.

5. What factors appear to be most important to business executives when they are deciding where to locate industrial plants, and what can state and local government officials do to influence business leaders' location choices?

Glossary

Clean Air Act Amendments of 1990 453
Clear Skies 458
demand-side policies 466
Energy Independence Act of 2007 459

environmental impact statement (EIS) 449
environmental justice 461
market-based incentives 455
National Environmental Policy Act 448

Safe Drinking Water Act of 1974 451
supply-side incentives 464
technology-forcing standards 454
Water Pollution Control Act of 1972 451

Endnotes

1. Office of Air Quality Planning and Standards, U.S. Environmental Protection Agency, *Air Emission Trends—Continued Progress through* 2005, April 2006, www.epa.gov/airtrends/2006/econ-emissions.html.

2. Ibid.

3. Federal Highway Administration, *Our Nation's Highways: Selected Facts and Figures* (Washington, D.C.: U.S. Department of Transportation, 2000), 8.

4. Doug Brandow, "Environmentalism: The Triumph of Politics," *The Freeman* 43, no. 9 (September 1993), 332.

5. Walter A. Rosenbaum, *Environmental Politics and Policy*, 3d ed. (Washington, D.C.: Congressional Quarterly Press, 1995), 35.

6. Riley E. Dunlap, "Public Opinion and Environmental Policy," in James Lester, ed., *Environmental Politics and Policy: Theories and Evidence* (Durham, N.C.: Duke University Press, 1989), 131.

7. Norman J. Vig and Michael E. Kraft, "Environmental Policy from the Seventies to the Eighties," in Norman J. Vig and Michael, eds., *Environmental Policy in the 1980s: Reagan's New Agenda* (Washington, D.C.: Congressional Quarterly Press, 1984), 17.

8. The Council on Environmental Quality, *Environmental Quality, 1981* (Washington, D.C.: U.S. Government Printing Office, 1981), 33, 243, 246.

9. Susan Welch et al., *American Government*, 4th ed. (St. Paul, Minn.: West Publishing, 1992), 574.

10. Helen M. Ingram and Dean E. Mann, "Preserving the Clean Water Act: The Appearance of Environmental Victory," in Norman J. Vig and Michael E. Kraft, eds., *Environmental Policy in the 1980s: Reagan's New Agenda* (Washington, D.C.: Congressional Quarterly Press, 1984), 255–256.

11. Ingram and Mann, "Preserving the Clean Water Act," 255.

12. The Council on Environmental Quality, *Environmental Quality, 1980* (Washington, D.C.: U.S. Government Printing Office, 1980), iv.

13. Michael E. Kraft, "A New Environmental Policy Agenda: The 1980 Presidential Campaign and Its Aftermath," in Norman J. Vig and Michael E. Kraft, eds., *Environmental Policy in the 1980s: Reagan's New Agenda* (Washington, D.C.: Congressional Quarterly Press, 1984), 29–50.

14. Norman J. Vig, "The President and the Environment: Revolution or Retreat," in Norman J. Vig and Michael E. Kraft, eds., *Environmental Policy in the 1980s: Reagan's New Agenda* (Washington, D.C.: Congressional Quarterly Press, 1984), 87.

15. Ibid.

16. Welch et al., *American Government*, 578.

17. Robert V. Bartlett, "The Budgetary Process and Environmental Policy," in Norman J. Vig and Michael E. Kraft, eds., *Environmental Policy in the 1980s: Reagan's New Agenda* (Washington, D.C.: Congressional Quarterly Press, 1984), 131.

18. Tom Arrandale, "A Guide to Environmental Mandates," *Governing* (March 1994), 78–79.

19. Jackie Cummins and Larry Morandi, "Now You See It, Now You Don't," *State Legislatures* 19, no. 10 (October 1993), 34.

20. Ibid., 31–32.

21. R. Shep Melnick, "Pollution Deadlines and the Coalition for Failure," in Michael S. Greve and Fred L. Smith, *Environmental Politics* (New York: Greenwood Publishing, 1993), 89–104.

22. Kelly Robinson, "The Regional Economic Impacts of Marketable Permit Programs: The Case of Los Angeles," *Proceedings of a Conference on Cost Effective Control of Urban Smog*, 166–188; David Harrison Jr. and Albert Nichols, *An Economic Analysis of the RECLAIM Trading Program for the South Coast Air Basin* (Cambridge, Mass.: National Economic Research Associates, 1992).

23. William Fulton, "The Air Pollution Trading Game," *Governing* (March 1992), 40–45; Thomas H. Klier and Richard H. Mattoon, "How Regions Can Benefit from Flexible Environmental Compliance," *Chicago Fed Letter*, no. 73 (September 1993).

24. William Fulton, "The Big Green Bazaar," *Governing* 9, no. 9 (June 1996), 38–42.

25. Tom Arrandale, "A '70s-Style Cleanup Isn't the Answer for the '90s," *Governing* (March 1993), 58.

26. Susan Biemesderfer, "Stopping Pollution Before It Starts," *State Legislatures* 17, no. 8 (August 1991), 36–39.

27. Deb Waldman and Kristin Rahenkemp, "How Green Was My Label," *State Legislatures* 17, no. 8 (August 1991), 39–41; Tom Arrandale, "The Role of Government in Marketing of the 'Green'," *Governing* (September 1991), 77.

28. Tom Arrandale, "Complaining Alone Won't Cure the Mandate Blues," *Governing* (September 1993), 80.

29. Oral Testimony of Fred Hanson, Deputy Administrator, Environmental Protection Agency, Before the Subcommittee on Commercial and Administrative Law, Committee on the Judiciary, U.S. House of Representatives, July 20, 1997; Jackie Cummins Radcliffe and Jeff Dale, "Defining Dirty Air," *State Legislatures* 23, no. 5 (May 1997), 20–25.

30. Tom Arrandale, "The Selling of the Garbage Glut," *Governing* (April 1993), 28–32.

31. National Conference of State Legislatures, Air Quality, www.ncsl.org/programs/esnr/cleanair.htm, April 27, 2000; Sierra Club, Clean Air Program, www.sierraclub.org/cleanair/standards.asp.

32. White Paper on the Clear Skies Initiative and the Current Clean Air Act (Washington, D.C.: U.S. Environmental Protection Agency, 2002).

33. James E. McCarthy, "Clean Air Act Issues in the 109th Congress," *CRS Issue Brief for Congress*, Updated May 3, 2006, www.ncseonline.org/NLE/CRSreports/06apr/IB10137.pdf.

34. National Resources Defense Council, *Rewriting the Rules (2005 Special Edition)*, www.nrdc.org/legislation /rollbacks/execsum.asp.

35. James E. McCarthy, "Clean Air Act Issues in the 109th Congress."

36. Tom Arrandale, "The Pollution Puzzle," *Governing* (August 2002), 25

37. Steven Brown, "The States Protect the Environment," *ECOStates* (Summer 1999), 1–6.

38. California Air Resources Board, www.arb.ca.gov/html/brochure/history.htm.

39. James M. Taylor, "Auto Manufacturers' Association Suit Challenging California Greenhouse Gas Law," *Environment News*, February 1, 2005, www.heartland.org/article.cfm?artId=16377.

40. www.pewclimate.org.

41. *Massachusetts et al. v. Environmental Protection Agency et al.*, 549 US 05-1120 (2007).

42. www.whitehouse.gov/news/releases/2—7/12/20071219-6.html.

43. Regional Greenhouse Gas Initiative, www.rggi.org

44. Barry R. Gabe, "Statehouse and Greenhouse," *Brookings Review* 20 (Spring 2002): 13.

45. Barry Rabe, "Environmental Policy and the Bush Era: The Collision between the Administrative Presidency and State Experimentation," *Publius* 37, no. 3 (Summer 2007): 413–431.

46. *A Primer on Solid Waste* (Washington, D.C.: U.S. Department of Energy, 2002), 7–8.

47. Zero Waste America, www.zerowasteamerica.org.

48. Cited in David Nagub Pellow, *Garbage Wars* (Cambridge, Mass.: MIT Press, 2002), 9.

49. *State Air Pollution Control Standards*, 1999 (Lexington, Ky.: Council of State Governments, 1999.

50. Lawrence Lund, *Factors in Corporate Locational Decision* (New York: The Conference Board, 1979); Advisory Commission on Intergovernmental Relations, *Regional Growth: Interstate Tax Competition* (Washington, D.C.: U.S. Government Printing Office, 1981); Michael Kieschnick, "Taxes and Growth: Business Incentives and Economic Development," in Michael Barker, ed., *State Taxation Policy* (Durham, N.C.: Duke University Press, 1983), 155–280.

51. Roger Schmennee, *Making Business Locational Decisions* (Englewood Cliffs, N.J.: Prentice Hall, 1982); Peter K. Eisinger, *The Rise of the Entrepreneurial State* (Madison: University of Wisconsin Press, 1988).

52. Dan Pilcher, "The Third Wave of Economic Development," *State Legislatures* 17, no. 11 (November 1991), 36.

53. Eisinger, *The Rise of the Entrepreneurial State*, 128–172.

54. Ibid., 229.

55. Ibid., 305–306; Richard H. Mattoon, "Economic Development Policy in the 1990s: Are State Economic Development Agencies Ready?" *Economic Perspectives 17*, no. 3 (May/June 1993), 12.

56. U.S. General Accounting Office, *Air Pollution: States Assigned a Major Role in EPA's Air Toxic Strategy* (Washington, D.C.: U.S. Government Printing Office, 1987).

18

Fiscal Policy and Financial Management

LEARNING OBJECTIVES

- Know the different revenue sources available to state and local governments and the extent of their use.
- Identify the criteria that can be used to evaluate state and local taxes.
- Understand the issues and politics involved in state financial management, including revenue and expenditure estimating, cash flow management, budget balancing, and capital budgeting and debt management.

California has had a deplorable record of failing to pass budgets before the new fiscal year begins. Not surprisingly, politics usually got in the way, exacerbated by a constitutional provision in California that the state budget required a two-thirds, super majority vote for approval. Voters, tired of recurring budget stalemates, approved a constitutional amendment in November 2011, which lowered the bar of approval to a simple majority. That change paved the way for majority-party Democrats in the legislature to pass a budget on the day before the new 2011–2012 fiscal year began.

The legislature's action eliminated $15 billion of budget deficit, but not without deep cuts to a wide swath of state programs, including the University of California, which saw its budget cut by $650 million, or about a fifth of its state appropriation. In addition, the university got no new funding from the legislature to cover about $350 million of mandatory spending increases. Despite the efforts of Democratic Governor Jerry Brown to win legislative approval of an extension of tax increases scheduled to expire, the measure failed, amidst hardened Republican opposition. Unlike most state operations, which have no recourse facing appropriations reductions but to cut programs, typically resulting in position cuts, furloughed employees, and reduced aid payments, the Regents of the University of California possess independent authority to raise tuition to close budget gaps. And they made use of it, increasing tuition by 9.6 percent for the 2011–2012 school year, on top of an 8 percent increase approved the preceding fall. Budget cuts can entail pain, but the pain in this instance was felt directly by students and their parents, who were faced with footing the bill for a valued higher education.

When state legislatures, city councils, county boards, and local school districts enact budgets, they are establishing priorities among public programs—deciding who should benefit from those programs, and who should pay for them. Those who determine which programs should be supported and at what levels do not have to pay for them by themselves. The public pays. Although the public also benefits from government programs, those benefits are not distributed evenly across society; neither is the burden to pay for them. Some state and local residents invariably pay more and benefit less, and vice versa. From the taxpayer's perspective, the optimal situation is to benefit the most and pay the least. The worst is to pay heavily while realizing disproportionately few benefits in return.

The public pays taxes and fees to different levels of government concomitantly. Taxpayers not only pay their state's income and sales taxes, they also pay property taxes in support of their municipality, county, and school district. Some cities, counties, and school districts, if they have received the state's permission, also levy local income or sales taxes on top of the property tax. But it does not end there. Property owners also pay fees to special-purpose districts to cover the costs of water and sewerage services. In addition, municipalities and counties may charge fees for the use of their golf courses, zoos, museums, swimming pools, and other public attractions.

The link between payment and benefit in these latter examples is direct and clear. The payee directly gets something in return: drinkable tap water, raw sewage removal and treatment, a round of golf, a visit to the zoo or museum, or the pleasure of a cold swim on a hot afternoon. In other words, the recipient pays a fee for use. User fees are not limited to local governments; states charge them as well. When you register your car or truck, obtain a driver's license, buy gasoline or diesel fuel, or get a hunting or fishing license, you are paying a user fee of sorts. If you do not drive a motor vehicle, you have no need to register it, obtain a driver's license, or purchase fuel. Similarly, if you do not hunt or fish, it makes no sense for you to acquire a hunting or fishing license. Only those who engage in those activities pay the associated fee or tax.

Similarly, benefits from taxpayer-supported public spending can be individualized by way of a payment to low-income families with dependent children, a government-financed medical service, a higher education tuition grant, or a hot meal delivered to the homebound elderly. However, unlike the direct fee-for-use relationship previously discussed, the users do not pay directly for these benefits. As taxpayers, if they pay any taxes at all, they contribute to the general support of government services, but the value of benefits received often exceeds their tax contribution. Those who fail to receive these benefits pay for them nonetheless.

The circle of those who benefit from government programs can be drawn even wider. Although bus and light rail riders pay a fare to support their personal mobility, total fare revenue falls short of covering the costs of transit operations. Both local governments and states commonly subsidize mass transit. When they do, the rider benefits because the subsidy lowers the fare that has to be charged. It can be argued that a general taxpayer subsidy is appropriate because of the indirect or spillover benefits that mass transit provides to the public at large. Even those who never ride buses or light rail benefit from mass transit. The displacement of automobile drivers cuts down on vehicular congestion and reduces air pollution. In a somewhat different sense, all municipal residents benefit from the availability of police and fire protection, even though some actually use these services more than others do.

Some benefits can be thought of as indivisible because it cannot be said that one person benefits more than another. Government measures to purify water benefit us all. We all drink water; therefore, we have a common stake in ensuring that it meets acceptable standards for human consumption. However, some of us use more water than others, providing a rationale to graduate water charges based on use. In this case, fees can be set to combine both charges: base fees applied to all residents, and graduated fees based on usage.

Within this broad spectrum, from individualized to indivisible benefits, state and local policymakers not only determine what public services should be provided and for whom, they also decide who should pay for them and what type of tax or fee should be employed. That latter consideration is important because different tax and fee instruments impose different burdens on different groups of payers.

Beyond deciding whether new government programs should be created or existing ones expanded, and who should pay for them, state and local policymakers must accommodate forces that push up public expenditures with no accompanying change in policy, including inflation and growth in the number of persons who meet eligibility requirements. In either case, someone has to pay to finance spending increases. Rising demands on the public treasury mean additional revenues have to be raised or offsetting cuts must be made elsewhere in the budget. The quest for additional revenues raises the question of who should pay to support increased spending, and the prospect of budget cuts focuses interest on whose benefits should be reduced or eliminated. Some cuts can be accommodated by realizing greater administrative efficiencies, but after a point, services themselves must be cut back to make fiscal ends meet.

State and local governments are constrained in making fiscal ends meet by requirements that they balance their budgets—that expenditures not exceed available revenues. Because local governments are legally creatures of their states, local governments are subject to state constitutional or statutory requirements that they balance their budgets for each fiscal year, requirements that also apply to all state governments except Vermont. However, the way in which the **balanced budget requirement** applies to states and local governments varies considerably. For some, the budget must be in balance when enacted by the state legislature or local legislative body; for others, the chief executive must submit a balanced budget for legislative consideration; some require that, when the books are closed at fiscal year-end, actual expenditures must fall within actual revenues received.

Revenues can fall short of projections during the course of the fiscal year. In a similar vein, expenditures can increase beyond planned levels on a monthly or quarterly basis. These warning signs can alert policymakers to a looming **budget deficit** and give them an opportunity to prevent it. Executives can impose reductions or freezes on discretionary spending,

---

balanced budget requirement The requirement that expenditures not exceed revenues in a given fiscal period. It is applied to most state and local governments, but not to the federal government.

budget deficit The condition existing when expenditures exceed revenues at the close of a given fiscal period.

and legislative bodies can pass interim tax or fee increases. Even with such actions, a state or local government can close the fiscal year in the red, particularly when facing a rapidly deteriorating economy, which reduces revenues below expected levels and increases social welfare expenditures. Faced with a prospective deficit, local governments possess less flexibility than states to correct the situation through interim budget cuts. Because all but about one-quarter of local government budgets cover the salaries and fringe benefits of employees, who often have civil service protection, program administrators have limited flexibility to reduce expenditures after the budget has been enacted, unless steps are taken to lay off government workers. State budgets provide far greater flexibility because of the higher percentage of expenditures devoted to financial aid for individuals and local units of government. No mid-year benefit reduction, however, can escape the political fallout of disgruntled recipients, nor is the alternative, a highly visible interim tax increase, palatable to those asked to pay.

Rather than risk budget deficits, state and local policymakers have an incentive to build a politically acceptable surplus into the budget. A **budget surplus** provides a cushion against the eroding effects of higher-than-expected levels of inflation or unexpected claims against the public purse, such as those occasioned by unfavorable court judgments or financial aid cuts imposed by higher levels of government. It also provides a contingency against revenues falling short of projections. But a surplus, just as a deficit, can spell political problems. Political opponents can take advantage of the situation, suggesting that current leaders "stole" from the people by taking more of their personal resources, through taxation, than was necessary. A call to "give it back," through tax cuts, can prove politically appealing to the electorate in the next election.

Elected public officials face contradictory pressures to keep taxes low while increasing the services and benefits enjoyed by special-interest groups and the general public. The favorite tax cut for most taxpayers always seems to be the next one. The favorite spending cut is in someone else's program. At the same time, government bureaucrats have the incentive to expand their agency's programs, adding responsibility and staff members. If their programs become bigger, they have a claim to greater funding and higher job classifications for themselves and their workers, which in turn can justify higher salaries. In contrast, business leaders strive to maximize profits by operating as lean as possible. The incentive for low-production costs is increased profit, which means higher returns to stockholders as well as the prospect of bonuses to managers and workers. It is within the incentive system of the public sector that we examine state and local government taxing and spending.

THE ECONOMY, TAXING, AND SPENDING

The condition of the economy at state and local levels affects taxing and spending. A robust economy means industrial and business expansion, job growth, and rising levels of personal income. Industrial and business expansion brings with it an expanded tax base, allowing local governments to raise additional property tax revenues without increasing the taxes of existing property taxpayers. New jobs reduce unemployment and increase

---

budget surplus The condition existing when revenues exceed expenditures at the close of a given fiscal period.

aggregate personal income, allowing states and local governments (where permitted) to tax that additional income. A healthy economy also encourages and provides the where-withal for heightened consumer spending. That added spending generates increased sales tax revenues. Increased revenues give governors, mayors, and school administrators the opportunity to advance new programs and improve services without feeling the political sting of an accompanying tax increase.

A sagging economy works in the opposite direction. Firms stop expanding or, in deep recessions, even close plants. Unemployment rises and personal income drops. With a steady or shrinking property tax base, local governments are faced with raising rates or cutting back on services. With rising unemployment, unemployment compensation and public assistance costs increase. With declining personal income, both income and sales tax collections fall below projected levels. Faced with these events, state and local poli-cymakers confront the tough choices of pursuing tax increases to make up for evaporated revenues, or cutting expenditures. Cuts in the state budget can add to the woes of local governments when those cuts come in the form of reduced aid from the state. Similarly, a bad economy can prompt the federal government to cut back on its financial assistance to state and local governments, making their predicament worse.

Taxing and spending decisions at the federal level can be used as instruments of national fiscal policy. **Keynesian economics** suggests that the national government can smooth out the ups and downs of the business cycle by increasing federal spending to stimulate aggregate demand for goods and services, thus increasing employment and rais-ing aggregate income.

Unlike the federal government, state and local governments are not well positioned to influence the course of the economy. As noted earlier, they generally are not permit-ted to run deficits, which means that they must increase taxes if they are to increase spending significantly—hardly a Keynesian prescription for increasing demand. The choice to increase taxes by a state or local government could also place it at a com-petitive disadvantage vis-à-vis other states or communities. Governments improve their competitive position not by raising taxes, but by lowering them and offering other incen-tives for industry to locate within their borders.

State and local economies are easily penetrated by national and regional economic forces. International developments can also affect a state's or region's economic fortunes. A major drop in the international price of oil, for example, can result in plummeting rev-enues to America's oil-producing states. The weather, too, can differentially affect the economy of agricultural states. Favorable conditions can increase agricultural yields, whereas severe droughts or floods can impose hardship. If farmers are hard hit, so are their rural communities because the economic troubles spread to related agribusinesses and to rural main streets. Under these conditions, states and local governments can do little to employ taxing or spending as tools of economic management. At best, they can use the

---

Keynesian economics An economic theory that accords government the role of using fiscal policy to manage the economy, particularly increasing government spending in bad economic times to stimulate demand for goods and services, thus increasing employment and raising aggregate demand.

powers of government to soften the blow on individuals by providing services, financial assistance, and loan guarantees to help people get back on their feet economically.

Nevertheless, the financial choices of state and local governments, in the aggregate, can help cushion the effects of the business cycle of expansion and contraction. State and local governments, particularly states, build up reserves during periods of expansion and draw them down during contractions, providing resources that allow spending to rise relative to revenue receipts.

Given the length of many state legislative sessions and the time requirements of the legislative process, actions to cut spending and raise taxes, following the depletion of available reserves, usually take effect during the last stages of economic downturn or after recovery has already begun. With recovery, these higher tax rates and lowered expenditure levels produce an improved revenue–expenditure balance. State treasuries grow, and financial commitments shrink. But these conditions themselves do not promote economic development. Recovering businesses and industries are likely faced with higher tax burdens, as are consumers of their goods and services. As a result, disposable income drops temporarily, until full-blown economic recovery expands personal income and increases purchasing power.

One study has found that state and local governments have adopted countercyclical measures during all nine of the business cycle contractions since World War II. In each case, expenditures rose relative to revenues, from peak to trough, over each contraction, the result of revenue growth falling short of expenditure growth that was fueled by increased claims against recession-sensitive social welfare programs. Looking at expansions, from trough to peak, the converse can be found: the growth of receipts outstripped the growth of expenditures.[1]

Governments can temporarily spend beyond their means. Drawing down available balances in the general fund is not their only option; they have others. They can temporarily transfer money from segregated funds (such as a highway fund or a natural resources conservation fund), which might be in a more favorable financial position; engage in the questionable practice of short-term borrowing to meet operational requirements; or push major expenditure obligations into the next fiscal year (easily done when payments are scheduled for the last day of the fiscal year) or move up tax payments (always a more precarious endeavor).

TAXING AND SPENDING COMPARISONS AMONG THE STATES

State spending varies considerably, both in total spending and by major spending categories. Because states vary greatly in their population, it is not surprising that aggregate state spending also varies. One way to control for population difference is to divide a state's spending by its population, yielding per capita spending amounts. These amounts yield useful comparisons because they factor in the size of the population to be served by state governments.

As Table 18.1 illustrates, Alaska, Wyoming, Vermont, Hawaii, and New Mexico lead the nation in per capita state spending from general-purpose revenue sources. Florida, Georgia, Tennessee, Texas, Nevada, and Arizona bring up the rear. Note that Alaska spends almost four times more per person than does Florida.

Eight major programs account for 70 to 85 percent of state expenditures, depending on the state in question. They include school aid, state revenue sharing, public colleges and

Table 18.1 States Ranked by Total and per Capita General Expenditures, 2009

From All Revenue Sources

Rank	Total Spending ($ Billions)	Rank	Per Capita Spending ($)
United States	1,826.7		5,950
1 California	254.3	1 Alaska	16,232
2 New York	163.7	2 Wyoming	10,249
3 Texas	110.7	3 Vermont	8,764
4 Pennsylvania	77.6	4 Hawaii	8,647
5 Florida	75.7	5 New Mexico	8,515
6 Ohio	71.6	6 New York	8,377
7 Illinois	68.4	7 Delaware	8,316
8 New Jersey	62.0	8 Connecticut	7,300
9 Michigan	59.2	9 Massachusetts	7,266
10 North Carolina	48.6	10 New Jersey	7,125
11 Massachusetts	47.9	11 Rhode Island	6,976
12 Washington	43.4	12 North Dakota	6,936
13 Virginia	42.1	13 Louisiana	6,923
14 Georgia	41.5	14 Minnesota	6,895
15 Minnesota	36.3	15 California	6,881
16 Maryland	36.0	16 Maine	6,660
17 Wisconsin	35.6	17 Mississippi	6,520
18 Indiana	32.7	18 Washington	6,519
19 Arizona	31.5	19 Montana	6,429
20 Louisiana	31.1	20 Oregon	6,373
21 South Carolina	28.7	21 Maryland	6,320
22 Missouri	28.7	22 West Virginia	6,309
23 Tennessee	27.8	23 Wisconsin	6,304
24 Kentucky	26.9	24 South Carolina	6,284
25 Alabama	26.4	25 Kentucky	6,224
26 Connecticut	25.7	26 Ohio	6,203
27 Colorado	24.9	27 Pennsylvania	6,154
28 Oregon	24.4	28 Iowa	6,085
29 Oklahoma	21.4	29 Michigan	5,937
30 Mississippi	19.2	30 Oklahoma	5,792
31 Iowa	18.3	31 Kansas	5,617
32 New Mexico	17.1	32 Alabama	5,611
33 Arkansas	16.2	33 Arkansas	5,596
34 Kansas	15.8	34 Utah	5,591
35 Utah	15.6	35 Virginia	5,335
36 Nevada	12.1	36 Idaho	5,316
37 West Virginia	11.5	37 Illinois	5,302
38 Alaska	11.3	38 New Hampshire	5,252
39 Hawaii	11.2	39 North Carolina	5,179
40 Nebraska	9.0	40 Indiana	5,094

Table 18.1 States Ranked by Total and per Capita General Expenditures, 2009 (*continued*)

From All Revenue Sources

Rank	Total Spending ($ Billions)	Rank	Per Capita Spending ($)
41 Maine	8.8	41 South Dakota	5,059
42 Idaho	8.2	42 Nebraska	5,028
43 Delaware	7.4	43 Colorado	4,953
44 Rhode Island	7.3	44 Missouri	4,785
45 New Hampshire	7.0	45 Arizona	4,778
46 Montana	6.3	46 Nevada	4,561
47 Wyoming	5.6	47 Texas	4,468
48 Vermont	5.4	48 Tennessee	4,418
49 North Dakota	4.5	49 Georgia	4,217
50 South Dakota	4.1	50 Florida	4,083

Source: Bureau of the Census, U.S. Department of Commerce, *2009 Annual Survey of Government Finances*, January 2011.

universities, Medicaid, TANF, community social service assistance, corrections, and property tax credits. Everything else falls within the remaining 15 to 30 percent. In 2009, 21.7 percent went toward funding public education at the K–12 level, and 10.4 percent went toward higher education. Medicaid and the Children's Health Insurance Program accounted for 21.1 percent. Transportation came to 7.8 percent, corrections totaled 3.5 percent, and assistance to the poor came to about 1.7 percent.[2] The specific mix of spending on each area varies considerably from state to state. For example, Alaska spends 10 percent on K–12 education while Texas spends 31 percent. Alaska, Texas, and Wyoming spend 10 percent or less on Medicaid, but Illinois, Missouri, and Pennsylvania spend 30 percent.[3]

States also differ in the extent to which they tax their residents. Table 18.2 ranks states by the total revenue they raise per resident *through taxes*. (For comparison, note that Table 18.1 includes spending from general-purpose revenues, which include tax revenue.) Table 18.2 also ranks the states in their relative tax effort—taxes paid by state residents as a percent of their personal income. Alaska, Wyoming, Vermont, North Dakota, and Hawaii lead the nation in state tax revenue raised per capita. South Dakota, New Hampshire, Texas, Missouri and Tennessee fall at the bottom. New Hampshire, Colorado, South Dakota, Texas, and Florida exact the lowest tax bite.

By comparing the two rankings, some interesting contrasts become apparent. Some states rank comparatively low in per capita tax collection but make a substantial effort to raise that tax revenue. Idaho, for instance, ranks 37th in taxes collected per resident but 20th in tax collection as a percentage of personal income. Utah looks similar, ranking 38th in tax collection per resident but 24th in tax effort. Arkansas ranks 7th in tax effort but 16th in taxes collected per resident. In contrast, wealthy states like Massachusetts and Maryland are able to raise tax revenues with comparatively much lower tax effort. Massachusetts ranks 11th

Table 18.2 State Tax Revenue, Per Capita and Per $100 of Personal Income, 2009
Revenue from Taxes Only

	Tax Revenue		
Rank	Per Capita ($)	Rank	Per $100 of Personal Income ($)
United States	3,660		9.4
1 Alaska	7,092	1 Alaska	16.6
2 Wyoming	5,072	2 Wyoming	11.1
3 Vermont	4,030	3 Vermont	10.5
4 North Dakota	3,732	4 North Dakota	9.4
5 Connecticut	3,764	5 Hawaii	8.7
6 Hawaii	3,639	6 West Virginia	8.2
7 New York	3,328	7 Arkansas	8.1
8 Minnesota	3,259	8 Delaware	8.0
9 Delaware	3,170	9 Minnesota	7.8
10 New Jersey	3,109	10 New Mexico	7.3
11 Massachusetts	2,988	11 Mississippi	7.3
12 California	2,733	12 Montana	7.3
13 Maryland	2,654	13 Maine	7.2
14 Maine	2,647	14 Kentucky	7.1
15 West Virginia	2,631	15 New York	7.1
16 Arkansas	2,584	16 Wisconsin	6.9
17 Wisconsin	2,547	17 Indiana	6.9
18 Montana	2,469	18 Connecticut	6.8
19 Washington	2,462	19 Michigan	6.7
20 Rhode Island	2,456	20 Idaho	6.5
21 New Mexico	2,414	21 California	6.5
22 Pennsylvania	2,386	22 North Carolina	6.3
23 Kansas	2,375	23 Iowa	6.3
24 Iowa	2,322	24 Utah	6.3
25 Indiana	2,320	25 Louisiana	6.3
26 Michigan	2,283	26 Oklahoma	6.3
27 Illinois	2,267	27 Kansas	6.3
28 Kentucky	2,261	28 New Jersey	6.2
29 Louisiana	2,229	29 Pennsylvania	6.0
30 Nebraska	2,227	30 Massachusetts	6.0
31 Oklahoma	2,213	31 Rhode Island	6.0
32 Mississippi	2,192	32 Washington	5.9
33 North Carolina	2,185	33 Ohio	5.9
34 Nevada	2,105	34 Nebraska	5.8
35 Ohio	2,075	35 Maryland	5.5
36 Virginia	2,072	36 Illinois	5.5
37 Idaho	2,052	37 Arizona	5.5
38 Utah	1,947	38 Nevada	5.5
39 Oregon	1,939	39 Oregon	5.4

Table 18.2 State Tax Revenue, Per Capita and Per $100 of Personal Income, 2009 (*continued*)

Revenue from Taxes Only

	Tax Revenue		
Rank	**Per Capita ($)**	**Rank**	**Per $100 of Personal Income ($)**
40 Arizona	1,799	40 Alabama	5.3
41 Alabama	1,764	41 South Carolina	6.2
42 Colorado	1,728	42 Tennessee	4.9
43 Missouri	1,728	43 Missouri	4.8
44 Florida	1,724	44 Georgia	4.8
45 Tennessee	1,659	45 Virginia	4.7
46 Texas	1,646	46 Florida	4.6
47 South Dakota	1,642	47 Texas	4.5
48 Georgia	1,636	48 South Dakota	4.5
49 New Hampshire	1,605	49 Colorado	4.2
50 South Carolina	1,567	50 New Hampshire	3.7

Source: Bureau of the Census and Bureau of Economic Analysis, U.S. Department of Commerce.

in taxes collected per resident but 30th in tax effort. Comparable rankings for Maryland are 13th and 35th. Note that Alaska, Wyoming, and Vermont make from 4.4 to 2.5 times the tax effort than New Hampshire does.

States have come to devote less of their budgets to pay for the general operations of government, and more to aiding local governments and providing direct financial assistance to individuals. On the average, between 30 and 30 percent of all state expenditures goes to assisting municipalities, counties, school districts, and other special districts, with the largest share devoted to school districts.[4]

FINANCING STATE AND LOCAL GOVERNMENTS

States and local governments differ in the **revenue instruments** they use to pay for the services they provide, and their relative reliance has changed over time (see Figure 18.1). States today rely heavily on general **sales taxes** and the individual **income tax**. That, however, has not always been the case. In 1955, for example, only 9 percent of state revenues came from the individual income tax, compared with 36 percent 52 years later. Although the relative contribution of sales taxes has fallen a bit over the past four decades, they still comprise a third of all state tax revenues.

---

revenue instruments The devices governments use to raise revenues, including taxes and user fees of various kinds.

sales tax A tax based on the value of transfers of goods or services.

income tax A tax on income, whether personal or corporate.

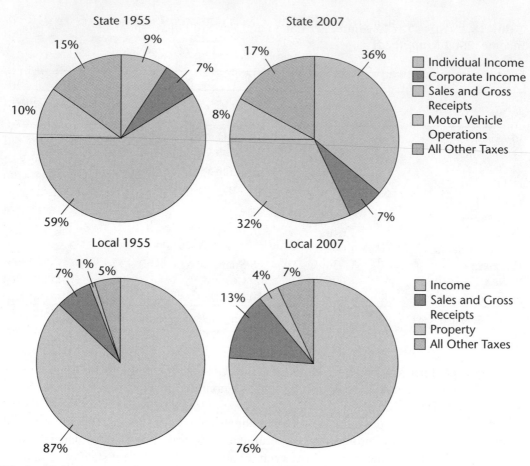

Figure 18.1 Sources of Tax Revenue, 1955 and 2007 Compared
Source: Bureau of the Census, U.S. Department of Commerce; *Significant Features of Fiscal Federalism,* 1989 ed., vol. 2 (Washington, D.C.: Advisory Commission on Intergovernmental Relations, 1989), 32–33.

Every state except Alaska employs either the sales tax or the individual income tax. Only five states do not use the general sales tax (Alaska, Delaware, Montana, New Hampshire, and Oregon), and seven states have no individual income tax (Alaska, Florida, Nevada, South Dakota, Texas, Washington, and Wyoming). New Hampshire taxes dividends and interest income only.

Local governments, in comparison, remain dependent on the **property tax**. About 75 percent of locally raised revenues still comes from property tax, down from 87 percent in 1955. To fill the gap, cities and counties have increased their use of sales taxes, the personal income tax, and a variety of **user fees**. Nonetheless, local property taxes still bring in more revenue than does any single state tax.

---

property tax A tax on the value of property, most commonly placed on real estate and motor vehicles.
user fees Fees charged in return for service. With user fees, only those who receive the service bear the cost of its provision.

Governments commonly tax three major classes of property: real estate, personal property, and public utilities. Local governments—municipalities, counties, school districts, and other special-purpose districts—rely heavily on real estate taxes, whereas states tend to tax personal property (such as industrial machinery, equipment, and inventories). Yet states have significantly reduced their taxation of personal property over the past several decades.

However, states used to depend heavily on real estate taxes. As recently as 1932, state governments collected more revenue from the property tax than from all other tax instruments combined. The Great Depression not only reduced the market value of real estate but also greatly weakened property owners' ability to pay their tax bills. Although total personal income dropped significantly during the depression, the imposition of payroll taxes on income provided a way for states to capture tax revenues before taxpayers received their payroll checks. Between 1931 and 1937, 16 states adopted the personal income tax. But none of them was the first state to do so. That honor goes to Wisconsin, which instituted the personal income tax in 1911, two decades before Congress enacted the federal income tax.

Mississippi was the first state to adopt the general sales tax, in 1932. In the following five years, 23 states followed suit. Because the general sales tax was originally designed to be applied to the sale of manufactured goods, it provided a sure way of capturing needed government revenues during the depression. The tax had to be paid when something was purchased.

The 1960s witnessed a second wave of state adoption of income and sales taxes, providing a means for states to take further financial advantage of that decade's economic prosperity. States needed the newfound revenue to meet rising demands for financial aid to local school districts, as well as to come up with state matching funds for federal Great Society programs. Between 1961 and 1971, 10 states added the individual income tax, and 10 adopted the general sales tax. The Nebraska legislature enacted both. Since 1971, however, only two states have adopted major new taxes: New Jersey (in 1976) and Connecticut (in 1991) added the individual income tax.[5] The Michigan legislature, however, in 1993, approved a large sales tax increase of up to 6 percent, to replace almost $7 billion in property tax revenues that originally had gone to local school districts. In approving the swap, recommended by the state's Republican governor, the legislature eliminated local property taxes as a source of K–12 education funding, beginning with the 1994–1995 school year. It dedicated the new sales tax revenues to take the place of property taxes.

States also make use of other taxes, which in the aggregate nationally bring in far less revenue than do income and sales taxes. Yet one such instrument, the **severance tax**, is highly important to a number of states that have substantial deposits of petroleum, natural gas, coal, or minerals within their borders. Those states tax these resources when they are extracted, or severed, from the land for sale. Although the severance tax accounts for only about 1 percent of state revenues nationally, it generates a large share of tax revenues in a few states. Taxes on petroleum and natural gas contribute 64.4 percent of state tax revenues in Alaska, providing almost $2.2 billion annually to its treasury. The severance tax generates almost 40 percent of Wyoming's tax revenues, raising over $800 million a year. Oklahoma's severance tax yields over $940 million annually, or about 10.6 percent of its tax revenue.[6]

---

severance tax A tax on the extraction of natural resources such as oil and natural gas.

Motor fuel taxes produce another 5 percent of tax revenues across the states. They also vary considerably—for example, gasoline is taxed at 35.3 cents a gallon in California and 8 cents in Alaska.[7]

Beyond taxes, states have increasingly come to rely on lotteries to generate additional revenues. In 2009, lotteries added $52 billion to state treasuries. Currently, 42 states operate lotteries, with most Southern states among those that have not yet taken the plunge. Net proceeds from lotteries in 2009 amounted to $2.5 billion in New York, $1.2 billion in Florida, and $1 billion in California and Texas.[8]

Cities and counties, which had become increasingly dependent on federal and state aid during the 1960s and 1970s, were forced to become more self-sufficient during the subsequent two decades. Budget cuts initiated by the Reagan administration forced municipalities and counties to cope with constant-dollar reductions in federal grants-in-aid during most of the 1980s, although federal aid recovered during the second half of the George H. W. Bush administration. But that was the same time that the early 1990s recession forced many states to pull back on their financial commitments to general-purpose local governments. The combined effects squeezed local governments fiscally. However, the economic recovery and sustained growth that followed put local governments on an improved fiscal footing, that is, until they once again faced revenue constraints in the early 2000s.

Not all local units of government were forced to become more self-reliant. The dependency of school districts increased during the 1980s and into the 1990s as states expanded general school aid, several responding to court orders that mandated additional financial assistance to poor districts (see Chapter 15). In contrast, municipalities and counties, faced with an embattled property tax, found themselves having to look to new revenue sources to close the gap. As Figure 18.1 illustrates, they found them in income and sales taxes. In one dramatic case, the California legislature, in 1993, expanded its municipalities' and counties' sales tax authority, but not without a catch. In exchange, the legislature shifted existing local property tax revenues to California's underfunded school districts, inviting municipalities to use their newly obtained additional authority to fill in the gap.

Not all cities and counties, however, hold the option of levying income or sales taxes. Those not given the authority in state constitutions or by their state legislatures find themselves between the proverbial rock and a hard place, between taxpayer opposition to property tax increases and the need to be more reliant on locally generated revenues. Figure 18.2 shows the states that have extended income and sales tax options to their cities or counties. Only five states (Alabama, California, Missouri, New York, and Ohio) permit local governments to use both the income tax and the sales tax. Ohio limits the income tax to cities and the sales tax to counties.

Local income taxes provide a sizable share of own-source revenues for many major cities in the eastern half of the nation, most notably those in New York, Ohio, Pennsylvania, and Maryland. This heavy reliance on the income tax not only shifts a significant burden away from the property tax, it also shifts part of the tax burden to nonresidents: those who work in the city and use its services but live in the suburbs. Compared with the income tax,

---

motor fuel taxes A tax on motor fuel, including gasoline and diesel fuel.

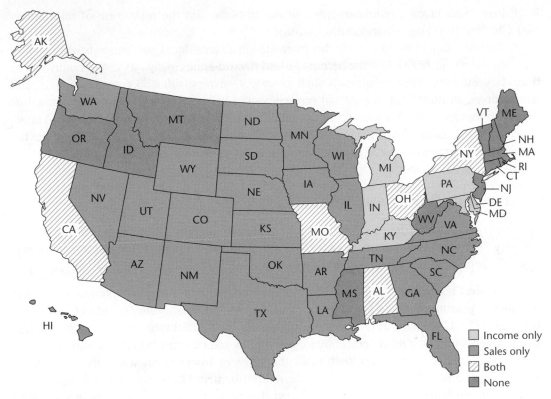

Figure 18.2 States in Which Cities or Counties Levy Income or Sales Tax
Source: Bureau of the Census, U.S. Department of Commerce.

the local sales tax is used more widely nationally. About twice as many local governments use the sales tax than use the income tax.

In their search for new revenues, cities and counties have increasingly turned to user fees, which now constitute another major element of revenue diversification. Cities and counties have applied them to services as diverse as garbage collection, boat launching privileges, admission to zoos and museums, and ambulance transportation. Since the mid-1970s, revenues from user fees charged by local governments have increased over eight-fold, rising from $26 billion in 1976 to $222 billion in 2006, far outstripping the overall growth in local tax revenues.[9]

In addition to relying more heavily on nonproperty tax revenues, local governments have made concerted efforts to expand their property tax base, enabling additional revenues to be collected without corresponding increases in the tax rate. Growing regional and intercity competition for economic development has prompted local legislative bodies to approve a variety of incentives to lure industrial firms to locate within their boundaries and to entice existing firms to expand there. These incentives are based on the theory that firms will choose to locate their operations in settings that reduce operating costs and offer the prospect of increased profits. Such incentives include offers of inexpensive or free land, loan guarantees, tax abatements and exemptions, and the relaxation of regulations (see Chapter 17 for an expanded discussion).

When developers are already highly interested in an area, local governments increasingly have used their authority to issue permits geared toward enticing developers to contribute to necessary infrastructure investments such as streets, sewers, sidewalks, traffic signals, and fire stations. In other instances, local governments have entered into equity arrangements with developers, through which cities or counties receive a percentage of developers' after-tax profits. The rationale, of course, is that new developments, although they expand the tax base, place an increased burden on local governments to provide expanded services.

EVALUATING STATE AND LOCAL TAXES[10]

Several criteria can be used to evaluate both taxes and user fees. Other criteria are appropriate only for evaluating one or the other. Those applicable to both include yield, elasticity, ease of administration, effects on economic behavior, political acceptability, and equity.

1. Yield. The primary purpose of a tax or user fee is to generate revenue to support the operations and program activities of government. Yield is a function of tax rate times tax base. The higher the rate and the broader the base, the more revenue is generated. Governments can expand revenues by increasing tax rates even when bases remain stable. Conversely, governments can keep rates the same or lower them when the tax base is enlarging. The latter option is clearly preferred politically. Those that produce high yields at low administrative costs also are preferred. In contrast, taxes or user fees that produce relatively little revenue in relation to the cost of administration are normally to be avoided, unless they have been instituted largely for other purposes, for example, to bias individual choices in what are deemed to be socially desirable directions (as is discussed under the criterion of effects on economic behavior).

2. Elasticity. Elasticity refers to the relative ability of a tax to respond to changing economic conditions. A tax that responds quickly is considered elastic; one that responds slowly is regarded as inelastic. For instance, income and sales taxes respond more quickly to changing economic conditions than does the property tax. As people's incomes rise, so do income tax revenues. Also, with more income in their pockets, people tend to spend more, generating higher sales tax revenues. In contrast, changes in property taxes lag behind economic change. Although property values tend to rise in a growing economy that creates jobs and attracts workers to fill them, the rather cumbersome process of property tax administration slows responsiveness to change. Even when real estate sales are active, higher selling prices do not get translated into increased real estate tax revenues until local assessors revise the taxable value of properties within their jurisdiction. With that happening no more frequently than once a year, and sometimes less often than that, significant time lags exist between changes in market value, higher property assessment, and the collection of increased property taxes. Therefore, most authorities on tax policy regard property taxes as inelastic compared to the more elastic income and sales taxes. However, the federal income tax is more elastic than are state income taxes because of its more steeply graduated tax rates. More progressive tax rates capture larger sums of tax revenue than do rates that flatten relatively low on the income ladder.

3. Ease of Administration. Taxes or fees should be calculated unambiguously, so that taxpayers and tax collectors alike can readily determine what is owed. They also should be collectible: it does little good to establish taxes or fees that can be evaded easily. Some taxes become difficult to collect because of the lack of valid and reliable information about transactions subject to taxation.

4. Effects on Economic Behavior. Taxes and fees shift resources from private to public use. Economists argue that revenue-generating instruments should not alter the payers' behavior in ways that jeopardize the attainment of economic goals. In other words, they should capture revenues while distorting economic activity as little as possible.[11] Governments also may institute taxes and user fees to bias individual choice. For example, a surcharge on downtown parking not only raises municipal revenue but may also serve to discourage drivers from bringing their cars into an already congested central business district and prompt commuters and shoppers to make greater use of mass transit. Other effects on individual behavior may not be the result of policy design. For instance, high income tax rates can depress entrepreneurial activity and remove any significant economic gain from additional income earned at the highest tax bracket. When individuals choose leisure over work, potential tax revenues are foregone.

5. Political Acceptability. A tax or fee that meets the criteria listed here but encounters widespread opposition is not likely to be adopted. Taxes have to be tolerated.

6. Equity. Equity can be defined as treating similar cases alike and different cases in an appropriately different manner. Under this definition, government policymakers must give good reasons for different treatment, to show that it is appropriate and not just arbitrary. Put differently, people expect taxation to be fair.

Economists speak of both horizontal and vertical equity.[12] **Horizontal equity** presumes equal treatment of taxpayers who have equal capacity to pay. **Vertical equity** concerns the appropriate relative taxes to be paid by persons with different abilities to pay. Here the comparison is of unequals (rather than equals, as with horizontal equity), and the focus is on the extent to which their tax obligations should differ. The vertical equity criterion looks at the relationship between income and the relative incidence of the tax burden. A **progressive tax** increases as a percentage of income as that income rises. Those with progressively higher incomes thus pay a higher proportion of receipts than those with lower incomes. A **proportional tax**, or flat tax as it is sometimes called, applies the same rate to all levels of income. Unlike a progressive tax, it does not gradually increase as

---

horizontal equity Presumes equal treatment of taxpayers who have an equal capacity to pay taxes.

vertical equity Concerns the appropriate relationship between the relative taxes to be paid by persons with different abilities to pay. The comparison is of unequals, and the focus is the extent to which their tax obligations should differ.

progressive tax A tax that increases as ability to pay rises. It is most typically associated with the income tax, for which rates increase as income rises.

proportional tax A tax that applies the same rate to all levels of income; also referred to as a flat tax.

incomes rise above set brackets; the same rate is applied to all income levels. As a consequence, those with higher incomes pay greater amounts in taxes, but they pay less than they would under progressive taxation.

The individual income tax that incorporates progressive tax rates is considered the fairest tax, scoring highest on vertical equity. The individual income tax is further related to the ability to pay by the existence of personal deductions, through which tax liability is reduced for every person financially dependent on the income earner or earners—disproportionately benefiting those with relatively lower incomes.

The sales tax tends to place a greater burden on those with lower incomes because they are likely to spend a relatively higher percentage of their incomes on items subject to a sales tax, particularly when the tax is applied to necessities such as food and utilities. Thus, sales taxes are examples of a **regressive tax**. Exempting these necessities makes a sales tax less regressive.

Finally, the property tax (limited here to real property taxes imposed on land and structures built on the land) is progressive in the sense that it increases as the value of the property increases. Indeed, the value of real property can be used as a measure of wealth,

DEBATING THE ISSUES

What can you do if you think your taxes are too high?

With income and sales taxes, you can do very little if you think they are too high, short of trying to get elected officials to change the law. Legislative bodies set tax rates, and only they can change them. You can personally lobby for lower rates, or you can join organizations that work to keep taxes down, such as the local chapter of your state's taxpayers association.

With property taxes, in comparison, you have a better chance of getting your tax bill lowered through a little personal effort. Because the amount of property tax owed is the product of the legislatively approved tax rate applied to the assessed value of your property, your tax liability will drop if you can get the authorities to reduce the value of your property. The alternative is to convince policymakers to lower the tax rate itself—typically a difficult political sell.

To be successful in appealing your assessment, you'll have to do some homework. You'll have to show that your property is assessed too high in relation to comparable properties. You'll have to put together the comparisons, taking into account location (neighborhood), lot size, the square footage of your house, amenities, and condition. You might strengthen your case by submitting accompanying photographs, which you'll probably have to take.

Although not many people take the appeals route, a thorough, well-documented case can win approval. While pursuing your appeal, you are participating face to face with government, and you are helping to ensure that its representatives are treating taxpayers fairly.

Although property assessment is administratively located differently among the states, it is best to check with your county government for information about how to appeal your assessment. Try your county government's Internet homepage as a starting point, or check the government section of your local phone directory.

---

regressive tax A tax carrying a burden that is inversely related to the ability to pay.

and property taxes are the closest approximation of any tax in the United States to a wealth tax. However, the value of real property is not always a good indicator of its owner's ability to pay. Many elderly citizens own houses bought when their incomes were much higher. In such cases, the tax can be considered regressive.

Compared to taxes at the state and local levels, federal taxation is the most progressive overall because about three-fourths of federal general tax revenues come from the individual income tax. By comparison, both state and local taxes are more regressive. As Figure 18.1 shows, states rely most heavily on the sales tax, and local governments place greatest reliance on the property tax. State programs of circuit-breaker property tax relief reduce the burden of property taxes on lower-income taxpayers. The most common form of circuit-breaker relief allows those with lower incomes to take a special credit on their income taxes for a certain percentage of their paid property taxes.

Compared to local taxation, state taxes are more progressive. States, on the whole, make greater use of the more progressive income tax, and they commonly use income-based property tax relief programs to reduce the otherwise regressive nature of local property taxes.

EXECUTIVE AND LEGISLATIVE BALANCE IN FISCAL POLICY MAKING

Executives greatly influence state and local government fiscal policy agendas. They propose taxing and spending levels and set policy priorities for legislative bodies to consider. Governors, for example, may place educational reform at the top of their policy agendas. Policy initiatives may include increased state support for primary and secondary schools in order to reduce class size, perhaps accompanied by requirements that school districts adopt regularly scheduled assessments of student performance and test teachers on their subject-matter competence. A mayor may emphasize programs aimed at reducing gang-related violence and property damage. A county executive may push for a countrywide mass transit system. In each case, it is the chief executive who sets the agenda, focusing both legislative deliberation and the broader public debate. See Debating the Issues/Exploring the Web for the citizen's role in raising taxes to finance the budget.

Governors use the budget as a vehicle for realizing their policy preferences. The executive budget sets spending priorities: some programs are favored more than others, and others may be cut back or eliminated altogether. Adding policy initiatives to the budget gives the governor a tactical advantage; the governors of 44 states can use the line-item veto to remove objectionable budget actions taken by their legislatures. Where governors have the greatest flexibility in using the line-item veto, they also have the greatest incentive to put policy initiatives into the budget rather than floating them as separate legislation. However, states differ in the extent to which substantive policy initiatives can be included in the budget. State law in some states allows only appropriations to be included in the budget. Other states permit expressions of legislative intent to accompany appropriations, allowing policymakers to specify spending purposes or make them conditional on certain restrictions that must be met. Still other states allow state statutory law to be created, changed, or repealed right within the budget bill itself. This last situation gives the governor the greatest latitude to use the budget as a policy vehicle.

Mayors and county chief executives enjoy less flexibility. Only strong mayors of unreformed cities and popularly elected county executives (discussed in detail in Chapter 11) possess veto power over legislation, and most city and county charters restrict budgets to appropriations alone. Nevertheless, because budgets provide spending authority, mayors or county executives can still channel resources consistent with their policy priorities. Executive budget documents can be used to communicate the rationale underlying those priorities, providing a clear expression of executive intent.

Studies of state budgeting suggest that governors, assisted by their budget offices, exercise considerable influence in state budgeting. Legislatures tend to follow a governor's recommendations rather than agency requests.[13] Yet a number of studies have shown that state legislatures do not just rubber-stamp governor's recommendations; they change them selectively.[14] Governors set the agenda, but legislatures put their own distinctive stamp on the final budget product, which is built on the influence of budget and finance committees and legislative leadership, and assisted by increasingly sophisticated budget staffs.

Mayors and county chief executives are in the budgetary driver's seat. They have their own budget staffs and can rely on resources within the executive branch agencies. In contrast, city council and county board budget staff support is typically very small or nonexistent. Lacking staff resources, legislative bodies seldom offer major budgetary alternatives to a chief executive's recommendations. If they propose spending increases, they have to show how they will be accommodated, either by raising taxes or by offsetting cuts. The former is not an attractive alternative for local legislative bodies because chief executives usually mold public expectations about the required level of taxes. Research consistently has shown that the chief executive's recommendations regularly shape the approved local budget.[15]

STATE AND LOCAL FINANCIAL MANAGEMENT

Several issues confront state and local budgeters and financial managers; some are perennial, and others are products of current times. However, they are all issues that today must be addressed as state and local policymakers chart the fiscal course of their jurisdictions, reconciling revenue and spending policies, managing the public purse, and ensuring that budgets are executed according to legislative intent.

Estimating Revenues and Expenditures

Both state and local governments estimate the revenues they can expect to collect during the coming budget year. The task is easier for most local governments because they rely primarily on the property tax. Those that also collect income and sales taxes face a more formidable challenge. States, with their diverse revenue sources, have the most difficult job of revenue estimating.

Budgets are spending plans for a fiscal year or biennium. They *presume* the availability of revenues to finance planned expenditures. The amount of planned spending is constrained by the size of expected available revenue. Revenue estimating and budget planning go hand in hand.

Exploring the Web

Keeping State and Local Finances in Line

Government financial management is not an exciting topic to most people, but without proper controls and sound cash management practices, you, as citizens, have no assurance that your tax dollars are being spent efficiently and for the purposes intended. It is the job of state and local government financial managers and auditors to exercise the controls and reviews that provide that assurance. Check the following websites and learn more about the contributions that financial managers make.

■ At the state level, find the National Association of State Auditors, Comptrollers and Treasurers at www.nasact.org. The site offers the states' views on a variety of management and audit topics and provides updates on financial issues and innovative auditing practices.

■ At the local level, go to the homepage of the National Association of Local Government Auditors, at www.governmentauditors.org, which offers a forum for local government auditing issues. The association publishes the *Local Government Auditing Quarterly* and *Audit Abstracts*, both of which can be accessed online.

■ The Government Finance Officers Association is a broad-based organization of officials from both state and local governments. Its website, at www.gfoa.org, contains a wide array of resources for financial professionals and students of financial management. It publishes a bimonthly professional magazine, *Government Finance Review*, and issues reports on accounting, auditing, and financial reporting; capital finance and debt management; and cash management. The association also offers training and technical assistance to its members.

Accuracy is important in these projections, on both the expenditure and revenue sides. Errors that overestimate can create situations in which actual revenues prove to be insufficient to cover budgeted expenditures, necessitating subsequent budget cuts or tax increases during the course of the fiscal year or biennium. Conversely, with underestimation, executives and legislators may find themselves sitting on unexpectedly high revenue balances, having lost the opportunity to initiate new programs or expand existing high-priority programs. Revenue and expenditure projections can be a precarious business, especially on the revenue side. One thing is known from the start: revenue projections are always going to be in error; it is just a matter of to what extent they will miss the mark. This is particularly true for state governments, which can be on an annual or biennial budget period. Given the time between initial revenue estimates and the end of the prospective fiscal period, 19 to 31 months will have elapsed. A lot can happen to the economy during the intervening period, which can significantly alter the revenue and expenditure picture.

Because of the time dimensions involved, another revenue projection is usually made while the budget is being considered by the legislature, but that revised projection puts the estimate only a few months closer to the start of the fiscal year. This time-lag problem is particularly acute with biennial budgeting and frequently requires the legislature to make adjustments for the second year. A recent analysis of 23 years, 1987 to 2009, of states' revenue projections revealed that their annual estimates have worsened and that revenues "have become more difficult to predict accurately." Furthermore, the study found that the problem of overestimating revenue is greater in times of fiscal crisis.[16]

Revenue and expenditure estimating can be employed as a tool of political strategy. An administration that wants to hold the line on public spending might estimate revenues conservatively. Similarly, that administration might also project the costs of budget continuation on the high side, leaving little room for the legislature to pursue new spending initiatives.

Legislatures at the state level have gotten into the revenue-estimating business. To achieve some independence from the executive branch's budget forecasts, legislative staffs in 30 states make separate revenue estimates.[17] Most also make independent assessments of the costs of budget continuation. Legislatures, like governors, can use revenue estimates to their political advantage. They can come in with initial estimates lower than the administration's, inviting the governor to be a little more careful about spending; then, after the budget is in the legislative arena, subsequent estimates may "find additional revenues" that can be used to finance new legislative spending.

Local government property tax revenues are relatively easy to forecast. Financial staff members apply the existing mill rate, or tax rate per $1,000 of value, to the updated assessed value of all taxable property within the local jurisdiction, yielding the property tax revenue that can be expected to be collected without any change in the tax rate. Projected revenues can then be compared with what the current budget will cost next year without any policy changes, taking into account the eroding effects of inflation and any mandatory spending. That comparison shows how much spending room is available to finance new program initiatives or the expansion of existing programs. If desired spending increases outstrip forecasted revenues, local chief executives can decide whether to recommend an increase in the mill rate, thereby producing added revenues.

Managing Cash Flow

Revenue collection and expenditures do not coincide with each other during the course of the fiscal year. When managing state and local fiscal resources, executive branch financial administrators must make sure that enough cash is available to pay the bills when they are due. On the other hand, they do not want to have too much cash on hand, in excess of what they need to meet their financial obligations, because cash accounts yield lower rates of return than do other less liquid investments such as bonds and stocks. The key for financial managers is to increase investment yields to the maximum extent possible while ensuring that just enough cash is available to pay the bills.

The optimal strategy for increasing revenue yield involves speeding up tax and other revenue collections and slowing cash outflows to the extent feasible and appropriate. But if payments are too slow in coming, private vendors, clients, and other units of government can be quick to voice their displeasure, even taking their case to their elected representative. Such pressures for timely payment have prompted states and local governments to enact laws stipulating maximum time limits for the payment of debts. In addition, state statutes often specify payment dates for major local assistance payments such as state revenue sharing, school aid, and transportation aid. Because these payments are most often made quarterly, state cash managers know in advance when funds must be available. Hence, they can anticipate the need to move funds out of higher-interest-bearing investments into a cash account for payment.

In addition to implementing an investment strategy that optimally mixes high yield with the necessary liquidity, financial managers want to ensure that payments received earn as much interest as possible. Two factors relate to interest yield: the timeliness of deposit and the rate of interest earned. Regarding the timeliness factor, states and the larger local governments have adopted the practice of using lock-box deposits, whereby those owing the state money remit their payments not to a state agency office but directly to the state's bank account.

States have addressed the second factor, the rate of return, by pooling financial resources across funds for investment purposes and using these larger cash reserves to obtain higher bids or negotiated interest rates. States have also established investment pools for local units of government, enabling their pooled resources to earn higher rates of return. With this practice, fewer banks get a piece of a state's investment action, but yields are maximized.

Capital Finance and Debt Management

States and local governments do not pay for all their expenses with current revenues. Major capital projects, such as the construction of university and school buildings, government office facilities, prisons, and major non-federally-aided highway or bridge projects, are usually funded from bond revenues. Bond purchases lend governments the necessary funds to pay for these types of projects upfront. The governments, in turn, pledge to pay back to the bondholders the principal amount of the loan plus a guaranteed rate of interest.

States and local governments commonly use two forms of financing to pay bondholders: general obligation bonds and revenue bonds. **General obligation bonds** draw on general-purpose revenues of the general fund. With this device, states and local governments pledge their "full faith and credit" behind their promise to pay bondholders. Not only do they commit general-purpose revenues to retire bonded indebtedness, but they also stipulate that bondholders will have "first claim" to available revenues. Because of the security that this commitment affords, prospective bond purchasers are willing to accept lower rates of return than they could get from less secure investments.

Unlike general obligation bonds, state and local treasuries do not stand behind **revenue bonds**. Instead, future earmarked revenues are committed to debt retirement, to the extent that they are expected to be available. For example, a state may garner sufficient funds, through the sale of bonds, to construct a new toll road in a highly congested urban

---

general obligation bonds Debt instruments pledging the full faith and credit of a government's general treasury to repay bondholders.

revenue bonds Debt instruments pledging specified earmarked revenues as the source of repayment to bondholders.

corridor. Rather than paying back the bondholders with general revenues, the state pledges the expected future toll receipts. No other revenue source is available as a backup should actual toll revenues fall significantly short of projections. To attract investors, the state has to make a strong case that the toll revenue forecasts are so sound that prospective investors have little to worry about in making the investment. Because of this higher element of risk, revenue bonds carry higher rates of return than do general obligation bonds; they also cost the states more in interest.

The interest rates that governments have to pay in the bond market are very much influenced by bond ratings made by two major private Wall Street corporations: Moody's Investors Services and Standard and Poor's Corporation. In rating major bond offerings nationwide, the two corporations make judgments about their relative security. For general obligation bonds, the raters look at the basic financial condition of the state or local unit of government as well as the relative quality of its financial management systems. For revenue bonds, they assess the probability that sufficient revenues will be generated and available to repay the bondholders on schedule. Ratings range from AAA for the most secure bonds to C for the least secure. States and local governments with an AAA rating pay the lowest interest rates and are best able to attract investors compared to those with lower ratings. As a rule of thumb, general obligation bonds usually win higher ratings than do revenue bonds, but very strong revenue bonds can carry higher ratings than general obligation bonds offered by a state deep in economic trouble.

According to the established principles of public finance, **long-term debt** (10 to 25 years) is appropriately employed as an instrument to finance the acquisition of fixed assets whose useful lives extend well beyond the upcoming fiscal year or biennium. As the theory goes, future generations who will benefit from a capital project should help pay for it by contributing to the debt service costs. A new university campus or county courthouse, for example, will benefit current and future students; therefore, in financing its construction with long-term general obligation bonds, future taxpayers (and students, through their tuition payments into the general fund) share the financial obligations.

In addition to incurring long-term bonded indebtedness, states and local governments may go into **short-term debt**, usually for one year or less. Financial managers normally resort to short-term borrowing only to cover emergencies or a temporary inability to meet statutorily required payment dates because of cash flow problems. It is considered bad practice for government managers to use short-term borrowing to balance operating budgets—a lesson driven home by New York City's fiscal difficulty in the 1970s.

No widely accepted standards exist among states or local governments for what constitutes imprudent or excessive debt. Defaults remain rare, and the interest paid on debt comprises approximately 4 percent of all state and local government expenditures, compared to a figure of 7 percent at the federal level. However, the bond market itself may exert a practical constraint on a state or local government's appetite for borrowing. Too much "bond paper" offered by a state in a given year, or even over a few years, may

---

long-term debt Debt issued to be repaid over 10 years or more.
short-term debt Debt issued to be repaid over one year or less.

prompt rating firms and investors to worry about the state's longer-term ability to manage its increased debt service requirements.

Government debt has grown dramatically over the past three decades. State debt grew by 614 percent between 1980 and 2006, and local debt increased by 522 percent during that same period.[18] Most of the new long-term debt assumed by state and local governments has not been backed by the full faith and credit of the borrowing government. By 2008, state and local debt reached $2.6 trillion, with states accounting for 39.4 percent of the total and local governments at 60.6 percent.[19]

Two factors help to explain this growth phenomenon. First, state constitutions or statutory law commonly place limits on general obligation debt. Revenue bond indebtedness typically falls outside those limitations. Second, state constitutions or statutes also usually require local voters to approve bond issues carrying the full faith and credit guarantee.

The American Recovery and Reinvestment Act of 2009

As the scope of what came to be known as the Great Recession was becoming clearer in 2008, Congress passed the American Recovery and Reinvestment Act, which President Obama signed on February 17, 2009. Often referred to as the "Stimulus Bill," the act's primary goal was to stimulate the economy by "making supplemental appropriations for job preservation and creation, infrastructure investment, energy efficiency and science, assistance to the unemployed, and State and local fiscal stabilization, for the fiscal year ending September 30, 2009, and for other purposes."[20] To help stabilize fiscal situations, it increased federal funding for state and local governments by $224 billion, with another $275 billion available through federal contracts, grants, and loans.[21] The increase in federal funds allowed states to use the funds to prevent cuts in state programs. This was particularly helpful in 2009 as states faced significant shortfalls due to the effects of the recession that caused declines in tax revenues while also increasing the need for social services.

In addition to using funds from the American Recovery and Reinvestment Act, states engaged in other methods to close their budget gaps, such as reducing funding for local governments, increasing taxes, and cutting a broad range of services, including health care, education, corrections, and public assistance. The Center on Budget and Policy Priorities estimated that funds from the act would fill about 30 percent of state budget gaps through fiscal year 2011.[22] Even with this support, state policymakers expected to see continued shortfalls in 2012 and several years beyond. The continued high rate of unemployment has long-term effects on family incomes that keep state revenues depressed while increasing the need for public services. In the meantime, the cost of health care continues to rise, putting more financial pressure on governments, businesses, and individuals alike. Medicaid is the largest portion of state expenditures and accounted for 22 percent of total spending in fiscal 2010.[23]

The slow recovery from the Great Recession and the wind-down of Recovery Act spending in 2012 are expected to cause continued gaps between state revenues and budgetary needs. The National Association of State Budget Officers reported that 10 states had $12.1 billion in budget gaps that still needed to be closed by the end of fiscal 2011, after beginning the year with shortfalls of $89.3 billion. The Center on Budget and Policy Priorities found that, as of June 2011, 42 states and the District of Columbia had shortfalls of $103 billion for fiscal 2012, and that 24 states have projected gaps totaling $46 billion for 2013. Only 8 states saw no shortfalls in fiscal year 2012: Alaska, Arkansas, Delaware, Indiana, Montana, North Dakota, West Virginia, and Wyoming.[24]

These gaps remained after states made deep cuts in programs. For example, in K–12 education, Washington's budget cuts amounted to $1,100 per student for fiscal 2012, and Michigan's cuts came to $470 per student. For Medicaid, Arizona froze enrollment in part of its program, a change meaning that 100,000 low-income individuals who would have qualified previously would no longer be eligible, and an additional 150,000 would face more stringent rules to qualify. Florida's budget reduced Medicaid payments to hospitals by 12 percent. For higher education, California reduced funding by more than $1 billion. North Carolina's biennial budget reduced higher education funding by close to half a billion for each year.[25] Coping with budget deficits after making significant cuts in programs will require more tough choices on the part of lawmakers; more than half of the states have put together restructuring commissions to evaluate current operations and make recommendations to improve efficiency and cut costs.[26]

SUMMARY AND CONCLUSIONS

State legislatures, city councils, county boards, and local school districts enact budgets that establish spending priorities among public programs. In doing so, they determine who should benefit from public spending and who should pay for it. Therein lies the political tension in public budgeting.

The condition of the economy affects taxing and spending choices. A growing economy provides the wherewithal for states and local governments to increase spending, whereas a recessionary economy reduces revenues and pushes up unemployment compensation and public assistance costs. Economic recession can also prompt the federal government and the states to cut back on the financial assistance they provide to other governments.

Although taxing and spending decisions at the federal level can be used as instruments of national fiscal policy, state and local governments are not well positioned to influence the course of the economy. They are too easily penetrated by national and regional economic forces and, with few exceptions, are not permitted to run deficits. Nevertheless, state and local governments can help to cushion the effects of the business cycle by drawing down revenues in bad economic times. They can also soften the blow on individuals by providing services, financial assistance, and loan guarantees to help people get back on their feet economically.

States and local governments differ in the revenue instruments they use to pay for the services they provide, and their relative reliance has changed over time. Today states make little use of property taxes, preferring to support their spending through sales taxes and the income tax. Local governments, in comparison, rely heavily on the property tax, although they have increasingly turned to sales and income taxes as well as user fees, when permitted by their states. In addition, local governments have made efforts to expand their property tax bases by attracting economic development, using incentives such as offers of free land, loan guarantees, tax concessions, and the relaxation of regulations. They also have used their authority to issue permits to entice developers to contribute toward infrastructure investments such as streets, sewers, and traffic signals.

Beyond exercising controls over how revenues are spent, state and local financial managers face other significant challenges, including accurately estimating revenues and expenditures and prudently managing cash flow and debt. All are important elements of sound budget and financial management, aimed at ensuring that public monies are not only used as the people's representatives intend but also managed wisely.

Discussion Questions

1. Discuss the relationship between benefiting from and paying for public programs.

2. What constraints and opportunities do balanced budget requirements pose for state and local government budget makers?

3. How does the condition of the economy at the state and local level affect taxing and spending?

4. Compare and contrast the revenue sources relied on by state and local governments to finance their public programs. What criteria can be used to evaluate state and local taxes? Apply them to the income tax and the property tax.

5. Compare and contrast preaudit and postaudit financial controls. What are their functions in the control of budget execution and state financial management?

6. What is the optimal strategy for cash flow management, and what mechanisms are employed to realize optimal management practices?

Glossary

balanced budget requirement 476

budget deficit 476

budget surplus 477

general obligation bonds 495

horizontal equity 489

income tax 483

Keynesian economics 478

long-term debt 496

motor fuel taxes 486

progressive tax 489

property tax 484

proportional tax 489

regressive tax 490

revenue bonds 495

revenue instruments 483

sales tax 483

severance tax 485

short-term debt 496

user fees 484

vertical equity 489

Endnotes

1. Richard Mattoon and William A. Testa, "State and Local Governments' Reaction to Recession," *Economic Perspectives* 16, no. 2 (March/April 1992), 19–27; Corina Eckl, "Let the Good Times Roll," *State Legislatures* 23, no. 9 (October/November 1997), 25–31.

2. National Association of State Budget Offices, *State Expenditure Report: 2009*, http://nasbo.org/Publications/StateExpenditureReport/tabid/79/Default.aspx.

3. Center on Budget and Policy Priorities, "Policy Basics: Where Do Our State Tax Dollars Go?," www.cbpp.org/.

4. Congressional Budget Office, *Fiscal Stress Faces by Local Governments,* December 9, 2010, www.cbo.gov.

5. Ronald K. Sneel, "Our Outmoded Tax Systems," *State Legislatures* 20, no. 8 (August 1994), 17–22.

6. National Conference of State Legislatures, "State Energy Revenues Update, 2007," http://www.ncsl.org/default.aspx?tabid=12674.

7. As of January 1, 2011. See Federation of Tax Administrators, http://www.taxadmin.org/fta/rate/mf.pdf.

8. U.S. Census Bureau, 2009 Survey of Government Finances, January 2009, http://www.census.gov/govs/state/09lottery.html.

9. Bureau of the Census, U.S. Department of Commerce, State and Local Government Finance: 2007–2008, http://www.census.gov/govs/estimate.

10. This section incorporates material presented in James J. Gosling, *Budgetary Politics in American Governments*, 4th ed. (New York: Routledge, 2006), 96–99, and is included with permission of the publisher.

11. John Mikesell, *Fiscal Administration: Analysis and Applications for the Public Sector*, 4th ed. (Belmont, Calif.: Wadsworth Publishing Co., 1995), 294–295.

12. Mikesell, *Fiscal Administration*, 282–283.

13. Ira Sharkansky, "Agency Requests, Gubernatorial Support, and Budget Success in State Legislatures," *American Political Science Review* 62 (December 1968), 1220–1231; Joel A. Thompson, "Agency Requests, Gubernatorial Support, and Budget Success in State Legislatures Revisited," *Journal of Politics* 49 (August 1987), 756–779.

14. Richard Sheriden, *State Budgeting in Ohio* (Columbus: Ohio Legislative Budget Office, 1978); James J. Gosling, "Patterns of Influence and Choice in the Wisconsin Budgetary Process," *Legislative Studies Quarterly* 10 (November 1985), 457–482; Eagleton Institute of Politics, Rutgers University, "The Role of the New York Legislature in the Budget Process," August 22, 1977, cited in Alan Rosenthal, *Legislative Life* (New York: Harper Collins, 1981), 301–302; Thomas Lauth, "The Executive Budget in Georgia," *State and Local Government Review* 18 (Spring 1986), 56–64; Thomas Lauth, "Exploring the Budgetary Base in Georgia," *Public Budgeting and Finance* 7 (Winter 1987), 72–82.

15. Thomas J. Anton, *Budgeting in Three Illinois Cities* (Urbana, Ill.: Institute of Government and Public Affairs, 1964); John Crecine, *Government Problem Solving: A Computer Simulation of Municipal Budgeting* (Chicago, Ill.: Rand-McNally, 1969); Arnold J. Meltsner, *The Politics of City Revenue* (Berkeley: University of California Press, 1971); Paul Peterson, *City Limits* (Chicago, Ill.: University of Chicago Press, 1981).

16. "States' Revenue Estimating: Cracks in the Crystal Ball," Pew Center on the States, http://www.pewcenteronthestates.org/uploadedFiles/States_Revenue_Estimating_final.pdf.

17. *Legislative Budget Procedure: A Guide to Appropriations and Budget Processes in the States, Commonwealths and Territories, 1998* (Denver, Colo.: National Conference of State Legislatures, 1998), 158–159.

18. Bureau of the Census, U.S. Department of Commerce, State and Local Government Finances by Level of Government and by State: 2005–2006, table 1.

19. "State and Local Government Finances Summary: 2008," U.S. Census Bureau, http://www2.census.gov/govs/estimate/08statesummaryreport.pdf.

20. *American Recovery and Reinvestment Act of 2009,* Public Law 111-5, 111th Congress, H.R. 1 (February 17, 2009), http://frwebgate.access.gpo.gov/cgi-bin/getdoc.cgi?dbname=111_cong_public_laws&docid=f:publ005.pdf.

21. "The Recovery Act," http://www.recovery.gov/About/Pages/The_Act.aspx.

22. Katharine Bradbury, "State Government Budgets and the Recovery Act," Federal Reserve Bank of Boston: Public Policy Brief 10-1, February 17, 2010.

23. "Fiscal Survey of the States: Spring 2011," National Association of State Budget Officers, http://www.nasbo.org.

24. Elizabeth McNichol, Phil Oliff, and Nicholas Johnson, "States Continue to Feel Recession's Impact," Center on Budget and Policy Priorities, June 17, 2011, www.cbpp.org.

25. Erica Williams, Michael Leachman, and Nicholas Johnson, "State Budget Cuts in the New Fiscal Year Are Unnecessarily Harmful: Cuts Are Hitting Hard at Education, Health Care, and State Economies," Center on Budget and Policy Priorities, July 28, 2011; Michael Leachman, Erica Williams, and Nicholas Johnson, "New Fiscal Year Brings Further Budget Cuts to Most States, Slowing Economic Recovery," Center on Budget and Policy Priorities, June 28, 2011, www.cbpp.org.

26. To follow the progress of the restructuring commissions, go to the National Association of State Budget Officers' web site at http://nasbo.org/Resources/ResponsestotheEconomicDownturn/tabid/138/Default.aspx.

Index